Compound Interest and Annuity Tables

JACK C. ESTES

McGRAW-HILL BOOK COMPANY

New York   *St. Louis*   *San Francisco*   *Auckland*   *Bogota*   *Düsseldorf*
Johannesburg   *London*   *Madrid*   *Mexico*   *Montreal*   *New Delhi*
Panama   *Paris*   *São Paulo*   *Singapore*   *Sydney*   *Tokyo*   *Toronto*

11 12 13 14 15 BKP BKP 8 7 6

Estes, Jack C   1922-1975.
    Compound interest and annuity tables.

    (McGraw-Hill paperbacks)
    1. Interest and usury—Tables, etc.   2. Annu-
ities—Tables.   I. Title.
HG1626.E82   1976   332.8′021′2   76-28364
ISBN 0-07-019683-4

These tables have been prepared as accurately as possible; the
publishers do not, however, guarantee complete freedom from
error.

Preface

This book is concerned with the effects that compound interest and time have on money. It is intended primarily for people in real estate, banking, and finance who are involved in making investment decisions and need tools and methods to evaluate investment opportunities. It is also useful for students of business administration and those nonmathematically inclined members of the public who want to be able to easily measure or evaluate financial opportunities.

Although books similar to this one are on the market, most of them presuppose that the user is skilled in higher mathematics. Perhaps the most welcome feature of this book is that the tables are explained in such a way that anyone with the ability to add, subtract, multiply, and divide can understand their makeup and learn how to use them effectively. There are no complicated formulas—only straightforward, simple explanations.

After an easy-to-understand discussion of compound interest, each table is described and explained. Some typical problems and their solutions are given, which serve not only to illustrate how to use each table but also to introduce the techniques of problem solving.

The tables show the effect of compound interest and time on one monetary unit under six different situations. In the United States, the monetary unit is $1, but the tables can just as easily be used for any other monetary unit. The amounts given can be multiplied by any amount larger than $1 to assist in determining values. Tables such as these are nothing more than precomputed series of calculations set forth in an orderly manner for easy use. Each table is presented for monthly, quarterly, semiannual, and annual compounding periods, with the entire span of interest rates covered in each of the compounding periods.

The rate coverage for all compounding periods is from 5 through 22½ percent in increments of ½ percent, with additional coverage from 23 to 30 percent in increments of 1 percent in the annual tables.

The amounts are presented with ten decimal places for extreme accuracy when needed.

The key to using these tables successfully is in being able to select the proper table for the problem being solved. A short time spent with the instructions and practice problems should give you a clear understanding of the construction and use of each table and enable you to answer questions such as the following:

1. If your savings institution pays 6 percent interest, compounded annually, what will be the value at the end of 15 years of an initial deposit of $1,000 made today?

2. Your savings bank pays 6½ percent interest, compounded monthly. If you deposit $10 at the end of each month for the next 10 years, how much money will you have?

3. You will need $20,000 in 20 years, and you can get 7 percent interest, compounded quarterly. How much must you deposit at the end of each quarter to accumulate the required amount?

4. If you want 8 percent interest, compounded twice a year, what should you pay today so that 25 years from now you will receive $17,500?

5. If current interest rates are 8½ percent, compounded monthly, what should you pay today to receive $100 at the end of each month for the next 60 months?

6. If you borrow $25,000 for 30 years at 10 percent, compounded monthly, how much must you pay back at the end of each month to fully repay both the amount borrowed and the interest?

I wish to express may deep appreciation to Robert A. Arnold of Computer Sciences Corporation and to Sandor Rosenberg, a computer programmer, whose knowledge and dedication to precision and accuracy have made these tables possible. I would also like to express my indebtedness to W. Z. Smith, Jr., Director, Systems, Airline Tariff Publishing Company, for the use of unique printing equipment which made possible presentation of these tables in clear, easy-to-read type.

Jack C. Estes

Contents

Explanation of Tables

Tables such as the ones presented here are generally called compound interest and annuity tables. The names of the six tables vary from one text to another; we chose the name that seemed most descriptive of the function of each table. Regardless of the names used, the amounts shown are standard.

Before the individual tables are discussed, we present a review of compound interest and annuity and clarify a few terms.

An *annuity* is generally thought of as a regular series of payments, of equal amounts, made or received at regular intervals of time, such as monthly, quarterly, semiannually, or annually.

Simple interest is interest earned on the original principal only, during the entire life of the loan.

Compound interest is interest earned and then added to the original investment so that it, too, begins to earn interest. Simply stated, it is interest on interest.

The number of times per year that interest is earned and converted or added to the principal is called the *frequency of compounding*. The time span between compoundings is called the *interest period* (or the period). For instance, if interest is added only once a year, it is compounded annually. If interest is added twice a year, it is said to be compounded semiannually. Four interest additions per year would be quarterly compounding, and interest added once per month would be monthly compounding. The more times interest is compounded in a year, the greater will be the amount of interest earned in a year.

Interest rates are generally stated on an annual basis. If someone *simply* says "10 percent interest," 10 percent per annum is meant. This would mean that $1 deposited for one year would earn 10 cents interest. The interest rate shown at the top of each column in the tables in this book is the *annual rate* (also called the nominal rate or the nominal annual rate). The monthly, quarterly, and semi-annual compounding tables have been computed using the rate per conversion period, which is the annual rate divided by the number of compoundings per year. For example, 12 percent interest compounded monthly would be 1 percent per compounding period, or 1 percent per month (.12 ÷ 12); quarterly compounding would be 3 percent (.12 ÷ 4); and semiannual compounding would be 6 percent (.12 ÷ 2). Refer to the conversion table, pages 19–20, which shows the annual percentage rate, as well as the fractional rate and its decimal equivalent per compounding period, for the monthly, quarterly, and semiannual tables.

Let's compare $1 deposited at 12 percent for one year under four different circumstances—at simple interest, annual compounding, semiannual compounding, and quarterly compounding.

Simple interest
$1.00 × .12   .12

Annual compounding
$1.00 × .12   .12

Semiannual compounding
First period
$1.00 × .06   .06

Second period
$1.00 + .06 = $1.06
$1.06 × .06   <u>.0636</u>
Total interest for year   .1236

Quarterly compounding
First period
$1.00 × .03   .03

Second period
$1.00 + .03 = $1.03
$1.03 × .03   .0309

Third period
$1.03 + .0309 = $1.0609
$1.0609 × .03   .031827

Fourth period
$1.0609 + .031827 = $1.092727
$1.092727 × .03   <u>.03278181</u>
Total interest for year   .12550881

As you can see, the amounts earned by simple interest and by annual compounding for one year are the same (but only for one year). In fact, until interest earned is added to the principal and begins to earn interest, it is simple interest. The only difference is in what happens to the 12 cents. Under simple interest, it would generally be paid to the investor. Under compound interest, it would be added to the original deposit and it, too, would earn interest for the second interest period. You will see how this takes place in the semiannual and quarterly compounding examples. You will also see that semiannual compounding results in more interest than annual compounding and that quarterly compounding results in more interest than semiannual compounding. Again, monthly compounding results in more total interest than quarterly compounding. In this example, the 12 percent interest compounded semiannually results in actual earnings of .1236, or an effective rate of 12.36 percent. Quarterly compounding results in an effective rate of 12.55 percent. Keep in mind that interest compounded more often than annually will actually earn more than the annual rate quoted. Always make certain you select the proper compounding period suitable for the problem you are solving.

The procedure used in the foregoing semiannual and quarterly compounding examples is the one that is used to make up Table 1—Future Worth of One Dollar with Interest. The other five tables are variations of Table 1. All tables are designed to assist you in calculating values under six different circumstances, which are described and illustrated in the instructions to follow. The compound interest and annuity tables provide answers related to the growth or the diminishment of an investment. In the final analysis, however, the user must rely on his or her judgment concerning selection of the rates to be used, depending on the risk of the particular investment being considered.

Each of these circumstances and its associated table, is concerned with the calculation of a value. There are two major categories of value: future value and present value. Tables 1, 2, and 3 are associated with the calculation of future value; Tables 4, 5, and 6 are concerned with the calculation of present value.

Future value pertains to the value that will exist at some time in the future. *Present value* is the value as of today of a sum or sums of money to be collected or paid in the future. In the example of quarterly compounding, an original deposit of $1 was shown to grow to $1.12550881. This is future value. Now the present value of $1.12550881 payable one year from now (and taken at 12 percent interest compounded quarterly) is $1.00.

A word here about rounding and accuracy is in order. The most frequently used rounding procedure is as follows:

1. Decide on the number of digits to be retained.
2. If the next digit to the right is above 5, add 1 to the last digit retained.
3. If the next digit to the right is below 5, leave the last digit as it is.
4. When the next digit to the right is 5 followed by zeros, if the preceding number is even, leave it as is. If the preceding number is odd, add 1 to it.

EXAMPLE: Round to six decimals:

5.1234 567 435	rounded to	5.123457
1.4364 534 628	rounded to	1.436453
3.2396 545 000	rounded to	3.239654
7.8943 635 000	rounded to	7.894364

The tables in the book are carried to ten decimals to provide extreme accuracy when desired. For most purposes, fewer decimals would be accurate enough. To save time, never use more decimals than needed. The ten decimals are arranged so that it is easy to use four decimals or seven, for example, 1.1234 567 890. Just round to the number of decimals you need and proceed. A general rule to follow is to use one more digit in the factor than the number of digits expected in the answer.

1. Estimate the number of digits expected in the answer.
2. Use one more digit than that expected in the answer.
3. Round as discussed above.

EXAMPLE: How many decimals should you use to multiply $1,000 by a factor of 2.1589 249 973? The factor is more than 2 and less than 3; therefore, the answer will be between $2,000 and $3,000. In any event, it will contain six digits, so round the factor to seven digits and proceed:

2.1589 249 973 rounded to 2.1589 250

$1,000 × 2.1589 250 = $2,158.9250 rounded to $2,158.92

If the amount to be multiplied by the factor had been $15.00, we would have needed only five digits; if it were $6.00, we would have used only four digits.

When computing long-term payments, it is desirable to deviate from normally mathematical correct rounding and round up *any* fractional portion of a cent. Perhaps the importance of this can best be explained by quoting from the preface of *Interest Amortization Tables**:

> One deviation from absolute accuracy has been made in the rounding procedure. Normally, when computing payments or interest, any half cent or greater would be rounded up, and anything less than a half cent would be dropped. In these tables any portion of a cent has been rounded up. This was done to ensure that any loan would be fully paid within the time periods specified, without a large lump sum payment becoming necessary at the end.

TABLE 1—FUTURE WORTH OF ONE DOLLAR WITH INTEREST

This table is also called "Amount of 1," "Amount of 1 at Compound Interest," and "Compound Amount of 1." It shows the future growth, with interest, of a *single* deposit of $1 made at the beginning of the first period. Note that, in this table, the deposit is made only once, at the *beginning* of the first period. For *all* other tables, the deposit or payment will be made periodically or repeatedly at the *end* of the period.

Let's work another example, but here we will multiply the principal amount at the beginning of each period by 1 plus the rate per period. The end result will be the same as multiplying the principal by the rate per period to get the interest and then adding it to the principal amount.

EXAMPLE: If $1.00 were to be deposited at the beginning of the first year at 6 percent interest compounded annually, what would be the value of the deposit at the end of the fifth year?

Beginning of first year—deposit	= $1.00
End of first year: $1.00 × 1.06	= $1.06
End of second year: $1.06 × 1.06	= $1.1236
End of third year: $1.1236 × 1.06	= $1.1910 160
End of fourth year: $1.1910 160 × 1.06	= $1.2624 769 600
End of fifth year: $1.2624 769 600 × 1.06	= $1.3382 255 776

*By Jack C. Estes, McGraw-Hill, New York, 1976.

Our original deposit has now grown to the figure above, which is the amount shown in the annual section, Table 1, at 6 percent for five years, page 183. If our deposit had been other than $1, we could have obtained the answer by multiplying the specific deposit by the amount shown above. For example, had our deposit been $500, we would have multiplied $500 × 1.3382 255 776, which comes to $669.1127, or $669.11.

Using the techniques shown above, we could if necessary devise a future worth table for as many time periods as we desired. However, even with an electronic calculator, this would require considerable time and effort. Instead, by referring to Table 1, we find that all the information we need is supplied.

Let's now do the previous example using the full 10 decimals, then seven decimals rounded, then four decimals:

$$\$500 \times 1.3382\ 255\ 776 = \$669.11$$
$$\$500 \times 1.3382\ 256 = \$669.11$$
$$\$500 \times 1.3382 = \$669.10$$

As you can see, the variation is not great. Of course, working with larger sums would produce larger variations.

PROBLEM: If your savings institution pays 6 percent interest, compounded annually, what will be the value at the end of 15 years of an initial deposit of $1,000 made today?

SOLUTION: Referring to the annual compounding section, Future Worth of One Dollar with Interest, Table 1, under the 6 percent column, page 183, we find opposite 15 years the amount 2.3965 581 931. This amount multiplied by your original deposit of $1,000 equals $2,396.56, the future worth of your investment.

TABLE 2—FUTURE WORTH OF ONE DOLLAR PER PERIOD WITH INTEREST

This table is also called "Amount of 1 per Period," "Accumulation of 1 per Period," "Compound Amount of 1 per Period," and "Amount of Annuity of 1 per Period." It shows the future growth of a *series* of deposits of $1, made at the *end* of each period.

Remember that in Table 1 the deposit is made at the beginning of the period, whereas the other five tables are based on the deposit being made at the end of the period. The first figure shown in Table 2 is $1, which represents the deposit just made at the end of the first period and which, obviously, did not earn any interest.

The amounts to which a series of deposits will grow, as shown in Table 2, can be broken down into how much a deposit of $1 will grow in one period, how much a deposit of $1 will grow in two periods, how much in three periods, and so on, as shown in Table 1. Considered in this manner, then, Table 2 is nothing more than an addition of the amounts shown in Table 1. However, to compensate for the difference between the time of deposit of Table 1 and of Table 2, it is only necessary to add four time periods from Table 1 plus the deposit just made to construct Table 2 for five periods. For example, to obtain the amount to which $1, deposited at the end of each year for five years at 6 percent, compounded annually, will grow, add the first four years from Table 1, then add $1.

FROM TABLE 1:

First deposit: value at end of fourth year after deposit	=	$1.2624 769 600
Second deposit: value at end of third year after deposit	=	1.1910 160 000
Third deposit: value at end of second year after deposit	=	1.1236 000 000
Fourth deposit: value at end of first year after deposit	=	1.0600 000 000
Fifth deposit: value at time of deposit	=	1.0000 000 000
		$5.6370 929 600

which is the future worth of $1 deposited at the end of each year at 6 percent, compounded annually for five years, as shown in Table 2.

Perhaps this can be more clearly seen by the following table, which shows how $1 deposited at the end of each year will grow. Each periodic deposit is indicated by an asterisk, with its successive values shown to the right along the same horizontal line. The five-year column is then added to determine the amount to which the five separate deposits will grow by the end of the fifth year, which results in the same amount as the previous example.

First year	Second year	Third year	Fourth year	Fifth year
$1.00*	$1.06	$1.1236	$1.1910 160	$1.2624 769 600
	1.00*	1.0600	1.1236 000	1.1910 160 000
		1.00*	1.0600 000	1.1236 000 000
			1.00*	1.0600 000 000
				1.00*
				$5.6370 929 600

Note: In both examples, the final figure is the exact amount that is shown in the annual compounding section of Table 2 under 6 percent for five years, page 194. However, this will not always be the case. Each amount shown in the tables has been individually computed using 18 decimals before rounding to 10 places. This will often cause a variation in figures obtained by adding amounts from another table.

Had our annual deposit been $500 at 6 percent compounded annually for five years, we would have $500 × 5.6370 929 600 = $2,818.5464, or $2,818.55.

PROBLEM: Your savings bank pays 6½ percent interest, compounded monthly. If you deposit $10 at the end of each month for the next ten years, how much money will you have?

SOLUTION: Referring to the monthly compounding section, Future Worth of One Dollar per Period with Interest, Table 2, under the 6½ percent column, page 30, we find opposite 120 periods (10 years) the amount 168.4031 542 385. This multiplied by your regular deposit of $10 is $1,684.03, which is the amount you will have in 10 years.

TABLE 3—SINKING FUND FACTORS

This table is also called "Sinking Fund Payment," "Annuity Whose Accumulation at Compound Interest Is 1," and "Periodic Payment of Annuity Whose Amount Is 1." It shows the amount of regular deposits which must be made at the *end* of each period to accumulate $1 by some future date.

A sinking fund table is used when it is desired to accumulate a stipulated amount through regular deposits over a certain period of time. Some practical examples would be a person needing to accumulate money to pay off a note coming due; parents wishing to set up a college education fund; an apartment house owner desiring to put aside a sum each month for equipment replacement at some future date.

Without taking interest into consideration, if you needed $1 five years from now, you could divide $1 by five and determine that you would need to deposit 20 cents each year to accumulate the $1. For our purposes, however, we wish to determine the amount to be deposited each year, with interest, in order to accumulate $1. The amount we need then will be less than the 20 cents required when interest is not taken into account.

Table 2 shows the amount to which a series of deposits of $1, with interest, will grow in a certain period of time. We need to determine the amount of deposit necessary to accumulate $1, just the reciprocal of Table 2. Therefore, if we divide $1 by the amount shown in Table 2, we should have the periodic payment needed to accumulate $1 within a comparable period of time, as shown in Table 3.

Let's assume we wish to accumulate $500 in five years through regular payments annually. Also assume that we can get 6 percent compounded annually. If our reasoning is correct, we can divide $1 by the amount to which a series of annual deposits of $1 will grow at the above rates and time from Table 2, then multiply the result by $500 to determine the amount of the annual deposits required to accumulate the $500: $\dfrac{1}{5.6370\ 929\ 600} = .1773\ 964\ 004$, which is the annual deposit needed to accumulate $1. This is the amount shown in the annual compounding section, Table 3, at 6 percent for five years, page 205. Thus, .1773 964 004 × $500 = $88.6982, rounded to $88.70. In this case, we would have rounded up any fractional part of a cent to assure accumulating the required amount within the time period.

Now, let's check to see if our procedure has been correct.

		Balance at end of each year
First year		
Initial deposit made at *end* of year		$ 88.70
Second year		
$88.70 × 1.06	$ 94.02	
Plus another deposit	88.70	
		$182.72
Third year		
$182.72 × 1.06	$193.69	
Plus another deposit	88.70	
		$282.39
Fourth year		
$282.39 × 1.06	$299.33	
Plus another deposit	88.70	
		$388.03
Fifth year		
$388.03 × 1.06	$411.31	
Plus another deposit	88.70	
		$500.01

We have accumulated the required amount; therefore, our procedure was correct. Note that we have actually accumulated 1 cent more than required. Some variation is to be expected because of rounding of the annual deposit and the interest.

PROBLEM: You will need $20,000 in 20 years, and you can get 7 percent interest, compounded quarterly. How much must you deposit at the end of each quarter to accumulate the required amount?

SOLUTION: Referring to the quarterly compounding section, Sinking Fund Factors, Table 3, under the 7 percent column, page 94, we find opposite 80 periods (20 years) the amount .0058 209 310. This multiplied by your future need of $20,000 is $116.42, which must be your regular quarterly deposit to accumulate the needed amount in 20 years.

TABLE 4—PRESENT WORTH OF ONE DOLLAR

This table is also called "Present Worth of 1," "Present Value Reversion of 1," "Present Value of 1," and "Present Value of 1 at Compound Interest." It shows the present worth of $1 which is to be collected in one lump sum at the *end* of a given time.

To determine the present value of a lump sum payment to be received in the future requires nothing more than a reversal of the compounding procedure. Instead of adding interest each conversion period, it is necessary to subtract or discount interest from the amount to be received in the future.

Table 1 shows how much a single deposit of $1 will grow, with interest. The present value of a single $1 future payment, as shown in Table 2, is just the reciprocal of Table 1. Therefore, if we divide $1 by the amount shown in Table 1, we should have the discounted amount for a comparable period and rate for Table 4.

Let's try another example to see if this reasoning is valid. Assume that a friend wants to borrow money to be repaid, with interest, in one lump sum of $500 at the end of five years. If you expect 6 percent, compounded annually, what amount would you be justified in lending your friend today?

Referring to the example in Table 1, we see that $1 deposited at the beginning of the first period will grow to 1.3382 255 776 in five years, when compounded annually at 6 percent. So, let's divide $1 by that amount: $\frac{1}{1.3382\ 255\ 776}$ = .7472 581 729, which is the present worth of $1 to be received five years from now. This amount times $500 equals $373.6291, or $373.63, which is the amount you should lead your friend to achieve the return you want on your investment.

If our calculations are correct, we should be able to deposit the $373.63 in a bank at the rates and terms specified and have $500 at the end of the five years. Remember: in Table 1 the deposit is made at the beginning of the first period.

	Balance at end of each year
First year $373.63 × 1.06	$396.05
Second year $396.05 × 1.06	$419.81
Third year $419.91 × 1.06	$445.00
Fourth year $445.00 × 1.06	$471.70
Fifth year $471.70 × 1.06	$500.00

We have accumulated the required amount; therefore, our procedure must have been correct. In this example, we ended up with exactly the amount desired without variation, but, again, variation caused by rounding is not unusual.

PROBLEM: If you want 8 percent interest, compounded twice a year, what should you pay today so that 25 years from now you will receive $17,500?

SOLUTION: Referring to the semiannual compounding section, Present Worth of One Dollar, Table 4, under the 8 percent column, page 157, opposite 50 periods (25 years), we find .1407 126 153. This amount times the future receipt of $17,500 is $2,462.47, which is the present worth of that future payment.

TABLE 5—PRESENT WORTH OF ONE DOLLAR PER PERIOD

This table is also called "Present Worth of 1 per Period," "Present Value of Ordinary Annuity 1 per Period," and "Present Value of 1 per Period at Compound Interest." It shows the present worth of a *series* of receipts of $1 at the *end* of each period for a specified number of periods into the future. The most common use of this table is to measure the present worth of a specific number of future periodic payments, such as those from annuities and investment income.

You will recall that Table 2 was concerned with determining the total amount that would be accumulated at some time in the future by making a specific number of equal deposits. That amount to be collected in the future is the future worth. Now we want to determine the present value—or the value today—of the same series of future deposits. In other words, what should you be willing to pay in cash today for the right to receive a certain series of payments of $1 each? For example, the present worth of $1 to be received at the end of each of the next five years is equal to the present worth of $1 to be received one year from now, plus the sum of the present worths of $1 to be received two, three, four, and five years from now. Therefore, if we add the amounts shown in Table 4 for the first five years, we should obtain the desired amount for Table 5 for five years. Referring to the annual compounding section, Table 4 at 6 percent, page 216, we see:

FROM TABLE 4:		*For Table 5:* *cumulative total*
First year	.9433 962 264	.9433 962 264
Second year	.8899 964 400	1.8333 926 664
Third year	.8396 192 830	2.6730 119 495
Fourth year	.7920 936 632	3.4651 056 127
Fifth year	.7472 581 729	4.2123 637 856

which is a variation of 1 in the tenth decimal place from that amount shown for the comparable compounding period, rate and term, Table 5, page 227.

Accordingly, the right to receive $1 at the end of each year for five years is today worth $4.2123 637 856, or $4.21, if we are to obtain 6 percent, compounded annually on our investment. Stated another way, if we place $4.21 in the bank today under the above conditions, we would be able to withdraw $1 at the end of each of the next five years, at which time our funds would be exhausted. Let's use an example of 6 percent, annual compounding for five years, and $500 to see if we can verify our procedure.

The right to receive $500 at the end of each year for five years is worth $500 × 4.2123 637 856 (from previous example), which equals $2,106.18. Let's deposit this amount in the bank today and see if we can withdraw $500 at the end of each of the next five years.

Keep in mind that, in Table 5, payments (in this case, withdrawals) are made at the end of the year. However, the initial deposit would be in the bank at the beginning of the first year.

		Balance at end of each year
First year		
$2,106.18 × 1.06	$2,232.55	
Minus $500	500.00	
		$1,732.55
Second year		
$1,732.55 × 1.06	$1,836.50	
Minus $500	500.00	
		$1,336.50
Third year		
$1,336.50 × 1.06	$1,416.69	
Minus $500	500.00	
		$ 916.69
Fourth year		
$916.69 × 1.06	$ 971.69	
Minus $500	500.00	
		$ 471.69
Fifth year		
$471.69 × 1.06	$ 499.99	
	500.00	
		$ −.01

We have again determined that our construction of a table is valid, even though we are 1 cent short because of rounding.

PROBLEM: If current interest rates are 8½ percent, compounded monthly, what should you pay today to receive $100 at the end of each month for the next 60 months?

SOLUTION: Referring to the monthly compounding section, Present Worth of One Dollar per Period, Table 5, under the 8½ percent column, page 58, opposite 60 months, we find 48.7411 826 131. When this amount is multiplied by the regular payment to be received ($100), it is equal to $4,874.12, which is the present worth of such a series of payments.

TABLE 6—PARTIAL PAYMENT TO AMORTIZE 1

This table is also called "Periodic Payment to Amortize 1," "Investment to Amortize 1," "Annuity Whose Present Value at Compound Interest is 1," or just "Partial Payment." It shows the amount of the equal, regular payment required to repay both principal amount and the interest on a loan with payments made at the end of each period. Its most common use is to determine the amounts of regular payments necessary to repay a mortgage or other long-term loan.

Table 5 shows the amount you must deposit today to be able to withdraw a series of $1 amounts. Table 6 shows how much you can withdraw at the end of each time period in the future if you have $1 today. Therefore, Table 6 is just the reciprocal of Table 5. If we divide $1 by the amount shown in Table 5, we should obtain the corresponding entry for Table 6. Let's use another example and see.

If you borrow $500 at 6 percent compounded annually to be repaid in equal annual payments for five years, how much will your payments be? We saw in the example used in the discussion of Table 5 that the present worth of $1 per period for five years at 6 percent compounded annually was 4.2123 637 856.

So, let's divide 1 by that amount: $\dfrac{1}{4.2123\ 637\ 856} = .2373\ 964\ 4004$, which

is the annual payment required to repay $1 under the terms and conditions outlined. Thus, $500 × .2373 964 4004 = $118.6982 2002, or $118.70, per annum payment required to repay a $500 loan in five years at 6 percent, compounded annually. Let's see if this will fully repay both principal and interest.

		Balance at end of each year
First year		
$500 × 1.06	$530.00	
Less payment	118.70	
		$411.30
Second year		
$411.30 × 1.06	$435.98	
Less payment	118.70	
		$317.28
Third year		
$317.28 × 1.06	$336.31	
Less payment	118.70	
		$217.61
Fourth year		
$217.61 × 1.06	$230.67	
Less payment	118.70	
		$111.97
Fifth year		
$111.97 × 1.06	$118.69	
Less payment	118.70	
		$ −.01

Again our procedure is correct.

PROBLEM: If you borrow $25,000 for 30 years at 10 percent, compounded monthly, how much must you pay back at the end of each month to fully repay both the amount borrowed and interest?

SOLUTION: Referring to the monthly compounding section, Partial Payment to Amortize 1, Table 6, under the 10 percent column, page 68, opposite 360 periods (30 years), we find .0087 757 157. This is then multiplied by $25,000, and it equals $219.40, which is the monthly payment required.

Practice Problems and Solutions

One of the best ways to develop an understanding of these tables is to work some practice problems. The following problems, with suggested solutions, were developed for this purpose.

Many of the practice problems require the use of two or more tables, and these may seem unduly complicated. Just break the problem into individual steps and work on one at a time. That way, solving a complex problem becomes no more than solving a series of individual simple problems.

Another good way to become more familiar with these tables is to take an actual or simulated situation, develop a problem concerning it, work it out, then prove it in a way similar to that of some of the examples used in explaining the tables.

PROBLEM: You deposit $750 in a savings account at 6 percent compounded monthly. If the interest rate changes to 6½ percent at the end of the sixth year, how much will you have at the end of 10 years?

SOLUTION: Solving this type of problem requires nothing more than measuring the growth of the initial deposit for the first six years and then depositing that amount for an additional four-year period.

Refer to the monthly compounding section, Table 1, 6 percent opposite six years. The amount there, 1.4320 442 785, times $750 equals $1,074.03 as the amount to be deposited for an additional four years at 6½ percent. The total amount you have at the end of 10 years is 1.2960 204 354 × $1,074.03 = $1,391.96.

PROBLEM: You originate a $25,000, 30-year loan, to be repaid in equal monthly payments at 10 percent, compounded monthly. What is the unpaid balance at the end of the first five years?

SOLUTION: This problem requires the use of three separate tables.

First, you must determine the amount of the regular monthly payment required to amortize the loan. Refer to the monthly compounding section, Table 6, 10 percent column, 360 months, page 68. The amount there, .0087 757 157, times $25,000 equals $219.392892500, rounded up to $219.40, the monthly payment required to amortize the loan.

Second, consider how much the original loan would have grown if no payments had been made. Refer to the monthly compounding section, Table 1, 10 percent, 60 months, page 23. The amount there, 1.6453 089 348, times $25,000 equals $41,132.72, which is the amount now owed.

Third, assume that the regular monthly payments had been deposited into a savings account at 10 percent, compounded monthly for 60 months. Refer to Table 2, page 32. That amount, 77.4370 721 734, multiplied by $219.40 equals $16,989.69, the amount your regular monthly payments have accumulated.

Now, if you subtract the result obtained in the third step from that of the second step, you should have the unpaid balance at the end of the fifth year.

Result from second step	$41,132.72
Result from third step	16,989.69
Unpaid balance	$24,143.03

Note: Because of the variation caused by rounding, the actual balance could vary slightly.

ALTERNATIVE
SOLUTION: First, compute the monthly payment as above.

Second, assume the principal reduction is deposited into a savings account at the same interest rate and compounding periods as those on the loan, and also assume that this same amount is deposited into a savings account each time period for the time span you are working with. $25,000 × 10 percent = $2500 per annum interest ÷ 12 months = 208.33333333 as the first month's interest.

Regular monthly payment	$219.40
First month's interest	208.33333333
Principal reduction	$ 11.06666667

Third, refer to the monthly compounding section, Table 2, 10 percent, for 60 months, page 32. That amount is 77.4370 721 734 times 11.0666 666 667 equals 856.97, the amount of principal reduction at the end of the first five years.

Original loan balance	$25,000.00
Principal reduction	856.97
Loan balance	$24,143.03

PROBLEM: If you expect 8½ percent, compounded annually, on your investments, what should you pay for the right to receive $1,600 at the beginning of each year for the next 15 years?

SOLUTION: This is a little different from any problems thus far. Table 5 is constructed with payments at the end of each period. In this problem you will, in effect, have $1,600 of your initial investment returned to you immediately. Then you will receive $1,600 at the end of each of the next 14 years. Refer to the annual compounding section, Table 5, 8½ percent, for 14 years. The amount is $1,600 × 8.0100 966 847 = $12,816.15. To this add the immediate return of $1,600 = $14,416.15 as the amount you should pay for the income.

Another, perhaps more direct, solution would be to add 1 to the 14-year amount: thus, 8.0100 966 847 + 1 = 9.0100 966 847 × $1,600 = $14,416.15.

PROBLEM: You have inherited a parcel of land containing a small store which is under lease for 18 more years at a monthly rental of $325. Because of the changing character of the area, you expect the property to be worth $65,000 when the lease expires. What is the value of your inheritance if current interest rates are 7½ percent compounded monthly?

SOLUTION: In this problem, there are two values: the rental income and the right to receive $65,000 at the end of the lease period.

Refer to the monthly compounding section, Table 5, 7½ percent opposite 18 years (216 months). The amount, 118.3469 302 617, times $325 equals $38,462.75, the present worth of the series of rent payments. Now refer to the monthly compounding section, Table 4, 7½ percent, opposite 18 years (216 months). The amount, .2603 316 859, multiplied by $65,000 equals $16,921.56, which is the present worth of $65,000 to be received 18 years from now. Add these two values together: $38,462.75 + $16,921.56 = $55,384.31. This is the total value of your inheritance.

PROBLEM: You will start receiving income from a trust fund starting five years from now. This income will be $4,150 every six months, and it will continue for 20 years from the time you start receiving it. If the current interest rates are 5½ percent compounded semiannually, what is the present worth of your future receipts?

SOLUTION: The easiest way to solve this problem is to consider the present worth of the future income as if it were to start today and rerun a full 25 years. Then subtract from that value the present worth of the receipts for the first five years which you will *not* receive. Refer to the semiannual compounding section, Table 5, 5½ percent column, opposite 25 years (50 periods). That amount is 26.9971 699 802. Subtract from this the amount shown in the same table opposite five years (10 periods): 8.6400 761 634. Then 26.9971 699 802 minus 8.6400 761 634 equals 18.3570 938 168. Multiplying by $4,150, we arrive at $76,181.94 as the present worth of $4,150 every six months for the next 20 years, but delayed five years in starting.

ALTERNATIVE
SOLUTION: Another way to solve this problem is to estimate the present worth of the series of receipts for the 20-year period, then to discount the receipt of that worth because it will be delayed for five years. Refer to the semiannual compounding section, Table 5, 5½ percent, opposite 20 years (40 periods). That amount, 24.0781 010 600, times $4,150 equals $99,924.12. Now consider this as a lump sum payment you will receive five years (10 periods) from now. Refer to the semiannual compounding section, Table 4, 5½ percent, opposite 10 periods. The amount, .7623 979 055, times $99,924.12 equals $76,181.94, the present worth of your receipts.

PROBLEM: You plan to retire as soon as you can accumulate $80,000. You can get 7 percent, compounded annually. If you deposit $1,750 at the end of each year, how long will it be before you are able to retire?

SOLUTION: To solve this type of problem, you must first determine how much each $1 of your annual deposits will have to grow in order to reach your desired objective. You would therefore divide the $80,000 by the annual deposits of $1,750, making 45.7142 857 143 the amount that each $1 of the annual deposits will have to amount to.

Refer to the annual compounding section, Table 2, 7 percent column, and follow it down to the figure closest to 45.7142 857 143. The amount falls between 21 and 22 years and is closer to 21 years. For our purposes, let's use the 21-year amount of 44.8651 767 837. Multiplying that by $1,750, we obtain $78,514.06, the amount you will have at the end of 21 years.

ADDITIONAL

PROBLEM: Suppose that you were not able to start your retirement plan for five years but had some money now, and that you still wanted to have approximately $80,000 by the end of the original 21-year period, and that after five years you could make the annual deposits of $1,750. How much would you have to deposit today to start your program?

SOLUTION: Consider how much you would now have if you had made the regular deposits each year for five years. Refer to the annual compounding section, Table 2, 7 percent, opposite five years. You will see that each $1 deposited would have amounted to $5.7507 390 100. This amount times $1,750 equals $10,063.79, the amount you would now have. If you deposit that amount now, then make your regular deposits of $1,750 each year for the next 16 years, you should accumulate $78,514.06 by the end of the original 21-year period.

You can test this by referring to the same table opposite 16 years. That amount, 27.8880 535 509, times $1,750 equals $48,804.09, which is the amount now accumulated from the annual deposits for 16 years. Now add the amount your $10,063.79 initial deposit would have grown by referring to Table 1, annual compounding, 7 percent. This amount, 2.9521 637 486, multiplied by $10,063.79, will equal $29,709.96. Thus, $29,709.96 + $48,804.09 = $78,514.05.

Conversion Table

**Showing the Rate per Conversion Period
and Its Decimal Equivalent**

Annual	Semiannual	Quarterly	Monthly
5 .050000	2 1/2 .025000	1 1/4 .012500	5/12 .004167
5 1/2 .055000	2 3/4 .027500	1 3/8 .013750	11/24 .004583
6 .060000	3 .030000	1 1/2 .015000	1/2 .005000
6 1/2 .065000	3 1/4 .032500	1 5/8 .016250	13/24 .005417
7 .070000	3 1/2 .035000	1 3/4 .017500	7/12 .005833
7 1/2 .075000	3 3/4 .037500	1 7/8 .018750	5/8 .006250
8 .080000	4 .040000	2 .020000	2/3 .006667
8 1/2 .085000	4 1/4 .042500	2 1/8 .021250	17/24 .007083
9 .090000	4 1/2 .045000	2 1/4 .022500	3/4 .007500
9 1/2 .095000	4 3/4 .047500	2 3/8 .023750	19/24 .007917
10 .100000	5 .050000	2 1/2 .025000	5/6 .008333
10 1/2 .105000	5 1/4 .052500	2 5/8 .026250	7/8 .008750
11 .110000	5 1/2 .055000	2 3/4 .027500	11/12 .009167
11 1/2 .115000	5 3/4 .057500	2 7/8 .028750	23/24 .009583
12 .120000	6 .060000	3 .030000	1 .010000
12 1/2 .125000	6 1/4 .062500	3 1/8 .031250	1 1/24 .010417
13 .130000	6 1/2 .065000	3 1/4 .032500	1 1/12 .010833
13 1/2 .135000	6 3/4 .067500	3 3/8 .033750	1 1/8 .011250
14 .140000	7 .070000	3 1/2 .035000	1 1/6 .011667
14 1/2 .145000	7 1/4 .072500	3 5/8 .036250	1 5/24 .012083

Annual	Semiannual	Quarterly	Monthly
15 .150000	7 1/2 .075000	3 3/4 .037500	1 1/4 .012500
15 1/2 .155000	7 3/4 .077500	3 7/8 .038750	1 7/24 .012917
16 .160000	8 .080000	4 .040000	1 1/3 .013333
16 1/2 .165000	8 1/4 .082500	4 1/8 .041250	1 3/8 .013750
17 .170000	8 1/2 .085000	4 1/4 .042500	1 5/12 .014167
17 1/2 .175000	8 3/4 .087500	4 3/8 .043750	1 11/24 .014583
18 .180000	9 .090000	4 1/2 .045000	1 1/2 .015000
18 1/2 .185000	9 1/4 .092500	4 5/8 .046250	1 13/24 .015417
19 .190000	9 1/2 .095000	4 3/4 .047500	1 7/12 .015833
19 1/2 .195000	9 3/4 .097500	4 7/8 .048750	1 5/8 .016250
20 .200000	10 .100000	5 .050000	1 2/3 .016667
20 1/2 .205000	10 1/4 .102500	5 1/8 .051250	1 17/24 .017083
21 .210000	10 1/2 .105000	5 1/4 .052500	1 3/4 .017500
21 1/2 .215000	10 3/4 .107500	5 3/8 .053750	1 19/24 .017917
22 .220000	11 .110000	5 1/2 .055000	1 5/6 .018333
22 1/2 .225000	11 1/4 .112500	5 5/8 .056250	1 7/8 .018750
23 .230000			
24 .240000			
25 .250000			
26 .260000			
27 .270000			
28 .280000			
29 .290000			
30 .300000			

Table 1.   FUTURE WORTH OF ONE DOLLAR WITH INTEREST
PAYABLE AT BEGINNING OF EACH PERIOD

	5% NOMINAL ANNUAL RATE	5½% NOMINAL ANNUAL RATE	6% NOMINAL ANNUAL RATE	6½% NOMINAL ANNUAL RATE	
MONTHS					**MONTHS**
1	1.0041 666 667	1.0045 833 333	1.0050 000 000	1.0054 166 667	1
2	1.0083 506 944	1.0091 876 736	1.0100 250 000	1.0108 626 736	2
3	1.0125 521 557	1.0138 131 171	1.0150 751 250	1.0163 381 798	3
4	1.0167 711 230	1.0184 597 606	1.0201 505 006	1.0218 433 449	4
5	1.0210 076 693	1.0231 277 011	1.0252 512 531	1.0273 783 297	5
6	1.0252 618 680	1.0278 170 364	1.0303 775 094	1.0329 432 956	6
7	1.0295 337 924	1.0325 278 645	1.0355 293 969	1.0385 384 052	7
8	1.0338 235 165	1.0372 602 839	1.0407 070 439	1.0441 638 215	8
9	1.0381 311 145	1.0420 143 935	1.0459 105 791	1.0498 197 089	9
10	1.0424 566 608	1.0467 902 928	1.0511 401 320	1.0555 062 323	10
11	1.0468 002 303	1.0515 880 817	1.0563 958 327	1.0612 235 577	11
YEARS					
1	1.0511 618 979	1.0564 078 604	1.0616 778 119	1.0669 718 520	12
2	1.1049 413 356	1.1159 975 675	1.1271 597 762	1.1384 289 330	24
3	1.1614 722 313	1.1789 486 025	1.1966 805 248	1.2146 716 270	36
4	1.2208 953 550	1.2454 505 706	1.2704 891 611	1.2960 204 354	48
5	1.2833 586 785	1.3157 037 725	1.3488 501 525	1.3828 173 242	60
6	1.3490 177 442	1.3899 198 072	1.4320 442 785	1.4754 271 614	72
7	1.4180 360 522	1.4683 222 097	1.5203 696 361	1.5742 392 509	84
8	1.4905 854 679	1.5511 471 239	1.6141 427 085	1.6796 689 690	96
9	1.5668 466 494	1.6386 440 143	1.7136 994 988	1.7921 595 106	108
10	1.6470 094 977	1.7310 764 171	1.8193 967 340	1.9121 837 521	120
11	1.7312 736 294	1.8287 227 339	1.9316 131 435	2.0402 462 394	132
12	1.8198 488 741	1.9318 770 706	2.0507 343 156	2.1768 853 086	144
13	1.9129 557 963	2.0408 501 227	2.1772 366 385	2.3226 753 493	156
14	2.0108 262 454	2.1559 701 114	2.3115 238 303	2.4782 292 190	168
15	2.1137 039 324	2.2775 837 725	2.4540 935 622	2.6442 008 195	180
16	2.2218 450 372	2.4060 573 999	2.6054 566 833	2.8212 878 455	192
17	2.3355 188 461	2.5417 779 498	2.7661 555 504	3.0102 347 175	204
18	2.4550 084 228	2.6851 542 056	2.9367 659 720	3.2118 357 115	216
19	2.5806 113 130	2.8366 180 091	3.1178 992 711	3.4269 382 974	228
20	2.7126 402 855	2.9966 255 617	3.3102 044 758	3.6564 467 019	240
21	2.8514 241 108	3.1656 587 980	3.5143 706 447	3.9013 257 093	252
22	2.9973 083 799	3.3442 268 375	3.7311 293 361	4.1626 047 173	264
23	3.1506 563 652	3.5328 675 181	3.9612 572 294	4.4413 820 644	276
24	3.3118 499 244	3.7321 490 158	4.2055 789 075	4.7388 296 467	288
25	3.4812 904 520	3.9426 715 564	4.4649 698 122	5.0561 978 444	300
26	3.6593 998 786	4.1650 692 231	4.7403 593 802	5.3948 207 781	312
27	3.8466 217 215	4.4000 118 664	5.0327 343 742	5.7561 219 169	324
28	4.0434 221 892	4.6482 071 214	5.3431 424 181	6.1416 200 620	336
29	4.2502 913 424	4.9104 025 398	5.6726 957 510	6.5529 357 319	348
30	4.4677 443 140	5.1873 878 407	6.0225 752 123	6.9917 979 739	360
31	4.6963 225 924	5.4799 972 898	6.3940 344 731	7.4600 516 330	372
32	4.9365 953 693	5.7891 122 118	6.7884 045 284	7.9596 651 069	384
33	5.1891 609 574	6.1156 636 452	7.2070 984 658	8.4927 386 204	396
34	5.4546 482 804	6.4606 351 463	7.6516 165 291	9.0615 130 544	408
35	5.7337 184 387	6.8250 657 516	8.1235 514 938	9.6683 793 656	420
36	6.0270 663 560	7.2100 531 076	8.6245 943 745	10.3158 886 376	432
37	6.3354 225 094	7.6167 567 767	9.1565 404 837	11.0067 628 047	444
38	6.6595 547 489	8.0464 017 295	9.7212 958 650	11.7439 060 943	456
39	7.0002 702 089	8.5002 820 349	10.3208 841 225	12.5304 172 352	468
40	7.3584 173 184	8.9797 647 572	10.9574 536 717	13.3696 024 838	480
41	7.7348 879 138	9.4862 940 739	11.6332 854 377	14.2649 895 226	492
42	8.1306 194 594	10.0213 956 256	12.3508 010 283	15.2203 422 898	504
43	8.5465 973 819	10.5866 811 109	13.1125 714 105	16.2396 768 010	516
44	8.9838 575 244	11.1838 531 409	13.9213 261 230	17.3272 780 323	528
45	9.4434 887 256	11.8147 103 675	14.7799 630 566	18.4877 179 323	540
46	9.9266 355 315	12.4811 529 004	15.6915 588 373	19.7258 746 415	552
47	10.4345 010 448	13.1851 880 307	16.6593 798 512	21.0469 529 996	564
48	10.9683 499 217	13.9289 362 762	17.6868 939 474	22.4565 064 200	576
49	11.5295 115 204	14.7146 377 690	18.7777 828 648	23.9604 602 444	588
50	12.1193 832 114	15.5446 590 019	19.9359 554 235	25.5651 366 418	600

Table 1.   FUTURE WORTH OF ONE DOLLAR WITH INTEREST
PAYABLE AT BEGINNING OF EACH PERIOD

MONTHS	7% NOMINAL ANNUAL RATE	7½% NOMINAL ANNUAL RATE	8% NOMINAL ANNUAL RATE	8½% NOMINAL ANNUAL RATE	MONTHS
1	1.0058 333 333	1.0062 500 000	1.0066 666 667	1.0070 833 333	1
2	1.0117 006 944	1.0125 390 625	1.0133 777 778	1.0142 168 403	2
3	1.0176 022 818	1.0188 674 316	1.0201 336 296	1.0214 008 762	3
4	1.0235 382 951	1.0252 353 531	1.0269 345 205	1.0286 357 991	4
5	1.0295 089 352	1.0316 430 740	1.0337 807 506	1.0359 219 693	5
6	1.0355 144 040	1.0380 908 433	1.0406 726 223	1.0432 597 500	6
7	1.0415 549 047	1.0445 789 110	1.0476 104 398	1.0506 495 065	7
8	1.0476 306 416	1.0511 075 292	1.0545 945 094	1.0580 916 072	8
9	1.0537 418 204	1.0576 769 513	1.0616 251 394	1.0655 864 227	9
10	1.0598 886 476	1.0642 874 322	1.0687 026 404	1.0731 343 266	10
11	1.0660 713 314	1.0709 392 287	1.0758 273 246	1.0807 356 947	11

YEARS					
1	1.0722 900 809	1.0776 325 989	1.0829 995 068	1.0883 909 059	12
2	1.1498 060 175	1.1612 920 181	1.1728 879 317	1.1845 947 640	24
3	1.2329 255 875	1.2514 461 355	1.2702 370 516	1.2893 021 683	36
4	1.3220 538 779	1.3485 991 513	1.3756 661 004	1.4032 647 550	48
5	1.4176 252 596	1.4532 944 083	1.4898 457 083	1.5273 005 979	60
6	1.5201 055 043	1.5661 174 301	1.6135 021 673	1.6623 000 813	72
7	1.6299 940 541	1.6876 991 963	1.7474 220 514	1.8092 322 913	84
8	1.7478 264 560	1.8187 196 710	1.8924 572 199	1.9691 519 725	96
9	1.8741 769 719	1.9599 116 057	2.0495 302 358	2.1432 070 992	108
10	2.0096 613 767	2.1120 646 371	2.2196 402 345	2.3326 471 162	120
11	2.1549 399 601	2.2760 297 039	2.4038 692 793	2.5388 319 080	132
12	2.3107 207 441	2.4527 238 048	2.6033 892 439	2.7632 415 602	144
13	2.4777 629 335	2.6431 351 281	2.8194 692 672	3.0074 869 849	156
14	2.6568 806 163	2.8483 285 772	3.0534 838 258	3.2733 214 840	168
15	2.8489 467 309	3.0694 517 271	3.3069 214 774	3.5626 533 352	180
16	3.0548 973 204	3.3077 412 417	3.5813 943 291	3.8775 594 909	192
17	3.2757 360 947	3.5645 297 906	3.8786 482 921	4.2203 004 870	204
18	3.5125 393 219	3.8412 535 020	4.2005 741 874	4.5933 366 702	216
19	3.7664 610 734	4.1394 599 942	4.5492 197 733	4.9993 458 595	228
20	4.0387 388 490	4.4608 170 314	4.9268 027 708	5.4412 425 689	240
21	4.3306 996 069	4.8071 218 506	5.3357 249 709	5.9221 989 288	252
22	4.6437 662 317	5.1803 112 129	5.7785 875 120	6.4456 674 569	264
23	4.9794 644 680	5.5824 722 352	6.2582 074 255	7.0154 058 425	276
24	5.3394 303 571	6.0158 540 628	6.7776 355 553	7.6355 039 202	288
25	5.7254 182 093	6.4828 804 481	7.3401 759 637	8.3104 130 286	300
26	6.1393 091 546	6.9861 633 053	7.9494 069 486	9.0449 779 646	312
27	6.5831 203 098	7.5285 173 188	8.6092 038 048	9.8444 717 606	324
28	7.0590 146 093	8.1129 756 838	9.3237 634 746	10.7146 335 376	336
29	7.5693 113 461	8.7428 070 705	10.0976 312 445	11.6617 097 023	348
30	8.1164 974 754	9.4215 339 047	10.9357 296 578	12.6924 987 871	360
31	8.7032 397 341	10.1529 520 670	11.8433 898 259	13.8144 002 530	372
32	9.3323 976 341	10.9411 521 220	12.8263 853 404	15.0354 676 057	384
33	10.0070 374 181	11.7905 421 957	13.8909 689 978	16.3644 662 079	396
34	10.7304 469 621	12.7058 726 283	15.0439 125 737	17.8109 362 004	408
35	11.5061 518 407	13.6922 625 411	16.2925 498 978	19.3852 609 860	420
36	12.3379 324 876	14.7552 284 664	17.6448 235 039	21.0987 417 655	432
37	13.2298 426 247	15.9007 151 990	19.1093 351 524	22.9636 786 633	444
38	14.1862 290 177	17.1351 290 435	20.6954 005 455	24.9934 590 230	456
39	15.2117 526 605	18.4653 736 429	22.4131 085 840	27.2026 535 075	468
40	16.3114 114 903	19.8988 885 877	24.2733 855 425	29.6071 206 937	480
41	17.4905 647 458	21.4436 910 231	26.2880 645 710	32.2241 209 126	492
42	18.7549 590 855	23.1084 204 863	28.4699 609 654	35.0724 401 517	504
43	20.1107 565 942	24.9023 872 241	30.8329 536 843	38.1725 249 086	516
44	21.5645 648 145	26.8356 242 620	33.3920 736 335	41.5466 289 655	528
45	23.1234 689 486	28.9189 435 154	36.1635 992 764	45.2189 731 365	540
46	24.7950 663 885	31.1639 962 567	39.1651 601 807	49.2159 191 356	552
47	26.5875 037 426	33.5833 382 768	42.4158 491 597	53.5661 588 123	564
48	28.5095 165 379	36.1905 001 055	45.5363 437 208	58.3009 201 149	576
49	30.5704 717 936	39.0000 626 826	49.7490 375 942	63.4541 912 582	588
50	32.7804 136 714	42.0277 389 042	53.8781 831 787	69.0629 647 062	600

Table 1. FUTURE WORTH OF ONE DOLLAR WITH INTEREST
PAYABLE AT BEGINNING OF EACH PERIOD

MONTHS	9% NOMINAL ANNUAL RATE	9½% NOMINAL ANNUAL RATE	10% NOMINAL ANNUAL RATE	10½% NOMINAL ANNUAL RATE	MONTHS
1	1.0075 000 000	1.0079 166 667	1.0083 333 333	1.0087 500 000	1
2	1.0150 562 500	1.0158 960 069	1.0167 361 111	1.0175 765 625	2
3	1.0226 691 719	1.0239 385 170	1.0252 089 120	1.0264 803 574	3
4	1.0303 391 907	1.0320 446 969	1.0337 523 196	1.0354 620 605	4
5	1.0380 667 346	1.0402 150 508	1.0423 669 223	1.0445 223 536	5
6	1.0458 522 351	1.0484 500 866	1.0510 533 133	1.0536 619 242	6
7	1.0536 961 269	1.0567 503 164	1.0598 120 909	1.0628 814 660	7
8	1.0615 988 478	1.0651 162 565	1.0686 438 584	1.0721 816 788	8
9	1.0695 608 392	1.0735 484 268	1.0775 492 238	1.0815 632 685	9
10	1.0775 825 455	1.0820 473 519	1.0865 288 007	1.0910 269 471	10
11	1.0856 644 146	1.0906 135 601	1.0955 832 074	1.1005 734 329	11
YEARS					
1	1.0938 068 977	1.0992 475 841	1.1047 130 674	1.1102 034 505	12
2	1.1964 135 294	1.2083 452 511	1.2203 909 614	1.2325 517 014	24
3	1.3086 453 709	1.3282 705 980	1.3481 818 424	1.3683 831 517	36
4	1.4314 053 333	1.4600 982 459	1.4893 540 986	1.5191 836 966	48
5	1.5656 810 269	1.6050 094 693	1.6453 089 348	1.6866 029 818	60
6	1.7125 527 068	1.7643 027 816	1.8175 942 802	1.8724 724 500	72
7	1.8732 019 633	1.9394 055 702	2.0079 201 527	2.0788 253 749	84
8	2.0489 212 282	2.1318 868 876	2.2181 756 310	2.3079 191 041	96
9	2.2411 241 722	2.3434 715 107	2.4504 476 055	2.5622 597 527	108
10	2.4513 570 781	2.5760 553 965	2.7070 414 909	2.8446 296 184	120
11	2.6813 112 807	2.8317 226 711	2.9905 041 091	3.1581 176 176	132
12	2.9328 367 736	3.1127 643 050	3.3036 489 675	3.5061 530 760	144
13	3.2079 570 928	3.4216 986 421	3.6495 841 847	3.8925 432 428	156
14	3.5088 855 955	3.7612 939 658	4.0317 433 395	4.3215 149 391	168
15	3.8380 432 675	4.1345 933 049	4.4539 195 517	4.7977 607 966	180
16	4.1980 781 995	4.5449 417 016	4.9203 031 301	5.3264 905 908	192
17	4.5918 868 916	4.9960 161 852	5.4355 231 636	5.9134 882 328	204
18	5.0226 375 554	5.4918 587 216	6.0046 934 672	6.5651 750 402	216
19	5.4937 956 026	6.0369 124 319	6.6334 633 392	7.2886 799 825	228
20	6.0091 515 245	6.6360 614 060	7.3280 736 332	8.0919 176 658	240
21	6.5728 513 866	7.2946 744 684	8.0954 187 018	8.9836 749 133	252
22	7.1894 301 840	8.0186 532 861	8.9431 148 263	9.9737 068 865	264
23	7.8638 483 256	8.8144 852 523	9.8795 758 123	11.0728 437 992	276
24	8.6015 315 408	9.6893 016 185	10.9140 945 006	12.2931 093 922	288
25	9.4084 145 299	10.6509 413 955	12.0569 450 235	13.6478 524 640	300
26	10.2909 887 089	11.7080 215 972	13.3194 647 209	15.1518 928 968	312
27	11.2563 544 337	12.8700 144 551	14.7141 867 285	16.8216 837 749	324
28	12.3122 781 222	14.1473 322 969	16.2549 543 557	18.6754 913 693	336
29	13.4672 547 361	15.5514 208 486	17.9570 604 874	20.7335 949 570	348
30	14.7305 761 230	17.0948 617 968	19.8373 993 733	23.0185 086 616	360
31	16.1124 057 700	18.7914 855 303	21.9146 343 117	25.5552 277 403	372
32	17.6238 605 694	20.6564 950 705	24.2093 828 924	28.3715 020 144	384
33	19.2771 002 544	22.7066 023 018	26.7444 216 359	31.4981 394 309	396
34	21.0854 252 253	24.9601 777 230	29.5449 120 623	34.9693 430 790	408
35	23.0633 835 518	27.4374 150 602	32.6386 504 317	38.8230 853 463	420
36	25.2268 880 125	30.1605 122 184	36.0563 436 355	43.1015 233 086	432
37	27.5933 441 149	33.1538 701 907	39.8319 139 783	47.8514 598 970	444
38	30.1817 901 227	36.4443 117 101	44.0028 358 730	53.1248 558 868	456
39	33.0130 502 203	40.0613 216 008	48.6105 077 934	58.9793 983 103	468
40	36.1099 020 441	44.0373 109 848	53.7006 631 743	65.4791 315 096	480
41	39.4972 599 300	48.4079 077 094	59.3238 243 389	72.6951 577 346	492
42	43.2023 753 506	53.2122 756 000	65.5358 039 578	80.7064 149 481	504
43	47.2550 561 542	58.4934 653 968	72.3982 590 175	89.6005 403 490	516
44	51.6879 063 713	64.2988 005 219	79.9793 027 966	99.4748 290 578	528
45	56.5365 885 151	70.6803 011 330	88.3541 809 243	110.4372 984 530	540
46	61.8401 104 886	77.6951 502 626	97.6060 182 301	122.6078 698 011	552
47	67.6411 394 052	85.4062 062 210	107.8266 437 997	136.1196 801 058	564
48	73.9863 448 477	93.8825 658 539	119.1175 024 239	151.1205 385 278	576
49	80.9267 743 279	103.2001 837 022	131.5906 614 886	167.7745 433 077	588
50	88.5182 639 661	113.4425 526 114	145.3699 232 997	186.2638 768 782	600

23

Table 1. FUTURE WORTH OF ONE DOLLAR WITH INTEREST
PAYABLE AT BEGINNING OF EACH PERIOD

MONTHS	11% NOMINAL ANNUAL RATE	11½% NOMINAL ANNUAL RATE	12% NOMINAL ANNUAL RATE	12½% NOMINAL ANNUAL RATE	MONTHS
1	1.0091 666 667	1.0095 833 333	1.0100 000 000	1.0104 166 667	1
2	1.0184 173 611	1.0192 585 069	1.0201 000 000	1.0209 418 403	2
3	1.0277 528 536	1.0290 264 010	1.0303 010 000	1.0315 766 511	3
4	1.0371 739 214	1.0388 879 040	1.0406 040 100	1.0423 222 412	4
5	1.0466 813 490	1.0488 439 131	1.0510 100 501	1.0531 797 646	5
6	1.0562 759 281	1.0588 953 339	1.0615 201 506	1.0641 503 871	6
7	1.0659 584 574	1.0690 430 808	1.0721 353 521	1.0752 352 870	7
8	1.0757 297 433	1.0792 880 770	1.0828 567 056	1.0864 356 546	8
9	1.0855 905 992	1.0896 312 544	1.0936 852 727	1.0977 526 926	9
10	1.0955 418 464	1.1000 735 540	1.1046 221 254	1.1091 876 165	10
11	1.1055 843 133	1.1106 159 255	1.1156 683 467	1.1207 416 542	11

YEARS					
1	1.1157 188 362	1.1212 593 281	1.1268 250 301	1.1324 160 464	12
2	1.2448 285 214	1.2572 224 809	1.2697 346 485	1.2823 661 022	24
3	1.3888 786 292	1.4096 724 343	1.4307 687 836	1.4521 719 515	36
4	1.5495 980 478	1.5806 083 666	1.6122 260 777	1.6444 628 200	48
5	1.7289 157 305	1.7722 718 752	1.8166 966 986	1.8622 160 851	60
6	1.9289 838 467	1.9871 763 720	2.0470 993 121	2.1088 033 767	72
7	2.1522 036 124	2.2281 400 438	2.3067 227 440	2.3880 427 825	84
8	2.4012 541 097	2.4983 228 085	2.5992 729 256	2.7042 579 664	96
9	2.6791 244 407	2.8012 677 537	2.9289 257 927	3.0623 451 148	108
10	2.9891 496 030	3.1409 475 995	3.3003 868 946	3.4678 487 477	120
11	3.3350 505 163	3.5218 167 951	3.7189 585 619	3.9270 475 684	132
12	3.7209 786 807	3.9488 699 335	4.1906 155 936	4.4470 516 815	144
13	4.1515 660 031	4.4277 072 485	4.7220 905 425	5.0359 126 834	156
14	4.6319 803 894	4.9646 080 547	5.3209 698 179	5.7027 483 310	168
15	5.1679 877 693	5.5666 130 918	5.9958 019 754	6.4578 837 187	180
16	5.7660 212 995	6.2416 168 554	6.7562 197 415	7.3130 111 489	192
17	6.4332 585 737	6.9984 711 217	7.6130 775 138	8.2813 711 727	204
18	7.1777 077 688	7.8471 010 280	8.5786 062 989	9.3779 576 023	216
19	8.0083 037 584	8.7986 352 264	9.6665 883 013	10.6197 496 714	228
20	8.9350 153 492	9.8655 518 225	10.8925 536 539	12.0259 749 368	240
21	9.9689 649 268	11.0618 420 082	12.2740 020 992	13.6184 069 922	252
22	11.1225 619 462	12.4031 935 381	13.8306 527 853	15.4217 026 046	264
23	12.4096 518 701	13.9071 964 533	15.5847 257 416	17.4637 834 925	276
24	13.8456 823 421	15.5935 737 515	17.5612 590 533	19.7762 686 580	288
25	15.4478 885 890	17.4844 400 279	19.7884 662 619	22.3949 639 666	300
26	17.2355 002 782	19.6045 914 786	22.2981 390 919	25.3604 165 546	312
27	19.2299 723 117	21.9818 310 697	25.1261 012 541	28.7185 426 503	324
28	21.4552 423 276	24.6473 331 364	28.3127 198 027	32.5213 385 268	336
29	23.9380 180 001	27.6360 521 929	31.9034 813 448	36.8276 855 987	348
30	26.7080 975 839	30.9871 813 142	35.9496 413 277	41.7042 621 243	360
31	29.7987 275 532	34.7446 661 013	40.5089 556 723	47.2265 756 334	372
32	33.2470 016 258	38.9577 809 691	45.6465 051 961	53.4801 320 645	384
33	37.0943 059 609	43.6817 753 152	51.4356 245 930	60.5617 597 143	396
34	41.3868 158 762	48.9785 980 418	57.9589 492 318	68.5811 084 996	408
35	46.1760 500 432	54.9177 099 335	65.3095 947 146	77.6623 477 459	420
36	51.5194 888 143	61.5769 945 429	73.5924 860 322	87.9460 887 897	432
37	57.4812 641 013	69.0437 795 299	82.9258 552 907	99.5915 621 650	444
38	64.1329 290 861	77.4159 818 478	93.4429 293 866	112.7790 830 832	456
39	71.5543 170 017	86.8033 917 938	105.2938 317 217	127.7128 433 834	468
40	79.8344 992 099	97.3291 127 629	118.6477 251 025	144.6240 731 807	480
41	89.0728 546 360	109.1311 755 848	133.6952 264 137	163.7746 211 677	492
42	99.3802 617 110	122.3643 486 151	150.6511 275 322	185.4610 090 059	504
43	110.8804 299 370	137.2021 673 162	169.7574 613 208	210.0190 225 827	516
44	123.7113 842 461	153.8392 099 440	191.2869 564 680	237.8289 112 251	528
45	138.0271 216 552	172.4936 491 831	215.5469 304 859	269.3212 753 727	540
46	153.9994 505 365	193.4101 131 911	242.8836 764 396	304.9837 338 731	552
47	171.8200 977 688	216.8628 935 718	273.6874 060 226	345.3684 741 336	564
48	191.7029 195 175	243.1595 423 444	308.3978 195 382	391.1008 020 348	576
49	213.8865 582 593	272.6449 050 794	347.5103 822 937	442.8888 239 901	588
50	238.6372 618 589	305.7056 430 896	391.5833 969 993	501.5344 110 644	600

Table 1. FUTURE WORTH OF ONE DOLLAR WITH INTEREST
PAYABLE AT BEGINNING OF EACH PERIOD

MONTHS	13% NOMINAL ANNUAL RATE	13½% NOMINAL ANNUAL RATE	14% NOMINAL ANNUAL RATE	14½% NOMINAL ANNUAL RATE	MONTHS
1	1.0108 333 333	1.0112 500 000	1.0116 666 667	1.0120 833 333	1
2	1.0217 840 278	1.0226 265 625	1.0234 694 444	1.0243 126 736	2
3	1.0328 533 547	1.0341 311 113	1.0354 099 213	1.0366 897 851	3
4	1.0440 425 994	1.0457 650 863	1.0474 897 037	1.0492 164 533	4
5	1.0553 530 609	1.0575 299 436	1.0597 104 169	1.0618 944 855	5
6	1.0667 860 524	1.0694 271 554	1.0720 737 051	1.0747 257 105	6
7	1.0783 429 013	1.0814 582 109	1.0845 812 317	1.0877 119 795	7
8	1.0900 249 494	1.0936 246 158	1.0972 346 794	1.1008 551 659	8
9	1.1018 335 530	1.1059 278 927	1.1100 357 506	1.1141 571 658	9
10	1.1137 700 832	1.1183 695 815	1.1229 861 677	1.1276 198 983	10
11	1.1258 359 258	1.1309 512 393	1.1360 876 730	1.1412 453 054	11

YEARS					
1	1.1380 324 816	1.1436 744 407	1.1493 420 292	1.1550 353 528	12
2	1.2951 179 292	1.3079 912 264	1.3209 871 001	1.3341 066 662	24
3	1.4738 862 710	1.4959 161 344	1.5182 659 942	1.5409 403 639	36
4	1.6773 304 506	1.7108 410 484	1.7450 069 186	1.7798 405 969	48
5	1.9088 565 351	1.9566 451 792	2.0056 097 928	2.0557 788 117	60
6	2.1723 407 397	2.2377 650 810	2.3051 316 291	2.3744 972 051	72
7	2.4721 943 229	2.5592 747 276	2.6493 846 642	2.7426 282 170	84
8	2.8134 374 404	2.9269 770 928	3.0450 491 461	3.1678 325 503	96
9	3.2017 831 971	3.3475 088 896	3.4998 029 646	3.6589 585 873	108
10	3.6437 332 717	3.8284 603 572	4.0224 706 412	4.2262 265 228	120
11	4.1466 868 176	4.3785 122 580	4.6231 945 691	4.8814 410 428	132
12	4.7190 642 895	5.0075 925 579	5.3136 318 275	5.6382 369 771	144
13	5.3704 484 442	5.7270 556 181	6.1071 803 871	6.5123 630 360	156
14	6.1117 447 704	6.5498 871 312	7.0192 390 988	7.5220 095 369	168
15	6.9553 640 680	7.4909 385 017	8.0675 065 093	8.6881 869 392	180
16	7.9154 302 308	8.5671 949 015	9.2723 243 021	10.0351 630 666	192
17	9.0080 167 087	9.7980 818 377	10.6570 720 288	11.5909 681 130	204
18	10.2514 156 094	11.2058 157 661	12.2486 207 910	13.3879 779 438	216
19	11.6664 439 460	12.8158 050 794	14.0778 546 749	15.4635 878 276	228
20	13.2767 921 555	14.6571 087 068	16.1802 700 590	17.8609 906 221	240
21	15.1094 207 245	16.7629 606 032	18.5966 644 227	20.6300 756 046	252
22	17.1950 115 629	19.1713 695 930	21.3739 280 241	23.8284 666 543	264
23	19.5684 816 803	21.9258 053 976	24.5659 538 073	27.5227 213 889	276
24	22.2695 677 681	25.0759 832 259	28.2346 831 983	31.7897 162 095	288
25	25.3434 914 715	28.6787 610 920	32.4513 080 812	36.7182 460 776	300
26	28.8417 164 921	32.7991 660 531	37.2976 522 804	42.4108 723 126	312
27	32.8228 101 935	37.5115 678 926	42.8677 593 567	48.9860 568 643	324
28	37.3534 241 381	42.9010 214 309	49.2697 175 266	56.5806 274 727	336
29	42.5094 099 686	49.0648 016 923	56.6277 571 204	65.3526 250 149	348
30	48.3770 893 186	56.1141 596 356	65.0846 612 783	75.4845 922 907	360
31	55.0546 990 105	64.1763 301 390	74.8045 366 638	87.1873 726 877	372
32	62.6540 357 394	73.3968 284 807	85.9759 979 631	100.7044 497 724	384
33	71.3023 277 756	83.9420 767 649	98.8158 279 620	116.3172 551 135	396
34	81.1443 650 233	96.0024 076 989	113.5731 842 276	134.3505 417 973	408
35	92.3449 230 965	109.7954 999 350	130.5344 340 237	155.1796 254 442	420
36	105.0915 219 959	125.5703 069 842	150.0287 112 822	179.2379 534 229	432
37	119.5975 655 736	143.6115 506 141	172.4343 034 644	207.0261 727 677	444
38	136.1059 143 447	164.2448 598 328	198.1859 922 487	239.1225 485 024	456
39	154.8929 514 640	187.8426 482 141	227.7834 904 916	276.1949 971 729	468
40	176.2732 099 391	214.8308 356 439	261.8011 391 815	319.0149 860 023	480
41	200.6046 385 490	245.6965 358 093	300.8990 525 556	368.4735 869 069	492
42	228.2945 946 312	280.9968 481 842	345.8359 276 508	425.6000 194 520	504
43	259.8066 640 672	321.3689 131 975	397.4837 668 589	491.5830 686 211	516
44	295.6684 226 482	367.5414 120 733	456.8447 991 785	567.7958 230 973	528
45	336.4802 687 612	420.3477 189 027	525.0709 285 205	655.8242 488 518	540
46	382.9254 752 724	480.7409 423 335	603.4860 864 635	757.5001 926 499	552
47	435.7816 288 975	549.8111 283 655	693.6119 232 142	874.9395 022 665	564
48	495.9336 485 759	628.8049 347 475	797.1973 353 093	1010.5860 566 825	576
49	564.3886 008 047	719.1481 320 836	916.2524 030 429	1167.2626 225 191	588
50	642.2925 599 683	822.4713 377 719	1053.0873 961 793	1348.2295 950 162	600

Table 1.   FUTURE WORTH OF ONE DOLLAR WITH INTEREST PAYABLE AT BEGINNING OF EACH PERIOD

MONTHS	15% NOMINAL ANNUAL RATE	15½% NOMINAL ANNUAL RATE	16% NOMINAL ANNUAL RATE	16½% NOMINAL ANNUAL RATE	MONTHS
1	1.0125 000 000	1.0129 166 667	1.0133 333 333	1.0137 500 000	1
2	1.0251 562 500	1.0260 001 736	1.0268 444 444	1.0276 890 625	2
3	1.0379 707 031	1.0392 526 759	1.0405 357 037	1.0418 197 871	3
4	1.0509 453 369	1.0526 763 563	1.0544 095 131	1.0561 448 092	4
5	1.0640 821 536	1.0662 734 259	1.0684 683 066	1.0706 668 003	5
6	1.0773 831 805	1.0800 461 243	1.0827 145 507	1.0853 884 688	6
7	1.0908 504 703	1.0939 967 200	1.0971 507 447	1.1003 125 603	7
8	1.1044 861 012	1.1081 275 110	1.1117 794 213	1.1154 418 580	8
9	1.1182 921 774	1.1224 408 247	1.1266 031 469	1.1307 791 835	9
10	1.1322 708 297	1.1369 390 187	1.1416 245 222	1.1463 273 973	10
11	1.1464 242 150	1.1516 244 810	1.1568 461 825	1.1620 893 990	11

YEARS	15%	15½%	16%	16½%	MONTHS
1	1.1607 545 177	1.1664 996 305	1.1722 707 983	1.1780 681 282	12
2	1.3473 510 504	1.3607 213 881	1.3742 188 245	1.3878 445 148	24
3	1.5639 438 187	1.5872 809 965	1.6109 565 983	1.6349 753 898	36
4	1.8153 548 531	1.8515 626 959	1.8884 773 775	1.9261 123 971	48
5	2.1071 813 470	2.1598 472 008	2.2138 068 828	2.2690 916 265	60
6	2.4459 202 681	2.5194 609 617	2.5951 811 617	2.6731 445 252	72
7	2.8391 130 012	2.9389 502 810	3.0422 550 920	3.1491 463 673	84
8	3.2955 132 425	3.4282 844 170	3.5663 468 052	3.7099 089 664	96
9	3.8252 818 844	3.9990 925 059	4.1807 242 162	4.3705 255 120	108
10	4.4402 132 289	4.6649 399 306	4.9009 409 143	5.1487 768 093	120
11	5.1539 975 651	5.4416 507 056	5.7452 299 178	6.0656 098 584	132
12	5.9825 259 581	6.3476 835 377	6.7349 652 619	7.1457 016 524	144
13	6.9442 440 332	7.4045 705 015	7.8952 031 038	8.4181 233 706	156
14	8.0605 626 337	8.6374 287 544	9.2553 160 449	9.9171 228 424	168
15	9.3563 344 925	10.0755 574 509	10.8497 367 281	11.6830 463 444	180
16	10.8604 075 315	11.7531 340 440	12.7188 295 352	13.7634 245 389	192
17	12.6062 671 065	13.7100 265 201	14.9099 124 521	16.2142 517 846	204
18	14.6327 814 955	15.9927 408 706	17.4784 549 722	19.1014 932 506	216
19	16.9850 672 278	18.6555 263 170	20.4894 823 626	22.5028 604 002	228
20	19.7154 935 184	21.7616 645 564	24.0192 218 451	26.5099 026 315	240
21	22.8848 481 707	25.3849 736 652	28.1570 323 660	31.2304 713 727	252
22	26.5636 909 015	29.6115 624 019	33.0076 668 083	36.7916 229 538	264
23	30.8339 242 213	34.5418 766 018	38.6939 239 180	43.3430 383 878	276
24	35.7906 168 390	40.2930 862 944	45.3597 570 791	51.0610 521 053	288
25	41.5441 201 880	47.0018 702 761	53.1739 186 399	60.1533 980 793	300
26	48.2225 251 931	54.8276 643 121	62.3342 320 506	70.8648 010 820	312
27	55.9745 139 739	63.9564 501 639	73.0725 999 648	83.4835 635 681	324
28	64.9726 699 725	74.6051 754 873	85.6608 750 916	98.3493 254 708	336
29	75.4173 201 991	87.0269 096 429	100.4177 424 232	115.8622 057 702	348
30	87.5409 951 357	101.5168 579 462	117.7167 870 698	136.4935 718 845	360
31	101.6136 055 807	118.4193 772 887	137.9959 519 467	160.7987 267 456	372
32	117.9484 517 504	138.1361 598 570	161.7686 247 451	189.4318 550 392	384
33	136.9091 982 277	161.1357 794 385	189.6366 348 632	223.1636 308 934	396
34	158.9179 703 606	187.9648 271 832	222.3054 893 302	262.9019 609 359	408
35	184.4647 520 434	219.2609 014 652	260.6022 334 344	309.7164 210 281	420
36	214.1182 942 951	255.7677 605 528	305.4963 882 162	364.8670 444 031	432
37	248.5387 774 302	298.3529 981 910	358.1244 948 794	429.8382 360 533	444
38	288.4925 087 314	348.0286 621 627	419.8188 874 884	506.3787 261 896	456
39	334.8689 828 392	405.9753 058 330	492.1414 223 601	596.5486 381 384	468
40	388.7006 846 759	473.5700 442 658	576.9230 180 464	702.7749 375 307	480
41	451.1860 757 796	552.4192 816 748	676.3100 068 991	827.9167 552 248	492
42	523.7162 757 949	644.3968 879 813	792.8184 716 581	975.3423 421 591	504
43	607.9060 331 340	751.6887 317 565	929.3979 426 450	1149.0197 274 122	516
44	705.6296 743 113	876.8446 278 812	1089.5060 681 247	1353.6235 195 735	528
45	819.0628 322 963	1022.8389 344 716	1277.1961 481 884	1594.6607 260 339	540
46	950.7308 828 869	1193.1412 391 713	1497.2197 481 700	1878.6189 766 829	552
47	1103.5651 674 498	1391.7988 146 851	1755.1469 893 562	2213.1411 415 208	564
48	1280.9682 537 191	1623.5328 031 275	2057.5075 622 742	2607.2310 421 034	576
49	1486.8896 875 641	1893.8504 150 311	2411.9560 324 509	3071.4957 936 376	588
50	1725.9139 221 958	2209.1758 094 472	2827.4656 235 265	3618.4313 004 813	600

Table 1.   FUTURE WORTH OF ONE DOLLAR WITH INTEREST
PAYABLE AT BEGINNING OF EACH PERIOD

MONTHS	17% NOMINAL ANNUAL RATE	17½% NOMINAL ANNUAL RATE	18% NOMINAL ANNUAL RATE	18½% NOMINAL ANNUAL RATE	MONTHS
1	1.0141 666 667	1.0145 833 333	1.0150 000 000	1.0154 166 667	1
2	1.0285 340 278	1.0293 793 403	1.0302 250 000	1.0310 710 069	2
3	1.0431 049 265	1.0443 911 223	1.0456 783 750	1.0469 666 850	3
4	1.0578 822 463	1.0596 218 262	1.0613 635 506	1.0631 074 214	4
5	1.0728 689 115	1.0750 746 445	1.0772 840 039	1.0794 969 941	5
6	1.0880 678 877	1.0907 528 164	1.0934 432 639	1.0961 392 394	6
7	1.1034 821 828	1.1066 596 283	1.1098 449 129	1.1130 380 527	7
8	1.1191 148 470	1.1227 984 145	1.1264 925 866	1.1301 973 894	8
9	1.1349 689 740	1.1391 725 581	1.1433 899 754	1.1476 212 658	9
10	1.1510 477 012	1.1557 854 912	1.1605 408 250	1.1653 137 603	10
11	1.1673 542 103	1.1726 406 963	1.1779 489 374	1.1832 790 141	11
YEARS					
1	1.1838 917 282	1.1897 417 065	1.1956 181 715	1.2015 212 322	12
2	1.4015 996 242	1.4154 853 281	1.4295 028 119	1.4436 532 715	24
3	1.6593 422 014	1.6840 619 297	1.7091 395 381	1.7345 800 577	36
4	1.9644 815 065	2.0035 987 140	2.0434 782 893	2.0841 347 683	48
5	2.3257 334 059	2.3837 649 531	2.4432 197 757	2.5041 321 749	60
6	2.7534 165 413	2.8360 645 831	2.9211 579 607	3.0087 679 764	72
7	3.2597 470 677	3.3741 843 167	3.4925 895 395	3.6150 986 065	84
8	3.8591 875 896	4.0144 078 069	4.1758 035 189	4.3436 177 323	96
9	4.5688 602 650	4.7761 083 946	4.9926 665 676	5.2189 489 301	108
10	5.4090 358 752	5.6823 353 516	5.9693 228 723	6.2706 779 494	120
11	6.4037 128 304	6.7605 113 578	7.1370 308 975	7.5343 526 966	132
12	7.5813 026 500	8.0432 623 194	8.5331 638 313	9.0526 847 361	144
13	8.9754 414 966	9.5694 046 374	10.2024 057 368	10.8769 929 191	156
14	10.6259 509 451	11.3851 198 031	12.1981 816 915	13.0689 379 350	168
15	12.5799 754 286	13.5453 518 628	14.5843 676 891	15.7026 064 116	180
16	14.8933 288 514	16.1154 700 398	17.4373 350 284	18.8670 150 048	192
17	17.6320 888 331	19.1732 468 255	20.8483 946 218	22.6691 191 169	204
18	20.8744 841 211	22.8112 113 966	24.9267 194 557	27.2374 279 348	216
19	24.7131 290 823	27.1394 495 733	29.8028 387 361	32.7263 479 749	228
20	29.2576 690 994	32.2889 350 477	35.6328 155 540	39.3214 019 451	240
21	34.6379 124 344	38.4154 926 834	42.6032 417 767	47.2454 993 178	252
22	41.0075 380 146	45.7045 138 196	50.9372 100 314	56.7664 705 575	264
23	48.5484 850 509	54.3765 662 646	60.9014 539 171	68.2061 196 533	276
24	57.4761 498 704	64.6940 687 390	72.8148 849 717	81.9511 009 311	288
25	68.0455 384 026	76.9692 317 393	87.0587 996 251	98.4659 877 730	300
26	80.5585 500 585	91.5735 051 143	104.0890 828 174	118.3089 749 613	312
27	95.3726 010 533	108.9488 182 411	124.4507 988 672	142.1507 453 788	324
28	112.9108 334 877	129.6209 529 308	148.7956 365 786	170.7971 387 493	336
29	133.6742 017 948	154.2154 537 327	177.9027 669 275	205.2163 886 106	348
30	158.2557 817 840	183.4765 570 863	212.7037 808 918	246.5718 481 162	360
31	187.3577 110 003	218.2897 121 230	254.3125 055 728	296.2613 107 807	372
32	221.8112 442 752	259.7083 746 036	304.0606 528 928	355.9642 551 899	384
33	262.6004 973 280	308.9858 847 824	363.5404 418 251	427.6986 105 239	396
34	310.8905 566 184	367.6133 938 327	434.6555 583 072	513.8889 615 377	408
35	368.0607 583 685	437.3649 864 956	519.6820 838 389	617.4484 982 938	420
36	435.7440 873 222	520.3513 653 785	621.3413 428 208	741.8774 805 056	432
37	515.8738 206 103	619.0837 214 035	742.8870 001 568	891.3815 445 373	444
38	610.7387 490 361	736.5497 231 434	888.2091 967 300	1071.0138 517 754	456
39	723.0485 530 996	876.3039 245 042	1061.9590 556 697	1286.8458 829 155	468
40	856.0112 011 306	1042.5753 265 160	1269.6975 443 068	1546.1726 509 246	480
41	1013.4245 802 993	1240.3953 480 809	1518.0734 562 333	1857.7592 687 720	492
42	1199.7849 778 116	1475.7500 781 091	1815.0362 098 859	2232.1372 057 929	504
43	1420.4155 108 978	1755.7614 162 360	2170.0902 744 003	2681.9602 460 002	516
44	1681.6181 740 159	2088.9025 834 868	2594.5993 657 850	3222.4321 795 534	528
45	1990.8538 462 756	2485.2545 243 035	3102.1501 493 951	3871.8206 831 394	540
46	2356.9554 007 406	2956.8109 587 289	3708.9870 892 189	4652.0747 581 610	552
47	2790.3800 027 676	3517.8413 157 137	4434.5323 615 863	5589.5665 958 297	564
48	3303.5078 039 231	4185.3225 300 079	5302.0074 734 468	6715.9829 438 266	576
49	3910.9955 632 411	4979.4527 689 314	6339.1764 804 779	8069.3961 022 705	588
50	4630.1952 965 049	5924.2626 345 386	7579.2345 921 609	9695.5507 481 140	600

27

Table 1. FUTURE WORTH OF ONE DOLLAR WITH INTEREST
PAYABLE AT BEGINNING OF EACH PERIOD

MONTHS	19% NOMINAL ANNUAL RATE	19½% NOMINAL ANNUAL RATE	20% NOMINAL ANNUAL RATE	20½% NOMINAL ANNUAL RATE	MONTHS
1	1.0158 333 333	1.0162 500 000	1.0166 666 667	1.0170 833 333	1
2	1.0319 173 611	1.0327 640 625	1.0336 111 111	1.0344 585 069	2
3	1.0482 560 527	1.0495 464 785	1.0508 379 630	1.0521 305 064	3
4	1.0648 534 402	1.0666 016 088	1.0683 519 290	1.0701 044 026	4
5	1.0817 136 196	1.0839 338 849	1.0861 577 945	1.0883 853 528	5
6	1.0988 407 519	1.1015 478 106	1.1042 604 244	1.1069 786 026	6
7	1.1162 390 638	1.1194 479 625	1.1226 647 648	1.1258 894 870	7
8	1.1339 128 490	1.1376 389 919	1.1413 758 442	1.1451 234 324	8
9	1.1518 664 691	1.1561 256 255	1.1603 987 750	1.1646 859 577	9
10	1.1701 043 549	1.1749 126 669	1.1797 387 545	1.1845 826 762	10
11	1.1886 310 072	1.1940 049 977	1.1994 010 671	1.2048 192 969	11

YEARS					
1	1.2074 509 981	1.2134 075 790	1.2193 910 849	1.2254 016 266	12
2	1.4579 379 129	1.4723 579 527	1.4869 146 179	1.5016 091 464	24
3	1.7603 885 881	1.7865 702 987	1.8131 304 291	1.8400 742 904	36
4	2.1255 829 578	2.1678 379 408	2.2109 150 811	2.2548 300 285	48
5	2.5665 372 640	2.6304 709 873	2.6959 701 393	2.7630 723 846	60
6	3.0989 679 812	3.1918 334 323	3.2874 419 531	3.3858 733 944	72
7	3.7418 519 821	3.8729 948 775	4.0086 774 097	4.1490 547 648	84
8	4.5181 029 106	4.6995 213 376	4.8881 454 957	5.0842 584 575	96
9	5.4553 878 691	5.7024 348 085	5.9605 610 391	6.2302 585 837	108
10	6.5871 135 277	6.9193 776 152	7.2682 549 922	7.6345 690 024	120
11	7.9536 168 038	8.3960 252 400	8.8628 453 403	9.3554 132 736	132
12	9.6036 025 485	10.1878 006 593	10.8072 745 948	11.4641 386 427	144
13	11.5958 794 828	12.3619 545 330	13.1782 942 930	14.0481 741 399	156
14	14.0014 562 557	15.0000 893 210	16.0694 945 752	17.2146 554 413	168
15	16.9060 723 312	18.2012 220 672	19.5949 984 239	21.0948 667 785	180
16	20.4132 539 108	22.0855 008 027	23.8939 663 868	25.8496 840 626	192
17	24.6480 038 097	26.7987 140 591	29.1360 895 951	31.6762 448 965	204
18	29.7612 568 019	32.5177 627 457	35.5282 879 013	38.8161 220 196	216
19	35.9352 592 310	39.4572 997 664	43.3228 775 288	47.5653 390 598	228
20	43.3900 646 265	47.8777 865 819	52.8275 306 311	58.2866 438 519	240
21	52.3913 768 422	58.0952 691 022	64.4174 198 891	71.4245 481 831	252
22	63.2600 202 615	70.4932 398 303	78.5500 275 253	87.5237 575 203	264
23	76.3833 746 065	85.5370 314 755	95.7832 032 835	107.2517 548 284	276
24	92.2291 819 092	103.7912 822 741	116.7971 841 675	131.4264 748 187	288
25	111.3622 177 529	125.9411 285 414	142.4214 451 159	161.0502 160 165	300
26	134.4644 209 797	152.8179 198 748	173.6674 404 736	197.3511 966 652	312
27	162.3591 993 249	185.4304 221 769	211.7685 286 519	241.8344 773 980	324
28	196.0407 772 804	225.0026 796 391	258.2286 559 016	296.3443 619 630	336
29	236.7096 322 013	273.0199 567 603	314.8817 208 735	363.1408 631 727	348
30	285.8152 816 684	331.2844 847 402	383.9639 632 327	444.9934 044 040	360
31	345.1079 471 312	401.9831 045 755	468.2022 336 909	545.2956 415 672	372
32	416.7009 352 261	487.7693 457 056	570.9216 296 953	668.2061 661 352	384
33	503.1459 601 604	591.8630 208 633	696.1767 454 301	818.8209 228 626	396
34	607.5240 918 006	718.1710 752 214	848.9117 168 958	1003.3844 907 411	408
35	733.5555 710 326	871.4342 256 632	1035.1553 794 543	1229.5489 870 240	420
36	885.7324 064 269	1057.4048 939 845	1262.2592 411 983	1506.6913 286 403	432
37	1069.4784 782 161	1283.0631 123 897	1539.1876 655 564	1846.3020 048 468	444
38	1291.3428 560 003	1556.8785 048 570	1876.8717 173 756	2262.4614 798 691	456
39	1559.2332 204 053	1889.1281 773 127	2288.6406 396 785	2772.4239 774 717	468
40	1882.6977 082 955	2292.2824 479 773	2790.7479 925 758	3397.3328 515 210	480
41	2273.2652 270 580	2781.4728 954 916	3403.0132 223 641	4163.0972 022 357	492
42	2744.8563 674 249	3375.0602 920 601	4149.6039 851 654	5101.4660 831 669	504
43	3314.2795 605 700	4095.3237 378 312	5059.9901 053 980	6251.3448 361 776	516
44	4001.8301 634 914	4969.2968 617 774	6170.1068 242 310	7660.4081 304 693	528
45	4832.0138 252 535	6029.7824 741 806	7523.7732 543 802	9387.0765 832 270	540
46	5834.4199 162 791	7316.5837 536 482	9174.4220 312 396	11502.9389 137 744	552
47	7044.7761 514 194	8877.9981 787 690	11187.2084 340 517	14095.7200 552 142	564
48	8506.2219 956 322	10772.6302 761 074	13641.5822 294 593	17272.9182 832 610	576
49	10270.8462 389 395	13071.5912 223 579	16634.4237 546 043	21166.2621 598 283	588
50	12401.5435 428 448	15861.1678 582 702	20283.8680 289 003	25937.1720 789 498	600

28

Table 1. FUTURE WORTH OF ONE DOLLAR WITH INTEREST PAYABLE AT BEGINNING OF EACH PERIOD

	21% NOMINAL ANNUAL RATE	**21½%** NOMINAL ANNUAL RATE	**22%** NOMINAL ANNUAL RATE	**22½%** NOMINAL ANNUAL RATE	
MONTHS					**MONTHS**
1	1.0175 000 000	1.0179 166 667	1.0183 333 333	1.0187 500 000	1
2	1.0353 062 500	1.0361 543 403	1.0370 027 778	1.0378 515 625	2
3	1.0534 241 094	1.0547 187 722	1.0560 144 954	1.0573 112 793	3
4	1.0718 590 313	1.0736 158 169	1.0753 747 611	1.0771 358 658	4
5	1.0906 165 643	1.0928 514 336	1.0950 899 651	1.0973 321 633	5
6	1.1097 023 542	1.1124 316 884	1.1151 666 144	1.1179 071 413	6
7	1.1291 221 454	1.1323 627 562	1.1356 113 357	1.1388 679 002	7
8	1.1488 817 830	1.1526 509 222	1.1564 308 769	1.1602 216 734	8
9	1.1689 872 142	1.1733 025 846	1.1776 321 096	1.1819 758 297	9
10	1.1894 444 904	1.1943 242 559	1.1992 220 316	1.2041 378 765	10
11	1.2102 597 690	1.2157 225 655	1.2212 077 688	1.2267 154 617	11
YEARS					
1	1.2314 393 149	1.2375 042 615	1.2435 965 779	1.2497 163 766	12
2	1.5164 427 864	1.5314 167 971	1.5465 324 487	1.5617 910 220	24
3	1.8674 072 660	1.8951 348 125	1.9232 624 609	1.9517 958 171	36
4	2.2995 987 244	2.3452 374 066	2.3917 626 148	2.4391 911 965	48
5	2.8318 162 778	2.9022 412 847	2.9743 878 030	3.0482 971 840	60
6	3.4872 098 972	3.5915 359 577	3.6989 384 933	3.8095 069 117	72
7	4.2942 873 669	4.4445 410 528	4.5999 872 523	4.7608 031 744	84
8	5.2881 542 933	5.5001 384 931	5.7205 284 056	5.9496 536 930	96
9	6.5120 411 002	6.8064 448 238	7.1140 295 492	7.4353 796 554	108
10	8.0191 834 313	8.4230 044 749	8.8469 828 028	9.2921 157 218	120
11	9.8751 377 511	10.4235 039 320	11.0020 775 387	11.6125 091 912	132
12	12.1606 328 672	12.8991 305 352	13.6821 459 774	14.5123 429 100	144
13	14.9750 814 073	15.9627 290 065	17.0150 699 164	18.1363 125 979	156
14	18.4409 039 894	19.7539 451 701	21.1598 827 216	22.6652 468 654	168
15	22.7088 541 757	24.4455 913 287	26.3143 577 422	28.3251 301 881	180
16	27.9645 758 293	30.2515 234 432	32.7244 452 391	35.3983 790 663	192
17	34.4366 781 020	37.4363 891 767	40.6960 081 144	44.2379 340 254	204
18	42.4066 792 909	46.3276 911 399	50.6094 164 271	55.2848 706 200	216
19	52.2212 520 950	57.3307 152 093	62.9376 970 805	69.0904 081 938	228
20	64.3073 029 055	70.9470 043 842	78.2691 047 130	86.3434 145 881	240
21	79.1905 410 359	87.7972 202 634	97.3351 907 799	107.9047 792 251	252
22	97.5183 456 033	108.6494 342 204	121.0457 101 674	134.8503 697 146	264
23	120.0879 247 043	134.4541 378 532	150.5320 309 391	168.5247 154 274	276
24	147.8809 917 310	166.3875 685 646	187.2011 185 469	210.6080 967 370	288
25	182.1064 671 506	205.9053 251 529	232.8026 704 123	263.2003 875 437	300
26	224.2530 631 549	254.8087 173 345	289.5126 042 611	328.9258 346 495	312
27	276.1540 384 657	315.3268 735 591	360.0368 839 309	411.0640 022 592	324
28	340.0669 399 475	390.2183 497 829	447.7406 367 902	513.7134 154 677	336
29	418.7717 995 643	482.8968 707 570	556.8087 237 190	641.9960 682 060	348
30	515.6920 579 737	597.5869 354 084	692.4454 233 866	802.3130 001 711	360
31	635.0434 745 936	739.5163 791 619	861.1227 589 369	1002.6636 954 994	372
32	782.0175 013 137	915.1546 706 338	1070.8893 162 040	1253.0452 405 209	384
33	963.0070 960 925	1132.5078 048 062	1331.7542 889 886	1565.9511 577 411	396
34	1185.8847 986 992	1401.4832 345 867	1656.1650 764 491	1956.9948 068 365	408
35	1460.3451 641 136	1734.3414 751 686	2059.6012 215 833	2445.6884 590 893	420
36	1798.3264 484 789	2146.2549 663 514	2561.3130 310 912	3056.4169 194 663	432
37	2214.5298 897 620	2655.9996 670 439	3185.2401 205 096	3819.6542 780 753	444
38	2727.0591 703 733	3286.8109 064 085	3961.1537 137 973	4773.4845 043 871	456
39	3358.2078 765 784	4067.4425 033 003	4926.0772 031 904	5965.5017 587 365	468
40	4135.4292 069 759	5033.4774 310 859	6126.0527 525 779	7455.1852 427 262	480
41	5092.5301 096 411	6228.9497 709 416	7618.3382 394 132	9316.8670 886 677	492
42	6271.1417 895 521	7708.3518 859 730	9474.1393 641 579	11643.4413 796 213	504
43	7722.5305 492 477	9539.1183 077 403	11782.0072 922 358	14550.9993 724 793	516
44	9509.8277 292 059	11804.6995 564 189	14652.0639 499 414	18184.6222 121 642	528
45	11710.7757 440 963	14608.3660 063 471	18221.2565 879 709	22725.6201 814 263	540
46	14421.1096 597 820	18077.9151 858 512	22659.8923 386 489	28400.5797 098 703	552
47	17758.7214 001 856	22371.4970 808 396	28179.7645 689 342	35492.6695 692 965	564
48	21868.7877 153 400	27684.8229 728 239	35044.2587 852 078	44355.7704 111 744	576
49	26930.0849 628 513	34260.0864 066 909	43580.9203 018 852	55432.1326 810 191	588
50	33162.7653 780 587	42397.0029 263 365	54197.0833 510 957	69274.4440 031 641	600

Table 2.   FUTURE WORTH OF ONE DOLLAR PER PERIOD WITH INTEREST
PAYABLE AT END OF EACH PERIOD

MONTHS	5% NOMINAL ANNUAL RATE	5½% NOMINAL ANNUAL RATE	6% NOMINAL ANNUAL RATE	6½% NOMINAL ANNUAL RATE	MONTHS
1	1.0000 000 000	1.0000 000 000	1.0000 000 000	1.0000 000 000	1
2	2.0041 666 667	2.0045 833 333	2.0050 000 000	2.0054 166 667	2
3	3.0125 173 611	3.0137 710 069	3.0150 250 000	3.0162 793 403	3
4	4.0250 695 168	4.0275 841 241	4.0301 001 250	4.0326 175 200	4
5	5.0418 406 398	5.0460 438 846	5.0502 506 256	5.0544 608 649	5
6	6.0628 483 091	6.0691 715 858	6.0755 018 788	6.0818 391 946	6
7	7.0881 101 771	7.0969 886 222	7.1058 793 881	7.1147 824 903	7
8	8.1176 439 695	8.1295 164 867	8.1414 087 851	8.1533 208 954	8
9	9.1514 674 860	9.1667 767 706	9.1821 158 290	9.1974 847 169	9
10	10.1895 986 005	10.2087 911 641	10.2280 264 082	10.2473 044 258	10
11	11.2320 552 614	11.2555 814 570	11.2791 665 402	11.3028 106 581	11
YEARS					
1	12.2788 554 916	12.3071 695 387	12.3355 623 729	12.3640 342 159	12
2	25.1859 205 340	25.3085 601 784	25.4319 552 411	25.5561 107 014	24
3	38.7533 355 200	39.0433 314 462	39.3361 049 647	39.6316 849 809	36
4	53.0148 852 061	53.5528 517 740	54.0978 322 191	54.6499 265 379	48
5	68.0060 828 408	68.8808 230 988	69.7700 305 099	70.6739 675 458	60
6	83.7642 585 981	85.0734 124 901	86.4088 556 983	87.7711 682 565	72
7	100.3286 525 342	102.1793 912 030	104.0739 272 164	106.0134 001 630	84
8	117.7405 123 014	120.2502 815 749	122.8285 416 922	125.4773 481 248	96
9	136.0431 958 600	139.3405 122 080	142.7398 997 512	146.2448 327 290	108
10	155.2822 794 457	159.5075 819 053	163.8793 468 065	168.4031 542 385	120
11	175.5056 710 611	180.8122 328 545	186.3226 287 002	192.0454 595 767	132
12	196.7637 297 732	203.3186 335 800	210.1501 631 121	217.2711 338 891	144
13	219.1093 911 143	227.0945 722 155	235.4473 277 088	244.1862 183 282	156
14	242.5982 988 991	252.2116 606 780	262.3047 660 641	272.9038 558 190	168
15	267.2889 437 852	278.7455 503 598	290.8187 124 494	303.5447 666 777	180
16	293.2428 089 237	306.7761 599 862	321.0913 366 555	336.2377 560 837	192
17	320.5245 230 600	336.3879 163 270	353.2311 100 819	371.1202 555 376	204
18	349.2020 214 691	367.6700 084 852	387.3531 944 072	408.3389 005 825	216
19	379.3467 151 232	400.7166 565 304	423.5798 542 298	448.0501 472 150	228
20	411.0336 685 157	435.6273 952 848	462.0408 951 615	490.4209 295 799	240
21	444.3417 865 818	472.5073 741 168	502.8741 289 399	535.6293 617 105	252
22	479.3540 111 832	511.4676 736 448	546.2258 672 290	583.8654 862 671	264
23	516.1575 276 441	552.6256 403 112	592.2514 458 764	635.3320 734 186	276
24	554.8439 818 560	596.1052 398 140	641.1157 815 046	690.2454 732 279	288
25	595.5097 084 876	642.0374 304 952	692.9939 624 325	748.8365 251 222	300
26	638.2559 708 724	690.5605 577 755	748.0718 760 435	811.3515 282 726	312
27	683.1892 131 682	741.8207 708 449	806.5468 748 481	878.0532 769 620	324
28	730.4213 254 178	795.9724 628 565	868.6284 836 278	949.2221 652 929	336
29	780.0699 221 711	853.1787 359 507	934.5391 501 941	1025.1573 658 803	348
30	832.2586 353 615	913.6118 925 108	1004.5150 424 526	1106.1780 874 832	360
31	887.1174 221 666	977.4539 541 288	1078.8068 946 290	1192.6249 168 624	372
32	944.7828 886 203	1044.8972 098 452	1157.6809 056 869	1284.8612 505 050	384
33	1005.3986 297 799	1116.1447 953 140	1241.4196 931 599	1383.2748 222 334	396
34	1069.1155 872 987	1191.4113 046 368	1330.3233 058 124	1488.2793 331 227	408
35	1136.0924 252 915	1270.9234 367 092	1424.7102 987 602	1600.3161 905 749	420
36	1206.4959 254 301	1354.9206 780 264	1524.9188 749 014	1719.8563 638 633	432
37	1280.5014 022 533	1443.6560 240 047	1631.3080 967 491	1847.4023 639 454	444
38	1358.2931 397 244	1537.3967 409 902	1744.2591 730 064	1983.4903 558 685	456
39	1440.0648 501 240	1636.4251 712 518	1864.1768 244 949	2128.6924 126 461	468
40	1526.0201 564 208	1741.0395 833 818	1991.4907 343 311	2283.6189 200 806	480
41	1616.3730 993 206	1851.5550 706 655	2126.6570 875 460	2448.9211 426 423	492
42	1711.3486 702 585	1968.3045 001 264	2270.1602 056 649	2625.2939 611 891	504
43	1811.1833 716 579	2091.6395 151 044	2422.5142 821 050	2813.4787 940 369	516
44	1916.1258 058 554	2221.9315 943 880	2584.2652 246 087	3014.2667 136 593	528
45	2026.4372 941 547	2359.5731 710 891	2755.9926 113 130	3228.5017 721 185	540
46	2142.3925 275 536	2504.9788 146 320	2938.3117 674 664	3457.0845 492 067	552
47	2264.2802 507 625	2658.5864 794 151	3131.8759 702 323	3700.9759 382 123	564
48	2392.4039 812 193	2820.8588 239 075	3337.3787 894 801	3961.2011 852 270	576
49	2527.0827 648 899	2992.2846 041 525	3555.5565 729 512	4238.8541 989 722	588
50	2668.6519 707 375	3173.3801 458 759	3787.1910 847 041	4535.1021 492 620	600

30

Table 2. FUTURE WORTH OF ONE DOLLAR PER PERIOD WITH INTEREST
PAYABLE AT END OF EACH PERIOD

MONTHS	7% NOMINAL ANNUAL RATE	7½% NOMINAL ANNUAL RATE	8% NOMINAL ANNUAL RATE	8½% NOMINAL ANNUAL RATE	MONTHS
1	1.0000 000 000	1.0000 000 000	1.0000 000 000	1.0000 000 000	1
2	2.0058 333 333	2.0062 500 000	2.0066 666 667	2.0070 833 333	2
3	3.0175 340 278	3.0187 890 625	3.0200 444 444	3.0213 001 736	3
4	4.0351 363 096	4.0376 564 941	4.0401 780 741	4.0427 010 498	4
5	5.0586 746 047	5.0628 918 472	5.0671 125 946	5.0713 368 489	5
6	6.0881 835 399	6.0945 349 213	6.1008 933 452	6.1072 588 183	6
7	7.1236 979 439	7.1326 257 645	7.1415 659 675	7.1505 185 683	7
8	8.1652 528 486	8.1772 046 756	8.1891 764 073	8.2011 680 748	8
9	9.2128 834 902	9.2283 122 048	9.2437 709 167	9.2592 596 820	9
10	10.2666 253 106	10.2859 891 561	10.3053 960 561	10.3248 461 047	10
11	11.3265 139 582	11.3502 765 883	11.3740 986 965	11.3979 804 313	11
YEARS					
1	12.3925 852 896	12.4212 158 170	12.4499 260 211	12.4787 161 260	12
2	25.6810 315 719	25.8067 228 988	25.9331 897 618	26.0604 372 748	24
3	39.9301 007 103	40.2313 816 823	40.5355 577 431	40.8426 590 595	36
4	55.2092 362 089	55.7758 642 148	56.3499 150 651	56.9314 948 188	48
5	71.5929 016 481	72.5271 053 242	73.4768 562 452	74.4424 373 457	60
6	89.1609 435 866	90.5787 888 150	92.0253 250 965	93.5011 879 456	72
7	107.9989 806 974	110.0318 714 089	112.1133 077 144	114.2445 587 761	84
8	128.1988 210 340	130.9951 473 604	133.8685 829 824	136.8214 549 457	96
9	149.8589 094 619	153.5858 569 044	157.4295 353 681	161.3939 434 199	108
10	173.0848 074 335	177.9303 419 404	182.9460 351 817	188.1384 164 104	120
11	197.9897 074 475	204.1647 526 176	210.5803 918 953	217.2468 575 961	132
12	224.6949 846 973	232.4358 087 750	240.5083 865 871	248.9282 202 674	144
13	253.3307 885 987	262.9016 204 944	272.9203 900 780	283.4099 272 851	156
14	284.0366 770 795	295.7325 723 538	308.0225 738 733	320.9395 036 228	168
15	316.9622 967 213	331.1122 763 290	346.0382 216 115	361.7863 532 108	180
16	352.2681 120 693	369.2385 986 705	387.2091 493 629	406.2436 928 367	192
17	390.1261 876 635	410.3247 665 002	431.7972 438 125	454.6306 569 857	204
18	430.7210 266 035	454.6005 603 156	480.0861 281 110	507.2945 887 293	216
19	474.2504 697 328	502.3135 990 713	532.3829 659 904	564.6135 331 075	228
20	520.9266 598 255	553.7307 250 249	589.0204 156 215	626.9989 509 042	240
21	570.9770 754 741	609.1394 960 920	650.3587 456 387	694.8986 722 943	252
22	624.6456 397 168	668.8497 940 564	716.7881 267 593	768.8001 115 680	264
23	682.1939 088 081	733.1955 576 303	788.7311 138 265	849.2337 660 059	276
24	743.9023 469 251	802.5366 500 558	866.6453 332 989	936.7770 240 238	288
25	810.0716 930 231	877.2608 716 938	951.0263 945 609	1032.0583 099 227	300
26	881.0244 265 007	957.7861 288 550	1042.4110 422 915	1135.7615 949 968	312
27	957.1063 388 184	1044.5627 710 033	1141.3805 707 135	1248.6313 073 827	324
28	1038.6882 187 293	1138.0761 094 015	1248.5645 211 836	1371.4776 758 941	336
29	1126.1676 593 353	1238.8491 312 872	1364.6446 866 803	1505.1825 462 040	348
30	1219.9709 957 759	1347.4454 247 566	1490.3594 486 634	1650.7057 111 227	360
31	1320.5553 829 925	1464.4723 307 141	1626.5084 738 895	1809.0918 004 170	372
32	1428.4110 236 938	1590.5843 395 171	1773.9578 010 617	1981.4777 796 249	384
33	1544.0635 573 822	1726.4867 513 105	1933.6453 496 682	2169.1011 116 981	396
34	1668.0766 220 821	1872.9396 205 222	2106.5868 860 525	2373.3086 400 598	408
35	1801.0546 012 565	2030.7620 065 807	2293.8824 846 631	2595.5662 568 435	420
36	1943.6455 692 975	2200.8365 546 266	2496.7235 255 857	2837.4694 257 163	432
37	2096.5444 499 475	2384.1144 318 366	2716.4002 728 651	3100.7546 348 240	444
38	2260.4964 030 425	2581.6206 469 672	2954.3100 818 258	3387.3118 620 729	456
39	2436.3004 560 833	2794.4597 828 686	3211.9662 875 950	3699.1981 422 284	468
40	2624.8133 983 333	3023.8221 740 283	3491.0078 313 688	4038.6523 332 224	480
41	2826.9539 564 210	3270.9905 636 936	3793.2096 856 547	4408.1111 876 673	492
42	3043.7072 717 972	3537.3472 778 037	4120.4941 448 027	4810.2268 449 467	504
43	3276.1297 018 678	3824.3819 558 528	4474.9430 526 457	5247.8858 694 467	516
44	3525.3539 682 009	4133.6998 819 208	4858.8110 450 281	5724.2299 715 942	528
45	3792.5946 768 987	4467.0309 624 621	5274.5398 914 574	6242.6785 604 472	540
46	4079.1542 380 362	4826.2394 010 654	5724.7740 271 061	6806.9532 897 277	552
47	4386.4292 130 186	5213.3341 242 884	6212.3773 739 614	7421.1047 735 016	564
48	4715.9171 207 875	5630.4800 168 787	6740.4515 581 235	8089.5416 632 818	576
49	5069.2237 360 502	6080.0100 292 129	7312.3556 391 288	8817.0622 952 813	588
50	5448.0709 150 972	6564.4382 246 684	7931.7274 767 987	9608.8891 349 990	600

31

Table 2.   FUTURE WORTH OF ONE DOLLAR PER PERIOD WITH INTEREST
PAYABLE AT END OF EACH PERIOD

MONTHS	9% NOMINAL ANNUAL RATE	9½% NOMINAL ANNUAL RATE	10% NOMINAL ANNUAL RATE	10½% NOMINAL ANNUAL RATE	MONTHS
1	1.0000 000 000	1.0000 000 000	1.0000 000 000	1.0000 000 000	1
2	2.0075 000 000	2.0079 166 667	2.0083 333 333	2.0087 500 000	2
3	3.0225 562 500	3.0238 126 736	3.0250 694 444	3.0263 265 625	3
4	4.0452 254 219	4.0477 511 906	4.0502 783 565	4.0528 069 199	4
5	5.0755 646 125	5.0797 958 875	5.0840 306 761	5.0882 689 805	5
6	6.1136 313 471	6.1200 109 383	6.1263 975 984	6.1327 913 341	6
7	7.1594 835 822	7.1684 610 249	7.1774 509 117	7.1864 532 582	7
8	8.2131 797 091	8.2252 113 414	8.2372 630 027	8.2493 347 242	8
9	9.2747 785 569	9.2903 275 978	9.3059 068 610	9.3215 164 031	9
10	10.3443 393 961	10.3638 760 246	10.3834 560 849	10.4030 796 716	10
11	11.4219 219 416	11.4459 233 765	11.4699 848 856	11.4941 066 187	11

YEARS

YEARS	9%	9½%	10%	10½%	MONTHS
1	12.5075 863 561	12.5365 369 365	12.5655 680 930	12.5946 800 516	12
2	26.1884 705 857	26.3172 948 768	26.4469 153 651	26.5773 373 023	24
3	41.1527 161 222	41.4657 597 494	41.7818 210 903	42.1009 316 285	36
4	57.5207 111 085	58.1176 731 632	58.7224 918 329	59.3352 796 128	48
5	75.4241 369 255	76.4222 487 536	77.4370 721 734	78.4689 122 113	60
6	95.0070 275 762	96.5435 092 490	98.1113 136 273	99.7111 371 418	72
7	116.4269 284 462	118.6617 562 372	120.9504 183 209	123.2943 285 550	84
8	139.8561 637 652	142.9751 858 031	146.1810 757 246	149.4764 690 345	96
9	165.4832 229 643	169.7016 645 141	174.0537 126 585	178.5439 717 351	108
10	193.5142 770 833	199.0806 816 682	204.8449 789 035	210.8148 135 293	120
11	224.1748 374 277	231.3754 952 975	238.8604 930 874	246.6420 134 382	132
12	257.7115 698 188	266.8754 911 579	276.4378 761 020	286.4174 943 971	144
13	294.3942 790 335	305.8987 758 423	317.9501 021 586	330.5763 706 011	156
14	334.5180 793 979	348.7950 272 545	363.8092 007 418	379.6017 073 308	168
15	378.4057 689 972	395.9486 279 855	414.4703 462 078	434.0298 053 277	180
16	426.4104 266 037	447.7821 096 698	470.4363 756 157	494.4560 675 254	192
17	478.9182 522 141	504.7599 391 858	532.2627 796 353	561.5415 123 152	204
18	536.3516 740 485	567.3926 806 274	600.5632 160 687	636.0200 045 959	216
19	599.1727 470 077	636.2415 703 415	676.1350 000 086	718.7062 837 104	228
20	667.8868 699 297	711.9235 460 264	759.3688 359 900	810.5048 760 883	240
21	743.0468 515 491	795.1167 749 564	851.4502 442 188	912.4199 900 929	252
22	825.2573 578 732	886.5667 308 697	953.1737 791 575	1025.5665 013 140	264
23	915.1797 767 516	987.0928 739 716	1065.5490 974 707	1151.1821 484 782	276
24	1013.5375 387 760	1097.5959 939 134	1189.6915 800 691	1290.6410 733 907	288
25	1121.1219 373 178	1219.0662 815 429	1326.8334 028 201	1445.4688 530 249	300
26	1238.7984 945 246	1352.5922 017 572	1478.3357 665 060	1617.3591 882 005	312
27	1367.5139 244 916	1499.3702 469 650	1645.7024 074 179	1808.1924 314 118	324
28	1508.3037 496 261	1660.7156 585 557	1830.5945 226 872	2020.0561 564 858	336
29	1662.3006 314 802	1838.0742 124 494	2034.8472 584 919	2255.2679 950 887	348
30	1830.7434 830 720	2033.0351 743 332	2260.4879 247 961	2516.4009 898 926	360
31	2014.9874 360 065	2247.3455 406 740	2509.7561 174 085	2806.3117 417 508	372
32	2216.5147 425 804	2482.9256 931 177	2785.1259 470 848	3128.1716 587 869	384
33	2436.9467 005 800	2741.8866 065 488	3089.3305 963 074	3485.5016 492 424	396
34	2678.0566 967 071	3026.5487 650 094	3425.3894 474 799	3882.2106 375 961	408
35	2941.7844 735 683	3339.4629 549 765	3796.6380 517 995	4322.6383 252 916	420
36	3230.2517 350 066	3683.4331 223 225	4206.7612 362 608	4811.6026 638 457	432
37	3545.7792 153 200	4061.5414 977 735	4659.8296 773 957	5354.4525 596 563	444
38	3890.9053 496 915	4477.1762 160 089	5160.3403 047 628	5957.1263 870 626	456
39	4268.4066 960 336	4934.0616 758 893	5713.2609 352 084	6626.2169 497 462	468
40	4681.3202 725 427	5436.2919 138 645	6324.0795 809 196	7369.0436 011 022	480
41	5132.9679 906 704	5988.3672 896 112	6998.8589 206 735	8193.7323 125 252	492
42	5626.9833 800 757	6595.2348 126 314	7744.2964 749 391	9109.3045 654 957	504
43	6167.3408 205 630	7262.3324 711 686	8567.7910 820 977	10125.7760 398 815	516
44	6758.3875 161 757	7995.6379 606 617	9477.5163 355 933	11254.2661 780 305	528
45	7404.8784 686 826	8801.7222 483 803	10482.5017 109 113	12507.1198 232 043	540
46	8112.0147 318 165	9687.8084 542 207	11592.7221 876 124	13898.0422 629 875	552
47	8885.4852 540 257	10661.8365 752 782	12819.1972 559 650	15442.2491 549 456	564
48	9731.5126 463 632	11732.5346 341 777	14174.1002 908 651	17156.6329 746 090	576
49	10656.9032 437 206	12909.4968 887 031	15670.8793 786 351	19059.9478 065 981	588
50	11669.1018 621 500	14203.2698 035 448	17324.3907 959 676	21173.0145 003 684	600

32

Table 2.   FUTURE WORTH OF ONE DOLLAR PER PERIOD WITH INTEREST
PAYABLE AT END OF EACH PERIOD

	11% NOMINAL ANNUAL RATE	**11½%** NOMINAL ANNUAL RATE	**12%** NOMINAL ANNUAL RATE	**12½%** NOMINAL ANNUAL RATE	
MONTHS					**MONTHS**
1	1.0000 000 000	1.0000 000 000	1.0000 000 000	1.0000 000 000	1
2	2.0091 666 667	2.0095 833 333	2.0100 000 000	2.0104 166 667	2
3	3.0275 840 278	3.0288 418 403	3.0301 000 000	3.0313 585 069	3
4	4.0553 368 814	4.0578 682 412	4.0604 010 000	4.0629 351 581	4
5	5.0925 108 028	5.0967 561 452	5.1010 050 100	5.1052 573 993	5
6	6.1391 921 518	6.1456 000 583	6.1520 150 601	6.1584 371 639	6
7	7.1954 680 799	7.2044 953 922	7.2135 352 107	7.2225 875 510	7
8	8.2614 265 373	8.2735 384 730	8.2856 705 628	8.2978 228 380	8
9	9.3371 562 805	9.3528 265 501	9.3685 272 684	9.3842 584 925	9
10	10.4227 468 798	10.4424 578 045	10.4622 125 411	10.4820 111 852	10
11	11.5182 887 262	11.5425 313 584	11.5668 346 665	11.5911 988 017	11
YEARS					
1	12.6238 730 395	12.6531 472 840	12.6825 030 132	12.7119 404 559	12
2	26.7085 659 754	26.8406 067 064	26.9734 648 532	27.1071 458 092	24
3	42.4231 231 859	42.7484 279 264	43.0768 783 592	43.4085 073 427	36
4	59.9561 506 683	60.5852 208 597	61.2226 077 682	61.8684 307 217	48
5	79.5180 796 858	80.5848 913 202	81.6696 698 564	82.7727 441 716	60
6	101.3436 923 630	103.0097 083 837	104.7099 312 100	106.4451 241 616	72
7	125.6949 395 385	128.1537 436 980	130.6722 744 040	133.2521 071 191	84
8	152.8640 846 970	156.3467 278 412	159.9272 925 559	163.6087 647 762	96
9	183.1772 117 136	187.9583 742 997	192.8925 792 665	197.9851 310 227	108
10	216.9981 385 101	223.4032 277 692	230.0386 894 574	236.9134 797 776	120
11	254.7327 835 945	263.1461 003 563	271.8958 561 925	280.9965 665 680	132
12	296.8340 378 923	307.7081 669 716	319.0615 593 601	330.9169 614 251	144
13	343.8072 003 398	357.6737 998 452	372.2090 542 531	387.4476 176 047	156
14	396.2160 424 781	413.6982 317 909	432.0969 817 873	451.4638 397 768	168
15	454.6895 748 350	476.5161 487 138	499.5801 975 356	523.9568 369 953	180
16	519.9295 963 045	546.9513 240 377	575.6219 741 546	606.0490 702 984	192
17	592.7191 171 318	625.9274 213 987	661.3077 513 846	699.0116 325 768	204
18	673.9317 565 964	714.4801 072 646	757.8606 298 936	804.2839 298 168	216
19	764.5422 281 843	813.7706 323 234	866.6588 301 289	923.4959 684 543	228
20	865.6380 380 913	925.1010 597 414	989.2553 653 874	1058.4935 939 333	240
21	978.4325 374 650	1049.9313 399 894	1127.4002 099 240	1211.3670 712 537	252
22	1104.2794 850 355	1189.8984 561 515	1283.0652 785 316	1384.4834 500 427	264
23	1244.6892 949 175	1346.8378 907 808	1458.4725 741 559	1580.5232 152 806	276
24	1401.3471 645 895	1522.8076 958 117	1656.1259 053 330	1802.5217 911 715	288
25	1576.1333 006 207	1720.1154 811 732	1878.8466 261 924	2053.9165 407 916	300
26	1771.1454 848 966	1941.3486 760 240	2129.8139 091 858	2338.5999 892 461	312
27	1988.7242 521 807	2189.4084 594 443	2412.6101 254 070	2660.9800 944 247	324
28	2231.4809 811 957	2467.5478 055 402	2731.2719 802 717	3026.0484 985 740	336
29	2502.3292 363 709	2779.4411 418 724	3090.3481 344 814	3439.4578 174 720	348
30	2804.5197 364 205	3129.0971 806 171	3494.9641 327 685	3907.6091 639 296	360
31	3141.6793 694 450	3521.1825 497 013	3950.8955 672 302	4437.7512 608 091	372
32	3517.8547 228 152	3960.8119 272 133	4464.6505 196 056	5038.0926 781 957	384
33	3937.5606 502 827	4453.7504 676 722	5043.5624 592 965	5717.9289 325 720	396
34	4405.8344 592 210	5006.4624 043 605	5695.8949 231 825	6487.7864 159 625	408
35	4928.2963 683 503	5626.1958 191 455	6430.9594 714 568	7359.5853 836 069	420
36	5511.2169 615 603	6321.0776 914 319	7259.2486 032 150	8346.8245 238 156	432
37	6161.5924 474 109	7100.2204 726 871	8192.5855 290 664	9464.7899 678 372	444
38	6887.2286 275 740	7973.8415 841 209	9244.2929 386 622	10730.7919 759 851	456
39	7696.8345 820 067	8953.3974 045 744	10429.3831 721 700	12164.4329 648 057	468
40	8600.1271 952 630	10051.7335 056 897	11764.7725 102 515	13787.9110 253 447	480
41	9607.9477 784 692	11283.2531 044 960	13269.5226 413 731	15626.3636 321 023	492
42	10732.3921 866 575	12664.1059 424 423	14965.1127 532 153	17708.2568 645 686	504
43	11986.9559 931 275	14212.4000 677 755	16875.7461 320 834	20065.8261 679 368	516
44	13386.6964 632 150	15948.4392 985 066	19028.6956 467 975	22735.5754 776 071	528
45	14948.4132 714 763	17894.9894 799 774	21454.6930 485 879	25758.8424 357 838	540
46	16690.8501 312 561	20077.5770 286 403	24188.3676 439 604	29182.4384 518 201	552
47	18634.9197 565 932	22524.8236 770 565	27268.7406 022 620	33059.3735 168 231	564
48	20803.9548 564 569	25268.8218 098 476	30739.7819 538 180	37449.6769 953 426	576
49	23223.9881 737 433	28345.5553 126 330	34651.0382 293 743	42421.3271 030 508	588
50	25924.0649 300 597	31795.3714 528 258	39058.3396 999 319	48051.3034 621 818	600

Table 2.   FUTURE WORTH OF ONE DOLLAR PER PERIOD WITH INTEREST
PAYABLE AT END OF EACH PERIOD

MONTHS	13% NOMINAL ANNUAL RATE	13½% NOMINAL ANNUAL RATE	14% NOMINAL ANNUAL RATE	14½% NOMINAL ANNUAL RATE	MONTHS
1	1.0000 000 000	1.0000 000 000	1.0000 000 000	1.0000 000 000	1
2	2.0108 333 333	2.0112 500 000	2.0116 666 667	2.0120 833 333	2
3	3.0326 173 611	3.0338 765 625	3.0351 361 111	3.0363 960 069	3
4	4.0654 707 159	4.0680 076 738	4.0705 460 324	4.0730 857 920	4
5	5.1095 133 153	5.1137 727 602	5.1180 357 361	5.1223 022 453	5
6	6.1648 663 762	6.1713 027 037	6.1777 461 530	6.1841 967 308	6
7	7.2316 524 286	7.2407 298 591	7.2498 198 582	7.2589 224 413	7
8	8.3099 953 299	8.3221 880 700	8.3344 010 898	8.3466 344 208	8
9	9.4000 202 793	9.4158 126 858	9.4316 357 692	9.4474 895 867	9
10	10.5018 538 323	10.5217 405 785	10.5416 715 199	10.5616 467 526	10
11	11.6156 239 155	11.6401 101 601	11.6646 576 876	11.6892 666 508	11

YEARS	13%	13½%	14%	14½%	MONTHS
1	12.7414 598 413	12.7710 613 994	12.8007 453 606	12.8305 119 562	12
2	27.2416 550 038	27.3769 979 030	27.5131 800 087	27.6502 068 602	24
3	43.7433 480 886	44.0814 341 652	44.4227 995 018	44.7674 783 920	36
4	62.5228 108 206	63.1858 709 654	63.8577 358 831	64.5385 321 549	48
5	83.8944 493 969	85.0351 270 386	86.1951 251 010	87.3747 982 131	60
6	108.2160 682 821	110.0235 627 587	111.8684 253 520	113.7514 928 365	72
7	135.8948 605 789	138.6021 980 059	141.3758 283 589	144.2175 076 166	84
8	167.3942 252 644	171.2868 526 895	175.2899 268 075	179.4068 317 466	96
9	203.2415 254 268	208.6674 568 556	214.2688 255 371	220.0517 451 581	108
10	244.0369 173 897	251.4186 984 199	259.0689 120 993	266.9980 570 600	120
11	290.4633 985 437	300.3122 007 070	310.5595 344 973	321.2227 069 905	132
12	343.2982 421 040	356.2304 495 911	369.7398 709 293	383.8540 946 536	144
13	403.4260 102 365	420.1827 216 110	437.7583 188 933	456.1955 615 996	156
14	471.8533 634 184	493.3233 005 476	515.9347 798 998	539.7525 133 960	168
15	549.7259 139 701	576.9723 112 585	605.7862 722 292	636.2637 466 934	180
16	638.3474 059 242	672.6395 468 020	709.0563 687 503	747.7376 330 946	192
17	739.2015 423 369	782.0517 189 096	827.7490 310 424	876.4939 128 024	204
18	853.9768 254 798	907.1836 236 552	964.1674 963 731	1025.2119 677 605	216
19	984.5948 257 828	1050.2937 848 341	1120.9589 721 377	1196.9865 788 373	228
20	1133.2423 528 111	1213.9652 183 851	1301.1660 050 553	1395.3923 273 452	240
21	1302.4080 668 808	1401.1520 536 171	1508.2855 219 463	1624.5579 810 713	252
22	1494.9241 442 676	1615.2328 527 155	1746.3366 877 781	1889.2524 127 734	264
23	1714.0136 935 666	1860.0715 908 980	2019.9388 977 704	2194.9838 390 797	276
24	1963.3447 170 510	2140.0873 978 611	2334.4014 169 985	2548.1144 449 267	288
25	2247.0915 204 504	2460.3343 192 888	2695.8264 069 578	2955.9927 788 370	300
26	2570.0045 992 729	2826.5925 380 521	3111.2273 383 237	3427.1066 741 462	312
27	2937.4901 717 109	3245.4727 015 637	3588.6650 877 144	3971.2598 784 256	324
28	3355.7006 896 699	3724.5352 383 061	4137.4043 594 191	4599.7760 667 098	336
29	3831.6378 432 597	4272.4268 170 957	4768.0934 674 659	5325.7344 839 877	348
30	4373.2697 832 517	4899.0364 120 556	5492.9709 667 073	6164.2421 206 092	360
31	4989.6645 240 422	5615.6737 901 354	6326.1031 426 120	7132.7480 845 033	372
32	5691.1417 605 578	6435.2736 427 262	7283.6569 682 640	8251.4067 122 024	384
33	6489.4456 408 252	7372.6290 457 708	8384.2138 253 140	9543.4969 749 141	396
34	7397.9413 867 680	8444.6584 621 250	9649.1300 766 537	11035.9609 073 598	408
35	8431.8390 550 589	9670.7111 053 337	11102.9514 877 456	12759.6931 402 105	420
36	9608.4481 842 387	11072.9161 763 765	12773.8895 384 748	14750.7271 798 298	432
37	10947.4675 914 089	12676.5822 768 080	14694.3688 683 793	17050.4418 842 263	444
38	12471.3151 702 798	14510.6542 073 572	16901.6564 784 622	19706.6936 691 673	456
39	14205.5032 120 626	16608.2253 968 100	19438.5848 992 786	22774.7583 867 230	468
40	16179.0655 328 400	19007.1853 905 699	22354.3833 584 131	26318.4816 001 903	480
41	18425.0435 583 727	21750.8031 830 531	25705.6330 761 938	30411.6071 922 972	492
42	20981.0395 044 200	24888.6087 274 831	29557.3652 272 078	35139.3119 546 474	504
43	23889.8459 138 952	28477.2367 286 687	33984.3228 736 167	40599.9780 927 817	516
44	27200.1620 906 046	32581.4588 509 583	39072.4113 581 545	46907.2405 321 864	528
45	30967.4094 241 117	37275.3527 913 519	44920.3653 017 587	54192.3516 291 115	540
46	35254.6592 559 161	42643.6393 185 373	51641.6645 540 107	62606.9124 951 647	552
47	40133.6888 213 032	48783.2114 102 628	59366.7362 755 026	72326.0277 737 770	564
48	45686.1829 454 681	55804.8830 886 669	68245.4858 836 529	83551.9495 185 516	576
49	52005.1016 127 380	63835.3895 185 448	78450.2059 751 066	96518.2860 015 772	588
50	59196.2363 047 674	73019.6744 686 164	90178.9196 725 090	111494.8630 358 240	600

34

Table 2. FUTURE WORTH OF ONE DOLLAR PER PERIOD WITH INTEREST
PAYABLE AT END OF EACH PERIOD

	15% NOMINAL ANNUAL RATE	**15½%** NOMINAL ANNUAL RATE	**16%** NOMINAL ANNUAL RATE	**16½%** NOMINAL ANNUAL RATE	
MONTHS					**MONTHS**
1	1.0000 000 000	1.0000 000 000	1.0000 000 000	1.0000 000 000	1
2	2.0125 000 000	2.0129 166 667	2.0133 333 333	2.0137 500 000	2
3	3.0376 562 500	3.0389 168 403	3.0401 777 778	3.0414 390 625	3
4	4.0756 269 531	4.0781 695 161	4.0807 134 815	4.0832 588 496	4
5	5.1265 722 900	5.1308 458 724	5.1351 229 946	5.1394 036 588	5
6	6.1906 544 437	6.1971 192 982	6.2035 913 012	6.2100 704 591	6
7	7.2680 376 242	7.2771 654 225	7.2863 058 518	7.2954 589 279	7
8	8.3588 880 945	8.3711 621 425	8.3834 565 965	8.3957 714 882	8
9	9.4633 741 957	9.4792 896 536	9.4952 360 178	9.5112 133 461	9
10	10.5816 663 731	10.6017 304 782	10.6218 391 647	10.6419 925 296	10
11	11.7139 372 028	11.7386 694 969	11.7634 636 869	11.7883 199 269	11
YEARS					
1	12.8603 614 178	12.8902 939 779	12.9203 098 694	12.9504 093 259	12
2	27.7880 840 331	27.9268 171 408	28.0664 118 338	28.2068 738 003	24
3	45.1155 054 982	45.4669 158 551	45.8217 448 741	46.1800 283 471	36
4	65.2283 882 442	65.7294 345 250	66.6358 033 106	67.3536 288 825	48
5	88.5745 077 561	89.7946 219 944	91.0355 162 089	92.2975 728 331	60
6	115.6736 214 508	117.6356 873 596	119.6385 871 255	121.6832 381 938	72
7	147.1290 400 983	150.1122 798 221	153.1691 319 016	156.3015 539 820	84
8	183.6410 594 001	187.9962 129 312	192.4760 103 924	197.0842 884 651	96
9	226.0225 507 560	232.1878 069 066	238.5543 162 178	245.1291 281 419	108
10	275.2170 583 151	283.7372 849 522	292.5705 685 701	301.7292 224 910	120
11	332.3198 052 116	343.8697 320 474	355.8922 438 341	368.4079 896 986	132
12	398.6020 766 460	414.0142 093 679	430.1223 946 430	446.9601 201 757	144
13	475.5395 226 585	495.8377 162 473	517.1402 327 866	539.4998 814 954	156
14	564.8450 106 995	591.2848 067 922	619.1487 033 319	648.5180 249 002	168
15	668.5067 594 006	702.6238 026 498	738.7302 546 098	776.9488 250 445	180
16	788.8326 025 204	832.5007 001 832	878.9122 151 389	928.2490 573 776	192
17	928.5013 685 206	984.0020 531 727	1043.2434 339 097	1106.4910 388 834	204
18	1090.6225 196 401	1160.7283 254 625	1235.8841 229 171	1316.4722 364 081	216
19	1278.8053 782 205	1366.8794 567 967	1461.7111 771 969	1563.8443 927 398	228
20	1497.2394 814 758	1607.3546 753 352	1726.4416 383 860	1855.2656 459 261	240
21	1750.7878 536 541	1887.8689 289 162	2036.7774 274 475	2198.5797 361 941	252
22	2045.0952 721 214	2215.0887 020 820	2400.5750 106 190	2603.0271 239 116	264
23	2386.7139 377 067	2596.7904 465 880	2827.0442 938 481	3079.4937 009 281	276
24	2783.2493 471 233	3042.0453 905 338	3326.9817 809 319	3640.8037 894 787	288
25	3243.5296 150 408	3561.4351 181 463	3913.0438 979 952	4302.0653 148 549	300
26	3777.8020 154 448	4167.3030 435 168	4600.0674 037 942	5081.0764 423 263	312
27	4397.9611 179 084	4874.0477 546 224	5405.4449 973 569	5998.8046 231 380	324
28	5117.8135 978 001	5698.4651 990 190	6349.5656 318 690	7079.9509 433 320	336
29	5953.3856 159 285	6660.1478 433 250	7456.3306 817 376	8353.6419 651 073	348
30	6923.2796 108 540	7781.9502 926 126	8753.7590 302 321	9854.0779 552 357	360
31	8049.0884 471 761	9090.5324 352 546	10274.6963 960 054	11621.7255 814 969	372
32	9355.8761 400 295	10616.9930 211 884	12057.6468 558 822	13704.1349 119 391	384
33	10872.7358 582 139	12397.6087 307 265	14147.7476 147 381	16157.3549 740 647	396
34	12633.4376 288 485	14474.6962 980 508	16597.9116 997 816	19047.4513 407 929	408
35	14677.1801 634 754	16897.6181 779 509	19470.1675 075 816	22452.1033 475 000	420
36	17049.4635 436 063	19723.9556 557 013	22837.2291 162 161	26463.0577 747 735	432
37	19803.1021 944 124	23020.8772 793 015	26784.3371 159 569	31188.2353 493 330	444
38	22999.4006 985 123	26866.7351 351 774	31411.4165 616 271	36754.8164 501 554	456
39	26709.5186 271 375	31352.9269 031 974	36835.6066 770 100	43312.6282 282 496	468
40	31016.0547 740 743	36586.0679 431 607	43194.2263 534 779	51038.1772 749 629	480
41	36014.8860 623 685	42690.5250 328 844	50648.2505 174 356	60139.4003 799 844	492
42	41817.3020 635 912	49811.3719 727 440	59386.3853 743 591	70861.2612 479 335	504
43	48552.4826 507 186	58111.8372 972 802	69629.8456 983 786	83492.3438 117 960	516
44	56370.3739 449 069	67807.3260 295 127	81637.9551 093 500	98372.6196 053 419	528
45	65445.0265 837 034	79110.1110 558 624	95714.7111 141 294	115902.5982 570 117	540
46	75978.4706 309 533	92294.8056 132 644	112216.4811 127 476	136554.1073 951 209	552
47	88205.2133 959 811	107674.7469 433 640	131561.0242 017 121	160882.9921 106 071	564
48	102397.4602 975 240	125615.4428 227 774	154238.0671 705 657	189544.0757 893 378	576
49	118871.1750 051 302	146543.2579 378 899	180821.7024 338 145	223308.7849 918 238	588
50	137993.1137 756 640	170955.5465 378 485	211984.9217 644 860	263085.9127 622 745	600

Table 2.   FUTURE WORTH OF ONE DOLLAR PER PERIOD WITH INTEREST
PAYABLE AT END OF EACH PERIOD

MONTHS	17% NOMINAL ANNUAL RATE	17½% NOMINAL ANNUAL RATE	18% NOMINAL ANNUAL RATE	18½% NOMINAL ANNUAL RATE	MONTHS
1	1.0000 000 000	1.0000 000 000	1.0000 000 000	1.0000 000 000	1
2	2.0141 666 667	2.0145 833 333	2.0150 000 000	2.0154 166 667	2
3	3.0427 006 944	3.0439 626 736	3.0452 250 000	3.0464 876 736	3
4	4.0858 056 209	4.0883 537 959	4.0909 033 750	4.0934 543 586	4
5	5.1436 878 672	5.1479 756 221	5.1522 669 256	5.1565 617 799	5
6	6.2165 567 787	6.2230 502 666	6.2295 509 295	6.2360 587 740	6
7	7.3046 246 664	7.3138 030 830	7.3229 941 935	7.3321 980 135	7
8	8.4081 068 492	8.4204 627 113	8.4328 391 064	8.4452 360 662	8
9	9.5272 216 962	9.5432 611 258	9.5593 316 929	9.5754 334 555	9
10	10.6621 906 702	10.6824 336 839	10.7027 216 683	10.7230 547 213	10
11	11.8132 383 714	11.8382 191 751	11.8632 624 934	11.8883 684 816	11

YEARS					
1	12.9805 925 817	13.0108 598 714	13.0412 114 308	13.0716 474 957	12
2	28.3482 087 667	28.4904 224 974	28.6335 207 953	28.7775 095 019	24
3	46.5418 024 510	46.9071 037 512	47.2759 692 065	47.6484 361 728	36
4	68.0810 475 208	68.8181 975 335	69.5652 192 875	70.3222 552 397	48
5	93.5811 815 914	94.8867 396 403	96.2146 517 126	97.5653 302 641	60
6	123.7705 793 867	125.9015 714 114	128.0771 973 793	130.2984 633 371	72
7	159.5115 577 170	162.8012 102 883	166.1726 359 673	169.6280 177 216	84
8	201.8250 063 215	206.7022 496 134	211.7202 345 929	216.8833 123 685	96
9	251.9195 481 177	258.9331 470 553	266.1777 711 761	273.6615 522 218	108
10	311.2260 617 802	321.0744 241 078	331.2881 914 881	341.8818 129 339	120
11	381.4385 527 360	395.0064 931 097	409.1353 931 646	423.8499 046 474	132
12	464.5625 399 976	482.9665 590 640	502.2109 220 864	522.3363 072 062	144
13	562.9723 409 350	587.6163 179 933	613.4937 157 837	640.6698 109 661	156
14	679.4788 902 426	712.1225 007 837	746.5454 460 992	782.8500 282 172	168
15	817.4100 302 536	860.2526 991 615	905.6245 126 089	953.6825 780 469	180
16	980.7055 659 704	1036.4893 741 574	1095.8223 352 269	1158.9415 138 224	192
17	1174.0297 999 837	1246.1654 966 078	1323.2263 081 215	1405.5644 832 606	204
18	1402.9047 614 897	1495.6259 243 355	1595.1146 303 768	1701.8872 173 951	216
19	1673.8679 352 179	1792.4193 993 141	1920.1892 490 734	2057.9252 740 487	228
20	1994.6589 952 525	2145.5269 747 010	2308.8543 702 680	2485.7125 585 982	240
21	2374.4408 777 207	2565.6337 840 052	2773.5494 517 816	2999.7080 638 605	252
22	2824.0615 069 104	3065.4523 762 018	3329.1473 354 280	3617.2845 767 015	264
23	3356.3636 506 541	3660.1074 010 014	3993.4302 611 412	4359.3158 694 036	276
24	3986.5517 555 567	4367.5932 849 608	4787.6589 981 156	5250.8822 225 607	288
25	4732.6262 401 862	5209.3187 478 380	5737.2533 083 391	6322.1181 258 167	300
26	5615.8976 511 901	6210.7546 364 112	6872.6055 211 588	7609.2308 083 008	312
27	6661.5953 684 685	7402.2046 793 912	8230.0532 578 151	9155.7240 245 719	324
28	7899.5882 461 940	8819.7224 866 864	9853.0424 385 707	11013.8684 594 139	336
29	9365.2377 737 533	10506.2025 416 734	11793.5177 951 676	13246.4684 504 179	348
30	11100.4081 259 298	12512.6782 002 020	14113.5853 927 881	15928.9847 426 752	360
31	13154.6619 529 589	14899.8659 741 476	16887.5003 715 223	19152.0850 236 126	372
32	15586.6760 664 843	17740.0028 299 588	20204.0435 261 863	23024.7084 447 502	384
33	18465.9174 584 501	21119.0320 993 677	24169.3627 883 389	27677.7477 096 599	396
34	21874.6275 260 050	25139.2041 485 279	28910.3705 538 150	33268.4731 808 269	408
35	25910.1711 789 518	29922.1705 025 531	34578.8055 892 585	39985.8485 379 767	420
36	30687.8179 286 274	35612.6650 545 253	41356.0895 213 839	48056.9176 544 191	432
37	36344.0343 960 214	42382.8837 533 823	49459.1333 437 873	57754.4785 645 824	444
38	43040.3822 849 045	50437.6953 012 586	59147.2797 820 020	69406.3038 989 417	456
39	50968.1331 599 712	60020.8405 374 317	70730.6037 113 118	83406.2194 323 548	468
40	60353.7318 445 108	71422.3081 039 573	84579.8362 871 199	100227.4151 951 112	480
41	71465.2644 917 182	84987.1095 826 882	101138.2304 155 531	120438.4390 554 811	492
42	84620.1160 808 167	101125.7196 417 662	120935.7473 257 298	144722.4133 487 274	504
43	100194.0360 633 764	120326.4971 133 242	144606.0182 933 541	173900.1240 648 759	516
44	118631.8711 070 018	143170.4628 676 682	172906.6243 856 641	208957.7629 980 555	528
45	140460.2715 018 050	170348.8816 665 241	206743.3432 930 049	251080.2605 279 587	540
46	166302.7341 699 252	202684.1800 271 225	247199.1392 812 578	301691.3356 644 945	552
47	196897.4119 600 659	241154.8330 775 100	295568.8241 057 536	362501.6170 267 916	564
48	233118.1979 239 842	286924.9734 862 562	353400.4982 297 880	435566.4612 211 852	576
49	275999.6868 170 216	341379.6184 410 095	422545.0986 985 254	523355.4228 499 815	588
50	326766.7268 121 076	406166.5806 540 768	505215.6394 773 956	628835.7242 019 912	600

Table 2. **FUTURE WORTH OF ONE DOLLAR PER PERIOD WITH INTEREST PAYABLE AT END OF EACH PERIOD**

MONTHS	19% NOMINAL ANNUAL RATE	19½% NOMINAL ANNUAL RATE	20% NOMINAL ANNUAL RATE	20½% NOMINAL ANNUAL RATE	MONTHS
1	1.0000 000 000	1.0000 000 000	1.0000 000 000	1.0000 000 000	1
2	2.0158 333 333	2.0162 500 000	2.0166 666 667	2.0170 833 333	2
3	3.0477 506 944	3.0490 140 625	3.0502 777 778	3.0515 418 403	3
4	4.0960 067 471	4.0985 605 410	4.1011 157 407	4.1036 723 467	4
5	5.1608 601 873	5.1651 621 498	5.1694 676 698	5.1737 767 493	5
6	6.2425 738 069	6.2490 960 347	6.2556 254 642	6.2621 621 021	6
7	7.3414 145 588	7.3506 438 453	7.3598 858 887	7.3691 407 047	7
8	8.4576 536 227	8.4700 918 078	8.4825 506 535	8.4950 301 917	8
9	9.5915 664 717	9.6077 307 997	9.6239 264 977	9.6401 536 242	9
10	10.7434 329 409	10.7638 564 252	10.7843 252 726	10.8048 395 819	10
11	11.9135 372 958	11.9387 690 921	11.9640 640 272	11.9894 222 581	11
YEARS					
1	13.1021 683 029	13.1327 740 898	13.1634 650 943	13.1942 415 550	12
2	28.9223 944 980	29.0681 817 032	29.2148 770 768	29.3624 866 178	24
3	48.0245 424 078	48.4043 260 750	48.7878 257 483	49.1750 804 165	36
4	71.0894 499 680	71.8669 502 037	72.6549 048 638	73.4534 650 838	48
5	98.9391 956 233	100.3366 761 437	101.7582 083 598	103.2042 371 455	60
6	132.5663 988 124	134.8820 573 702	137.2465 171 842	139.6608 816 215	72
7	173.1695 988 674	176.7996 847 684	180.5206 445 830	184.3349 130 615	84
8	222.1959 733 011	227.6628 515 455	233.2887 297 402	239.0785 438 532	96
9	281.3929 180 458	289.3806 036 026	297.6336 623 484	306.1614 780 694	108
10	352.8703 280 640	364.2693 917 052	376.0952 995 296	388.3650 147 728	120
11	439.1757 981 342	455.1400 147 678	471.7707 204 155	489.0973 623 584	132
12	543.3854 241 145	565.4031 174 969	588.4364 756 883	612.5349 449 376	144
13	669.2134 410 191	699.1972 020 279	730.6976 575 817	763.7955 594 093	156
14	821.1446 056 233	861.5439 582 178	904.1696 745 105	949.1505 624 181	168
15	1004.5940 419 717	1058.5367 425 981	1115.6999 054 341	1176.2848 845 969	180
16	1226.1002 469 969	1297.5692 801 655	1373.6379 832 103	1454.6156 524 437	192
17	1493.5581 353 465	1587.6131 728 677	1688.1653 757 081	1795.6826 280 860	204
18	1816.5004 295 919	1939.5546 305 035	2071.6972 740 785	2213.6266 548 057	216
19	2206.4374 251 168	2366.6030 625 489	2539.3726 517 281	2725.7759 449 610	228
20	2677.2672 395 711	2884.7868 665 755	3109.6518 378 637	3353.3645 181 614	240
21	3245.7711 689 831	3513.5550 216 755	3805.0451 933 445	4122.4125 765 745	252
22	3932.2118 059 905	4276.5070 664 823	4653.0016 515 201	5064.8053 182 605	264
23	4761.0552 383 062	5202.2788 600 335	5686.9921 970 073	6219.6149 167 852	276
24	5761.8430 679 467	6325.6173 707 155	6947.8310 500 506	7634.7204 771 901	288
25	6970.2453 317 622	7688.6814 333 142	8485.2867 069 538	9368.7931 326 711	300
26	8429.3318 513 486	9342.6412 230 646	10360.0464 284 186	11493.7285 852 789	312
27	10191.1073 257 809	11349.5644 416 563	12646.1117 191 123	14097.6279 452 497	324
28	12318.3648 808 646	13784.7802 854 855	15433.7193 540 954	17288.4504 563 688	336
29	14886.9241 390 296	16739.6896 467 901	18832.9032 524 076	21198.4895 515 737	348
30	17988.3335 790 564	20325.1990 609 357	22977.8377 939 629	25989.8578 187 695	360
31	21733.1335 030 258	24675.8833 584 907	28032.1340 214 512	31861.2082 868 621	372
32	26254.7959 090 190	29955.0366 588 044	34195.2977 817 206	39055.9707 005 945	384
33	31714.4816 943 412	36360.8012 838 943	41710.6047 258 041	47872.4442 651 292	396
34	38306.7847 453 035	44133.6046 290 093	50874.7030 137 419	58676.1653 116 753	408
35	46266.6676 441 619	53565.1831 177 341	62049.3227 672 574	71915.0626 550 648	420
36	55877.8361 953 844	65009.5319 375 047	75675.5544 718 952	88138.0289 935 782	432
37	67482.8512 557 516	78896.1915 316 710	92291.2599 333 837	108017.6783 324 979	444
38	81495.3382 737 029	95746.3695 296 639	112552.3030 425 338	132378.2329 679 472	456
39	98414.7297 098 086	116192.5032 192 459	137258.4383 807 121	162229.6962 422 465	468
40	118844.0657 870 827	141001.9967 986 050	167384.8795 545 488	198809.7278 939 112	480
41	143511.4880 247 157	171106.0243 379 476	204120.7933 418 473	243634.9581 796 516	492
42	173296.1916 268 343	207634.4795 113 930	248916.2391 099 262	298563.8682 829 379	504
43	209259.7617 202 116	251958.3838 665 360	303539.4063 238 775	365873.8440 689 345	516
44	252684.0103 257 699	305741.3453 401 447	370146.4094 538 574	448355.5978 811 296	528
45	305116.6626 475 865	371001.9984 111 112	451366.3952 628 099	549428.8731 645 077	540
46	368426.5210 281 551	450189.7694 552 718	550405.3218 743 760	673284.2290 989 872	552
47	444870.0727 212 269	546276.8110 011 701	671172.5060 431 024	825056.7837 198 559	564
48	537171.9155 136 109	662869.5554 527 645	818434.9337 675 577	1011039.1190 201 578	576
49	648621.8677 224 921	804344.0752 220 234	998005.4252 762 586	1238942.1752 094 606	588
50	783192.2237 586 206	976010.3297 397 051	1216972.0817 340 191	1518214.9509 629 128	600

Table 2. FUTURE WORTH OF ONE DOLLAR PER PERIOD WITH INTEREST
PAYABLE AT END OF EACH PERIOD

	21% NOMINAL ANNUAL RATE	21½% NOMINAL ANNUAL RATE	22% NOMINAL ANNUAL RATE	22½% NOMINAL ANNUAL RATE	
MONTHS					**MONTHS**
1	1.0000 000 000	1.0000 000 000	1.0000 000 000	1.0000 000 000	1
2	2.0175 000 000	2.0179 166 667	2.0183 333 333	2.0187 500 000	2
3	3.0528 062 500	3.0540 710 069	3.0553 361 111	3.0566 015 625	3
4	4.1062 303 594	4.1087 897 792	4.1113 506 065	4.1139 128 418	4
5	5.1780 893 907	5.1824 055 960	5.1867 253 676	5.1910 487 076	5
6	6.2687 059 550	6.2752 570 296	6.2818 153 327	6.2883 808 708	6
7	7.3784 083 092	7.3876 887 181	7.3969 819 471	7.4062 880 122	7
8	8.5075 304 546	8.5200 514 743	8.5325 932 828	8.5451 559 124	8
9	9.6564 122 376	9.6727 023 965	9.6890 241 597	9.7053 775 858	9
10	10.8253 994 517	10.8460 049 811	10.8666 562 692	10.8873 534 155	10
11	12.0148 439 421	12.0403 292 370	12.0658 783 009	12.0914 912 920	11
YEARS					
1	13.2251 037 111	13.2560 518 025	13.2870 860 697	13.3182 067 538	12
2	29.5110 163 652	29.6604 723 983	29.8108 608 368	29.9621 878 413	24
3	49.5661 294 873	49.9610 127 924	50.3597 705 920	50.7624 435 788	36
4	74.2627 842 514	75.0830 180 401	75.9143 244 439	76.7568 638 121	48
5	104.6752 158 756	106.1716 065 906	107.6938 801 651	109.2425 164 788	60
6	142.1262 798 406	144.6438 674 047	147.2148 269 086	149.8403 686 219	72
7	188.2449 923 937	192.2534 541 102	196.3629 410 360	200.5761 693 012	84
8	245.0373 881 863	251.1705 205 447	257.4833 675 771	263.9815 302 918	96
9	314.9737 771 551	324.0806 413 302	333.4925 208 662	343.2202 482 881	108
10	401.0961 960 765	414.3072 265 060	428.0172 437 890	442.2461 718 315	120
11	507.1507 286 346	525.9630 101 582	545.5678 657 470	566.0004 901 948	132
12	637.7504 495 547	664.1375 182 446	691.7534 169 491	720.6582 885 325	144
13	798.5760 804 165	835.1290 608 271	873.5492 681 690	913.9366 718 892	156
14	996.6230 851 105	1046.7318 234 468	1099.6299 666 306	1155.4798 328 191	168
15	1240.5059 528 977	1308.5911 439 258	1380.7831 495 767	1457.3402 766 970	180
16	1540.8329 045 325	1632.6431 689 222	1730.4242 857 667	1834.5802 168 689	192
17	1910.6673 201 130	2033.6589 307 906	2165.2368 062 412	2306.0231 480 218	204
18	2366.0959 594 784	2529.9176 450 162	2705.9681 687 507	2895.1930 997 315	216
19	2926.9286 911 449	3144.0399 186 579	3378.4198 407 548	3631.4884 370 031	228
20	3617.5601 660 269	3904.0188 493 484	4214.6784 388 921	4551.6487 780 300	240
21	4468.0309 163 348	4844.4960 146 992	5254.6467 698 123	5701.5882 253 396	252
22	5515.3340 344 746	6008.3405 146 285	6547.9478 273 153	7138.6863 847 787	264
23	6805.0242 688 163	7448.6030 429 701	8156.2925 966 780	8934.6514 894 588	276
24	8393.1995 274 849	9230.9340 594 169	10156.4246 480 123	11179.0984 926 391	288
25	10348.9409 800 321	11436.5762 876 058	12643.7820 224 888	13984.0206 689 984	300
26	12757.3178 945 659	14166.0679 442 500	15737.0511 415 128	17489.3778 479 757	312
27	15723.0879 123 284	17543.8255 009 723	19583.8300 325 923	21870.0801 204 918	324
28	19375.2537 112 855	21723.8148 716 015	24367.6710 976 479	27344.7154 916 087	336
29	23872.6742 608 181	26896.5695 306 212	30316.8394 755 813	34186.4569 709 879	348
30	29410.9747 413 531	33297.8754 646 554	37715.2049 119 948	42736.6933 424 575	360
31	36231.0556 910 615	41219.5188 369 448	46915.7868 511 013	53422.0637 599 663	372
32	44629.5715 036 385	51022.5862 679 352	58357.5990 656 721	66775.7461 611 172	384
33	54971.8340 624 313	63153.9239 891 853	72586.5975 811 957	83464.0617 461 916	396
34	67707.7027 828 103	78166.5061 164 670	90281.7314 426 779	104319.7230 312 792	408
35	83391.1522 350 606	96744.6404 745 266	112287.3393 590 867	130383.3844 847 646	420
36	102704.3684 845 110	119735.1609 126 390	139653.4380 595 208	162955.5690 382 040	432
37	126487.4222 721 147	148186.0279 280 324	173685.8247 550 715	203661.5614 973 505	444
38	155774.8097 356 167	183394.0971 018 707	216008.3843 889 418	254532.5069 006 461	456
39	191840.4500 901 941	226964.2327 423 448	268640.5747 194 741	318106.7604 659 491	468
40	236253.0975 414 802	280882.4612 699 091	334093.7865 042 469	397556.5462 787 286	480
41	290944.5776 937 765	347606.4988 432 523	415491.1766 952 657	496846.2447 289 451	492
42	358293.8165 458 369	430177.7796 822 156	516716.6925 904 285	620930.2069 131 351	504
43	441230.3170 998 712	532360.0915 948 089	642600.3977 583 178	775999.9665 322 300	516
44	543361.5845 260 495	658811.1380 326 832	799148.9427 240 772	969793.1846 487 592	528
45	669130.0425 197 859	815294.8468 658 828	993832.1775 256 835	1211979.7430 094 011	540
46	824006.2662 732 554	1008944.1033 963 474	1235939.5821 081 234	1514644.2511 930 846	552
47	1014726.9371 534 641	1248585.8835 817 467	1537023.5219 418 659	1892889.0436 958 134	564
48	1249587.8694 479 993	1545143.6077 855 200	1911450.4791 931 507	2365587.7552 626 332	576
49	1538804.8550 200 767	1912135.0552 571 643	2377086.5619 210 136	2956327.0763 210 176	588
50	1894958.0216 033 534	2366288.5354 234 345	2956150.0009 688 579	3694583.6801 687 537	600

Table 3. SINKING FUND FACTORS
PAYABLE AT END OF EACH PERIOD

MONTHS	5% NOMINAL ANNUAL RATE	5½% NOMINAL ANNUAL RATE	6% NOMINAL ANNUAL RATE	6½% NOMINAL ANNUAL RATE	MONTHS
1	1.0000 000 000	1.0000 000 000	1.0000 000 000	1.0000 000 000	1
2	0.4989 604 990	0.4988 567 865	0.4987 531 172	0.4986 494 910	2
3	0.3319 482 944	0.3318 102 131	0.3316 722 084	0.3315 342 802	3
4	0.2484 429 140	0.2482 877 996	0.2481 327 930	0.2479 778 940	4
5	0.1983 402 633	0.1981 750 502	0.1980 099 750	0.1978 450 376	5
6	0.1649 389 774	0.1647 671 327	0.1645 954 556	0.1644 239 461	6
7	0.1410 813 285	0.1409 048 335	0.1407 285 355	0.1405 524 345	7
8	0.1231 884 527	0.1230 085 457	0.1228 288 649	0.1226 494 103	8
9	0.1092 720 923	0.1090 895 988	0.1089 073 606	0.1087 253 777	9
10	0.0981 392 927	0.0979 547 905	0.0977 705 727	0.0975 866 392	10
11	0.0890 309 010	0.0888 448 104	0.0886 590 331	0.0884 735 691	11

YEARS					
1	0.0814 408 151	0.0812 534 512	0.0810 664 297	0.0808 797 503	12
2	0.0397 047 231	0.0395 123 228	0.0393 206 103	0.0391 295 848	24
3	0.0258 042 304	0.0256 125 685	0.0254 219 375	0.0252 323 362	36
4	0.0188 626 269	0.0186 731 419	0.0184 850 290	0.0182 982 863	48
5	0.0147 045 670	0.0145 178 288	0.0143 328 015	0.0141 494 816	60
6	0.0119 382 660	0.0117 545 538	0.0115 728 879	0.0113 932 630	72
7	0.0099 672 424	0.0097 867 093	0.0096 085 545	0.0094 327 698	84
8	0.0084 932 533	0.0083 159 888	0.0081 414 302	0.0079 695 659	96
9	0.0073 506 065	0.0071 766 637	0.0070 057 496	0.0068 378 484	108
10	0.0064 398 849	0.0062 692 945	0.0061 020 502	0.0059 381 311	120
11	0.0056 978 216	0.0055 305 993	0.0053 670 346	0.0052 071 005	132
12	0.0050 822 375	0.0049 183 884	0.0047 585 021	0.0046 025 442	144
13	0.0045 639 303	0.0044 034 518	0.0042 472 344	0.0040 952 352	156
14	0.0041 220 404	0.0039 649 237	0.0038 123 592	0.0036 642 941	168
15	0.0037 412 696	0.0035 875 012	0.0034 385 683	0.0032 944 070	180
16	0.0034 101 433	0.0032 597 057	0.0031 143 786	0.0029 740 860	192
17	0.0031 198 861	0.0029 727 584	0.0028 310 077	0.0026 945 444	204
18	0.0028 636 719	0.0027 198 302	0.0025 816 232	0.0024 489 462	216
19	0.0026 361 109	0.0024 955 289	0.0023 608 299	0.0022 318 930	228
20	0.0024 328 907	0.0022 955 397	0.0021 643 106	0.0020 390 647	240
21	0.0022 505 198	0.0021 163 691	0.0019 885 692	0.0018 669 626	252
22	0.0020 861 409	0.0019 551 578	0.0018 307 445	0.0017 127 233	264
23	0.0019 373 930	0.0018 095 433	0.0016 884 720	0.0015 739 800	276
24	0.0018 023 085	0.0016 775 561	0.0015 597 807	0.0014 487 600	288
25	0.0016 792 337	0.0015 575 416	0.0014 430 140	0.0013 354 049	300
26	0.0015 667 695	0.0014 480 989	0.0013 367 699	0.0012 325 114	312
27	0.0014 637 233	0.0013 480 345	0.0012 398 535	0.0011 388 831	324
28	0.0013 690 728	0.0012 563 249	0.0011 512 402	0.0010 534 942	336
29	0.0012 819 364	0.0011 720 873	0.0010 700 461	0.0009 754 600	348
30	0.0012 015 496	0.0010 945 567	0.0009 955 053	0.0009 040 136	360
31	0.0011 272 465	0.0010 230 661	0.0009 269 500	0.0008 384 866	372
32	0.0010 584 442	0.0009 570 319	0.0008 637 959	0.0007 782 942	384
33	0.0009 946 304	0.0008 959 411	0.0008 055 294	0.0007 229 221	396
34	0.0009 353 526	0.0008 393 407	0.0007 516 970	0.0006 719 169	408
35	0.0008 802 101	0.0007 868 295	0.0007 018 971	0.0006 248 765	420
36	0.0008 288 466	0.0007 380 506	0.0006 557 726	0.0005 814 439	432
37	0.0007 809 441	0.0006 926 858	0.0006 130 050	0.0005 413 006	444
38	0.0007 362 181	0.0006 504 502	0.0005 733 093	0.0005 041 618	456
39	0.0006 944 132	0.0006 110 881	0.0005 364 298	0.0004 697 720	468
40	0.0006 552 993	0.0005 743 695	0.0005 021 364	0.0004 379 014	480
41	0.0006 186 690	0.0005 400 866	0.0004 702 216	0.0004 083 431	492
42	0.0005 843 345	0.0005 080 515	0.0004 404 975	0.0003 809 097	504
43	0.0005 521 252	0.0004 780 939	0.0004 127 943	0.0003 554 319	516
44	0.0005 218 864	0.0004 500 589	0.0003 869 572	0.0003 317 556	528
45	0.0004 934 769	0.0004 238 055	0.0003 628 457	0.0003 097 412	540
46	0.0004 667 679	0.0003 992 050	0.0003 403 315	0.0002 892 611	552
47	0.0004 416 414	0.0003 761 397	0.0003 192 974	0.0002 701 990	564
48	0.0004 179 896	0.0003 545 020	0.0002 996 364	0.0002 524 487	576
49	0.0003 957 132	0.0003 341 928	0.0002 812 499	0.0002 359 128	588
50	0.0003 747 210	0.0003 151 214	0.0002 640 479	0.0002 205 022	600

39

Table 3.   SINKING FUND FACTORS
PAYABLE AT END OF EACH PERIOD

	7% NOMINAL ANNUAL RATE	7½% NOMINAL ANNUAL RATE	8% NOMINAL ANNUAL RATE	8½% NOMINAL ANNUAL RATE	
MONTHS					MONTHS
1	1.0000 000 000	1.0000 000 000	1.0000 000 000	1.0000 000 000	1
2	0.4985 459 078	0.4984 423 676	0.4983 388 704	0.4982 354 162	2
3	0.3313 964 286	0.3312 586 535	0.3311 209 548	0.3309 833 325	3
4	0.2478 231 027	0.2476 684 189	0.2475 138 426	0.2473 593 738	4
5	0.1976 802 380	0.1975 155 761	0.1973 510 518	0.1971 866 649	5
6	0.1642 526 040	0.1640 814 292	0.1639 104 215	0.1637 395 810	6
7	0.1403 765 303	0.1402 008 227	0.1400 253 116	0.1398 499 970	7
8	0.1224 701 817	0.1222 911 789	0.1221 124 018	0.1219 338 503	8
9	0.1085 436 499	0.1083 621 769	0.1081 809 587	0.1079 999 951	9
10	0.0974 029 898	0.0972 196 242	0.0970 365 423	0.0968 537 439	10
11	0.0882 884 181	0.0881 035 799	0.0879 190 542	0.0877 348 409	11
YEARS					
1	0.0806 934 128	0.0805 074 169	0.0803 217 624	0.0801 364 491	12
2	0.0389 392 458	0.0387 495 927	0.0385 606 248	0.0383 723 415	24
3	0.0250 437 635	0.0248 562 182	0.0246 696 988	0.0244 842 041	36
4	0.0181 129 113	0.0179 289 019	0.0177 462 557	0.0175 649 700	48
5	0.0139 678 652	0.0137 879 486	0.0136 097 276	0.0134 331 980	60
6	0.0112 156 731	0.0110 401 123	0.0108 665 739	0.0106 950 513	72
7	0.0092 593 466	0.0090 882 759	0.0089 195 477	0.0087 531 521	84
8	0.0078 003 837	0.0076 338 706	0.0074 700 126	0.0073 087 952	96
9	0.0066 729 433	0.0065 110 162	0.0063 520 482	0.0061 960 194	108
10	0.0057 775 146	0.0056 201 769	0.0054 660 928	0.0053 152 356	120
11	0.0050 507 676	0.0048 980 051	0.0047 487 802	0.0046 030 585	132
12	0.0044 504 776	0.0043 022 631	0.0041 578 592	0.0040 172 223	144
13	0.0039 474 081	0.0038 037 042	0.0036 640 721	0.0035 284 579	156
14	0.0035 206 721	0.0033 814 334	0.0032 465 153	0.0031 158 520	168
15	0.0031 549 494	0.0030 201 236	0.0028 898 542	0.0027 640 622	180
16	0.0028 387 469	0.0027 082 759	0.0025 825 836	0.0024 615 767	192
17	0.0025 632 732	0.0024 370 939	0.0023 159 018	0.0021 995 877	204
18	0.0023 216 884	0.0021 997 333	0.0020 829 596	0.0019 712 412	216
19	0.0021 085 904	0.0019 907 882	0.0018 783 471	0.0017 711 230	228
20	0.0019 196 560	0.0018 059 319	0.0016 977 340	0.0015 948 990	240
21	0.0017 513 838	0.0016 416 601	0.0015 376 129	0.0014 390 587	252
22	0.0016 009 077	0.0014 951 040	0.0013 951 124	0.0013 007 282	264
23	0.0014 658 589	0.0013 638 926	0.0012 678 592	0.0011 775 321	276
24	0.0013 442 625	0.0012 460 490	0.0011 538 746	0.0010 674 899	288
25	0.0012 344 586	0.0011 399 118	0.0010 514 955	0.0009 689 375	300
26	0.0011 350 423	0.0010 440 744	0.0009 593 145	0.0008 804 665	312
27	0.0010 448 160	0.0009 573 384	0.0008 761 320	0.0008 008 769	324
28	0.0009 627 528	0.0008 786 759	0.0008 009 198	0.0007 291 406	336
29	0.0008 879 673	0.0008 072 008	0.0007 327 915	0.0006 643 712	348
30	0.0008 196 916	0.0007 421 451	0.0006 709 791	0.0006 058 015	360
31	0.0007 572 571	0.0006 828 398	0.0006 148 139	0.0005 527 635	372
32	0.0007 000 786	0.0006 286 998	0.0005 637 113	0.0005 046 738	384
33	0.0006 476 417	0.0005 792 109	0.0005 171 579	0.0004 610 205	396
34	0.0005 994 928	0.0005 339 200	0.0004 747 015	0.0004 213 527	408
35	0.0005 552 303	0.0004 924 260	0.0004 359 421	0.0003 852 724	420
36	0.0005 144 971	0.0004 543 727	0.0004 005 249	0.0003 524 267	432
37	0.0004 769 753	0.0004 194 430	0.0003 681 343	0.0003 225 021	444
38	0.0004 423 807	0.0003 873 536	0.0003 384 885	0.0002 952 193	456
39	0.0004 104 584	0.0003 578 509	0.0003 113 358	0.0002 703 289	468
40	0.0003 809 795	0.0003 307 073	0.0002 864 502	0.0002 476 073	480
41	0.0003 537 376	0.0003 057 178	0.0002 636 290	0.0002 268 545	492
42	0.0003 285 467	0.0002 826 977	0.0002 426 893	0.0002 078 904	504
43	0.0003 052 382	0.0002 614 802	0.0002 234 665	0.0001 905 529	516
44	0.0002 836 595	0.0002 419 140	0.0002 058 117	0.0001 746 960	528
45	0.0002 636 717	0.0002 238 623	0.0001 895 900	0.0001 601 876	540
46	0.0002 451 489	0.0002 072 007	0.0001 746 794	0.0001 469 086	552
47	0.0002 279 759	0.0001 918 158	0.0001 609 690	0.0001 347 508	564
48	0.0002 120 478	0.0001 776 040	0.0001 483 580	0.0001 236 164	576
49	0.0001 972 689	0.0001 644 734	0.0001 367 548	0.0001 134 165	588
50	0.0001 835 512	0.0001 523 360	0.0001 260 759	0.0001 040 703	600

Table 3.   SINKING FUND FACTORS
PAYABLE AT END OF EACH PERIOD

	9% NOMINAL ANNUAL RATE	**9½%** NOMINAL ANNUAL RATE	**10%** NOMINAL ANNUAL RATE	**10½%** NOMINAL ANNUAL RATE	
MONTHS					**MONTHS**
1	1.0000 000 000	1.0000 000 000	1.0000 000 000	1.0000 000 000	1
2	0.4981 320 050	0.4980 286 366	0.4979 253 112	0.4978 220 286	2
3	0.3308 457 866	0.3307 083 169	0.3305 709 235	0.3304 336 063	3
4	0.2472 050 123	0.2470 507 580	0.2468 966 110	0.2467 425 712	4
5	0.1970 224 155	0.1968 583 034	0.1966 943 285	0.1965 304 908	5
6	0.1635 689 074	0.1633 984 008	0.1632 280 609	0.1630 578 876	6
7	0.1396 748 786	0.1394 999 563	0.1393 252 301	0.1391 506 998	7
8	0.1217 555 241	0.1215 774 232	0.1213 995 474	0.1212 218 965	8
9	0.1078 192 858	0.1076 388 308	0.1074 586 298	0.1072 786 826	9
10	0.0966 712 287	0.0964 889 967	0.0963 070 477	0.0961 253 813	10
11	0.0875 509 398	0.0873 673 505	0.0871 840 730	0.0870 011 070	11
YEARS					
1	0.0799 514 768	0.0797 668 451	0.0795 825 539	0.0793 986 029	12
2	0.0381 847 423	0.0379 978 263	0.0378 115 930	0.0376 260 416	24
3	0.0242 997 327	0.0241 162 831	0.0239 338 539	0.0237 524 435	36
4	0.0173 850 424	0.0172 064 700	0.0170 292 501	0.0168 533 798	48
5	0.0132 583 552	0.0130 851 946	0.0129 137 114	0.0127 439 004	60
6	0.0105 255 372	0.0103 580 241	0.0101 925 044	0.0100 289 700	72
7	0.0085 890 783	0.0084 273 150	0.0082 678 507	0.0081 106 731	84
8	0.0071 502 033	0.0069 942 207	0.0068 408 308	0.0066 900 162	96
9	0.0060 429 087	0.0058 926 941	0.0057 453 529	0.0056 008 612	108
10	0.0051 675 774	0.0050 230 891	0.0048 817 404	0.0047 434 997	120
11	0.0044 608 039	0.0043 219 789	0.0041 865 441	0.0040 544 593	132
12	0.0038 803 070	0.0037 470 657	0.0036 174 493	0.0034 914 068	144
13	0.0033 968 051	0.0032 690 553	0.0031 451 476	0.0030 250 196	156
14	0.0029 893 750	0.0028 670 134	0.0027 486 935	0.0026 343 401	168
15	0.0026 426 658	0.0025 255 802	0.0024 127 178	0.0023 039 892	180
16	0.0023 451 584	0.0022 332 290	0.0021 256 860	0.0020 224 244	192
17	0.0020 880 390	0.0019 811 398	0.0018 787 712	0.0017 808 122	204
18	0.0018 644 484	0.0017 624 478	0.0016 651 036	0.0015 722 776	216
19	0.0016 689 678	0.0015 717 301	0.0014 792 558	0.0013 913 890	228
20	0.0014 972 596	0.0014 046 452	0.0013 168 831	0.0012 337 989	240
21	0.0013 458 102	0.0012 576 769	0.0011 744 667	0.0010 959 865	252
22	0.0012 117 432	0.0011 279 467	0.0010 491 266	0.0009 750 708	264
23	0.0010 926 815	0.0010 130 759	0.0009 384 833	0.0008 686 723	276
24	0.0009 866 433	0.0009 110 820	0.0008 405 540	0.0007 748 088	288
25	0.0008 919 636	0.0008 202 999	0.0007 536 741	0.0006 918 171	300
26	0.0008 072 338	0.0007 393 211	0.0006 764 363	0.0006 182 918	312
27	0.0007 312 540	0.0006 669 467	0.0006 076 433	0.0005 530 385	324
28	0.0006 629 964	0.0006 021 500	0.0005 462 706	0.0004 950 357	336
29	0.0006 015 759	0.0005 440 477	0.0004 914 374	0.0004 434 063	348
30	0.0005 462 262	0.0004 918 754	0.0004 423 824	0.0003 973 929	360
31	0.0004 962 810	0.0004 449 694	0.0003 984 451	0.0003 563 396	372
32	0.0004 511 587	0.0004 027 507	0.0003 590 502	0.0003 196 756	384
33	0.0004 103 496	0.0003 647 124	0.0003 236 947	0.0002 869 027	396
34	0.0003 734 051	0.0003 304 093	0.0002 919 376	0.0002 575 852	408
35	0.0003 399 297	0.0002 994 493	0.0002 633 909	0.0002 313 402	420
36	0.0003 095 734	0.0002 714 859	0.0002 377 126	0.0002 078 310	432
37	0.0002 820 255	0.0002 462 119	0.0002 146 001	0.0001 867 605	444
38	0.0002 570 096	0.0002 233 551	0.0001 937 857	0.0001 678 662	456
39	0.0002 342 795	0.0002 026 728	0.0001 750 314	0.0001 509 157	468
40	0.0002 136 150	0.0001 839 489	0.0001 581 258	0.0001 357 028	480
41	0.0001 948 191	0.0001 669 904	0.0001 428 804	0.0001 220 445	492
42	0.0001 777 151	0.0001 516 246	0.0001 291 273	0.0001 097 779	504
43	0.0001 621 444	0.0001 376 968	0.0001 167 162	0.0000 987 579	516
44	0.0001 479 643	0.0001 250 682	0.0001 055 129	0.0000 888 552	528
45	0.0001 350 461	0.0001 136 141	0.0000 953 971	0.0000 799 545	540
46	0.0001 232 739	0.0001 032 225	0.0000 862 610	0.0000 719 526	552
47	0.0001 125 431	0.0000 937 925	0.0000 780 080	0.0000 647 574	564
48	0.0001 027 589	0.0000 852 331	0.0000 705 512	0.0000 582 865	576
49	0.0000 938 359	0.0000 774 624	0.0000 638 126	0.0000 524 660	588
50	0.0000 856 964	0.0000 704 063	0.0000 577 221	0.0000 472 299	600

41

Table 3.   SINKING FUND FACTORS
PAYABLE AT END OF EACH PERIOD

MONTHS	11% NOMINAL ANNUAL RATE	11½% NOMINAL ANNUAL RATE	12% NOMINAL ANNUAL RATE	12½% NOMINAL ANNUAL RATE	MONTHS
1	1.0000 000 000	1.0000 000 000	1.0000 000 000	1.0000 000 000	1
2	0.4977 187 889	0.4976 155 920	0.4975 124 378	0.4974 093 264	2
3	0.3302 963 653	0.3301 592 004	0.3300 221 115	0.3298 850 986	3
4	0.2465 886 384	0.2464 348 127	0.2462 810 939	0.2461 274 820	4
5	0.1963 667 901	0.1962 032 264	0.1960 397 996	0.1958 765 096	5
6	0.1628 878 809	0.1627 180 406	0.1625 483 667	0.1623 788 590	6
7	0.1389 763 652	0.1388 022 263	0.1386 282 829	0.1384 545 349	7
8	0.1210 444 704	0.1208 672 690	0.1206 902 920	0.1205 135 395	8
9	0.1070 989 892	0.1069 195 494	0.1067 403 628	0.1065 614 295	9
10	0.0959 439 974	0.0957 628 959	0.0955 820 766	0.0954 015 391	10
11	0.0868 184 523	0.0866 361 086	0.0864 540 757	0.0862 723 535	11
YEARS					
1	0.0792 149 919	0.0790 317 205	0.0788 487 887	0.0786 661 960	12
2	0.0374 411 715	0.0372 569 820	0.0370 734 722	0.0368 906 416	24
3	0.0235 720 505	0.0233 926 731	0.0232 143 098	0.0230 369 589	36
4	0.0166 788 559	0.0165 056 756	0.0163 338 354	0.0161 633 322	48
5	0.0125 757 564	0.0124 092 740	0.0122 444 477	0.0120 812 716	60
6	0.0098 674 123	0.0097 078 228	0.0095 501 925	0.0093 945 120	72
7	0.0079 557 698	0.0078 031 275	0.0076 527 328	0.0075 045 718	84
8	0.0065 417 590	0.0063 960 405	0.0062 528 414	0.0061 121 420	96
9	0.0054 591 944	0.0053 203 269	0.0051 842 326	0.0050 508 844	108
10	0.0046 083 345	0.0044 762 111	0.0043 470 948	0.0042 209 502	120
11	0.0039 256 824	0.0038 001 703	0.0036 778 788	0.0035 587 623	132
12	0.0033 688 859	0.0032 498 325	0.0031 341 914	0.0030 219 061	144
13	0.0029 086 069	0.0027 958 436	0.0026 866 622	0.0025 809 941	156
14	0.0025 238 756	0.0024 172 209	0.0023 142 953	0.0022 150 168	168
15	0.0021 993 027	0.0020 985 648	0.0020 016 806	0.0019 085 542	180
16	0.0019 233 373	0.0018 283 163	0.0017 372 513	0.0016 500 314	192
17	0.0016 871 398	0.0015 979 293	0.0015 121 553	0.0014 305 914	204
18	0.0014 838 298	0.0013 996 191	0.0013 195 038	0.0012 433 420	216
19	0.0013 079 722	0.0012 288 475	0.0011 538 566	0.0010 828 418	228
20	0.0011 552 173	0.0010 809 630	0.0010 108 613	0.0009 447 388	240
21	0.0010 220 429	0.0009 524 432	0.0008 869 965	0.0008 255 136	252
22	0.0009 055 679	0.0008 404 078	0.0007 793 836	0.0007 222 910	264
23	0.0008 034 134	0.0007 424 799	0.0006 856 488	0.0006 327 019	276
24	0.0007 135 990	0.0006 566 817	0.0006 038 188	0.0005 547 783	288
25	0.0006 344 641	0.0005 813 563	0.0005 322 414	0.0004 868 747	300
26	0.0005 646 064	0.0005 151 058	0.0004 695 246	0.0004 276 063	312
27	0.0005 028 349	0.0004 567 444	0.0004 144 889	0.0003 758 014	324
28	0.0004 481 329	0.0004 052 606	0.0003 661 298	0.0003 304 640	336
29	0.0003 996 277	0.0003 597 881	0.0003 235 881	0.0002 907 435	348
30	0.0003 565 673	0.0003 195 810	0.0002 861 260	0.0002 559 110	360
31	0.0003 183 011	0.0002 839 955	0.0002 531 072	0.0002 253 394	372
32	0.0002 842 642	0.0002 524 735	0.0002 239 817	0.0001 984 878	384
33	0.0002 539 643	0.0002 245 299	0.0001 982 726	0.0001 748 885	396
34	0.0002 269 718	0.0001 997 418	0.0001 755 650	0.0001 541 358	408
35	0.0002 029 099	0.0001 777 400	0.0001 554 978	0.0001 358 772	420
36	0.0001 814 481	0.0001 582 009	0.0001 377 553	0.0001 198 060	432
37	0.0001 622 957	0.0001 408 407	0.0001 220 616	0.0001 056 547	444
38	0.0001 451 963	0.0001 254 101	0.0001 081 748	0.0000 931 898	456
39	0.0001 299 235	0.0001 116 894	0.0000 958 829	0.0000 822 069	468
40	0.0001 162 774	0.0000 994 853	0.0000 849 995	0.0000 725 273	480
41	0.0001 040 805	0.0000 886 269	0.0000 753 607	0.0000 639 944	492
42	0.0000 931 759	0.0000 789 633	0.0000 668 221	0.0000 564 708	504
43	0.0000 834 240	0.0000 703 611	0.0000 592 566	0.0000 498 360	516
44	0.0000 747 010	0.0000 627 021	0.0000 525 522	0.0000 439 839	528
45	0.0000 668 967	0.0000 558 816	0.0000 466 098	0.0000 388 216	540
46	0.0000 599 131	0.0000 498 068	0.0000 413 422	0.0000 342 672	552
47	0.0000 536 627	0.0000 443 955	0.0000 366 720	0.0000 302 486	564
48	0.0000 480 678	0.0000 395 745	0.0000 325 311	0.0000 267 025	576
49	0.0000 430 589	0.0000 352 789	0.0000 288 592	0.0000 235 730	588
50	0.0000 385 742	0.0000 314 511	0.0000 256 027	0.0000 208 111	600

Table 3.　SINKING FUND FACTORS
PAYABLE AT END OF EACH PERIOD

MONTHS	13% NOMINAL ANNUAL RATE	13½% NOMINAL ANNUAL RATE	14% NOMINAL ANNUAL RATE	14½% NOMINAL ANNUAL RATE	MONTHS
1	1.0000 000 000	1.0000 000 000	1.0000 000 000	1.0000 000 000	1
2	0.4973 062 578	0.4972 032 318	0.4971 002 486	0.4969 973 079	2
3	0.3297 481 617	0.3296 113 007	0.3294 745 156	0.3293 378 063	3
4	0.2459 739 769	0.2458 205 786	0.2456 672 869	0.2455 141 019	4
5	0.1957 133 563	0.1955 503 396	0.1953 874 595	0.1952 247 158	5
6	0.1622 095 174	0.1620 403 419	0.1618 713 322	0.1617 024 884	6
7	0.1382 809 821	0.1381 076 244	0.1379 344 618	0.1377 614 940	7
8	0.1203 370 111	0.1201 607 067	0.1199 846 263	0.1198 087 696	8
9	0.1063 827 492	0.1062 043 217	0.1060 261 469	0.1058 482 246	9
10	0.0952 212 834	0.0950 413 092	0.0948 616 164	0.0946 822 047	10
11	0.0860 909 416	0.0859 098 399	0.0857 290 481	0.0855 485 660	11

YEARS					
1	0.0784 839 424	0.0783 020 274	0.0781 204 509	0.0779 392 127	12
2	0.0367 084 893	0.0365 271 145	0.0363 462 166	0.0361 660 947	24
3	0.0228 606 187	0.0226 852 873	0.0225 109 631	0.0223 376 441	36
4	0.0159 941 626	0.0158 263 230	0.0156 598 098	0.0154 946 195	48
5	0.0119 197 397	0.0117 598 460	0.0116 015 842	0.0114 449 477	60
6	0.0092 407 719	0.0090 889 622	0.0089 390 728	0.0087 910 934	72
7	0.0073 586 300	0.0072 148 928	0.0070 733 449	0.0069 339 709	84
8	0.0059 739 217	0.0058 381 597	0.0057 048 344	0.0055 739 237	96
9	0.0049 202 544	0.0047 923 141	0.0046 670 345	0.0045 443 857	108
10	0.0040 977 407	0.0039 774 289	0.0038 599 768	0.0037 453 456	120
11	0.0034 427 746	0.0033 298 680	0.0032 199 945	0.0031 131 050	132
12	0.0029 129 191	0.0028 071 716	0.0027 046 042	0.0026 051 565	144
13	0.0024 787 693	0.0023 799 170	0.0022 843 655	0.0021 920 424	156
14	0.0021 193 025	0.0020 270 683	0.0019 382 295	0.0018 527 010	168
15	0.0018 190 883	0.0017 331 854	0.0016 507 472	0.0015 716 753	180
16	0.0015 665 451	0.0014 866 804	0.0014 103 251	0.0013 373 675	192
17	0.0013 528 110	0.0012 786 878	0.0012 080 956	0.0011 409 092	204
18	0.0011 709 920	0.0011 023 127	0.0010 371 642	0.0009 754 080	216
19	0.0010 156 462	0.0009 521 146	0.0008 920 933	0.0008 354 313	228
20	0.0008 824 238	0.0008 237 468	0.0007 685 414	0.0007 166 443	240
21	0.0007 678 085	0.0007 136 984	0.0006 630 044	0.0006 155 521	252
22	0.0006 689 303	0.0006 191 058	0.0005 726 273	0.0005 293 099	264
23	0.0005 834 259	0.0005 376 137	0.0004 950 645	0.0004 555 842	276
24	0.0005 093 349	0.0004 672 706	0.0004 283 753	0.0003 924 471	288
25	0.0004 450 197	0.0004 064 488	0.0003 709 438	0.0003 382 958	300
26	0.0003 891 044	0.0003 537 829	0.0003 214 166	0.0002 917 913	312
27	0.0003 404 267	0.0003 081 215	0.0002 786 551	0.0002 518 093	324
28	0.0002 980 004	0.0002 684 899	0.0002 416 974	0.0002 174 019	336
29	0.0002 609 850	0.0002 340 590	0.0002 097 274	0.0001 877 675	348
30	0.0002 286 619	0.0002 041 218	0.0001 820 508	0.0001 622 259	360
31	0.0002 004 143	0.0001 780 730	0.0001 580 752	0.0001 401 984	372
32	0.0001 757 117	0.0001 553 935	0.0001 372 937	0.0001 211 915	384
33	0.0001 540 964	0.0001 356 368	0.0001 192 718	0.0001 047 834	396
34	0.0001 351 727	0.0001 184 181	0.0001 036 363	0.0000 906 133	408
35	0.0001 185 981	0.0001 034 050	0.0000 900 661	0.0000 783 718	420
36	0.0001 040 751	0.0000 903 104	0.0000 782 847	0.0000 677 933	432
37	0.0000 913 453	0.0000 788 856	0.0000 680 533	0.0000 586 495	444
38	0.0000 801 840	0.0000 689 149	0.0000 591 658	0.0000 507 442	456
39	0.0000 703 953	0.0000 602 111	0.0000 514 441	0.0000 439 083	468
40	0.0000 618 083	0.0000 526 117	0.0000 447 340	0.0000 379 961	480
41	0.0000 542 740	0.0000 459 753	0.0000 389 020	0.0000 328 822	492
42	0.0000 476 621	0.0000 401 790	0.0000 338 325	0.0000 284 582	504
43	0.0000 418 588	0.0000 351 158	0.0000 294 253	0.0000 246 306	516
44	0.0000 367 645	0.0000 306 923	0.0000 255 935	0.0000 213 187	528
45	0.0000 322 920	0.0000 268 274	0.0000 222 616	0.0000 184 528	540
46	0.0000 283 650	0.0000 234 502	0.0000 193 642	0.0000 159 727	552
47	0.0000 249 167	0.0000 204 989	0.0000 168 444	0.0000 138 263	564
48	0.0000 218 885	0.0000 179 196	0.0000 146 530	0.0000 119 686	576
49	0.0000 192 289	0.0000 156 653	0.0000 127 469	0.0000 103 607	588
50	0.0000 168 930	0.0000 136 949	0.0000 110 891	0.0000 089 690	600

43

Table 3.   SINKING FUND FACTORS
PAYABLE AT END OF EACH PERIOD

MONTHS	15% NOMINAL ANNUAL RATE	15½% NOMINAL ANNUAL RATE	16% NOMINAL ANNUAL RATE	16½% NOMINAL ANNUAL RATE	MONTHS
1	1.0000 000 000	1.0000 000 000	1.0000 000 000	1.0000 000 000	1
2	0.4968 944 099	0.4967 915 545	0.4966 887 417	0.4965 859 714	2
3	0.3292 011 728	0.3290 646 150	0.3289 281 329	0.3287 917 264	3
4	0.2453 610 233	0.2452 080 513	0.2450 551 857	0.2449 024 264	4
5	0.1950 621 084	0.1948 996 374	0.1947 373 025	0.1945 751 037	5
6	0.1615 338 102	0.1613 652 976	0.1611 969 505	0.1610 287 688	6
7	0.1375 887 209	0.1374 161 424	0.1372 437 584	0.1370 715 687	7
8	0.1196 331 365	0.1194 577 268	0.1192 825 404	0.1191 075 771	8
9	0.1056 705 546	0.1054 931 368	0.1053 159 709	0.1051 390 568	9
10	0.0945 030 740	0.0943 242 240	0.0941 456 545	0.0939 673 653	10
11	0.0853 683 935	0.0851 885 301	0.0850 089 758	0.0848 297 303	11

YEARS					
1	0.0777 583 123	0.0775 777 497	0.0773 975 245	0.0772 176 365	12
2	0.0359 866 480	0.0358 078 758	0.0356 297 772	0.0354 523 513	24
3	0.0221 653 285	0.0219 940 144	0.0218 236 997	0.0216 543 826	36
4	0.0153 307 483	0.0151 681 922	0.0150 069 475	0.0148 470 100	48
5	0.0112 899 301	0.0111 365 244	0.0109 847 238	0.0108 345 211	60
6	0.0086 450 133	0.0085 008 217	0.0083 585 073	0.0082 180 587	72
7	0.0067 967 547	0.0066 616 802	0.0065 287 306	0.0063 978 890	84
8	0.0054 454 053	0.0053 192 561	0.0051 954 527	0.0050 739 712	96
9	0.0044 243 373	0.0043 068 584	0.0041 919 174	0.0040 794 825	108
10	0.0036 334 957	0.0035 243 870	0.0034 179 788	0.0033 142 299	120
11	0.0030 091 496	0.0029 080 780	0.0028 098 393	0.0027 143 820	132
12	0.0025 087 677	0.0024 153 760	0.0023 249 196	0.0022 373 361	144
13	0.0021 028 746	0.0020 167 889	0.0019 337 115	0.0018 535 685	156
14	0.0017 703 972	0.0016 912 324	0.0016 151 209	0.0015 419 772	168
15	0.0014 958 712	0.0014 232 367	0.0013 536 741	0.0012 870 861	180
16	0.0012 676 961	0.0012 012 002	0.0011 377 701	0.0010 772 971	192
17	0.0010 770 043	0.0010 162 580	0.0009 585 490	0.0009 037 579	204
18	0.0009 169 075	0.0008 615 280	0.0008 091 373	0.0007 596 058	216
19	0.0007 819 798	0.0007 315 934	0.0006 841 297	0.0006 394 498	228
20	0.0006 678 958	0.0006 221 402	0.0005 792 261	0.0005 390 064	240
21	0.0005 711 714	0.0005 296 978	0.0004 909 717	0.0004 548 391	252
22	0.0004 889 748	0.0004 514 492	0.0004 165 669	0.0003 841 681	264
23	0.0004 189 861	0.0003 850 908	0.0003 537 263	0.0003 247 287	276
24	0.0003 592 923	0.0003 287 262	0.0003 005 727	0.0002 746 646	288
25	0.0003 083 061	0.0002 807 857	0.0002 555 555	0.0002 324 465	300
26	0.0002 647 042	0.0002 399 634	0.0002 173 881	0.0001 968 087	312
27	0.0002 273 781	0.0002 051 683	0.0001 849 986	0.0001 666 999	324
28	0.0001 953 959	0.0001 754 858	0.0001 574 911	0.0001 412 439	336
29	0.0001 679 716	0.0001 501 468	0.0001 341 142	0.0001 197 087	348
30	0.0001 444 402	0.0001 285 025	0.0001 142 366	0.0001 014 808	360
31	0.0001 242 377	0.0001 100 046	0.0000 973 265	0.0000 860 457	372
32	0.0001 068 847	0.0000 941 886	0.0000 829 349	0.0000 729 707	384
33	0.0000 919 732	0.0000 806 607	0.0000 706 826	0.0000 618 913	396
34	0.0000 791 550	0.0000 690 861	0.0000 602 485	0.0000 525 006	408
35	0.0000 681 330	0.0000 591 799	0.0000 513 606	0.0000 445 393	420
36	0.0000 586 529	0.0000 506 998	0.0000 437 881	0.0000 377 885	432
37	0.0000 504 971	0.0000 434 388	0.0000 373 353	0.0000 320 634	444
38	0.0000 434 794	0.0000 372 207	0.0000 318 356	0.0000 272 073	456
39	0.0000 374 398	0.0000 318 949	0.0000 271 476	0.0000 230 880	468
40	0.0000 322 414	0.0000 273 328	0.0000 231 512	0.0000 195 932	480
41	0.0000 277 663	0.0000 234 244	0.0000 197 440	0.0000 166 280	492
42	0.0000 239 135	0.0000 200 757	0.0000 168 389	0.0000 141 121	504
43	0.0000 205 963	0.0000 172 064	0.0000 143 617	0.0000 119 771	516
44	0.0000 177 398	0.0000 147 477	0.0000 122 492	0.0000 101 654	528
45	0.0000 152 800	0.0000 126 406	0.0000 104 477	0.0000 086 279	540
46	0.0000 131 616	0.0000 108 348	0.0000 089 113	0.0000 073 231	552
47	0.0000 113 372	0.0000 092 872	0.0000 076 010	0.0000 062 157	564
48	0.0000 097 659	0.0000 079 608	0.0000 064 835	0.0000 052 758	576
49	0.0000 084 125	0.0000 068 239	0.0000 055 303	0.0000 044 781	588
50	0.0000 072 467	0.0000 058 495	0.0000 047 173	0.0000 038 010	600

44

Table 3.   SINKING FUND FACTORS
PAYABLE AT END OF EACH PERIOD

MONTHS	17% NOMINAL ANNUAL RATE	17½% NOMINAL ANNUAL RATE	18% NOMINAL ANNUAL RATE	18½% NOMINAL ANNUAL RATE	MONTHS
1	1.0000 000 000	1.0000 000 000	1.0000 000 000	1.0000 000 000	1
2	0.4964 832 437	0.4963 805 584	0.4962 779 156	0.4961 753 153	2
3	0.3286 553 955	0.3285 191 401	0.3283 829 602	0.3282 468 558	3
4	0.2447 497 734	0.2445 972 266	0.2444 447 860	0.2442 924 514	4
5	0.1944 130 410	0.1942 511 141	0.1940 893 231	0.1939 276 678	5
6	0.1608 607 523	0.1606 929 009	0.1605 252 146	0.1603 576 933	6
7	0.1368 995 733	0.1367 277 719	0.1365 561 645	0.1363 847 510	7
8	0.1189 328 368	0.1187 583 194	0.1185 840 246	0.1184 099 523	8
9	0.1049 623 943	0.1047 859 832	0.1046 098 234	0.1044 339 146	9
10	0.0937 893 563	0.0936 116 272	0.0934 341 779	0.0932 570 080	10
11	0.0846 507 933	0.0844 721 647	0.0842 938 442	0.0841 158 315	11
YEARS					
1	0.0770 380 854	0.0768 588 710	0.0766 799 929	0.0765 014 510	12
2	0.0352 755 974	0.0350 995 146	0.0349 241 020	0.0347 493 587	24
3	0.0214 860 609	0.0213 187 326	0.0211 523 955	0.0209 870 476	36
4	0.0146 883 756	0.0145 310 403	0.0143 749 996	0.0142 202 493	48
5	0.0106 859 091	0.0105 388 804	0.0103 934 274	0.0102 495 425	60
6	0.0080 794 645	0.0079 427 126	0.0078 077 911	0.0076 746 876	72
7	0.0062 691 382	0.0061 424 605	0.0060 178 380	0.0058 952 525	84
8	0.0049 547 874	0.0048 378 767	0.0047 232 141	0.0046 107 743	96
9	0.0039 695 213	0.0038 620 007	0.0037 568 877	0.0036 541 487	108
10	0.0032 130 985	0.0031 145 427	0.0030 185 199	0.0029 249 874	120
11	0.0026 216 542	0.0025 316 040	0.0024 441 787	0.0023 593 258	132
12	0.0021 525 627	0.0020 705 367	0.0019 911 952	0.0019 144 754	144
13	0.0017 762 862	0.0017 017 907	0.0016 300 085	0.0015 608 664	156
14	0.0014 717 161	0.0014 042 528	0.0013 395 032	0.0012 773 839	168
15	0.0012 233 762	0.0011 624 491	0.0011 042 104	0.0010 485 669	180
16	0.0010 196 740	0.0009 647 952	0.0009 125 567	0.0008 628 563	192
17	0.0008 517 671	0.0008 024 616	0.0007 557 286	0.0007 114 579	204
18	0.0007 128 068	0.0006 686 164	0.0006 269 142	0.0005 875 830	216
19	0.0005 974 187	0.0005 579 051	0.0005 207 820	0.0004 859 263	228
20	0.0005 013 388	0.0004 660 860	0.0004 331 152	0.0004 022 991	240
21	0.0004 211 518	0.0003 897 672	0.0003 605 488	0.0003 333 658	252
22	0.0003 540 999	0.0003 262 161	0.0003 003 772	0.0002 764 505	264
23	0.0002 979 415	0.0002 732 160	0.0002 504 113	0.0002 293 938	276
24	0.0002 508 434	0.0002 289 590	0.0002 088 703	0.0001 904 442	288
25	0.0002 112 992	0.0001 919 637	0.0001 742 994	0.0001 581 748	300
26	0.0001 780 659	0.0001 610 110	0.0001 455 052	0.0001 314 193	312
27	0.0001 501 142	0.0001 350 949	0.0001 215 059	0.0001 092 213	324
28	0.0001 265 889	0.0001 133 823	0.0001 014 915	0.0000 907 946	336
29	0.0001 067 779	0.0000 951 819	0.0000 847 923	0.0000 754 918	348
30	0.0000 900 868	0.0000 799 189	0.0000 708 537	0.0000 627 786	360
31	0.0000 760 187	0.0000 671 147	0.0000 592 154	0.0000 522 136	372
32	0.0000 641 574	0.0000 563 698	0.0000 494 950	0.0000 434 316	384
33	0.0000 541 538	0.0000 473 507	0.0000 413 747	0.0000 361 301	396
34	0.0000 457 151	0.0000 397 785	0.0000 345 897	0.0000 300 585	408
35	0.0000 385 949	0.0000 334 200	0.0000 289 194	0.0000 250 088	420
36	0.0000 325 862	0.0000 280 799	0.0000 241 802	0.0000 208 087	432
37	0.0000 275 148	0.0000 235 944	0.0000 202 187	0.0000 173 147	444
38	0.0000 232 340	0.0000 198 264	0.0000 169 069	0.0000 144 079	456
39	0.0000 196 201	0.0000 166 609	0.0000 141 382	0.0000 119 895	468
40	0.0000 165 690	0.0000 140 012	0.0000 118 231	0.0000 099 773	480
41	0.0000 139 928	0.0000 117 665	0.0000 098 875	0.0000 083 030	492
42	0.0000 118 175	0.0000 098 887	0.0000 082 689	0.0000 069 098	504
43	0.0000 099 806	0.0000 083 107	0.0000 069 153	0.0000 057 504	516
44	0.0000 084 294	0.0000 069 847	0.0000 057 835	0.0000 047 857	528
45	0.0000 071 195	0.0000 058 703	0.0000 048 369	0.0000 039 828	540
46	0.0000 060 131	0.0000 049 338	0.0000 040 453	0.0000 033 146	552
47	0.0000 050 788	0.0000 041 467	0.0000 033 833	0.0000 027 586	564
48	0.0000 042 897	0.0000 034 852	0.0000 028 297	0.0000 022 959	576
49	0.0000 036 232	0.0000 029 293	0.0000 023 666	0.0000 019 107	588
50	0.0000 030 603	0.0000 024 620	0.0000 019 794	0.0000 015 902	600

Table 3.   SINKING FUND FACTORS
PAYABLE AT END OF EACH PERIOD

MONTHS	19% NOMINAL ANNUAL RATE	19½% NOMINAL ANNUAL RATE	20% NOMINAL ANNUAL RATE	20½% NOMINAL ANNUAL RATE	MONTHS
1	1.0000 000 000	1.0000 000 000	1.0000 000 000	1.0000 000 000	1
2	0.4960 727 573	0.4959 702 418	0.4958 677 686	0.4957 653 377	2
3	0.3281 108 267	0.3279 748 730	0.3278 389 946	0.3277 031 915	3
4	0.2441 402 228	0.2439 881 002	0.2438 360 835	0.2436 841 725	4
5	0.1937 661 482	0.1936 047 642	0.1934 435 156	0.1932 824 025	5
6	0.1601 903 367	0.1600 231 449	0.1598 561 176	0.1596 892 549	6
7	0.1362 135 311	0.1360 425 047	0.1358 716 718	0.1357 010 322	7
8	0.1182 361 024	0.1180 624 747	0.1178 890 691	0.1177 158 853	8
9	0.1042 582 568	0.1040 828 496	0.1039 076 930	0.1037 327 867	9
10	0.0930 801 175	0.0929 035 060	0.0927 271 734	0.0925 511 196	10
11	0.0839 381 265	0.0837 607 288	0.0835 836 383	0.0834 068 547	11
YEARS					
1	0.0763 232 449	0.0761 453 744	0.0759 678 392	0.0757 906 391	12
2	0.0345 752 839	0.0344 018 766	0.0342 291 360	0.0340 570 611	24
3	0.0208 226 867	0.0206 593 105	0.0204 969 167	0.0203 355 031	36
4	0.0140 667 849	0.0139 146 019	0.0137 636 957	0.0136 140 616	48
5	0.0101 072 178	0.0099 664 454	0.0098 272 170	0.0096 895 247	60
6	0.0075 433 896	0.0074 138 845	0.0072 861 594	0.0071 602 011	72
7	0.0057 746 857	0.0056 561 187	0.0055 395 326	0.0054 249 083	84
8	0.0045 005 316	0.0043 924 601	0.0042 865 337	0.0041 827 258	96
9	0.0035 537 497	0.0034 556 566	0.0033 598 350	0.0032 662 502	108
10	0.0028 339 022	0.0027 452 210	0.0026 589 006	0.0025 748 972	120
11	0.0022 769 925	0.0021 971 261	0.0021 196 737	0.0020 445 827	132
12	0.0018 403 144	0.0017 686 496	0.0016 994 188	0.0016 325 599	144
13	0.0014 942 916	0.0014 302 117	0.0013 685 551	0.0013 092 509	156
14	0.0012 178 123	0.0011 607 069	0.0011 059 871	0.0010 535 736	168
15	0.0009 954 270	0.0009 447 003	0.0008 962 984	0.0008 501 342	180
16	0.0008 155 940	0.0007 706 718	0.0007 279 938	0.0006 874 668	192
17	0.0006 695 421	0.0006 298 764	0.0005 923 590	0.0005 568 913	204
18	0.0005 505 091	0.0005 155 823	0.0004 826 960	0.0004 517 474	216
19	0.0004 532 193	0.0004 225 466	0.0003 937 981	0.0003 668 680	228
20	0.0003 735 152	0.0003 466 461	0.0003 215 794	0.0002 982 080	240
21	0.0003 080 932	0.0002 846 120	0.0002 628 090	0.0002 425 764	252
22	0.0002 543 098	0.0002 338 357	0.0002 149 150	0.0001 974 410	264
23	0.0002 100 375	0.0001 922 235	0.0001 758 399	0.0001 607 817	276
24	0.0001 735 556	0.0001 580 873	0.0001 439 298	0.0001 309 806	288
25	0.0001 433 670	0.0001 300 613	0.0001 178 511	0.0001 067 373	300
26	0.0001 186 334	0.0001 070 361	0.0000 965 247	0.0000 870 040	312
27	0.0000 981 248	0.0000 881 091	0.0000 790 757	0.0000 709 339	324
28	0.0000 811 796	0.0000 725 438	0.0000 647 932	0.0000 578 421	336
29	0.0000 671 730	0.0000 597 383	0.0000 530 986	0.0000 471 732	348
30	0.0000 555 916	0.0000 492 000	0.0000 435 202	0.0000 384 765	360
31	0.0000 460 127	0.0000 405 254	0.0000 356 733	0.0000 313 861	372
32	0.0000 380 883	0.0000 333 834	0.0000 292 438	0.0000 256 043	384
33	0.0000 315 313	0.0000 275 021	0.0000 239 747	0.0000 208 888	396
34	0.0000 261 050	0.0000 226 585	0.0000 196 561	0.0000 170 427	408
35	0.0000 216 138	0.0000 186 688	0.0000 161 162	0.0000 139 053	420
36	0.0000 178 962	0.0000 153 824	0.0000 132 143	0.0000 113 458	432
37	0.0000 148 186	0.0000 126 749	0.0000 108 353	0.0000 092 577	444
38	0.0000 122 706	0.0000 104 443	0.0000 088 848	0.0000 075 541	456
39	0.0000 101 611	0.0000 086 064	0.0000 072 855	0.0000 061 641	468
40	0.0000 084 144	0.0000 070 921	0.0000 059 743	0.0000 050 299	480
41	0.0000 069 681	0.0000 058 443	0.0000 048 991	0.0000 041 045	492
42	0.0000 057 705	0.0000 048 162	0.0000 040 174	0.0000 033 494	504
43	0.0000 047 787	0.0000 039 689	0.0000 032 945	0.0000 027 332	516
44	0.0000 039 575	0.0000 032 707	0.0000 027 016	0.0000 022 304	528
45	0.0000 032 774	0.0000 026 954	0.0000 022 155	0.0000 018 201	540
46	0.0000 027 142	0.0000 022 213	0.0000 018 168	0.0000 014 853	552
47	0.0000 022 478	0.0000 018 306	0.0000 014 899	0.0000 012 120	564
48	0.0000 018 616	0.0000 015 086	0.0000 012 218	0.0000 009 891	576
49	0.0000 015 417	0.0000 012 432	0.0000 010 020	0.0000 008 071	588
50	0.0000 012 768	0.0000 010 246	0.0000 008 217	0.0000 006 587	600

46

Table 3.   SINKING FUND FACTORS
             PAYABLE AT END OF EACH PERIOD

	21% NOMINAL ANNUAL RATE	21½% NOMINAL ANNUAL RATE	22% NOMINAL ANNUAL RATE	22½% NOMINAL ANNUAL RATE	
MONTHS					**MONTHS**
1	1.0000 000 000	1.0000 000 000	1.0000 000 000	1.0000 000 000	1
2	0.4956 629 492	0.4955 606 029	0.4954 582 989	0.4953 560 372	2
3	0.3275 674 635	0.3274 318 108	0.3272 962 331	0.3271 607 305	3
4	0.2435 323 673	0.2433 806 677	0.2432 290 738	0.2430 775 854	4
5	0.1931 214 246	0.1929 605 820	0.1927 998 745	0.1926 393 021	5
6	0.1595 225 565	0.1593 560 224	0.1591 896 525	0.1590 234 467	6
7	0.1355 305 857	0.1353 603 323	0.1351 902 718	0.1350 204 041	7
8	0.1175 429 233	0.1173 701 829	0.1171 976 639	0.1170 253 662	8
9	0.1035 581 306	0.1033 837 245	0.1032 095 682	0.1030 356 615	9
10	0.0923 753 442	0.0921 998 470	0.0920 246 279	0.0918 496 867	10
11	0.0832 303 778	0.0830 542 073	0.0828 783 430	0.0827 027 846	11
YEARS					
1	0.0756 137 738	0.0754 372 429	0.0752 610 463	0.0750 851 837	12
2	0.0338 856 510	0.0337 149 047	0.0335 448 213	0.0333 753 599	24
3	0.0201 750 673	0.0200 156 071	0.0198 571 198	0.0196 996 033	36
4	0.0134 656 950	0.0133 185 909	0.0131 727 445	0.0130 281 508	48
5	0.0095 533 598	0.0094 187 140	0.0092 855 787	0.0091 539 451	60
6	0.0070 359 964	0.0069 135 320	0.0067 927 940	0.0066 737 690	72
7	0.0053 122 263	0.0052 014 670	0.0050 926 106	0.0049 856 371	84
8	0.0040 810 099	0.0039 813 590	0.0038 837 460	0.0037 881 438	96
9	0.0031 748 675	0.0030 856 518	0.0029 985 680	0.0029 135 810	108
10	0.0024 931 675	0.0024 136 678	0.0023 363 545	0.0022 611 841	120
11	0.0019 718 004	0.0019 012 744	0.0018 329 525	0.0017 667 829	132
12	0.0015 680 114	0.0015 057 123	0.0014 456 018	0.0013 876 202	144
13	0.0012 522 288	0.0011 974 197	0.0011 447 551	0.0010 941 677	156
14	0.0010 033 884	0.0009 553 545	0.0009 093 968	0.0008 654 413	168
15	0.0008 061 227	0.0007 641 806	0.0007 242 267	0.0006 861 815	180
16	0.0006 489 996	0.0006 125 037	0.0005 778 930	0.0005 450 838	192
17	0.0005 233 774	0.0004 917 245	0.0004 618 432	0.0004 336 470	204
18	0.0004 226 371	0.0003 952 698	0.0003 695 535	0.0003 454 001	216
19	0.0003 416 551	0.0003 180 621	0.0002 959 964	0.0002 753 692	228
20	0.0002 764 294	0.0002 561 463	0.0002 372 660	0.0002 197 006	240
21	0.0002 238 122	0.0002 064 198	0.0001 903 077	0.0001 753 897	252
22	0.0001 813 127	0.0001 664 353	0.0001 527 196	0.0001 400 818	264
23	0.0001 469 502	0.0001 342 534	0.0001 226 047	0.0001 119 238	276
24	0.0001 191 441	0.0001 083 314	0.0000 984 598	0.0000 894 527	288
25	0.0000 966 282	0.0000 874 388	0.0000 790 903	0.0000 715 102	300
26	0.0000 783 864	0.0000 705 912	0.0000 635 443	0.0000 571 776	312
27	0.0000 636 007	0.0000 570 001	0.0000 510 625	0.0000 457 246	324
28	0.0000 516 122	0.0000 460 324	0.0000 410 380	0.0000 365 701	336
29	0.0000 418 889	0.0000 371 795	0.0000 329 850	0.0000 292 513	348
30	0.0000 340 009	0.0000 300 319	0.0000 265 145	0.0000 233 991	360
31	0.0000 276 006	0.0000 242 604	0.0000 213 148	0.0000 187 189	372
32	0.0000 224 067	0.0000 195 992	0.0000 171 357	0.0000 149 755	384
33	0.0000 181 911	0.0000 158 343	0.0000 137 766	0.0000 119 812	396
34	0.0000 147 694	0.0000 127 932	0.0000 110 764	0.0000 095 859	408
35	0.0000 119 917	0.0000 103 365	0.0000 089 057	0.0000 076 697	420
36	0.0000 097 367	0.0000 083 518	0.0000 071 606	0.0000 061 366	432
37	0.0000 079 059	0.0000 067 483	0.0000 057 575	0.0000 049 101	444
38	0.0000 064 195	0.0000 054 527	0.0000 046 294	0.0000 039 288	456
39	0.0000 052 127	0.0000 044 060	0.0000 037 224	0.0000 031 436	468
40	0.0000 042 327	0.0000 035 602	0.0000 029 932	0.0000 025 154	480
41	0.0000 034 371	0.0000 028 768	0.0000 024 068	0.0000 020 127	492
42	0.0000 027 910	0.0000 023 246	0.0000 019 353	0.0000 016 105	504
43	0.0000 022 664	0.0000 018 784	0.0000 015 562	0.0000 012 887	516
44	0.0000 018 404	0.0000 015 179	0.0000 012 513	0.0000 010 311	528
45	0.0000 014 945	0.0000 012 266	0.0000 010 062	0.0000 008 251	540
46	0.0000 012 136	0.0000 009 911	0.0000 008 091	0.0000 006 602	552
47	0.0000 009 855	0.0000 008 009	0.0000 006 506	0.0000 005 283	564
48	0.0000 008 003	0.0000 006 472	0.0000 005 232	0.0000 004 227	576
49	0.0000 006 499	0.0000 005 230	0.0000 004 207	0.0000 003 383	588
50	0.0000 005 277	0.0000 004 226	0.0000 003 383	0.0000 002 707	600

Table 4.   PRESENT WORTH OF ONE DOLLAR
PAYABLE AT END OF EACH PERIOD

MONTHS	5% NOMINAL ANNUAL RATE	5½% NOMINAL ANNUAL RATE	6% NOMINAL ANNUAL RATE	6½% NOMINAL ANNUAL RATE	MONTHS
1	0.9958 506 224	0.9954 375 778	0.9950 248 756	0.9946 125 155	1
2	0.9917 184 621	0.9908 959 712	0.9900 745 031	0.9892 540 561	2
3	0.9876 034 478	0.9863 750 854	0.9851 487 593	0.9839 244 652	3
4	0.9835 055 082	0.9818 748 258	0.9802 475 217	0.9786 235 875	4
5	0.9794 245 724	0.9773 950 983	0.9753 706 684	0.9733 512 681	5
6	0.9753 605 701	0.9729 358 091	0.9705 180 780	0.9681 073 533	6
7	0.9713 134 308	0.9684 968 652	0.9656 896 298	0.9628 916 899	7
8	0.9672 830 846	0.9640 781 736	0.9608 852 038	0.9577 041 259	8
9	0.9632 694 618	0.9596 796 419	0.9561 046 804	0.9525 445 098	9
10	0.9592 724 931	0.9553 011 781	0.9513 479 407	0.9474 126 911	10
11	0.9552 921 093	0.9509 426 908	0.9466 148 664	0.9423 085 199	11

YEARS	5%	5½%	6%	6½%	MONTHS
1	0.9513 282 416	0.9466 040 887	0.9419 053 397	0.9372 318 474	12
2	0.9050 254 234	0.8960 593 008	0.8871 856 689	0.8784 035 358	24
3	0.8609 762 447	0.8482 133 979	0.8356 449 188	0.8232 677 687	36
4	0.8190 710 169	0.8029 222 705	0.7870 984 111	0.7715 927 717	48
5	0.7792 053 903	0.7600 495 042	0.7413 721 962	0.7231 613 189	60
6	0.7412 800 939	0.7194 659 683	0.6983 024 303	0.6777 698 189	72
7	0.7052 006 883	0.6810 494 273	0.6577 347 878	0.6352 274 595	84
8	0.6708 773 308	0.6446 841 725	0.6195 239 087	0.5953 554 054	96
9	0.6382 245 514	0.6102 606 736	0.5835 328 777	0.5579 860 465	108
10	0.6071 610 403	0.5776 752 488	0.5496 327 334	0.5229 622 932	120
11	0.5776 094 449	0.5468 297 525	0.5177 020 064	0.4901 369 162	132
12	0.5494 961 775	0.5176 312 796	0.4876 262 842	0.4593 719 274	144
13	0.5227 512 324	0.4899 918 857	0.4592 978 008	0.4305 380 002	156
14	0.4973 080 107	0.4638 283 224	0.4326 150 511	0.4035 139 253	168
15	0.4731 031 554	0.4390 617 865	0.4074 824 267	0.3781 861 017	180
16	0.4500 763 929	0.4156 176 823	0.3838 098 735	0.3544 480 588	192
17	0.4281 703 835	0.3934 253 974	0.3615 125 693	0.3322 000 089	204
18	0.4073 305 781	0.3724 180 898	0.3405 106 193	0.3113 484 281	216
19	0.3875 050 826	0.3525 324 865	0.3207 287 706	0.2918 056 624	228
20	0.3686 445 289	0.3337 086 931	0.3020 961 416	0.2734 895 601	240
21	0.3507 019 514	0.3158 900 134	0.2845 459 689	0.2563 231 257	252
22	0.3336 326 708	0.2990 227 782	0.2680 153 674	0.2402 341 366	264
23	0.3173 941 821	0.2830 561 845	0.2524 451 057	0.2251 551 399	276
24	0.3019 460 491	0.2679 421 416	0.2377 793 930	0.2110 225 677	288
25	0.2872 498 040	0.2536 351 268	0.2239 656 800	0.1977 770 710	300
26	0.2732 688 509	0.2400 920 480	0.2109 544 699	0.1853 629 696	312
27	0.2599 683 755	0.2272 721 143	0.1986 991 416	0.1737 280 785	324
28	0.2473 152 575	0.2151 367 127	0.1871 557 824	0.1628 234 879	336
29	0.2352 779 891	0.2036 492 919	0.1762 830 308	0.1526 033 584	348
30	0.2238 265 956	0.1927 752 523	0.1660 419 280	0.1430 247 275	360
31	0.2129 325 617	0.1824 818 421	0.1563 957 786	0.1340 473 296	372
32	0.2025 687 595	0.1727 380 578	0.1473 100 190	0.1256 334 266	384
33	0.1927 093 818	0.1635 145 518	0.1387 520 935	0.1177 476 483	396
34	0.1833 298 773	0.1547 835 433	0.1306 913 377	0.1103 568 459	408
35	0.1744 068 898	0.1465 187 350	0.1230 988 689	0.1034 299 506	420
36	0.1659 181 998	0.1386 952 336	0.1159 474 819	0.0969 378 437	432
37	0.1578 426 693	0.1312 894 752	0.1092 115 523	0.0908 532 343	444
38	0.1501 601 890	0.1242 791 540	0.1028 669 443	0.0851 505 446	456
39	0.1428 516 286	0.1176 431 554	0.0968 909 241	0.0798 058 023	468
40	0.1358 987 887	0.1113 614 919	0.0912 620 788	0.0747 965 395	480
41	0.1292 843 557	0.1054 152 435	0.0859 602 393	0.0701 016 989	492
42	0.1229 918 587	0.0997 865 005	0.0809 664 084	0.0657 015 447	504
43	0.1170 056 287	0.0944 583 094	0.0762 626 924	0.0615 775 802	516
44	0.1113 107 590	0.0894 146 219	0.0718 322 372	0.0577 124 692	528
45	0.1058 930 687	0.0846 402 467	0.0676 591 678	0.0540 899 641	540
46	0.1007 390 668	0.0801 208 036	0.0637 285 314	0.0506 948 370	552
47	0.0958 359 193	0.0758 426 803	0.0600 262 440	0.0475 128 158	564
48	0.0911 714 166	0.0717 929 912	0.0565 390 398	0.0445 305 241	576
49	0.0867 339 434	0.0679 595 390	0.0532 544 234	0.0417 354 254	588
50	0.0825 124 499	0.0643 307 775	0.0501 606 258	0.0391 157 698	600

48

Table 4.   PRESENT WORTH OF ONE DOLLAR
PAYABLE AT END OF EACH PERIOD

MONTHS	7% NOMINAL ANNUAL RATE	7½% NOMINAL ANNUAL RATE	8% NOMINAL ANNUAL RATE	8½% NOMINAL ANNUAL RATE	MONTHS
1	0.9942 004 971	0.9937 888 199	0.9933 774 834	0.9929 664 874	1
2	0.9884 346 284	0.9876 162 185	0.9867 988 246	0.9859 824 451	2
3	0.9827 021 989	0.9814 819 563	0.9802 637 331	0.9790 475 251	3
4	0.9770 030 147	0.9753 857 951	0.9737 719 203	0.9721 613 820	4
5	0.9713 368 829	0.9693 274 982	0.9673 230 996	0.9653 236 726	5
6	0.9657 036 118	0.9633 068 305	0.9609 169 864	0.9585 340 564	6
7	0.9601 030 109	0.9573 235 583	0.9545 532 977	0.9517 921 950	7
8	0.9545 348 907	0.9513 774 492	0.9482 317 527	0.9450 977 526	8
9	0.9489 990 628	0.9454 682 725	0.9419 520 722	0.9384 503 956	9
10	0.9434 953 400	0.9395 957 988	0.9357 139 790	0.9318 497 929	10
11	0.9380 235 361	0.9337 598 000	0.9295 171 977	0.9252 956 156	11

YEARS					
1	0.9325 834 658	0.9279 600 497	0.9233 614 547	0.9187 875 373	12
2	0.8697 119 208	0.8611 098 539	0.8525 963 759	0.8441 705 386	24
3	0.8110 789 574	0.7990 755 428	0.7872 546 299	0.7756 133 702	36
4	0.7563 988 251	0.7415 101 804	0.7269 205 803	0.7126 238 983	48
5	0.7054 050 379	0.6880 918 239	0.6712 104 444	0.6547 499 565	60
6	0.6578 490 751	0.6385 217 231	0.6197 698 523	0.6015 761 000	72
7	0.6134 991 704	0.5925 226 499	0.5722 715 924	0.5527 206 234	84
8	0.5721 391 827	0.5498 373 476	0.5284 135 300	0.5078 328 204	96
9	0.5335 675 419	0.5102 270 924	0.4879 166 858	0.4665 904 664	108
10	0.4975 962 675	0.4734 703 581	0.4505 234 607	0.4286 975 055	120
11	0.4640 500 517	0.4393 615 770	0.4159 959 980	0.3938 819 253	132
12	0.4327 654 056	0.4077 099 908	0.3841 146 699	0.3618 938 041	144
13	0.4035 898 618	0.3783 385 834	0.3546 766 803	0.3325 035 171	156
14	0.3763 812 321	0.3510 830 906	0.3274 947 755	0.3055 000 876	168
15	0.3510 069 139	0.3257 910 822	0.3023 960 523	0.2806 896 731	180
16	0.3273 432 443	0.3023 211 089	0.2792 208 587	0.2578 941 735	192
17	0.3052 748 973	0.2805 419 112	0.2578 217 783	0.2369 499 525	204
18	0.2846 943 218	0.2603 316 859	0.2380 626 922	0.2177 066 633	216
19	0.2655 012 173	0.2415 774 042	0.2198 179 138	0.2000 261 690	228
20	0.2476 020 454	0.2241 741 800	0.2029 713 887	0.1837 815 512	240
21	0.2309 095 737	0.2080 246 832	0.1874 159 567	0.1688 561 989	252
22	0.2153 424 505	0.1930 385 953	0.1730 526 704	0.1551 429 711	264
23	0.2008 248 089	0.1791 321 045	0.1597 901 655	0.1425 434 283	276
24	0.1872 858 963	0.1662 274 366	0.1475 440 796	0.1309 671 255	288
25	0.1746 597 302	0.1542 524 204	0.1362 365 160	0.1203 309 627	300
26	0.1628 847 766	0.1431 400 837	0.1257 955 476	0.1105 585 889	312
27	0.1519 036 495	0.1328 282 791	0.1161 547 598	0.1015 798 536	324
28	0.1416 628 319	0.1232 593 365	0.1072 528 280	0.0933 303 035	336
29	0.1321 124 148	0.1143 797 400	0.0990 331 273	0.0857 507 197	348
30	0.1232 058 536	0.1061 398 293	0.0914 433 724	0.0787 866 926	360
31	0.1148 997 420	0.0984 935 212	0.0844 352 854	0.0723 882 312	372
32	0.1071 535 996	0.0913 980 529	0.0779 642 879	0.0665 094 047	384
33	0.0999 296 753	0.0848 137 417	0.0719 892 183	0.0611 080 122	396
34	0.0931 927 629	0.0787 037 639	0.0664 720 694	0.0561 452 800	408
35	0.0869 100 299	0.0730 339 487	0.0613 777 467	0.0515 855 835	420
36	0.0810 508 569	0.0677 725 867	0.0566 738 454	0.0473 961 913	432
37	0.0755 866 890	0.0628 902 529	0.0523 304 444	0.0435 470 298	444
38	0.0704 908 964	0.0583 596 422	0.0483 199 152	0.0400 104 683	456
39	0.0657 386 445	0.0541 554 165	0.0446 167 472	0.0367 611 196	468
40	0.0613 067 729	0.0502 540 630	0.0411 973 846	0.0337 756 586	480
41	0.0571 736 828	0.0466 337 628	0.0380 400 770	0.0310 326 542	492
42	0.0533 192 312	0.0432 742 688	0.0351 247 408	0.0285 124 159	504
43	0.0497 246 334	0.0401 567 926	0.0324 328 318	0.0261 968 524	516
44	0.0463 723 710	0.0372 638 993	0.0299 472 267	0.0240 693 415	528
45	0.0432 461 065	0.0345 794 098	0.0276 521 148	0.0221 146 110	540
46	0.0403 306 039	0.0320 883 109	0.0255 328 970	0.0203 186 290	552
47	0.0376 116 543	0.0297 766 706	0.0235 760 929	0.0186 685 031	564
48	0.0350 760 069	0.0276 315 607	0.0217 692 554	0.0171 523 880	576
49	0.0327 113 041	0.0256 409 844	0.0201 008 914	0.0157 594 003	588
50	0.0305 060 214	0.0237 938 092	0.0185 603 883	0.0144 795 406	600

49

Table 4.   PRESENT WORTH OF ONE DOLLAR
PAYABLE AT END OF EACH PERIOD

	9% NOMINAL ANNUAL RATE	9½% NOMINAL ANNUAL RATE	10% NOMINAL ANNUAL RATE	10½% NOMINAL ANNUAL RATE	
MONTHS					**MONTHS**
1	0.9925 558 313	0.9921 455 147	0.9917 355 372	0.9913 258 984	1
2	0.9851 670 782	0.9843 527 223	0.9835 393 757	0.9827 270 368	2
3	0.9778 333 282	0.9766 211 383	0.9754 109 511	0.9742 027 626	3
4	0.9705 541 719	0.9689 502 819	0.9673 497 036	0.9657 524 289	4
5	0.9633 292 029	0.9613 396 761	0.9593 550 780	0.9573 753 942	5
6	0.9561 580 178	0.9537 888 477	0.9514 265 236	0.9490 710 227	6
7	0.9490 402 162	0.9462 973 272	0.9435 634 945	0.9408 386 843	7
8	0.9419 754 006	0.9388 646 488	0.9357 654 491	0.9326 777 539	8
9	0.9349 631 768	0.9314 903 502	0.9280 318 503	0.9245 876 123	9
10	0.9280 031 532	0.9241 739 729	0.9203 621 656	0.9165 676 454	10
11	0.9210 949 411	0.9169 150 620	0.9127 558 667	0.9086 172 445	11
YEARS					
1	0.9142 381 550	0.9097 131 661	0.9052 124 298	0.9007 358 062	12
2	0.8358 314 040	0.8275 780 445	0.8194 095 430	0.8113 249 926	24
3	0.7641 489 606	0.7528 586 430	0.7417 397 035	0.7307 894 713	36
4	0.6986 141 359	0.6848 854 197	0.6714 319 992	0.6582 482 436	48
5	0.6386 996 086	0.6230 492 836	0.6077 885 915	0.5929 077 624	60
6	0.5839 236 340	0.5667 961 364	0.5501 777 877	0.5340 532 514	72
7	0.5338 452 658	0.5156 219 077	0.4980 277 720	0.4810 408 859	84
8	0.4880 617 108	0.4690 680 382	0.4508 209 296	0.4332 907 502	96
9	0.4462 046 380	0.4267 173 701	0.4080 887 091	0.3902 804 932	108
10	0.4079 373 050	0.3881 904 098	0.3694 069 719	0.3515 396 147	120
11	0.3729 518 490	0.3531 419 267	0.3343 917 826	0.3166 443 183	132
12	0.3409 668 104	0.3212 578 602	0.3026 955 981	0.2852 128 753	144
13	0.3117 248 676	0.2922 525 051	0.2740 038 178	0.2569 014 492	156
14	0.2849 907 678	0.2658 659 517	0.2480 316 617	0.2314 003 339	168
15	0.2605 494 337	0.2418 617 567	0.2245 213 431	0.2084 305 663	180
16	0.2382 042 336	0.2200 248 244	0.2032 395 106	0.1877 408 742	192
17	0.2177 753 990	0.2001 594 797	0.1839 749 312	0.1691 049 277	204
18	0.1990 985 790	0.1820 877 140	0.1665 363 945	0.1523 188 634	216
19	0.1820 235 175	0.1656 475 908	0.1507 508 143	0.1371 990 542	228
20	0.1664 128 448	0.1506 917 942	0.1364 615 109	0.1235 801 007	240
21	0.1521 409 722	0.1370 863 092	0.1235 266 559	0.1113 130 216	252
22	0.1390 930 817	0.1247 092 204	0.1118 178 643	0.1002 636 243	264
23	0.1271 642 024	0.1134 496 197	0.1012 189 206	0.0903 110 365	276
24	0.1162 583 658	0.1032 066 128	0.0916 246 251	0.0813 463 842	288
25	0.1062 878 338	0.0938 884 144	0.0829 397 495	0.0732 716 010	300
26	0.0971 723 931	0.0854 115 268	0.0750 780 922	0.0659 983 546	312
27	0.0888 387 094	0.0776 999 904	0.0679 616 222	0.0594 470 811	324
28	0.0812 197 377	0.0706 847 043	0.0615 197 052	0.0535 461 145	336
29	0.0742 541 832	0.0643 028 061	0.0556 884 018	0.0482 309 027	348
30	0.0678 860 074	0.0584 971 094	0.0504 098 335	0.0434 433 010	360
31	0.0620 639 782	0.0532 155 906	0.0456 316 079	0.0391 309 367	372
32	0.0567 412 569	0.0484 109 234	0.0413 062 987	0.0352 466 358	384
33	0.0518 750 220	0.0440 400 544	0.0373 909 750	0.0317 479 070	396
34	0.0474 261 244	0.0400 638 173	0.0338 467 753	0.0285 964 766	408
35	0.0433 587 725	0.0364 465 821	0.0306 385 217	0.0257 578 704	420
36	0.0396 402 442	0.0331 559 356	0.0277 343 707	0.0232 010 361	432
37	0.0362 406 237	0.0301 623 911	0.0251 054 971	0.0208 980 040	444
38	0.0331 325 609	0.0274 391 243	0.0227 258 080	0.0188 235 805	456
39	0.0302 910 514	0.0249 617 327	0.0205 716 839	0.0169 550 729	468
40	0.0276 932 349	0.0227 080 169	0.0186 217 440	0.0152 720 413	480
41	0.0253 182 120	0.0206 577 819	0.0168 566 341	0.0137 560 744	492
42	0.0231 468 754	0.0187 926 562	0.0152 588 347	0.0123 905 888	504
43	0.0211 617 567	0.0170 959 268	0.0138 124 868	0.0111 606 470	516
44	0.0193 468 854	0.0155 523 897	0.0125 032 348	0.0100 527 944	528
45	0.0176 876 608	0.0141 482 136	0.0113 180 835	0.0090 549 118	540
46	0.0161 707 344	0.0128 708 162	0.0102 452 699	0.0081 560 833	552
47	0.0147 839 024	0.0117 087 510	0.0092 741 457	0.0073 464 763	564
48	0.0135 160 076	0.0106 516 049	0.0083 950 719	0.0066 172 342	576
49	0.0123 568 499	0.0096 899 052	0.0075 993 235	0.0059 603 798	588
50	0.0112 971 036	0.0088 150 344	0.0068 790 020	0.0053 687 275	600

Table 4. **PRESENT WORTH OF ONE DOLLAR**
PAYABLE AT END OF EACH PERIOD

MONTHS	11% NOMINAL ANNUAL RATE	11½% NOMINAL ANNUAL RATE	12% NOMINAL ANNUAL RATE	12½% NOMINAL ANNUAL RATE	MONTHS
1	0.9909 165 979	0.9905 076 352	0.9900 990 099	0.9896 907 216	1
2	0.9819 157 039	0.9811 053 753	0.9802 960 494	0.9794 877 245	2
3	0.9729 965 687	0.9717 923 652	0.9705 901 479	0.9693 899 129	3
4	0.9641 584 496	0.9625 677 575	0.9609 803 445	0.9593 962 025	4
5	0.9554 006 106	0.9534 307 131	0.9514 656 876	0.9495 055 200	5
6	0.9467 223 227	0.9443 804 010	0.9420 452 353	0.9397 168 033	6
7	0.9381 228 631	0.9354 159 977	0.9327 180 547	0.9300 290 012	7
8	0.9296 015 159	0.9265 366 877	0.9234 832 225	0.9204 410 733	8
9	0.9211 575 715	0.9177 416 635	0.9143 398 242	0.9109 519 901	9
10	0.9127 903 268	0.9090 301 248	0.9052 869 547	0.9015 607 325	10
11	0.9044 990 852	0.9004 012 792	0.8963 237 175	0.8922 662 919	11

YEARS					
1	0.8962 831 563	0.8918 543 417	0.8874 492 253	0.8830 676 704	12
2	0.8033 234 962	0.7954 041 669	0.7875 661 274	0.7798 085 105	24
3	0.7200 053 187	0.7093 846 596	0.6989 249 496	0.6886 236 847	36
4	0.6453 286 395	0.6326 677 886	0.6202 604 051	0.6081 013 130	48
5	0.5783 971 899	0.5642 475 142	0.5504 496 159	0.5369 946 098	60
6	0.5184 076 589	0.5032 265 953	0.4884 960 852	0.4742 025 791	72
7	0.4646 400 527	0.4488 048 239	0.4335 154 724	0.4187 529 668	84
8	0.4164 490 530	0.4002 685 308	0.3847 229 701	0.3697 872 068	96
9	0.3732 562 716	0.3569 812 270	0.3414 221 017	0.3265 471 273	108
10	0.3345 433 092	0.3183 752 573	0.3029 947 797	0.2883 632 110	120
11	0.2998 455 331	0.2839 443 555	0.2688 924 825	0.2546 442 289	132
12	0.2687 465 008	0.2532 370 062	0.2386 284 253	0.2248 680 860	144
13	0.2408 729 620	0.2258 505 235	0.2117 706 111	0.1985 737 369	156
14	0.2158 903 786	0.2014 257 700	0.1879 356 648	0.1753 540 472	168
15	0.1934 989 100	0.1796 424 475	0.1667 833 601	0.1548 494 900	180
16	0.1734 298 137	0.1602 148 967	0.1480 117 637	0.1367 425 783	192
17	0.1554 422 209	0.1428 883 513	0.1313 529 250	0.1207 529 501	204
18	0.1393 202 443	0.1274 355 965	0.1165 690 516	0.1066 330 263	216
19	0.1248 703 883	0.1136 539 900	0.1034 491 145	0.0941 641 782	228
20	0.1119 192 258	0.1013 628 044	0.0918 058 365	0.0831 533 414	240
21	0.1003 113 169	0.0904 008 572	0.0814 730 185	0.0734 300 275	252
22	0.0899 073 437	0.0806 243 970	0.0723 031 671	0.0648 436 833	264
23	0.0805 824 378	0.0719 052 052	0.0641 653 897	0.0572 613 604	276
24	0.0722 246 817	0.0641 289 813	0.0569 435 253	0.0505 656 561	288
25	0.0647 337 657	0.0571 937 104	0.0505 344 875	0.0446 528 961	300
26	0.0580 197 838	0.0510 084 590	0.0448 467 917	0.0394 315 290	312
27	0.0520 021 550	0.0454 921 156	0.0397 992 506	0.0348 207 084	324
28	0.0466 086 556	0.0405 723 408	0.0353 198 141	0.0307 490 419	336
29	0.0417 745 529	0.0361 846 183	0.0313 445 417	0.0271 534 848	348
30	0.0374 418 282	0.0322 714 089	0.0278 166 892	0.0239 783 645	360
31	0.0335 584 799	0.0287 813 962	0.0246 858 993	0.0211 745 185	372
32	0.0300 779 003	0.0256 688 131	0.0219 074 822	0.0186 985 327	384
33	0.0269 583 154	0.0228 928 424	0.0194 417 781	0.0165 120 697	396
34	0.0241 622 840	0.0204 170 809	0.0172 535 909	0.0145 812 750	408
35	0.0216 562 482	0.0182 090 623	0.0153 116 859	0.0128 762 525	420
36	0.0194 101 305	0.0162 398 312	0.0135 883 438	0.0113 706 023	432
37	0.0173 969 730	0.0144 835 640	0.0120 589 652	0.0100 410 113	444
38	0.0155 926 139	0.0129 172 294	0.0107 017 193	0.0088 668 924	456
39	0.0139 753 972	0.0115 202 872	0.0094 972 325	0.0078 300 661	468
40	0.0125 259 131	0.0102 744 181	0.0084 283 116	0.0069 144 782	480
41	0.0112 267 649	0.0091 632 844	0.0074 796 986	0.0061 059 521	492
42	0.0100 623 603	0.0081 723 150	0.0066 378 527	0.0053 919 689	504
43	0.0090 187 240	0.0072 885 146	0.0058 907 573	0.0047 614 734	516
44	0.0080 833 305	0.0065 002 934	0.0052 277 480	0.0042 047 033	528
45	0.0072 449 529	0.0057 973 149	0.0046 393 609	0.0037 130 375	540
46	0.0064 935 293	0.0051 703 605	0.0041 171 972	0.0032 788 634	552
47	0.0058 200 409	0.0046 112 084	0.0036 538 035	0.0028 954 583	564
48	0.0052 164 046	0.0041 125 262	0.0032 425 651	0.0025 568 856	576
49	0.0046 753 756	0.0036 677 744	0.0028 776 119	0.0022 579 030	588
50	0.0041 904 604	0.0032 711 205	0.0025 537 344	0.0019 938 811	600

Table 4. PRESENT WORTH OF ONE DOLLAR
PAYABLE AT END OF EACH PERIOD

MONTHS	**13%** NOMINAL ANNUAL RATE	**13½%** NOMINAL ANNUAL RATE	**14%** NOMINAL ANNUAL RATE	**14½%** NOMINAL ANNUAL RATE	MONTHS
1	0.9892 827 700	0.9888 751 545	0.9884 678 748	0.9880 609 304	1
2	0.9786 803 990	0.9778 740 712	0.9770 687 395	0.9762 644 022	2
3	0.9681 916 561	0.9669 953 733	0.9658 010 605	0.9646 087 136	3
4	0.9578 153 234	0.9562 376 991	0.9546 633 217	0.9530 921 831	4
5	0.9475 501 963	0.9455 997 025	0.9436 540 248	0.9417 131 492	5
6	0.9373 950 829	0.9350 800 519	0.9327 716 884	0.9304 699 704	6
7	0.9273 488 042	0.9246 774 308	0.9220 148 485	0.9193 610 247	7
8	0.9174 101 937	0.9143 905 373	0.9113 820 578	0.9083 847 094	8
9	0.9075 780 977	0.9042 180 838	0.9008 718 858	0.8975 394 412	9
10	0.8978 513 744	0.8941 587 974	0.8904 829 184	0.8868 236 553	10
11	0.8882 288 947	0.8842 114 189	0.8802 137 579	0.8762 358 060	11

YEARS					
1	0.8787 095 414	0.8743 747 035	0.8700 630 227	0.8657 743 658	12
2	0.7721 304 581	0.7645 371 221	0.7570 096 634	0.7495 652 524	24
3	0.6784 784 007	0.6684 866 732	0.6586 461 159	0.6489 543 810	36
4	0.5961 854 444	0.5845 078 366	0.5730 636 305	0.5618 480 676	48
5	0.5238 738 384	0.5110 788 663	0.4986 014 745	0.4864 336 544	60
6	0.4603 329 403	0.4468 744 322	0.4338 147 060	0.4211 417 886	72
7	0.4044 989 468	0.3907 356 992	0.3774 461 344	0.3646 137 649	84
8	0.3554 370 841	0.3416 494 111	0.3284 019 246	0.3156 732 511	96
9	0.3123 259 571	0.2987 296 025	0.2857 303 711	0.2733 018 087	108
10	0.2744 437 986	0.2612 016 076	0.2486 034 304	0.2366 177 001	120
11	0.2411 563 844	0.2283 880 782	0.2163 006 521	0.2048 575 392	132
12	0.2119 064 159	0.1996 967 582	0.1881 951 992	0.1773 604 061	144
13	0.1862 041 895	0.1746 097 937	0.1637 416 838	0.1535 540 931	156
14	0.1636 193 980	0.1526 743 866	0.1424 655 844	0.1329 431 976	168
15	0.1437 739 262	0.1334 946 215	0.1239 540 370	0.1150 988 126	180
16	0.1263 355 207	0.1167 243 201	0.1078 478 241	0.0996 496 014	192
17	0.1110 122 275	0.1020 607 928	0.0938 344 038	0.0862 740 705	204
18	0.0975 475 035	0.0892 393 754	0.0816 418 450	0.0746 938 787	216
19	0.0857 159 221	0.0780 286 524	0.0710 335 504	0.0646 680 454	228
20	0.0753 193 986	0.0682 262 798	0.0618 036 656	0.0559 879 360	240
21	0.0661 838 742	0.0596 553 332	0.0537 730 841	0.0484 729 198	252
22	0.0581 564 017	0.0521 611 143	0.0467 859 721	0.0419 666 114	264
23	0.0511 025 851	0.0456 083 588	0.0407 067 443	0.0363 336 164	276
24	0.0449 043 291	0.0398 787 952	0.0354 174 330	0.0314 567 137	288
25	0.0394 578 624	0.0348 690 097	0.0308 153 988	0.0272 344 163	300
26	0.0346 720 002	0.0304 885 801	0.0268 113 390	0.0235 788 595	312
27	0.0304 666 174	0.0266 584 431	0.0233 275 547	0.0204 139 721	324
28	0.0267 713 074	0.0233 094 683	0.0202 964 427	0.0176 738 938	336
29	0.0235 242 032	0.0203 812 095	0.0176 591 843	0.0153 016 042	348
30	0.0206 709 418	0.0178 208 140	0.0153 646 033	0.0132 477 367	360
31	0.0181 637 538	0.0155 820 689	0.0133 681 732	0.0114 695 508	372
32	0.0159 606 638	0.0136 245 669	0.0116 311 532	0.0099 300 431	384
33	0.0140 247 876	0.0119 129 766	0.0101 198 363	0.0085 971 767	396
34	0.0123 237 146	0.0104 164 054	0.0088 048 953	0.0074 432 152	408
35	0.0108 289 656	0.0091 078 414	0.0076 608 138	0.0064 441 450	420
36	0.0095 155 154	0.0079 636 661	0.0066 653 909	0.0055 791 755	432
37	0.0083 613 742	0.0069 632 282	0.0057 993 101	0.0048 303 071	444
38	0.0073 472 193	0.0060 884 706	0.0050 457 653	0.0041 819 561	456
39	0.0064 560 717	0.0053 236 047	0.0043 901 338	0.0036 206 304	468
40	0.0056 730 118	0.0046 548 198	0.0038 196 931	0.0031 346 490	480
41	0.0049 849 296	0.0040 700 615	0.0033 233 737	0.0027 138 987	492
42	0.0043 803 052	0.0035 587 588	0.0028 915 446	0.0023 496 240	504
43	0.0038 490 160	0.0031 116 887	0.0025 158 260	0.0020 342 442	516
44	0.0033 821 671	0.0027 207 818	0.0021 889 272	0.0017 611 965	528
45	0.0029 719 425	0.0023 789 828	0.0019 045 046	0.0015 247 988	540
46	0.0026 114 742	0.0020 801 224	0.0016 570 390	0.0013 201 317	552
47	0.0022 947 273	0.0018 188 064	0.0014 417 284	0.0011 429 362	564
48	0.0020 163 988	0.0015 903 183	0.0012 543 946	0.0009 895 248	576
49	0.0017 718 288	0.0013 905 341	0.0010 914 023	0.0008 567 052	588
50	0.0015 569 229	0.0012 158 478	0.0009 495 888	0.0007 417 134	600

52

Table 4.   PRESENT WORTH OF ONE DOLLAR
PAYABLE AT END OF EACH PERIOD

MONTHS	15% NOMINAL ANNUAL RATE	15½% NOMINAL ANNUAL RATE	16% NOMINAL ANNUAL RATE	16½% NOMINAL ANNUAL RATE	MONTHS
1	0.9876 543 210	0.9872 480 461	0.9868 421 053	0.9864 364 982	1
2	0.9754 610 578	0.9746 587 045	0.9738 573 407	0.9730 569 649	2
3	0.9634 183 287	0.9622 299 016	0.9610 434 283	0.9598 589 049	3
4	0.9515 242 752	0.9499 595 902	0.9483 981 201	0.9468 398 569	4
5	0.9397 770 619	0.9378 457 493	0.9359 191 974	0.9339 973 928	5
6	0.9281 748 760	0.9258 863 835	0.9236 044 712	0.9213 291 174	6
7	0.9167 159 269	0.9140 795 230	0.9114 517 807	0.9088 326 682	7
8	0.9053 984 463	0.9024 232 230	0.8994 589 942	0.8965 057 146	8
9	0.8942 206 877	0.8909 155 637	0.8876 240 074	0.8843 459 577	9
10	0.8831 809 262	0.8795 546 494	0.8759 447 441	0.8723 511 297	10
11	0.8722 774 579	0.8683 386 091	0.8644 191 554	0.8605 189 935	11

YEARS

	15%	15½%	16%	16½%	MONTHS
1	0.8615 086 004	0.8572 655 951	0.8530 452 191	0.8488 473 426	12
2	0.7421 970 686	0.7349 043 006	0.7276 861 459	0.7205 418 110	24
3	0.6394 091 578	0.6300 081 726	0.6207 491 878	0.6116 300 014	36
4	0.5508 564 886	0.5400 843 310	0.5295 271 269	0.5191 805 013	48
5	0.4745 676 026	0.4629 957 155	0.4517 105 841	0.4407 049 889	60
6	0.4088 440 711	0.3969 102 976	0.3853 295 542	0.3740 912 587	72
7	0.3522 226 835	0.3402 575 424	0.3287 035 340	0.3175 463 708	84
8	0.3034 428 711	0.2916 910 846	0.2803 989 782	0.2695 483 930	96
9	0.2614 186 432	0.2500 567 313	0.2391 930 078	0.2288 054 371	108
10	0.2252 144 094	0.2143 650 325	0.2040 424 517	0.1942 208 872	120
11	0.1940 241 506	0.1837 677 672	0.1740 574 380	0.1648 638 840	132
12	0.1671 534 745	0.1575 377 843	0.1484 788 653	0.1399 442 698	144
13	0.1440 041 558	0.1350 517 224	0.1266 591 862	0.1187 913 215	156
14	0.1240 608 188	0.1157 751 952	0.1080 460 132	0.1008 356 976	168
15	0.1068 794 623	0.0992 500 916	0.0921 681 350	0.0855 941 139	180
16	0.0920 775 760	0.0850 836 888	0.0786 235 870	0.0726 563 362	192
17	0.0793 256 236	0.0729 393 192	0.0670 694 750	0.0616 741 379	204
18	0.0683 397 070	0.0625 283 688	0.0572 132 950	0.0523 519 280	216
19	0.0588 752 453	0.0536 034 193	0.0488 055 277	0.0444 387 950	228
20	0.0507 215 302	0.0459 523 672	0.0416 333 221	0.0377 217 530	240
21	0.0436 970 345	0.0393 933 834	0.0355 151 064	0.0320 200 098	252
22	0.0376 453 710	0.0337 705 923	0.0302 959 917	0.0271 801 002	264
23	0.0324 318 109	0.0289 503 669	0.0258 438 509	0.0230 717 559	276
24	0.0279 402 840	0.0248 181 535	0.0220 459 734	0.0195 843 987	288
25	0.0240 707 950	0.0212 757 491	0.0188 062 122	0.0166 241 648	300
26	0.0207 371 969	0.0182 389 677	0.0160 425 494	0.0141 113 781	312
27	0.0178 652 735	0.0156 356 395	0.0136 850 201	0.0119 784 058	324
28	0.0153 910 868	0.0134 038 958	0.0116 739 410	0.0101 678 379	336
29	0.0132 595 536	0.0114 906 987	0.0099 583 995	0.0086 309 422	348
30	0.0114 232 195	0.0098 505 807	0.0084 949 651	0.0073 263 523	360
31	0.0098 412 018	0.0084 445 639	0.0072 465 894	0.0062 189 547	372
32	0.0084 782 800	0.0072 392 341	0.0061 816 684	0.0052 789 432	384
33	0.0073 041 111	0.0062 059 463	0.0052 732 427	0.0044 810 169	396
34	0.0062 925 546	0.0053 201 443	0.0044 983 145	0.0038 036 993	408
35	0.0054 210 899	0.0045 607 767	0.0038 372 657	0.0032 287 600	420
36	0.0046 703 156	0.0039 097 969	0.0032 733 611	0.0027 407 244	432
37	0.0040 235 170	0.0033 517 344	0.0027 923 251	0.0023 264 566	444
38	0.0034 662 945	0.0028 733 266	0.0023 819 795	0.0019 748 065	456
39	0.0029 862 425	0.0024 632 040	0.0020 319 363	0.0016 763 092	468
40	0.0025 726 736	0.0021 116 200	0.0017 333 335	0.0014 229 307	480
41	0.0022 163 805	0.0018 102 192	0.0014 786 119	0.0012 078 509	492
42	0.0019 094 308	0.0015 518 387	0.0012 613 228	0.0010 252 810	504
43	0.0016 449 911	0.0013 303 379	0.0010 759 654	0.0008 703 071	516
44	0.0014 171 740	0.0011 404 529	0.0009 178 471	0.0007 387 578	528
45	0.0012 209 076	0.0009 776 710	0.0007 829 651	0.0006 270 926	540
46	0.0010 518 224	0.0008 381 237	0.0006 679 046	0.0005 323 059	552
47	0.0009 061 540	0.0007 184 946	0.0005 697 529	0.0004 518 465	564
48	0.0007 806 595	0.0006 159 407	0.0004 860 249	0.0003 835 487	576
49	0.0006 725 448	0.0005 280 248	0.0004 146 013	0.0003 255 743	588
50	0.0005 794 032	0.0004 526 575	0.0003 536 736	0.0002 763 629	600

Table 4.   PRESENT WORTH OF ONE DOLLAR
PAYABLE AT END OF EACH PERIOD

MONTHS	17% NOMINAL ANNUAL RATE	17½% NOMINAL ANNUAL RATE	18% NOMINAL ANNUAL RATE	18½% NOMINAL ANNUAL RATE	MONTHS
1	0.9860 312 243	0.9856 262 834	0.9852 216 749	0.9848 173 984	1
2	0.9722 575 753	0.9714 591 705	0.9706 617 486	0.9698 653 083	2
3	0.9586 763 274	0.9574 956 916	0.9563 169 937	0.9551 402 297	3
4	0.9452 847 928	0.9437 329 199	0.9421 842 303	0.9406 387 162	4
5	0.9320 803 216	0.9301 679 703	0.9282 603 254	0.9263 573 733	5
6	0.9190 603 007	0.9167 979 995	0.9145 421 925	0.9122 928 584	6
7	0.9062 221 535	0.9036 202 048	0.9010 267 907	0.8984 418 795	7
8	0.8935 633 395	0.8906 318 241	0.8877 111 238	0.8848 011 944	8
9	0.8810 813 537	0.8778 301 346	0.8745 922 402	0.8713 676 104	9
10	0.8687 737 259	0.8652 124 530	0.8616 672 317	0.8581 379 832	10
11	0.8566 380 206	0.8527 761 344	0.8489 332 332	0.8451 092 161	11
YEARS					
1	0.8446 718 362	0.8405 185 719	0.8363 874 219	0.8322 782 596	12
2	0.7134 705 109	0.7064 744 196	0.6995 439 195	0.6926 871 014	24
3	0.6026 484 466	0.5938 023 907	0.5850 897 353	0.5765 084 152	36
4	0.5090 401 700	0.4991 019 374	0.4893 616 953	0.4798 154 204	48
5	0.4299 718 951	0.4195 044 477	0.4092 959 667	0.3993 399 430	60
6	0.3631 851 502	0.3526 012 792	0.3423 299 984	0.3323 619 527	72
7	0.3067 722 677	0.2963 679 237	0.2863 205 048	0.2766 176 276	84
8	0.2591 218 946	0.2491 027 439	0.2394 748 688	0.2302 228 376	96
9	0.2188 729 666	0.2093 754 826	0.2002 937 682	0.1916 094 626	108
10	0.1848 758 306	0.1759 839 816	0.1675 231 884	0.1594 723 901	120
11	0.1561 594 073	0.1479 178 049	0.1401 142 876	0.1327 254 033	132
12	0.1319 304 533	0.1243 276 621	0.1171 898 278	0.1104 644 676	144
13	0.1114 151 321	0.1044 997 090	0.0980 160 979	0.0919 371 749	156
14	0.0941 092 242	0.0878 339 462	0.0819 794 315	0.0765 173 119	168
15	0.0794 914 112	0.0738 260 630	0.0685 665 653	0.0636 836 952	180
16	0.0671 441 563	0.0620 521 770	0.0573 482 128	0.0530 025 550	192
17	0.0567 147 778	0.0521 560 072	0.0479 653 239	0.0441 128 742	204
18	0.0479 053 755	0.0438 380 927	0.0401 175 936	0.0367 141 862	216
19	0.0404 643 215	0.0368 467 311	0.0335 538 507	0.0305 566 190	228
20	0.0341 790 727	0.0309 703 618	0.0280 640 186	0.0254 314 432	240
21	0.0288 701 001	0.0260 311 643	0.0234 723 922	0.0211 660 373	252
22	0.0243 857 605	0.0218 796 770	0.0196 320 136	0.0176 160 327	264
23	0.0205 979 651	0.0183 902 749	0.0164 199 692	0.0146 614 410	276
24	0.0173 985 210	0.0154 573 676	0.0137 334 557	0.0122 023 986	288
25	0.0146 960 407	0.0129 922 045	0.0114 864 896	0.0101 557 911	300
26	0.0124 133 317	0.0109 201 892	0.0096 071 555	0.0084 524 441	312
27	0.0104 851 916	0.0091 786 218	0.0080 353 040	0.0070 347 855	324
28	0.0088 565 461	0.0077 148 021	0.0067 206 272	0.0058 548 990	336
29	0.0074 808 750	0.0064 844 344	0.0056 210 480	0.0048 729 052	348
30	0.0063 188 845	0.0054 502 876	0.0047 013 739	0.0040 556 130	360
31	0.0053 373 837	0.0045 810 679	0.0039 321 700	0.0033 753 986	372
32	0.0045 083 377	0.0038 504 727	0.0032 888 175	0.0028 092 708	384
33	0.0038 080 659	0.0032 363 938	0.0027 507 256	0.0023 380 950	396
34	0.0032 165 660	0.0027 202 491	0.0023 006 723	0.0019 459 457	408
35	0.0027 169 427	0.0022 864 199	0.0019 242 534	0.0016 195 683	420
36	0.0022 949 250	0.0019 217 784	0.0016 094 213	0.0013 479 315	432
37	0.0019 384 585	0.0016 152 904	0.0013 460 997	0.0011 218 541	444
38	0.0016 373 613	0.0013 576 816	0.0011 258 609	0.0009 336 947	456
39	0.0013 830 330	0.0011 411 566	0.0009 416 559	0.0007 770 938	468
40	0.0011 682 090	0.0009 591 633	0.0007 875 891	0.0006 467 583	480
41	0.0009 867 533	0.0008 061 946	0.0006 587 297	0.0005 382 829	492
42	0.0008 334 827	0.0006 776 215	0.0005 509 532	0.0004 480 011	504
43	0.0007 040 193	0.0005 695 535	0.0004 608 103	0.0003 728 616	516
44	0.0005 946 653	0.0004 787 203	0.0003 854 160	0.0003 103 246	528
45	0.0005 022 970	0.0004 023 733	0.0003 223 571	0.0002 582 764	540
46	0.0004 242 762	0.0003 382 022	0.0002 696 154	0.0002 149 579	552
47	0.0003 583 741	0.0002 842 652	0.0002 255 029	0.0001 789 047	564
48	0.0003 027 085	0.0002 389 302	0.0001 886 078	0.0001 488 985	576
49	0.0002 556 894	0.0002 008 253	0.0001 577 492	0.0001 239 250	588
50	0.0002 159 736	0.0001 687 974	0.0001 319 394	0.0001 031 401	600

Table 4. PRESENT WORTH OF ONE DOLLAR
PAYABLE AT END OF EACH PERIOD

	19% NOMINAL ANNUAL RATE	19½% NOMINAL ANNUAL RATE	20% NOMINAL ANNUAL RATE	20½% NOMINAL ANNUAL RATE	
MONTHS					MONTHS
1	0.9844 134 537	0.9840 098 401	0.9836 065 574	0.9832 036 051	1
2	0.9690 698 477	0.9682 753 654	0.9674 818 597	0.9666 893 290	2
3	0.9539 653 956	0.9527 924 875	0.9516 215 014	0.9504 524 333	3
4	0.9390 963 698	0.9375 571 833	0.9360 211 489	0.9344 882 589	4
5	0.9244 591 007	0.9225 654 940	0.9206 765 399	0.9187 922 250	5
6	0.9100 499 761	0.9078 135 242	0.9055 834 818	0.9033 598 280	6
7	0.8958 654 399	0.8932 974 408	0.8907 378 510	0.8881 866 396	7
8	0.8819 019 917	0.8790 134 719	0.8761 355 911	0.8732 683 060	8
9	0.8681 561 855	0.8649 579 059	0.8617 727 126	0.8586 005 467	9
10	0.8546 246 288	0.8511 270 907	0.8476 452 911	0.8441 791 528	10
11	0.8413 039 824	0.8375 174 324	0.8337 494 666	0.8299 999 864	11
YEARS					
1	0.8281 909 589	0.8241 253 947	0.8200 814 426	0.8160 589 788	12
2	0.6859 002 645	0.6791 824 663	0.6725 335 725	0.6659 522 569	24
3	0.5680 563 977	0.5597 316 829	0.5515 323 023	0.5434 563 187	36
4	0.4704 591 728	0.4612 890 942	0.4523 014 061	0.4434 924 085	48
5	0.3896 300 334	0.3801 600 568	0.3709 239 896	0.3619 159 620	60
6	0.3226 880 710	0.3132 995 569	0.3041 878 805	0.2953 447 703	72
7	0.2672 473 430	0.2581 981 210	0.2494 588 359	0.2410 187 517	84
8	0.2213 318 332	0.2127 876 284	0.2045 765 620	0.1966 855 164	96
9	0.1833 050 232	0.1753 636 882	0.1677 694 421	0.1605 069 816	108
10	0.1518 115 630	0.1445 216 688	0.1375 846 061	0.1309 831 635	120
11	0.1257 289 639	0.1191 039 773	0.1128 305 822	0.1068 899 867	132
12	0.1041 275 912	0.0981 566 123	0.0925 302 666	0.0872 285 334	144
13	0.0862 375 296	0.0808 933 569	0.0758 823 546	0.0711 836 279	156
14	0.0714 211 423	0.0666 662 697	0.0622 297 108	0.0580 900 387	168
15	0.0591 503 444	0.0549 413 658	0.0510 334 310	0.0474 048 976	180
16	0.0489 877 804	0.0452 785 748	0.0418 515 697	0.0386 851 923	192
17	0.0405 712 368	0.0373 152 233	0.0343 216 957	0.0315 693 986	204
18	0.0336 007 315	0.0307 524 232	0.0281 465 857	0.0257 624 911	216
19	0.0278 278 221	0.0253 438 529	0.0230 824 926	0.0210 237 122	228
20	0.0230 467 506	0.0208 865 128	0.0189 295 238	0.0171 565 891	240
21	0.0190 871 105	0.0172 131 056	0.0155 237 512	0.0140 007 886	252
22	0.0158 077 724	0.0141 857 574	0.0127 307 403	0.0114 254 692	264
23	0.0130 918 542	0.0116 908 429	0.0104 402 439	0.0093 238 568	276
24	0.0108 425 552	0.0096 347 205	0.0085 618 502	0.0076 088 170	288
25	0.0089 797 062	0.0079 402 179	0.0070 214 145	0.0062 092 435	300
26	0.0074 369 115	0.0065 437 352	0.0057 581 317	0.0050 671 089	312
27	0.0061 591 829	0.0053 928 583	0.0047 221 370	0.0041 350 597	324
28	0.0051 009 796	0.0044 443 915	0.0038 725 369	0.0033 744 526	336
29	0.0042 245 852	0.0036 627 359	0.0031 757 957	0.0027 537 523	348
30	0.0034 987 632	0.0030 185 537	0.0026 044 111	0.0022 472 243	360
31	0.0028 976 441	0.0024 876 667	0.0021 358 292	0.0018 338 676	372
32	0.0023 998 026	0.0020 501 493	0.0017 515 539	0.0014 965 641	384
33	0.0019 874 948	0.0016 895 801	0.0014 364 168	0.0012 212 683	396
34	0.0016 460 253	0.0013 924 259	0.0011 779 788	0.0009 966 269	408
35	0.0013 632 232	0.0011 475 335	0.0009 660 385	0.0008 133 064	420
36	0.0011 290 092	0.0009 457 115	0.0007 922 303	0.0006 637 060	432
37	0.0009 350 352	0.0007 793 849	0.0006 496 934	0.0005 416 232	444
38	0.0007 743 877	0.0006 423 109	0.0005 328 015	0.0004 419 965	456
39	0.0006 413 409	0.0005 293 447	0.0004 369 406	0.0003 606 952	468
40	0.0005 311 527	0.0004 362 464	0.0003 583 269	0.0002 943 486	480
41	0.0004 398 959	0.0003 595 217	0.0002 938 572	0.0002 402 058	492
42	0.0003 643 178	0.0002 962 910	0.0002 409 869	0.0001 960 221	504
43	0.0003 017 247	0.0002 441 809	0.0001 976 288	0.0001 599 656	516
44	0.0002 498 857	0.0002 012 357	0.0001 620 717	0.0001 305 413	528
45	0.0002 069 531	0.0001 658 435	0.0001 329 120	0.0001 065 294	540
46	0.0001 713 966	0.0001 366 758	0.0001 089 987	0.0000 869 343	552
47	0.0001 419 492	0.0001 126 380	0.0000 893 878	0.0000 709 435	564
48	0.0001 175 610	0.0000 928 278	0.0000 733 053	0.0000 578 941	576
49	0.0000 973 630	0.0000 765 018	0.0000 601 163	0.0000 472 450	588
50	0.0000 806 351	0.0000 630 471	0.0000 493 003	0.0000 385 547	600

55

Table 4. PRESENT WORTH OF ONE DOLLAR PAYABLE AT END OF EACH PERIOD

MONTHS	21% NOMINAL ANNUAL RATE	21½% NOMINAL ANNUAL RATE	22% NOMINAL ANNUAL RATE	22½% NOMINAL ANNUAL RATE	MONTHS
1	0.9828 009 828	0.9823 986 901	0.9819 967 267	0.9815 950 920	1
2	0.9658 977 718	0.9651 071 864	0.9643 175 712	0.9635 289 247	2
3	0.9492 852 794	0.9481 200 357	0.9469 566 984	0.9457 952 635	3
4	0.9329 585 056	0.9314 318 812	0.9299 083 781	0.9283 879 887	4
5	0.9169 125 362	0.9150 374 600	0.9131 669 834	0.9113 010 932	5
6	0.9011 425 417	0.8989 316 022	0.8967 269 886	0.8945 286 805	6
7	0.8856 437 756	0.8831 092 285	0.8805 829 676	0.8780 649 624	7
8	0.8704 115 731	0.8675 653 493	0.8647 295 917	0.8619 042 576	8
9	0.8554 413 495	0.8522 950 628	0.8491 616 285	0.8460 409 890	9
10	0.8407 285 990	0.8372 935 533	0.8338 739 396	0.8304 696 825	10
11	0.8262 688 934	0.8225 560 900	0.8188 614 792	0.8151 849 644	11

YEARS	21%	21½%	22%	22½%	MONTHS
1	0.8120 578 805	0.8080 780 254	0.8041 192 922	0.8001 815 602	12
2	0.6594 380 012	0.6529 900 951	0.6466 078 360	0.6402 905 292	24
3	0.5355 018 255	0.5276 669 466	0.5199 498 354	0.5123 486 746	36
4	0.4348 584 774	0.4263 960 643	0.4181 016 936	0.4099 719 618	48
5	0.3531 302 535	0.3445 612 897	0.3362 036 379	0.3280 520 040	60
6	0.2867 622 052	0.2784 324 066	0.2703 478 314	0.2625 011 644	72
7	0.2328 675 085	0.2249 951 093	0.2173 919 068	0.2100 485 912	84
8	0.1891 018 954	0.1818 136 036	0.1748 090 262	0.1680 770 095	96
9	0.1535 616 844	0.1469 195 778	0.1405 673 104	0.1344 921 237	108
10	0.1247 009 759	0.1187 224 823	0.1130 328 862	0.1076 181 173	120
11	0.1012 644 102	0.0959 370 291	0.0908 919 244	0.0861 140 330	132
12	0.0822 325 623	0.0775 246 050	0.0730 879 499	0.0689 068 613	144
13	0.0667 776 003	0.0626 459 298	0.0587 714 306	0.0551 379 998	156
14	0.0542 272 765	0.0506 227 992	0.0472 592 411	0.0441 204 107	168
15	0.0440 356 872	0.0409 071 716	0.0380 020 675	0.0353 043 391	180
16	0.0357 595 268	0.0330 561 865	0.0305 581 956	0.0282 498 811	192
17	0.0290 388 056	0.0267 119 779	0.0245 724 347	0.0226 050 339	204
18	0.0235 811 909	0.0215 853 623	0.0197 591 688	0.0180 881 313	216
19	0.0191 492 919	0.0174 426 570	0.0158 887 288	0.0144 737 891	228
20	0.0155 503 334	0.0140 950 278	0.0127 764 334	0.0115 816 592	240
21	0.0126 277 708	0.0113 898 822	0.0102 737 765	0.0092 674 301	252
22	0.0102 544 808	0.0092 039 136	0.0082 613 419	0.0074 156 267	264
23	0.0083 272 319	0.0074 374 803	0.0066 431 044	0.0059 338 477	276
24	0.0067 621 943	0.0060 100 644	0.0053 418 484	0.0047 481 555	288
25	0.0054 912 932	0.0048 566 010	0.0042 954 834	0.0037 993 865	300
26	0.0044 592 479	0.0039 245 125	0.0034 540 810	0.0030 401 990	312
27	0.0036 211 674	0.0031 713 123	0.0027 774 932	0.0024 327 112	324
28	0.0029 405 975	0.0025 626 678	0.0022 334 359	0.0019 466 106	336
29	0.0023 879 354	0.0020 708 355	0.0017 959 489	0.0015 576 419	348
30	0.0019 391 418	0.0016 733 967	0.0014 441 571	0.0012 463 964	360
31	0.0015 746 953	0.0013 522 351	0.0011 612 746	0.0009 973 434	372
32	0.0012 787 438	0.0010 927 115	0.0009 338 033	0.0007 980 558	384
33	0.0010 384 139	0.0008 829 961	0.0007 508 893	0.0006 385 895	396
34	0.0008 432 522	0.0007 135 298	0.0006 038 045	0.0005 109 876	408
35	0.0006 847 696	0.0005 765 877	0.0004 855 309	0.0004 088 828	420
36	0.0005 560 726	0.0004 659 279	0.0003 904 248	0.0003 271 805	432
37	0.0004 515 631	0.0003 765 061	0.0003 139 481	0.0002 618 038	444
38	0.0003 666 954	0.0003 042 463	0.0002 524 517	0.0002 094 906	456
39	0.0002 977 779	0.0002 458 547	0.0002 030 013	0.0001 676 305	468
40	0.0002 418 129	0.0001 986 698	0.0001 632 372	0.0001 341 348	480
41	0.0001 963 660	0.0001 605 407	0.0001 312 622	0.0001 073 322	492
42	0.0001 594 606	0.0001 297 294	0.0001 055 505	0.0000 858 853	504
43	0.0001 294 912	0.0001 048 315	0.0000 848 752	0.0000 687 238	516
44	0.0001 051 544	0.0000 847 120	0.0000 682 498	0.0000 549 915	528
45	0.0000 853 914	0.0000 684 539	0.0000 548 810	0.0000 440 032	540
46	0.0000 693 428	0.0000 553 161	0.0000 441 308	0.0000 352 105	552
47	0.0000 563 104	0.0000 446 997	0.0000 354 865	0.0000 281 748	564
48	0.0000 457 273	0.0000 361 209	0.0000 285 353	0.0000 225 450	576
49	0.0000 371 332	0.0000 291 885	0.0000 229 458	0.0000 180 401	588
50	0.0000 301 543	0.0000 235 866	0.0000 184 512	0.0000 144 353	600

Table 5. PRESENT WORTH OF ONE DOLLAR PER PERIOD
PAYABLE AT END OF EACH PERIOD

MONTHS	5% NOMINAL ANNUAL RATE	5½% NOMINAL ANNUAL RATE	6% NOMINAL ANNUAL RATE	6½% NOMINAL ANNUAL RATE	MONTHS
1	0.9958 506 224	0.9954 375 778	0.9950 248 756	0.9946 125 155	1
2	1.9875 690 846	1.9863 335 490	1.9850 993 787	1.9838 665 716	2
3	2.9751 725 323	2.9727 086 344	2.9702 481 380	2.9677 910 368	3
4	3.9586 780 405	3.9545 834 602	3.9504 956 597	3.9464 146 243	4
5	4.9381 026 129	4.9319 785 585	4.9258 663 281	4.9197 658 924	5
6	5.9134 631 830	5.9049 143 677	5.8963 844 061	5.8878 732 456	6
7	6.8847 766 138	6.8734 112 328	6.8620 740 359	6.8507 649 355	7
8	7.8520 596 984	7.8374 894 064	7.8229 592 397	7.8084 690 615	8
9	8.8153 291 602	8.7971 690 483	8.7790 639 201	8.7610 135 713	9
10	9.7746 016 533	9.7524 702 264	9.7304 118 608	9.7084 262 624	10
11	10.7298 937 626	10.7034 129 172	10.6770 267 272	10.6507 347 823	11

YEARS					
1	11.6812 220 043	11.6500 170 059	11.6189 320 668	11.5879 666 297	12
2	22.7938 983 940	22.6779 707 374	22.5628 662 218	22.4485 780 020	24
3	33.3657 012 837	33.1170 768 299	32.8710 162 393	32.6274 888 625	36
4	43.4229 559 379	42.9987 773 396	42.5803 177 828	42.1674 882 931	48
5	52.9907 063 239	52.3528 354 457	51.7255 607 511	51.1086 795 838	60
6	62.0927 774 752	61.2074 250 950	60.3395 139 355	59.4886 488 154	72
7	70.7518 348 188	69.5892 158 610	68.4530 424 355	67.3426 228 596	84
8	78.9894 406 159	77.5234 532 710	76.0952 182 532	74.7036 174 627	96
9	86.8261 076 543	85.0340 348 441	83.2934 244 626	81.6025 760 334	108
10	94.2813 503 282	92.1435 820 700	90.0734 533 272	88.0684 997 199	120
11	101.3737 332 323	98.8735 085 429	96.4595 987 178	94.1285 693 219	132
12	108.1209 173 896	105.2440 844 590	102.4747 431 612	99.8082 595 505	144
13	114.5397 042 300	111.2744 976 687	108.1404 398 312	105.1314 461 163	156
14	120.6460 774 284	116.9829 114 697	113.4769 897 777	110.1205 060 955	168
15	126.4552 427 061	122.3865 193 138	118.5035 146 676	114.7964 119 967	180
16	131.9816 656 951	127.5015 965 929	123.2380 253 014	119.1788 199 228	192
17	137.2391 079 599	132.3435 496 595	127.6974 861 481	123.2861 521 196	204
18	142.2406 612 652	136.9269 622 297	131.8978 761 316	127.1356 748 173	216
19	146.9987 801 767	141.2656 393 089	135.8542 458 858	130.7435 700 121	228
20	151.5253 130 743	145.3726 487 718	139.5807 716 829	134.1250 042 907	240
21	155.8315 316 566	149.2603 607 218	143.0908 062 297	137.2941 921 866	252
22	159.9281 590 086	152.9404 847 494	146.3969 265 116	140.2644 560 132	264
23	163.8253 963 041	156.4241 052 010	149.5109 788 588	143.0482 818 666	276
24	167.5329 482 076	159.7217 145 640	152.4441 213 926	145.6573 721 142	288
25	171.0600 470 409	162.8432 450 700	155.2068 640 072	148.1026 945 870	300
26	174.4154 757 721	165.7980 986 101	157.8091 060 280	150.3945 286 857	312
27	177.6075 898 869	168.5951 750 527	160.2601 716 825	152.5425 085 920	324
28	180.6643 381 949	171.2428 990 497	162.5688 435 103	154.5556 637 679	336
29	183.5332 826 230	173.7492 454 111	164.7433 938 325	156.4424 569 125	348
30	186.2816 170 461	176.1217 631 246	166.7916 143 923	158.2108 195 371	360
31	188.8961 852 002	178.3675 980 928	168.7208 442 745	159.8681 853 067	372
32	191.3834 977 250	180.4935 146 562	170.5379 962 019	161.4215 212 887	384
33	193.7497 483 756	182.5059 159 674	172.2495 813 053	162.8773 572 409	396
34	196.0008 294 463	184.4108 632 768	173.8617 324 535	164.2418 130 599	408
35	198.1423 464 432	186.2140 941 887	175.3802 262 283	165.5206 245 078	420
36	200.1796 320 423	187.9210 399 427	176.8105 036 231	166.7191 673 237	432
37	202.1177 593 690	189.5368 417 728	178.1576 895 384	167.8424 798 212	444
38	203.9615 546 308	191.0663 663 916	179.4266 111 456	168.8952 840 685	456
39	205.7156 091 351	192.5142 206 497	180.6218 151 830	169.8820 057 382	468
40	207.3842 907 225	193.8847 654 102	181.7475 842 478	170.8067 927 115	480
41	208.9717 546 429	195.1821 286 843	182.8079 521 412	171.6735 325 150	492
42	210.4819 539 030	196.4102 180 641	183.8067 183 220	172.4858 686 623	504
43	211.9186 491 096	197.5727 324 923	184.7474 615 208	173.2472 159 703	516
44	213.2854 178 344	198.6731 734 033	185.6335 525 630	173.9607 749 144	528
45	214.5856 635 220	199.7148 552 690	186.4681 664 471	174.6295 450 817	540
46	215.8226 239 657	200.7009 155 823	187.2542 937 210	175.2563 377 812	552
47	216.9993 793 696	201.6343 243 065	187.9947 511 980	175.8437 878 609	564
48	218.1188 600 188	202.5178 928 213	188.6921 920 494	176.3943 647 843	576
49	219.1838 535 765	203.3542 823 901	189.3491 153 114	176.9103 830 114	588
50	220.1970 120 250	204.1460 121 757	189.9678 748 396	177.3940 117 277	600

57

Table 5. PRESENT WORTH OF ONE DOLLAR PER PERIOD
PAYABLE AT END OF EACH PERIOD

MONTHS	7% NOMINAL ANNUAL RATE	7½% NOMINAL ANNUAL RATE	8% NOMINAL ANNUAL RATE	8½% NOMINAL ANNUAL RATE	MONTHS
1	0.9942 004 971	0.9937 888 199	0.9933 774 834	0.9929 664 874	1
2	1.9826 351 255	1.9814 050 384	1.9801 763 081	1.9789 489 324	2
3	2.9653 373 245	2.9628 869 947	2.9604 400 411	2.9579 964 575	3
4	3.9423 403 392	3.9382 727 897	3.9342 119 614	3.9301 578 395	4
5	4.9136 772 220	4.9076 002 879	4.9015 350 610	4.8954 815 121	5
6	5.8793 808 338	5.8709 071 184	5.8624 520 473	5.8540 155 685	6
7	6.8394 838 447	6.8282 306 767	6.8170 053 450	6.8058 077 635	7
8	7.7940 187 355	7.7796 081 259	7.7652 370 977	7.7509 055 161	8
9	8.7430 177 983	8.7250 763 984	8.7071 891 699	8.6893 559 117	9
10	9.6865 131 383	9.6646 721 972	9.6429 031 489	9.6212 057 047	10
11	10.6245 366 744	10.5984 319 972	10.5724 203 466	10.5465 013 203	11

YEARS					
1	11.5571 201 402	11.5263 920 469	11.4957 818 013	11.4652 888 576	12
2	22.3350 992 958	22.2224 233 837	22.1105 436 077	21.9994 533 710	24
3	32.3864 644 516	32.1479 131 547	31.9118 055 101	31.6781 124 414	36
4	41.7602 014 051	41.3583 711 359	40.9619 129 579	40.5707 437 726	48
5	50.5019 935 012	49.9053 081 820	49.3184 333 356	48.7411 826 131	60
6	58.6544 442 718	57.8365 243 081	57.0345 221 475	56.2480 799 938	72
7	66.2572 850 667	65.1963 760 188	64.1592 611 371	63.1453 237 506	84
8	73.3475 686 854	72.0260 243 780	70.7379 704 946	69.4824 253 558	96
9	79.9598 499 565	78.3636 652 089	76.8124 971 368	75.3048 753 330	108
10	86.1263 541 414	84.2447 427 094	82.4214 808 934	80.6544 698 084	120
11	91.8771 339 863	89.7021 476 791	87.6006 002 941	85.5696 105 417	132
12	97.2402 161 854	94.7664 014 660	92.3827 995 177	90.0855 805 914	144
13	102.2417 379 053	99.4658 266 618	96.7984 979 493	94.2347-975 917	156
14	106.9060 744 910	103.8267 055 002	100.8757 836 765	98.0470 464 609	168
15	111.2559 576 093	107.8734 268 437	104.6405 921 566	101.5496 932 109	180
16	115.3125 866 838	111.6286 225 829	108.1168 711 913	104.7678 813 922	192
17	119.0957 318 858	115.1132 942 076	111.3267 332 575	107.7247 125 858	204
18	122.6238 305 501	118.3469 302 617	114.2905 961 643	110.4414 122 362	216
19	125.9140 770 302	121.3476 153 352	117.0273 129 293	112.9374 820 174	228
20	128.9825 064 963	124.1321 312 052	119.5542 917 024	115.2308 398 246	240
21	131.8440 730 824	126.7160 506 903	121.8876 064 982	117.2739 483 963	252
22	134.5127 227 670	129.1138 247 442	124.0420 994 423	119.2739 334 916	264
23	137.0014 613 390	131.3388 632 743	126.0314 751 811	121.0526 924 695	276
24	139.3224 177 821	133.4036 101 394	127.8683 880 572	122.6869 940 502	288
25	141.4869 033 859	135.3196 127 429	129.5645 226 026	124.1885 699 746	300
26	143.5054 668 720	137.0975 866 142	131.1306 678 637	125.5681 992 203	312
27	145.3879 458 040	138.7474 753 361	132.5767 860 302	126.8357 853 772	324
28	147.1435 145 307	140.2785 061 565	133.9120 758 040	128.0004 277 406	336
29	148.7807 288 984	141.6992 415 927	135.1450 309 120	129.0704 866 294	348
30	150.3075 679 478	143.0176 273 187	136.2834 941 340	130.0536 434 006	360
31	151.7314 728 003	144.2410 366 025	137.3347 071 907	130.9569 555 892	372
32	153.0593 829 226	145.3763 115 423	138.3053 568 079	131.7869 075 703	384
33	154.2977 699 469	146.4298 013 319	139.2016 172 505	132.5494 571 070	396
34	155.4526 692 100	147.4073 977 694	140.0291 895 964	133.2500 781 179	408
35	156.5297 091 675	148.3145 682 082	140.7933 380 016	133.8937 999 711	420
36	157.5341 388 240	149.1563 861 336	141.4989 231 846	134.4852 435 872	432
37	158.4708 533 142	149.9375 595 376	142.1504 333 456	135.0286 546 108	444
38	159.3444 177 600	150.6624 572 483	142.7520 127 156	135.5279 338 868	456
39	160.1590 895 185	151.3351 333 640	143.3074 879 177	135.9866 654 632	468
40	160.9188 389 305	151.9593 499 257	143.8203 923 084	136.4081 423 185	480
41	161.6273 686 704	152.5385 979 574	144.2939 884 526	136.7953 900 005	492
42	162.2881 317 909	153.0761 169 897	144.7312 888 773	137.1511 883 445	504
43	162.9043 485 519	153.5749 131 776	145.1350 752 336	137.4780 914 287	516
44	163.4790 221 145	154.0377 761 129	145.5079 159 909	137.7784 459 084	528
45	164.0149 531 774	154.4672 944 254	145.8521 827 749	138.0544 078 611	540
46	164.5147 536 254	154.8658 702 600	146.1700 654 534	138.3079 582 640	552
47	164.9808 592 594	155.2357 327 112	146.4635 860 658	138.5409 172 143	564
48	165.4155 416 671	155.5789 502 899	146.7346 116 854	138.7549 569 945	576
49	165.8209 192 933	155.8974 424 913	146.9848 662 958	138.9516 140 770	588
50	166.1989 677 650	156.1929 905 303	147.2159 417 569	139.1323 001 535	600

58

Table 5. PRESENT WORTH OF ONE DOLLAR PER PERIOD
PAYABLE AT END OF EACH PERIOD

MONTHS	9% NOMINAL ANNUAL RATE	9½% NOMINAL ANNUAL RATE	10% NOMINAL ANNUAL RATE	10½% NOMINAL ANNUAL RATE	MONTHS
1	0.9925 558 313	0.9921 455 147	0.9917 355 372	0.9913 258 984	1
2	1.9777 229 094	1.9764 982 370	1.9752 749 129	1.9740 529 352	2
3	2.9555 562 377	2.9531 193 752	2.9506 858 640	2.9482 556 978	3
4	3.9261 104 096	3.9220 696 571	3.9180 355 677	3.9140 081 267	4
5	4.8894 396 125	4.8834 093 332	4.8773 906 456	4.8713 835 209	5
6	5.8455 976 303	5.8371 981 810	5.8288 171 692	5.8204 545 437	6
7	6.7946 378 464	6.7834 955 082	6.7723 806 637	6.7612 932 279	7
8	7.7366 132 471	7.7223 601 570	7.7081 461 127	7.6939 709 818	8
9	8.6715 764 239	8.6538 505 071	8.6361 779 630	8.6185 585 941	9
10	9.5995 795 771	9.5780 244 800	9.5565 401 286	9.5351 262 395	10
11	10.5206 745 182	10.4949 395 419	10.4692 959 953	10.4437 434 841	11
YEARS					
1	11.4349 126 731	11.4046 527 080	11.3745 084 251	11.3444 792 903	12
2	21.8891 461 374	21.7796 154 308	21.6708 548 343	21.5628 579 898	24
3	31.4468 052 513	31.2178 556 172	30.9912 355 853	30.7669 175 659	36
4	40.1847 818 852	39.8039 469 792	39.4281 600 915	39.0573 435 886	48
5	48.1733 735 210	47.6148 273 362	47.0653 690 238	46.5248 271 560	60
6	55.4768 487 987	54.7204 880 355	53.9786 654 781	53.2510 569 874	72
7	62.1539 645 614	61.1846 011 272	60.2366 673 594	59.3096 130 374	84
8	68.2584 3R5 567	67.0650 899 136	65.9014 884 480	64.7667 714 055	96
9	73.8393 815 990	72.4146 479 855	71.0293 549 100	69.6822 293 478	108
10	78.9416 926 690	77.2812 113 962	75.6711 633 697	74.1097 583 204	120
11	83.6064 201 276	81.7083 882 043	79.8729 860 841	78.0977 921 990	132
12	87.8710 919 527	85.7358 492 351	83.6765 282 329	81.6899 571 099	144
13	91.7700 176 535	89.3996 835 607	87.1195 418 633	84.9255 486 669	156
14	95.3345 642 925	92.7327 218 849	90.2362 005 974	87.8399 618 366	168
15	98.5934 088 351	95.7648 307 314	93.0574 388 230	90.4650 781 326	180
16	101.5727 688 569	98.5231 800 700	95.6112 587 322	92.8296 143 759	192
17	104.2966 134 662	101.0324 867 800	97.9230 082 574	94.9594 368 354	204
18	106.7868 561 361	103.3152 361 317	100.0156 326 622	96.8778 441 854	216
19	109.0635 310 001	105.3918 832 718	101.9099 022 844	98.6058 223 765	228
20	111.1449 540 271	107.2810 365 164	103.6246 186 917	100.1622 742 056	240
21	113.0478 703 751	108.9996 240 957	105.1768 012 971	101.5642 260 987	252
22	114.7875 891 060	110.5630 458 436	106.5818 562 849	102.8270 143 674	264
23	116.3781 063 488	111.9853 111 918	107.8537 295 244	103.9644 529 767	276
24	117.8322 178 982	113.2791 647 047	109.0050 449 899	104.9889 846 594	288
25	119.1616 221 582	114.4562 002 803	110.0472 300 573	105.9118 170 306	300
26	120.3770 142 561	115.5269 650 404	110.9906 289 393	106.7430 451 905	312
27	121.4881 720 852	116.5010 538 404	111.8446 053 313	107.4917 621 573	324
28	122.5040 349 687	117.3871 952 467	112.6176 353 760	108.1661 583 380	336
29	123.4327 755 771	118.1933 297 510	113.3173 917 811	108.7736 111 255	348
30	124.2818 656 772	118.9266 809 231	113.9508 199 769	109.3207 656 018	360
31	125.0581 362 438	119.5938 201 398	114.5242 070 530	109.8136 072 301	372
32	125.7678 324 144	120.2007 254 688	115.0432 441 614	110.2575 273 315	384
33	126.4166 637 319	120.7528 352 371	115.5130 830 035	110.6573 820 619	396
34	127.0098 500 785	121.2550 967 625	115.9383 869 633	111.0175 455 349	408
35	127.5521 636 696	121.7120 106 849	116.3233 773 942	111.3419 576 712	420
36	128.0479 674 465	122.1276 712 959	116.6718 755 176	111.6341 672 982	432
37	128.5012 501 767	122.5058 032 263	116.9873 403 506	111.8973 709 722	444
38	128.9156 585 436	122.8497 948 219	117.2729 030 387	112.1344 479 457	456
39	129.2945 264 844	123.1627 285 055	117.5313 979 333	112.3479 916 646	468
40	129.6409 020 116	123.4474 083 975	117.7653 907 251	112.5403 381 384	480
41	129.9575 717 344	123.7063 854 434	117.9772 039 086	112.7135 914 945	492
42	130.2470 832 776	123.9419 802 718	118.1689 398 351	112.8696 469 959	504
43	130.5117 657 767	124.1563 039 890	118.3425 015 791	113.0102 117 738	516
44	130.7537 486 163	124.3512 770 963	118.4996 118 270	113.1368 235 023	528
45	130.9749 785 610	124.5286 466 991	118.6418 299 763	113.2508 672 197	540
46	131.1772 354 176	124.6900 021 620	118.7705 676 128	113.3535 904 794	552
47	131.3621 463 530	124.8367 893 511	118.8871 025 215	113.4461 169 975	564
48	131.5311 989 853	124.9703 235 895	118.9925 913 694	113.5294 589 454	576
49	131.6857 533 520	125.0918 014 444	119.0880 811 857	113.6045 280 221	588
50	131.8270 528 511	125.2023 114 483	119.1745 197 543	113.6721 454 274	600

Table 5. PRESENT WORTH OF ONE DOLLAR PER PERIOD
PAYABLE AT END OF EACH PERIOD

MONTHS	11% NOMINAL ANNUAL RATE	11½% NOMINAL ANNUAL RATE	12% NOMINAL ANNUAL RATE	12½% NOMINAL ANNUAL RATE	MONTHS
1	0.9909 165 979	0.9905 076 352	0.9900 990 099	0.9896 907 216	1
2	1.9728 323 018	1.9716 130 105	1.9703 950 593	1.9691 784 462	2
3	2.9458 288 704	2.9434 053 756	2.9409 852 072	2.9385 683 591	3
4	3.9099 873 200	3.9059 731 331	3.9019 655 517	3.8979 645 616	4
5	4.8653 879 306	4.8594 038 462	4.8534 312 393	4.8474 700 816	5
6	5.8121 102 533	5.8037 842 472	5.7954 764 746	5.7871 868 848	6
7	6.7502 331 164	6.7392 002 449	6.7281 945 293	6.7172 158 860	7
8	7.6798 346 323	7.6657 369 326	7.6516 777 518	7.6376 569 594	8
9	8.6009 922 038	8.5834 785 960	8.5660 175 760	8.5486 089 495	9
10	9.5137 825 306	9.4925 087 208	9.4713 045 307	9.4501 696 820	10
11	10.4182 816 157	10.3929 100 000	10.3676 282 482	10.3424 359 739	11
YEARS					
1	11.3145 647 720	11.2847 643 417	11.2550 774 735	11.2255 036 443	12
2	21.4556 185 975	21.3491 304 152	21.2433 872 576	21.1383 829 962	24
3	30.5448 743 280	30.3250 789 945	30.1075 050 373	29.8921 262 721	36
4	38.6914 211 422	38.3303 177 061	37.9739 594 935	37.6222 739 539	48
5	45.9930 338 334	45.4698 246 076	44.9550 384 062	44.4485 174 588	60
6	52.5373 463 020	51.8372 248 355	51.1503 914 789	50.4765 524 081	72
7	58.4029 033 369	57.5160 183 742	56.6484 527 634	55.7997 151 877	84
8	63.6601 033 094	62.5806 750 475	61.5277 029 908	60.5004 281 425	96
9	68.3720 430 938	67.0976 110 909	65.8577 898 250	64.6514 757 806	108
10	72.5952 753 558	71.1260 601 126	69.7005 220 314	68.3171 317 480	120
11	76.3804 872 972	74.7188 498 629	73.1107 517 508	71.5541 540 235	132
12	79.7731 090 032	77.9230 950 007	76.1371 574 733	74.4126 637 432	144
13	82.8138 586 938	80.7808 149 387	78.8229 388 871	76.9369 212 622	156
14	85.5392 314 238	83.3294 848 729	81.2064 335 219	79.1660 114 689	168
15	87.9819 370 963	85.6025 272 193	83.3216 639 891	81.1344 489 648	180
16	90.1712 930 463	87.6297 499 049	85.1988 236 284	82.8727 124 785	192
17	92.1335 759 073	89.4377 372 587	86.8647 074 960	84.4077 167 901	204
18	93.8923 369 834	91.0501 986 300	88.3430 948 437	85.7632 294 715	216
19	95.4686 849 118	92.4882 793 048	89.6550 885 500	86.9602 388 973	228
20	96.8815 390 084	93.7708 377 984	90.8194 163 483	88.0172 792 223	240
21	98.1478 563 375	94.9146 931 594	91.8526 981 508	88.9507 173 596	252
22	99.2828 352 300	95.9348 455 295	92.7696 832 859	89.7750 064 010	264
23	100.3000 976 940	96.8446 728 449	93.5834 610 337	90.5029 094 044	276
24	101.2118 529 060	97.6561 062 959	94.3056 474 655	91.1456 970 139	288
25	102.0290 437 452	98.3797 867 143	94.9465 512 548	91.7133 219 708	300
26	102.7614 781 298	99.0252 042 817	95.5153 208 262	92.2145 732 191	312
27	103.4179 467 318	99.6008 227 206	96.0200 749 416	92.6572 119 913	324
28	104.0063 284 824	100.1141 905 245	96.4680 185 903	93.0480 919 806	336
29	104.5336 851 348	100.5720 398 293	96.8655 458 343	93.3932 654 621	348
30	105.0063 460 198	100.9803 747 196	97.2183 310 791	93.6980 770 044	360
31	105.4299 840 096	101.3445 499 644	97.5314 100 712	93.9672 462 229	372
32	105.8096 836 042	101.6693 412 377	97.8092 517 802	94.2049 408 576	384
33	106.1500 019 553	101.9590 077 449	98.0558 221 896	94.4148 413 049	396
34	106.4550 235 611	102.2173 480 770	98.2746 409 083	94.6001 976 040	408
35	106.7284 092 888	102.4477 500 238	98.4688 314 108	94.7638 797 592	420
36	106.9734 403 116	102.6532 350 004	98.6411 656 218	94.9084 221 786	432
37	107.1930 574 901	102.8364 976 690	98.7941 034 838	95.0360 629 162	444
38	107.3898 966 680	102.9999 412 756	98.9298 280 709	95.1487 783 251	456
39	107.5663 203 077	103.1457 091 658	99.0502 767 506	95.2483 136 585	468
40	107.7244 458 443	103.2757 128 016	99.1571 688 381	95.3362 100 936	480
41	107.8661 710 993	103.3916 572 788	99.2520 301 384	95.4138 285 937	492
42	107.9931 970 582	103.4950 627 840	99.3362 147 258	95.4823 709 818	504
43	108.1070 482 856	103.5872 854 328	99.4109 242 727	95.5428 985 488	516
44	108.2090 912 230	103.6695 346 025	99.4772 252 021	95.5963 484 864	528
45	108.3005 505 890	103.7428 888 816	99.5360 639 107	95.6435 483 982	540
46	108.3825 240 783	103.8083 102 138	99.5882 802 769	95.6852 291 144	552
47	108.4559 955 359	103.8666 565 131	99.6346 196 507	95.7220 360 074	564
48	108.5218 467 659	103.9186 929 134	99.6757 434 921	95.7545 389 846	576
49	108.5808 681 141	103.9651 018 029	99.7122 388 133	95.7832 413 129	588
50	108.6337 679 544	104.0064 917 726	99.7446 265 578	95.8085 874 112	600

Table 5.   PRESENT WORTH OF ONE DOLLAR PER PERIOD
PAYABLE AT END OF EACH PERIOD

	13% NOMINAL ANNUAL RATE	**13½%** NOMINAL ANNUAL RATE	**14%** NOMINAL ANNUAL RATE	**14½%** NOMINAL ANNUAL RATE	
ONTHS					**MONTHS**
1	0.9892 827 700	0.9888 751 545	0.9884 678 748	0.9880 609 304	1
2	1.9679 631 690	1.9667 492 257	1.9655 366 143	1.9643 253 327	2
3	2.9361 548 251	2.9337 445 990	2.9313 376 748	2.9289 340 463	3
4	3.8939 701 484	3.8899 822 981	3.8860 009 965	3.8820 262 293	4
5	4.8415 203 447	4.8355 820 006	4.8296 550 212	4.8237 393 785	5
6	5.7789 154 276	5.7706 620 525	5.7624 267 096	5.7542 093 489	6
7	6.7062 642 317	6.6953 394 833	6.6844 415 581	6.6735 703 735	7
8	7.6236 744 255	7.6097 300 206	7.5958 236 159	7.5819 550 829	8
9	8.5312 525 231	8.5139 481 044	8.4966 595 017	8.4794 945 241	9
10	9.4291 038 976	9.4081 069 018	9.3871 784 202	9.3663 181 794	10
11	10.3173 327 923	10.2923 183 207	10.2673 921 781	10.2425 539 854	11
YEARS					
1	11.1960 423 337	11.1666 930 242	11.1374 552 007	11.1083 283 512	12
2	21.0341 115 581	20.9305 669 260	20.8277 431 374	20.7256 342 841	24
3	29.6789 168 543	29.4678 512 737	29.2589 043 500	29.0520 512 284	36
4	37.2751 897 516	36.9326 367 438	36.5945 459 592	36.2608 495 774	48
5	43.9501 072 254	43.4596 563 256	42.9770 164 708	42.5020 423 958	60
6	49.8154 208 975	49.1667 171 372	48.5301 680 561	47.9055 071 498	72
7	54.9693 279 845	54.1568 267 420	53.3617 599 097	52.5836 884 201	84
8	59.4981 153 172	58.5200 523 480	57.5655 493 222	56.6339 378 422	96
9	63.4776 039 573	62.3351 464 435	61.2231 110 449	60.1405 399 668	108
10	66.9744 185 952	65.6709 682 119	64.4054 202 530	63.1764 661 972	120
11	70.0471 029 820	68.5877 263 816	67.1742 298 217	65.8048 933 038	132
12	72.7471 000 704	71.1380 659 413	69.5832 686 441	68.0805 181 150	144
13	75.1196 132 736	73.3680 183 376	71.6792 842 436	70.0506 957 426	156
14	77.2043 632 624	75.3178 323 029	73.5029 499 117	71.7564 250 285	168
15	79.0362 529 689	77.0227 003 106	75.0896 539 752	73.2332 017 192	180
16	80.6459 519 328	78.5133 937 693	76.4701 865 088	74.5117 571 219	192
17	82.0604 097 711	79.8168 184 203	77.6713 368 178	75.6186 976 148	204
18	83.3033 073 695	80.9564 999 630	78.7164 132 863	76.5770 583 180	216
19	84.3954 533 482	81.9530 086 739	79.6256 956 774	77.4067 824 480	228
20	85.3551 324 403	82.8243 306 826	80.4168 286 631	78.1251 363 303	240
21	86.1984 116 152	83.5861 926 055	81.1051 642 199	78.7470 687 072	252
22	86.9394 090 722	84.2523 453 985	81.7040 595 351	79.2855 218 164	264
23	87.5905 306 078	84.8348 125 493	82.2251 362 033	79.7517 007 154	276
24	88.1626 773 137	85.3441 070 916	82.6785 057 442	80.1553 064 561	288
25	88.6654 280 833	85.7894 213 560	83.0729 658 174	80.5047 379 602	300
26	89.1071 999 815	86.1787 928 839	83.4161 709 410	80.8072 667 991	312
27	89.4953 891 635	86.5192 494 981	83.7147 810 282	81.0691 885 127	324
28	89.8364 947 016	86.8169 361 492	83.9745 906 233	81.2959 536 181	336
29	90.1362 273 926	87.0772 258 265	84.2006 413 449	81.4922 810 335	348
30	90.3996 053 680	87.3048 165 359	84.3973 197 191	81.6622 562 770	360
31	90.6310 381 080	87.5038 160 950	84.5684 422 997	81.8094 164 857	372
32	90.8344 002 648	87.6778 162 754	84.7173 297 295	81.9368 240 220	384
33	91.0130 965 324	87.8299 576 316	84.8468 711 767	82.0471 302 009	396
34	91.1701 186 477	87.9629 861 848	84.9595 803 998	82.1426 304 630	408
35	91.3080 954 786	88.0793 029 865	85.0576 445 272	82.2253 121 419	420
36	91.4293 370 365	88.1810 074 556	85.1429 664 982	82.2968 958 200	432
37	91.5358 731 501	88.2699 352 705	85.2172 019 903	82.3588 711 334	444
38	91.6294 874 497	88.3476 915 024	85.2817 915 469	82.4125 277 712	456
39	91.7117 472 280	88.4156 795 845	85.3379 885 317	82.4589 823 127	468
40	91.7840 296 800	88.4751 266 437	85.3868 834 502	82.4992 014 638	480
41	91.8475 449 603	88.5271 056 485	85.4294 251 108	82.5340 221 740	492
42	91.9033 564 431	88.5725 547 753	85.4664 390 365	82.5641 690 522	504
43	91.9523 985 255	88.6122 943 421	85.4986 434 847	82.5902 694 466	516
44	91.9954 922 713	88.6470 416 141	85.5266 633 842	82.6128 664 989	528
45	92.0333 591 569	88.6774 237 497	85.5510 424 626	82.6324 304 476	540
46	92.0666 331 506	88.7039 891 205	85.5722 537 973	82.6493 684 129	552
47	92.0958 713 263	88.7272 172 087	85.5907 089 953	82.6640 328 690	564
48	92.1215 631 903	88.7475 272 615	85.6067 661 806	82.6767 289 793	576
49	92.1441 388 763	88.7652 858 579	85.6207 369 438	82.6877 209 460	588
50	92.1639 763 470	88.7808 135 253	85.6328 923 883	82.6972 375 091	600

Table 5.   PRESENT WORTH OF ONE DOLLAR PER PERIOD
PAYABLE AT END OF EACH PERIOD

MONTHS	15% NOMINAL ANNUAL RATE	15½% NOMINAL ANNUAL RATE	16% NOMINAL ANNUAL RATE	16½% NOMINAL ANNUAL RATE	MONTHS
1	0.9876 543 210	0.9872 480 461	0.9868 421 053	0.9864 364 982	1
2	1.9631 153 788	1.9619 067 505	1.9606 994 460	1.9594 934 630	2
3	2.9265 337 074	2.9241 366 521	2.9217 428 743	2.9193 523 680	3
4	3.8780 579 826	3.8740 962 423	3.8701 409 944	3.8661 922 249	4
5	4.8178 350 446	4.8119 419 916	4.8060 601 918	4.8001 896 176	5
6	5.7460 099 206	5.7378 283 751	5.7296 646 630	5.7215 187 350	6
7	6.6627 258 475	6.6519 078 981	6.6411 164 438	6.6303 514 032	7
8	7.5681 242 938	7.5543 311 211	7.5405 754 379	7.5268 571 179	8
9	8.4623 449 815	8.4452 466 847	8.4281 994 453	8.4112 030 756	9
10	9.3455 259 077	9.3248 013 342	9.3041 441 895	9.2835 542 053	10
11	10.2178 033 656	10.1931 399 432	10.1685 633 449	10.1440 731 988	11

YEARS					
1	11.0793 119 660	11.0504 055 384	11.0216 085 640	10.9929 205 413	12
2	20.6242 345 116	20.5235 380 186	20.4235 390 568	20.3242 319 298	24
3	28.8472 673 749	28.6445 285 721	28.4438 109 145	28.2450 908 044	36
4	35.9314 809 083	35.6063 743 719	35.2854 654 789	34.9686 908 109	48
5	42.0345 917 945	41.5745 252 547	41.1217 061 961	40.6760 008 089	60
6	47.2924 743 123	46.6908 156 731	46.1002 834 378	45.5206 357 338	72
7	51.8221 853 215	51.0768 354 234	50.3472 349 519	49.6329 912 154	84
8	55.7245 703 133	54.8368 192 550	53.9700 766 370	53.1237 532 377	96
9	59.0865 085 459	58.0601 240 320	57.0605 244 161	56.0868 773 038	108
10	61.9828 472 474	60.8233 523 199	59.6968 161 192	58.6021 172 930	120
11	64.4780 679 485	63.1921 728 627	61.9456 921 528	60.7371 720 737	132
12	66.6277 220 424	65.2228 812 150	63.8640 851 016	62.5495 076 505	144
13	68.4796 675 323	66.9637 376 192	65.5005 610 351	64.0879 038 887	156
14	70.0751 344 993	68.4561 139 206	66.8965 490 064	65.3937 674 472	168
15	71.1496 430 131	69.7354 767 788	68.0873 898 714	66.5022 462 587	180
16	72.6337 939 191	70.8322 305 407	69.1032 309 779	67.4431 755 521	192
17	73.6539 501 088	71.7724 398 072	69.9697 893 773	68.2418 808 823	204
18	74.5328 234 400	72.5784 488 636	70.7090 028 770	68.9198 597 793	216
19	75.2899 803 735	73.2694 126 970	71.3395 854 189	69.4953 603 644	228
20	75.9422 775 836	73.8617 522 188	71.8775 008 415	69.9838 725 067	240
21	76.5042 372 401	74.3695 445 115	72.3363 670 210	70.3985 447 404	252
22	76.9883 703 173	74.8048 573 736	72.7278 006 217	70.7505 381 641	264
23	77.4054 551 271	75.1780 361 133	73.0617 111 834	71.0493 268 464	276
24	77.7647 772 778	75.4999 494 077	73.3465 519 917	71.3029 528 253	288
25	78.0743 364 015	75.7722 000 684	73.5895 340 814	71.5182 425 636	300
26	78.3410 242 479	76.0073 057 243	73.7968 087 914	71.7009 906 857	312
27	78.5707 781 217	76.2088 537 143	73.9736 234 918	71.8561 159 436	324
28	78.7687 130 599	76.3816 338 719	74.1244 544 266	71.9877 936 065	336
29	78.9392 357 115	76.5297 523 565	74.2531 200 345	72.0995 678 407	348
30	79.0861 424 425	76.6567 292 374	74.3628 776 161	72.1944 471 024	360
31	79.2127 038 546	76.7655 821 487	74.4565 057 964	72.2749 851 116	372
32	79.3217 375 997	76.8588 980 045	74.5363 748 680	72.3433 495 866	384
33	79.4156 711 088	76.9388 944 772	74.6045 067 977	72.4013 805 896	396
34	79.4965 956 347	77.0074 727 010	74.6626 264 146	72.4506 400 522	408
35	79.5663 128 098	77.0662 624 528	74.7122 050 759	72.4924 538 162	420
36	79.6263 747 558	77.1166 608 844	74.7544 979 159	72.5279 473 186	432
37	79.6781 186 388	77.1598 657 258	74.7905 756 208	72.5580 758 838	444
38	79.7226 964 390	77.1969 037 499	74.8213 515 346	72.5836 504 364	456
39	79.7611 005 972	77.2286 551 737	74.8476 047 807	72.6053 593 273	468
40	79.7941 861 099	77.2558 745 769	74.8699 999 867	72.6237 868 617	480
41	79.8226 895 636	77.2792 088 347	74.8891 041 102	72.6394 290 253	492
42	79.8472 455 341	77.2992 124 912	74.9054 007 914	72.6527 068 343	504
43	79.8684 007 139	77.3163 609 377	74.9193 025 973	72.6639 776 672	516
44	79.8866 260 832	77.3310 617 109	74.9311 614 665	72.6735 448 837	528
45	79.9023 273 956	77.3436 641 779	74.9412 776 181	72.6816 659 900	540
46	79.9158 542 113	77.3544 678 393	74.9499 071 528	72.6885 595 696	552
47	79.9275 076 793	77.3637 294 466	74.9572 685 362	72.6944 111 662	564
48	79.9375 472 423	77.3716 691 038	74.9635 481 291	72.6993 782 785	576
49	79.9461 964 121	77.3784 754 988	74.9689 049 058	72.7035 945 986	588
50	79.9536 477 463	77.3843 103 871	74.9734 744 786	72.7071 736 106	600

Table 5.   PRESENT WORTH OF ONE DOLLAR PER PERIOD
PAYABLE AT END OF EACH PERIOD

MONTHS	17% NOMINAL ANNUAL RATE	17½% NOMINAL ANNUAL RATE	18% NOMINAL ANNUAL RATE	18½% NOMINAL ANNUAL RATE	MONTHS
1	0.9860 312 243	0.9856 262 834	0.9852 216 749	0.9848 173 984	1
2	1.9582 887 997	1.9570 854 538	1.9558 834 235	1.9546 827 067	2
3	2.9169 651 270	2.9145 811 455	2.9122 004 173	2.9098 229 364	3
4	3.8622 499 198	3.8583 140 653	3.8543 846 476	3.8504 616 526	4
5	4.7943 302 414	4.7884 820 357	4.7826 449 730	4.7768 190 260	5
6	5.7133 905 421	5.7052 800 351	5.6971 871 655	5.6891 118 844	6
7	6.6196 126 955	6.6089 002 400	6.5982 139 561	6.5875 537 639	7
8	7.5131 760 350	7.4995 320 640	7.4859 250 799	7.4723 549 583	8
9	8.3942 573 887	8.3773 621 986	8.3605 173 201	8.3437 225 687	9
10	9.2630 311 146	9.2425 746 516	9.2221 845 519	9.2018 605 519	10
11	10.1196 691 352	10.0953 507 860	10.0711 177 851	10.0469 697 679	11

YEARS					
1	10.9643 409 714	10.9358 693 579	10.9075 052 070	10.8792 480 275	12
2	20.2256 109 929	20.1276 706 527	20.0304 053 663	19.9338 096 413	24
3	28.0483 449 478	27.8535 503 498	27.6606 843 109	27.4697 244 225	36
4	34.6559 880 019	34.3472 957 192	34.0425 536 456	33.7417 024 609	48
5	40.2372 779 936	39.8054 093 032	39.3802 688 853	38.9617 334 268	60
6	44.9516 364 595	44.3390 551 379	43.8446 667 735	43.3062 517 140	72
7	48.9337 222 816	48.2490 566 631	47.5786 330 136	46.9220 998 328	84
8	52.2972 780 250	51.4900 975 581	50.7016 754 105	49.9314 916 120	96
9	55.1383 788 310	54.2142 526 226	53.3137 487 893	52.4361 429 644	108
10	57.5381 766 658	56.5039 555 469	55.4984 541 085	54.5207 098 328	120
11	59.5652 183 095	58.4284 933 788	57.3257 141 579	56.2556 495 180	132
12	61.2774 032 969	60.0461 031 688	58.8540 114 798	57.6996 020 996	144
13	62.7236 377 341	61.4057 342 394	60.1322 601 368	58.9013 724 412	156
14	63.9452 312 318	62.5485 294 050	61.2013 712 355	59.9015 797 695	168
15	64.9770 768 547	63.5090 699 656	62.0955 623 111	60.7340 305 839	180
16	65.8486 477 916	64.3164 221 458	62.8434 524 795	61.4268 612 989	192
17	66.5848 392 154	64.9950 166 473	63.4689 784 093	62.0034 892 406	204
18	67.2066 793 771	65.5653 879 285	63.9921 604 291	62.4834 041 403	216
19	67.7319 302 484	66.0447 955 833	64.4297 432 898	62.8828 268 778	228
20	68.1755 948 663	66.4477 466 206	64.7957 320 905	63.2152 577 386	240
21	68.5503 458 737	66.7864 344 510	65.1018 405 200	63.4919 327 168	252
22	68.8668 874 954	67.0711 078 626	65.3578 657 601	63.7222 032 862	264
23	69.1342 612 881	67.3103 811 519	65.5720 020 507	63.9138 524 749	276
24	69.3601 044 006	67.5114 947 953	65.7511 029 506	64.0733 579 281	288
25	69.5508 677 172	67.6805 345 476	65.9009 006 906	64.2061 108 491	300
26	69.7120 001 181	67.8226 155 989	66.0261 896 362	64.3165 982 191	312
27	69.8481 041 190	67.9420 373 611	66.1309 797 344	64.4085 544 552	324
28	69.9630 673 354	68.0424 135 702	66.2186 248 544	64.4850 876 312	336
29	70.0601 735 264	68.1267 816 381	66.2919 301 304	64.5487 845 298	348
30	70.1421 963 912	68.1976 945 661	66.3532 417 412	64.6017 980 737	360
31	70.2114 787 949	68.2572 981 990	66.4045 220 013	64.6459 200 938	372
32	70.2699 996 901	68.3073 961 594	66.4474 121 659	64.6826 418 919	384
33	70.3194 306 421	68.3495 044 255	66.4832 849 600	64.7132 046 460	396
34	70.3611 835 751	68.3848 972 053	66.5132 885 138	64.7386 413 619	408
35	70.3964 511 017	68.4146 454 939	66.5383 831 088	64.7598 117 875	420
36	70.4262 405 882	68.4396 494 830	66.5593 719 124	64.7774 314 725	432
37	70.4514 029 284	68.4606 658 003	66.5769 266 838	64.7920 959 532	444
38	70.4726 568 485	68.4783 304 052	66.5916 092 738	64.8043 008 817	456
39	70.4906 094 362	68.4931 778 337	66.6038 896 073	64.8144 587 784	468
40	70.5057 734 815	68.5056 573 731	66.6141 607 238	64.8229 129 749	480
41	70.5185 821 234	68.5161 466 577	66.6227 513 565	64.8299 492 189	492
42	70.5294 012 225	68.5249 630 963	66.6299 364 536	64.8358 053 318	504
43	70.5385 398 108	68.5323 734 766	66.6359 459 785	64.8406 792 473	516
44	70.5462 589 190	68.5386 020 389	66.6409 722 695	64.8447 357 012	528
45	70.5527 790 323	68.5438 372 612	66.6451 761 960	64.8481 117 995	540
46	70.5582 863 883	68.5482 375 628	66.6486 923 073	64.8509 216 528	552
47	70.5629 382 969	68.5519 360 979	66.6516 331 386	64.8532 602 326	564
48	70.5668 676 330	68.5550 447 855	66.6540 928 129	64.8552 065 817	576
49	70.5701 866 326	68.5576 576 950	66.6561 500 535	64.8568 264 858	588
50	70.5729 900 980	68.5598 538 941	66.6578 707 037	64.8581 746 967	600

Table 5. PRESENT WORTH OF ONE DOLLAR PER PERIOD
PAYABLE AT END OF EACH PERIOD

	19% NOMINAL ANNUAL RATE	19½% NOMINAL ANNUAL RATE	20% NOMINAL ANNUAL RATE	20½% NOMINAL ANNUAL RATE	
MONTHS					MONTHS
1	0.9844 134 537	0.9840 098 401	0.9836 065 574	0.9832 036 051	1
2	1.9534 833 014	1.9522 852 055	1.9510 884 171	1.9498 929 341	2
3	2.9074 486 970	2.9050 776 930	2.9027 099 185	2.9003 453 674	3
4	3.8465 450 668	3.8426 348 763	3.8387 310 673	3.8348 336 263	4
5	4.7710 041 675	4.7652 003 702	4.7594 076 072	4.7536 258 514	5
6	5.6810 541 435	5.6730 138 945	5.6649 910 891	5.6569 856 793	6
7	6.5769 195 835	6.5663 113 353	6.5557 289 401	6.5451 723 189	7
8	7.4588 215 752	7.4453 248 071	7.4318 645 312	7.4184 406 249	8
9	8.3269 777 606	8.3102 827 131	8.2936 372 438	8.2770 411 715	9
10	9.1816 023 895	9.1614 098 037	9.1412 825 349	9.1212 203 243	10
11	10.0229 063 719	9.9989 272 362	9.9750 320 015	9.9512 203 107	11
YEARS					
1	10.8510 973 308	10.8230 526 309	10.7951 134 441	10.7672 792 895	12
2	19.8378 780 347	19.7426 051 527	19.6479 856 504	19.5540 142 310	24
3	27.2806 485 635	27.0934 348 957	26.9080 618 605	26.7245 081 743	36
4	33.4446 838 248	33.1514 403 594	32.8619 156 322	32.5760 541 393	48
5	38.5496 820 988	38.1439 965 036	37.7445 606 223	37.3512 607 639	60
6	42.7775 955 146	42.2584 888 067	41.7487 271 695	41.2481 110 055	72
7	46.2791 151 808	45.6493 464 002	45.0324 698 479	44.4281 706 343	84
8	49.1790 421 107	48.4438 382 529	47.7254 062 807	47.0232 868 474	96
9	51.5807 353 757	50.7648 499 542	49.9338 334 754	49.1410 547 342	108
10	53.5697 960 239	52.6448 203 816	51.7449 236 351	50.8692 782 333	120
11	55.2171 180 695	54.2089 860 093	53.2301 650 659	52.2796 105 371	132
12	56.5814 152 940	55.4980 546 247	54.4481 840 011	53.4305 248 767	144
13	57.7113 139 207	56.5604 088 062	55.4470 587 266	54.3697 388 573	156
14	58.6470 857 479	57.4359 218 654	56.2662 173 524	55.1361 928 593	168
15	59.4220 835 147	58.1574 544 110	56.9379 941 400	55.7616 645 294	180
16	60.0639 296 584	58.7520 877 049	57.4889 058 171	56.2720 863 018	192
17	60.5955 008 317	59.2421 401 029	57.9406 982 600	56.6886 205 721	204
18	61.0357 432 714	59.6460 047 289	58.3112 048 583	57.0285 371 034	216
19	61.4003 480 796	59.9788 398 233	58.6150 504 444	57.3059 290 408	228
20	61.7023 104 855	60.2531 376 768	58.8642 285 702	57.5322 972 220	240
21	61.9523 930 199	60.4791 935 036	59.0685 749 274	57.7170 270 087	252
22	62.1595 091 139	60.6664 918 511	59.2361 555 828	57.8677 774 099	264
23	62.3310 407 904	60.8190 250 502	59.3735 853 684	57.9907 986 283	276
24	62.4731 017 740	60.9455 556 586	59.4862 889 852	58.0911 911 982	288
25	62.5907 553 963	61.0498 327 462	59.5787 151 299	58.1731 174 562	300
26	62.6881 950 626	61.1357 701 421	59.6545 120 960	58.2399 741 147	312
27	62.7688 937 132	61.2065 933 325	59.7166 717 813	58.2945 330 911	324
28	62.8357 276 060	61.2649 605 222	59.7676 477 857	58.3390 564 337	336
29	62.8910 788 318	61.3130 624 055	59.8094 522 609	58.3753 901 072	348
30	62.9369 202 166	61.3527 043 890	59.8437 353 352	58.4050 405 277	360
31	62.9748 856 370	61.3853 743 544	59.8718 502 483	58.4292 370 196	372
32	63.0063 282 550	61.4122 985 024	59.8949 067 667	58.4489 827 840	384
33	63.0323 687 469	61.4344 873 766	59.9138 149 897	58.4650 964 924	396
34	63.0539 352 469	61.4527 737 913	59.9293 212 724	58.4782 462 288	408
35	63.0717 964 271	61.4678 440 900	59.9420 376 871	58.4889 771 892	420
36	63.0865 888 952	61.4802 639 059	59.9524 661 828	58.4977 342 858	432
37	63.0988 398 835	61.4904 993 915	59.9610 183 986	58.5048 805 932	444
38	63.1089 860 412	61.4989 347 152	59.9680 319 121	58.5107 124 014	456
39	63.1173 889 973	61.5058 864 796	59.9737 835 644	58.5154 715 009	468
40	63.1243 482 496	61.5116 156 052	59.9785 003 877	58.5193 552 068	480
41	63.1301 118 394	61.5163 371 231	59.9823 685 669	58.5225 245 399	492
42	63.1348 851 923	61.5202 282 460	59.9855 407 889	58.5251 109 026	504
43	63.1388 384 401	61.5234 350 191	59.9881 422 693	58.5272 215 270	516
44	63.1421 124 842	61.5260 778 022	59.9902 756 951	58.5289 439 211	528
45	63.1448 240 179	61.5282 557 870	59.9920 252 780	58.5303 499 963	540
46	63.1470 696 856	61.5300 507 195	59.9934 600 785	58.5314 965 285	552
47	63.1489 295 272	61.5315 299 689	59.9946 367 317	58.5324 325 744	564
48	63.1504 698 313	61.5327 490 560	59.9956 016 832	58.5331 964 431	576
49	63.1517 454 972	61.5337 537 366	59.9963 930 220	58.5338 198 050	588
50	63.1528 019 922	61.5345 817 194	59.9970 419 843	58.5343 285 051	600

Table 5.   PRESENT WORTH OF ONE DOLLAR PER PERIOD
PAYABLE AT END OF EACH PERIOD

MONTHS	21% NOMINAL ANNUAL RATE	21½% NOMINAL ANNUAL RATE	22% NOMINAL ANNUAL RATE	22½% NOMINAL ANNUAL RATE	MONTHS
1	0.9828 009 828	0.9823 986 901	0.9819 967 267	0.9815 950 920	1
2	1.9486 987 546	1.9475 058 765	1.9463 142 979	1.9451 240 167	2
3	2.8979 840 340	2.8956 259 123	2.8932 709 963	2.8909 192 802	3
4	3.8309 425 396	3.8270 577 935	3.8231 793 744	3.8193 072 689	4
5	4.7478 550 757	4.7420 952 535	4.7363 463 579	4.7306 083 621	5
6	5.6489 976 174	5.6410 268 557	5.6330 733 465	5.6251 370 426	6
7	6.5346 413 930	6.5241 360 842	6.5136 563 141	6.5032 020 050	7
8	7.4050 529 661	7.3917 014 335	7.3783 859 058	7.3651 062 626	8
9	8.2604 943 156	8.2439 964 962	8.2275 475 343	8.2111 472 516	9
10	9.1012 229 146	9.0812 900 495	9.0614 214 740	9.0416 169 341	10
11	9.9274 918 080	9.9038 461 395	9.8802 829 532	9.8568 018 985	11

YEARS

MONTHS	21% NOMINAL ANNUAL RATE	21½% NOMINAL ANNUAL RATE	22% NOMINAL ANNUAL RATE	22½% NOMINAL ANNUAL RATE	MONTHS
1	10.7395 496 884	10.7119 241 649	10.6844 022 453	10.6569 834 586	12
2	19.4606 856 454	19.3679 946 921	19.2759 362 161	19.1845 051 091	24
3	26.5427 528 258	26.3627 750 712	26.1845 544 313	26.0080 706 875	36
4	32.2938 012 895	32.0151 033 880	31.7399 076 204	31.4681 620 379	48
5	36.9639 855 154	36.5826 256 930	36.2070 742 946	35.8372 264 532	60
6	40.7564 454 191	40.2735 400 980	39.7992 091 986	39.3332 712 334	72
7	43.8361 423 702	43.2560 869 223	42.6877 141 750	42.1307 418 000	84
8	46.3370 345 488	45.6662 174 707	45.0104 167 521	44.3692 261 625	96
9	48.3679 037 506	47.6137 910 052	46.8781 467 042	46.1604 200 720	108
10	50.0170 870 901	49.1875 823 812	48.3800 243 913	47.5937 004 090	120
11	51.3563 194 172	50.4593 286 086	49.5877 132 140	48.7405 849 053	132
12	52.4438 535 822	51.4869 987 889	50.5588 390 953	49.6583 007 308	144
13	53.3269 942 712	52.3174 364 789	51.3397 401 515	50.3926 400 118	156
14	54.0441 556 272	52.9884 949 277	51.9676 777 561	50.9802 447 634	168
15	54.6265 321 579	53.5307 625 139	52.4726 144 982	51.4504 352 503	180
16	55.0994 556 090	53.9689 570 341	52.8786 438 739	51.8266 730 076	192
17	55.4834 968 244	54.3230 523 968	53.2051 399 281	52.1277 315 233	204
18	55.7953 605 197	54.6091 890 783	53.4676 817 040	52.3686 329 961	216
19	56.0486 118 912	54.8404 098 428	53.6787 966 111	52.5613 979 124	228
20	56.2542 666 631	55.0272 542 616	53.8485 581 807	52.7156 448 439	240
21	56.4212 702 412	55.1782 391 307	53.9850 667 339	52.8390 703 941	252
22	56.5568 868 130	55.3002 466 855	54.0948 358 951	52.9378 332 435	264
23	56.6670 153 188	55.3988 383 095	54.1831 033 953	53.0168 614 544	276
24	56.7564 460 398	55.4785 080 343	54.2540 809 951	53.0800 983 715	288
25	56.8290 689 615	55.5428 873 882	54.3111 554 524	53.1306 993 865	300
26	56.8880 429 774	55.5949 109 294	54.3570 501 246	53.1711 893 856	312
27	56.9359 332 917	55.6369 500 099	54.3939 549 159	53.2035 887 363	324
28	56.9748 229 989	55.6709 208 670	54.4236 307 706	53.2295 140 992	336
29	57.0064 036 921	55.6983 719 701	54.4474 936 978	53.2502 590 966	348
30	57.0320 490 428	55.7205 546 033	54.4666 823 380	53.2668 588 610	360
31	57.0528 745 520	55.7384 799 018	54.4821 122 937	53.2801 416 864	372
32	57.0697 860 709	55.7529 649 415	54.4945 198 188	53.2907 703 583	384
33	57.0835 192 030	55.7646 699 839	54.5044 969 491	53.2992 752 255	396
34	57.0946 713 012	55.7741 285 714	54.5125 197 521	53.3060 806 635	408
35	57.1037 274 504	55.7817 718 481	54.5189 710 427	53.3115 262 495	420
36	57.1110 815 677	55.7879 482 120	54.5241 586 500	53.3158 837 069	432
37	57.1170 535 367	55.7929 391 960	54.5283 301 051	53.3193 704 641	444
38	57.1219 031 211	55.7969 723 005	54.5316 844 526	53.3221 605 028	456
39	57.1258 412 644	55.8002 313 626	54.5343 817 481	53.3243 930 404	468
40	57.1290 392 646	55.8028 649 409	54.5365 506 955	53.3261 794 758	480
41	57.1316 362 260	55.8049 930 768	54.5382 947 879	53.3276 089 484	492
42	57.1337 451 089	55.8067 127 767	54.5396 972 463	53.3287 527 861	504
43	57.1354 576 438	55.8081 024 284	54.5408 249 901	53.3296 680 639	516
44	57.1368 483 214	55.8092 253 754	54.5417 318 307	53.3304 004 523	528
45	57.1379 776 320	55.8101 328 042	54.5424 610 387	53.3309 864 960	540
46	57.1388 946 976	55.8108 660 774	54.5430 474 089	53.3314 554 374	552
47	57.1396 394 080	55.8114 586 194	54.5435 189 205	53.3318 306 756	564
48	57.1402 441 559	55.8119 374 396	54.5438 980 721	53.3321 309 343	576
49	57.1407 352 462	55.8123 243 637	54.5442 029 552	53.3323 711 958	588
50	57.1411 340 400	55.8126 370 285	54.5444 481 176	53.3325 634 487	600

Table 6.   PARTIAL PAYMENT TO AMORTIZE 1
PAYABLE AT END OF EACH PERIOD

MONTHS	5% NOMINAL ANNUAL RATE	5½% NOMINAL ANNUAL RATE	6% NOMINAL ANNUAL RATE	6½% NOMINAL ANNUAL RATE	MONTHS
1	1.0041 666 667	1.0045 833 333	1.0050 000 000	1.0054 166 667	1
2	0.5031 271 656	0.5034 401 199	0.5037 531 172	0.5040 661 576	2
3	0.3361 149 611	0.3363 935 464	0.3366 722 084	0.3369 509 469	3
4	0.2526 095 807	0.2528 711 330	0.2531 327 930	0.2533 945 607	4
5	0.2025 069 300	0.2027 583 835	0.2030 099 750	0.2032 617 043	5
6	0.1691 056 440	0.1693 504 660	0.1695 954 556	0.1698 406 128	6
7	0.1452 479 951	0.1454 881 668	0.1457 285 355	0.1459 691 012	7
8	0.1273 551 193	0.1275 918 790	0.1278 288 649	0.1280 660 770	8
9	0.1134 387 590	0.1136 729 321	0.1139 073 606	0.1141 420 444	9
10	0.1023 059 594	0.1025 381 239	0.1027 705 727	0.1030 033 059	10
11	0.0931 975 677	0.0934 281 437	0.0936 590 331	0.0938 902 358	11
YEARS					
1	0.0856 074 818	0.0858 367 846	0.0860 664 297	0.0862 964 170	12
2	0.0438 713 897	0.0440 956 562	0.0443 206 103	0.0445 462 514	24
3	0.0299 708 971	0.0301 959 018	0.0304 219 375	0.0306 490 029	36
4	0.0230 292 936	0.0232 564 752	0.0234 850 290	0.0237 149 529	48
5	0.0188 712 336	0.0191 011 622	0.0193 328 015	0.0195 661 482	60
6	0.0161 049 327	0.0163 378 871	0.0165 728 879	0.0168 099 296	72
7	0.0141 339 091	0.0143 700 427	0.0146 085 545	0.0148 494 365	84
8	0.0126 599 200	0.0128 993 222	0.0131 414 302	0.0133 862 326	96
9	0.0115 172 732	0.0117 599 971	0.0120 057 496	0.0122 545 151	108
10	0.0106 065 515	0.0108 526 278	0.0111 020 502	0.0113 547 977	120
11	0.0098 644 882	0.0101 139 326	0.0103 670 346	0.0106 237 671	132
12	0.0092 489 041	0.0095 017 217	0.0097 585 021	0.0100 192 109	144
13	0.0087 305 970	0.0089 867 851	0.0092 472 344	0.0095 119 019	156
14	0.0082 887 071	0.0085 482 571	0.0088 123 592	0.0090 809 608	168
15	0.0079 079 363	0.0081 708 345	0.0084 385 683	0.0087 110 737	180
16	0.0075 768 100	0.0078 430 390	0.0081 143 786	0.0083 907 527	192
17	0.0072 865 528	0.0075 560 917	0.0078 310 077	0.0081 112 110	204
18	0.0070 303 385	0.0073 031 636	0.0075 816 232	0.0078 656 129	216
19	0.0068 027 775	0.0070 788 622	0.0073 608 299	0.0076 485 597	228
20	0.0065 995 574	0.0068 788 731	0.0071 643 106	0.0074 557 314	240
21	0.0064 171 865	0.0066 997 024	0.0069 885 692	0.0072 836 293	252
22	0.0062 528 075	0.0065 384 911	0.0068 307 445	0.0071 293 899	264
23	0.0061 040 597	0.0063 928 766	0.0066 884 720	0.0069 906 467	276
24	0.0059 689 751	0.0062 608 895	0.0065 597 807	0.0068 654 266	288
25	0.0058 459 004	0.0061 408 749	0.0064 430 140	0.0067 520 716	300
26	0.0057 334 362	0.0060 314 323	0.0063 367 699	0.0066 491 781	312
27	0.0056 303 900	0.0059 313 678	0.0062 398 535	0.0065 555 497	324
28	0.0055 357 395	0.0058 396 582	0.0061 512 402	0.0064 701 608	336
29	0.0054 486 030	0.0057 554 207	0.0060 700 461	0.0063 921 267	348
30	0.0053 682 162	0.0056 778 900	0.0059 955 053	0.0063 206 802	360
31	0.0052 939 132	0.0056 063 994	0.0059 269 500	0.0062 551 533	372
32	0.0052 251 109	0.0055 403 653	0.0058 637 959	0.0061 949 608	384
33	0.0051 612 970	0.0054 792 744	0.0058 055 294	0.0061 395 888	396
34	0.0051 020 192	0.0054 226 740	0.0057 516 970	0.0060 885 835	408
35	0.0050 468 767	0.0053 701 628	0.0057 018 971	0.0060 415 432	420
36	0.0049 955 132	0.0053 213 839	0.0056 557 726	0.0059 981 106	432
37	0.0049 476 108	0.0052 760 191	0.0056 130 050	0.0059 579 673	444
38	0.0049 028 848	0.0052 337 835	0.0055 733 093	0.0059 208 284	456
39	0.0048 610 798	0.0051 944 215	0.0055 364 298	0.0058 864 386	468
40	0.0048 219 660	0.0051 577 028	0.0055 021 364	0.0058 545 681	480
41	0.0047 853 357	0.0051 234 199	0.0054 702 216	0.0058 250 097	492
42	0.0047 510 011	0.0050 913 848	0.0054 404 975	0.0057 975 764	504
43	0.0047 187 919	0.0050 614 272	0.0054 127 943	0.0057 720 985	516
44	0.0046 885 531	0.0050 333 922	0.0053 869 572	0.0057 484 223	528
45	0.0046 601 436	0.0050 071 388	0.0053 628 457	0.0057 264 079	540
46	0.0046 334 345	0.0049 825 383	0.0053 403 315	0.0057 059 277	552
47	0.0046 083 081	0.0049 594 731	0.0053 192 974	0.0056 868 657	564
48	0.0045 846 563	0.0049 378 353	0.0052 996 364	0.0056 691 153	576
49	0.0045 623 799	0.0049 175 261	0.0052 812 499	0.0056 525 795	588
50	0.0045 413 877	0.0048 984 547	0.0052 640 479	0.0056 371 689	600

Table 6. PARTIAL PAYMENT TO AMORTIZE 1
PAYABLE AT END OF EACH PERIOD

MONTHS	7% NOMINAL ANNUAL RATE	7½% NOMINAL ANNUAL RATE	8% NOMINAL ANNUAL RATE	8½% NOMINAL ANNUAL RATE	MONTHS
1	1.0058 333 333	1.0062 500 000	1.0066 666 667	1.0070 833 333	1
2	0.5043 792 411	0.5046 923 676	0.5050 055 371	0.5053 187 496	2
3	0.3372 297 619	0.3375 086 535	0.3377 876 215	0.3380 666 659	3
4	0.2536 564 360	0.2539 184 189	0.2541 805 093	0.2544 427 071	4
5	0.2035 135 714	0.2037 655 761	0.2040 177 184	0.2042 699 983	5
6	0.1700 859 373	0.1703 314 292	0.1705 770 882	0.1708 229 143	6
7	0.1462 098 636	0.1464 508 227	0.1466 919 783	0.1469 333 303	7
8	0.1283 035 150	0.1285 411 789	0.1287 790 685	0.1290 171 836	8
9	0.1143 769 832	0.1146 121 769	0.1148 476 254	0.1150 833 284	9
10	0.1032 363 231	0.1034 696 242	0.1037 032 089	0.1039 370 772	10
11	0.0941 217 514	0.0943 535 799	0.0945 857 209	0.0948 181 743	11

YEARS					
1	0.0865 267 461	0.0867 574 169	0.0869 884 291	0.0872 197 825	12
2	0.0447 725 791	0.0449 995 927	0.0452 272 915	0.0454 556 749	24
3	0.0308 770 969	0.0311 062 182	0.0313 363 655	0.0315 675 374	36
4	0.0239 462 447	0.0241 789 019	0.0244 129 223	0.0246 483 034	48
5	0.0198 011 985	0.0200 379 486	0.0202 763 943	0.0205 165 313	60
6	0.0170 490 065	0.0172 901 123	0.0175 332 406	0.0177 783 846	72
7	0.0150 926 800	0.0153 382 759	0.0155 862 144	0.0158 364 854	84
8	0.0136 337 171	0.0138 838 706	0.0141 366 793	0.0143 921 286	96
9	0.0125 062 766	0.0127 610 162	0.0130 187 149	0.0132 793 527	108
10	0.0116 108 479	0.0118 701 769	0.0121 327 594	0.0123 985 689	120
11	0.0108 841 009	0.0111 480 051	0.0114 154 469	0.0116 863 919	132
12	0.0102 838 110	0.0105 522 631	0.0108 245 258	0.0111 005 556	144
13	0.0097 807 414	0.0100 537 042	0.0103 307 388	0.0106 117 912	156
14	0.0093 540 054	0.0096 314 334	0.0099 131 820	0.0101 991 854	168
15	0.0089 882 827	0.0092 701 236	0.0095 565 208	0.0098 473 956	180
16	0.0086 720 802	0.0089 582 759	0.0092 492 503	0.0095 449 100	192
17	0.0083 966 065	0.0086 870 939	0.0089 825 684	0.0092 829 210	204
18	0.0081 550 217	0.0084 497 333	0.0087 496 262	0.0090 545 745	216
19	0.0079 419 238	0.0082 407 882	0.0085 450 138	0.0088 544 563	228
20	0.0077 529 894	0.0080 559 319	0.0083 644 007	0.0086 782 323	240
21	0.0075 847 171	0.0078 916 601	0.0082 042 796	0.0085 223 921	252
22	0.0074 342 410	0.0077 451 040	0.0080 617 791	0.0083 840 616	264
23	0.0072 991 922	0.0076 138 926	0.0079 345 259	0.0082 608 654	276
24	0.0071 775 958	0.0074 960 490	0.0078 205 412	0.0081 508 232	288
25	0.0070 677 920	0.0073 899 118	0.0077 181 622	0.0080 522 708	300
26	0.0069 683 756	0.0072 940 744	0.0076 259 811	0.0079 637 998	312
27	0.0068 781 493	0.0072 073 384	0.0075 427 986	0.0078 842 103	324
28	0.0067 960 861	0.0071 286 759	0.0074 675 864	0.0078 124 739	336
29	0.0067 213 006	0.0070 572 008	0.0073 994 581	0.0077 477 046	348
30	0.0066 530 250	0.0069 921 451	0.0073 376 457	0.0076 891 348	360
31	0.0065 905 905	0.0069 328 398	0.0072 814 806	0.0076 360 969	372
32	0.0065 334 119	0.0068 786 998	0.0072 303 779	0.0075 880 072	384
33	0.0064 809 751	0.0068 292 109	0.0071 838 246	0.0075 443 538	396
34	0.0064 328 262	0.0067 839 200	0.0071 413 682	0.0075 046 860	408
35	0.0063 885 636	0.0067 424 260	0.0071 026 088	0.0074 686 057	420
36	0.0063 478 304	0.0067 043 727	0.0070 671 916	0.0074 357 600	432
37	0.0063 103 087	0.0066 694 430	0.0070 348 009	0.0074 058 355	444
38	0.0062 757 140	0.0066 373 536	0.0070 051 552	0.0073 785 527	456
39	0.0062 437 917	0.0066 078 509	0.0069 780 024	0.0073 536 622	468
40	0.0062 143 128	0.0065 807 073	0.0069 531 169	0.0073 309 407	480
41	0.0061 870 710	0.0065 557 178	0.0069 302 956	0.0073 101 879	492
42	0.0061 618 800	0.0065 326 977	0.0069 093 560	0.0072 912 237	504
43	0.0061 385 716	0.0065 114 802	0.0068 901 332	0.0072 738 863	516
44	0.0061 169 928	0.0064 919 140	0.0068 724 783	0.0072 580 293	528
45	0.0060 970 051	0.0064 738 623	0.0068 562 567	0.0072 435 210	540
46	0.0060 784 822	0.0064 572 007	0.0068 413 461	0.0072 302 419	552
47	0.0060 613 092	0.0064 418 158	0.0068 276 356	0.0072 180 842	564
48	0.0060 453 812	0.0064 276 048	0.0068 150 247	0.0072 069 497	576
49	0.0060 306 022	0.0064 144 734	0.0068 034 215	0.0071 967 498	588
50	0.0060 168 845	0.0064 023 360	0.0067 927 426	0.0071 874 036	600

67

Table 6. PARTIAL PAYMENT TO AMORTIZE 1
PAYABLE AT END OF EACH PERIOD

MONTHS	9% NOMINAL ANNUAL RATE	9½% NOMINAL ANNUAL RATE	10% NOMINAL ANNUAL RATE	10½% NOMINAL ANNUAL RATE	MONTHS
1	1.0075 000 000	1.0079 166 667	1.0083 333 333	1.0087 500 000	1
2	0.5056 320 050	0.5059 453 033	0.5062 586 445	0.5065 720 286	2
3	0.3383 457 866	0.3386 249 836	0.3389 042 569	0.3391 836 063	3
4	0.2547 050 123	0.2549 674 247	0.2552 299 444	0.2554 925 712	4
5	0.2045 224 155	0.2047 749 701	0.2050 276 619	0.2052 804 908	5
6	0.1710 689 074	0.1713 150 674	0.1715 613 942	0.1718 078 876	6
7	0.1471 748 786	0.1474 166 230	0.1476 585 635	0.1479 006 998	7
8	0.1292 555 241	0.1294 940 898	0.1297 328 807	0.1299 718 965	8
9	0.1153 192 858	0.1155 554 974	0.1157 919 631	0.1160 286 826	9
10	0.1041 712 287	0.1044 056 634	0.1046 403 810	0.1048 753 813	10
11	0.0950 509 398	0.0952 840 172	0.0955 174 064	0.0957 511 070	11

YEARS					
1	0.0874 514 768	0.0876 835 118	0.0879 158 872	0.0881 486 029	12
2	0.0456 847 423	0.0459 144 930	0.0461 449 263	0.0463 760 416	24
3	0.0317 997 327	0.0320 329 497	0.0322 671 872	0.0325 024 435	36
4	0.0248 850 424	0.0251 231 367	0.0253 625 834	0.0256 033 798	48
5	0.0207 583 552	0.0210 018 613	0.0212 470 447	0.0214 939 004	60
6	0.0180 255 372	0.0182 746 908	0.0185 258 378	0.0187 789 700	72
7	0.0160 890 783	0.0163 439 817	0.0166 011 840	0.0168 606 731	84
8	0.0146 502 033	0.0149 108 873	0.0151 741 641	0.0154 400 162	96
9	0.0135 429 087	0.0138 093 608	0.0140 786 862	0.0143 508 612	108
10	0.0126 675 774	0.0129 397 558	0.0132 150 737	0.0134 934 997	120
11	0.0119 608 039	0.0122 386 455	0.0125 198 775	0.0128 044 593	132
12	0.0113 803 070	0.0116 637 324	0.0119 507 826	0.0122 414 068	144
13	0.0108 968 051	0.0111 857 219	0.0114 784 809	0.0117 750 196	156
14	0.0104 893 750	0.0107 836 800	0.0110 820 269	0.0113 843 401	168
15	0.0101 426 658	0.0104 422 468	0.0107 460 512	0.0110 539 892	180
16	0.0098 451 584	0.0101 498 957	0.0104 590 193	0.0107 724 244	192
17	0.0095 880 390	0.0098 978 065	0.0102 121 046	0.0105 308 122	204
18	0.0093 644 484	0.0096 791 145	0.0099 984 370	0.0103 222 776	216
19	0.0091 689 678	0.0094 883 967	0.0098 125 891	0.0101 413 890	228
20	0.0089 972 596	0.0093 213 119	0.0096 502 165	0.0099 837 989	240
21	0.0088 458 102	0.0091 743 436	0.0095 078 001	0.0098 459 865	252
22	0.0087 117 432	0.0090 446 133	0.0093 824 600	0.0097 250 708	264
23	0.0085 926 815	0.0089 297 426	0.0092 718 166	0.0096 186 723	276
24	0.0084 866 433	0.0088 277 487	0.0091 738 873	0.0095 248 088	288
25	0.0083 919 636	0.0087 369 666	0.0090 870 075	0.0094 418 171	300
26	0.0083 072 338	0.0086 559 878	0.0090 097 696	0.0093 682 918	312
27	0.0082 312 540	0.0085 836 133	0.0089 409 766	0.0093 030 385	324
28	0.0081 629 964	0.0085 188 167	0.0088 796 040	0.0092 450 357	336
29	0.0081 015 759	0.0084 607 143	0.0088 247 707	0.0091 934 063	348
30	0.0080 462 262	0.0084 085 421	0.0087 757 157	0.0091 473 929	360
31	0.0079 962 810	0.0083 616 361	0.0087 317 784	0.0091 063 396	372
32	0.0079 511 587	0.0083 194 173	0.0086 923 835	0.0090 696 756	384
33	0.0079 103 496	0.0082 813 791	0.0086 570 281	0.0090 369 027	396
34	0.0078 734 051	0.0082 470 760	0.0086 252 709	0.0090 075 852	408
35	0.0078 399 297	0.0082 161 160	0.0085 967 243	0.0089 813 402	420
36	0.0078 095 734	0.0081 881 525	0.0085 710 459	0.0089 578 310	432
37	0.0077 820 255	0.0081 628 786	0.0085 479 335	0.0089 367 605	444
38	0.0077 570 096	0.0081 400 217	0.0085 271 190	0.0089 178 662	456
39	0.0077 342 795	0.0081 193 394	0.0085 083 647	0.0089 009 157	468
40	0.0077 136 150	0.0081 006 156	0.0084 914 591	0.0088 857 028	480
41	0.0076 948 191	0.0080 836 571	0.0084 762 138	0.0088 720 445	492
42	0.0076 777 151	0.0080 682 913	0.0084 624 606	0.0088 597 779	504
43	0.0076 621 444	0.0080 543 635	0.0084 500 495	0.0088 487 579	516
44	0.0076 479 643	0.0080 417 349	0.0084 388 462	0.0088 388 552	528
45	0.0076 350 461	0.0080 302 808	0.0084 287 304	0.0088 299 545	540
46	0.0076 232 739	0.0080 198 892	0.0084 195 943	0.0088 219 526	552
47	0.0076 125 431	0.0080 104 591	0.0084 113 413	0.0088 147 574	564
48	0.0076 027 589	0.0080 018 997	0.0084 038 845	0.0088 082 865	576
49	0.0075 938 359	0.0079 941 290	0.0083 971 460	0.0088 024 660	588
50	0.0075 856 964	0.0079 870 730	0.0083 910 554	0.0087 972 299	600

Table 6.   PARTIAL PAYMENT TO AMORTIZE 1
PAYABLE AT END OF EACH PERIOD

MONTHS	11% NOMINAL ANNUAL RATE	11½% NOMINAL ANNUAL RATE	12% NOMINAL ANNUAL RATE	12½% NOMINAL ANNUAL RATE	MONTHS
1	1.0091 666 667	1.0095 833 333	1.0100 000 000	1.0104 166 667	1
2	0.5068 854 556	0.5071 989 253	0.5075 124 378	0.5078 259 931	2
3	0.3394 630 320	0.3397 425 337	0.3400 221 115	0.3403 017 653	3
4	0.2557 553 051	0.2560 181 460	0.2562 810 939	0.2565 441 487	4
5	0.2055 334 568	0.2057 865 598	0.2060 397 996	0.2062 931 763	5
6	0.1720 545 476	0.1723 013 740	0.1725 483 667	0.1727 955 257	6
7	0.1481 430 319	0.1483 855 597	0.1486 282 829	0.1488 712 015	7
8	0.1302 111 371	0.1304 506 023	0.1306 902 920	0.1309 302 061	8
9	0.1162 656 559	0.1165 028 827	0.1167 403 628	0.1169 780 962	9
10	0.1051 106 641	0.1053 462 293	0.1055 820 766	0.1058 182 058	10
11	0.0959 851 189	0.0962 194 419	0.0964 540 757	0.0966 890 201	11
YEARS					
1	0.0883 816 585	0.0886 150 539	0.0888 487 887	0.0890 828 627	12
2	0.0466 078 382	0.0468 403 153	0.0470 734 722	0.0473 073 082	24
3	0.0327 387 171	0.0329 760 064	0.0332 143 098	0.0334 536 256	36
4	0.0258 455 226	0.0260 890 089	0.0263 338 354	0.0265 799 989	48
5	0.0217 424 231	0.0219 926 074	0.0222 444 477	0.0224 979 382	60
6	0.0190 340 790	0.0192 911 562	0.0195 501 925	0.0198 111 787	72
7	0.0171 224 364	0.0173 864 608	0.0176 527 328	0.0179 212 384	84
8	0.0157 084 257	0.0159 793 738	0.0162 528 414	0.0165 288 086	96
9	0.0146 258 610	0.0149 036 603	0.0151 842 326	0.0154 675 510	108
10	0.0137 750 011	0.0140 595 444	0.0143 470 948	0.0146 376 169	120
11	0.0130 923 490	0.0133 835 037	0.0136 778 788	0.0139 754 290	132
12	0.0125 355 526	0.0128 331 658	0.0131 341 914	0.0134 385 728	144
13	0.0120 752 736	0.0123 791 769	0.0126 866 622	0.0129 979 607	156
14	0.0116 905 423	0.0120 005 542	0.0123 142 953	0.0126 316 835	168
15	0.0113 659 693	0.0116 818 981	0.0120 016 806	0.0123 252 208	180
16	0.0110 900 040	0.0114 116 496	0.0117 372 513	0.0120 666 981	192
17	0.0108 538 064	0.0111 809 627	0.0115 121 553	0.0118 472 580	204
18	0.0106 504 964	0.0109 829 524	0.0113 195 038	0.0116 600 087	216
19	0.0104 746 389	0.0108 121 808	0.0111 538 566	0.0114 995 084	228
20	0.0103 218 839	0.0106 642 963	0.0110 108 613	0.0113 614 055	240
21	0.0101 887 095	0.0105 357 766	0.0108 869 965	0.0112 421 803	252
22	0.0100 722 345	0.0104 237 412	0.0107 793 836	0.0111 389 577	264
23	0.0099 700 800	0.0103 258 132	0.0106 856 488	0.0110 493 685	276
24	0.0098 802 657	0.0102 400 151	0.0106 038 188	0.0109 714 450	288
25	0.0098 011 308	0.0101 646 896	0.0105 322 414	0.0109 035 414	300
26	0.0097 312 730	0.0100 984 392	0.0104 695 246	0.0108 442 729	312
27	0.0096 695 016	0.0100 400 777	0.0104 144 889	0.0107 924 680	324
28	0.0096 147 995	0.0099 885 940	0.0103 661 298	0.0107 471 306	336
29	0.0095 662 943	0.0099 431 214	0.0103 235 881	0.0107 074 102	348
30	0.0095 232 340	0.0099 029 143	0.0102 861 260	0.0106 725 776	360
31	0.0094 849 678	0.0098 673 288	0.0102 531 072	0.0106 420 060	372
32	0.0094 509 308	0.0098 358 068	0.0102 239 817	0.0106 151 545	384
33	0.0094 206 310	0.0098 078 020	0.0101 982 726	0.0105 915 552	396
34	0.0093 936 384	0.0097 830 752	0.0101 755 650	0.0105 708 024	408
35	0.0093 695 765	0.0097 610 733	0.0101 554 978	0.0105 525 439	420
36	0.0093 481 148	0.0097 415 342	0.0101 377 553	0.0105 364 727	432
37	0.0093 289 624	0.0097 241 740	0.0101 220 616	0.0105 223 214	444
38	0.0093 118 630	0.0097 087 434	0.0101 081 748	0.0105 098 564	456
39	0.0092 965 902	0.0096 950 228	0.0100 958 829	0.0104 988 735	468
40	0.0092 829 440	0.0096 828 187	0.0100 849 995	0.0104 891 940	480
41	0.0092 707 472	0.0096 719 603	0.0100 753 607	0.0104 806 611	492
42	0.0092 598 425	0.0096 622 967	0.0100 668 221	0.0104 731 375	504
43	0.0092 500 907	0.0096 536 944	0.0100 592 566	0.0104 665 026	516
44	0.0092 413 677	0.0096 460 354	0.0100 525 522	0.0104 606 506	528
45	0.0092 335 634	0.0096 392 149	0.0100 466 098	0.0104 554 883	540
46	0.0092 265 797	0.0096 331 401	0.0100 413 422	0.0104 509 339	552
47	0.0092 203 294	0.0096 277 288	0.0100 366 720	0.0104 469 153	564
48	0.0092 147 345	0.0096 229 078	0.0100 325 311	0.0104 433 692	576
49	0.0092 097 256	0.0096 186 122	0.0100 288 592	0.0104 402 397	588
50	0.0092 052 409	0.0096 147 845	0.0100 256 027	0.0104 374 778	600

Table 6.   PARTIAL PAYMENT TO AMORTIZE 1
PAYABLE AT END OF EACH PERIOD

	13% NOMINAL ANNUAL RATE	13½% NOMINAL ANNUAL RATE	14% NOMINAL ANNUAL RATE	14½% NOMINAL ANNUAL RATE	
MONTHS					**MONTHS**
1	1.0108 333 333	1.0112 500 000	1.0116 666 667	1.0120 833 333	1
2	0.5081 395 911	0.5084 532 318	0.5087 669 152	0.5090 806 413	2
3	0.3405 814 950	0.3408 613 007	0.3411 411 823	0.3414 211 396	3
4	0.2568 073 102	0.2570 705 786	0.2573 339 536	0.2575 974 352	4
5	0.2065 466 896	0.2068 003 396	0.2070 541 261	0.2073 080 491	5
6	0.1730 428 508	0.1732 903 419	0.1735 379 989	0.1737 858 217	6
7	0.1491 143 154	0.1493 576 244	0.1496 011 284	0.1498 448 273	7
8	0.1311 703 444	0.1314 107 067	0.1316 512 929	0.1318 921 029	8
9	0.1172 160 825	0.1174 543 217	0.1176 928 136	0.1179 315 580	9
10	0.1060 546 167	0.1062 913 092	0.1065 282 831	0.1067 655 381	10
11	0.0969 242 749	0.0971 598 399	0.0973 957 148	0.0976 318 994	11
YEARS					
1	0.0893 172 757	0.0895 520 274	0.0897 871 176	0.0900 225 460	12
2	0.0475 418 226	0.0477 770 145	0.0480 128 833	0.0482 494 280	24
3	0.0336 939 520	0.0339 352 873	0.0341 776 298	0.0344 209 774	36
4	0.0268 274 959	0.0270 763 230	0.0273 264 765	0.0275 779 529	48
5	0.0227 530 730	0.0230 098 460	0.0232 682 508	0.0235 282 811	60
6	0.0200 741 052	0.0203 389 622	0.0206 057 395	0.0208 744 268	72
7	0.0181 919 633	0.0184 648 928	0.0187 400 116	0.0190 173 042	84
8	0.0168 072 551	0.0170 881 597	0.0173 715 010	0.0176 572 571	96
9	0.0157 535 877	0.0160 423 141	0.0163 337 012	0.0166 277 190	108
10	0.0149 310 740	0.0152 274 289	0.0155 266 435	0.0158 286 789	120
11	0.0142 761 079	0.0145 798 680	0.0148 866 612	0.0151 964 383	132
12	0.0137 462 524	0.0140 571 716	0.0143 712 708	0.0146 884 899	144
13	0.0133 121 026	0.0136 299 170	0.0139 510 322	0.0142 753 757	156
14	0.0129 526 358	0.0132 770 683	0.0136 048 961	0.0139 360 343	168
15	0.0126 524 217	0.0129 831 854	0.0133 174 139	0.0136 550 086	180
16	0.0123 998 784	0.0127 366 804	0.0130 769 918	0.0134 207 008	192
17	0.0121 861 444	0.0125 286 878	0.0128 747 623	0.0132 242 426	204
18	0.0120 043 253	0.0123 523 127	0.0127 038 309	0.0130 587 414	216
19	0.0118 489 795	0.0122 021 146	0.0125 587 600	0.0129 187 646	228
20	0.0117 157 571	0.0120 737 468	0.0124 352 081	0.0127 999 777	240
21	0.0116 011 418	0.0119 636 984	0.0123 296 711	0.0126 988 854	252
22	0.0115 022 636	0.0118 691 058	0.0122 392 939	0.0126 126 432	264
23	0.0114 167 592	0.0117 876 137	0.0121 617 311	0.0125 389 176	276
24	0.0113 426 682	0.0117 172 706	0.0120 950 420	0.0124 757 804	288
25	0.0112 783 530	0.0116 564 488	0.0120 376 104	0.0124 216 292	300
26	0.0112 224 377	0.0116 037 829	0.0119 880 832	0.0123 751 247	312
27	0.0111 737 600	0.0115 581 215	0.0119 453 218	0.0123 351 426	324
28	0.0111 313 337	0.0115 184 899	0.0119 083 641	0.0123 007 352	336
29	0.0110 943 183	0.0114 840 590	0.0118 763 941	0.0122 711 009	348
30	0.0110 619 952	0.0114 541 218	0.0118 487 175	0.0122 455 593	360
31	0.0110 337 476	0.0114 280 730	0.0118 247 761	0.0122 235 318	372
32	0.0110 090 450	0.0114 053 935	0.0118 039 603	0.0122 045 248	384
33	0.0109 874 297	0.0113 856 368	0.0117 859 384	0.0121 881 167	396
34	0.0109 685 061	0.0113 684 181	0.0117 703 030	0.0121 739 466	408
35	0.0109 519 314	0.0113 534 050	0.0117 567 328	0.0121 617 051	420
36	0.0109 374 084	0.0113 403 104	0.0117 449 514	0.0121 511 266	432
37	0.0109 246 787	0.0113 288 856	0.0117 347 199	0.0121 419 828	444
38	0.0109 135 173	0.0113 189 149	0.0117 258 325	0.0121 340 775	456
39	0.0109 037 286	0.0113 102 111	0.0117 181 107	0.0121 272 416	468
40	0.0108 951 416	0.0113 026 117	0.0117 114 006	0.0121 213 294	480
41	0.0108 876 073	0.0112 959 753	0.0117 055 686	0.0121 162 155	492
42	0.0108 809 954	0.0112 901 790	0.0117 004 992	0.0121 117 915	504
43	0.0108 751 921	0.0112 851 158	0.0116 960 920	0.0121 079 639	516
44	0.0108 700 978	0.0112 806 923	0.0116 922 602	0.0121 046 520	528
45	0.0108 656 253	0.0112 768 274	0.0116 889 283	0.0121 017 861	540
46	0.0108 616 984	0.0112 734 502	0.0116 860 309	0.0120 993 060	552
47	0.0108 582 501	0.0112 704 989	0.0116 835 111	0.0120 971 596	564
48	0.0108 552 218	0.0112 679 196	0.0116 813 197	0.0120 953 019	576
49	0.0108 525 622	0.0112 656 653	0.0116 794 136	0.0120 936 941	588
50	0.0108 502 263	0.0112 636 949	0.0116 777 557	0.0120 923 024	600

70

Table 6.   PARTIAL PAYMENT TO AMORTIZE 1
PAYABLE AT END OF EACH PERIOD

MONTHS	15% NOMINAL ANNUAL RATE	15½% NOMINAL ANNUAL RATE	16% NOMINAL ANNUAL RATE	16½% NOMINAL ANNUAL RATE	MONTHS
1	1.0125 000 000	1.0129 166 667	1.0133 333 333	1.0137 500 000	1
2	0.5093 944 099	0.5097 082 212	0.5100 220 751	0.5103 359 714	2
3	0.3417 011 728	0.3419 812 816	0.3422 614 662	0.3425 417 264	3
4	0.2578 610 233	0.2581 247 180	0.2583 885 190	0.2586 524 264	4
5	0.2075 621 084	0.2078 163 041	0.2080 706 358	0.2083 251 037	5
6	0.1740 338 102	0.1742 819 643	0.1745 302 839	0.1747 787 688	6
7	0.1500 887 209	0.1503 328 091	0.1505 770 917	0.1508 215 687	7
8	0.1321 331 365	0.1323 743 934	0.1326 158 737	0.1328 575 771	8
9	0.1181 705 546	0.1184 098 034	0.1186 493 042	0.1188 890 568	9
10	0.1070 030 740	0.1072 408 906	0.1074 789 878	0.1077 173 653	10
11	0.0978 683 935	0.0981 051 968	0.0983 423 091	0.0985 797 303	11
YEARS					
1	0.0902 583 123	0.0904 944 164	0.0907 308 579	0.0909 676 365	12
2	0.0484 866 480	0.0487 245 425	0.0489 631 105	0.0492 023 513	24
3	0.0346 653 285	0.0349 106 810	0.0351 570 330	0.0354 043 826	36
4	0.0278 307 483	0.0280 848 589	0.0283 402 808	0.0285 970 100	48
5	0.0237 899 301	0.0240 531 911	0.0243 180 571	0.0245 845 211	60
6	0.0211 450 133	0.0214 174 883	0.0216 918 406	0.0219 680 587	72
7	0.0192 967 547	0.0195 783 469	0.0198 620 639	0.0201 478 890	84
8	0.0179 454 053	0.0182 359 228	0.0185 287 860	0.0188 239 712	96
9	0.0169 243 373	0.0172 235 250	0.0175 252 508	0.0178 294 825	108
10	0.0161 334 957	0.0164 410 537	0.0167 513 121	0.0170 642 299	120
11	0.0155 091 496	0.0158 247 447	0.0161 431 726	0.0164 643 820	132
12	0.0150 087 677	0.0153 320 427	0.0156 582 530	0.0159 873 361	144
13	0.0146 028 746	0.0149 334 556	0.0152 670 448	0.0156 035 685	156
14	0.0142 703 972	0.0146 078 990	0.0149 484 542	0.0152 919 772	168
15	0.0139 958 712	0.0143 399 034	0.0146 870 074	0.0150 370 861	180
16	0.0137 676 961	0.0141 178 669	0.0144 711 034	0.0148 272 971	192
17	0.0135 770 043	0.0139 329 247	0.0142 918 824	0.0146 537 579	204
18	0.0134 169 075	0.0137 781 947	0.0141 424 707	0.0145 096 058	216
19	0.0132 819 798	0.0136 482 601	0.0140 174 630	0.0143 894 498	228
20	0.0131 678 958	0.0135 388 069	0.0139 125 594	0.0142 890 064	240
21	0.0130 711 714	0.0134 463 645	0.0138 243 050	0.0142 048 391	252
22	0.0129 889 748	0.0133 681 159	0.0137 499 002	0.0141 341 681	264
23	0.0129 189 861	0.0133 017 574	0.0136 870 597	0.0140 747 287	276
24	0.0128 592 923	0.0132 453 929	0.0136 339 061	0.0140 246 646	288
25	0.0128 083 061	0.0131 974 524	0.0135 888 889	0.0139 824 465	300
26	0.0127 647 042	0.0131 566 300	0.0135 507 215	0.0139 468 087	312
27	0.0127 273 781	0.0131 218 349	0.0135 183 320	0.0139 166 999	324
28	0.0126 953 959	0.0130 921 525	0.0134 908 244	0.0138 912 439	336
29	0.0126 679 716	0.0130 668 135	0.0134 674 476	0.0138 697 087	348
30	0.0126 444 402	0.0130 451 692	0.0134 475 700	0.0138 514 808	360
31	0.0126 242 377	0.0130 266 712	0.0134 306 598	0.0138 360 457	372
32	0.0126 068 847	0.0130 108 553	0.0134 162 683	0.0138 229 707	384
33	0.0125 919 732	0.0129 973 274	0.0134 040 160	0.0138 118 913	396
34	0.0125 791 550	0.0129 857 527	0.0133 935 819	0.0138 025 006	408
35	0.0125 681 330	0.0129 758 466	0.0133 846 940	0.0137 945 393	420
36	0.0125 586 529	0.0129 673 664	0.0133 771 215	0.0137 877 885	432
37	0.0125 504 971	0.0129 601 055	0.0133 706 686	0.0137 820 634	444
38	0.0125 434 794	0.0129 538 874	0.0133 651 689	0.0137 772 073	456
39	0.0125 374 398	0.0129 485 616	0.0133 604 810	0.0137 730 880	468
40	0.0125 322 414	0.0129 439 995	0.0133 564 846	0.0137 695 932	480
41	0.0125 277 663	0.0129 400 911	0.0133 530 774	0.0137 666 280	492
42	0.0125 239 135	0.0129 367 424	0.0133 501 722	0.0137 641 121	504
43	0.0125 205 963	0.0129 338 731	0.0133 476 950	0.0137 619 771	516
44	0.0125 177 398	0.0129 314 143	0.0133 455 825	0.0137 601 654	528
45	0.0125 152 800	0.0129 293 073	0.0133 437 810	0.0137 586 279	540
46	0.0125 131 616	0.0129 275 015	0.0133 422 447	0.0137 573 231	552
47	0.0125 113 372	0.0129 259 539	0.0133 409 344	0.0137 562 157	564
48	0.0125 097 659	0.0129 246 275	0.0133 398 168	0.0137 552 758	576
49	0.0125 084 125	0.0129 234 906	0.0133 388 636	0.0137 544 781	588
50	0.0125 072 467	0.0129 225 161	0.0133 380 506	0.0137 538 010	600

Table 6. PARTIAL PAYMENT TO AMORTIZE 1
PAYABLE AT END OF EACH PERIOD

MONTHS	17% NOMINAL ANNUAL RATE	17½% NOMINAL ANNUAL RATE	18% NOMINAL ANNUAL RATE	18½% NOMINAL ANNUAL RATE	MONTHS
1	1.0141 666 667	1.0145 833 333	1.0150 000 000	1.0154 166 667	1
2	0.5106 499 104	0.5109 638 918	0.5112 779 156	0.5115 919 819	2
3	0.3428 220 621	0.3431 024 734	0.3433 829 602	0.3436 635 224	3
4	0.2589 164 401	0.2591 805 600	0.2594 447 860	0.2597 091 181	4
5	0.2085 797 076	0.2088 344 474	0.2090 893 231	0.2093 443 345	5
6	0.1750 274 189	0.1752 762 343	0.1755 252 146	0.1757 743 599	6
7	0.1510 662 400	0.1513 111 053	0.1515 561 645	0.1518 014 176	7
8	0.1330 995 035	0.1333 416 527	0.1335 840 246	0.1338 266 190	8
9	0.1191 290 609	0.1193 693 165	0.1196 098 234	0.1198 505 813	9
10	0.1079 560 230	0.1081 949 606	0.1084 341 779	0.1086 736 747	10
11	0.0988 174 600	0.0990 554 980	0.0992 938 442	0.0995 324 982	11
YEARS					
1	0.0912 047 521	0.0914 422 043	0.0916 799 929	0.0919 181 176	12
2	0.0494 422 641	0.0496 828 479	0.0499 241 020	0.0501 660 254	24
3	0.0356 527 275	0.0359 020 659	0.0361 523 955	0.0364 037 143	36
4	0.0288 550 423	0.0291 143 736	0.0293 749 996	0.0296 369 160	48
5	0.0248 525 758	0.0251 222 137	0.0253 934 274	0.0256 662 092	60
6	0.0222 461 311	0.0225 260 460	0.0228 077 911	0.0230 913 543	72
7	0.0204 358 049	0.0207 257 938	0.0210 178 380	0.0213 119 192	84
8	0.0191 214 541	0.0194 212 100	0.0197 232 141	0.0200 274 410	96
9	0.0181 361 879	0.0184 453 341	0.0187 568 877	0.0190 708 153	108
10	0.0173 797 652	0.0176 978 760	0.0180 185 199	0.0183 416 541	120
11	0.0167 883 209	0.0171 149 373	0.0174 441 787	0.0177 759 924	132
12	0.0163 192 294	0.0166 538 701	0.0169 911 952	0.0173 311 420	144
13	0.0159 429 529	0.0162 851 241	0.0166 300 085	0.0169 775 331	156
14	0.0156 383 827	0.0159 875 861	0.0163 395 032	0.0166 940 505	168
15	0.0153 900 429	0.0157 457 825	0.0161 042 104	0.0164 652 336	180
16	0.0151 863 407	0.0155 481 286	0.0159 125 567	0.0162 795 230	192
17	0.0150 184 338	0.0153 857 950	0.0157 557 286	0.0161 281 246	204
18	0.0148 794 734	0.0152 519 497	0.0156 269 142	0.0160 042 497	216
19	0.0147 640 854	0.0151 412 385	0.0155 207 820	0.0159 025 930	228
20	0.0146 680 055	0.0150 494 193	0.0154 331 152	0.0158 189 658	240
21	0.0145 878 184	0.0149 731 006	0.0153 605 488	0.0157 500 324	252
22	0.0145 207 666	0.0149 095 495	0.0153 003 772	0.0156 931 171	264
23	0.0144 646 082	0.0148 565 494	0.0152 504 113	0.0156 460 605	276
24	0.0144 175 100	0.0148 122 924	0.0152 088 703	0.0156 071 109	288
25	0.0143 779 612	0.0147 752 970	0.0151 742 994	0.0155 748 415	300
26	0.0143 447 326	0.0147 443 444	0.0151 455 052	0.0155 480 860	312
27	0.0143 167 809	0.0147 184 282	0.0151 215 059	0.0155 258 880	324
28	0.0142 932 555	0.0146 967 156	0.0151 014 915	0.0155 074 613	336
29	0.0142 734 445	0.0146 785 152	0.0150 847 923	0.0154 921 585	348
30	0.0142 567 534	0.0146 632 523	0.0150 708 537	0.0154 794 453	360
31	0.0142 426 853	0.0146 504 480	0.0150 592 154	0.0154 688 803	372
32	0.0142 308 240	0.0146 397 031	0.0150 494 950	0.0154 600 983	384
33	0.0142 208 205	0.0146 306 840	0.0150 413 747	0.0154 527 968	396
34	0.0142 123 817	0.0146 231 118	0.0150 345 897	0.0154 467 252	408
35	0.0142 052 615	0.0146 167 534	0.0150 289 194	0.0154 416 755	420
36	0.0141 992 529	0.0146 114 132	0.0150 241 802	0.0154 374 753	432
37	0.0141 941 815	0.0146 069 278	0.0150 202 187	0.0154 339 813	444
38	0.0141 899 007	0.0146 031 598	0.0150 169 069	0.0154 310 746	456
39	0.0141 862 868	0.0145 999 942	0.0150 141 382	0.0154 286 562	468
40	0.0141 832 357	0.0145 973 346	0.0150 118 231	0.0154 266 440	480
41	0.0141 806 595	0.0145 950 998	0.0150 098 875	0.0154 249 697	492
42	0.0141 784 842	0.0145 932 220	0.0150 082 689	0.0154 235 764	504
43	0.0141 766 473	0.0145 916 441	0.0150 069 153	0.0154 224 171	516
44	0.0141 750 961	0.0145 903 180	0.0150 057 835	0.0154 214 523	528
45	0.0141 737 861	0.0145 892 036	0.0150 048 369	0.0154 206 495	540
46	0.0141 726 798	0.0145 882 671	0.0150 040 453	0.0154 199 813	552
47	0.0141 717 455	0.0145 874 800	0.0150 033 833	0.0154 194 253	564
48	0.0141 709 563	0.0145 868 186	0.0150 028 297	0.0154 189 625	576
49	0.0141 702 899	0.0145 862 626	0.0150 023 666	0.0154 185 774	588
50	0.0141 697 270	0.0145 857 954	0.0150 019 794	0.0154 182 569	600

Table 6.   PARTIAL PAYMENT TO AMORTIZE 1
             PAYABLE AT END OF EACH PERIOD

	19% NOMINAL ANNUAL RATE	**19½%** NOMINAL ANNUAL RATE	**20%** NOMINAL ANNUAL RATE	**20½%** NOMINAL ANNUAL RATE	
MONTHS					**MONTHS**
1	1.0158 333 333	1.0162 500 000	1.0166 666 667	1.0170 833 333	1
2	0.5119 060 907	0.5122 202 418	0.5125 344 353	0.5128 486 711	2
3	0.3439 441 601	0.3442 248 730	0.3445 056 613	0.3447 865 248	3
4	0.2599 735 562	0.2602 381 002	0.2605 027 501	0.2607 675 058	4
5	0.2095 994 816	0.2098 547 642	0.2101 101 823	0.2103 657 358	5
6	0.1760 236 700	0.1762 731 449	0.1765 227 843	0.1767 725 882	6
7	0.1520 468 644	0.1522 925 047	0.1525 383 385	0.1527 843 655	7
8	0.1340 694 358	0.1343 124 747	0.1345 557 358	0.1347 992 187	8
9	0.1200 915 901	0.1203 328 496	0.1205 743 597	0.1208 161 201	9
10	0.1089 134 508	0.1091 535 060	0.1093 938 401	0.1096 344 529	10
11	0.0997 714 598	0.1000 107 288	0.1002 503 049	0.1004 901 880	11
YEARS					
1	0.0921 565 782	0.0923 953 744	0.0926 345 059	0.0928 739 724	12
2	0.0504 086 172	0.0506 518 766	0.0508 958 026	0.0511 403 944	24
3	0.0366 560 200	0.0369 093 105	0.0371 635 834	0.0374 188 364	36
4	0.0299 001 182	0.0301 646 019	0.0304 303 623	0.0306 973 950	48
5	0.0259 405 511	0.0262 164 454	0.0264 938 837	0.0267 728 580	60
6	0.0233 767 230	0.0236 638 845	0.0239 528 261	0.0242 435 344	72
7	0.0216 080 190	0.0219 061 187	0.0222 061 993	0.0225 082 416	84
8	0.0203 338 649	0.0206 424 601	0.0209 532 004	0.0212 660 592	96
9	0.0193 870 830	0.0197 056 566	0.0200 265 017	0.0203 495 836	108
10	0.0186 672 355	0.0189 952 210	0.0193 255 672	0.0196 582 306	120
11	0.0181 103 258	0.0184 471 261	0.0187 863 404	0.0191 279 160	132
12	0.0176 736 477	0.0180 186 496	0.0183 660 855	0.0187 158 933	144
13	0.0173 276 249	0.0176 802 117	0.0180 352 218	0.0183 925 842	156
14	0.0170 511 456	0.0174 107 069	0.0177 726 538	0.0181 369 070	168
15	0.0168 287 603	0.0171 947 003	0.0175 629 650	0.0179 334 675	180
16	0.0166 489 273	0.0170 206 718	0.0173 946 605	0.0177 708 002	192
17	0.0165 028 754	0.0168 798 764	0.0172 590 257	0.0176 402 246	204
18	0.0163 838 424	0.0167 655 823	0.0171 493 627	0.0175 350 807	216
19	0.0162 865 526	0.0166 725 466	0.0170 604 647	0.0174 502 013	228
20	0.0162 068 485	0.0165 966 461	0.0169 882 461	0.0173 815 413	240
21	0.0161 414 265	0.0165 346 120	0.0169 294 756	0.0173 259 097	252
22	0.0160 876 431	0.0164 838 357	0.0168 815 817	0.0172 807 743	264
23	0.0160 433 708	0.0164 422 235	0.0168 425 065	0.0172 441 150	276
24	0.0160 068 889	0.0164 080 873	0.0168 105 965	0.0172 143 139	288
25	0.0159 768 003	0.0163 800 613	0.0167 845 177	0.0171 900 707	300
26	0.0159 519 667	0.0163 570 361	0.0167 631 913	0.0171 703 373	312
27	0.0159 314 581	0.0163 381 091	0.0167 457 424	0.0171 542 673	324
28	0.0159 145 129	0.0163 225 438	0.0167 314 599	0.0171 411 754	336
29	0.0159 005 064	0.0163 097 383	0.0167 197 652	0.0171 305 065	348
30	0.0158 889 249	0.0162 992 000	0.0167 101 869	0.0171 218 099	360
31	0.0158 793 460	0.0162 905 254	0.0167 023 400	0.0171 147 195	372
32	0.0158 714 216	0.0162 833 834	0.0166 959 105	0.0171 089 376	384
33	0.0158 648 647	0.0162 775 021	0.0166 906 414	0.0171 042 222	396
34	0.0158 594 384	0.0162 726 585	0.0166 863 228	0.0171 003 760	408
35	0.0158 549 472	0.0162 686 688	0.0166 827 829	0.0170 972 386	420
36	0.0158 512 295	0.0162 653 824	0.0166 798 810	0.0170 946 792	432
37	0.0158 481 519	0.0162 626 749	0.0166 775 019	0.0170 925 911	444
38	0.0158 456 040	0.0162 604 443	0.0166 755 514	0.0170 908 874	456
39	0.0158 434 944	0.0162 586 064	0.0166 739 522	0.0170 894 974	468
40	0.0158 417 477	0.0162 570 921	0.0166 726 409	0.0170 883 633	480
41	0.0158 403 014	0.0162 558 443	0.0166 715 657	0.0170 874 378	492
42	0.0158 391 038	0.0162 548 162	0.0166 706 841	0.0170 866 827	504
43	0.0158 381 171	0.0162 539 689	0.0166 699 611	0.0170 860 665	516
44	0.0158 372 908	0.0162 532 707	0.0166 693 683	0.0170 855 637	528
45	0.0158 366 108	0.0162 526 954	0.0166 688 822	0.0170 851 534	540
46	0.0158 360 476	0.0162 522 213	0.0166 684 835	0.0170 848 186	552
47	0.0158 355 812	0.0162 518 306	0.0166 681 566	0.0170 845 454	564
48	0.0158 351 949	0.0162 515 086	0.0166 678 885	0.0170 843 224	576
49	0.0158 348 751	0.0162 512 432	0.0166 676 687	0.0170 841 405	588
50	0.0158 346 102	0.0162 510 246	0.0166 674 884	0.0170 839 920	600

73

Table 6.   PARTIAL PAYMENT TO AMORTIZE 1
PAYABLE AT END OF EACH PERIOD

	21% NOMINAL ANNUAL RATE	21½% NOMINAL ANNUAL RATE	22% NOMINAL ANNUAL RATE	22½% NOMINAL ANNUAL RATE	
MONTHS					**MONTHS**
1	1.0175 000 000	1.0179 166 667	1.0183 333 333	1.0187 500 000	1
2	0.5131 629 492	0.5134 772 696	0.5137 916 323	0.5141 060 372	2
3	0.3450 674 635	0.3453 484 774	0.3456 295 664	0.3459 107 305	3
4	0.2610 323 673	0.2612 973 344	0.2615 624 071	0.2618 275 854	4
5	0.2106 214 246	0.2108 772 487	0.2111 332 078	0.2113 893 021	5
6	0.1770 225 565	0.1772 726 891	0.1775 229 859	0.1777 734 467	6
7	0.1530 305 857	0.1532 769 990	0.1535 236 051	0.1537 704 041	7
8	0.1350 429 233	0.1352 868 496	0.1355 309 973	0.1357 753 662	8
9	0.1210 581 306	0.1213 003 912	0.1215 429 016	0.1217 856 615	9
10	0.1098 753 442	0.1101 165 137	0.1103 579 613	0.1105 996 867	10
11	0.1007 303 778	0.1009 708 739	0.1012 116 763	0.1014 527 846	11
YEARS					
1	0.0931 137 738	0.0933 539 096	0.0935 943 796	0.0938 351 837	12
2	0.0513 856 510	0.0516 315 714	0.0518 781 546	0.0521 253 599	24
3	0.0376 750 673	0.0379 322 737	0.0381 904 532	0.0384 496 033	36
4	0.0309 656 950	0.0312 352 576	0.0315 060 778	0.0317 781 508	48
5	0.0270 533 598	0.0273 353 807	0.0276 189 120	0.0279 039 451	60
6	0.0245 359 964	0.0248 301 986	0.0251 261 274	0.0254 237 690	72
7	0.0228 122 263	0.0231 181 337	0.0234 259 440	0.0237 356 371	84
8	0.0215 018 099	0.0218 980 256	0.0222 170 793	0.0225 381 438	96
9	0.0206 748 675	0.0210 023 184	0.0213 319 013	0.0216 635 810	108
10	0.0199 931 675	0.0203 303 344	0.0206 696 878	0.0210 111 841	120
11	0.0194 718 004	0.0198 179 411	0.0201 662 859	0.0205 167 829	132
12	0.0190 680 114	0.0194 223 789	0.0197 789 352	0.0201 376 202	144
13	0.0187 522 288	0.0191 140 864	0.0194 780 885	0.0198 441 677	156
14	0.0185 033 884	0.0188 720 212	0.0192 427 302	0.0196 154 413	168
15	0.0183 061 227	0.0186 808 473	0.0190 575 600	0.0194 361 815	180
16	0.0181 489 996	0.0185 291 704	0.0189 112 263	0.0192 950 838	192
17	0.0180 233 774	0.0184 083 912	0.0187 951 766	0.0191 836 470	204
18	0.0179 226 371	0.0183 119 365	0.0187 028 868	0.0190 954 001	216
19	0.0178 416 551	0.0182 347 288	0.0186 293 297	0.0190 253 692	228
20	0.0177 764 294	0.0181 728 130	0.0185 705 594	0.0189 697 006	240
21	0.0177 238 122	0.0181 230 865	0.0185 236 411	0.0189 253 897	252
22	0.0176 813 127	0.0180 831 020	0.0184 860 529	0.0188 900 818	264
23	0.0176 469 502	0.0180 509 200	0.0184 559 381	0.0188 619 238	276
24	0.0176 191 441	0.0180 249 981	0.0184 317 932	0.0188 394 527	288
25	0.0175 966 282	0.0180 041 054	0.0184 124 236	0.0188 215 102	300
26	0.0175 783 864	0.0179 872 579	0.0183 968 776	0.0188 071 776	312
27	0.0175 636 007	0.0179 736 660	0.0183 843 959	0.0187 957 246	324
28	0.0175 516 122	0.0179 626 991	0.0183 743 713	0.0187 865 701	336
29	0.0175 418 889	0.0179 538 461	0.0183 663 183	0.0187 792 513	348
30	0.0175 340 009	0.0179 466 986	0.0183 598 478	0.0187 733 991	360
31	0.0175 276 006	0.0179 409 270	0.0183 546 481	0.0187 687 189	372
32	0.0175 224 067	0.0179 362 658	0.0183 504 691	0.0187 649 755	384
33	0.0175 181 911	0.0179 325 010	0.0183 471 100	0.0187 619 812	396
34	0.0175 147 694	0.0179 294 599	0.0183 444 098	0.0187 595 859	408
35	0.0175 119 917	0.0179 270 032	0.0183 422 391	0.0187 576 697	420
36	0.0175 097 367	0.0179 250 184	0.0183 404 939	0.0187 561 366	432
37	0.0175 079 059	0.0179 234 149	0.0183 390 909	0.0187 549 101	444
38	0.0175 064 195	0.0179 221 194	0.0183 379 628	0.0187 539 288	456
39	0.0175 052 127	0.0179 210 726	0.0183 370 558	0.0187 531 436	468
40	0.0175 042 327	0.0179 202 269	0.0183 363 265	0.0187 525 154	480
41	0.0175 034 371	0.0179 195 435	0.0183 357 401	0.0187 520 127	492
42	0.0175 027 910	0.0179 189 913	0.0183 352 686	0.0187 516 105	504
43	0.0175 022 664	0.0179 185 451	0.0183 348 895	0.0187 512 887	516
44	0.0175 018 404	0.0179 181 846	0.0183 345 847	0.0187 510 311	528
45	0.0175 014 945	0.0179 178 932	0.0183 343 395	0.0187 508 251	540
46	0.0175 012 136	0.0179 176 578	0.0183 341 424	0.0187 506 602	552
47	0.0175 009 855	0.0179 174 676	0.0183 339 839	0.0187 505 283	564
48	0.0175 008 003	0.0179 173 139	0.0183 338 565	0.0187 504 227	576
49	0.0175 006 499	0.0179 171 896	0.0183 337 540	0.0187 503 383	588
50	0.0175 005 277	0.0179 170 893	0.0183 336 716	0.0187 502 707	600

74

Table 1. FUTURE WORTH OF ONE DOLLAR WITH INTEREST
PAYABLE AT BEGINNING OF EACH PERIOD

QUARTERS	5% NOMINAL ANNUAL RATE	5½% NOMINAL ANNUAL RATE	6% NOMINAL ANNUAL RATE	6½% NOMINAL ANNUAL RATE	QUARTERS
1	1.0125 000 000	1.0137 500 000	1.0150 000 000	1.0162 500 000	1
2	1.0251 562 500	1.0276 890 625	1.0302 250 000	1.0327 640 625	2
3	1.0379 707 031	1.0418 197 871	1.0456 783 750	1.0495 464 785	3
YEARS					
1	1.0509 453 369	1.0561 448 092	1.0613 635 506	1.0666 016 088	4
2	1.1044 861 012	1.1154 418 580	1.1264 925 866	1.1376 389 919	8
3	1.1607 545 177	1.1780 681 282	1.1956 181 715	1.2134 075 790	12
4	1.2198 895 477	1.2442 105 385	1.2689 855 477	1.2942 224 758	16
5	1.2820 372 317	1.3140 665 018	1.3468 550 066	1.3804 197 749	20
6	1.3473 510 504	1.3878 445 148	1.4295 028 119	1.4723 579 527	24
7	1.4159 923 036	1.4657 647 802	1.5172 221 801	1.5704 193 610	28
8	1.4881 305 086	1.5480 598 641	1.6103 243 202	1.6750 118 170	32
9	1.5639 438 187	1.6349 753 898	1.7091 395 381	1.7865 702 987	36
10	1.6436 194 635	1.7267 707 710	1.8140 184 087	1.9055 587 548	40
11	1.7273 542 108	1.8237 199 865	1.9253 330 191	2.0324 720 336	44
12	1.8153 548 531	1.9261 123 971	2.0434 782 893	2.1678 379 408	48
13	1.9078 387 177	2.0342 536 101	2.1688 733 728	2.3122 194 353	52
14	2.0050 342 039	2.1484 663 909	2.3019 631 438	2.4662 169 695	56
15	2.1071 813 470	2.2690 916 265	2.4432 197 757	2.6304 709 873	60
16	2.2145 324 106	2.3964 893 428	2.5931 444 161	2.8056 645 870	64
17	2.3273 525 104	2.5310 397 797	2.7522 689 647	2.9925 263 622	68
18	2.4459 202 681	2.6731 445 252	2.9211 579 607	3.1918 334 323	72
19	2.5705 285 003	2.8232 277 144	3.1004 105 851	3.4044 146 738	76
20	2.7014 849 408	2.9817 372 958	3.2906 627 870	3.6311 541 681	80
21	2.8391 130 012	3.1491 463 673	3.4925 895 395	3.8729 948 775	84
22	2.9837 525 696	3.3259 545 891	3.7069 072 345	4.1309 425 672	88
23	3.1357 608 495	3.5126 896 749	3.9343 762 243	4.4060 699 880	92
24	3.2955 132 425	3.7099 089 664	4.1758 035 189	4.6995 213 376	96
25	3.4634 042 749	3.9182 010 974	4.4320 456 495	5.0125 170 192	100
26	3.6398 485 726	4.1381 877 503	4.7040 117 071	5.3463 587 168	104
27	3.8252 818 844	4.3705 255 120	4.9926 665 676	5.7024 348 085	108
28	4.0201 621 588	4.6159 078 328	5.2990 343 153	6.0822 261 408	112
29	4.2249 706 745	4.8750 670 973	5.6242 018 758	6.4873 121 868	116
30	4.4402 132 289	5.1487 768 093	5.9693 228 723	6.9193 776 152	120
31	4.6664 213 879	5.4378 539 007	6.3356 217 186	7.3802 192 962	124
32	4.9041 537 976	5.7431 611 703	6.7243 979 627	7.8717 537 746	128
33	5.1539 975 651	6.0656 098 584	7.1370 308 975	8.3960 252 400	132
34	5.4165 697 076	6.4061 623 664	7.5749 844 543	8.9552 140 284	136
35	5.6925 186 762	6.7658 351 301	8.0398 123 963	9.5516 456 898	140
36	5.9825 259 581	7.1457 016 524	8.5331 638 313	10.1878 006 593	144
37	6.2873 077 586	7.5468 957 082	9.0567 890 620	10.8663 245 733	148
38	6.6076 167 707	7.9706 147 276	9.6125 457 962	11.5900 392 715	152
39	6.9442 440 332	8.4181 233 706	10.2024 057 368	12.3619 545 330	156
40	7.2980 208 851	8.8907 573 009	10.8284 615 777	13.1852 805 927	160
41	7.6698 210 179	9.3899 271 730	11.4929 344 279	14.0634 414 925	164
42	8.0605 626 337	9.9171 228 424	12.1981 816 915	15.0000 893 210	168
43	8.4712 107 128	10.4739 178 120	12.9467 054 312	15.9991 194 018	172
44	8.9027 793 967	11.0619 739 289	13.7411 612 454	17.0646 864 932	176
45	9.3563 344 925	11.6830 463 444	14.5843 676 891	18.2012 220 672	180
46	9.8329 961 055	12.3389 887 520	15.4793 162 742	19.4134 527 389	184
47	10.3339 414 050	13.0317 589 210	16.4291 820 820	20.7064 199 235	188
48	10.8604 075 315	13.7634 245 389	17.4373 350 284	22.0855 008 027	192
49	11.4136 946 522	14.5361 693 834	18.5073 518 192	23.5564 306 871	196
50	11.9951 691 717	15.3522 998 396	19.6430 286 395	25.1253 268 683	200
51	12.6062 671 065	16.2142 517 846	20.8483 946 218	26.7987 140 591	204
52	13.2484 976 315	17.1245 978 571	22.1277 261 406	28.5835 515 290	208
53	13.9234 468 069	18.0860 551 361	23.4855 619 839	30.4872 620 458	212
54	14.6327 814 955	19.1014 932 506	24.9267 194 557	32.5177 627 457	216
55	15.3782 534 788	20.1739 429 443	26.4563 114 669	34.6834 980 588	220
56	16.1617 037 834	21.3066 051 213	28.0797 646 749	36.9934 748 281	224
57	16.9850 612 278	22.5028 604 002	29.8028 387 361	39.4572 997 664	228
58	17.8503 772 002	23.7662 792 034	31.6316 467 397	42.0852 194 094	232
59	18.7597 706 807	25.1006 324 142	33.5726 768 957	44.8881 627 284	236
60	19.7154 935 184	26.5099 026 315	35.6328 155 540	47.8777 865 819	240

75

Table 1.   FUTURE WORTH OF ONE DOLLAR WITH INTEREST
PAYABLE AT BEGINNING OF EACH PERIOD

QUARTERS	7% NOMINAL ANNUAL RATE	7½% NOMINAL ANNUAL RATE	8% NOMINAL ANNUAL RATE	8½% NOMINAL ANNUAL RATE	QUARTERS
1	1.0175 000 000	1.0187 500 000	1.0200 000 000	1.0212 500 000	1
2	1.0353 062 500	1.0378 515 625	1.0404 000 000	1.0429 515 625	2
3	1.0534 241 094	1.0573 112 793	1.0612 080 000	1.0651 142 832	3
YEARS					
1	1.0718 590 313	1.0771 358 658	1.0824 321 600	1.0877 479 617	4
2	1.1488 817 830	1.1602 216 734	1.1716 593 810	1.1831 956 282	8
3	1.2314 393 149	1.2497 163 766	1.2682 417 946	1.2870 186 329	12
4	1.3199 293 512	1.3461 143 313	1.3727 857 051	1.3999 518 947	16
5	1.4147 781 958	1.4499 480 257	1.4859 473 960	1.5227 948 199	20
6	1.5164 427 864	1.5617 910 220	1.6084 372 495	1.6564 169 615	24
7	1.6254 128 960	1.6822 611 247	1.7410 242 062	1.8017 641 736	28
8	1.7422 134 922	1.8120 237 930	1.8845 405 921	1.9598 653 074	32
9	1.8674 072 660	1.9517 958 171	2.0398 873 437	2.1318 394 933	36
10	2.0015 973 432	2.1023 492 773	2.2080 396 636	2.3189 040 636	40
11	2.1454 301 893	2.2645 158 090	2.3900 531 425	2.5223 831 686	44
12	2.2995 987 244	2.4391 911 965	2.5870 703 855	2.7437 171 503	48
13	2.4648 456 611	2.6273 403 212	2.8003 281 854	2.9844 727 378	52
14	2.6419 670 826	2.8300 024 916	3.0311 652 865	3.2463 541 373	56
15	2.8318 162 778	3.0482 971 840	3.2810 307 884	3.5312 150 959	60
16	3.0353 078 523	3.2834 302 264	3.5514 932 433	3.8410 720 230	64
17	3.2534 221 343	3.5367 004 597	3.8442 505 025	4.1781 182 638	68
18	3.4872 098 972	3.8095 069 117	4.1611 403 751	4.5447 396 253	72
19	3.7377 974 223	4.1033 565 255	4.5041 521 642	4.9435 312 640	76
20	4.0063 919 242	4.4198 724 837	4.8754 391 561	5.3773 160 561	80
21	4.2942 873 669	4.7608 031 744	5.2773 321 367	5.8491 645 796	84
22	4.6028 706 972	5.1280 318 491	5.7123 540 237	6.3624 168 492	88
23	4.9336 285 266	5.5235 870 255	6.1832 357 046	6.9207 059 593	92
24	5.2881 542 933	5.9496 536 930	6.6929 331 795	7.5279 838 009	96
25	5.6681 559 381	6.4085 853 817	7.2446 461 183	8.1885 490 353	100
26	6.0754 641 330	6.9029 171 636	7.8418 379 462	8.9070 775 226	104
27	6.5120 411 002	7.4353 796 554	8.4882 575 865	9.6886 554 201	108
28	6.9799 900 654	8.0089 141 026	9.1879 629 940	10.5388 151 851	112
29	7.4815 653 899	8.6266 886 258	9.9453 466 296	11.4635 747 365	116
30	8.0191 834 313	9.2921 157 218	10.7651 630 342	12.4694 800 537	120
31	8.5954 341 844	10.0088 711 130	11.6525 586 759	13.5636 515 121	124
32	9.2130 937 584	10.7809 140 518	12.6131 042 570	14.7538 342 858	128
33	9.8751 377 511	11.6125 091 912	13.6528 296 853	16.0484 531 720	132
34	10.5847 555 837	12.5082 501 415	14.7782 619 263	17.4566 722 266	136
35	11.3453 658 664	13.4730 848 456	15.9964 659 780	18.9884 596 329	140
36	12.1606 328 672	14.5123 429 100	17.3150 892 209	20.6546 582 619	144
37	13.0344 841 649	15.6317 650 449	18.7424 094 260	22.4670 624 245	148
38	13.9711 295 703	16.8375 347 754	20.2873 867 185	24.4385 013 581	152
39	14.9750 814 073	18.1363 125 979	21.9597 198 265	26.5829 300 398	156
40	16.0511 762 507	19.5352 727 723	23.7699 069 648	28.9155 279 673	160
41	17.2045 982 271	21.0421 429 509	25.7293 117 389	31.4528 066 086	164
42	18.4409 039 894	22.6652 468 654	27.8502 344 809	34.2127 262 789	168
43	19.7660 494 862	24.4135 503 055	30.1459 894 656	37.2148 232 748	172
44	21.1864 186 547	26.2967 106 452	32.6309 884 926	40.4803 481 629	176
45	22.7088 541 757	28.3251 301 881	35.3208 313 570	44.0324 162 040	180
46	24.3406 904 385	30.5100 136 286	38.2324 037 787	47.8961 709 756	184
47	26.0897 888 743	32.8634 299 449	41.3839 834 042	52.0989 623 529	188
48	27.9645 758 293	35.3983 790 663	44.7953 545 456	56.6705 401 072	192
49	29.9740 831 588	38.1288 636 829	48.4879 323 788	61.6432 644 912	196
50	32.1279 917 384	41.0699 665 944	52.4848 973 787	67.0523 353 042	200
51	34.4366 781 020	44.2379 340 254	56.8113 408 370	72.9360 410 557	204
52	36.9112 644 312	47.6502 653 669	61.4944 223 747	79.3360 299 944	208
53	39.5636 721 369	51.3258 098 408	66.5635 404 390	86.2976 049 175	212
54	42.4066 792 909	55.2848 706 200	72.0505 168 546	93.8700 438 504	216
55	45.4539 821 849	59.5493 169 800	77.9897 965 881	102.1069 488 649	220
56	48.7202 613 129	64.1427 051 021	84.4186 639 788	111.0666 255 054	224
57	52.2212 520 950	69.0900 081 938	91.3774 767 949	120.8124 955 088	228
58	55.9738 206 833	74.4197 566 472	98.9099 195 824	131.4135 457 401	232
59	59.9960 452 151	80.1601 890 076	107.0632 778 990	142.9448 165 213	236
60	64.3073 029 055	86.3434 145 881	115.8887 351 529	155.4879 328 097	240

76

Table 1. FUTURE WORTH OF ONE DOLLAR WITH INTEREST
PAYABLE AT BEGINNING OF EACH PERIOD

QUARTERS	9% NOMINAL ANNUAL RATE	9½% NOMINAL ANNUAL RATE	10% NOMINAL ANNUAL RATE	10½% NOMINAL ANNUAL RATE	QUARTERS
1	1.0225 000 000	1.0237 500 000	1.0250 000 000	1.0262 500 000	1
2	1.0455 062 500	1.0480 640 625	1.0506 250 000	1.0531 890 625	2
3	1.0690 301 406	1.0729 555 840	1.0768 906 250	1.0808 352 754	3
YEARS					
1	1.0930 833 188	1.0984 382 791	1.1038 128 906	1.1092 072 014	4
2	1.1948 311 418	1.2065 666 530	1.2184 028 975	1.2303 406 156	8
3	1.3060 499 899	1.3253 389 979	1.3448 888 242	1.3647 026 709	12
4	1.4276 214 575	1.4558 030 881	1.4845 056 207	1.5137 380 303	16
5	1.5605 092 007	1.5991 098 388	1.6386 164 045	1.6790 491 242	20
6	1.7057 665 761	1.7565 234 595	1.8087 259 496	1.8624 133 800	24
7	1.8645 449 901	1.9294 326 060	1.9964 950 188	2.0658 023 331	28
8	2.0381 030 258	2.1193 626 314	2.2037 569 378	2.2914 028 244	32
9	2.2278 164 194	2.3279 890 417	2.4325 353 157	2.5416 405 141	36
10	2.4351 889 654	2.5571 522 767	2.6850 638 384	2.8192 059 615	40
11	2.6618 644 362	2.8088 739 462	2.9638 080 770	3.1270 835 547	44
12	2.9096 396 121	3.0853 746 637	3.2714 895 607	3.4685 835 981	48
13	3.1804 785 237	3.3890 936 360	3.6111 123 486	3.8473 779 056	52
14	3.4765 280 200	3.7227 101 812	3.9859 923 599	4.2675 392 793	56
15	3.8001 347 859	4.0891 673 651	4.3997 897 488	4.7335 853 007	60
16	4.1538 639 437	4.4916 979 635	4.8565 446 408	5.2505 269 039	64
17	4.5405 193 853	4.9338 529 812	5.3607 165 784	5.8239 222 527	68
18	4.9631 659 988	5.4195 329 781	5.9172 280 622	6.4599 365 030	72
19	5.4251 539 616	5.9530 224 780	6.5315 126 118	7.1654 080 895	76
20	5.9301 452 973	6.5390 277 662	7.2095 678 162	7.9479 222 536	80
21	6.4821 429 025	7.1827 184 065	7.9580 138 914	8.8158 925 996	84
22	7.0855 222 767	7.8897 728 457	8.7841 583 171	9.7786 515 580	88
23	7.7450 662 056	8.6664 285 072	9.6960 671 837	10.8465 507 278	92
24	8.4660 026 722	9.5195 368 154	10.7026 439 457	12.0310 721 773	96
25	9.2540 462 979	10.4566 236 374	11.8137 163 511	13.3449 518 993	100
26	10.1154 436 395	11.4859 556 735	13.0401 323 945	14.8023 167 486	104
27	11.0570 227 045	12.6166 133 838	14.3938 662 325	16.4188 363 345	108
28	12.0862 470 737	13.8585 710 934	15.8881 350 934	18.2118 915 004	112
29	13.2112 750 631	15.2227 849 827	17.5375 283 240	20.2007 612 028	116
30	14.4410 243 914	16.7212 897 396	19.3581 498 338	22.4068 297 992	120
31	15.7852 428 684	18.3673 047 260	21.3677 753 252	24.8538 169 732	124
32	17.2545 856 625	20.1753 505 950	23.5860 258 479	27.5680 327 682	128
33	18.8606 997 603	22.1613 773 878	26.0345 593 695	30.5786 604 741	132
34	20.6163 162 887	24.3429 052 405	28.7372 822 338	33.9180 704 061	136
35	22.5353 514 300	26.7391 789 407	31.7205 825 712	37.6221 679 510	140
36	24.6330 167 312	29.3713 377 003	35.0135 879 403	41.7307 796 224	144
37	26.9259 396 803	32.2626 016 385	38.6484 497 155	46.2880 812 759	148
38	29.4322 955 073	35.4384 766 232	42.6606 569 986	51.3430 730 888	152
39	32.1719 512 527	38.9269 792 761	47.0893 831 176	56.9501 064 105	156
40	35.1666 232 472	42.7588 841 268	51.9778 680 968	63.1694 681 493	160
41	38.4400 492 497	46.9679 950 966	57.3738 408 325	70.0680 289 779	164
42	42.0181 766 083	51.5914 437 069	63.3299 850 955	77.7199 623 281	168
43	45.9293 679 364	56.6700 166 419	69.9044 539 116	86.2075 419 045	172
44	50.2046 259 338	62.2485 155 569	77.1614 373 397	95.6220 262 929	176
45	54.8778 391 343	68.3761 523 051	85.1717 891 947	106.0646 401 736	180
46	59.9860 505 289	75.1069 830 698	94.0137 188 307	117.6476 626 912	184
47	65.5697 511 932	82.5003 852 319	103.7735 547 409	130.4956 346 814	188
48	71.6732 012 464	90.6215 811 795	114.5465 874 290	144.7466 977 359	192
49	78.3447 806 867	99.5422 136 805	126.4379 997 812	160.5540 795 032	196
50	85.6373 728 828	109.3409 778 934	139.5638 940 234	178.0877 411 942	200
51	93.6087 837 631	120.1043 155 928	154.0524 252 888	197.5362 050 082	204
52	102.3222 000 236	131.9271 777 327	170.0450 528 658	219.1085 811 264	208
53	111.8466 899 876	144.9138 620 757	187.6979 213 403	243.0368 160 673	212
54	122.2577 510 872	159.1789 332 768	207.1833 851 189	269.5781 865 797	216
55	133.6379 083 060	174.8482 335 382	228.6916 912 176	299.0180 658 864	220
56	146.0773 683 272	192.0599 927 520	252.4328 367 448	331.6729 920 208	224
57	159.6747 345 711	210.9660 479 233	278.6386 192 160	367.8940 712 493	228
58	174.5377 887 917	231.7331 826 302	307.5648 997 166	408.0707 531 709	232
59	190.7843 454 265	254.5445 983 396	339.4941 010 109	452.6350 180 855	236
60	208.5431 854 718	279.6015 305 554	374.7379 649 870	502.0660 216 525	240

Table 1.   FUTURE WORTH OF ONE DOLLAR WITH INTEREST
PAYABLE AT BEGINNING OF EACH PERIOD

QUARTERS	11% NOMINAL ANNUAL RATE	11½% NOMINAL ANNUAL RATE	12% NOMINAL ANNUAL RATE	12½% NOMINAL ANNUAL RATE	QUARTERS
1	1.0275 000 000	1.0287 500 000	1.0300 000 000	1.0312 500 000	1
2	1.0557 562 500	1.0583 265 625	1.0609 000 000	1.0634 765 625	2
3	1.0847 895 469	1.0887 534 512	1.0927 270 000	1.0967 102 051	3
YEARS					
1	1.1146 212 594	1.1200 551 129	1.1255 088 100	1.1309 823 990	4
2	1.2423 805 519	1.2545 234 559	1.2667 700 814	1.2791 211 868	8
3	1.3847 837 755	1.4051 354 110	1.4257 608 868	1.4466 635 485	12
4	1.5435 094 358	1.5738 291 014	1.6047 064 391	1.6361 510 106	16
5	1.7204 284 313	1.7627 753 319	1.8061 112 347	1.8504 579 950	20
6	1.9176 261 048	1.9744 055 234	2.0327 941 065	2.0928 354 224	24
7	2.1374 268 240	2.2114 430 014	2.2879 276 757	2.3669 600 268	28
8	2.3824 213 785	2.4769 380 406	2.5750 827 557	2.6769 901 294	32
9	2.6554 975 174	2.7743 071 167	2.8982 783 280	3.0276 287 186	36
10	2.9598 739 872	3.1073 768 707	3.2620 377 920	3.4241 947 914	40
11	3.2991 384 713	3.4804 333 518	3.6714 522 734	3.8727 040 398	44
12	3.6772 898 779	3.8982 771 707	4.1322 518 793	4.3799 601 055	48
13	4.0987 854 749	4.3662 852 765	4.6508 858 952	4.9536 577 875	52
14	4.5685 934 281	4.8904 801 483	5.2346 130 494	5.6024 997 683	56
15	5.0922 513 606	5.4776 072 947	5.8916 031 040	6.3363 286 283	60
16	5.6759 316 248	6.1352 220 568	6.6310 511 986	7.1662 761 528	64
17	6.3265 140 559	6.8717 868 335	7.4633 065 436	8.1049 321 951	68
18	7.0516 670 447	7.6967 799 775	8.4000 172 666	9.1665 356 576	72
19	7.8599 380 247	8.6208 177 666	9.4542 934 377	10.3671 904 885	76
20	8.7608 540 200	9.6557 910 168	10.6408 905 564	11.7251 099 694	80
21	9.7650 341 413	10.8150 180 974	11.9764 160 675	13.2608 930 016	84
22	10.8843 146 528	12.1134 163 161	13.4795 617 962	14.9978 365 796	88
23	12.1318 885 061	13.5676 938 794	15.1713 655 566	16.9622 891 944	92
24	13.5224 608 458	15.1965 648 998	17.0755 055 936	19.1840 505 254	96
25	15.0724 223 383	17.0209 902 144	19.2186 319 809	21.6968 234 855	100
26	16.8000 423 691	19.0644 471 162	21.6307 396 106	24.5387 254 760	104
27	18.7256 843 837	21.3532 314 670	24.3455 879 985	27.7528 666 070	108
28	20.8720 459 111	23.9167 960 814	27.4011 737 770	31.3880 036 539	112
29	23.2644 261 000	26.7881 297 349	30.8402 624 903	35.4992 796 719	116
30	25.9310 239 192	30.0041 816 745	34.7109 871 356	40.1490 604 856	120
31	28.9032 705 387	33.6063 370 927	39.0675 218 249	45.4078 807 451	124
32	32.2161 998 090	37.6409 496 862	43.9708 399 988	51.3555 138 980	128
33	35.9088 612 046	42.1599 381 502	49.4895 678 018	58.0821 823 096	132
34	40.0247 801 000	47.2214 542 844	55.7009 445 640	65.6899 258 869	136
35	44.6124 708 029	52.8906 313 095	62.6919 038 321	74.2941 499 688	140
36	49.7260 083 919	59.2404 220 223	70.5602 900 787	84.0253 759 624	144
37	55.4256 660 994	66.3525 375 761	79.4162 281 197	95.0312 212 817	148
38	61.7786 257 516	74.3184 989 655	89.3836 644 057	107.4786 386 239	152
39	68.8597 696 401	83.2408 147 488	100.6021 017 587	121.5564 485 507	156
40	76.7525 631 592	93.2343 001 608	113.2285 518 339	137.4782 037 941	160
41	85.5500 386 117	104.4275 545 921	127.4397 326 326	155.4854 287 355	164
42	95.3558 917 803	116.9646 164 479	143.4345 418 221	175.8512 831 988	168
43	106.2857 041 887	131.0068 166 800	161.4368 404 790	198.8847 061 371	172
44	118.4683 054 606	146.7348 548 463	181.6985 862 177	224.9351 020 687	176
45	132.0472 918 331	164.3511 244 102	204.5033 595 526	254.3976 413 540	180
46	147.1827 187 252	184.0823 172 054	230.1703 328 510	287.7192 547 151	184
47	164.0529 873 095	206.1823 405 791	259.0587 374 245	325.4054 129 324	188
48	182.8569 473 256	230.9355 847 538	291.5728 912 787	368.0277 945 616	192
49	203.8162 409 206	258.6605 824 525	328.1678 578 914	416.2329 579 871	196
50	227.1779 151 440	289.7141 078 798	369.3558 152 156	470.7521 493 616	200
51	253.2173 338 889	324.4957 678 080	415.7132 240 499	532.4123 952 132	204
52	282.2414 236 047	363.4531 438 456	467.8888 961 016	602.1490 479 885	208
53	314.5922 910 371	407.0875 520 613	526.6130 746 636	681.0199 748 417	212
54	350.6552 536 377	455.9604 940 814	592.7076 549 950	770.2216 049 044	216
55	390.8433 441 740	510.7008 826 731	667.0976 874 514	871.1070 784 662	220
56	435.6423 005 168	572.0131 347 970	750.8243 243 571	985.2067 733 782	224
57	485.5761 696 561	640.6862 362 713	845.0593 918 262	1114.2515 200 533	228
58	541.2335 217 636	717.6038 946 959	951.1217 904 737	1260.1988 572 246	232
59	603.2703 896 652	803.7559 112 862	1070.4959 545 611	1425.2627 267 443	236
60	672.4180 014 958	900.2509 179 541	1204.8526 279 279	1611.9470 578 797	240

78

Table 1. FUTURE WORTH OF ONE DOLLAR WITH INTEREST
PAYABLE AT BEGINNING OF EACH PERIOD

QUARTERS	13% NOMINAL ANNUAL RATE	13½% NOMINAL ANNUAL RATE	14% NOMINAL ANNUAL RATE	14½% NOMINAL ANNUAL RATE	QUARTERS
1	1.0325 000 000	1.0337 500 000	1.0350 000 000	1.0362 500 000	1
2	1.0660 562 500	1.0686 390 625	1.0712 250 000	1.0738 140 625	2
3	1.1007 030 781	1.1047 056 309	1.1087 178 750	1.1127 398 223	3
YEARS					
1	1.1364 759 282	1.1419 894 459	1.1475 230 006	1.1530 766 408	4
2	1.2915 775 353	1.3041 398 945	1.3168 090 370	1.3295 857 396	8
3	1.4678 467 782	1.4893 139 956	1.5110 686 573	1.5331 142 583	12
4	1.6681 725 297	1.7007 808 646	1.7339 860 398	1.7677 982 390	16
5	1.8958 379 240	1.9422 737 971	1.9897 888 635	2.0384 068 551	20
6	2.1545 741 643	2.2180 561 774	2.2833 284 872	2.3504 393 291	24
7	2.4486 216 732	2.5329 967 449	2.6201 719 571	2.7102 366 860	28
8	2.7827 995 888	2.8926 555 492	3.0067 075 863	3.1251 106 137	32
9	3.1625 847 456	3.3033 821 079	3.4502 661 115	3.6034 920 487	36
10	3.5942 014 341	3.7724 275 029	3.9592 597 212	4.1551 025 067	40
11	4.0847 234 108	4.3080 723 938	4.5433 415 955	4.7911 516 407	44
12	4.6421 898 296	4.9197 732 059	5.2135 889 805	5.5245 650 396	48
13	5.2757 369 953	5.6183 290 773	5.9827 132 710	6.3702 468 978	52
14	5.9957 480 985	6.4160 725 099	6.8653 010 846	7.3453 828 942	56
15	6.8140 233 853	7.3270 870 905	7.8780 909 008	8.4697 894 331	60
16	7.7439 735 513	8.3674 561 265	9.0402 905 096	9.7663 163 481	64
17	8.8008 395 294	9.5555 465 855	10.3739 412 921	11.2613 112 478	68
18	10.0019 422 729	10.9123 333 505	11.9043 362 399	12.9851 549 449	72
19	11.3669 666 280	12.4617 695 164	13.6604 996 424	14.9728 788 444	76
20	12.9182 839 489	14.2312 092 650	15.6757 375 397	17.2648 768 414	80
21	14.6813 187 412	16.2518 907 830	17.9882 693 786	19.9077 261 925	84
22	16.6849 653 430	18.5594 877 501	20.6419 528 533	22.9551 340 444	88
23	18.9620 614 746	21.1947 391 320	23.6871 156 770	26.4690 288 536	92
24	21.5499 264 143	24.2041 683 973	27.1815 100 579	30.5208 188 764	96
25	24.4909 726 235	27.6409 048 566	31.1914 079 831	35.1928 433 051	100
26	27.8334 008 440	31.5656 216 213	35.7928 580 825	40.5800 455 392	104
27	31.6319 900 581	36.0476 067 449	41.0731 279 078	46.7919 025 948	108
28	35.9489 952 610	41.1659 864 526	47.1323 589 818	53.9546 498 618	112
29	40.8551 677 558	47.0111 220 590	54.0854 660 053	62.2138 464 194	116
30	46.4309 146 955	53.5862 052 313	62.0643 162 406	71.7373 330 419	120
31	52.7676 168 741	61.3090 797 647	71.2202 304 042	82.7186 430 055	124
32	59.9691 263 640	70.0143 220 291	81.7268 524 986	95.3809 350 102	128
33	68.1534 685 457	79.9556 168 192	93.7834 430 108	109.9815 281 401	132
34	77.4547 764 231	91.3084 705 480	107.6186 579 327	126.8171 310 204	136
35	88.0254 889 262	104.2733 096 872	123.4948 852 742	146.2298 714 358	140
36	100.0388 492 295	119.0790 191 519	141.7132 213 117	168.6142 489 431	144
37	113.6917 440 305	135.9869 830 997	162.6191 809 478	194.4251 517 662	148
38	129.2079 303 217	155.2956 994 798	186.6092 504 804	224.1871 008 900	152
39	146.8417 025 385	177.3460 497 997	214.1384 070 557	258.5049 092 100	156
40	166.8820 601 856	202.5273 171 434	245.7287 474 136	298.0759 723 481	160
41	189.6574 442 434	231.2840 586 844	281.9793 895 719	343.7044 409 051	164
42	215.5411 199 798	264.1239 540 227	323.5778 352 359	396.3175 621 547	168
43	244.9572 943 865	301.6267 679 036	371.3130 084 256	456.9845 232 684	172
44	278.3880 684 985	344.4545 855 471	426.0902 175 997	526.9381 789 983	176
45	316.3813 385 366	393.3635 012 869	488.9483 250 369	607.6001 053 606	180
46	359.5597 753 672	449.2169 668 723	561.0794 490 970	700.6094 884 528	184
47	408.6310 294 409	513.0010 350 877	643.8515 730 168	807.8564 354 737	188
48	464.3993 284 604	585.8417 678 064	738.8344 890 253	931.5203 848 830	192
49	527.7786 578 508	669.0251 158 029	847.8295 698 116	1074.1143 962 588	196
50	599.8077 400 462	764.0196 212 895	972.9039 319 688	1238.5362 198 975	200
51	681.6670 580 890	872.5023 439 738	1116.4296 393 327	1428.1271 839 767	204
52	774.6982 025 406	996.3884 683 418	1281.1286 897 137	1646.7400 959 675	208
53	880.4258 587 793	1137.8651 148 637	1470.1246 382 071	1898.8175 381 664	212
54	1000.5827 950 359	1299.4299 520 331	1687.0018 361 281	2189.4821 484 442	216
55	1137.1382 606 934	1483.9352 909 093	1935.8734 090 536	2524.6407 208 695	220
56	1292.3302 602 724	1694.6384 406 183	2221.4592 631 874	2911.1042 417 045	224
57	1468.7022 320 376	1935.2592 138 040	2549.1755 994 590	3356.7263 001 095	228
58	1669.1447 323 516	2210.0455 972 466	2925.2376 330 112	3870.5626 862 917	232
59	1896.9428 089 394	2523.8487 470 154	3356.7774 661 742	4463.0554 204 031	236
60	2155.8298 394 636	2882.2086 321 417	3851.9793 504 146	5146.2449 519 642	240

79

Table 1.   FUTURE WORTH OF ONE DOLLAR WITH INTEREST
PAYABLE AT BEGINNING OF EACH PERIOD

QUARTERS	15% NOMINAL ANNUAL RATE	15½% NOMINAL ANNUAL RATE	16% NOMINAL ANNUAL RATE	16½% NOMINAL ANNUAL RATE	QUARTERS
1	1.0375 000 000	1.0387 500 000	1.0400 000 000	1.0412 500 000	1
2	1.0764 062 500	1.0790 015 625	1.0816 000 000	1.0842 015 625	2
3	1.1167 714 844	1.1208 128 730	1.1248 640 000	1.1289 248 770	3
YEARS					
1	1.1586 504 150	1.1642 443 719	1.1698 585 600	1.1754 930 281	4
2	1.3424 707 843	1.3554 649 574	1.3685 690 504	1.3817 838 592	8
3	1.5554 543 314	1.5780 924 480	1.6010 322 186	1.6242 772 928	12
4	1.8022 278 066	1.8372 852 509	1.8729 812 457	1.9093 266 335	16
5	2.0881 519 961	2.1390 490 129	2.1911 231 430	2.2444 001 461	20
6	2.4194 381 770	2.4903 757 744	2.5633 041 649	2.6382 767 240	24
7	2.8032 830 479	2.8994 059 792	2.9987 033 192	3.1012 758 954	28
8	3.2480 250 670	3.3756 170 931	3.5080 587 468	3.6455 281 933	32
9	3.7633 255 919	3.9300 432 022	4.1039 325 540	4.2852 929 751	36
10	4.3603 787 590	4.5755 306 794	4.8010 206 279	5.0373 320 157	40
11	5.0521 546 588	5.3270 358 419	5.6165 150 783	5.9213 486 648	44
12	5.8536 810 923	6.2019 714 977	6.5705 282 418	6.9605 040 726	48
13	6.7823 700 270	7.2206 104 107	7.6865 887 073	8.1820 240 096	52
14	7.8583 958 468	8.4065 550 322	8.9922 215 965	9.6179 121 792	56
15	9.1051 336 094	9.7872 843 831	10.5196 274 081	11.3057 887 118	60
16	10.5496 668 355	11.3947 907 590	12.3064 761 713	13.2898 758 083	64
17	12.2233 758 575	13.2663 210 099	14.3968 364 925	15.6221 563 573	68
18	14.1626 195 105	15.4452 395 713	16.8422 624 076	18.3637 358 823	72
19	16.4095 249 739	17.9820 332 432	19.7030 648 473	21.5864 435 000	76
20	19.0129 029 216	20.9354 809 983	23.0497 990 699	25.3747 138 364	80
21	22.0293 078 612	24.3740 159 248	26.9650 047 482	29.8277 992 054	84
22	25.5242 666 964	28.3773 108 605	31.5452 416 251	35.0623 700 103	88
23	29.5737 022 013	33.0381 244 583	36.9034 709 424	41.2155 714 967	92
24	34.2655 823 298	38.4644 504 580	43.1718 413 757	48.4486 169 447	96
25	39.7018 311 880	44.7820 199 631	50.5049 481 843	56.9510 114 409	100
26	46.0005 431 838	52.1372 147 033	59.0836 459 557	66.9455 168 936	104
27	53.2985 484 519	60.7004 587 837	69.1195 089 773	78.6939 883 728	108
28	61.7543 852 848	70.6701 675 093	80.8600 492 401	92.5042 346 877	112
29	71.5517 441 407	82.2773 447 823	94.5948 207 656	108.7380 829 477	116
30	82.9034 580 454	95.7909 355 958	110.6625 608 043	127.8208 583 970	120
31	96.0561 260 725	111.5240 576 443	129.4595 440 284	150.2525 278 949	124
32	111.2954 703 409	129.8412 564 413	151.4493 557 553	176.6207 989 990	128
33	128.9525 429 025	151.1669 520 493	177.1743 252 368	207.6165 178 456	132
34	149.4109 173 543	175.9952 731 373	207.2689 009 905	244.0517 692 516	136
35	173.1150 214 039	204.9015 062 271	242.4752 980 455	286.8811 532 574	140
36	200.5797 913 991	238.5554 254 141	283.6618 030 071	337.2267 955 553	144
37	232.4018 585 531	277.7368 114 192	331.8441 883 929	396.4077 470 730	148
38	269.2725 098 683	323.3535 195 580	388.2107 643 777	465.9745 429 800	152
39	311.9927 053 176	376.4625 152 721	454.1516 857 914	547.7498 265 579	156
40	361.4904 775 054	438.2943 646 284	531.2932 371 615	643.8761 022 768	160
41	418.8410 917 943	510.2817 472 442	621.5379 413 635	756.8718 692 042	164
42	485.2904 048 428	594.0926 523 009	727.1114 810 689	889.6976 054 353	168
43	562.2819 289 856	691.6690 268 151	850.6175 902 027	1045.8333 323 309	172
44	651.4881 903 881	805.2717 716 714	995.1022 691 852	1229.3697 907 383	176
45	754.8470 621 863	937.5331 280 002	1164.1289 076 818	1445.1156 180 033	180
46	874.6038 618 931	1091.5176 677 229	1361.8661 675 950	1698.7233 338 010	184
47	1013.3601 275 773	1270.7933 014 511	1593.1907 937 354	1996.8374 356 005	188
48	1174.1301 324 014	1479.5139 490 340	1863.8078 877 645	2347.2684 838 523	192
49	1360.4063 652 168	1722.5157 882 770	2180.3916 116 968	2759.1977 379 116	196
50	1576.2353 996 802	2005.4293 119 716	2550.7497 910 957	3243.4177 041 401	200
51	1826.3058 000 387	2334.8097 896 609	2984.0164 775 316	3812.6148 985 218	204
52	2116.0499 732 031	2718.2891 570 171	3490.8772 194 213	4481.7022 321 472	208
53	2451.7621 796 952	3164.7528 521 926	4083.8325 970 491	5268.2097 280 322	212
54	2840.7352 670 809	3684.5456 965 484	4777.5065 212 649	6192.7438 060 150	216
55	3291.4190 962 194	4289.7115 901 317	5589.0068 993 575	7279.5271 689 501	220
56	3813.6041 019 021	4994.2725 757 882	6538.3475 631 125	8557.0334 351 651	224
57	4418.6339 754 636	5814.5537 379 833	7648.9418 649 623	10058.7331 444 900	228
58	5119.6520 895 766	6769.5614 644 240	8948.1801 156 685	11823.9706 831 424	232
59	5931.8870 184 435	7881.4238 350 364	10468.1051 047 365	13898.9951 028 171	236
60	6872.9833 558 844	9175.9033 423 218	12246.2023 637 557	16338.1718 413 390	240

80

Table 1.   FUTURE WORTH OF ONE DOLLAR WITH INTEREST
PAYABLE AT BEGINNING OF EACH PERIOD

QUARTERS	17% NOMINAL ANNUAL RATE	17½% NOMINAL ANNUAL RATE	18% NOMINAL ANNUAL RATE	18½% NOMINAL ANNUAL RATE	QUARTERS
1	1.0425 000 000	1.0437 500 000	1.0450 000 000	1.0462 500 000	1
2	1.0868 062 500	1.0894 140 625	1.0920 250 000	1.0946 390 625	2
3	1.1329 955 156	1.1370 759 277	1.1411 661 250	1.1452 661 191	3
YEARS					
1	1.1811 478 250	1.1868 229 996	1.1925 186 006	1.1982 346 772	4
2	1.3951 101 846	1.4085 488 323	1.4221 006 128	1.4357 663 415	8
3	1.6478 313 602	1.6716 981 502	1.6958 814 328	1.7203 850 187	12
4	1.9463 324 272	1.9840 098 130	2.0223 701 530	2.0614 249 875	16
5	2.2989 063 131	2.3546 684 775	2.4117 140 248	2.4700 709 043	20
6	2.7153 481 917	2.7945 747 054	2.8760 138 340	2.9597 246 126	24
7	3.2072 276 109	3.3166 655 344	3.4296 999 927	3.5464 446 656	28
8	3.7882 099 170	3.9362 949 381	4.0899 810 359	4.2494 729 789	32
9	4.4744 359 043	4.6716 853 657	4.8773 784 615	5.0918 658 830	36
10	5.2849 702 366	5.5444 636 388	5.8163 645 376	6.1012 502 724	40
11	6.2423 311 004	6.5802 969 668	6.9361 228 991	7.3107 296 503	44
12	7.3731 158 024	7.8096 477 842	8.2714 555 734	8.7599 697 823	48
13	8.7087 396 937	9.2686 696 088	9.8638 646 255	10.4964 995 640	52
14	10.2863 089 481	11.0002 702 672	11.7628 420 400	12.5772 697 662	56
15	12.1496 514 417	13.0553 737 547	14.0274 079 289	15.0705 207 778	60
16	14.3505 343 753	15.4944 178 400	16.7279 448 738	18.0580 205 987	64
17	16.9501 024 656	18.3891 314 576	19.9483 854 122	21.6377 464 820	68
18	20.0205 766 614	21.8246 441 560	23.7888 206 565	25.9270 981 702	72
19	23.6472 605 797	25.9019 896 418	28.3686 111 198	31.0667 481 054	76
20	27.9309 104 018	30.7410 770 416	33.8300 964 342	37.2252 548 862	80
21	32.9905 340 725	36.4842 172 646	40.3430 192 587	44.6045 912 704	84
22	38.9666 975 666	43.3003 081 711	48.1098 008 714	53.4467 680 203	88
23	46.0254 300 797	51.3898 016 260	57.3718 324 115	64.0417 708 236	92
24	54.3628 366 351	60.9905 985 132	68.4169 773 027	76.7370 705 870	96
25	64.2105 462 545	72.3850 450 732	81.5885 180 320	91.9490 190 003	100
26	75.8421 470 531	85.9082 363 180	97.2958 253 506	110.1765 030 962	104
27	89.5807 870 381	101.9578 707 149	116.0270 814 938	132.0173 066 170	108
28	105.8081 517 753	121.0059 459 519	138.3644 528 575	158.1877 147 726	112
29	124.9750 683 408	143.6126 397 408	165.0021 836 979	189.5460 053 398	116
30	147.6140 301 548	170.4427 838 737	196.7681 732 035	227.1205 965 135	120
31	174.3539 906 626	202.2854 160 126	234.6497 065 562	272.1437 746 377	124
32	205.9378 368 580	240.0769 842 019	279.8241 396 994	326.0921 079 416	128
33	243.2430 280 981	284.9288 865 188	333.6954 914 955	390.7348 716 809	132
34	287.3059 735 940	338.1601 557 632	397.9380 805 531	468.1920 728 201	136
35	339.3508 258 313	401.3362 503 989	474.5485 629 565	561.0039 772 202	140
36	400.8234 898 558	476.3150 925 357	565.9079 882 255	672.2144 195 249	144
37	473.4317 932 678	565.3017 068 649	674.8558 022 012	805.4706 279 555	148
38	559.1929 329 226	670.9130 674 051	804.7780 968 647	965.1428 378 428	152
39	660.4895 164 987	796.2550 591 102	959.7128 498 867	1156.4676 167 071	156
40	780.1357 558 735	945.0138 176 782	1144.4754 247 487	1385.7196 013 404	160
41	921.4556 512 852	1121.5641 337 345	1364.8082 319 710	1660.4172 791 338	164
42	1088.3753 383 855	1331.0981 094 120	1627.5592 029 116	1989.5695 623 986	168
43	1285.5321 637 602	1579.7778 509 380	1940.8946 230 905	2383.9712 422 700	172
44	1518.4035 192 431	1874.9166 877 088	2314.5529 398 884	2856.5570 118 183	176
45	1793.4590 142 857	2225.1942 472 556	2760.1474 329 482	3422.8256 688 192	180
46	2118.3402 140 202	2640.9117 111 599	3291.5271 542 581	4101.3484 102 213	184
47	2502.0729 364 828	3134.2947 586 456	3925.2073 559 150	4914.3778 882 048	188
48	2955.3180 070 157	3719.8531 070 010	4680.8827 832 388	5888.5780 022 705	192
49	3490.6674 362 854	4414.8072 224 209	5582.0397 863 575	7055.8983 614 284	196
50	4122.9942 503 032	5239.5947 502 490	6656.6862 746 602	8454.6220 951 156	200
51	4869.8656 913 942	6218.4715 580 362	7938.2222 010 574	10130.6213 765 735	204
52	5752.0312 696 226	7380.2250 672 664	9466.4776 306 553	12138.8618 344 963	208
53	6793.9992 236 714	8759.0208 518 551	11288.9506 569 569	14545.2051 912 368	212
54	8024.7174 063 565	10395.4074 007 190	13462.2836 399 589	17428.5692 464 149	216
55	9478.3775 110 711	12337.5085 931 021	16054.0236 475 406	20883.5160 441 798	220
56	11195.3649 821 008	14642.4389 557 201	19144.7218 145 658	25023.3531 049 729	224
57	13223.3809 991 269	17377.9833 224 887	22830.4368 676 609	29983.8494 289 697	228
58	15618.7677 067 816	20624.5902 933 213	27225.7206 250 804	35927.6881 402 620	232
59	18448.0735 066 554	24477.7381 168 787	32467.1782 608 281	43049.8017 995 244	236
60	21789.9018 985 468	29050.7425 746 303	38717.7139 858 451	51583.7653 606 624	240

Table 1.   FUTURE WORTH OF ONE DOLLAR WITH INTEREST
PAYABLE AT BEGINNING OF EACH PERIOD

QUARTERS	19% NOMINAL ANNUAL RATE	19½% NOMINAL ANNUAL RATE	20% NOMINAL ANNUAL RATE	20½% NOMINAL ANNUAL RATE	QUARTERS
1	1.0475 000 000	1.0487 500 000	1.0500 000 000	1.0512 500 000	1
2	1.0972 562 500	1.0998 765 625	1.1025 000 000	1.1051 265 625	2
3	1.1493 759 219	1.1534 955 449	1.1576 250 000	1.1617 642 988	3
YEARS					
1	1.2039 712 782	1.2097 284 527	1.2155 062 500	1.2213 047 191	4
2	1.4495 468 386	1.4634 429 294	1.4774 554 438	1.4915 852 170	8
3	1.7452 127 601	1.7703 685 506	1.7958 563 260	1.8216 800 645	12
4	2.1011 860 374	2.1416 652 075	2.1828 745 884	2.2248 264 596	16
5	2.5297 676 391	2.5908 333 377	2.6532 977 051	2.7171 910 544	20
6	3.0457 675 779	3.1342 048 050	3.2250 999 437	3.3185 182 575	24
7	3.6670 166 838	3.7915 367 293	3.9201 291 385	4.0529 220 084	28
8	4.4149 827 639	4.5867 298 610	4.7649 414 686	4.9498 527 752	32
9	5.3155 124 413	5.5486 976 179	5.7918 161 360	6.0452 785 535	36
10	6.3997 243 080	6.7124 173 840	7.0399 887 121	7.3831 272 259	40
11	7.7050 842 550	8.1202 022 960	8.5571 502 795	9.0170 481 230	44
12	9.2767 001 389	9.8232 397 595	10.4012 696 469	11.0125 634 253	48
13	1.1688 805 234	11.8834 526 351	12.6428 082 638	13.4496 956 812	52
14	3.4470 113 594	14.3757 507 695	15.3674 124 622	16.4261 768 065	56
15	6.1898 154 538	17.3907 547 353	18.6791 858 941	20.0613 672 513	60
16	19.4920 728 052	21.0380 908 178	22.7046 671 992	24.5010 424 965	64
17	23.4678 958 093	25.4503 770 536	27.5976 648 848	29.9232 388 249	68
18	28.2546 725 134	30.7880 452 546	33.5451 341 529	36.5453 927 888	72
19	34.0178 141 800	37.2451 743 486	40.7743 202 199	44.6330 606 759	76
20	40.9564 712 187	45.0565 471 367	49.5614 410 668	54.5105 676 333	80
21	49.3104 150 023	54.5061 870 533	60.2422 413 758	66.5740 134 937	84
22	59.3683 233 771	65.9376 853 286	73.2248 209 062	81.3071 568 522	88
23	71.4777 561 787	79.7666 940 496	89.0052 274 667	99.3008 143 637	92
24	86.0571 654 668	96.4960 393 725	108.1864 102 684	121.2765 531 971	96
25	103.6103 555 023	116.7340 044 053	131.5012 578 463	148.1156 267 411	100
26	124.7438 921 451	141.2164 465 310	159.8406 007 950	180.8943 139 177	104
27	150.1880 632 691	170.8335 533 630	194.2872 492 701	220.9270 792 539	108
28	180.8221 144 991	206.6622 101 853	236.1573 657 832	269.8192 844 792	112
29	217.7046 323 138	250.0051 557 667	287.0507 540 930	329.5315 654 503	116
30	262.1101 244 290	302.4383 502 619	348.9119 856 672	402.4584 559 910	120
31	315.5730 615 286	365.8682 775 106	424.1046 992 784	491.5244 115 609	124
32	379.9409 022 427	442.6012 652 583	515.5019 126 273	600.3010 834 133	128
33	457.4379 337 000	535.4273 438 003	626.5957 966 854	733.1505 460 794	132
34	550.7421 337 175	647.7216 921 685	761.6311 017 904	895.4002 217 691	136
35	663.0777 106 706	783.5673 604 711	925.7673 708 682	1093.5565 163 683	140
36	798.3265 188 382	947.9037 305 978	1125.2760 253 363	1335.5657 340 903	144
37	961.1621 992 779	1146.7061 133 595	1367.7800 417 715	1631.1327 337 702	148
38	1157.2116 815 876	1387.2030 122 583	1662.5451 893 985	1992.1101 053 023	152
39	1393.2496 273 874	1678.1389 536 511	2020.8340 686 213	2432.9734 726 583	156
40	1677.4325 346 872	2030.0924 398 777	2456.3364 406 221	2971.4019 837 075	160
41	2019.5805 928 213	2455.8605 862 059	2985.6922 956 789	3628.9872 651 730	164
42	2431.5170 276 944	2970.9204 270 882	3629.1276 459 746	4432.0992 726 659	168
43	2927.4766 637 109	3594.0118 103 795	4411.2273 357 299	5412.9437 574 175	172
44	3524.5978 206 035	4347.7783 464 882	5361.8743 967 505	6610.8537 553 899	176
45	4243.5145 430 863	5259.6311 719 398	6517.3918 409 652	8073.8668 890 224	180
46	5109.0696 283 474	6362.7254 795 971	7921.9305 163 922	9860.6517 332 960	184
47	6151.1730 906 706	7697.1700 496 221	9629.1560 547 405	12042.8604 957 007	188
48	7405.8357 281 831	9311.4856 145 815	11704.2993 667 624	14708.0023 553 808	192
49	8916.4135 075 337	11264.3690 852 088	14226.6490 321 707	17962.9526 857 939	196
50	10735.1057 673 046	13626.8277 845 061	17292.5808 151 600	21938.2388 849 038	200
51	12924.7590 118 882	16484.7612 914 616	21019.2400 594 571	26793.2746 798 209	204
52	15561.0386 275 055	19942.0847 708 556	25549.0176 625 204	32722.7528 077 617	208
53	18735.0435 659 181	24124.5073 541 936	31054.9906 501 540	39964.4524 274 713	212
54	22556.4543 485 178	29184.1029 546 265	37747.5352 289 537	48808.7743 476 393	216
55	27157.3231 728 343	35304.8397 118 123	45882.3649 928 884	59610.3864 463 610	220
56	32696.6370 919 119	42709.2691 186 920	55770.3014 136 371	72802.4462 768 825	224
57	39365.8119 512 156	51666.6180 484 756	67789.1499 326 597	88913.9712 031 162	228
58	47395.3069 308 712	62502.5779 099 264	82398.1354 253 349	108591.0526 281 165	232
59	57062.5882 645 390	75611.1468 670 376	100155.4485 978 410	132622.7650 314 318	236
60	68701.7173 282 067	91468.9557 091 176	121739.5737 422 295	161972.8087 986 897	240

82

Table 1.　FUTURE WORTH OF ONE DOLLAR WITH INTEREST
PAYABLE AT BEGINNING OF EACH PERIOD

QUARTERS	21% NOMINAL ANNUAL RATE	21½% NOMINAL ANNUAL RATE	22% NOMINAL ANNUAL RATE	22½% NOMINAL ANNUAL RATE	QUARTERS
1	1.0525 000 000	1.0537 500 000	1.0550 000 000	1.0562 500 000	1
2	1.1077 562 500	1.1103 890 625	1.1130 250 000	1.1156 640 625	2
3	1.1659 134 531	1.1700 724 746	1.1742 413 750	1.1784 201 660	3
YEARS					
1	1.2271 239 094	1.2329 638 701	1.2388 246 506	1.2447 063 004	4
2	1.5058 330 891	1.5201 999 050	1.5346 865 150	1.5492 937 741	8
3	1.8478 437 872	1.8743 515 582	1.9012 074 858	1.9284 157 218	12
4	2.2675 332 921	2.3110 077 512	2.3552 626 993	2.4003 111 986	16
5	2.7825 443 181	2.8493 890 608	2.9177 574 906	2.9876 824 717	20
6	3.4145 266 618	3.5131 937 639	3.6145 899 039	3.7187 871 960	24
7	4.1900 473 060	4.3316 409 796	4.4778 430 749	4.6287 978 525	28
8	5.1417 072 308	5.3407 568 262	5.5472 623 828	5.7614 938 501	32
9	6.3095 118 781	6.5849 602 058	6.8720 853 833	7.1713 676 947	36
10	7.7425 528 823	8.1190 180 200	8.5133 087 740	8.9262 465 517	40
11	9.5010 717 618	10.0104 558 795	10.5464 967 676	11.1105 553 214	44
12	11.6589 923 240	12.3425 304 228	13.0652 601 734	13.8293 782 090	48
13	14.3070 282 404	15.2178 940 772	16.1855 663 697	17.2135 141 867	52
14	17.5564 964 265	18.7631 135 764	20.0510 786 031	21.4257 695 594	56
15	21.5439 965 304	23.1342 411 307	24.8397 704 451	26.6687 903 605	60
16	26.4371 532 468	28.5236 834 768	30.7721 199 432	33.1948 113 846	64
17	32.4416 628 460	35.1686 711 696	38.1212 607 377	41.3177 908 694	68
18	39.8099 401 395	43.3617 009 122	47.2255 575 147	51.4285 146 119	72
19	48.8517 293 775	53.4634 105 717	58.5041 847 888	64.0133 961 553	76
20	59.9471 251 354	65.9184 536 083	72.4764 262 841	79.6778 775 015	80
21	73.5625 505 543	81.2750 716 732	89.7855 834 662	99.1755 561 250	84
22	90.2703 646 227	100.2092 269 144	111.2285 940 687	123.4444 395 499	88
23	110.7729 227 400	123.5543 562 381	137.7927 241 866	153.6520 716 514	92
24	135.9321 020 099	152.3380 572 375	170.7010 233 992	191.2517 016 470	96
25	166.8055 324 333	187.8273 206 181	211.4686 356 738	238.0521 979 934	100
26	204.6910 570 714	231.5843 001 434	261.9725 587 067	296.3050 706 555	104
27	251.1812 901 756	285.5350 749 638	324.5380 635 132	368.8127 882 718	108
28	308.2305 667 720	352.0544 310 823	402.0457 531 462	459.0636 012 130	112
29	378.2370 980 981	434.0703 938 399	498.0661 896 767	571.3993 566 931	116
30	464.1437 865 036	535.1931 126 933	617.0141 957 650	711.2243 792 941	120
31	569.5619 378 245	659.8737 714 876	764.3723 954 993	885.2654 658 727	124
32	698.9230 717 967	813.6005 190 838	946.9233 658 018	1101.8955 028 576	128
33	857.6652 122 428	1003.1400 447 410	1173.0720 078 080	1371.5362 747 386	132
34	1052.4614 882 159	1236.8354 318 358	1453.2305 202 307	1707.1598 423 312	136
35	1291.5006 559 272	1524.9734 007 373	1800.2977 915 024	2124.9126 114 609	140
36	1584.8313 339 122	1880.2371 060 026	2230.2532 825 789	2644.8921 151 871	144
37	1944.7844 222 323	2318.2644 189 595	2762.8927 435 961	3292.1138 795 300	148
38	2386.4914 631 772	2858.3362 699 609	3422.7396 377 998	4097.7148 873 339	152
39	2928.5207 340 774	3524.2253 495 143	4240.1742 359 777	5100.4515 373 189	156
40	3593.6578 120 011	4345.2425 261 109	5252.8323 664 742	6348.5641 631 511	160
41	4409.8634 233 592	5357.5270 416 021	6507.3382 211 890	7902.0978 120 758	164
42	5411.4488 440 547	6605.6372 754 843	8061.4509 983 632	9835.7909 327 043	168
43	6640.5182 611 106	8144.5120 997 875	9986.7242 165 779	12242.6709 429 018	172
44	8148.7387 291 095	10041.8891 587 902	12371.8001 384 903	15238.5296 557 908	176
45	9999.5121 260 586	12381.2865 205 343	15326.4909 841 676	18967.4938 706 941	180
46	12270.6404 123 623	15265.6789 454 180	18986.8348 387 686	23608.9591 227 789	184
47	15057.5962 338 322	18822.0305 925 463	23521.3590 356 121	29386.2201 649 231	188
48	18477.5363 568 387	23206.8836 828 959	29138.8393 895 173	36577.2133 828 696	192
49	22674.2266 505 444	28613.2491 190 794	36097.9125 263 368	45527.8879 470 506	196
50	27824.0856 503 565	35279.1023 705 572	44718.9838 737 310	56668.8489 695 050	200
51	34143.6007 591 372	43497.8585 931 488	55398.9795 736 798	70536.0733 461 524	204
52	41898.4288 450 254	53631.2880 729 251	68629.6215 153 454	87796.6948 961 880	208
53	51414.5638 026 145	66125.4405 018 944	85020.0668 962 738	109281.0992 875 434	212
54	63092.0405 342 831	81530.2790 345 810	105324.9546 688 905	136022.8727 928 167	216
55	77421.7514 333 399	100523.8883 704 102	130479.1501 697 822	169308.5267 574 702	220
56	95006.0822 925 639	123942.3224 446 545	161640.7876 229 274	210739.3899 586 776	224
57	116584.2351 209 651	152816.4055 529 762	200244.5922 537 229	262308.6464 143 253	228
58	143063.3023 776 870	188417.1068 083 683	248067.9370 382 638	326497.2248 292 413	232
59	175556.3989 073 934	232311.4852 071 893	307312.6754 326 916	406393.1527 930 544	236
60	215429.4545 498 952	286431.6678 742 950	380706.5177 755 382	505840.1177 022 422	240

83

Table 2. FUTURE WORTH OF ONE DOLLAR PER PERIOD WITH INTEREST PAYABLE AT END OF EACH PERIOD

QUARTERS	5% NOMINAL ANNUAL RATE	5½% NOMINAL ANNUAL RATE	6% NOMINAL ANNUAL RATE	6½% NOMINAL ANNUAL RATE	QUARTERS
1	1.0000 000 000	1.0000 000 000	1.0000 000 000	1.0000 000 000	1
2	2.0125 000 000	2.0137 500 000	2.0150 000 000	2.0162 500 000	2
3	3.0376 562 500	3.0414 390 625	3.0452 250 000	3.0490 140 625	3
YEARS					
1	4.0756 269 531	4.0832 588 496	4.0909 033 750	4.0985 605 410	4
2	8.3588 880 945	8.3957 714 882	8.4328 391 064	8.4700 918 078	8
3	12.8603 614 178	12.9504 093 259	13.0412 114 308	13.1327 740 898	12
4	17.5911 638 162	17.7607 664 360	17.9323 698 436	18.1059 985 131	16
5	22.5629 785 367	22.8412 001 280	23.1236 671 033	23.4104 476 839	20
6	27.7880 840 331	28.2068 738 003	28.6335 207 953	29.0681 817 032	24
7	33.2793 842 895	33.8738 021 971	34.4814 786 732	35.1027 299 103	28
8	39.0504 406 876	39.8588 992 073	40.6882 880 103	41.5391 887 363	32
9	45.1155 054 982	46.1800 283 471	47.2759 692 065	48.4043 260 750	36
10	51.4895 570 790	52.8560 560 763	54.2678 939 113	55.7266 926 051	40
11	58.1883 368 650	59.9069 081 085	61.6888 679 416	63.5367 405 262	44
12	65.2283 882 442	67.3536 288 825	69.5652 192 875	71.8669 502 037	48
13	72.6270 974 128	75.2184 443 735	77.9248 915 180	80.7519 652 472	52
14	80.4027 363 127	83.5248 284 294	86.7975 429 186	90.2287 365 867	56
15	88.5745 077 561	92.2975 728 331	96.2146 517 126	100.3366 761 437	60
16	97.1625 928 489	101.5628 612 974	106.2096 277 389	111.1178 207 366	64
17	106.1882 008 301	111.3483 476 146	116.8179 309 825	122.6170 069 041	68
18	115.6736 214 508	121.6832 381 938	128.0771 973 793	134.8820 573 702	72
19	125.6422 800 208	132.5983 792 324	140.0273 723 395	147.9639 799 291	76
20	136.1187 952 603	144.1263 487 819	152.7108 524 660	161.9171 795 766	80
21	147.1290 400 983	156.3015 539 820	166.1726 359 673	176.7996 847 684	84
22	158.7002 055 690	169.1603 337 548	180.4604 823 019	192.6733 887 488	88
23	170.8608 679 632	182.7410 672 642	195.6250 816 185	209.6043 069 518	92
24	183.6410 594 001	197.0842 884 651	211.7202 345 929	227.6628 515 455	96
25	197.0723 419 957	212.2328 070 834	228.8030 433 017	246.9241 242 615	100
26	211.1878 858 082	228.2318 363 889	246.9341 138 075	267.4682 287 277	104
27	226.0225 507 560	245.1291 281 419	266.1777 711 761	289.3806 036 026	108
28	241.6129 727 076	262.9751 151 160	286.6022 876 880	312.7523 778 966	112
29	257.9976 539 581	281.8230 616 234	308.2801 250 527	337.6807 499 589	116
30	275.2170 385 151	301.7292 224 910	331.2881 914 881	364.2693 917 052	120
31	293.3137 110 286	322.7530 109 620	355.7081 145 729	392.6288 797 672	124
32	312.3323 038 116	344.9571 760 251	381.6265 308 443	422.8771 553 588	128
33	332.3198 052 116	368.4079 896 986	409.1353 931 646	455.1400 147 678	132
34	353.3255 766 044	393.1754 448 310	438.3322 969 505	489.5516 325 178	136
35	375.4014 940 980	419.3334 640 058	469.3208 264 200	526.2551 193 710	140
36	398.6020 766 460	446.9601 201 757	502.2109 220 864	565.4031 174 969	144
37	422.9846 206 885	476.1378 696 846	537.1192 708 033	607.1584 352 789	148
38	448.6093 416 521	506.9537 983 720	574.1697 197 439	651.6947 244 008	152
39	475.5395 226 585	539.4998 814 954	613.4937 157 837	699.1972 020 279	156
40	503.8416 708 094	573.8732 582 453	655.2307 718 453	749.8634 210 865	160
41	533.5856 814 332	610.1765 216 738	699.5289 618 595	803.9040 918 457	164
42	564.8450 106 995	648.5180 249 002	746.5454 460 992	861.5439 582 178	168
43	597.6968 570 269	689.0122 045 090	796.4470 287 498	923.0227 324 207	172
44	632.2223 517 338	731.7799 221 049	849.4107 496 936	988.5960 918 920	176
45	668.5067 594 006	776.9488 250 445	905.6245 126 089	1058.5367 425 981	180
46	706.6396 884 407	824.6537 274 205	965.2877 516 106	1133.1355 531 610	184
47	746.7153 123 983	875.0370 124 374	1028.6121 387 992	1212.7027 645 214	188
48	788.8326 025 204	928.2490 573 776	1095.8223 352 269	1297.5692 801 655	192
49	833.0955 721 777	984.4486 834 954	1167.1567 879 456	1388.0880 422 839	196
50	879.6135 337 370	1043.8036 247 013	1242.8685 759 650	1484.6354 995 853	200
51	928.5013 685 206	1106.4910 388 834	1323.2263 081 215	1587.6131 728 677	204
52	979.8798 105 182	1172.6980 259 728	1408.5150 760 432	1697.4493 248 603	208
53	1033.8757 445 534	1242.6221 917 189	1499.0374 655 931	1814.6007 412 790	212
54	1090.6225 196 401	1316.4722 364 081	1595.1146 303 768	1939.5546 305 035	216
55	1150.2602 783 023	1394.4685 777 644	1697.0874 311 256	2072.8306 497 751	220
56	1212.9363 026 724	1476.8440 088 230	1805.3176 449 955	2214.9830 663 434	224
57	1278.8053 782 205	1563.8443 927 398	1920.1892 490 734	2366.6030 625 489	228
58	1348.0301 760 146	1655.7293 966 103	2042.1097 826 435	2528.3211 944 265	232
59	1420.7816 544 551	1752.7732 664 899	2171.5117 930 475	2700.8100 140 580	236
60	1497.2394 814 758	1855.2656 459 261	2308.8543 702 680	2884.7868 665 755	240

Table 2.   FUTURE WORTH OF ONE DOLLAR PER PERIOD WITH INTEREST
PAYABLE AT END OF EACH PERIOD

QUARTERS	7% NOMINAL ANNUAL RATE	7½% NOMINAL ANNUAL RATE	8% NOMINAL ANNUAL RATE	8½% NOMINAL ANNUAL RATE	QUARTERS
1	1.0000 000 000	1.0000 000 000	1.0000 000 000	1.0000 000 000	1
2	2.0175 000 000	2.0187 500 000	2.0200 000 000	2.0212 500 000	2
3	3.0528 062 500	3.0566 015 625	3.0604 000 000	3.0642 015 625	3
YEARS					
1	4.1062 303 594	4.1139 128 418	4.1216 080 000	4.1293 158 457	4
2	8.5075 304 546	8.5451 559 124	8.5829 690 501	8.6209 707 402	8
3	13.2251 037 111	13.3182 067 538	13.4120 897 281	13.5067 591 964	12
4	18.2816 772 119	18.4594 310 042	18.6392 852 545	18.8212 656 310	16
5	23.7016 111 860	23.9972 280 384	24.2973 697 989	24.6021 091 729	20
6	29.5110 163 652	29.9621 878 413	30.4218 624 738	30.8902 099 525	24
7	35.7378 797 730	36.3872 599 830	37.0512 103 087	37.7300 787 587	28
8	42.4121 995 532	43.3079 356 271	44.2270 296 051	45.1701 321 111	32
9	49.5661 294 873	50.7624 435 788	51.9943 671 858	53.2630 349 802	36
10	57.2341 338 963	58.7919 614 554	60.4019 831 807	62.0660 735 805	40
11	65.4531 536 742	67.4408 431 451	69.5026 571 226	71.6415 608 749	44
12	74.2627 842 514	76.7568 638 121	79.3535 192 750	82.0572 776 619	48
13	83.7054 663 479	86.7914 837 989	90.0164 092 724	93.3869 523 668	52
14	93.8266 904 326	97.6001 328 862	101.5582 643 242	105.7107 829 341	56
15	104.6752 158 756	109.2425 164 788	114.0515 394 183	119.1160 045 142	60
16	116.3033 058 477	121.7829 454 095	127.5746 621 638	133.6975 069 644	64
17	128.7669 791 010	135.2906 911 832	142.2125 251 273	149.5585 065 334	68
18	142.1262 798 406	149.8403 686 219	158.0570 187 526	166.8112 764 855	72
19	156.4455 669 901	165.5123 480 267	175.2076 082 115	185.5779 418 349	76
20	171.7938 242 428	182.3931 991 314	193.7719 578 048	205.9913 438 171	80
21	188.2449 923 937	200.5761 693 012	213.8666 068 341	228.1959 802 149	84
22	205.8783 255 515	220.1616 986 177	235.6117 011 873	252.3490 281 975	88
23	224.7787 729 485	241.2579 746 947	259.1617 852 304	278.6214 569 098	92
24	245.0373 881 863	263.9815 302 918	284.6466 589 764	307.1992 376 912	96
25	266.7517 678 903	288.4578 870 236	312.2323 059 126	338.2846 604 866	100
26	290.0265 218 849	314.8222 487 231	342.0918 973 108	372.0977 657 715	104
27	314.9737 771 551	343.2202 482 881	374.4128 793 246	408.8779 021 247	108
28	341.7137 180 223	373.8087 521 361	409.3981 496 691	448.8854 204 747	112
29	370.3751 651 369	406.7567 267 114	447.2673 314 788	492.4035 170 134	116
30	401.0961 960 765	442.2461 718 315	488.2581 517 101	539.7402 378 213	120
31	434.0248 105 397	480.4731 260 270	532.6279 337 932	591.2306 593 948	124
32	469.3196 433 399	521.6487 494 307	580.6552 128 521	647.2392 605 094	128
33	507.1507 286 346	566.0004 901 948	632.6414 842 627	708.1625 022 108	132
34	547.7003 190 712	613.7733 408 818	688.9130 963 161	774.4316 341 929	136
35	591.1637 637 957	665.2311 917 674	749.8232 988 977	846.5157 474 314	140
36	637.7504 495 547	720.6582 885 325	815.7544 610 442	924.9250 946 791	144
37	687.6848 094 232	780.3608 023 945	887.1204 712 977	1010.2147 023 277	148
38	741.2074 040 199	844.6685 213 526	964.3693 359 270	1102.9882 992 034	152
39	798.5760 804 165	913.9366 718 892	1047.9859 913 252	1203.9025 901 065	156
40	860.0672 143 252	988.5478 811 886	1138.4953 482 399	1313.6719 043 449	160
41	925.9770 415 494	1068.9142 907 145	1236.4655 869 453	1433.0732 521 673	164
42	996.6230 851 105	1155.4798 328 191	1342.5117 240 428	1562.9518 248 879	168
43	1072.3456 849 262	1248.7226 829 610	1457.2994 732 810	1704.2269 776 359	172
44	1153.5096 374 114	1349.1579 010 768	1581.5494 246 304	1857.8987 370 794	176
45	1240.5059 528 977	1457.3402 766 970	1716.0415 678 495	2025.0548 801 882	180
46	1333.7537 393 407	1573.8673 935 233	1861.6201 889 371	2206.8786 341 440	184
47	1433.7022 213 872	1699.3829 303 932	2019.1991 702 108	2404.6570 519 019	188
48	1540.8329 045 325	1834.5802 168 689	2189.7677 272 814	2619.7901 226 904	192
49	1655.6618 947 898	1980.2060 630 808	2374.3966 189 395	2853.8006 819 395	196
50	1778.7423 850 510	2137.0648 850 368	2574.2448 689 354	3108.3451 907 840	200
51	1910.6673 201 130	2306.0231 480 218	2790.5670 418 507	3385.2254 614 469	204
52	2052.0722 532 113	2488.0141 529 035	3024.7211 187 353	3686.4014 115 012	208
53	2203.6384 078 216	2684.0431 915 116	3278.1770 219 502	4014.0049 372 923	212
54	2366.0959 594 784	2895.1930 997 315	3552.5258 427 319	4370.3550 047 241	216
55	2540.2275 534 229	3122.6302 389 320	3849.4898 294 042	4757.9740 642 324	220
56	2726.8720 750 250	3367.6109 387 762	4170.9331 989 400	5179.6059 061 368	224
57	2926.9286 911 449	3631.4884 370 031	4518.8738 397 443	5638.2350 827 650	228
58	3141.3611 819 021	3915.7203 545 166	4895.4959 791 219	6137.1080 348 283	232
59	3371.2025 837 220	4221.8767 470 709	5303.1638 949 523	6679.7560 715 929	236
60	3617.5601 660 269	4551.6487 780 300	5744.4367 576 472	7270.0203 675 157	240

85

Table 2.   FUTURE WORTH OF ONE DOLLAR PER PERIOD WITH INTEREST
PAYABLE AT END OF EACH PERIOD

QUARTERS	9% NOMINAL ANNUAL RATE	9½% NOMINAL ANNUAL RATE	10% NOMINAL ANNUAL RATE	10½% NOMINAL ANNUAL RATE	QUARTERS
1	1.0000 000 000	1.0000 000 000	1.0000 000 000	1.0000 000 000	1
2	2.0225 000 000	2.0237 500 000	2.0250 000 000	2.0262 500 000	2
3	3.0680 062 500	3.0718 140 625	3.0756 250 000	3.0794 390 625	3
YEARS					
1	4.1370 363 906	4.1447 696 465	4.1525 156 250	4.1602 743 379	4
2	8.6591 618 584	8.6975 432 843	8.7361 159 004	8.7748 805 932	8
3	13.6022 217 728	13.6984 841 241	13.7955 529 699	13.8934 350 830	12
4	19.0053 981 089	19.1917 089 741	19.3802 248 264	19.5709 725 837	16
5	24.9115 200 304	25.2256 774 250	25.5446 576 116	25.8685 380 655	20
6	31.3674 033 816	31.8536 193 465	32.3490 379 833	32.8538 430 491	24
7	38.4242 217 807	39.1340 044 646	39.8598 007 503	40.6019 936 406	28
8	46.1379 122 566	47.1310 581 651	48.1502 775 109	49.1962 980 740	32
9	54.5696 186 421	55.9153 280 697	57.3014 126 287	58.7291 624 423	36
10	63.7861 762 410	65.5643 063 869	67.4025 535 356	69.3030 842 493	40
11	73.8606 416 090	76.1631 135 247	78.5523 230 786	81.0317 544 643	44
12	84.8728 716 484	87.8052 489 978	90.8595 824 277	94.0412 799 293	48
13	96.9101 566 073	100.5934 162 519	104.4444 939 455	108.4715 392 615	52
14	110.0679 119 993	114.6404 286 834	119.4396 943 969	124.4776 868 304	56
15	124.4504 349 310	130.0702 048 453	135.9915 899 526	142.2318 209 800	60
16	140.1717 308 297	147.0188 616 194	154.2617 856 313	161.9248 344 329	64
17	157.3564 171 264	165.6359 149 995	174.4286 631 356	183.7684 667 714	68
18	176.1407 110 559	186.0855 990 764	196.6891 224 886	207.9975 810 654	72
19	196.6735 094 054	208.5483 148 620	221.2605 044 736	234.8726 891 231	76
20	219.1175 687 694	233.2222 217 335	248.3827 126 492	264.6827 525 183	80
21	243.6507 956 661	260.3249 855 363	278.3205 556 556	297.7482 895 095	84
22	270.4676 567 429	290.0956 987 661	311.3663 326 835	334.4248 212 573	88
23	299.7807 202 482	322.7969 897 753	347.8426 873 477	375.1066 943 932	92
24	331.8223 409 885	358.7173 395 952	388.1057 578 290	420.2313 210 408	96
25	366.8465 021 267	398.1736 268 362	432.5486 540 425	470.2838 818 775	100
26	405.1308 284 215	441.5139 230 930	481.6052 957 796	525.8025 428 044	104
27	446.9787 868 653	489.1205 635 293	535.7546 492 998	587.3842 413 150	108
28	492.7220 921 657	541.4135 197 240	595.5254 037 344	655.6911 047 756	112
29	542.7233 361 358	598.8541 045 357	661.5011 329 617	731.4575 696 289	116
30	597.3788 618 382	661.9460 416 671	734.3259 933 511	815.4982 780 666	120
31	657.1219 052 632	731.2549 358 298	814.7110 130 070	908.7168 370 739	124
32	722.4260 294 447	807.3831 829 457	903.4410 339 162	1012.1155 340 261	128
33	793.8088 782 356	891.0053 636 988	1001.3823 747 813	1126.8061 132 978	132
34	871.8362 794 966	982.8591 680 203	1109.4912 893 533	1254.0217 297 551	136
35	957.1267 302 235	1083.7549 027 683	1228.8233 028 493	1395.1302 076 562	140
36	1050.3562 991 651	1194.5826 400 138	1360.5435 176 105	1551.6487 475 185	144
37	1152.2639 857 930	1316.3200 689 907	1505.9379 886 197	1725.2602 390 816	148
38	1263.6575 781 023	1450.0411 209 787	1666.4262 799 453	1917.8313 557 638	152
39	1385.4200 556 757	1596.9254 432 044	1843.5753 247 049	2131.4326 251 636	156
40	1518.5165 887 655	1758.2688 053 373	2039.1147 238 725	2368.3606 914 036	160
41	1664.0021 888 747	1935.4945 303 835	2254.9536 332 987	2631.1630 086 835	164
42	1823.0300 714 780	2130.1660 508 161	2493.1994 038 218	2922.6652 315 470	168
43	1996.8607 971 741	2344.0007 007 107	2756.1781 564 620	3246.0015 963 624	172
44	2186.8722 637 255	2578.8848 655 538	3046.4574 935 868	3604.6486 206 804	176
45	2394.5706 281 914	2836.8906 233 727	3366.8715 677 873	4002.4624 828 037	180
46	2621.6022 457 289	3120.2940 239 903	3720.5487 532 274	4443.7204 834 755	184
47	2869.7667 196 968	3431.5951 676 569	4110.9421 896 362	4933.1670 354 827	188
48	3141.0311 665 072	3773.5402 601 891	4541.8634 971 596	5476.0646 756 545	192
49	3437.5458 082 962	4149.1458 391 783	5017.5199 912 489	6078.2506 477 397	196
50	3761.6610 170 125	4561.7253 849 851	5542.5557 609 342	6746.1996 645 404	200
51	4115.9459 450 261	5014.9185 512 745	6122.0970 115 520	7487.0935 241 235	204
52	4503.2088 899 361	5512.7232 729 552	6761.8021 146 329	8308.8983 286 236	208
53	4926.5195 550 024	6059.5310 347 680	7467.9168 536 121	9220.4501 358 953	212
54	5389.2333 816 519	6660.1656 116 544	8247.3354 047 578	10231.5499 649 425	216
55	5895.0181 469 354	7319.9256 226 598	9107.6676 487 046	11353.0691 766 253	220
56	6447.8830 367 646	8044.6312 737 702	10057.3134 697 934	12597.0663 626 982	224
57	7052.2104 253 809	8840.6757 020 328	11105.5447 686 394	13976.9169 999 738	228
58	7712.7906 129 649	9715.0813 739 040	12262.5959 886 622	15507.4572 636 545	232
59	8434.8597 967 354	10675.5620 353 530	13539.7640 404 368	17205.1435 461 152	236
60	9224.1415 765 266	11730.5907 602 277	14949.5185 994 799	19088.2293 962 871	240

86

Table 2. FUTURE WORTH OF ONE DOLLAR PER PERIOD WITH INTEREST
PAYABLE AT END OF EACH PERIOD

QUARTERS	11% NOMINAL ANNUAL RATE	11½% NOMINAL ANNUAL RATE	12% NOMINAL ANNUAL RATE	12½% NOMINAL ANNUAL RATE	QUARTERS
1	1.0000 000 000	1.0000 000 000	1.0000 000 000	1.0000 000 000	1
2	2.0275 000 000	2.0287 500 000	2.0300 000 000	2.0312 500 000	2
3	3.0832 562 500	3.0870 765 625	3.0909 000 000	3.0947 265 625	3
YEARS					
1	4.1680 457 969	4.1758 300 137	4.1836 270 000	4.1914 367 676	4
2	8.8138 382 523	8.8529 897 711	8.8923 360 463	8.9318 779 782	8
3	13.9921 372 899	14.0916 664 711	14.1920 295 615	14.2932 335 508	12
4	19.7639 794 848	19.9592 730 939	20.1568 813 033	20.3568 323 381	16
5	26.1973 975 013	26.5313 158 921	26.8703 744 890	27.2146 558 411	20
6	33.3682 219 932	33.8923 660 304	34.4264 702 153	34.9707 335 184	24
7	41.3609 754 193	42.1371 478 740	42.9309 225 246	43.7427 208 565	28
8	50.2698 683 093	51.3717 579 327	52.5027 585 228	53.6636 841 401	32
9	60.1999 097 224	61.7150 301 445	63.2759 442 668	64.8841 189 948	36
10	71.2681 449 883	73.3000 650 694	75.4012 597 333	77.5742 333 245	40
11	83.6050 353 198	86.2759 426 700	89.0484 091 149	91.9265 292 725	44
12	97.3559 955 584	100.8096 407 209	104.4083 959 753	108.1587 233 747	48
13	112.6831 081 777	117.0881 835 320	121.6961 965 082	126.5170 492 012	52
14	129.7670 337 485	135.3210 486 381	141.1537 083 135	147.2799 925 859	56
15	148.8091 403 841	155.7428 624 228	163.0534 368 015	170.7625 161 052	60
16	170.0338 772 641	178.6164 193 669	187.7017 066 209	197.3208 368 892	64
17	193.6914 202 161	204.2360 637 722	215.4435 514 539	227.3578 302 426	68
18	220.0606 205 358	232.9314 774 789	246.6672 422 190	261.3291 410 438	72
19	249.4522 918 060	265.0719 223 177	281.8097 812 559	299.7500 956 305	76
20	282.2128 734 534	301.0709 918 900	321.3630 185 477	343.2035 190 203	80
21	318.7285 142 283	341.3919 338 238	365.8805 355 836	392.3485 760 499	84
22	359.4296 237 372	386.5536 109 935	415.9853 932 069	447.9307 705 475	88
23	404.7959 456 776	437.1371 784 142	472.3788 518 856	510.7932 542 214	92
24	455.3622 125 737	493.7935 617 322	535.8501 864 550	581.8896 168 132	96
25	511.7244 486 654	557.2518 335 455	607.2877 326 952	662.2983 515 365	100
26	574.5469 952 412	628.3285 953 453	687.6913 203 534	753.2392 152 333	104
27	644.5703 412 252	707.9384 858 071	778.1862 666 183	856.0917 314 231	108
28	722.6198 513 143	797.1059 506 557	880.0391 258 999	972.4161 169 253	112
29	809.6154 945 464	896.9784 255 631	994.6754 163 450	1103.9769 495 012	116
30	906.5826 879 693	1008.8411 017 204	1123.6995 711 867	1252.7699 355 405	120
31	1014.6643 832 242	1134.1334 640 923	1268.9173 941 639	1421.0521 838 438	124
32	1135.1345 385 088	1274.4678 151 733	1432.3613 332 937	1611.3764 447 367	128
33	1269.4131 347 140	1431.6500 226 162	1616.3189 267 254	1826.6298 339 067	132
34	1419.0829 127 286	1607.7027 577 185	1823.3648 187 992	2070.0776 283 803	136
35	1585.9080 291 953	1804.8915 238 085	2056.3967 944 025	2345.4127 990 020	140
36	1771.8548 506 135	2025.7538 094 728	2318.6763 359 558	2656.8120 307 973	144
37	1979.1151 308 866	2273.1317 417 762	2613.8742 706 567	3008.9990 810 157	148
38	2210.1318 455 111	2550.2086 596 697	2946.1221 468 565	3407.3164 359 639	152
39	2467.6279 869 116	2860.5500 782 209	3320.0700 586 231	3857.8063 536 212	156
40	2754.6386 603 336	3208.1495 708 116	3740.9517 277 975	4367.3025 214 127	160
41	3074.5468 586 086	3597.4801 597 269	4214.6577 544 208	4943.5337 195 361	164
42	3431.1233 374 668	4033.5518 764 472	4747.8180 607 354	5595.2410 623 607	168
43	3828.5710 614 091	4521.9762 323 477	5347.8946 826 349	6332.3105 963 858	172
44	4271.5747 440 209	5069.0384 294 357	6023.2862 072 577	7165.9232 661 977	176
45	4765.3560 666 587	5681.7782 403 545	6783.4453 184 200	8108.7245 233 273	180
46	5315.7352 263 725	6368.0805 984 474	7639.0110 950 350	9175.0161 508 835	184
47	5929.1995 385 279	7136.7770 636 198	8601.9579 141 496	10380.9732 138 366	188
48	6612.9799 027 481	7997.7594 696 990	9685.7630 426 246	11744.8894 259 703	192
49	7375.1360 334 778	8962.1072 157 389	10905.5952 630 464	13287.4546 555 864	196
50	8224.6514 597 820	10042.2298 392 979	12278.5271 738 530	15032.0687 795 712	200
51	9171.5394 141 408	11252.0267 063 666	13823.7741 349 960	17005.1966 468 219	204
52	10226.9608 583 522	12607.0658 728 889	15562.9632 033 881	19236.7695 356 327	208
53	11403.3560 377 117	14124.7844 195 226	17520.4358 221 191	21760.6391 949 340	212
54	12714.5911 140 980	15824.7128 376 123	19723.5884 998 347	24615.0913 569 406	216
55	14176.1216 063 277	17728.7263 538 459	22203.2562 483 786	27843.4265 109 199	220
56	15805.1745 642 487	19861.3264 277 208	24994.1441 452 377	31494.6167 481 008	224
57	17620.9516 238 589	22249.9560 442 205	28135.3130 608 749	35624.0486 417 050	228
58	19644.8553 368 568	24925.3528 589 888	31670.7263 491 228	40294.3634 311 862	232
59	21900.7414 423 712	27921.9447 403 879	35649.8651 520 368	45576.4072 558 172	236
60	24415.2000 543 944	31278.2927 984 028	40128.4209 309 294	51550.3058 521 518	240

Table 2.   FUTURE WORTH OF ONE DOLLAR PER PERIOD WITH INTEREST
PAYABLE AT END OF EACH PERIOD

QUARTERS	13% NOMINAL ANNUAL RATE	13½% NOMINAL ANNUAL RATE	14% NOMINAL ANNUAL RATE	14½% NOMINAL ANNUAL RATE	QUARTERS
1	1.0000 000 000	1.0000 000 000	1.0000 000 000	1.0000 000 000	1
2	2.0325 000 000	2.0337 500 000	2.0350 000 000	2.0362 500 000	2
3	3.0985 562 500	3.1023 890 625	3.1062 250 000	3.1100 640 625	3
YEARS					
1	4.1992 593 281	4.2070 946 934	4.2149 428 750	4.2228 038 848	4
2	8.9716 164 707	9.0115 524 311	9.0516 867 704	9.0920 204 031	8
3	14.3952 854 837	14.4981 924 608	14.6019 616 385	14.7066 002 294	12
4	20.5591 547 595	20.7638 774 683	20.9710 297 094	21.1806 410 752	16
5	27.5642 438 156	27.9192 236 181	28.2796 818 133	28.6457 063 463	20
6	35.5253 589 026	36.0905 534 030	36.6665 282 061	37.2534 987 325	24
7	44.5729 745 604	45.4221 257 763	46.2906 273 446	47.1789 430 621	28
8	54.8553 719 627	56.0786 829 403	57.3345 024 663	58.6237 410 684	32
9	66.5410 690 942	68.2483 587 512	70.0076 031 845	71.8204 703 084	36
10	79.8215 825 880	82.1460 000 872	84.5502 777 478	87.0373 105 303	40
11	94.9145 664 873	98.0169 598 160	101.2383 312 998	104.5834 935 373	44
12	112.0673 793 731	116.1414 283 225	120.3882 565 864	124.8155 872 983	48
13	131.5611 383 180	136.8393 800 695	142.3632 363 131	148.1447 420 090	52
14	153.7153 261 084	160.4762 225 163	167.5800 309 877	175.0450 453 560	56
15	178.8930 272 403	187.4692 471 251	196.5168 828 788	206.0631 567 765	60
16	207.5068 785 031	218.2949 963 412	229.7225 859 896	241.8294 164 980	64
17	240.0258 316 753	253.4976 766 079	267.8268 940 611	283.0706 551 124	68
18	276.9828 391 647	293.6987 659 400	311.5524 639 960	330.6249 639 973	72
19	318.9835 885 533	339.6079 856 710	361.7285 612 119	385.4587 267 429	76
20	366.7164 291 984	392.0358 300 733	419.3067 868 486	448.6862 576 933	80
21	420.9636 535 744	451.9078 750 520	485.3791 251 019	521.5924 466 891	84
22	482.6143 182 474	520.2811 185 222	561.1986 529 527	605.6588 701 915	88
23	552.6788 146 036	598.3626 409 473	648.2033 050 580	702.5938 994 097	92
24	632.3054 281 314	687.5309 154 765	748.0431 445 102	814.3674 172 787	96
25	722.7991 576 469	789.3601 438 981	862.6116 566 603	943.2508 497 959	100
26	825.6431 028 911	905.6480 480 398	994.0816 594 999	1091.8633 252 207	104
27	942.5227 710 185	1038.4476 072 555	1144.9465 116 506	1263.2248 991 678	108
28	1075.3537 003 372	1190.1033 023 002	1318.0673 994 794	1460.8179 272 208	112
29	1226.3128 540 235	1363.2925 054 520	1516.7276 001 516	1688.6578 322 582	116
30	1397.8742 983 240	1561.0727 475 953	1744.6947 497 318	1951.3747 046 041	120
31	1592.8497 499 726	1786.9356 967 307	2006.2922 972 619	2254.3073 932 561	124
32	1814.4346 573 541	2044.8688 008 633	2306.4814 999 598	2603.6120 002 824	128
33	2066.2605 706 377	2339.4256 835 313	2650.9555 145 949	3006.3869 831 763	132
34	2352.4546 591 724	2675.8065 347 555	3046.2473 695 063	3470.8174 074 589	136
35	2677.7073 515 749	3059.9499 166 568	3499.8538 649 769	4006.3412 809 866	140
36	3047.3492 070 610	3498.6376 045 006	4020.3777 517 623	4623.8413 501 543	144
37	3467.4382 778 627	3999.6143 140 650	4617.6908 842 232	5335.8662 556 181	148
38	3944.8593 945 138	4571.7244 290 297	5303.1214 422 976	6156.8855 417 923	152
39	4487.4370 011 849	5225.0681 422 125	6089.6687 730 191	7103.5837 023 449	156
40	5104.0633 903 275	5971.1797 672 130	6992.2499 261 022	8195.1992 371 878	160
41	5804.8444 382 588	6823.2313 684 274	8027.9825 591 957	9453.9156 111 745	164
42	6601.2652 301 463	7796.2653 043 773	9216.5095 781 685	10905.3120 594 397	168
43	7506.3782 888 158	8907.4597 897 354	10580.3716 693 039	12578.8834 005 073	172
44	8535.0174 922 606	10176.4321 643 577	12145.4347 885 624	14508.6394 206 428	176
45	9704.0411 857 415	11625.5852 233 161	13941.3807 153 414	16733.7960 099 482	180
46	11032.6084 728 360	13280.5027 221 415	16002.2699 741 990	19299.5720 952 490	184
47	12542.4932 135 651	15170.4010 396 369	18367.1878 004 792	22258.1085 647 911	188
48	14258.4408 757 060	17328.6449 720 424	21080.9854 007 238	25669.5278 588 422	192
49	16208.5740 877 185	19793.3367 645 291	24195.1305 660 454	29603.1557 588 647	196
50	18424.8535 398 839	22607.9887 789 474	27768.6837 705 370	34138.9302 040 692	200
51	20943.6017 873 546	25822.2916 732 968	31869.4182 666 484	39369.0257 648 753	204
52	23806.0985 397 105	29492.9916 545 725	36575.1054 203 926	45399.7267 853 117	208
53	27059.2571 932 107	33684.8922 922 578	41974.9896 630 596	52353.5872 597 627	212
54	30756.3936 934 124	38471.9985 787 597	48171.4810 322 323	60371.9213 363 929	216
55	34958.1003 290 283	43938.8234 343 505	55282.0974 015 327	69617.6750 584 683	220
56	39733.2387 776 130	50181.8797 220 238	63441.6932 339 253	80278.7377 021 934	224
57	45160.0686 780 801	57311.3841 127 119	72805.0171 271 997	92571.7600 030 209	228
58	51327.5302 262 021	65453.2028 813 817	83549.6466 574 632	106746.5568 632 182	232
59	58336.7018 135 201	74751.0739 856 402	95879.3561 764 057	123091.1840 111 195	236
60	66302.4565 988 785	85369.1446 560 503	110027.9814 404 172	141937.7917 783 219	240

Table 2. FUTURE WORTH OF ONE DOLLAR PER PERIOD WITH INTEREST
PAYABLE AT END OF EACH PERIOD

QUARTERS	15% NOMINAL ANNUAL RATE	15½% NOMINAL ANNUAL RATE	16% NOMINAL ANNUAL RATE	16½% NOMINAL ANNUAL RATE	QUARTERS
1	1.0000 000 000	1.0000 000 000	1.0000 000 000	1.0000 000 000	1
2	2.0375 000 000	2.0387 500 000	2.0400 000 000	2.0412 500 000	2
3	3.1139 062 500	3.1177 515 625	3.1216 000 000	3.1254 515 625	3
YEARS					
1	4.2306 777 344	4.2385 644 355	4.2464 640 000	4.2543 764 395	4
2	9.1325 542 472	9.1732 892 245	9.2142 262 601	9.2553 662 831	8
3	14.8121 155 033	14.9185 147 867	15.0258 054 642	15.1339 949 780	12
4	21.3927 415 098	21.6073 613 128	21.8245 311 432	22.0442 820 238	16
5	29.0173 865 636	29.3948 132 351	29.7780 785 758	30.1672 762 685	20
6	37.8516 847 196	38.4613 103 069	39.0826 041 223	39.7157 993 706	24
7	48.0875 479 447	49.0169 284 954	49.9675 829 796	50.9400 217 061	28
8	59.9473 351 187	61.3062 475 630	62.7014 686 711	64.1340 168 077	32
9	73.6886 824 501	75.6140 181 217	77.5983 138 495	79.6434 660 627	36
10	89.6101 002 389	92.2717 594 687	95.0255 156 984	97.8747 155 320	40
11	108.0574 575 679	111.6654 410 803	115.4128 769 582	119.3054 221 773	44
12	129.4314 957 935	134.2444 257 465	139.2632 060 438	144.4970 684 267	48
13	154.1965 340 546	160.5318 815 668	167.1647 176 834	174.1096 729 598	52
14	182.8905 559 143	191.1369 040 566	199.8055 399 119	208.9190 831 333	56
15	216.1368 962 512	226.7686 292 415	237.9906 852 013	249.8373 021 054	60
16	254.6577 822 811	268.2526 647 483	282.6619 042 830	297.9363 832 306	64
17	299.2900 228 673	316.5502 196 099	334.9209 123 114	354.4765 177 525	68
18	351.0031 869 466	372.7803 760 329	396.0565 601 905	420.9390 516 924	72
19	410.9206 659 701	438.2460 191 782	467.5766 211 830	499.0652 969 704	76
20	480.3440 779 088	514.4640 257 615	551.2449 767 468	590.9021 536 085	80
21	560.7815 429 649	603.2004 109 618	649.1251 187 043	698.8557 383 118	84
22	653.9804 452 369	706.5112 480 120	763.6310 406 272	825.7544 244 918	88
23	761.9653 920 356	826.7903 086 016	897.5867 735 595	974.9229 453 750	92
24	887.0821 954 618	966.8245 279 477	1054.2960 343 913	1150.2695 016 892	96
25	1032.0488 316 799	1129.8585 796 918	1237.6237 046 067	1356.3881 561 427	100
26	1200.0144 849 009	1319.6700 568 591	1452.0911 488 931	1598.6791 974 199	104
27	1394.6279 587 177	1540.6570 008 690	1702.9877 244 328	1883.4906 272 189	108
28	1620.1169 409 277	1797.9398 066 908	1996.5012 310 027	2218.2844 772 786	112
29	1881.3798 437 521	2097.4798 653 498	2339.8705 191 390	2611.8323 138 838	116
30	2184.0922 145 438	2446.2176 927 953	2741.5640 201 064	3074.4450 520 478	120
31	2534.8300 285 992	2852.2337 456 594	3211.4886 007 095	3618.2431 004 826	124
32	2941.2125 424 243	3324.9356 500 985	3761.2338 938 824	4257.4739 151 269	128
33	3412.0678 107 324	3875.2761 819 174	4404.3581 309 205	5008.8852 811 056	132
34	3957.6244 627 809	4516.0070 487 035	5156.7225 247 629	5892.1641 030 693	136
35	4589.7339 041 042	5261.9743 542 475	6036.8824 511 387	6930.4522 001 802	140
36	5322.1277 706 435	6130.4625 913 316	7066.5450 751 784	8150.9526 195 217	144
37	6170.7162 280 814	7141.5951 033 986	8271.1047 098 233	9585.6423 532 843	148
38	7153.9335 964 892	8318.8005 047 222	9680.2691 094 431	11272.1101 328 483	152
39	8293.1388 084 685	9689.3552 328 295	11328.7921 447 856	13254.5412 498 873	156
40	9613.0794 001 429	11285.0158 613 786	13257.3309 290 382	15584.8752 067 096	160
41	11142.4291 145 134	13142.7547 675 932	15513.4485 340 881	18324.1665 261 628	164
42	12914.4107 958 087	15305.6168 335 713	18152.7870 267 224	21544.1843 741 900	168
43	14967.5181 062 831	17823.7168 210 336	21240.4397 550 682	25329.2929 049 920	172
44	17346.3517 436 839	20755.4005 592 612	24852.5567 296 308	29778.6615 936 554	176
45	20102.5883 249 673	24168.5968 516 173	29078.2226 920 442	35008.8634 667 478	180
46	23296.1029 838 172	28142.3914 251 059	34021.6541 898 742	41156.9293 042 670	184
47	26996.2700 687 269	32768.8593 922 870	39804.7698 433 842	48383.9378 327 393	188
48	31283.4701 973 714	38155.1986 847 489	46570.1971 941 128	56879.2359 721 761	192
49	36250.8364 057 809	44426.2138 910 200	54484.7902 924 209	66865.3997 069 480	196
50	42006.2773 248 056	51727.2080 508 790	63743.7447 773 934	78604.0655 549 115	200
51	48674.8213 343 663	60227.3494 106 049	74575.4119 382 890	92402.7854 187 102	204
52	56401.3326 187 501	70123.5911 488 285	87246.9304 855 336	108623.0844 156 893	208
53	65353.6581 252 054	81645.2348 952 939	102070.8149 262 264	127689.9328 007 808	212
54	75726.2737 888 246	95059.2437 818 931	119412.6630 316 217	150102.8801 458 188	216
55	87744.5092 325 177	110676.4281 324 303	139700.1724 839 383	176449.1434 896 984	220
56	101669.4427 173 898	128858.6471 171 156	163433.6890 778 116	207418.9923 676 384	224
57	117803.5726 790 283	150027.1932 382 787	191198.5466 240 564	243823.8338 058 174	228
58	136497.3890 553 749	174672.5539 206 709	223679.5028 917 115	286617.4711 064 817	232
59	158156.9871 584 929	203365.7763 880 355	261677.6276 184 135	336921.0934 016 271	236
60	183252.8894 902 498	236771.6991 566 922	306130.0590 938 934	396052.6506 991 266	240

89

Table 2. FUTURE WORTH OF ONE DOLLAR PER PERIOD WITH INTEREST
PAYABLE AT END OF EACH PERIOD

QUARTERS	17% NOMINAL ANNUAL RATE	17½% NOMINAL ANNUAL RATE	18% NOMINAL ANNUAL RATE	18½% NOMINAL ANNUAL RATE	QUARTERS
1	1.0000 000 000	1.0000 000 000	1.0000 000 000	1.0000 000 000	1
2	2.0425 000 000	2.0437 500 000	2.0450 000 000	2.0462 500 000	2
3	3.1293 062 500	3.1331 640 625	3.1370 250 000	3.1408 890 625	3
YEARS					
1	4.2623 017 656	4.2702 399 902	4.2781 911 250	4.2861 551 816	4
2	9.2967 102 258	9.3382 590 243	9.3800 136 186	9.4219 749 519	8
3	15.2430 908 288	15.3531 005 763	15.4640 318 393	15.5758 922 963	12
4	22.2666 453 449	22.4916 528 689	22.7193 367 340	22.9497 294 586	16
5	30.5625 014 857	30.9638 509 135	31.3714 227 742	31.7853 168 502	20
6	40.3611 339 232	41.0188 504 097	41.6891 963 113	42.3724 240 558	24
7	51.9347 673 151	52.9523 550 725	53.9933 331 713	55.0582 630 402	28
8	65.6049 392 238	67.1153 128 718	68.6662 452 415	70.2588 752 201	32
9	81.7514 330 416	83.9242 369 300	86.1639 658 106	88.4727 758 480	36
10	100.8228 290 966	103.8734 546 004	107.0303 230 577	110.2973 031 865	40
11	123.3489 670 674	127.5496 449 551	131.9138 422 022	136.4482 086 559	44
12	149.9556 659 380	155.6490 922 102	161.5879 016 311	167.7831 304 283	48
13	181.3821 104 406	188.9981 624 880	196.9747 694 560	205.3297 203 018	52
14	218.5013 870 136	228.5776 061 079	239.1742 675 551	250.3193 462 969	56
15	262.3447 398 047	275.5514 001 064	289.4979 539 753	304.2274 762 763	60
16	314.1302 205 964	331.3009 792 010	349.5098 860 835	368.8220 669 981	64
17	375.2965 286 021	397.4658 618 869	421.0752 313 819	446.2215 455 572	68
18	447.5429 802 687	475.5918 664 227	506.4182 368 104	538.9642 847 601	72
19	532.8767 195 215	569.1883 346 752	608.1913 582 171	650.0918 509 270	76
20	633.6684 800 424	679.7960 466 654	729.5576 985 382	783.2487 542 956	80
21	752.7184 487 635	811.0678 231 913	874.2893 168 610	942.8019 734 139	84
22	893.3340 603 895	966.8641 867 671	1046.8844 638 095	1133.9841 734 124	88
23	1059.4218 842 279	1151.7668 943 086	1252.7073 869 232	1363.0653 151 047	92
24	1255.5961 561 203	1371.2136 803 022	1498.1550 511 712	1637.5582 829 616	96
25	1487.3069 706 945	1631.6581 731 017	1790.8559 562 670	1966.4652 756 819	100
26	1760.9916 953 668	1940.7596 872 682	2139.9072 300 134	2360.5730 399 168	104
27	2084.2538 126 600	2307.6084 734 837	2556.1573 663 279	2832.8066 295 574	108
28	2466.0741 594 184	2742.9930 503 297	3052.5433 968 342	3398.6532 923 802	112
29	2917.0604 315 477	3259.7174 797 898	3644.4929 710 648	4076.6703 857 246	116
30	3449.7418 859 957	3872.9779 171 140	4350.4038 489 668	4889.0939 786 710	120
31	4078.9174 273 555	4600.8095 088 586	5192.2157 012 485	5862.5681 002 747	124
32	4822.0667 496 006	5464.6167 817 566	6196.0919 933 210	7029.0185 500 894	128
33	5699.8359 552 495	6489.8031 204 302	7393.2331 443 440	8426.6999 282 355	132
34	6736.6111 433 880	7706.5178 460 158	8820.8462 345 124	10101.4502 231 383	136
35	7961.1959 019 123	9150.5428 662 597	10523.3013 990 341	12108.1941 020 594	140
36	9407.6115 260 192	10864.3449 722 437	12553.5108 494 562	14512.7442 059 430	144
37	11116.0421 945 357	12898.3247 283 416	14974.5733 822 493	17393.9595 233 630	148
38	13133.9513 628 839	15312.2986 835 441	17861.7354 858 813	20846.3316 290 340	152
39	15517.4003 882 048	18177.2584 939 479	21304.7299 974 820	24983.0836 044 773	156
40	18332.6060 205 540	21577.4586 897 868	25410.5649 944 157	29939.8832 722 259	160
41	21657.7800 302 410	25612.8944 853 602	30306.8495 993 563	35879.2925 218 123	164
42	25585.3020 796 592	30402.2425 008 459	36145.7600 647 017	42996.0986 464 573	168
43	30224.2862 061 225	36086.3508 785 824	43108.7694 020 101	51523.7025 355 667	172
44	35703.6122 174 853	42832.3814 333 443	51412.2875 530 759	61741.7732 285 044	176
45	42175.5062 184 865	50838.7256 515 563	61314.3873 988 491	73985.4198 663 613	180
46	49819.7697 416 524	60340.8391 122 265	73122.8256 501 797	88656.1818 426 233	184
47	58848.7749 760 653	71618.1659 118 999	87204.6079 092 232	106235.1975 828 070	188
48	69513.3648 709 583	85002.3567 314 504	103997.3951 830 836	127298.9838 328 763	192
49	82109.8220 302 448	100887.0222 267 635	124023.1063 635 010	152538.3429 498 031	196
50	96988.1000 071 338	119739.3085 771 208	147904.1394 368 927	182781.0182 727 690	200
51	114561.5456 798 628	142113.6356 122 563	176382.7155 790 532	219018.8405 745 619	204
52	135318.3828 146 488	168668.0015 375 176	210343.9473 478 949	262440.2558 810 016	208
53	159835.2758 510 913	200183.3337 566 887	250843.3479 323 753	314469.3014 321 476	212
54	188793.3507 378 007	237586.4548 735 733	299139.6364 435 311	376812.3080 305 935	216
55	222997.1179 075 558	281977.3392 709 060	356733.8588 342 360	451513.8604 146 974	220
56	263396.8231 082 546	334661.4618 450 309	425416.0403 236 844	541023.8509 183 335	224
57	311114.8470 382 792	397188.1902 283 126	507320.8192 813 537	648277.8254 912 363	228
58	367476.8872 183 897	471396.3495 616 297	604993.7916 684 534	776793.2570 867 469	232
59	434048.7883 918 915	559468.2998 143 701	721470.6280 184 019	930784.9037 734 995	236
60	512680.0446 716 885	663994.1159 915 497	860371.4219 076 695	1115303.0348 251 327	240

Table 2. FUTURE WORTH OF ONE DOLLAR PER PERIOD WITH INTEREST
PAYABLE AT END OF EACH PERIOD

QUARTERS	19% NOMINAL ANNUAL RATE	19½% NOMINAL ANNUAL RATE	20% NOMINAL ANNUAL RATE	20½% NOMINAL ANNUAL RATE	QUARTERS
1	1.0000 000 000	1.0000 000 000	1.0000 000 000	1.0000 000 000	1
2	2.0475 000 000	2.0487 500 000	2.0500 000 000	2.0512 500 000	2
3	3.1447 562 500	3.1486 265 625	3.1525 000 000	3.1563 765 625	3
YEARS					
1	4.2941 321 719	4.3021 221 074	4.3101 250 000	4.3181 408 613	4
2	9.4661 439 715	9.5065 216 279	9.5491 088 758	9.5919 066 732	8
3	15.6886 896 859	15.8024 318 073	15.9171 265 204	16.0327 817 469	12
4	23.1828 639 457	23.4187 734 871	23.6574 917 676	23.8990 528 698	16
5	32.2056 345 081	32.6324 787 230	33.0659 541 029	33.5061 669 142	20
6	43.0687 911 147	43.7785 601 019	44.5019 988 743	45.2393 806 341	24
7	56.1477 196 592	57.2622 918 826	58.4025 827 692	59.5692 099 208	28
8	71.8943 739 760	73.5739 458 667	75.2988 293 721	77.0702 980 533	32
9	90.8528 935 006	93.3066 178 025	95.8363 227 194	98.4444 595 796	36
10	113.6784 064 847	117.1777 924 917	120.7997 742 425	124.5488 239 193	40
11	141.1596 685 269	146.0554 317 136	151.1430 055 903	156.4302 072 777	44
12	174.2463 187 134	180.9895 335 281	188.0253 929 388	195.3670 912 262	48
13	214.0816 952 286	223.2503 104 639	232.8561 652 759	242.9208 913 411	52
14	262.0423 444 078	274.3743 747 580	287.3482 492 439	300.9985 718 346	56
15	319.7855 885 017	336.2206 099 540	353.5837 178 825	371.9291 170 983	60
16	389.3067 958 987	411.0377 603 653	434.0933 439 844	458.5569 267 602	64
17	473.0083 328 280	501.5461 959 705	531.9532 976 964	564.3558 795 093	68
18	573.7825 792 290	611.0368 257 349	650.9026 830 581	693.5686 397 822	72
19	695.1118 774 745	743.4907 558 689	795.4864 043 989	851.3767 936 769	76
20	841.1888 677 618	903.7240 438 288	971.2288 213 368	1044.1086 367 478	80
21	1017.0613 684 685	1097.5628 113 495	1184.8448 275 151	1279.4929 462 195	84
22	1228.8068 079 382	1332.0550 836 628	1444.4964 181 247	1566.9689 141 895	88
23	1483.7422 353 419	1615.7270 574 270	1760.1045 493 332	1918.0646 705 114	92
24	1790.6771 677 225	1958.8931 153 938	2143.7282 053 680	2346.8595 745 785	96
25	2160.2180 105 739	2374.0308 595 967	2610.0251 569 261	2870.5488 144 602	100
26	2605.1345 714 755	2876.2348 006 368	3176.8120 159 009	3510.1329 544 920	104
27	3140.8013 319 807	3483.7651 971 896	3865.7449 854 026	4291.2600 830 021	108
28	3785.7287 262 960	4218.7120 038 020	4703.1473 156 630	5245.2543 313 020	112
29	4562.2027 855 529	5107.7980 670 090	5721.0150 818 591	6410.3720 087 861	116
30	5497.0552 511 377	6183.3507 746 023	6958.2397 133 440	7833.3357 266 544	120
31	6622.5907 690 226	7484.4774 873 961	8462.0939 855 679	9571.2080 304 563	124
32	7977.7032 051 095	9058.4874 924 786	10290.0382 525 452	11693.6796 763 576	128
33	9609.2196 568 411	10962.6121 805 194	12511.9159 337 077	14285.8643 137 443	132
34	11573.5186 045 781	13266.0859 932 009	15212.6221 418 963	17451.7116 442 747	136
35	13938.4781 193 813	16052.6638 045 359	18495.3474 173 634	21318.1759 291 381	140
36	16785.8214 492 252	19423.6662 686 730	22485.5205 067 265	26040.3070 066 398	144
37	20213.9410 374 293	23501.6638 637 855	27335.6008 354 293	31807.4679 760 047	148
38	24341.2985 597 386	28434.9335 847 854	33230.9037 879 695	38850.9288 839 479	152
39	29310.5184 713 135	34402.8503 313 040	40396.6813 724 256	47453.1409 299 185	156
40	35293.3165 197 305	41622.4090 231 320	49106.7288 124 419	57959.0630 967 318	160
41	42496.4335 330 806	50356.1145 888 398	59693.8459 135 782	70789.9954 180 106	164
42	51168.7795 304 091	60921.5267 095 025	72562.5529 194 913	86460.4736 129 938	168
43	61610.0350 254 936	73702.8063 667 585	88204.5467 145 974	105598.9025 837 552	172
44	74181.0067 495 481	89164.6840 305 273	107217.4879 350 101	128972.7562 027 305	176
45	89316.0956 439 222	107869.3573 731 244	130327.8368 193 044	157519.3539 321 443	180
46	107538.3079 652 086	130496.9329 148 119	158418.6103 278 446	192383.4484 545 560	184
47	129477.3282 246 446	157870.1548 640 429	192563.1210 948 096	234963.1316 234 275	188
48	155891.2784 880 651	190984.3202 991 077	234065.9873 352 480	286965.8996 171 868	192
49	187692.9159 480 774	231043.4684 145 395	284512.9806 434 147	350477.1255 764 670	196
50	225981.1740 485 186	279504.1596 821 758	345831.6163 031 996	428043.6855 590 976	200
51	272079.1370 923 823	338128.4367 479 300	420364.8011 891 411	522776.0913 135 780	204
52	327579.7605 790 626	409047.8927 354 993	510960.3532 504 084	638473.2255 173 008	208
53	394400.9171 772 234	494841.1764 962 782	621079.8130 030 792	779774.6815 116 360	212
54	474851.6704 951 121	598627.7529 154 160	754930.7045 790 740	952346.8165 393 040	216
55	571712.0667 965 122	724181.3274 217 908	917627.2998 577 681	1163109.9794 411 894	220
56	688329.2019 349 865	876067.0588 449 643	1115386.0282 727 412	1420516.0249 147 809	224
57	828732.8831 834 867	1059807.5497 123 195	1355762.9986 531 936	1734887.2429 876 329	228
58	997774.8827 551 830	1282083.6494 343 883	1647942.7085 066 985	2118830.2951 827 612	232
59	1201296.5950 429 272	1550977.3716 315 410	2003088.9719 568 201	2587741.7567 108 639	236
60	1446330.8911 201 411	1876265.7581 357 457	2434771.4748 445 896	3160425.5375 354 082	240

Table 2. FUTURE WORTH OF ONE DOLLAR PER PERIOD WITH INTEREST
PAYABLE AT END OF EACH PERIOD

QUARTERS	21% NOMINAL ANNUAL RATE	21½% NOMINAL ANNUAL RATE	22% NOMINAL ANNUAL RATE	22½% NOMINAL ANNUAL RATE	QUARTERS
1	1.0000 000 000	1.0000 000 000	1.0000 000 000	1.0000 000 000	1
2	2.0525 000 000	2.0537 500 000	2.0550 000 000	2.0562 500 000	2
3	3.1602 562 500	3.1641 390 625	3.1680 250 000	3.1719 140 625	3
YEARS					
1	4.3261 697 031	4.3342 115 371	4.3422 663 750	4.3503 342 285	4
2	9.6349 159 820	9.6781 377 678	9.7215 729 999	9.7652 226 514	8
3	16.1494 054 698	16.2670 057 349	16.3855 906 502	16.5051 683 871	12
4	24.1434 912 780	24.3908 418 832	24.6411 399 875	24.8944 213 083	16
5	33.9532 251 071	34.4072 383 409	34.8683 180 110	35.3365 772 746	20
6	45.9909 840 337	46.7570 932 821	47.5379 982 528	48.3339 945 952	24
7	60.7628 058 284	61.9840 182 257	63.2335 104 520	64.5119 618 224	28
8	78.8896 615 383	80.7582 665 343	82.6774 978 685	84.6487 795 571	32
9	101.1335 595 823	103.9062 363 874	106.7651 887 865	109.7132 034 605	36
10	128.4295 787 107	132.4468 468 828	136.6056 140 723	140.9110 498 078	40
11	161.9251 764 150	167.6363 884 549	173.5726 685 015	179.7432 057 138	44
12	203.0284 252 181	211.0238 218 194	219.3683 667 895	228.0778 348 263	48
13	253.4672 045 789	264.5189 595 749	276.1012 067 211	288.2402 522 079	52
14	315.3618 366 943	330.4765 316 546	346.3832 473 284	363.1247 921 673	56
15	391.3142 196 274	411.7998 349 897	433.4503 717 290	456.3340 508 539	60
16	484.5172 047 016	512.0685 298 007	541.3112 716 955	572.3522 023 925	64
17	598.8888 161 150	635.6962 078 066	674.9320 134 125	716.7607 265 679	68
18	739.2369 550 385	788.1246 681 347	840.0646 820 864	896.5069 264 339	72
19	911.4615 119 533	976.0634 524 972	1045.5306 325 233	1120.2381 538 718	76
20	1122.8023 835 317	1207.7851 834 104	1299.5713 869 284	1398.7178 222 497	80
21	1382.1438 200 820	1493.4897 055 480	1614.2833 357 488	1745.3432 200 001	84
22	1700.3878 975 746	1845.7530 588 733	2004.1562 557 938	2176.7900 364 428	88
23	2090.9128 140 953	2280.0810 462 907	2487.1404 397 566	2713.8146 071 367	92
24	2570.1352 763 797	2815.5917 625 581	3085.4731 527 118	3382.2524 737 243	96
25	3158.2006 177 771	3475.8571 277 777	3826.7024 667 960	4214.2612 976 610	100
26	3879.8296 585 037	4289.9404 677 849	4744.9556 128 494	5249.8679 227 653	104
27	4765.3579 081 068	5293.6758 132 799	5882.5102 456 943	6538.8940 137 208	108
28	5852.0107 956 564	6531.2452 294 374	7291.7409 662 953	8143.3529 104 539	112
29	7185.4685 352 023	8057.1236 063 246	9037.5307 213 937	10140.4330 078 766	116
30	8821.7864 095 923	9938.4765 152 233	11200.2581 048 183	12626.2111 874 502	120
31	10829.7511 966 579	12258.1166 788 399	13879.4980 999 864	15720.2749 488 480	124
32	13293.7727 961 275	15118.1491 922 576	17198.6066 509 410	19571.4756 063 569	128
33	16317.4326 141 495	18644.4659 486 689	21310.4001 419 637	24365.0893 286 856	132
34	20027.8378 707 788	22992.2871 039 216	26404.1912 769 222	30331.7305 303 316	136
35	24580.9648 748 042	28352.9935 020 899	32714.5053 000 438	37758.4464 259 721	140
36	30168.2158 840 426	34962.5508 093 506	40531.8778 650 715	47002.5264 922 151	144
37	37024.4651 853 768	43111.8961 666 882	50216.2317 017 473	58508.6911 916 447	148
38	45437.9326 319 476	53159.7445 574 125	62213.4479 599 962	72830.4868 859 355	152
39	55762.2996 967 115	65548.3785 956 154	77075.8951 995 939	90656.9162 190 020	156
40	68431.5773 714 503	80823.1167 648 537	95487.8612 086 210	112845.5851 226 854	160
41	83978.3509 211 281	99656.3170 530 617	118297.0585 670 734	140463.9611 035 691	164
42	103056.1684 581 839	122876.9725 671 489	146553.6545 156 948	174840.7276 925 207	168
43	126467.0144 973 440	151507.2018 565 125	181558.6221 195 976	217629.7056 515 878	172
44	155195.0234 116 088	186807.2401 635 386	224923.6388 816 619	270889.4161 029 473	176
45	190447.8500 201 634	230330.9120 099 406	278645.2906 212 287	337182.1132 567 844	180
46	233707.4364 259 491	283994.0268 914 972	345196.9970 685 202	419697.0510 716 253	184
47	286792.3092 158 522	350158.7086 985 354	427642.8915 565 837	522403.9140 430 767	188
48	351934.0258 445 464	431737.3708 445 751	529778.8979 912 245	650243.7934 732 375	192
49	431870.9838 198 926	532320.9138 433 379	656307.5004 788 513	809366.8968 364 550	196
50	529963.5361 972 671	656336.7882 894 365	813054.2522 496 549	1007428.4261 245 332	200
51	650335.2525 549 945	809243.8808 027 683	1007235.9922 487 244	1253956.8594 871 531	204
52	798046.2637 147 697	997772.8013 567 459	1247793.1184 608 262	1560812.3537 100 083	208
53	979305.9771 926 572	1230222.1488 724 543	1545801.2162 958 872	1942757.3206 674 379	212
54	1201734.1054 149 153	1516823.7959 922 046	1914980.9939 798 275	2418166.6274 278 524	216
55	1474680.9796 826 651	1870193.2720 076 321	2372330.0030 869 500	3009911.5867 994 696	220
56	1809620.6150 964 547	2305885.0687 377 590	2938905.2295 077 709	3746460.2659 320 455	224
57	2220633.0499 231 451	2843077.3126 135 110	3640792.5864 313 247	4663247.0473 657 825	228
58	2724996.2357 654 659	3505415.9406 208 056	4510307.9461 502 509	5804377.3302 976 240	232
59	3343912.3601 408 259	4322055.5387 384 049	5587485.0078 671 208	7224749.3829 876 341	236
60	4103399.1342 837 179	5328942.6581 264 185	6921918.5050 097 863	8992695.4258 176 389	240

92

Table 3. SINKING FUND FACTORS
PAYABLE AT END OF EACH PERIOD

QUARTERS	5% NOMINAL ANNUAL RATE	5½% NOMINAL ANNUAL RATE	6% NOMINAL ANNUAL RATE	6½% NOMINAL ANNUAL RATE	QUARTERS
1	1.0000 000 000	1.0000 000 000	1.0000 000 000	1.0000 000 000	1
2	0.4968 944 099	0.4965 859 714	0.4962 779 156	0.4959 702 418	2
3	0.3292 011 728	0.3287 917 264	0.3283 829 602	0.3279 748 730	3
YEARS					
1	0.2453 610 233	0.2449 024 264	0.2444 447 860	0.2439 881 002	4
2	0.1196 331 365	0.1191 075 771	0.1185 840 246	0.1180 624 747	8
3	0.0777 583 123	0.0772 176 365	0.0766 799 929	0.0761 453 744	12
4	0.0568 467 221	0.0563 038 765	0.0557 650 778	0.0552 303 149	16
5	0.0443 203 896	0.0437 805 367	0.0432 457 359	0.0427 159 708	20
6	0.0359 866 480	0.0354 523 513	0.0349 241 020	0.0344 018 766	24
7	0.0300 486 329	0.0295 210 391	0.0290 010 765	0.0284 878 128	28
8	0.0256 079 056	0.0250 885 002	0.0245 770 970	0.0240 736 526	32
9	0.0221 653 285	0.0216 543 826	0.0211 523 955	0.0206 593 105	36
10	0.0194 214 139	0.0189 193 079	0.0184 271 017	0.0179 447 219	40
11	0.0171 855 745	0.0166 925 657	0.0162 103 801	0.0157 389 251	44
12	0.0153 307 483	0.0148 470 100	0.0143 749 996	0.0139 146 019	48
13	0.0137 689 655	0.0132 946 116	0.0128 328 700	0.0123 835 995	52
14	0.0124 373 877	0.0119 724 879	0.0115 210 635	0.0110 829 436	56
15	0.0112 899 301	0.0108 345 211	0.0103 934 274	0.0099 664 454	60
16	0.0102 920 267	0.0098 461 188	0.0094 153 423	0.0089 994 566	64
17	0.0094 172 421	0.0089 808 248	0.0085 603 297	0.0081 554 755	68
18	0.0086 450 133	0.0082 180 587	0.0078 077 911	0.0074 138 845	72
19	0.0079 591 042	0.0075 415 703	0.0071 414 609	0.0067 584 016	76
20	0.0073 465 240	0.0069 383 566	0.0065 483 231	0.0061 759 969	80
21	0.0067 967 547	0.0063 978 890	0.0060 178 380	0.0056 561 187	84
22	0.0063 011 891	0.0059 115 514	0.0055 413 794	0.0051 901 303	88
23	0.0058 527 152	0.0054 722 237	0.0051 118 190	0.0047 708 943	92
24	0.0054 454 053	0.0050 739 712	0.0047 232 141	0.0043 924 601	96
25	0.0050 742 788	0.0047 118 069	0.0043 705 712	0.0040 498 271	100
26	0.0047 351 201	0.0043 815 097	0.0040 496 632	0.0037 387 618	104
27	0.0044 243 373	0.0040 794 825	0.0037 568 877	0.0034 556 566	108
28	0.0041 388 506	0.0038 026 412	0.0034 891 557	0.0031 974 177	112
29	0.0038 760 042	0.0035 483 257	0.0032 438 030	0.0029 613 770	116
30	0.0036 334 957	0.0033 142 299	0.0030 185 199	0.0027 452 210	120
31	0.0034 093 190	0.0030 983 444	0.0028 112 938	0.0025 469 344	124
32	0.0032 017 181	0.0028 989 106	0.0026 203 629	0.0023 647 529	128
33	0.0030 091 496	0.0027 143 820	0.0024 441 787	0.0021 971 261	132
34	0.0028 302 508	0.0025 433 938	0.0022 813 742	0.0020 426 855	136
35	0.0026 638 147	0.0023 847 369	0.0021 307 386	0.0019 002 190	140
36	0.0025 087 677	0.0022 373 361	0.0019 911 952	0.0017 686 496	144
37	0.0023 641 521	0.0021 002 320	0.0018 617 839	0.0016 470 166	148
38	0.0022 291 110	0.0019 725 663	0.0017 416 453	0.0015 344 608	152
39	0.0021 028 746	0.0018 535 685	0.0016 300 085	0.0014 302 117	156
40	0.0019 847 505	0.0017 425 450	0.0015 261 798	0.0013 335 762	160
41	0.0018 741 133	0.0016 388 700	0.0014 295 334	0.0012 439 295	164
42	0.0017 703 972	0.0015 419 772	0.0013 395 032	0.0011 607 069	168
43	0.0016 730 889	0.0014 513 531	0.0012 555 763	0.0010 833 969	172
44	0.0015 817 220	0.0013 665 311	0.0011 772 867	0.0010 115 355	176
45	0.0014 958 712	0.0012 870 861	0.0011 042 104	0.0009 447 003	180
46	0.0014 151 484	0.0012 126 302	0.0010 359 605	0.0008 825 069	184
47	0.0013 391 985	0.0011 428 088	0.0009 721 837	0.0008 246 044	188
48	0.0012 676 961	0.0010 772 971	0.0009 125 567	0.0007 706 718	192
49	0.0012 003 425	0.0010 157 970	0.0008 567 829	0.0007 204 154	196
50	0.0011 368 629	0.0009 580 346	0.0008 045 903	0.0006 735 660	200
51	0.0010 770 043	0.0009 037 579	0.0007 557 286	0.0006 298 764	204
52	0.0010 205 333	0.0008 527 344	0.0007 099 676	0.0005 891 192	208
53	0.0009 672 342	0.0008 047 498	0.0006 670 947	0.0005 510 854	212
54	0.0009 169 075	0.0007 596 058	0.0006 269 142	0.0005 155 823	216
55	0.0008 693 685	0.0007 171 191	0.0005 892 448	0.0004 824 321	220
56	0.0008 244 456	0.0006 771 196	0.0005 539 191	0.0004 514 707	224
57	0.0007 819 798	0.0006 394 498	0.0005 207 820	0.0004 225 466	228
58	0.0007 418 232	0.0006 039 634	0.0004 896 896	0.0003 955 194	232
59	0.0007 038 379	0.0005 705 244	0.0004 605 087	0.0003 702 593	236
60	0.0006 678 958	0.0005 390 064	0.0004 331 152	0.0003 466 461	240

93

Table 3.   SINKING FUND FACTORS
PAYABLE AT END OF EACH PERIOD

QUARTERS	7% NOMINAL ANNUAL RATE	7½% NOMINAL ANNUAL RATE	8% NOMINAL ANNUAL RATE	8½% NOMINAL ANNUAL RATE	QUARTERS
1	1.0000 000 000	1.0000 000 000	1.0000 000 000	1.0000 000 000	1
2	0.4956 629 492	0.4953 560 372	0.4950 495 050	0.4947 433 519	2
3	0.3275 674 635	0.3271 607 305	0.3267 546 726	0.3263 492 886	3
YEARS					
1	0.2435 323 673	0.2430 775 854	0.2426 237 527	0.2421 708 674	4
2	0.1175 429 233	0.1170 253 662	0.1165 097 991	0.1159 962 178	8
3	0.0756 137 738	0.0750 851 837	0.0745 595 966	0.0740 370 051	12
4	0.0546 995 764	0.0541 728 507	0.0536 501 259	0.0531 313 898	16
5	0.0421 912 246	0.0416 714 797	0.0411 567 181	0.0406 469 215	20
6	0.0338 856 510	0.0333 753 999	0.0328 710 973	0.0323 727 162	24
7	0.0279 815 145	0.0274 821 462	0.0269 896 716	0.0265 040 528	28
8	0.0235 781 216	0.0230 904 564	0.0226 106 073	0.0221 385 228	32
9	0.0201 750 673	0.0196 996 033	0.0192 328 526	0.0187 747 469	36
10	0.0174 720 911	0.0170 091 280	0.0165 557 478	0.0161 118 618	40
11	0.0152 781 026	0.0148 278 099	0.0143 879 391	0.0139 583 782	44
12	0.0134 656 950	0.0130 281 508	0.0126 018 355	0.0121 866 095	48
13	0.0119 466 511	0.0115 218 678	0.0111 090 856	0.0107 081 340	52
14	0.0106 579 481	0.0102 458 877	0.0098 465 645	0.0094 597 729	56
15	0.0095 533 598	0.0091 539 451	0.0087 679 658	0.0083 951 775	60
16	0.0085 982 079	0.0082 113 304	0.0078 385 471	0.0074 795 710	64
17	0.0077 659 661	0.0073 914 915	0.0070 317 294	0.0066 863 465	68
18	0.0070 359 964	0.0066 737 690	0.0063 268 307	0.0059 947 986	72
19	0.0063 919 996	0.0060 418 453	0.0057 075 147	0.0053 885 715	76
20	0.0058 209 310	0.0054 826 606	0.0051 607 055	0.0048 545 729	80
21	0.0053 122 263	0.0049 856 371	0.0046 758 118	0.0043 821 981	84
22	0.0048 572 379	0.0045 421 161	0.0042 441 633	0.0039 627 654	88
23	0.0044 488 187	0.0041 449 407	0.0038 585 936	0.0035 890 990	92
24	0.0040 810 099	0.0037 881 438	0.0035 131 275	0.0032 552 164	96
25	0.0037 488 036	0.0034 667 105	0.0032 027 435	0.0029 560 903	100
26	0.0034 479 605	0.0031 763 956	0.0029 231 911	0.0026 874 657	104
27	0.0031 748 675	0.0029 135 810	0.0026 708 483	0.0024 457 179	108
28	0.0029 264 263	0.0026 751 648	0.0024 426 100	0.0022 277 400	112
29	0.0026 999 650	0.0024 584 719	0.0022 357 993	0.0020 308 547	116
30	0.0024 931 675	0.0022 611 841	0.0020 480 969	0.0018 527 431	120
31	0.0023 040 158	0.0020 812 819	0.0018 774 832	0.0016 913 873	124
32	0.0021 307 440	0.0019 169 987	0.0017 221 924	0.0015 450 237	128
33	0.0019 718 004	0.0017 667 829	0.0015 806 741	0.0014 121 053	132
34	0.0018 258 160	0.0016 292 659	0.0014 515 619	0.0012 912 696	136
35	0.0016 915 786	0.0015 032 368	0.0013 336 475	0.0011 813 129	140
36	0.0015 680 114	0.0013 876 202	0.0012 258 591	0.0010 811 686	144
37	0.0014 541 546	0.0012 814 585	0.0011 272 426	0.0009 898 886	148
38	0.0013 491 500	0.0011 838 964	0.0010 369 471	0.0009 066 279	152
39	0.0012 522 288	0.0010 941 677	0.0009 542 112	0.0008 306 320	156
40	0.0011 626 998	0.0010 115 848	0.0008 783 523	0.0007 612 251	160
41	0.0010 799 404	0.0009 355 287	0.0008 087 568	0.0006 978 010	164
42	0.0010 033 884	0.0008 654 413	0.0007 448 725	0.0006 398 150	168
43	0.0009 325 351	0.0008 008 183	0.0006 862 008	0.0005 867 763	172
44	0.0008 669 195	0.0007 412 031	0.0006 322 913	0.0005 382 425	176
45	0.0008 061 227	0.0006 861 815	0.0005 827 365	0.0004 938 138	180
46	0.0007 497 636	0.0006 353 775	0.0005 371 665	0.0004 531 287	184
47	0.0006 974 949	0.0005 884 489	0.0004 952 458	0.0004 158 597	188
48	0.0006 489 996	0.0005 450 838	0.0004 566 694	0.0003 817 100	192
49	0.0006 039 881	0.0005 049 979	0.0004 211 596	0.0003 504 099	196
50	0.0005 621 950	0.0004 679 315	0.0003 884 634	0.0003 217 146	200
51	0.0005 233 774	0.0004 336 470	0.0003 583 501	0.0002 954 013	204
52	0.0004 873 123	0.0004 019 270	0.0003 306 090	0.0002 712 673	208
53	0.0004 537 950	0.0003 725 722	0.0003 050 476	0.0002 491 277	212
54	0.0004 226 371	0.0003 454 001	0.0002 814 899	0.0002 288 144	216
55	0.0003 936 655	0.0003 202 428	0.0002 597 747	0.0002 101 735	220
56	0.0003 667 205	0.0002 969 464	0.0002 397 545	0.0001 930 649	224
57	0.0003 416 551	0.0002 753 692	0.0002 212 941	0.0001 773 605	228
58	0.0003 183 333	0.0002 553 809	0.0002 042 694	0.0001 629 432	232
59	0.0002 966 301	0.0002 368 615	0.0001 885 667	0.0001 497 061	236
60	0.0002 764 294	0.0002 197 006	0.0001 740 815	0.0001 375 512	240

Table 3.   SINKING FUND FACTORS
            PAYABLE AT END OF EACH PERIOD

QUARTERS	9% NOMINAL ANNUAL RATE	9½% NOMINAL ANNUAL RATE	10% NOMINAL ANNUAL RATE	10½% NOMINAL ANNUAL RATE	QUARTERS
1	1.0000 000 000	1.0000 000 000	1.0000 000 000	1.0000 000 000	1
2	0.4944 375 773	0.4941 321 804	0.4938 271 605	0.4935 225 170	2
3	0.3259 445 772	0.3255 405 372	0.3251 371 672	0.3247 344 661	3
YEARS					
1	0.2417 189 277	0.2412 679 317	0.2408 178 777	0.2403 687 639	4
2	0.1154 846 181	0.1149 749 955	0.1144 673 458	0.1139 616 647	8
3	0.0735 174 015	0.0730 007 781	0.0724 871 270	0.0719 764 402	12
4	0.0526 166 300	0.0521 058 339	0.0515 989 886	0.0510 960 810	16
5	0.0401 420 708	0.0396 421 465	0.0391 471 287	0.0386 569 971	20
6	0.0318 802 289	0.0313 936 068	0.0309 128 204	0.0304 378 394	24
7	0.0260 252 506	0.0255 879 327	0.0250 879 327	0.0246 293 325	28
8	0.0216 741 493	0.0212 174 315	0.0207 683 123	0.0203 267 327	32
9	0.0183 252 151	0.0178 841 837	0.0174 515 767	0.0170 273 159	36
10	0.0156 773 781	0.0152 522 013	0.0148 362 332	0.0144 293 722	40
11	0.0135 390 105	0.0131 297 153	0.0127 303 683	0.0123 408 410	44
12	0.0117 823 279	0.0113 888 408	0.0110 059 938	0.0106 336 281	48
13	0.0103 188 359	0.0099 410 084	0.0095 744 635	0.0092 190 081	52
14	0.0090 853 000	0.0087 229 262	0.0083 724 260	0.0080 335 683	56
15	0.0080 353 275	0.0076 881 558	0.0073 533 959	0.0070 307 755	60
16	0.0071 341 061	0.0068 018 483	0.0064 824 869	0.0061 757 049	64
17	0.0063 549 998	0.0060 373 380	0.0057 330 027	0.0054 416 300	68
18	0.0056 772 792	0.0053 738 710	0.0050 841 652	0.0048 077 482	72
19	0.0050 845 689	0.0047 950 519	0.0045 195 594	0.0042 576 257	76
20	0.0045 637 600	0.0042 877 561	0.0040 260 451	0.0037 781 079	80
21	0.0041 042 345	0.0038 413 524	0.0035 929 793	0.0033 585 415	84
22	0.0036 972 998	0.0034 471 383	0.0032 116 510	0.0029 902 087	88
23	0.0033 357 716	0.0030 979 223	0.0028 748 628	0.0026 659 082	92
24	0.0030 136 609	0.0027 877 102	0.0025 766 173	0.0023 796 418	96
25	0.0027 259 358	0.0025 114 672	0.0023 118 787	0.0021 263 752	100
26	0.0024 683 384	0.0022 649 342	0.0020 763 891	0.0019 018 546	104
27	0.0022 372 426	0.0020 444 857	0.0018 665 260	0.0017 024 631	108
28	0.0020 295 416	0.0018 470 170	0.0016 791 895	0.0015 251 084	112
29	0.0018 425 594	0.0016 698 558	0.0015 117 132	0.0013 671 333	116
30	0.0016 739 796	0.0015 106 903	0.0013 617 930	0.0012 262 442	120
31	0.0015 217 877	0.0013 675 121	0.0012 274 291	0.0011 004 528	124
32	0.0013 842 248	0.0012 385 693	0.0011 068 791	0.0009 880 295	128
33	0.0012 597 491	0.0011 223 277	0.0009 986 195	0.0008 874 641	132
34	0.0011 470 043	0.0010 174 398	0.0009 013 140	0.0007 974 343	136
35	0.0010 447 937	0.0009 227 179	0.0008 137 867	0.0007 167 790	140
36	0.0009 520 579	0.0008 371 124	0.0007 350 004	0.0006 444 758	144
37	0.0008 678 567	0.0007 596 937	0.0006 640 380	0.0005 796 227	148
38	0.0007 913 536	0.0006 896 356	0.0006 000 866	0.0005 214 223	152
39	0.0007 218 027	0.0006 262 033	0.0005 424 243	0.0004 691 680	156
40	0.0006 585 374	0.0005 687 413	0.0004 904 089	0.0004 222 330	160
41	0.0006 009 607	0.0005 166 638	0.0004 434 681	0.0003 800 601	164
42	0.0005 485 373	0.0004 694 470	0.0004 010 911	0.0003 421 535	168
43	0.0005 007 860	0.0004 266 210	0.0003 628 212	0.0003 080 713	172
44	0.0004 572 741	0.0003 877 645	0.0003 282 501	0.0002 774 196	176
45	0.0004 176 114	0.0003 524 986	0.0002 970 116	0.0002 498 462	180
46	0.0003 814 461	0.0003 204 826	0.0002 687 776	0.0002 250 367	184
47	0.0003 484 604	0.0002 914 097	0.0002 432 532	0.0002 027 095	188
48	0.0003 183 668	0.0002 650 470	0.0002 201 739	0.0001 826 129	192
49	0.0002 909 052	0.0002 410 135	0.0001 993 016	0.0001 645 210	196
50	0.0002 658 400	0.0002 192 153	0.0001 804 222	0.0001 482 316	200
51	0.0002 429 575	0.0001 994 050	0.0001 633 427	0.0001 335 632	204
52	0.0002 220 639	0.0001 813 985	0.0001 478 896	0.0001 203 529	208
53	0.0002 029 831	0.0001 650 293	0.0001 339 062	0.0001 084 546	212
54	0.0001 855 551	0.0001 501 464	0.0001 212 513	0.0000 977 369	216
55	0.0001 696 348	0.0001 366 134	0.0001 097 976	0.0000 880 819	220
56	0.0001 550 897	0.0001 243 065	0.0000 994 301	0.0000 793 836	224
57	0.0001 417 995	0.0001 131 135	0.0000 900 451	0.0000 715 465	228
58	0.0001 296 548	0.0001 029 327	0.0000 815 488	0.0000 644 851	232
59	0.0001 185 556	0.0000 936 719	0.0000 738 565	0.0000 581 222	236
60	0.0001 084 112	0.0000 852 472	0.0000 668 918	0.0000 523 883	240

Table 3. SINKING FUND FACTORS
PAYABLE AT END OF EACH PERIOD

QUARTERS	11% NOMINAL ANNUAL RATE	11½% NOMINAL ANNUAL RATE	12% NOMINAL ANNUAL RATE	12½% NOMINAL ANNUAL RATE	QUARTER
1	1.0000 000 000	1.0000 000 000	1.0000 000 000	1.0000 000 000	1
2	0.4932 182 491	0.4929 143 561	0.4926 108 374	0.4923 076 923	2
3	0.3243 324 326	0.3239 310 654	0.3235 303 633	0.3231 303 250	3
YEARS					
1	0.2399 205 884	0.2394 733 494	0.2390 270 452	0.2385 816 739	4
2	0.1134 579 478	0.1129 561 906	0.1124 563 888	0.1119 585 380	8
3	0.0714 687 098	0.0709 639 277	0.0704 620 855	0.0699 631 750	12
4	0.0505 970 977	0.0501 020 250	0.0496 108 493	0.0491 235 563	16
5	0.0381 717 306	0.0376 913 080	0.0372 157 076	0.0367 449 071	20
6	0.0299 686 330	0.0295 051 694	0.0290 474 159	0.0285 953 396	24
7	0.0241 773 795	0.0237 320 286	0.0232 932 334	0.0228 609 465	28
8	0.0198 926 322	0.0194 659 486	0.0190 466 183	0.0186 345 760	32
9	0.0166 113 206	0.0162 035 082	0.0158 037 942	0.0154 120 918	36
10	0.0140 315 144	0.0136 425 527	0.0132 623 779	0.0128 908 783	40
11	0.0119 610 021	0.0115 907 166	0.0112 298 469	0.0108 782 525	44
12	0.0102 715 811	0.0099 196 862	0.0095 777 738	0.0092 456 713	48
13	0.0088 744 446	0.0085 405 715	0.0082 171 837	0.0079 040 731	52
14	0.0077 061 174	0.0073 898 334	0.0070 844 726	0.0067 897 885	56
15	0.0067 200 173	0.0064 208 400	0.0061 329 587	0.0058 560 861	60
16	0.0058 811 810	0.0055 985 894	0.0053 276 021	0.0050 678 885	64
17	0.0051 628 513	0.0048 962 949	0.0046 415 871	0.0043 983 530	68
18	0.0045 442 024	0.0042 931 080	0.0040 540 446	0.0038 265 920	72
19	0.0040 087 826	0.0037 725 610	0.0035 484 929	0.0033 361 124	76
20	0.0035 434 245	0.0033 214 758	0.0031 117 457	0.0029 137 230	80
21	0.0031 374 664	0.0029 291 846	0.0027 331 325	0.0025 487 540	84
22	0.0027 821 858	0.0025 869 633	0.0024 039 306	0.0022 324 878	88
23	0.0024 703 805	0.0022 876 114	0.0021 169 449	0.0019 577 392	92
24	0.0021 960 540	0.0020 251 378	0.0018 661 932	0.0017 185 390	96
25	0.0019 541 767	0.0017 945 208	0.0016 466 659	0.0015 098 935	100
26	0.0017 405 017	0.0015 915 239	0.0014 541 408	0.0013 275 995	104
27	0.0015 514 211	0.0014 125 521	0.0012 850 394	0.0011 680 991	108
28	0.0013 838 535	0.0012 545 384	0.0011 363 131	0.0010 283 663	112
29	0.0012 351 542	0.0011 148 540	0.0010 053 531	0.0009 058 160	116
30	0.0011 030 433	0.0009 912 364	0.0008 899 176	0.0007 982 312	120
31	0.0009 855 476	0.0008 817 304	0.0007 880 734	0.0007 037 039	124
32	0.0008 809 528	0.0007 846 412	0.0006 981 479	0.0006 205 875	128
33	0.0007 877 656	0.0006 984 947	0.0006 186 898	0.0005 474 563	132
34	0.0007 046 805	0.0006 220 055	0.0005 484 366	0.0004 830 737	136
35	0.0006 305 536	0.0005 540 499	0.0004 862 875	0.0004 263 642	140
36	0.0005 643 803	0.0004 936 434	0.0004 312 805	0.0003 763 909	144
37	0.0005 052 763	0.0004 399 217	0.0003 825 739	0.0003 323 364	148
38	0.0004 524 617	0.0003 921 248	0.0003 394 292	0.0002 934 861	152
39	0.0004 052 475	0.0003 495 831	0.0003 011 985	0.0002 592 147	156
40	0.0003 630 240	0.0003 117 062	0.0002 673 117	0.0002 289 743	160
41	0.0003 252 512	0.0002 779 723	0.0002 372 672	0.0002 022 845	164
42	0.0002 914 497	0.0002 479 205	0.0002 106 231	0.0001 787 233	168
43	0.0002 611 941	0.0002 211 423	0.0001 869 895	0.0001 579 202	172
44	0.0002 341 057	0.0001 972 761	0.0001 660 223	0.0001 395 494	176
45	0.0002 098 479	0.0001 760 012	0.0001 474 177	0.0001 233 240	180
46	0.0001 881 207	0.0001 570 232	0.0001 309 070	0.0001 089 916	184
47	0.0001 686 568	0.0001 401 193	0.0001 162 526	0.0000 963 301	188
48	0.0001 512 178	0.0001 250 350	0.0001 032 443	0.0000 851 434	192
49	0.0001 355 907	0.0001 115 809	0.0000 916 960	0.0000 752 590	196
50	0.0001 215 857	0.0000 995 795	0.0000 814 430	0.0000 665 244	200
51	0.0001 090 330	0.0000 888 729	0.0000 723 391	0.0000 588 056	204
52	0.0000 977 808	0.0000 793 206	0.0000 642 551	0.0000 519 838	208
53	0.0000 876 935	0.0000 707 975	0.0000 570 762	0.0000 459 545	212
54	0.0000 786 498	0.0000 631 923	0.0000 507 007	0.0000 406 255	216
55	0.0000 705 412	0.0000 564 056	0.0000 450 384	0.0000 359 151	220
56	0.0000 632 704	0.0000 503 491	0.0000 400 094	0.0000 317 515	224
57	0.0000 567 506	0.0000 449 439	0.0000 355 425	0.0000 280 709	228
58	0.0000 509 039	0.0000 401 198	0.0000 315 749	0.0000 248 174	232
59	0.0000 456 606	0.0000 358 141	0.0000 280 506	0.0000 219 412	236
60	0.0000 409 581	0.0000 319 711	0.0000 249 200	0.0000 193 985	240

Table 3.   SINKING FUND FACTORS
PAYABLE AT END OF EACH PERIOD

QUARTERS	**13%** NOMINAL ANNUAL RATE	**13½%** NOMINAL ANNUAL RATE	**14%** NOMINAL ANNUAL RATE	**14½%** NOMINAL ANNUAL RATE	QUARTERS
1	1.0000 000 000	1.0000 000 000	1.0000 000 000	1.0000 000 000	1
2	0.4920 049 200	0.4917 025 200	0.4914 004 914	0.4910 988 336	2
3	0.3227 309 493	0.3223 322 349	0.3219 341 806	0.3215 367 851	3

YEARS

1	0.2381 372 337	0.2376 937 228	0.2372 511 395	0.2368 094 819	4
2	0.1114 626 337	0.1109 686 713	0.1104 766 465	0.1099 865 548	8
3	0.0694 671 878	0.0689 741 154	0.0684 839 493	0.0679 966 807	12
4	0.0486 401 319	0.0481 605 616	0.0476 848 306	0.0472 129 241	16
5	0.0362 788 839	0.0358 176 149	0.0353 610 768	0.0349 092 457	20
6	0.0281 489 063	0.0277 080 816	0.0272 728 303	0.0268 431 163	24
7	0.0224 351 193	0.0220 157 023	0.0216 026 452	0.0211 958 966	28
8	0.0182 297 552	0.0178 320 878	0.0174 415 048	0.0170 579 356	32
9	0.0150 283 128	0.0146 523 670	0.0142 841 628	0.0139 236 070	36
10	0.0125 279 400	0.0121 734 473	0.0118 272 823	0.0114 893 256	40
11	0.0105 357 906	0.0102 023 160	0.0098 776 816	0.0095 617 383	44
12	0.0089 232 032	0.0086 101 920	0.0083 064 580	0.0080 118 199	48
13	0.0076 010 288	0.0073 078 378	0.0070 242 854	0.0067 501 552	52
14	0.0065 055 322	0.0062 314 528	0.0059 672 981	0.0057 128 152	56
15	0.0055 899 328	0.0053 342 082	0.0050 886 213	0.0048 528 811	60
16	0.0048 191 174	0.0045 809 570	0.0043 530 765	0.0041 351 462	64
17	0.0041 662 182	0.0039 448 093	0.0037 337 550	0.0035 326 869	68
18	0.0036 103 320	0.0034 048 492	0.0032 097 323	0.0030 245 750	72
19	0.0031 349 575	0.0029 445 715	0.0027 645 038	0.0025 943 115	76
20	0.0027 269 026	0.0025 507 873	0.0023 848 887	0.0022 287 288	80
21	0.0023 755 020	0.0022 128 404	0.0020 602 452	0.0019 172 057	84
22	0.0020 720 479	0.0019 220 378	0.0017 819 002	0.0016 510 945	88
23	0.0018 093 692	0.0016 712 273	0.0015 427 259	0.0014 232 970	92
24	0.0015 815 142	0.0014 544 800	0.0013 368 213	0.0012 279 470	96
25	0.0013 835 102	0.0012 668 489	0.0011 592 702	0.0010 601 634	100
26	0.0012 111 771	0.0011 041 817	0.0010 059 536	0.0009 158 655	104
27	0.0010 609 823	0.0009 629 759	0.0008 734 032	0.0007 916 247	108
28	0.0009 299 266	0.0008 402 632	0.0007 586 865	0.0006 845 094	112
29	0.0008 154 526	0.0007 335 183	0.0006 593 142	0.0005 921 863	116
30	0.0007 153 719	0.0006 405 851	0.0005 731 662	0.0005 124 592	120
31	0.0006 278 056	0.0005 596 172	0.0004 984 319	0.0004 435 952	124
32	0.0005 511 359	0.0004 890 289	0.0004 335 608	0.0003 840 818	128
33	0.0004 839 661	0.0004 274 553	0.0003 772 225	0.0003 326 252	132
34	0.0004 250 879	0.0003 737 191	0.0003 282 727	0.0002 881 166	136
35	0.0003 734 538	0.0003 268 027	0.0002 857 262	0.0002 496 043	140
36	0.0003 281 541	0.0002 858 255	0.0002 487 328	0.0002 162 704	144
37	0.0002 883 973	0.0002 500 241	0.0002 165 585	0.0001 874 110	148
38	0.0002 534 945	0.0002 187 358	0.0001 885 682	0.0001 624 198	152
39	0.0002 228 444	0.0001 913 851	0.0001 642 125	0.0001 407 740	156
40	0.0001 959 223	0.0001 674 711	0.0001 430 155	0.0001 220 227	160
41	0.0001 722 699	0.0001 465 581	0.0001 245 643	0.0001 057 763	164
42	0.0001 514 861	0.0001 282 665	0.0001 085 009	0.0000 916 984	168
43	0.0001 332 200	0.0001 122 655	0.0000 945 146	0.0000 794 983	172
44	0.0001 171 644	0.0000 982 663	0.0000 823 355	0.0000 689 245	176
45	0.0001 030 499	0.0000 860 172	0.0000 717 289	0.0000 597 593	180
46	0.0000 906 404	0.0000 752 984	0.0000 624 911	0.0000 518 146	184
47	0.0000 797 290	0.0000 659 178	0.0000 544 449	0.0000 449 274	188
48	0.0000 701 339	0.0000 577 079	0.0000 474 361	0.0000 389 567	192
49	0.0000 616 957	0.0000 505 221	0.0000 413 306	0.0000 337 802	196
50	0.0000 542 745	0.0000 442 322	0.0000 360 118	0.0000 292 921	200
51	0.0000 477 473	0.0000 387 262	0.0000 313 780	0.0000 254 007	204
52	0.0000 420 060	0.0000 339 064	0.0000 273 410	0.0000 220 266	208
53	0.0000 369 559	0.0000 296 869	0.0000 238 237	0.0000 191 009	212
54	0.0000 325 136	0.0000 259 929	0.0000 207 592	0.0000 165 640	216
55	0.0000 286 057	0.0000 227 589	0.0000 180 890	0.0000 143 642	220
56	0.0000 251 678	0.0000 199 275	0.0000 157 625	0.0000 124 566	224
57	0.0000 221 435	0.0000 174 485	0.0000 137 353	0.0000 108 024	228
58	0.0000 194 827	0.0000 152 781	0.0000 119 689	0.0000 093 680	232
59	0.0000 171 419	0.0000 133 777	0.0000 104 298	0.0000 081 241	236
60	0.0000 150 824	0.0000 117 138	0.0000 090 886	0.0000 070 453	240

Table 3. SINKING FUND FACTORS
PAYABLE AT END OF EACH PERIOD

QUARTERS	15% NOMINAL ANNUAL RATE	15½% NOMINAL ANNUAL RATE	16% NOMINAL ANNUAL RATE	16½% NOMINAL ANNUAL RATE	QUARTERS
1	1.0000 000 000	1.0000 000 000	1.0000 000 000	1.0000 000 000	1
2	0.4907 975 460	0.4904 966 278	0.4901 960 784	0.4898 958 971	2
3	0.3211 400 472	0.3207 439 656	0.3203 485 392	0.3199 537 667	3

YEARS

1	0.2363 687 482	0.2359 289 366	0.2354 900 454	0.2350 520 727	4
2	0.1094 983 915	0.1090 121 521	0.1085 278 320	0.1080 454 268	8
3	0.0675 123 010	0.0670 308 013	0.0665 521 727	0.0660 764 062	12
4	0.0467 448 270	0.0462 805 238	0.0458 199 992	0.0453 632 375	16
5	0.0344 620 973	0.0340 196 072	0.0335 817 503	0.0331 485 014	20
6	0.0264 189 033	0.0260 001 542	0.0255 868 313	0.0251 788 965	24
7	0.0207 954 043	0.0204 011 151	0.0200 129 752	0.0196 309 300	28
8	0.0166 813 087	0.0163 115 513	0.0159 485 897	0.0155 923 494	32
9	0.0135 706 050	0.0132 250 610	0.0128 868 780	0.0125 559 578	36
10	0.0111 594 563	0.0108 375 521	0.0105 234 893	0.0102 171 434	40
11	0.0092 543 358	0.0089 553 222	0.0086 645 444	0.0083 818 487	44
12	0.0077 260 947	0.0074 490 989	0.0071 806 476	0.0069 205 556	48
13	0.0064 852 301	0.0062 292 922	0.0059 821 236	0.0057 435 063	52
14	0.0054 677 509	0.0052 318 520	0.0050 048 662	0.0047 865 422	56
15	0.0046 266 973	0.0044 097 810	0.0042 018 451	0.0040 026 049	60
16	0.0039 268 386	0.0037 278 288	0.0035 377 955	0.0033 564 212	64
17	0.0033 412 407	0.0031 590 564	0.0029 857 795	0.0028 210 613	68
18	0.0028 489 770	0.0026 825 446	0.0025 248 919	0.0023 756 408	72
19	0.0024 335 598	0.0022 818 234	0.0021 386 869	0.0020 037 458	76
20	0.0020 818 410	0.0019 437 705	0.0018 140 755	0.0016 923 276	80
21	0.0017 832 256	0.0016 578 238	0.0015 405 351	0.0014 309 105	84
22	0.0015 290 977	0.0014 154 056	0.0013 095 329	0.0012 110 138	88
23	0.0013 123 956	0.0012 094 965	0.0011 140 984	0.0010 257 221	92
24	0.0011 272 913	0.0010 343 139	0.0009 485 002	0.0008 693 615	96
25	0.0009 689 464	0.0008 850 665	0.0008 080 041	0.0007 372 521	100
26	0.0008 333 233	0.0007 577 652	0.0006 886 620	0.0006 255 164	104
27	0.0007 170 371	0.0006 490 737	0.0005 872 033	0.0005 309 291	108
28	0.0006 172 394	0.0005 561 921	0.0005 008 762	0.0004 507 988	112
29	0.0005 315 248	0.0004 767 626	0.0004 273 741	0.0003 828 730	116
30	0.0004 578 561	0.0004 087 944	0.0003 647 553	0.0003 252 620	120
31	0.0003 945 038	0.0003 506 024	0.0003 113 821	0.0002 763 772	124
32	0.0003 399 958	0.0003 007 577	0.0002 658 702	0.0002 348 811	128
33	0.0002 930 774	0.0002 580 461	0.0002 270 478	0.0001 996 452	132
34	0.0002 526 768	0.0002 214 346	0.0001 939 216	0.0001 697 169	136
35	0.0002 178 776	0.0001 900 427	0.0001 656 484	0.0001 442 907	140
36	0.0001 878 948	0.0001 631 198	0.0001 415 119	0.0001 226 850	144
37	0.0001 620 557	0.0001 400 247	0.0001 209 028	0.0001 043 227	148
38	0.0001 397 832	0.0001 202 096	0.0001 033 029	0.0000 887 145	152
39	0.0001 205 816	0.0001 032 060	0.0000 882 707	0.0000 754 458	156
40	0.0001 040 249	0.0000 886 131	0.0000 754 300	0.0000 641 648	160
41	0.0000 897 470	0.0000 760 875	0.0000 644 602	0.0000 545 727	164
42	0.0000 774 329	0.0000 653 355	0.0000 550 880	0.0000 464 162	168
43	0.0000 668 113	0.0000 561 050	0.0000 470 800	0.0000 394 800	172
44	0.0000 576 490	0.0000 481 802	0.0000 402 373	0.0000 335 811	176
45	0.0000 497 448	0.0000 413 760	0.0000 343 900	0.0000 285 642	180
46	0.0000 429 256	0.0000 355 336	0.0000 293 930	0.0000 242 972	184
47	0.0000 370 422	0.0000 305 168	0.0000 251 226	0.0000 206 680	188
48	0.0000 319 658	0.0000 262 087	0.0000 214 730	0.0000 175 811	192
49	0.0000 275 856	0.0000 225 092	0.0000 183 537	0.0000 149 554	196
50	0.0000 238 060	0.0000 193 322	0.0000 156 878	0.0000 127 220	200
51	0.0000 205 445	0.0000 166 038	0.0000 134 092	0.0000 108 222	204
52	0.0000 177 301	0.0000 142 605	0.0000 114 617	0.0000 092 061	208
53	0.0000 153 014	0.0000 122 481	0.0000 097 971	0.0000 078 315	212
54	0.0000 132 055	0.0000 105 198	0.0000 083 743	0.0000 066 621	216
55	0.0000 113 967	0.0000 090 353	0.0000 071 582	0.0000 056 674	220
56	0.0000 098 358	0.0000 077 604	0.0000 061 187	0.0000 048 212	224
57	0.0000 084 887	0.0000 066 655	0.0000 052 302	0.0000 041 013	228
58	0.0000 073 261	0.0000 057 250	0.0000 044 707	0.0000 034 890	232
59	0.0000 063 228	0.0000 049 172	0.0000 038 215	0.0000 029 681	236
60	0.0000 054 569	0.0000 042 235	0.0000 032 666	0.0000 025 249	240

Table 3. SINKING FUND FACTORS
PAYABLE AT END OF EACH PERIOD

	17% NOMINAL ANNUAL RATE	17½% NOMINAL ANNUAL RATE	18% NOMINAL ANNUAL RATE	18½% NOMINAL ANNUAL RATE	QUARTERS
RTERS					
1	1.0000 000 000	1.0000 000 000	1.0000 000 000	1.0000 000 000	1
2	0.4895 960 832	0.4892 966 361	0.4889 975 550	0.4886 988 393	2
3	0.3195 596 468	0.3191 661 784	0.3187 733 601	0.3183 811 908	3
YEARS					
1	0.2346 150 167	0.2341 788 757	0.2337 436 479	0.2333 093 315	4
2	0.1075 649 316	0.1070 863 420	0.1066 096 533	0.1061 348 608	8
3	0.0656 034 928	0.0651 334 234	0.0646 661 886	0.0642 017 793	12
4	0.0449 102 226	0.0444 609 387	0.0440 153 694	0.0435 734 984	16
5	0.0327 198 348	0.0322 957 245	0.0318 761 443	0.0314 610 675	20
6	0.0247 763 108	0.0243 790 352	0.0239 870 299	0.0236 002 547	24
7	0.0192 549 240	0.0188 849 013	0.0185 208 051	0.0181 625 781	28
8	0.0152 427 548	0.0148 997 294	0.0145 631 962	0.0142 330 773	32
9	0.0122 322 015	0.0119 155 090	0.0116 057 796	0.0113 029 120	36
10	0.0099 183 886	0.0096 270 987	0.0093 431 466	0.0090 664 048	40
11	0.0081 070 805	0.0078 400 845	0.0075 807 056	0.0073 287 880	44
12	0.0066 686 377	0.0064 247 082	0.0061 885 821	0.0059 600 748	48
13	0.0055 132 229	0.0052 910 567	0.0050 767 923	0.0048 702 156	52
14	0.0045 766 300	0.0043 748 818	0.0041 810 518	0.0039 948 970	56
15	0.0038 117 784	0.0036 290 870	0.0034 542 558	0.0032 870 141	60
16	0.0031 833 932	0.0030 184 034	0.0028 611 494	0.0027 113 345	64
17	0.0026 645 597	0.0025 159 393	0.0023 748 725	0.0022 410 393	68
18	0.0022 344 223	0.0021 008 762	0.0019 746 524	0.0018 554 105	72
19	0.0018 766 067	0.0017 568 877	0.0016 442 194	0.0015 382 442	76
20	0.0015 781 123	0.0014 710 294	0.0013 706 935	0.0012 767 336	80
21	0.0013 285 180	0.0012 329 425	0.0011 437 861	0.0010 606 681	84
22	0.0011 194 021	0.0010 342 714	0.0009 552 152	0.0008 818 465	88
23	0.0009 439 110	0.0008 682 312	0.0007 982 710	0.0007 336 406	92
24	0.0007 964 344	0.0007 292 809	0.0006 674 877	0.0006 106 653	96
25	0.0006 723 562	0.0006 128 735	0.0005 583 922	0.0005 085 267	100
26	0.0005 678 618	0.0005 152 621	0.0004 673 100	0.0004 236 260	104
27	0.0004 797 880	0.0004 333 491	0.0003 912 122	0.0003 530 068	108
28	0.0004 055 028	0.0003 645 653	0.0003 275 957	0.0002 942 342	112
29	0.0003 428 109	0.0003 067 751	0.0002 743 866	0.0002 452 982	116
30	0.0002 898 768	0.0002 581 993	0.0002 298 637	0.0002 045 369	120
31	0.0002 451 631	0.0002 173 531	0.0001 925 960	0.0001 705 737	124
32	0.0002 073 800	0.0001 829 954	0.0001 613 921	0.0001 422 674	128
33	0.0001 754 436	0.0001 540 879	0.0001 352 588	0.0001 186 704	132
34	0.0001 484 426	0.0001 297 603	0.0001 133 678	0.0000 989 957	136
35	0.0001 256 093	0.0001 092 831	0.0000 950 272	0.0000 825 887	140
36	0.0001 062 969	0.0000 920 442	0.0000 796 590	0.0000 689 050	144
37	0.0000 899 601	0.0000 775 294	0.0000 667 799	0.0000 574 912	148
38	0.0000 761 385	0.0000 653 070	0.0000 559 856	0.0000 479 701	152
39	0.0000 644 438	0.0000 550 138	0.0000 469 379	0.0000 400 271	156
40	0.0000 545 476	0.0000 463 447	0.0000 393 537	0.0000 334 003	160
41	0.0000 461 728	0.0000 390 428	0.0000 329 958	0.0000 278 712	164
42	0.0000 390 849	0.0000 328 923	0.0000 276 658	0.0000 232 579	168
43	0.0000 330 860	0.0000 277 113	0.0000 231 971	0.0000 194 085	172
44	0.0000 280 084	0.0000 233 468	0.0000 194 506	0.0000 161 965	176
45	0.0000 237 104	0.0000 196 700	0.0000 163 094	0.0000 135 162	180
46	0.0000 200 724	0.0000 165 725	0.0000 136 756	0.0000 112 795	184
47	0.0000 169 927	0.0000 139 629	0.0000 114 673	0.0000 094 131	188
48	0.0000 143 857	0.0000 117 644	0.0000 096 156	0.0000 078 555	192
49	0.0000 121 788	0.0000 099 121	0.0000 080 630	0.0000 065 557	196
50	0.0000 103 105	0.0000 083 515	0.0000 067 611	0.0000 054 710	200
51	0.0000 087 289	0.0000 070 366	0.0000 056 695	0.0000 045 658	204
52	0.0000 073 900	0.0000 059 288	0.0000 047 541	0.0000 038 104	208
53	0.0000 062 564	0.0000 049 954	0.0000 039 866	0.0000 031 800	212
54	0.0000 052 968	0.0000 042 090	0.0000 033 429	0.0000 026 538	216
55	0.0000 044 844	0.0000 035 464	0.0000 028 032	0.0000 022 148	220
56	0.0000 037 966	0.0000 029 881	0.0000 023 506	0.0000 018 483	224
57	0.0000 032 142	0.0000 025 177	0.0000 019 711	0.0000 015 425	228
58	0.0000 027 213	0.0000 021 214	0.0000 016 529	0.0000 012 873	232
59	0.0000 023 039	0.0000 017 874	0.0000 013 861	0.0000 010 744	236
60	0.0000 019 505	0.0000 015 060	0.0000 011 623	0.0000 008 966	240

Table 3.   **SINKING FUND FACTORS**
PAYABLE AT END OF EACH PERIOD

QUARTERS	**19%** NOMINAL ANNUAL RATE	**19½%** NOMINAL ANNUAL RATE	**20%** NOMINAL ANNUAL RATE	**20½%** NOMINAL ANNUAL RATE	QUART
1	1.0000 000 000	1.0000 000 000	1.0000 000 000	1.0000 000 000	1
2	0.4884 004 884	0.4881 025 015	0.4878 048 780	0.4875 076 173	2
3	0.3179 896 693	0.3175 987 943	0.3172 085 646	0.3168 189 790	3
YEARS					
1	0.2328 759 246	0.2324 434 256	0.2320 118 326	0.2315 811 439	4
2	0.1056 619 598	0.1051 909 457	0.1047 218 136	0.1042 545 590	8
3	0.0637 401 861	0.0632 813 995	0.0628 254 100	0.0623 722 081	12
4	0.0431 353 090	0.0427 007 845	0.0422 699 080	0.0418 426 624	16
5	0.0310 504 673	0.0306 443 163	0.0302 425 872	0.0298 452 521	20
6	0.0232 186 689	0.0228 422 314	0.0224 709 008	0.0221 046 351	24
7	0.0178 101 623	0.0174 634 994	0.0171 225 304	0.0167 871 960	28
8	0.0139 092 942	0.0135 917 680	0.0132 804 189	0.0129 751 672	32
9	0.0110 068 041	0.0107 173 534	0.0104 344 571	0.0101 580 120	36
10	0.0087 967 454	0.0085 340 403	0.0082 781 612	0.0080 289 799	40
11	0.0070 841 765	0.0068 467 156	0.0066 162 506	0.0063 926 272	44
12	0.0057 390 022	0.0055 251 814	0.0053 184 306	0.0051 185 693	48
13	0.0046 711 140	0.0044 792 771	0.0042 944 966	0.0041 165 665	52
14	0.0038 161 771	0.0036 446 552	0.0034 800 978	0.0033 222 749	56
15	0.0031 270 953	0.0029 742 377	0.0028 281 845	0.0026 886 844	60
16	0.0025 686 682	0.0024 328 665	0.0023 036 520	0.0021 807 543	64
17	0.0021 141 277	0.0019 938 343	0.0018 798 643	0.0017 719 316	68
18	0.0017 428 204	0.0016 365 626	0.0015 363 280	0.0014 418 184	72
19	0.0014 386 173	0.0013 450 066	0.0012 570 925	0.0011 745 681	76
20	0.0011 887 937	0.0011 065 325	0.0010 296 235	0.0009 577 547	80
21	0.0009 822 248	0.0009 111 096	0.0008 439 924	0.0007 815 596	84
22	0.0008 137 976	0.0007 507 197	0.0006 922 828	0.0006 381 748	88
23	0.0006 739 715	0.0006 189 164	0.0005 681 481	0.0005 213 589	92
24	0.0005 584 480	0.0005 104 924	0.0004 664 770	0.0004 261 013	96
25	0.0004 629 162	0.0004 212 245	0.0003 831 381	0.0003 483 654	100
26	0.0003 838 573	0.0003 476 768	0.0003 147 810	0.0002 848 895	104
27	0.0003 183 901	0.0002 870 458	0.0002 586 824	0.0002 330 318	108
28	0.0002 641 499	0.0002 370 392	0.0002 126 236	0.0001 906 485	112
29	0.0002 191 924	0.0001 957 791	0.0001 747 942	0.0001 559 972	116
30	0.0001 819 156	0.0001 617 246	0.0001 437 145	0.0001 276 595	120
31	0.0001 509 983	0.0001 336 099	0.0001 181 741	0.0001 044 800	124
32	0.0001 253 494	0.0001 103 937	0.0000 971 814	0.0000 855 163	128
33	0.0001 040 667	0.0000 912 191	0.0000 799 238	0.0000 699 993	132
34	0.0000 864 041	0.0000 753 802	0.0000 657 349	0.0000 573 010	136
35	0.0000 717 438	0.0000 622 950	0.0000 540 677	0.0000 469 083	140
36	0.0000 595 741	0.0000 514 836	0.0000 444 731	0.0000 384 020	144
37	0.0000 494 708	0.0000 425 502	0.0000 365 823	0.0000 314 392	148
38	0.0000 410 824	0.0000 351 680	0.0000 300 925	0.0000 257 394	152
39	0.0000 341 174	0.0000 290 674	0.0000 247 545	0.0000 210 734	156
40	0.0000 283 340	0.0000 240 255	0.0000 203 638	0.0000 172 536	160
41	0.0000 235 314	0.0000 198 586	0.0000 167 521	0.0000 141 263	164
42	0.0000 195 432	0.0000 164 146	0.0000 137 812	0.0000 115 660	168
43	0.0000 162 311	0.0000 135 680	0.0000 113 373	0.0000 094 698	172
44	0.0000 134 805	0.0000 112 152	0.0000 093 268	0.0000 077 536	176
45	0.0000 111 962	0.0000 092 705	0.0000 076 730	0.0000 063 484	180
46	0.0000 092 990	0.0000 076 630	0.0000 063 124	0.0000 051 980	184
47	0.0000 077 234	0.0000 063 343	0.0000 051 931	0.0000 042 560	188
48	0.0000 064 147	0.0000 052 360	0.0000 042 723	0.0000 034 847	192
49	0.0000 053 279	0.0000 043 282	0.0000 035 148	0.0000 028 533	196
50	0.0000 044 251	0.0000 035 778	0.0000 028 916	0.0000 023 362	200
51	0.0000 036 754	0.0000 029 575	0.0000 023 789	0.0000 019 129	204
52	0.0000 030 527	0.0000 024 447	0.0000 019 571	0.0000 015 662	208
53	0.0000 025 355	0.0000 020 209	0.0000 016 101	0.0000 012 824	212
54	0.0000 021 059	0.0000 016 705	0.0000 013 246	0.0000 010 500	216
55	0.0000 017 491	0.0000 013 809	0.0000 010 898	0.0000 008 598	220
56	0.0000 014 528	0.0000 011 415	0.0000 008 966	0.0000 007 040	224
57	0.0000 012 067	0.0000 009 436	0.0000 007 376	0.0000 005 764	228
58	0.0000 010 022	0.0000 007 800	0.0000 006 068	0.0000 004 720	232
59	0.0000 008 324	0.0000 006 448	0.0000 004 992	0.0000 003 864	236
60	0.0000 006 914	0.0000 005 330	0.0000 004 107	0.0000 003 164	240

QUARTERLY
COMPOUNDING

Table 3.   SINKING FUND FACTORS
PAYABLE AT END OF EACH PERIOD

	21% NOMINAL ANNUAL RATE	21½% NOMINAL ANNUAL RATE	22% NOMINAL ANNUAL RATE	22½% NOMINAL ANNUAL RATE	
QUARTERS					QUARTERS
1	1.0000 000 000	1.0000 000 000	1.0000 000 000	1.0000 000 000	1
2	0.4872 107 186	0.4869 141 814	0.4866 180 049	0.4863 221 884	2
3	0.3164 300 363	0.3160 417 353	0.3156 540 747	0.3152 670 534	3
YEARS					
1	0.2311 513 576	0.2307 224 720	0.2302 944 853	0.2298 673 958	4
2	0.1037 891 770	0.1033 256 628	0.1028 640 118	0.1024 042 191	8
3	0.0619 217 842	0.0614 741 284	0.0610 292 312	0.0605 870 826	12
4	0.0414 190 304	0.0409 989 948	0.0405 825 380	0.0401 696 423	16
5	0.0294 522 832	0.0290 636 520	0.0286 793 300	0.0282 992 886	20
6	0.0217 433 921	0.0213 871 293	0.0210 358 037	0.0206 893 721	24
7	0.0164 574 362	0.0161 331 909	0.0158 143 996	0.0155 010 012	28
8	0.0126 759 322	0.0123 826 333	0.0120 951 895	0.0118 135 194	32
9	0.0098 879 146	0.0096 240 614	0.0093 663 488	0.0091 146 732	36
10	0.0077 863 683	0.0075 501 986	0.0073 203 434	0.0070 966 755	40
11	0.0061 756 919	0.0059 652 920	0.0057 612 757	0.0055 634 926	44
12	0.0049 254 187	0.0047 388 015	0.0045 585 424	0.0043 844 681	48
13	0.0039 452 836	0.0037 804 474	0.0036 218 603	0.0034 693 281	52
14	0.0031 709 607	0.0030 259 335	0.0028 869 756	0.0027 538 742	56
15	0.0025 554 911	0.0024 283 643	0.0023 070 692	0.0021 913 771	60
16	0.0020 639 102	0.0019 528 636	0.0018 473 659	0.0017 471 759	64
17	0.0016 697 590	0.0015 730 784	0.0014 816 307	0.0013 951 657	68
18	0.0013 527 462	0.0012 688 348	0.0011 898 180	0.0011 154 404	72
19	0.0010 971 390	0.0010 245 236	0.0009 564 521	0.0008 926 673	76
20	0.0008 906 287	0.0008 279 618	0.0007 694 845	0.0007 149 405	80
21	0.0007 235 137	0.0006 695 727	0.0006 194 699	0.0005 729 532	84
22	0.0005 881 011	0.0005 417 843	0.0004 989 631	0.0004 593 920	88
23	0.0004 782 600	0.0004 385 809	0.0004 020 682	0.0003 684 850	92
24	0.0003 890 846	0.0003 551 651	0.0003 240 994	0.0002 956 610	96
25	0.0003 166 360	0.0002 876 988	0.0002 613 216	0.0002 372 895	100
26	0.0002 577 433	0.0002 331 035	0.0002 107 501	0.0001 904 810	104
27	0.0002 098 478	0.0001 889 047	0.0001 699 955	0.0001 529 311	108
28	0.0001 708 814	0.0001 531 102	0.0001 371 415	0.0001 227 995	112
29	0.0001 391 698	0.0001 241 138	0.0001 106 497	0.0000 986 151	116
30	0.0001 133 557	0.0001 006 190	0.0000 892 837	0.0000 792 003	120
31	0.0000 923 382	0.0000 815 786	0.0000 720 487	0.0000 636 121	124
32	0.0000 752 232	0.0000 661 457	0.0000 581 442	0.0000 510 948	128
33	0.0000 612 842	0.0000 536 352	0.0000 469 254	0.0000 410 423	132
34	0.0000 499 305	0.0000 434 928	0.0000 378 728	0.0000 329 688	136
35	0.0000 406 819	0.0000 352 696	0.0000 305 675	0.0000 264 841	140
36	0.0000 331 475	0.0000 286 020	0.0000 246 719	0.0000 212 755	144
37	0.0000 270 092	0.0000 231 955	0.0000 199 139	0.0000 170 915	148
38	0.0000 220 080	0.0000 188 112	0.0000 160 737	0.0000 137 305	152
39	0.0000 179 333	0.0000 152 559	0.0000 129 742	0.0000 110 306	156
40	0.0000 146 131	0.0000 123 727	0.0000 104 725	0.0000 088 617	160
41	0.0000 119 078	0.0000 100 345	0.0000 084 533	0.0000 071 193	164
42	0.0000 097 034	0.0000 081 382	0.0000 068 234	0.0000 057 195	168
43	0.0000 079 072	0.0000 066 003	0.0000 055 079	0.0000 045 950	172
44	0.0000 064 435	0.0000 053 531	0.0000 044 460	0.0000 036 915	176
45	0.0000 052 508	0.0000 043 416	0.0000 035 888	0.0000 029 650	180
46	0.0000 042 789	0.0000 035 212	0.0000 028 969	0.0000 023 827	184
47	0.0000 034 868	0.0000 028 558	0.0000 023 384	0.0000 019 142	188
48	0.0000 028 414	0.0000 023 162	0.0000 018 876	0.0000 015 379	192
49	0.0000 023 155	0.0000 018 786	0.0000 015 237	0.0000 012 355	196
50	0.0000 018 869	0.0000 015 236	0.0000 012 299	0.0000 009 926	200
51	0.0000 015 377	0.0000 012 357	0.0000 009 928	0.0000 007 975	204
52	0.0000 012 531	0.0000 010 022	0.0000 008 014	0.0000 006 407	208
53	0.0000 010 211	0.0000 008 129	0.0000 006 469	0.0000 005 147	212
54	0.0000 008 321	0.0000 006 593	0.0000 005 222	0.0000 004 135	216
55	0.0000 006 781	0.0000 005 347	0.0000 004 215	0.0000 003 322	220
56	0.0000 005 526	0.0000 004 337	0.0000 003 403	0.0000 002 669	224
57	0.0000 004 503	0.0000 003 517	0.0000 002 747	0.0000 002 144	228
58	0.0000 003 670	0.0000 002 853	0.0000 002 217	0.0000 001 723	232
59	0.0000 002 991	0.0000 002 314	0.0000 001 790	0.0000 001 384	236
60	0.0000 002 437	0.0000 001 877	0.0000 001 445	0.0000 001 112	240

Table 4.   PRESENT WORTH OF ONE DOLLAR
PAYABLE AT END OF EACH PERIOD

QUARTERS	5% NOMINAL ANNUAL RATE	5½% NOMINAL ANNUAL RATE	6% NOMINAL ANNUAL RATE	6½% NOMINAL ANNUAL RATE	QUARTER
1	0.9876 543 210	0.9864 364 982	0.9852 216 749	0.9840 098 401	1
2	0.9754 610 578	0.9730 569 649	0.9706 617 486	0.9682 753 654	2
3	0.9634 183 287	0.9598 589 049	0.9563 169 937	0.9527 924 875	3
YEARS					
1	0.9515 242 752	0.9468 398 569	0.9421 842 303	0.9375 571 833	4
2	0.9053 984 463	0.8965 057 146	0.8877 111 238	0.8790 134 719	8
3	0.8615 086 004	0.8488 473 426	0.8363 874 219	0.8241 253 947	12
4	0.8197 463 466	0.8037 224 964	0.7880 310 393	0.7726 646 838	16
5	0.7800 085 483	0.7609 964 935	0.7424 704 182	0.7244 173 245	20
6	0.7421 970 686	0.7205 418 110	0.6995 439 195	0.6791 826 663	24
7	0.7062 185 278	0.6822 377 052	0.6590 992 494	0.6367 725 875	28
8	0.6719 840 728	0.6459 698 512	0.6209 929 189	0.5970 107 135	32
9	0.6394 091 578	0.6116 300 014	0.5850 897 353	0.5597 316 829	36
10	0.6084 133 355	0.5791 156 630	0.5512 623 219	0.5247 804 600	40
11	0.5789 200 581	0.5483 297 915	0.5193 906 665	0.4920 116 899	44
12	0.5508 564 886	0.5191 805 013	0.4893 616 953	0.4612 890 942	48
13	0.5241 533 211	0.4915 807 916	0.4610 688 722	0.4324 849 038	52
14	0.4987 446 090	0.4654 482 864	0.4344 118 205	0.4054 793 282	56
15	0.4745 676 026	0.4407 049 889	0.4092 959 667	0.3801 600 568	60
16	0.4515 625 941	0.4172 770 486	0.3856 322 054	0.3564 217 921	64
17	0.4296 727 700	0.3950 945 410	0.3633 365 826	0.3341 658 114	68
18	0.4088 440 711	0.3740 912 587	0.3423 299 984	0.3132 995 569	72
19	0.3890 250 584	0.3542 045 138	0.3225 379 260	0.2937 362 501	76
20	0.3701 667 868	0.3353 749 512	0.3038 901 476	0.2753 945 312	80
21	0.3522 226 835	0.3175 463 708	0.2863 205 048	0.2581 981 210	84
22	0.3351 484 336	0.3006 655 603	0.2697 666 644	0.2420 755 030	88
23	0.3189 018 704	0.2846 821 361	0.2541 698 971	0.2269 596 268	92
24	0.3034 428 711	0.2695 483 930	0.2394 748 688	0.2127 876 284	96
25	0.2887 332 580	0.2552 191 618	0.2256 294 450	0.1995 005 695	100
26	0.2747 367 040	0.2416 516 747	0.2125 845 049	0.1870 431 920	104
27	0.2614 186 432	0.2288 054 371	0.2002 937 682	0.1753 636 882	108
28	0.2487 461 850	0.2166 421 073	0.1887 136 298	0.1644 134 856	112
29	0.2366 880 334	0.2051 253 819	0.1778 030 060	0.1541 470 444	116
30	0.2252 144 094	0.1942 208 872	0.1675 231 884	0.1445 216 688	120
31	0.2142 969 777	0.1838 960 771	0.1578 377 063	0.1354 973 287	124
32	0.2039 087 764	0.1741 201 353	0.1487 121 978	0.1270 364 939	128
33	0.1940 241 506	0.1648 638 840	0.1401 142 876	0.1191 039 773	132
34	0.1846 186 893	0.1560 996 963	0.1320 134 722	0.1116 667 895	136
35	0.1756 691 645	0.1478 014 141	0.1243 810 117	0.1046 940 006	140
36	0.1671 534 745	0.1399 442 698	0.1171 898 278	0.0981 566 123	144
37	0.1590 505 886	0.1325 048 124	0.1104 144 077	0.0920 274 370	148
38	0.1513 404 961	0.1254 608 376	0.1040 307 137	0.0862 809 846	152
39	0.1440 041 558	0.1187 913 215	0.0980 160 979	0.0808 933 569	156
40	0.1370 234 500	0.1124 763 579	0.0923 492 218	0.0758 421 478	160
41	0.1303 811 390	0.1064 970 986	0.0870 099 805	0.0711 063 505	164
42	0.1240 608 188	0.1008 356 976	0.0819 794 315	0.0666 662 697	168
43	0.1180 468 807	0.0954 752 575	0.0772 397 275	0.0625 034 400	172
44	0.1123 244 726	0.0903 997 791	0.0727 740 532	0.0586 005 492	176
45	0.1068 794 623	0.0855 941 139	0.0685 665 653	0.0549 413 658	180
46	0.1016 984 029	0.0810 439 186	0.0646 023 366	0.0515 106 722	184
47	0.0967 684 991	0.0767 356 123	0.0608 673 028	0.0482 942 007	188
48	0.0920 775 760	0.0726 563 362	0.0573 482 128	0.0452 785 748	192
49	0.0876 140 488	0.0687 930 149	0.0540 325 817	0.0424 512 530	196
50	0.0833 668 943	0.0651 368 206	0.0509 086 464	0.0398 004 772	200
51	0.0793 256 236	0.0616 741 379	0.0479 653 239	0.0373 152 233	204
52	0.0754 802 565	0.0583 955 319	0.0451 921 717	0.0349 851 557	208
53	0.0718 212 964	0.0552 912 170	0.0425 793 515	0.0328 005 840	212
54	0.0683 397 070	0.0523 519 280	0.0401 175 936	0.0307 524 232	216
55	0.0650 268 902	0.0495 688 920	0.0377 981 640	0.0288 321 552	220
56	0.0618 746 645	0.0469 338 027	0.0356 128 341	0.0270 317 942	224
57	0.0588 752 453	0.0444 387 950	0.0335 538 507	0.0253 438 529	228
58	0.0560 212 251	0.0420 764 223	0.0316 139 090	0.0237 613 113	232
59	0.0533 055 556	0.0398 396 337	0.0297 861 265	0.0222 775 881	236
60	0.0507 215 302	0.0377 217 530	0.0280 640 186	0.0208 865 128	240

Table 4.   PRESENT WORTH OF ONE DOLLAR
PAYABLE AT END OF EACH PERIOD

QUARTERS	7% NOMINAL ANNUAL RATE	7½% NOMINAL ANNUAL RATE	8% NOMINAL ANNUAL RATE	8½% NOMINAL ANNUAL RATE	QUARTERS
1	0.9828 009 828	0.9815 950 920	0.9803 921 569	0.9791 921 665	1
2	0.9658 977 718	0.9635 289 247	0.9611 687 812	0.9588 172 989	2
3	0.9492 852 794	0.9457 952 635	0.9423 223 345	0.9388 663 881	3
YEARS					
1	0.9329 585 056	0.9283 879 887	0.9238 454 260	0.9193 306 126	4
2	0.8704 115 731	0.8619 042 576	0.8534 903 712	0.8451 687 753	8
3	0.8120 578 805	0.8001 815 602	0.7884 931 756	0.7769 895 279	12
4	0.7576 163 066	0.7428 789 492	0.7284 458 137	0.7143 102 587	16
5	0.7068 245 772	0.6896 798 935	0.6729 713 331	0.6566 872 877	20
6	0.6594 380 012	0.6402 905 292	0.6217 214 879	0.6037 127 265	24
7	0.6152 282 921	0.5944 380 366	0.5743 745 529	0.5550 115 907	28
8	0.5739 824 680	0.5518 691 332	0.5306 333 035	0.5102 391 456	32
9	0.5355 018 255	0.5123 486 746	0.4902 231 504	0.4690 784 663	36
10	0.4996 009 829	0.4756 583 555	0.4528 904 152	0.4312 381 938	40
11	0.4661 069 864	0.4415 955 040	0.4184 007 386	0.3964 504 729	44
12	0.4348 584 774	0.4099 719 618	0.3865 376 086	0.3644 690 561	48
13	0.4057 049 152	0.3806 130 450	0.3571 010 017	0.3350 675 606	52
14	0.3785 058 514	0.3533 565 794	0.3299 061 270	0.3080 378 658	56
15	0.3531 302 535	0.3280 520 040	0.3047 822 665	0.2831 886 398	60
16	0.3294 558 736	0.3045 595 402	0.2815 717 028	0.2603 439 857	64
17	0.3073 686 594	0.2827 494 190	0.2601 287 297	0.2393 421 959	68
18	0.2867 622 052	0.2625 011 644	0.2403 187 371	0.2200 346 076	72
19	0.2675 372 384	0.2437 029 280	0.2220 173 661	0.2022 845 506	76
20	0.2496 011 421	0.2262 508 712	0.2051 097 282	0.1859 663 798	80
21	0.2328 675 085	0.2100 485 912	0.1894 896 842	0.1709 645 859	84
22	0.2172 557 227	0.1950 065 892	0.1750 591 780	0.1571 729 775	88
23	0.2026 905 744	0.1810 417 751	0.1617 276 209	0.1444 939 296	92
24	0.1891 018 954	0.1680 770 095	0.1494 113 228	0.1328 376 929	96
25	0.1764 242 217	0.1560 406 768	0.1380 329 672	0.1221 217 576	100
26	0.1645 964 782	0.1448 662 900	0.1275 211 254	0.1122 702 702	104
27	0.1535 616 844	0.1344 921 237	0.1178 098 084	0.1032 134 963	108
28	0.1432 666 796	0.1248 608 712	0.1088 380 526	0.0948 873 267	112
29	0.1336 618 673	0.1159 193 340	0.1005 495 371	0.0872 328 242	116
30	0.1247 009 759	0.1076 181 173	0.0928 922 299	0.0801 958 057	120
31	0.1163 408 361	0.0999 113 675	0.0858 180 618	0.0737 264 592	124
32	0.1085 411 726	0.0927 565 135	0.0792 826 238	0.0677 789 909	128
33	0.1012 644 102	0.0861 140 330	0.0732 448 894	0.0623 113 012	132
34	0.0944 754 928	0.0799 472 339	0.0676 669 560	0.0572 846 867	136
35	0.0881 417 146	0.0742 220 517	0.0625 138 078	0.0526 635 662	140
36	0.0822 325 623	0.0689 068 613	0.0577 530 954	0.0484 152 285	144
37	0.0767 195 684	0.0639 723 024	0.0533 549 330	0.0445 096 017	148
38	0.0715 761 739	0.0593 911 171	0.0492 917 108	0.0409 190 394	152
39	0.0667 776 003	0.0551 379 998	0.0455 379 216	0.0376 181 256	156
40	0.0623 007 301	0.0511 894 567	0.0420 700 006	0.0345 834 944	160
41	0.0581 239 961	0.0475 236 768	0.0388 661 776	0.0317 936 651	164
42	0.0542 272 765	0.0441 204 107	0.0359 063 404	0.0292 288 896	168
43	0.0505 917 989	0.0409 608 593	0.0331 719 084	0.0268 710 130	172
44	0.0472 000 491	0.0380 275 698	0.0306 457 158	0.0247 033 448	176
45	0.0440 356 872	0.0353 043 391	0.0283 119 044	0.0227 105 411	180
46	0.0410 834 690	0.0327 761 243	0.0261 558 234	0.0208 784 957	184
47	0.0383 291 718	0.0304 289 601	0.0241 639 378	0.0191 942 402	188
48	0.0357 595 268	0.0282 498 811	0.0223 237 434	0.0176 458 526	192
49	0.0333 621 547	0.0262 268 503	0.0206 236 882	0.0162 223 725	196
50	0.0311 255 060	0.0243 486 928	0.0190 531 000	0.0149 137 237	200
51	0.0290 388 056	0.0226 050 339	0.0176 021 193	0.0137 106 427	204
52	0.0270 920 007	0.0209 862 420	0.0162 616 374	0.0126 046 136	208
53	0.0252 757 124	0.0194 833 750	0.0150 232 394	0.0115 878 071	212
54	0.0235 811 909	0.0180 881 313	0.0138 791 510	0.0106 530 258	216
55	0.0220 002 726	0.0167 928 039	0.0128 221 901	0.0097 936 527	220
56	0.0205 253 415	0.0155 902 374	0.0118 457 217	0.0090 036 048	224
57	0.0191 492 919	0.0144 737 891	0.0109 436 158	0.0082 772 895	228
58	0.0178 654 948	0.0134 372 920	0.0101 102 094	0.0076 095 656	232
59	0.0166 677 653	0.0124 750 205	0.0093 402 707	0.0069 957 066	236
60	0.0155 503 334	0.0115 816 592	0.0086 289 664	0.0064 313 673	240

103

Table 4. PRESENT WORTH OF ONE DOLLAR
PAYABLE AT END OF EACH PERIOD

QUARTERS	9% NOMINAL ANNUAL RATE	9½% NOMINAL ANNUAL RATE	10% NOMINAL ANNUAL RATE	10½% NOMINAL ANNUAL RATE	QUARTER
1	0.9779 951 100	0.9768 009 768	0.9756 097 561	0.9744 214 373	1
2	0.9564 744 352	0.9541 401 483	0.9518 143 962	0.9494 971 374	2
3	0.9354 273 205	0.9320 050 288	0.9285 994 109	0.9252 103 653	3
YEARS					
1	0.9148 433 453	0.9103 834 226	0.9059 506 448	0.9015 448 140	4
2	0.8369 383 464	0.8287 979 761	0.8207 465 708	0.8127 830 516	8
3	0.7656 674 765	0.7545 239 381	0.7435 558 850	0.7327 603 450	12
4	0.7004 657 956	0.6869 060 851	0.6736 249 335	0.6606 162 889	16
5	0.6408 164 717	0.6253 479 128	0.6102 709 429	0.5955 751 893	20
6	0.5862 466 846	0.5693 063 731	0.5528 753 542	0.5369 377 232	24
7	0.5363 238 781	0.5182 870 844	0.5008 777 836	0.4840 734 198	28
8	0.4906 523 308	0.4718 399 698	0.4537 705 510	0.4364 138 812	32
9	0.4488 700 197	0.4295 552 866	0.4110 937 233	0.3934 466 713	36
10	0.4106 457 504	0.3910 600 120	0.3724 306 237	0.3547 098 061	40
11	0.3756 765 320	0.3560 145 521	0.3374 037 637	0.3197 867 862	44
12	0.3436 851 753	0.3241 097 465	0.3056 711 573	0.2883 021 186	48
13	0.3144 180 954	0.2950 641 403	0.2769 229 820	0.2599 172 799	52
14	0.2876 433 022	0.2686 215 019	0.2508 785 541	0.2343 270 758	56
15	0.2631 485 609	0.2445 485 623	0.2272 835 879	0.2112 563 599	60
16	0.2407 397 097	0.2226 329 571	0.2059 077 130	0.1904 570 757	64
17	0.2202 391 214	0.2026 813 535	0.1865 422 253	0.1717 055 889	68
18	0.2014 842 946	0.1845 177 442	0.1689 980 493	0.1548 002 332	72
19	0.1843 265 660	0.1679 818 955	0.1531 038 918	0.1395 593 925	76
20	0.1686 299 323	0.1529 279 330	0.1387 045 695	0.1258 190 465	80
21	0.1542 699 714	0.1392 230 550	0.1256 594 941	0.1134 315 089	84
22	0.1411 328 567	0.1267 463 613	0.1138 412 997	0.1022 635 886	88
23	0.1291 144 547	0.1153 877 862	0.1031 345 989	0.0921 952 080	92
24	0.1181 194 997	0.1050 471 278	0.0934 348 564	0.0831 181 116	96
25	0.1080 608 382	0.0956 331 637	0.0846 473 684	0.0749 347 025	100
26	0.0988 587 387	0.0870 628 469	0.0766 863 380	0.0675 569 924	104
27	0.0904 402 593	0.0792 605 725	0.0694 740 373	0.0609 056 561	108
28	0.0827 386 693	0.0721 575 113	0.0629 400 489	0.0549 091 784	112
29	0.0756 929 210	0.0656 910 021	0.0570 205 779	0.0495 030 851	116
30	0.0692 471 651	0.0598 039 993	0.0516 578 293	0.0446 292 496	120
31	0.0633 503 082	0.0544 445 696	0.0467 994 438	0.0402 352 685	124
32	0.0579 556 078	0.0495 654 336	0.0423 979 863	0.0362 738 977	128
33	0.0530 203 021	0.0451 235 491	0.0384 104 830	0.0327 025 443	132
34	0.0485 052 706	0.0410 797 310	0.0347 980 018	0.0294 828 093	136
35	0.0443 747 240	0.0373 983 061	0.0315 252 722	0.0265 800 738	140
36	0.0405 959 210	0.0340 467 979	0.0285 603 407	0.0239 631 277	144
37	0.0371 389 081	0.0309 956 404	0.0258 742 591	0.0216 038 335	148
38	0.0339 762 829	0.0282 179 172	0.0234 408 017	0.0194 768 240	152
39	0.0310 829 764	0.0256 891 241	0.0212 362 094	0.0175 592 297	156
40	0.0284 360 541	0.0233 869 527	0.0192 389 576	0.0158 304 325	160
41	0.0260 145 348	0.0212 910 940	0.0174 295 460	0.0142 718 443	164
42	0.0237 992 241	0.0193 830 591	0.0157 903 085	0.0128 667 072	168
43	0.0217 725 618	0.0176 460 156	0.0143 052 401	0.0115 999 132	172
44	0.0199 184 832	0.0160 646 401	0.0129 598 415	0.0104 578 416	176
45	0.0182 222 918	0.0146 249 820	0.0117 409 768	0.0094 282 128	180
46	0.0166 705 424	0.0133 143 412	0.0106 367 455	0.0084 999 564	184
47	0.0152 509 348	0.0121 211 555	0.0096 363 664	0.0076 630 916	188
48	0.0139 522 162	0.0110 348 990	0.0087 300 724	0.0069 086 205	192
49	0.0127 640 921	0.0100 459 892	0.0079 090 147	0.0062 284 310	196
50	0.0116 771 448	0.0091 457 020	0.0071 651 770	0.0056 152 096	200
51	0.0106 827 582	0.0083 260 955	0.0064 912 967	0.0050 623 631	204
52	0.0097 730 502	0.0075 799 393	0.0058 807 944	0.0045 639 472	208
53	0.0089 408 100	0.0069 006 511	0.0053 277 095	0.0041 146 029	212
54	0.0081 794 405	0.0062 822 384	0.0048 266 419	0.0037 094 989	216
55	0.0074 829 067	0.0057 192 457	0.0043 726 993	0.0033 442 795	220
56	0.0068 456 874	0.0052 067 064	0.0039 614 498	0.0030 150 179	224
57	0.0062 627 316	0.0047 400 992	0.0035 888 780	0.0027 181 737	228
58	0.0057 294 183	0.0043 153 078	0.0032 513 463	0.0024 505 554	232
59	0.0052 415 202	0.0039 285 846	0.0029 455 593	0.0022 092 855	236
60	0.0047 951 699	0.0035 765 183	0.0026 685 313	0.0019 917 699	240

Table 4. PRESENT WORTH OF ONE DOLLAR
PAYABLE AT END OF EACH PERIOD

ARTERS	11% NOMINAL ANNUAL RATE	11½% NOMINAL ANNUAL RATE	12% NOMINAL ANNUAL RATE	12½% NOMINAL ANNUAL RATE	QUARTERS
1	0.9732 360 097	0.9720 534 629	0.9708 737 864	0.9696 969 697	1
2	0.9471 883 306	0.9448 879 348	0.9425 959 091	0.9403 122 130	2
3	0.9218 377 914	0.9184 815 891	0.9151 416 594	0.9118 179 036	3
YEARS					
1	0.8971 657 337	0.8928 132 094	0.8884 870 479	0.8841 870 580	4
2	0.8049 063 537	0.7971 154 268	0.7894 092 343	0.7817 867 535	8
3	0.7221 343 994	0.7116 751 824	0.7013 798 802	0.6912 457 296	12
4	0.6478 742 383	0.6353 930 036	0.6231 669 392	0.6111 905 280	16
5	0.5812 505 663	0.5672 872 668	0.5536 757 542	0.5404 067 548	20
6	0.5214 780 908	0.5064 815 653	0.4919 337 363	0.4778 206 586	24
7	0.4678 522 739	0.4521 934 318	0.4370 767 532	0.4224 828 424	28
8	0.4197 410 286	0.4037 242 691	0.3883 370 341	0.3735 538 615	32
9	0.3765 772 679	0.3604 503 604	0.3450 324 251	0.3302 914 898	36
10	0.3378 522 208	0.3218 148 431	0.3065 568 408	0.2920 394 606	40
11	0.3031 094 356	0.2873 205 429	0.2723 717 825	0.2582 175 115	44
12	0.2719 393 992	0.2565 235 760	0.2419 988 009	0.2283 125 818	48
13	0.2439 747 106	0.2290 276 371	0.2150 128 003	0.2018 710 300	52
14	0.2188 857 502	0.2044 788 998	0.1910 360 882	0.1784 917 521	56
15	0.1963 767 947	0.1825 614 627	0.1697 330 900	0.1578 200 972	60
16	0.1761 825 311	0.1629 932 854	0.1508 056 521	0.1395 424 874	64
17	0.1580 649 298	0.1455 225 583	0.1339 888 686	0.1233 816 614	68
18	0.1418 104 387	0.1299 244 623	0.1190 473 743	0.1090 924 682	72
19	0.1272 274 663	0.1159 982 762	0.1057 720 502	0.0964 581 485	76
20	0.1141 441 231	0.1035 647 932	0.0939 770 966	0.0852 870 466	80
21	0.1024 061 960	0.0924 640 154	0.0834 974 332	0.0754 097 028	84
22	0.0918 753 299	0.0825 530 943	0.0741 863 879	0.0666 762 833	88
23	0.0824 273 978	0.0737 044 931	0.0659 136 448	0.0589 543 067	92
24	0.0739 510 368	0.0658 043 450	0.0585 634 197	0.0521 266 350	96
25	0.0663 463 362	0.0587 509 885	0.0520 328 399	0.0460 896 961	100
26	0.0595 236 594	0.0524 536 586	0.0462 305 043	0.0407 519 128	104
27	0.0534 025 876	0.0468 313 193	0.0410 752 043	0.0360 323 139	108
28	0.0479 109 717	0.0418 116 204	0.0364 947 870	0.0318 593 056	112
29	0.0429 840 820	0.0373 299 670	0.0324 251 455	0.0281 695 857	116
30	0.0385 638 455	0.0333 286 877	0.0288 093 218	0.0249 071 831	120
31	0.0345 981 607	0.0297 562 926	0.0255 967 093	0.0220 226 089	124
32	0.0310 402 843	0.0265 668 111	0.0227 423 447	0.0194 721 058	128
33	0.0278 482 794	0.0237 191 999	0.0202 062 787	0.0172 169 839	132
34	0.0249 845 220	0.0211 768 150	0.0179 530 169	0.0152 230 344	136
35	0.0224 152 570	0.0189 069 401	0.0159 510 230	0.0134 600 100	140
36	0.0201 102 005	0.0168 803 659	0.0141 722 773	0.0119 011 666	144
37	0.0180 421 828	0.0150 710 137	0.0125 918 849	0.0105 228 575	148
38	0.0161 868 282	0.0134 556 001	0.0111 877 266	0.0093 041 744	152
39	0.0145 222 676	0.0120 133 375	0.0099 401 502	0.0082 266 306	156
40	0.0130 288 808	0.0107 256 664	0.0088 316 947	0.0072 738 803	160
41	0.0116 890 654	0.0095 760 166	0.0078 468 463	0.0064 314 708	164
42	0.0104 870 290	0.0085 495 941	0.0069 718 213	0.0056 866 233	168
43	0.0094 086 030	0.0076 331 906	0.0061 943 730	0.0050 280 387	172
44	0.0084 410 763	0.0068 150 134	0.0055 036 201	0.0044 457 267	176
45	0.0075 730 444	0.0060 845 340	0.0048 898 952	0.0039 308 541	180
46	0.0067 942 759	0.0054 323 523	0.0043 446 086	0.0034 756 103	184
47	0.0060 955 915	0.0048 500 759	0.0038 601 284	0.0030 730 896	188
48	0.0054 687 558	0.0043 302 118	0.0034 296 741	0.0027 171 861	192
49	0.0049 063 804	0.0038 660 703	0.0030 472 210	0.0024 025 008	196
50	0.0044 018 363	0.0034 516 786	0.0027 074 164	0.0021 242 601	200
51	0.0039 491 767	0.0030 817 043	0.0024 055 044	0.0018 782 433	204
52	0.0035 430 660	0.0027 513 863	0.0021 372 595	0.0016 607 184	208
53	0.0031 787 174	0.0024 564 740	0.0018 989 274	0.0014 683 857	212
54	0.0028 518 364	0.0021 931 725	0.0016 871 724	0.0012 983 276	216
55	0.0025 585 699	0.0019 580 933	0.0014 990 308	0.0011 479 645	220
56	0.0022 954 612	0.0017 482 116	0.0013 318 695	0.0010 150 154	224
57	0.0020 594 091	0.0015 608 264	0.0011 833 488	0.0008 974 634	228
58	0.0018 476 313	0.0013 935 264	0.0010 513 901	0.0007 935 256	232
59	0.0016 576 315	0.0012 441 588	0.0009 341 465	0.0007 016 250	236
60	0.0014 871 702	0.0011 108 014	0.0008 299 770	0.0006 203 678	240

Table 4.   PRESENT WORTH OF ONE DOLLAR
PAYABLE AT END OF EACH PERIOD

QUARTERS	13% NOMINAL ANNUAL RATE	13½% NOMINAL ANNUAL RATE	14% NOMINAL ANNUAL RATE	14½% NOMINAL ANNUAL RATE	QUARTE
1	0.9685 230 024	0.9673 518 742	0.9661 835 749	0.9650 180 941	1
2	0.9380 368 062	0.9357 696 486	0.9335 107 004	0.9312 599 219	2
3	0.9085 102 239	0.9052 185 234	0.9019 427 057	0.8986 826 750	3
YEARS					
1	0.8799 130 498	0.8756 648 352	0.8714 422 277	0.8672 450 422	4
2	0.7742 469 752	0.7667 889 037	0.7594 115 562	0.7521 139 632	8
3	0.6812 700 173	0.6714 500 790	0.6617 832 983	0.6522 671 057	12
4	0.5994 583 787	0.5879 652 228	0.5767 059 117	0.5656 754 136	16
5	0.5274 712 502	0.5148 604 700	0.5025 658 844	0.4905 791 979	20
6	0.4641 288 365	0.4508 452 086	0.4379 571 339	0.4254 523 772	24
7	0.4083 930 200	0.3947 892 953	0.3816 543 404	0.3689 714 648	28
8	0.3593 503 478	0.3457 031 032	0.3325 897 086	0.3199 886 736	32
9	0.3161 970 605	0.3027 200 510	0.2898 327 166	0.2775 085 907	36
10	0.2782 259 198	0.2650 813 035	0.2525 724 682	0.2406 679 494	40
11	0.2448 146 176	0.2321 223 760	0.2201 023 143	0.2087 180 860	44
12	0.2154 155 769	0.2032 614 021	0.1918 064 511	0.1810 097 253	48
13	0.1895 469 772	0.1779 888 622	0.1671 482 411	0.1569 797 868	52
14	0.1667 848 588	0.1558 585 877	0.1456 600 355	0.1361 399 418	56
15	0.1467 561 738	0.1364 798 845	0.1269 343 059	0.1180 666 896	60
16	0.1291 326 724	0.1195 106 356	0.1106 159 143	0.1023 927 512	64
17	0.1136 255 236	0.1046 512 610	0.0963 953 788	0.0887 996 058	68
18	0.0999 805 810	0.0916 394 292	0.0840 030 036	0.0770 110 179	72
19	0.0879 742 180	0.0802 454 257	0.0732 037 646	0.0667 874 235	76
20	0.0774 096 625	0.0702 680 975	0.0637 928 517	0.0579 210 619	80
21	0.0681 137 722	0.0615 313 020	0.0555 917 848	0.0502 317 538	84
22	0.0599 341 970	0.0538 807 974	0.0484 450 288	0.0435 632 394	88
23	0.0527 368 821	0.0471 815 196	0.0422 170 438	0.0377 800 034	92
24	0.0464 038 708	0.0413 151 976	0.0367 897 147	0.0327 645 206	96
25	0.0408 313 714	0.0361 782 657	0.0320 601 109	0.0284 148 681	100
26	0.0359 280 566	0.0316 800 351	0.0279 385 345	0.0246 426 535	104
27	0.0316 135 658	0.0277 410 927	0.0243 468 187	0.0213 712 190	108
28	0.0278 171 891	0.0242 918 994	0.0212 168 460	0.0185 340 838	112
29	0.0244 767 077	0.0212 715 621	0.0184 892 555	0.0160 735 923	116
30	0.0215 373 745	0.0186 267 589	0.0161 123 180	0.0139 397 432	120
31	0.0189 510 169	0.0163 107 977	0.0140 409 543	0.0120 891 732	124
32	0.0166 752 471	0.0142 827 920	0.0122 358 805	0.0104 842 755	128
33	0.0146 727 675	0.0125 069 387	0.0106 628 630	0.0090 924 359	132
34	0.0129 107 596	0.0109 518 864	0.0092 920 690	0.0078 853 700	136
35	0.0113 603 459	0.0095 901 818	0.0080 975 013	0.0068 385 480	140
36	0.0099 961 166	0.0083 977 850	0.0070 565 046	0.0059 306 969	144
37	0.0087 957 134	0.0073 536 450	0.0061 493 361	0.0051 433 675	148
38	0.0077 394 630	0.0064 393 283	0.0053 587 912	0.0044 605 599	152
39	0.0068 100 545	0.0056 386 934	0.0046 698 769	0.0038 683 985	156
40	0.0059 922 946	0.0049 376 055	0.0040 695 279	0.0033 548 494	160
41	0.0052 726 641	0.0043 236 875	0.0035 463 585	0.0029 094 765	164
42	0.0046 394 860	0.0037 861 011	0.0030 904 465	0.0025 232 291	168
43	0.0040 823 442	0.0033 153 556	0.0026 931 456	0.0021 882 579	172
44	0.0035 921 080	0.0029 031 403	0.0023 469 208	0.0018 977 558	176
45	0.0031 607 427	0.0025 421 779	0.0020 452 059	0.0016 458 193	180
46	0.0027 811 787	0.0022 260 958	0.0017 822 788	0.0014 273 287	184
47	0.0024 471 955	0.0019 493 138	0.0015 531 530	0.0012 378 437	188
48	0.0021 533 192	0.0017 069 456	0.0013 534 831	0.0010 735 138	192
49	0.0018 947 337	0.0014 947 122	0.0011 794 823	0.0009 309 995	196
50	0.0016 672 009	0.0013 088 669	0.0010 278 507	0.0008 074 047	200
51	0.0014 669 918	0.0011 461 287	0.0008 957 125	0.0007 002 177	204
52	0.0012 908 252	0.0010 036 246	0.0007 805 617	0.0006 072 604	208
53	0.0011 358 140	0.0008 788 388	0.0006 802 144	0.0005 266 435	212
54	0.0009 994 175	0.0007 695 682	0.0005 927 676	0.0004 567 290	216
55	0.0008 794 005	0.0006 738 838	0.0005 165 627	0.0003 960 960	220
56	0.0007 737 960	0.0005 900 964	0.0004 501 546	0.0003 435 123	224
57	0.0006 808 732	0.0005 167 266	0.0003 922 837	0.0002 979 093	228
58	0.0005 991 092	0.0004 524 794	0.0003 418 526	0.0002 583 604	232
59	0.0005 271 640	0.0003 962 203	0.0002 979 048	0.0002 240 617	236
60	0.0004 638 585	0.0003 469 561	0.0002 596 068	0.0001 943 164	240

Table 4. PRESENT WORTH OF ONE DOLLAR
PAYABLE AT END OF EACH PERIOD

QUARTERS	15% NOMINAL ANNUAL RATE	15½% NOMINAL ANNUAL RATE	16% NOMINAL ANNUAL RATE	16½% NOMINAL ANNUAL RATE	QUARTERS
1	0.9638 554 217	0.9626 955 475	0.9615 384 615	0.9603 841 537	1
2	0.9290 172 739	0.9267 827 172	0.9245 562 130	0.9223 377 226	2
3	0.8954 383 363	0.8922 095 954	0.8889 963 587	0.8857 985 331	3
YEARS					
1	0.8630 730 952	0.8589 262 050	0.8548 041 910	0.8507 068 745	4
2	0.7448 951 677	0.7377 542 256	0.7306 902 050	0.7237 021 864	8
3	0.6428 989 780	0.6336 764 372	0.6245 970 496	0.6156 584 251	12
4	0.5548 688 109	0.5442 812 974	0.5339 081 757	0.5237 448 546	16
5	0.4788 923 421	0.4674 974 692	0.4563 869 462	0.4455 533 483	20
6	0.4133 190 959	0.4015 458 271	0.3901 214 743	0.3790 352 964	24
7	0.3567 245 915	0.3448 982 334	0.3334 774 713	0.3224 479 323	28
8	0.3078 793 973	0.2962 421 307	0.2850 579 401	0.2743 086 727	32
9	0.2657 224 244	0.2544 501 291	0.2436 687 219	0.2333 562 736	36
10	0.2293 378 753	0.2185 538 837	0.2082 890 447	0.1985 177 862	40
11	0.1979 353 499	0.1877 216 579	0.1780 463 483	0.1688 804 454	44
12	0.1708 326 751	0.1612 390 512	0.1521 947 647	0.1436 677 559	48
13	0.1474 410 856	0.1384 924 464	0.1300 967 228	0.1222 191 476	52
14	0.1272 524 341	0.1189 547 914	0.1112 072 239	0.1039 726 691	56
15	0.1098 281 522	0.1021 733 875	0.0950 604 010	0.0884 502 643	60
16	0.0947 897 233	0.0877 594 000	0.0812 580 292	0.0752 452 479	64
17	0.0818 104 599	0.0753 788 484	0.0694 597 039	0.0640 116 497	68
18	0.0706 084 068	0.0647 448 682	0.0593 744 460	0.0544 551 504	72
19	0.0609 402 162	0.0556 110 639	0.0507 535 253	0.0463 253 708	76
20	0.0525 958 610	0.0477 658 001	0.0433 843 261	0.0394 093 114	80
21	0.0453 940 726	0.0410 272 974	0.0370 851 038	0.0335 257 722	84
22	0.0391 784 027	0.0352 394 208	0.0317 005 022	0.0285 206 048	88
23	0.0338 138 253	0.0302 680 620	0.0270 977 221	0.0242 626 746	92
24	0.0291 838 029	0.0259 980 316	0.0231 632 464	0.0206 404 241	96
25	0.0251 877 551	0.0223 303 907	0.0198 000 401	0.0175 589 507	100
26	0.0217 388 737	0.0191 801 577	0.0169 251 573	0.0149 375 200	104
27	0.0187 622 370	0.0164 743 401	0.0144 676 954	0.0127 074 510	108
28	0.0161 931 820	0.0141 502 424	0.0123 670 466	0.0108 103 159	112
29	0.0139 758 997	0.0121 540 140	0.0105 714 033	0.0091 964 101	116
30	0.0120 622 230	0.0104 394 011	0.0090 364 798	0.0078 234 493	120
31	0.0104 105 802	0.0089 666 752	0.0077 244 208	0.0066 554 621	124
32	0.0089 850 916	0.0077 017 123	0.0066 028 673	0.0056 618 473	128
33	0.0077 547 909	0.0066 152 025	0.0056 441 586	0.0048 165 724	132
34	0.0066 929 513	0.0056 819 708	0.0048 246 505	0.0040 974 913	136
35	0.0057 765 062	0.0048 803 936	0.0041 241 314	0.0034 857 640	140
36	0.0049 855 471	0.0041 918 980	0.0035 253 248	0.0029 653 634	144
37	0.0043 028 916	0.0036 005 310	0.0030 134 624	0.0025 226 550	148
38	0.0037 137 100	0.0030 925 904	0.0025 759 203	0.0021 460 400	152
39	0.0032 052 031	0.0026 563 070	0.0022 019 075	0.0018 256 510	156
40	0.0027 663 246	0.0022 815 717	0.0018 821 998	0.0015 530 938	160
41	0.0023 875 403	0.0019 597 017	0.0016 089 122	0.0013 212 276	164
42	0.0020 606 218	0.0016 832 391	0.0013 753 049	0.0011 239 774	168
43	0.0017 784 673	0.0014 457 782	0.0011 756 164	0.0009 561 753	172
44	0.0015 349 472	0.0012 418 168	0.0010 049 218	0.0008 134 249	176
45	0.0013 247 717	0.0010 666 290	0.0008 590 114	0.0006 919 862	180
46	0.0011 433 748	0.0009 161 556	0.0007 342 865	0.0005 886 774	184
47	0.0009 868 160	0.0007 869 100	0.0006 276 712	0.0005 007 919	188
48	0.0008 516 944	0.0006 758 976	0.0005 365 360	0.0004 260 271	192
49	0.0007 350 745	0.0005 805 462	0.0004 586 332	0.0003 624 242	196
50	0.0006 344 230	0.0004 986 463	0.0003 920 416	0.0003 083 167	200
51	0.0005 475 534	0.0004 283 004	0.0003 351 188	0.0002 622 872	204
52	0.0004 725 786	0.0003 678 784	0.0002 864 609	0.0002 231 295	208
53	0.0004 078 699	0.0003 159 804	0.0002 448 680	0.0001 898 178	212
54	0.0003 520 215	0.0002 714 039	0.0002 093 142	0.0001 614 793	216
55	0.0003 038 203	0.0002 331 159	0.0001 789 227	0.0001 373 716	220
56	0.0002 622 191	0.0002 002 294	0.0001 529 438	0.0001 168 629	224
57	0.0002 263 143	0.0001 719 822	0.0001 307 370	0.0000 994 161	228
58	0.0001 953 258	0.0001 477 201	0.0001 117 546	0.0000 845 740	232
59	0.0001 685 804	0.0001 268 806	0.0000 955 283	0.0000 719 476	236
60	0.0001 454 972	0.0001 089 811	0.0000 816 580	0.0000 612 064	240

Table 4. PRESENT WORTH OF ONE DOLLAR
PAYABLE AT END OF EACH PERIOD

QUARTERS	**17%** NOMINAL ANNUAL RATE	**17½%** NOMINAL ANNUAL RATE	**18%** NOMINAL ANNUAL RATE	**18½%** NOMINAL ANNUAL RATE	QUARTERS
1	0.9592 326 139	0.9580 838 323	0.9569 377 990	0.9557 945 042	1
2	0.9201 272 076	0.9179 246 298	0.9157 299 512	0.9135 431 342	2
3	0.8826 160 265	0.8794 487 471	0.8762 966 041	0.8731 595 070	3
YEARS					
1	0.8466 340 781	0.8425 856 260	0.8385 613 436	0.8345 610 581	4
2	0.7167 892 623	0.7099 505 371	0.7031 851 270	0.6964 921 597	8
3	0.6068 582 163	0.5981 941 177	0.5896 638 649	0.5812 652 337	12
4	0.5137 868 465	0.5040 297 651	0.4944 693 228	0.4851 013 285	16
5	0.4349 894 532	0.4246 882 351	0.4146 428 597	0.4048 466 780	20
6	0.3682 768 947	0.3578 362 024	0.3477 034 735	0.3378 692 719	24
7	0.3117 957 692	0.3015 076 406	0.2915 706 919	0.2819 725 371	28
8	0.2639 769 236	0.2540 460 041	0.2444 999 112	0.2353 232 989	32
9	0.2234 918 594	0.2140 555 114	0.2050 281 740	0.1963 916 613	36
10	0.1892 158 244	0.1803 600 971	0.1719 287 011	0.1639 008 327	40
11	0.1601 965 650	0.1519 688 253	0.1441 727 626	0.1367 852 523	44
12	0.1356 278 711	0.1280 467 478	0.1208 977 055	0.1141 556 449	48
13	0.1148 271 777	0.1078 903 491	0.1013 801 424	0.0952 698 558	52
14	0.0972 166 017	0.0909 068 574	0.0850 134 684	0.0795 085 117	56
15	0.0823 068 880	0.0765 968 113	0.0712 890 083	0.0663 547 076	60
16	0.0696 838 162	0.0645 393 722	0.0597 802 066	0.0553 770 550	64
17	0.0589 966 935	0.0543 799 473	0.0501 293 703	0.0462 155 336	68
18	0.0499 486 112	0.0458 197 620	0.0420 365 521	0.0385 696 846	72
19	0.0422 881 964	0.0386 070 728	0.0352 502 276	0.0321 887 568	76
20	0.0358 026 282	0.0325 297 646	0.0295 594 783	0.0268 634 830	80
21	0.0303 117 251	0.0274 091 121	0.0247 874 358	0.0224 192 168	84
22	0.0256 629 394	0.0230 945 239	0.0207 857 855	0.0187 102 053	88
23	0.0217 271 191	0.0194 591 138	0.0174 301 562	0.0156 148 087	92
24	0.0183 949 194	0.0163 959 696	0.0146 162 552	0.0130 315 113	96
25	0.0155 737 657	0.0138 150 083	0.0122 566 266	0.0108 755 918	100
26	0.0131 852 807	0.0116 403 274	0.0102 779 333	0.0090 763 454	104
27	0.0111 631 080	0.0098 079 726	0.0086 186 775	0.0075 747 644	108
28	0.0094 510 676	0.0082 640 567	0.0072 272 898	0.0063 216 034	112
29	0.0080 015 959	0.0069 631 754	0.0060 605 259	0.0052 757 640	116
30	0.0067 744 238	0.0058 670 715	0.0050 821 227	0.0044 029 472	120
31	0.0057 354 581	0.0049 435 101	0.0042 616 716	0.0036 745 283	124
32	0.0048 558 342	0.0041 653 306	0.0035 736 731	0.0030 666 182	128
33	0.0041 111 147	0.0035 096 477	0.0029 967 441	0.0025 592 801	132
34	0.0034 806 098	0.0029 571 787	0.0025 129 538	0.0021 358 755	136
35	0.0029 468 029	0.0024 916 762	0.0021 072 659	0.0017 825 186	140
36	0.0024 948 638	0.0020 994 506	0.0017 670 717	0.0014 876 206	144
37	0.0021 122 367	0.0017 689 669	0.0014 817 980	0.0012 415 102	148
38	0.0017 882 916	0.0014 905 061	0.0012 425 785	0.0010 361 161	152
39	0.0015 140 286	0.0012 558 790	0.0010 419 783	0.0008 647 021	156
40	0.0012 818 282	0.0010 581 856	0.0008 737 628	0.0007 216 467	160
41	0.0010 852 394	0.0008 916 120	0.0007 327 037	0.0006 022 582	164
42	0.0009 188 007	0.0007 512 594	0.0006 144 170	0.0005 026 213	168
43	0.0007 778 880	0.0006 330 004	0.0005 152 263	0.0004 194 681	172
44	0.0006 585 865	0.0005 333 570	0.0004 320 489	0.0003 500 718	176
45	0.0005 575 817	0.0004 493 990	0.0003 622 995	0.0002 921 563	180
46	0.0004 720 677	0.0003 786 571	0.0003 038 103	0.0002 438 223	184
47	0.0003 996 686	0.0003 190 510	0.0002 547 636	0.0002 034 846	188
48	0.0003 383 731	0.0002 688 278	0.0002 136 349	0.0001 698 203	192
49	0.0002 864 782	0.0002 265 105	0.0001 791 460	0.0001 417 254	196
50	0.0002 425 422	0.0001 908 545	0.0001 502 249	0.0001 182 785	200
51	0.0002 053 445	0.0001 608 112	0.0001 259 728	0.0000 987 106	204
52	0.0001 738 516	0.0001 354 972	0.0001 056 359	0.0000 823 800	208
53	0.0001 471 887	0.0001 141 680	0.0000 885 822	0.0000 687 512	212
54	0.0001 246 150	0.0000 961 963	0.0000 742 816	0.0000 573 771	216
55	0.0001 055 033	0.0000 810 536	0.0000 622 897	0.0000 478 847	220
56	0.0000 893 227	0.0000 682 946	0.0000 522 337	0.0000 399 627	224
57	0.0000 756 236	0.0000 575 441	0.0000 438 012	0.0000 333 513	228
58	0.0000 640 255	0.0000 484 858	0.0000 367 300	0.0000 278 337	232
59	0.0000 542 062	0.0000 408 534	0.0000 308 003	0.0000 232 289	236
60	0.0000 458 928	0.0000 344 225	0.0000 258 280	0.0000 193 859	240

Table 4.   PRESENT WORTH OF ONE DOLLAR
PAYABLE AT END OF EACH PERIOD

QUARTERS	19% NOMINAL ANNUAL RATE	19½% NOMINAL ANNUAL RATE	20% NOMINAL ANNUAL RATE	20½% NOMINAL ANNUAL RATE	QUARTERS
1	0.9546 539 379	0.9535 160 906	0.9523 809 524	0.9512 485 137	1
2	0.9113 641 412	0.9091 929 350	0.9070 294 785	0.9048 737 348	2
3	0.8700 373 663	0.8669 300 930	0.8638 375 985	0.8607 597 953	3
YEARS					
1	0.8305 845 979	0.8266 317 931	0.8227 024 748	0.8187 964 759	4
2	0.6898 707 743	0.6833 201 213	0.6768 393 620	0.6704 276 689	8
3	0.5729 960 397	0.5648 541 371	0.5568 374 182	0.5489 438 126	12
4	0.4759 216 853	0.4669 263 882	0.4581 115 220	0.4494 732 592	16
5	0.3952 932 216	0.3859 761 975	0.3768 894 829	0.3680 271 207	20
6	0.3283 244 615	0.3190 601 962	0.3100 679 103	0.3013 393 094	24
7	0.2727 012 409	0.2637 453 021	0.2550 936 371	0.2467 355 646	28
8	0.2265 014 505	0.2180 202 520	0.2098 661 666	0.2020 262 108	32
9	0.1881 286 162	0.1802 224 718	0.1726 574 146	0.1654 183 494	36
10	0.1562 567 311	0.1489 776 250	0.1420 456 823	0.1354 439 615	40
11	0.1297 844 341	0.1231 496 413	0.1168 613 344	0.1109 010 384	44
12	0.1077 969 520	0.1017 994 088	0.0961 421 090	0.0908 053 794	48
13	0.0895 344 881	0.0841 506 278	0.0790 963 510	0.0743 511 246	52
14	0.0743 659 668	0.0695 615 844	0.0650 727 637	0.0608 784 388	56
15	0.0617 672 266	0.0575 018 172	0.0535 355 237	0.0498 470 512	60
16	0.0513 029 071	0.0475 328 303	0.0440 438 079	0.0408 145 898	64
17	0.0426 114 045	0.0392 921 487	0.0362 349 497	0.0334 188 423	68
18	0.0353 923 762	0.0324 801 393	0.0298 105 828	0.0273 632 303	72
19	0.0293 963 626	0.0268 491 158	0.0245 252 403	0.0224 049 166	76
20	0.0244 161 660	0.0221 943 328	0.0201 769 759	0.0183 450 667	80
21	0.0202 796 914	0.0183 465 411	0.0165 996 480	0.0150 208 760	84
22	0.0168 439 993	0.0151 658 342	0.0136 565 715	0.0122 990 403	88
23	0.0139 903 664	0.0125 365 607	0.0112 352 951	0.0100 704 109	92
24	0.0116 201 829	0.0103 631 196	0.0092 433 051	0.0082 456 169	96
25	0.0096 515 449	0.0085 664 842	0.0076 044 900	0.0067 514 821	100
26	0.0080 164 246	0.0070 813 282	0.0062 562 327	0.0055 280 897	104
27	0.0066 583 188	0.0058 536 510	0.0051 470 182	0.0045 263 804	108
28	0.0055 302 970	0.0048 388 140	0.0042 344 646	0.0037 061 843	112
29	0.0045 933 795	0.0039 999 175	0.0034 837 045	0.0030 346 107	116
30	0.0038 151 903	0.0033 064 590	0.0028 660 523	0.0024 847 285	120
31	0.0031 688 383	0.0027 332 241	0.0023 579 083	0.0020 344 869	124
32	0.0026 319 883	0.0022 593 700	0.0019 398 570	0.0016 658 307	128
33	0.0021 860 889	0.0018 676 670	0.0015 959 252	0.0013 639 763	132
34	0.0018 157 318	0.0015 438 730	0.0013 129 716	0.0011 168 190	136
35	0.0015 081 189	0.0012 762 145	0.0010 801 850	0.0009 144 475	140
36	0.0012 526 203	0.0010 549 595	0.0008 886 708	0.0007 487 464	144
37	0.0010 404 071	0.0008 720 630	0.0007 311 117	0.0006 130 709	148
38	0.0008 641 461	0.0007 208 750	0.0006 014 874	0.0005 019 803	152
39	0.0007 177 465	0.0005 958 982	0.0004 948 452	0.0004 110 197	156
40	0.0005 961 492	0.0004 925 884	0.0004 071 104	0.0003 365 415	160
41	0.0004 951 523	0.0004 071 892	0.0003 349 307	0.0002 755 590	164
42	0.0004 112 659	0.0003 365 956	0.0002 755 483	0.0002 256 267	168
43	0.0003 415 911	0.0002 782 406	0.0002 266 943	0.0001 847 424	172
44	0.0002 837 203	0.0002 300 025	0.0001 865 019	0.0001 512 664	176
45	0.0002 356 537	0.0001 901 274	0.0001 534 356	0.0001 238 564	180
46	0.0001 957 304	0.0001 571 654	0.0001 262 319	0.0001 014 132	184
47	0.0001 625 706	0.0001 299 179	0.0001 038 513	0.0000 830 368	188
48	0.0001 350 286	0.0001 073 942	0.0000 854 387	0.0000 679 902	192
49	0.0001 121 527	0.0000 887 815	0.0000 702 906	0.0000 556 701	196
50	0.0000 931 523	0.0000 733 847	0.0000 578 283	0.0000 455 825	200
51	0.0000 773 709	0.0000 606 621	0.0000 475 755	0.0000 373 228	204
52	0.0000 642 631	0.0000 501 452	0.0000 391 404	0.0000 305 598	208
53	0.0000 533 759	0.0000 414 516	0.0000 322 009	0.0000 250 222	212
54	0.0000 443 332	0.0000 342 652	0.0000 264 918	0.0000 204 881	216
55	0.0000 368 225	0.0000 283 247	0.0000 217 949	0.0000 167 756	220
56	0.0000 305 842	0.0000 234 141	0.0000 179 307	0.0000 137 358	224
57	0.0000 254 028	0.0000 193 549	0.0000 147 516	0.0000 112 468	228
58	0.0000 210 991	0.0000 159 993	0.0000 121 362	0.0000 092 089	232
59	0.0000 175 246	0.0000 132 256	0.0000 099 845	0.0000 075 402	236
60	0.0000 145 557	0.0000 109 327	0.0000 082 143	0.0000 061 739	240

Table 4.   PRESENT WORTH OF ONE DOLLAR
PAYABLE AT END OF EACH PERIOD

QUARTERS	21% NOMINAL ANNUAL RATE	21½% NOMINAL ANNUAL RATE	22% NOMINAL ANNUAL RATE	22½% NOMINAL ANNUAL RATE	QUARTERS
1	0.9501 187 648	0.9489 916 963	0.9478 672 986	0.9467 455 621	1
2	0.9027 256 673	0.9005 852 397	0.8984 524 157	0.8963 271 594	2
3	0.8576 965 960	0.8546 479 143	0.8516 136 642	0.8485 937 604	3
YEARS					
1	0.8149 136 304	0.8110 537 739	0.8072 167 433	0.8034 023 767	4
2	0.6640 842 250	0.6578 082 242	0.6515 988 707	0.6454 553 789	8
3	0.5411 712 867	0.5335 178 428	0.5259 815 183	0.5185 603 855	12
4	0.4410 078 580	0.4327 116 599	0.4245 810 883	0.4166 126 461	16
5	0.3593 833 146	0.3509 524 248	0.3427 289 633	0.3347 075 901	20
6	0.2928 663 616	0.2846 412 886	0.2766 565 576	0.2689 048 734	24
7	0.2386 607 900	0.2308 593 913	0.2233 218 055	0.2160 388 144	28
8	0.1944 879 308	0.1872 393 806	0.1802 691 005	0.1735 660 969	32
9	0.1584 908 657	0.1518 612 063	0.1455 162 362	0.1394 434 148	36
10	0.1291 563 668	0.1231 676 044	0.1174 631 423	0.1120 291 709	40
11	0.1052 512 838	0.0998 955 504	0.0948 182 152	0.0900 045 021	44
12	0.0857 707 058	0.0810 206 632	0.0765 388 509	0.0723 098 309	48
13	0.0698 957 178	0.0657 121 146	0.0617 834 419	0.0580 938 900	52
14	0.0569 589 727	0.0532 960 586	0.0498 726 288	0.0466 727 693	56
15	0.0464 166 432	0.0432 259 694	0.0402 580 210	0.0374 970 138	60
16	0.0378 255 552	0.0350 585 856	0.0324 969 486	0.0301 251 900	64
17	0.0308 245 605	0.0284 343 982	0.0262 320 810	0.0242 026 492	68
18	0.0251 193 545	0.0230 618 260	0.0211 749 750	0.0194 444 659	72
19	0.0204 701 044	0.0187 043 810	0.0170 927 944	0.0156 217 301	76
20	0.0166 813 671	0.0151 702 588	0.0137 975 898	0.0125 505 351	80
21	0.0135 938 734	0.0123 038 956	0.0111 376 455	0.0100 831 297	84
22	0.0110 778 327	0.0099 791 210	0.0089 904 939	0.0081 008 104	88
23	0.0090 274 769	0.0080 936 037	0.0072 572 772	0.0065 082 103	92
24	0.0073 566 140	0.0065 643 479	0.0058 581 957	0.0052 287 116	96
25	0.0059 950 050	0.0053 240 391	0.0047 288 336	0.0042 007 594	100
26	0.0048 854 113	0.0043 180 820	0.0038 171 937	0.0033 749 001	104
27	0.0039 811 882	0.0035 021 967	0.0030 813 027	0.0027 114 027	108
28	0.0032 443 246	0.0028 404 699	0.0024 872 791	0.0021 783 474	112
29	0.0026 438 443	0.0023 037 738	0.0020 077 733	0.0017 500 895	116
30	0.0021 545 048	0.0018 684 844	0.0016 207 083	0.0014 060 260	120
31	0.0017 557 353	0.0015 154 414	0.0013 082 628	0.0011 296 047	124
32	0.0014 307 726	0.0012 291 044	0.0010 560 517	0.0009 075 271	128
33	0.0011 659 561	0.0009 968 698	0.0008 524 626	0.0007 291 094	132
34	0.0009 501 535	0.0008 085 150	0.0006 881 221	0.0005 857 682	136
35	0.0007 742 931	0.0006 557 491	0.0005 554 637	0.0004 706 076	140
36	0.0006 309 820	0.0005 318 478	0.0004 483 796	0.0003 780 873	144
37	0.0005 141 958	0.0004 313 572	0.0003 619 395	0.0003 037 562	148
38	0.0004 190 252	0.0003 498 539	0.0002 921 636	0.0002 440 385	152
39	0.0003 414 693	0.0002 837 503	0.0002 358 394	0.0001 960 611	156
40	0.0002 782 680	0.0002 301 368	0.0001 903 735	0.0001 575 159	160
41	0.0002 267 644	0.0001 866 533	0.0001 536 727	0.0001 265 487	164
42	0.0001 847 934	0.0001 513 858	0.0001 240 471	0.0001 016 695	168
43	0.0001 505 907	0.0001 227 821	0.0001 001 329	0.0000 816 815	172
44	0.0001 227 184	0.0000 995 829	0.0000 808 290	0.0000 656 231	176
45	0.0001 000 049	0.0000 807 671	0.0000 652 465	0.0000 527 218	180
46	0.0000 814 953	0.0000 655 064	0.0000 526 681	0.0000 423 568	184
47	0.0000 664 117	0.0000 531 292	0.0000 425 146	0.0000 340 296	188
48	0.0000 541 198	0.0000 430 907	0.0000 343 185	0.0000 273 394	192
49	0.0000 441 029	0.0000 349 488	0.0000 277 024	0.0000 219 646	196
50	0.0000 359 401	0.0000 283 454	0.0000 223 619	0.0000 176 464	200
51	0.0000 292 881	0.0000 229 896	0.0000 180 509	0.0000 141 771	204
52	0.0000 238 672	0.0000 186 458	0.0000 145 710	0.0000 113 900	208
53	0.0000 194 497	0.0000 151 228	0.0000 117 619	0.0000 091 507	212
54	0.0000 158 499	0.0000 122 654	0.0000 094 944	0.0000 073 517	216
55	0.0000 129 163	0.0000 099 479	0.0000 076 641	0.0000 059 064	220
56	0.0000 105 256	0.0000 080 683	0.0000 061 866	0.0000 047 452	224
57	0.0000 085 775	0.0000 065 438	0.0000 049 939	0.0000 038 123	228
58	0.0000 069 899	0.0000 053 074	0.0000 040 312	0.0000 030 628	232
59	0.0000 056 962	0.0000 043 046	0.0000 032 540	0.0000 024 607	236
60	0.0000 046 419	0.0000 034 912	0.0000 026 267	0.0000 019 769	240

Table 5.   PRESENT WORTH OF ONE DOLLAR PER PERIOD
PAYABLE AT END OF EACH PERIOD

QUARTERS	5% NOMINAL ANNUAL RATE	5½% NOMINAL ANNUAL RATE	6% NOMINAL ANNUAL RATE	6½% NOMINAL ANNUAL RATE	QUARTERS
1	0.9876 543 210	0.9864 364 982	0.9852 216 749	0.9840 098 401	1
2	1.9631 153 788	1.9594 934 630	1.9558 834 235	1.9522 852 055	2
3	2.9265 337 074	2.9193 523 680	2.9122 004 173	2.9050 776 930	3
YEARS					
1	3.8780 579 826	3.8661 922 249	3.8543 846 476	3.8426 348 763	4
2	7.5681 242 938	7.5268 571 179	7.4859 250 799	7.4453 248 071	8
3	11.0793 119 660	10.9929 205 413	10.9075 052 070	10.8230 526 309	12
4	14.4202 922 710	14.2747 275 372	14.1312 640 453	13.9898 656 152	16
5	17.5993 161 342	17.3820 732 036	17.1686 387 851	16.9589 338 766	20
6	20.6242 345 116	20.3242 319 298	20.0304 053 663	19.7426 051 527	24
7	23.5025 177 782	23.1099 850 770	22.7267 167 100	22.3524 561 535	28
8	26.2412 741 773	25.7476 471 884	25.2671 387 379	24.7993 407 065	32
9	28.8472 673 749	28.2450 908 044	27.6606 843 109	27.0934 348 957	36
10	31.3269 331 635	30.6097 699 605	29.9158 452 042	29.2442 793 820	40
11	33.6863 953 558	32.8487 424 343	32.0406 222 346	31.2608 190 801	44
12	35.9314 809 083	34.9686 908 109	34.0425 536 456	33.1514 403 594	48
13	38.0677 343 114	36.9759 424 286	35.9287 418 511	34.9240 059 207	52
14	40.1004 312 824	38.8764 882 630	37.7058 786 337	36.5858 874 954	56
15	42.0345 917 945	40.6760 008 089	39.3802 688 853	38.1439 965 036	60
16	43.8749 924 739	42.3798 510 103	40.9578 529 758	39.6048 127 965	64
17	45.6261 783 966	43.9931 242 913	42.4442 278 277	40.9744 116 053	68
18	47.2924 743 123	45.5206 357 338	43.8446 667 735	42.2584 888 067	72
19	48.8779 953 259	46.9669 444 494	45.1641 382 638	43.4623 846 107	76
20	50.3866 570 592	48.3363 671 868	46.4073 234 941	44.5911 057 697	80
21	51.8221 853 215	49.6329 912 154	47.5786 330 136	45.6493 464 002	84
22	53.1881 253 108	50.8606 865 252	48.6822 223 715	46.6415 075 049	88
23	54.4878 503 692	52.0231 173 767	49.7220 068 613	47.5717 152 756	92
24	55.7245 703 133	53.1237 532 377	50.7016 754 105	48.4438 382 529	96
25	56.9013 393 618	54.1658 791 389	51.6247 036 684	49.2615 034 150	100
26	58.0210 636 777	55.1526 054 780	52.4943 663 372	50.0281 112 612	104
27	59.0865 085 459	56.0868 773 038	53.3137 487 893	50.7468 499 542	108
28	60.1003 052 019	56.9714 831 056	54.0857 580 143	51.4207 085 787	112
29	61.0649 573 302	57.8090 631 364	54.8131 329 318	52.0524 895 725	116
30	61.9828 472 474	58.6021 172 930	55.4984 541 085	52.6448 203 816	120
31	62.8562 417 856	59.3530 125 770	56.1441 529 138	53.2001 643 865	124
32	63.6872 978 905	60.0639 901 604	56.7525 201 458	53.7208 311 475	128
33	64.4780 679 485	60.7371 720 737	57.3257 141 579	54.2089 860 093	132
34	65.2305 048 547	61.3745 675 401	57.8667 685 171	54.6666 591 066	136
35	65.9464 668 365	61.9780 789 723	58.3745 992 178	55.0957 538 065	140
36	66.6277 220 424	62.5495 076 505	58.8540 114 798	55.4980 546 247	144
37	67.2759 529 084	63.0905 590 983	59.3057 061 530	55.8752 346 467	148
38	67.8927 603 133	63.6028 481 738	59.7312 857 509	56.2288 624 856	152
39	68.4796 675 323	64.0879 038 887	60.1322 601 368	56.5604 088 062	156
40	69.0381 239 984	64.5471 739 723	60.5100 518 799	56.8712 524 407	160
41	69.5695 088 825	64.9820 291 927	60.8660 013 027	57.1626 861 231	164
42	70.0751 344 993	65.3937 674 472	61.2013 712 355	57.4359 218 654	168
43	70.5562 495 478	65.7836 176 373	61.5173 514 976	57.6920 959 984	172
44	71.0140 421 956	66.1527 433 355	61.8150 631 176	57.9322 738 969	176
45	71.4496 430 131	66.5022 462 587	62.0955 623 111	58.1574 544 110	180
46	71.8641 277 652	66.8331 695 565	62.3598 442 279	58.3685 740 194	184
47	72.2585 200 685	67.1465 009 245	62.6088 464 822	58.5665 107 249	188
48	72.6337 939 191	67.4431 755 521	62.8434 524 795	58.7520 877 049	192
49	72.9908 760 977	67.7240 789 140	63.0644 945 505	58.9260 767 355	196
50	73.3306 484 590	67.9900 494 131	63.2727 569 041	59.0892 014 010	200
51	73.6539 501 088	68.2418 808 823	63.4689 784 093	59.2421 401 029	204
52	73.9615 794 768	68.4803 249 546	63.6538 552 172	59.3855 288 815	208
53	74.2542 962 882	68.7060 933 059	63.8280 432 302	59.5199 640 609	212
54	74.5328 234 400	68.9198 597 793	63.9921 604 291	59.6460 047 289	216
55	74.7978 487 862	69.1222 623 965	64.1467 890 658	59.7641 750 627	220
56	75.0500 268 368	69.3139 052 615	64.2924 777 289	59.8749 665 079	224
57	75.2899 803 735	69.4953 603 644	64.4297 432 898	59.9788 398 233	228
58	75.5183 019 886	69.6671 692 881	64.5590 727 366	60.0762 269 962	232
59	75.7355 555 480	69.8298 448 248	64.6809 249 019	60.1675 330 398	236
60	75.9422 775 836	69.9838 725 067	64.7957 320 905	60.2531 376 768	240

Table 5.   PRESENT WORTH OF ONE DOLLAR PER PERIOD
PAYABLE AT END OF EACH PERIOD

QUARTERS	7% NOMINAL ANNUAL RATE	7½% NOMINAL ANNUAL RATE	8% NOMINAL ANNUAL RATE	8½% NOMINAL ANNUAL RATE	QUARTERS
1	0.9828 009 828	0.9815 950 920	0.9803 921 569	0.9791 921 665	1
2	1.9486 987 546	1.9451 240 167	1.9415 609 381	1.9380 094 653	2
3	2.8979 840 340	2.8909 192 802	2.8838 832 726	2.8768 758 534	3
YEARS					
1	3.8309 425 396	3.8193 072 689	3.8077 286 987	3.7962 064 660	4
2	7.4050 529 661	7.3651 062 626	7.3254 814 405	7.2861 752 820	8
3	10.7395 496 884	10.6569 834 586	10.5753 412 209	10.4946 104 515	12
4	13.8504 967 672	13.7131 227 078	13.5777 093 143	13.4442 231 214	16
5	16.7528 813 048	16.5504 056 785	16.3514 333 446	16.1558 923 441	20
6	19.4606 856 454	19.1845 051 091	18.9139 256 031	18.6488 128 718	24
7	21.9869 547 364	21.6299 713 815	21.2812 723 553	20.9406 310 277	28
8	24.3438 589 722	23.9003 128 956	23.4683 348 241	23.0475 696 169	32
9	26.5427 528 258	26.0080 706 875	25.4888 424 824	24.9845 427 608	36
10	28.5942 295 493	27.9648 877 047	27.3554 792 407	26.7652 614 677	40
11	30.5081 722 075	29.7815 731 195	29.0799 630 720	28.4023 306 875	44
12	32.2938 012 895	31.4681 620 379	30.6731 195 718	29.9073 385 361	48
13	33.9597 191 294	33.0339 709 316	32.1449 499 170	31.2909 383 236	52
14	35.5139 513 477	34.4876 491 011	33.5046 936 494	32.5629 239 638	56
15	36.9639 855 154	35.8372 264 532	34.7608 866 770	33.7322 993 016	60
16	38.3168 072 254	37.0901 578 566	35.9214 148 599	34.8073 418 473	64
17	39.5789 337 463	38.2533 643 223	36.9935 635 134	35.7956 613 694	68
18	40.7564 454 191	39.3332 712 334	37.9840 631 429	36.7042 537 610	72
19	41.8550 149 496	40.3358 438 386	38.8991 316 952	37.5395 505 611	76
20	42.8799 347 370	41.2666 202 031	39.7445 135 917	38.3074 644 800	80
21	43.8361 423 702	42.1307 418 000	40.5255 157 900	39.0134 312 534	84
22	44.7282 444 147	42.9329 819 114	41.2470 410 986	39.6624 481 198	88
23	45.5605 386 049	43.6777 719 949	41.9136 189 548	40.2591 091 931	92
24	46.3370 345 488	44.3692 261 625	42.5294 338 582	40.8076 379 831	96
25	47.0614 730 442	45.0111 639 064	43.0983 516 401	41.3119 172 916	100
26	47.7373 441 002	45.6071 311 974	43.6239 437 307	41.7755 166 973	104
27	48.3679 037 506	46.1604 200 720	44.1095 095 795	42.2017 178 229	108
28	48.9561 897 397	46.6740 868 175	44.5580 973 680	42.5935 375 648	112
29	49.5050 361 569	47.1509 688 542	44.9725 231 445	42.9537 494 482	116
30	50.0170 870 901	47.5937 004 090	45.3553 885 026	43.2849 032 595	120
31	50.4948 093 635	48.0047 270 668	45.7090 969 125	43.5893 430 958	124
32	50.9405 044 217	48.3863 192 790	46.0358 688 091	43.8692 239 570	128
33	51.3563 194 172	48.7405 849 053	46.3377 555 311	44.1265 270 006	132
34	51.7442 575 540	49.0694 808 576	46.6166 521 984	44.3630 735 652	136
35	52.1061 787 383	49.3748 239 092	46.8743 096 088	44.5805 380 634	140
36	52.4438 535 822	49.6583 007 308	47.1123 452 289	44.7804 598 338	144
37	52.7588 818 033	49.9214 772 070	47.3322 533 478	44.9642 540 374	148
38	53.0527 900 617	50.1658 070 865	47.5354 144 576	45.1332 216 752	152
39	53.3269 942 712	50.3926 400 118	47.7231 039 196	45.2885 587 972	156
40	53.5828 154 207	50.6032 289 752	47.8964 999 706	45.4313 649 686	160
41	53.8214 859 380	50.7987 372 393	48.0566 911 192	45.5626 510 538	164
42	54.0441 556 272	50.9802 447 634	48.2046 829 791	45.6833 463 708	168
43	54.2518 972 076	51.1487 541 687	48.3414 045 820	45.7943 052 706	172
44	54.4457 114 820	51.3051 962 765	48.4677 142 094	45.8963 131 839	176
45	54.6265 321 579	51.4504 352 503	48.5844 047 810	45.9900 921 813	180
46	54.7952 303 454	51.5852 733 691	48.6922 088 318	46.0763 060 845	184
47	54.9526 187 543	51.7104 554 590	48.7918 031 111	46.1555 651 649	188
48	55.0994 556 090	51.8266 730 076	48.8838 128 304	46.2284 304 638	192
49	55.2364 483 016	51.9345 679 839	48.9688 155 888	46.2954 177 637	196
50	55.3642 567 993	52.0347 363 839	49.0473 449 983	46.3570 012 392	200
51	55.4834 968 244	52.1277 315 233	49.1198 940 341	46.4136 168 134	204
52	55.5947 428 199	52.2140 670 937	49.1869 181 290	46.4656 652 439	208
53	55.6985 307 177	52.2942 200 003	49.2488 380 325	46.5135 149 594	212
54	55.7953 605 197	52.3686 329 961	49.3060 424 521	46.5575 046 677	216
55	55.8856 987 071	52.4377 171 275	49.3588 904 935	46.5979 457 532	220
56	55.9699 804 874	52.5018 540 053	49.4077 139 149	46.6351 244 811	224
57	56.0486 118 912	52.5613 979 124	49.4528 192 094	46.6693 040 237	228
58	56.1219 717 281	52.6166 777 605	49.4944 895 294	46.7007 263 236	232
59	56.1904 134 120	52.6679 989 074	49.5329 864 639	46.7296 138 059	236
60	56.2542 666 631	52.7156 448 439	49.5685 516 808	46.7561 709 526	240

112

Table 5.   PRESENT WORTH OF ONE DOLLAR PER PERIOD
PAYABLE AT END OF EACH PERIOD

QUARTERS	9% NOMINAL ANNUAL RATE	9½% NOMINAL ANNUAL RATE	10% NOMINAL ANNUAL RATE	10½% NOMINAL ANNUAL RATE	QUARTERS
1	0.9779 951 100	0.9768 009 768	0.9756 097 561	0.9744 214 373	1
2	1.9344 695 453	1.9309 411 251	1.9274 241 523	1.9239 185 747	2
3	2.8698 968 658	2.8629 461 539	2.8560 235 632	2.8491 289 400	3
YEARS					
1	3.7847 402 110	3.7733 295 765	3.7619 742 080	3.7506 737 540	4
2	7.2471 846 066	7.2085 062 708	7.1701 371 675	7.1320 742 257	8
3	10.4147 788 202	10.3358 341 868	10.2577 645 982	10.1805 582 849	12
4	13.3126 313 069	13.1829 016 785	13.0550 026 599	12.9289 032 789	16
5	15.9637 123 700	15.7748 247 258	15.5891 622 856	15.4066 594 553	20
6	18.3890 362 382	18.1344 685 006	17.8849 858 326	17.6404 676 863	24
7	20.6078 276 392	20.2826 490 763	19.9648 886 553	19.6543 459 123	28
8	22.6376 741 868	22.2383 170 611	21.8491 779 586	21.4699 473 830	32
9	24.4946 657 928	24.0187 247 745	23.5562 510 680	23.1067 934 731	36
10	26.1935 222 057	25.6395 784 422	25.1027 750 521	24.5824 835 768	40
11	27.7477 096 897	27.1151 767 517	26.5038 494 527	25.9128 843 369	44
12	29.1695 477 666	28.4585 369 910	27.7731 537 094	27.1123 002 426	48
13	30.4703 068 693	29.6815 098 833	28.9230 807 191	28.1936 274 321	52
14	31.6602 976 782	30.7948 841 308	29.9648 578 351	29.1684 923 521	56
15	32.7489 528 506	31.8084 815 887	30.9086 564 851	30.0473 767 650	60
16	33.7449 017 904	32.7312 439 116	31.7636 914 805	30.8397 304 495	64
17	34.6560 390 501	33.5713 114 334	32.5383 109 860	31.5540 728 046	68
18	35.4895 869 088	34.3360 949 790	33.2400 780 265	32.1980 844 502	72
19	36.2521 526 203	35.0323 412 407	32.8758 443 293	32.7786 898 094	76
20	36.9497 807 868	35.6661 922 954	34.4518 172 213	33.3021 315 600	80
21	37.5880 012 723	36.2432 397 880	34.9736 202 342	33.7740 377 557	84
22	38.1718 730 363	36.7685 742 593	35.4463 480 101	34.1994 823 390	88
23	38.7060 242 341	37.2468 300 533	35.8746 160 436	34.5830 396 968	92
24	39.1946 889 028	37.6822 261 999	36.2626 057 446	34.9288 338 435	96
25	39.6417 405 229	38.0786 036 339	36.6141 052 645	35.2405 827 632	100
26	40.0507 227 226	38.4394 590 790	36.9325 464 811	35.5216 383 850	104
27	40.4248 773 664	38.7679 758 941	37.2210 385 067	35.7750 226 233	108
28	40.7671 702 523	39.0670 521 566	37.4823 980 433	36.0034 598 692	112
29	41.0803 146 211	39.3393 262 281	37.7191 768 839	36.2094 062 836	116
30	41.3667 926 630	39.5872 000 292	37.9336 868 273	36.3950 762 055	120
31	41.6288 751 932	39.8128 602 286	38.1280 222 489	36.5624 659 606	124
32	41.8686 396 518	40.0182 975 332	38.3040 805 493	36.7133 753 263	128
33	42.0879 865 712	40.2053 242 497	38.4635 806 801	36.8494 268 823	132
34	42.2886 546 408	40.3755 902 720	38.6080 799 265	36.9720 834 570	136
35	42.4722 344 888	40.5305 976 361	38.7389 891 119	37.0826 638 559	140
36	42.6401 812 911	40.6717 137 708	38.8575 863 728	37.1823 570 410	144
37	42.7938 263 055	40.8001 835 605	38.9650 296 378	37.2722 349 150	148
38	42.9343 874 245	40.9171 403 273	39.0623 679 330	37.3532 638 463	152
39	43.0629 788 288	41.0236 158 289	39.1505 516 243	37.4263 150 590	156
40	43.1806 198 193	41.1205 493 606	39.2304 416 963	37.4921 740 010	160
41	43.2882 428 965	41.2087 960 408	39.3028 181 586	37.5515 487 886	164
42	43.3867 011 526	41.2891 343 557	39.3683 876 612	37.6050 778 204	168
43	43.4767 750 329	41.3622 730 257	39.4277 903 944	37.6533 366 414	172
44	43.5591 785 229	41.4288 572 584	39.4816 063 389	37.6968 441 313	176
45	43.6345 648 073	41.4894 744 401	39.5303 609 284	37.7360 680 831	180
46	43.7035 314 480	41.5446 593 174	39.5745 301 803	37.7714 302 335	184
47	43.7666 251 202	41.5948 987 149	39.6145 453 425	37.8033 107 968	188
48	43.8243 459 464	41.6406 358 295	39.6507 971 045	37.8320 525 532	192
49	43.8771 514 601	41.6822 741 405	39.6836 394 117	37.8579 645 347	196
50	43.9254 602 329	41.7201 809 685	39.7133 929 210	37.8813 253 473	200
51	43.9696 551 922	41.7546 907 163	39.7403 481 320	37.9023 861 667	204
52	44.0100 866 567	41.7861 078 187	39.7647 682 227	37.9213 734 392	208
53	44.0470 751 128	41.8147 094 279	39.7868 916 197	37.9384 913 162	212
54	44.0809 137 558	41.8407 478 587	39.8069 343 255	37.9539 238 495	216
55	44.1118 708 131	41.8644 528 145	39.8250 920 277	37.9678 369 699	220
56	44.1401 916 710	41.8860 334 133	39.8415 420 097	37.9803 802 714	224
57	44.1661 008 194	41.9056 080 327	39.8564 448 815	37.9916 886 198	228
58	44.1898 036 314	41.9235 659 893	39.8699 461 478	38.0018 836 027	232
59	44.2114 879 912	41.9398 490 677	39.8821 776 288	38.0110 748 366	236
60	44.2313 257 835	41.9546 729 123	39.8932 587 468	38.0193 611 459	240

113

Table 5.   PRESENT WORTH OF ONE DOLLAR PER PERIOD
PAYABLE AT END OF EACH PERIOD

QUARTERS	11% NOMINAL ANNUAL RATE	11½% NOMINAL ANNUAL RATE	12% NOMINAL ANNUAL RATE	12½% NOMINAL ANNUAL RATE	QUARTERS
1	0.9732 360 097	0.9720 534 629	0.9708 737 864	0.9696 969 697	1
2	1.9204 243 404	1.9169 413 978	1.9134 696 955	1.9100 091 827	2
3	2.8422 621 317	2.8354 229 869	2.8286 113 549	2.8218 270 863	3
YEARS					
1	3.7394 278 654	3.7282 361 962	3.7170 984 028	3.7060 141 443	4
2	7.0943 144 100	7.0568 547 199	7.0196 921 895	6.9828 238 874	8
3	10.1042 036 582	10.0286 893 066	9.9540 039 936	9.8801 366 537	12
4	12.8045 731 539	12.6819 824 818	12.5611 020 260	12.4419 031 047	16
5	15.2272 521 338	15.0508 776 768	14.8774 748 605	14.7069 838 462	20
6	17.4007 966 983	17.1658 585 985	16.9355 421 220	16.7097 389 232	24
7	19.3508 264 022	19.0541 415 030	18.7641 082 277	18.4805 490 426	28
8	21.1003 262 323	20.7400 254 231	20.3887 655 288	20.0462 764 323	32
9	22.6699 175 310	22.2452 048 564	21.8322 524 981	21.4306 723 267	36
10	24.0781 010 600	23.5890 489 369	23.1147 719 742	22.6547 372 596	40
11	25.3414 750 691	24.7888 506 833	24.2542 739 174	23.7370 396 314	44
12	26.4749 309 389	25.8600 495 311	25.2667 066 350	24.6939 973 814	48
13	27.4918 287 059	26.8164 300 123	26.1662 399 915	25.5401 270 390	52
14	28.4041 545 371	27.6702 991 390	26.9654 637 279	26.2882 639 316	56
15	29.2226 620 109	28.4326 447 744	27.6755 636 661	26.9497 568 896	60
16	29.9569 988 691	29.1132 770 278	28.3064 782 639	27.5346 404 021	64
17	30.6158 207 353	29.7209 544 944	28.8670 377 124	28.0517 868 343	68
18	31.2068 931 383	30.2634 969 636	29.3650 875 220	28.5090 410 167	72
19	31.7371 830 443	30.7478 860 467	29.8075 983 270	28.9133 392 470	76
20	32.2129 409 770	31.1803 550 186	30.2007 634 458	29.2708 145 098	80
21	32.6397 746 917	31.5664 690 293	30.5500 855 616	29.5868 895 107	84
22	33.0227 152 746	31.9111 967 184	30.8604 537 370	29.8663 589 358	88
23	33.3662 764 435	32.2189 741 542	31.1362 118 409	30.1134 621 847	92
24	33.6745 077 517	32.4937 619 119	31.3812 193 446	30.3319 476 793	96
25	33.9510 423 195	32.7390 960 529	31.5989 053 383	30.5251 297 260	100
26	34.1991 396 579	32.9581 336 147	31.7923 165 242	30.6959 387 915	104
27	34.4217 240 886	33.1536 932 432	31.9641 598 578	30.8469 659 566	108
28	34.6214 192 126	33.3282 914 628	32.1168 404 340	30.9805 022 214	112
29	34.8005 788 351	33.4841 750 596	32.2524 951 484	31.0985 732 585	116
30	34.9613 147 092	33.6233 499 939	32.3730 226 051	31.2029 701 414	120
31	35.1055 214 276	33.7476 072 136	32.4801 096 893	31.2952 765 142	124
32	35.2348 987 540	33.8585 457 008	32.5752 551 767	31.3768 926 144	128
33	35.3509 716 579	33.9575 930 476	32.6597 907 098	31.4490 565 139	132
34	35.4551 082 900	34.0460 238 271	32.7348 994 361	31.5128 628 999	136
35	35.5485 361 078	34.1249 759 952	32.8016 325 666	31.5692 796 807	140
36	35.6323 563 446	34.1954 655 338	32.8609 240 888	31.6191 626 680	144
37	35.7075 569 888	34.2583 995 250	32.9136 038 382	31.6632 685 599	148
38	35.7750 244 300	34.3145 878 236	32.9604 091 133	31.7022 664 186	152
39	35.8355 539 063	34.3647 534 788	33.0019 949 940	31.7367 478 206	156
40	35.8898 588 783	34.4095 420 385	33.0389 435 103	31.7672 358 300	160
41	35.9385 794 384	34.4495 298 561	33.0717 717 886	31.7941 929 333	164
42	35.9822 898 555	34.4852 315 080	33.1009 392 886	31.8180 280 552	168
43	36.0215 053 438	34.5171 064 143	33.1268 542 345	31.8391 027 615	172
44	36.0566 881 362	34.5455 647 518	33.1498 793 284	31.8577 367 440	176
45	36.0882 529 320	34.5709 727 314	33.1703 368 261	31.8742 126 703	180
46	36.1165 717 851	34.5936 573 112	33.1885 130 478	31.8887 804 710	184
47	36.1419 784 898	34.6139 104 037	33.2046 623 853	31.9016 611 318	188
48	36.1647 725 146	34.6319 926 322	33.2190 108 626	31.9130 500 455	192
49	36.1852 225 326	34.6481 366 846	33.2317 592 988	31.9231 199 755	196
50	36.2035 695 880	34.6625 503 079	33.2430 861 192	31.9320 236 773	200
51	36.2200 299 375	34.6754 189 812	33.2531 498 525	31.9398 962 153	204
52	36.2347 975 989	34.6869 083 027	33.2620 913 492	31.9468 570 114	208
53	36.2480 466 388	34.6971 661 207	33.2700 357 531	31.9530 116 572	212
54	36.2599 332 233	34.7063 244 361	33.2770 942 532	31.9584 535 155	216
55	36.2705 974 597	34.7145 011 010	33.2833 656 390	31.9632 651 361	220
56	36.2801 650 471	34.7218 013 355	33.2889 376 841	31.9675 195 087	224
57	36.2887 487 587	34.7283 190 813	33.2938 883 740	31.9712 811 700	228
58	36.2964 497 706	34.7341 382 108	33.2982 869 979	31.9746 071 822	232
59	36.3033 588 546	34.7393 336 065	33.3021 951 182	31.9775 479 991	236
60	36.3095 574 480	34.7439 721 244	33.3056 674 325	31.9801 482 314	240

Table 5. PRESENT WORTH OF ONE DOLLAR PER PERIOD
PAYABLE AT END OF EACH PERIOD

QUARTERS	13% NOMINAL ANNUAL RATE	13½% NOMINAL ANNUAL RATE	14% NOMINAL ANNUAL RATE	14½% NOMINAL ANNUAL RATE	QUARTERS
1	0.9685 230 024	0.9673 518 742	0.9661 835 749	0.9650 180 941	1
2	1.9065 598 086	1.9031 215 228	1.8996 942 752	1.8962 780 160	2
3	2.8150 700 326	2.8083 400 463	2.8016 369 809	2.7949 606 910	3
YEARS					
1	3.6949 830 824	3.6840 048 815	3.6730 792 086	3.6622 057 331	4
2	6.9462 469 155	6.9099 584 092	6.8739 555 367	6.8382 354 986	8
3	9.8070 763 906	9.7348 124 735	9.6633 343 346	9.5926 315 665	12
4	12.3243 575 791	12.2084 378 423	12.0941 168 081	11.9813 679 006	16
5	14.5393 461 469	14.3745 045 933	14.2124 033 020	14.0529 876 434	20
6	16.4883 434 930	16.2712 530 780	16.0583 676 030	15.8495 895 946	24
7	18.2032 916 918	17.9321 690 274	17.6670 188 458	17.4076 837 295	28
8	19.7122 969 917	19.3865 747 186	19.0688 654 684	18.7589 331 433	32
9	21.0400 904 474	20.6601 466 385	20.2904 938 121	19.9307 974 981	36
10	22.2084 332 365	21.7753 687 839	21.3550 723 373	20.9470 910 500	40
11	23.2364 733 033	22.7519 296 002	22.2827 910 189	21.8284 665 942	44
12	24.1410 591 738	23.6070 695 665	23.0912 442 535	22.5928 351 652	48
13	24.9370 116 860	24.3558 855 641	23.7957 645 412	23.2557 300 188	52
14	25.6373 889 601	25.0115 974 014	24.4097 132 702	23.8306 222 941	56
15	26.2536 561 917	25.5857 811 993	24.9447 341 182	24.3291 947 696	60
16	26.7959 177 710	26.0885 737 601	25.4109 738 780	24.7615 792 771	64
17	27.2730 608 111	26.5288 515 251	25.8172 748 928	25.1365 625 976	68
18	27.6929 051 987	26.9143 872 815	26.1713 427 543	25.4617 650 232	72
19	28.0623 317 542	27.2519 873 862	26.4798 924 403	25.7437 952 145	76
20	28.3873 950 014	27.5476 119 263	26.7487 756 660	25.9883 844 997	80
21	28.6734 223 945	27.8064 799 404	26.9830 918 632	26.2005 033 446	84
22	28.9251 016 304	28.0331 615 574	27.1872 848 921	26.3844 623 612	88
23	29.1465 574 744	28.2316 586 782	27.3652 273 200	26.5439 999 063	92
24	29.3414 193 615	28.4054 756 268	27.5202 938 659	26.6823 580 513	96
25	29.5128 808 789	28.5576 810 164	27.6554 254 020	26.8023 484 667	100
26	29.6637 521 056	28.6909 619 238	27.7731 847 289	26.9064 095 595	104
27	29.7965 056 668	28.8076 713 277	27.8758 051 790	26.9966 560 263	108
28	29.9133 172 577	28.9098 696 486	27.9652 329 727	27.0749 218 272	112
29	30.0161 013 009	28.9993 611 244	28.0431 641 285	27.1427 974 550	116
30	30.1065 423 219	29.0777 256 628	28.1110 766 284	27.2016 622 567	120
31	30.1861 225 564	29.1463 467 335	28.1702 584 487	27.2527 124 642	124
32	30.2561 462 433	29.2064 357 920	28.2218 319 860	27.2969 855 035	128
33	30.3177 609 992	29.2590 536 675	28.2667 753 442	27.3353 810 773	132
34	30.3719 766 270	29.3051 292 908	28.3059 408 844	27.3686 794 484	136
35	30.4196 816 654	29.3454 760 939	28.3400 713 901	27.3975 572 956	140
36	30.4616 579 512	29.3808 063 706	28.3698 141 539	27.4226 014 654	144
37	30.4985 934 329	29.4117 438 515	28.3957 332 543	27.4443 208 975	148
38	30.5310 934 452	29.4388 347 156	28.4183 202 529	27.4631 569 673	152
39	30.5596 906 302	29.4625 572 327	28.4380 035 172	27.4794 924 555	156
40	30.5848 536 664	29.4833 302 067	28.4551 563 450	27.4936 593 266	160
41	30.6069 949 504	29.5015 203 695	28.4701 040 434	27.5059 454 754	164
42	30.6264 773 551	29.5174 488 555	28.4831 300 990	27.5166 005 769	168
43	30.6436 201 772	29.5313 968 705	28.4944 815 539	27.5258 411 610	172
44	30.6587 043 701	29.5436 106 568	28.5043 736 911	27.5338 550 117	176
45	30.6719 771 483	29.5543 058 400	28.5129 941 171	27.5408 049 839	180
46	30.6836 560 390	29.5636 712 358	28.5205 063 204	27.5468 323 129	184
47	30.6939 324 474	29.5718 721 835	28.5270 527 715	27.5520 594 841	188
48	30.7029 747 032	29.5790 534 651	28.5327 576 255	27.5565 927 224	192
49	30.7109 312 713	29.5853 418 609	28.5377 290 762	27.5605 241 508	196
50	30.7179 322 802	29.5908 483 879	28.5420 614 082	27.5639 336 627	200
51	30.7240 925 593	29.5956 702 600	28.5458 367 853	27.5668 905 449	204
52	30.7295 130 693	29.5998 926 038	28.5491 268 083	27.5694 548 863	208
53	30.7342 826 467	29.6035 899 618	28.5519 938 733	27.5716 787 988	212
54	30.7384 794 602	29.6068 276 082	28.5544 923 548	27.5736 074 758	216
55	30.7421 722 911	29.6096 627 013	28.5566 696 371	27.5752 801 113	220
56	30.7454 216 612	29.6121 452 926	28.5585 670 128	27.5767 306 962	224
57	30.7482 808 244	29.6143 192 105	28.5602 204 661	27.5779 887 088	228
58	30.7507 966 394	29.6162 228 340	28.5616 613 552	27.5790 797 140	232
59	30.7530 103 378	29.6178 897 702	28.5629 170 067	27.5800 258 828	236
60	30.7549 581 999	29.6193 494 475	28.5640 112 345	27.5808 464 430	240

Table 5.   PRESENT WORTH OF ONE DOLLAR PER PERIOD
PAYABLE AT END OF EACH PERIOD

QUARTERS	**15%** NOMINAL ANNUAL RATE	**15½%** NOMINAL ANNUAL RATE	**16%** NOMINAL ANNUAL RATE	**16½%** NOMINAL ANNUAL RATE	QUARTERS
1	0.9638 554 217	0.9626 955 475	0.9615 384 615	0.9603 841 537	1
2	1.8928 726 956	1.8894 782 648	1.8860 946 746	1.8827 218 763	2
3	2.7883 110 319	2.7816 878 602	2.7750 910 332	2.7685 204 094	3
YEARS					
1	3.6513 841 271	3.6406 140 652	3.6298 952 243	3.6192 272 839	4
2	6.8027 955 276	6.7676 328 879	6.7327 448 750	6.6981 288 149	8
3	9.5226 939 194	9.4535 112 983	9.3850 737 605	9.3173 715 133	12
4	11.8701 650 431	11.7604 826 483	11.6522 956 079	11.5455 792 829	16
5	13.8962 042 118	13.7420 007 949	13.5903 263 450	13.4411 309 504	20
6	15.6448 241 082	15.4439 786 567	15.2469 631 414	15.0536 897 850	24
7	17.1540 108 946	16.9058 520 425	16.6630 632 180	16.4255 046 712	28
8	18.4565 494 056	18.1614 934 019	17.8735 514 984	17.5925 170 254	32
9	19.5807 353 499	19.2399 966 695	18.9082 819 537	18.5853 024 579	36
10	20.5509 899 925	20.1663 513 882	19.7927 738 834	19.4298 718 502	40
11	21.3883 906 701	20.9620 217 313	20.5488 412 919	20.1483 528 383	44
12	22.1111 286 648	21.6454 438 394	21.1951 308 814	20.7595 695 541	48
13	22.7349 043 829	22.2324 529 971	21.7475 819 311	21.2795 358 160	52
14	23.2732 684 227	22.7366 505 453	22.2198 194 037	21.7218 746 896	56
15	23.7379 159 409	23.1697 190 319	22.6234 899 745	22.0981 754 102	60
16	24.1389 407 126	23.5416 929 035	22.9685 492 702	22.4182 970 202	64
17	24.4850 544 036	23.8611 910 095	23.2635 074 023	22.6906 266 744	68
18	24.7837 758 182	24.1356 163 051	23.5156 388 498	22.9222 993 834	72
19	25.0415 942 341	24.3713 273 828	23.7311 618 678	23.1193 849 496	76
20	25.2641 103 723	24.5737 858 043	23.9153 918 468	23.2870 469 957	80
21	25.4561 580 645	24.7476 826 479	24.0728 724 050	23.4296 782 508	84
22	25.6219 092 606	24.8970 472 039	24.2074 874 462	23.5510 156 401	88
23	25.7649 646 584	25.0253 403 351	24.3225 569 476	23.6542 381 913	92
24	25.8884 319 234	25.1355 346 674	24.4209 188 396	23.7420 503 252	96
25	25.9949 931 980	25.2301 834 670	24.5049 989 972	23.8167 527 112	100
26	26.0869 633 671	25.3114 798 013	24.5768 710 682	23.8803 025 446	104
27	26.1663 403 456	25.3813 073 532	24.6383 076 158	23.9343 648 246	108
28	26.2348 484 801	25.4412 840 674	24.6908 238 341	23.9803 559 779	112
29	26.2939 760 078	25.4927 996 388	24.7357 149 176	24.0194 809 682	116
30	26.3450 073 862	25.5370 477 131	24.7740 880 039	24.0527 648 664	120
31	26.3890 511 958	25.5750 535 437	24.8068 894 790	24.0810 797 074	124
32	26.4270 642 230	25.6076 977 475	24.8349 283 173	24.1051 763 373	128
33	26.4598 722 440	25.6357 367 095	24.8588 960 338	24.1256 588 497	132
34	26.4881 879 642	25.6598 201 088	24.8793 837 383	24.1430 911 201	136
35	26.5126 265 005	25.6805 059 716	24.8968 967 140	24.1579 208 724	140
36	26.5337 187 436	25.6982 736 012	24.9118 668 790	24.1705 366 446	144
37	26.5519 228 912	25.7135 346 838	24.9246 634 388	24.1812 689 688	148
38	26.5676 344 013	25.7266 428 276	24.9356 019 918	24.1903 990 307	152
39	26.5811 945 828	25.7379 017 558	24.9449 523 127	24.1981 660 372	156
40	26.5928 980 107	25.7475 723 443	24.9529 450 062	24.2047 734 830	160
41	26.6029 989 244	25.7558 786 662	24.9597 771 941	24.2103 944 825	164
42	26.6117 167 513	25.7630 131 837	24.9656 173 769	24.2151 763 055	168
43	26.6192 408 731	25.7691 412 078	24.9706 095 897	24.2192 442 352	172
44	26.6257 347 403	25.7744 047 282	24.9748 769 541	24.2227 048 509	176
45	26.6313 394 222	25.7789 257 039	24.9785 247 151	24.2256 488 205	180
46	26.6361 766 725	25.7828 088 883	24.9816 428 364	24.2281 532 757	184
47	26.6403 515 730	25.7861 442 572	24.9843 082 196	24.2302 838 329	188
48	26.6439 548 173	25.7890 090 929	24.9865 866 004	24.2320 963 126	192
49	26.6470 646 806	25.7914 697 754	24.9885 341 698	24.2336 382 015	196
50	26.6497 487 198	25.7935 833 201	24.9901 989 603	24.2349 498 970	200
51	26.6520 652 419	25.7953 986 990	24.9916 220 302	24.2360 657 654	204
52	26.6540 645 698	25.7969 579 755	24.9928 384 763	24.2370 150 423	208
53	26.6557 901 359	25.7982 972 790	24.9938 782 995	24.2378 225 987	212
54	26.6572 794 256	25.7994 476 418	24.9947 671 448	24.2385 095 925	216
55	26.6585 647 915	25.8004 357 186	24.9955 269 334	24.2390 940 228	220
56	26.6596 741 562	25.8012 844 036	24.9961 764 039	24.2395 912 017	224
57	26.6606 316 190	25.8020 133 614	24.9967 315 741	24.2400 141 552	228
58	26.6614 579 794	25.8026 394 824	24.9972 061 358	24.2403 739 647	232
59	26.6621 711 888	25.8031 772 741	24.9976 117 932	24.2406 800 570	236
60	26.6627 867 407	25.8036 391 975	24.9979 585 508	24.2409 404 519	240

Table 5. PRESENT WORTH OF ONE DOLLAR PER PERIOD
PAYABLE AT END OF EACH PERIOD

QUARTERS	17% NOMINAL ANNUAL RATE	17½% NOMINAL ANNUAL RATE	18% NOMINAL ANNUAL RATE	18½% NOMINAL ANNUAL RATE	QUARTERS
1	0.9592 326 139	0.9580 838 323	0.9569 377 990	0.9557 945 042	1
2	1.8793 598 215	1.8760 084 621	1.8726 677 503	1.8693 376 384	2
3	2.7619 758 480	2.7554 572 092	2.7489 643 543	2.7424 971 454	3
YEARS					
1	3.6086 099 261	3.5980 428 352	3.5875 256 979	3.5770 582 035	4
2	6.6637 820 642	6.6297 020 097	6.5958 860 674	6.5623 316 827	8
3	9.2503 949 110	9.1841 344 529	9.1185 807 808	9.0537 246 761	12
4	11.4403 094 940	11.3364 625 121	11.2340 150 491	11.1329 442 489	16
5	13.2943 658 082	13.1499 831 971	13.0079 364 515	12.8681 799 355	20
6	14.8640 730 666	14.6780 296 587	14.4954 783 660	14.3163 400 661	24
7	16.1930 407 243	15.9655 396 430	15.7428 735 126	15.5249 181 170	28
8	17.3181 900 320	17.0503 770 491	16.7888 908 627	16.5335 502 940	32
9	18.2707 797 789	17.9644 454 540	17.6660 405 772	17.3753 154 308	36
10	19.0772 747 211	18.7346 263 531	18.4015 844 203	18.0778 198 341	40
11	19.7600 808 230	19.3835 697 080	19.0183 830 536	18.6641 026 521	44
12	20.3381 677 377	19.9303 600 510	19.5356 065 444	19.1533 914 611	48
13	20.8275 958 198	20.3910 777 343	19.9693 301 697	19.5617 328 473	52
14	21.2419 623 129	20.7792 718 320	20.3330 340 357	19.9025 186 666	56
15	21.5927 791 068	21.1063 585 987	20.6380 220 382	20.1869 252 405	60
16	21.8897 925 596	21.3819 572 069	20.8937 731 874	20.4242 798 918	64
17	22.1412 542 705	21.6141 726 326	21.1082 362 147	20.6223 668 406	68
18	22.3541 503 243	21.8098 340 124	21.2880 766 190	20.7876 824 943	72
19	22.5343 953 785	21.9746 954 787	21.4388 838 301	20.9256 485 012	76
20	22.6869 969 839	22.1136 053 804	21.5653 449 276	21.0407 895 578	80
21	22.8161 947 033	22.2306 488 668	21.6713 903 155	21.1368 817 999	84
22	22.9255 778 954	22.3292 680 262	21.7603 158 784	21.2170 766 431	88
23	23.0181 854 334	22.4123 631 123	21.8348 854 179	21.2840 041 363	92
24	23.0965 901 310	22.4823 778 374	21.8974 165 512	21.3398 592 158	96
25	23.1629 702 199	22.5413 712 384	21.9498 527 423	21.3864 736 901	100
26	23.2191 698 652	22.5910 782 301	21.9938 237 052	21.4253 763 151	104
27	23.2667 504 001	22.6329 606 268	22.0306 960 549	21.4578 429 310	108
28	23.3070 337 024	22.6682 501 323	22.0616 157 820	21.4849 383 043	112
29	23.3411 389 190	22.6979 845 623	22.0875 438 699	21.5075 510 477	116
30	23.3700 135 575	22.7230 383 657	22.1092 861 622	21.5264 227 627	120
31	23.3944 598 105	22.7441 483 402	22.1275 184 080	21.5421 723 612	124
32	23.4151 568 414	22.7619 353 014	22.1428 072 645	21.5553 163 628	128
33	23.4326 796 530	22.7769 223 392	22.1556 279 086	21.5662 858 347	132
34	23.4475 150 625	22.7895 502 018	22.1663 788 051	21.5754 405 287	136
35	23.4600 752 257	22.8001 902 573	22.1753 940 913	21.5830 806 798	140
36	23.4707 090 879	22.8091 554 152	22.1829 539 619	21.5894 568 525	144
37	23.4797 120 781	22.8167 093 283	22.1892 933 771	21.5947 781 578	148
38	23.4873 343 163	22.8230 741 470	22.1946 093 656	21.5992 191 121	152
39	23.4937 875 630	22.8284 370 516	22.1990 671 481	21.6029 253 596	156
40	23.4992 511 015	22.8329 557 580	22.2028 052 721	21.6060 184 494	160
41	23.5038 767 194	22.8367 631 551	22.2059 399 185	21.6085 998 217	164
42	23.5077 929 252	22.8399 712 131	22.2085 685 117	21.6107 541 345	168
43	23.5111 085 184	22.8426 742 767	22.2107 727 484	21.6125 520 401	172
44	23.5139 156 127	22.8449 518 393	22.2126 211 361	21.6140 525 020	176
45	23.5162 921 943	22.8468 708 807	22.2141 711 225	21.6153 047 292	180
46	23.5183 042 893	22.8484 878 375	22.2154 708 812	21.6163 497 892	184
47	23.5200 077 975	22.8498 502 620	22.2165 608 086	21.6172 219 556	188
48	23.5214 500 456	22.8509 982 213	22.2174 747 796	21.6179 498 317	192
49	23.5226 711 020	22.8519 654 753	22.2182 412 004	21.6185 572 887	196
50	23.5237 048 900	22.8527 804 696	22.2188 838 912	21.6190 642 487	200
51	23.5245 801 301	22.8534 671 721	22.2194 228 269	21.6194 873 378	204
52	23.5253 211 382	22.8540 457 778	22.2198 747 575	21.6198 404 314	208
53	23.5259 485 009	22.8545 333 026	22.2202 537 291	21.6201 351 097	212
54	23.5264 796 475	22.8549 440 840	22.2205 715 199	21.6203 810 366	216
55	23.5269 293 344	22.8552 902 025	22.2208 380 071	21.6205 862 777	220
56	23.5273 100 546	22.8555 818 370	22.2210 614 729	21.6207 575 639	224
57	23.5276 323 853	22.8558 275 640	22.2212 488 627	21.6209 005 127	228
58	23.5279 052 815	22.8560 346 100	22.2214 060 006	21.6210 198 122	232
59	23.5281 363 247	22.8562 090 640	22.2215 377 703	21.6211 193 749	236
60	23.5283 319 337	22.8563 560 565	22.2216 482 673	21.6212 024 661	240

117

Table 5.   PRESENT WORTH OF ONE DOLLAR PER PERIOD
PAYABLE AT END OF EACH PERIOD

QUARTERS	19% NOMINAL ANNUAL RATE	19½% NOMINAL ANNUAL RATE	20% NOMINAL ANNUAL RATE	20½% NOMINAL ANNUAL RATE	QUARTERS
1	0.9546 539 379	0.9535 160 906	0.9523 809 524	0.9512 485 137	1
2	1.8660 180 792	1.8627 090 256	1.8594 104 308	1.8561 222 484	2
3	2.7360 554 455	2.7296 391 186	2.7232 480 294	2.7168 820 437	3
YEARS					
1	3.5666 400 435	3.5562 709 116	3.5459 505 042	3.5356 785 196	4
2	6.5290 363 299	6.4959 975 119	6.4632 127 594	6.4306 796 312	8
3	8.9895 570 585	8.9260 689 826	8.8632 516 364	8.8010 963 391	12
4	11.0332 276 785	10.9348 433 196	10.8377 695 602	10.7419 851 858	16
5	12.7306 690 187	12.5953 600 518	12.4622 103 425	12.3311 781 336	20
6	14.1405 376 518	13.9679 959 754	13.7986 417 943	13.6324 037 187	24
7	15.3115 528 236	15.1026 604 702	14.8981 272 571	14.6978 426 421	28
8	16.2841 799 892	16.0406 102 161	15.8026 766 684	15.5702 202 779	32
9	17.0920 291 325	16.8159 492 963	16.5468 517 076	16.2845 200 116	36
10	17.7630 161 884	17.4568 692 304	17.1590 863 540	16.8693 861 164	40
11	18.3203 277 024	17.9866 740 247	17.6627 733 128	17.3482 724 218	44
12	18.7832 220 622	18.4246 275 118	18.0771 578 203	17.7403 828 410	48
13	19.1676 949 880	18.7866 537 882	18.4180 729 801	18.0614 414 704	52
14	19.4870 322 784	19.0859 162 181	18.6985 447 258	18.3243 231 447	56
15	19.7522 689 134	19.3332 960 571	18.9292 895 251	18.5395 697 332	60
16	19.9725 703 772	19.5377 880 971	19.1191 238 425	18.7158 128 813	64
17	20.1555 493 799	19.7068 277 187	19.2753 010 052	18.8601 201 498	68
18	20.3075 289 214	19.8465 612 442	19.4037 883 435	18.9782 784 328	72
19	20.4337 607 877	19.9620 694 190	19.5094 951 947	19.0750 260 185	76
20	20.5386 070 316	20.0575 521 486	19.5964 604 828	19.1542 426 006	80
21	20.6256 907 070	20.1364 812 086	19.6680 070 405	19.2191 048 590	84
22	20.6980 210 664	20.2017 264 790	19.7268 685 706	19.2722 138 475	88
23	20.7580 975 490	20.2556 602 938	19.7752 940 971	19.3156 993 002	92
24	20.8079 961 501	20.3002 436 999	19.8151 338 976	19.3513 050 356	96
25	20.8494 411 596	20.3370 977 608	19.8479 102 000	19.3804 588 862	100
26	20.8838 647 462	20.3675 624 992	19.8748 753 452	19.4043 299 564	104
27	20.9124 564 470	20.3927 456 206	19.8970 596 368	19.4238 755 045	108
28	20.9362 042 734	20.4135 627 893	19.9153 107 085	19.4398 793 304	112
29	20.9559 288 522	20.4307 709 229	19.9303 259 103	19.4529 832 067	116
30	20.9723 117 835	20.4449 957 132	19.9426 789 539	19.4637 126 144	120
31	20.9859 191 939	20.4567 543 771	19.9528 418 336	19.4724 978 156	124
32	20.9972 212 995	20.4664 744 625	19.9612 028 598	19.4796 911 074	128
33	21.0066 086 542	20.4745 093 941	19.9680 814 967	19.4855 809 494	132
34	21.0144 056 465	20.4811 513 241	19.9737 405 683	19.4904 035 313	136
35	21.0208 817 082	20.4866 417 546	19.9783 963 006	19.4943 522 443	140
36	21.0262 606 254	20.4911 803 189	19.9822 265 830	19.4975 854 366	144
37	21.0307 282 711	20.4949 320 405	19.9853 777 659	19.5002 327 631	148
38	21.0344 390 288	20.4980 333 329	19.9879 702 518	19.5024 003 847	152
39	21.0375 211 270	20.5005 969 598	19.9901 030 964	19.5041 752 256	156
40	21.0400 810 703	20.5027 161 353	19.9918 577 929	19.5056 284 591	160
41	21.0422 073 197	20.5044 679 131	19.9933 013 861	19.5068 183 615	164
42	21.0439 733 498	20.5059 159 883	19.9944 890 337	19.5077 926 495	168
43	21.0454 401 872	20.5071 130 133	19.9954 661 144	19.5085 903 930	172
44	21.0466 585 197	20.5081 025 123	19.9962 699 611	19.5092 435 826	176
45	21.0476 704 479	20.5089 204 636	19.9969 312 878	19.5097 784 119	180
46	21.0485 109 399	20.5095 966 081	19.9974 753 629	19.5102 163 283	184
47	21.0492 090 397	20.5101 555 307	19.9979 229 748	19.5105 748 927	188
48	21.0497 888 705	20.5106 175 539	19.9982 912 262	19.5108 684 839	192
49	21.0502 704 691	20.5109 994 769	19.9985 941 876	19.5111 088 754	196
50	21.0506 704 775	20.5113 151 866	19.9988 434 346	19.5113 057 071	200
51	21.0510 027 183	20.5115 761 623	19.9990 484 908	19.5114 668 722	204
52	21.0512 786 724	20.5117 918 932	19.9992 171 910	19.5115 988 336	208
53	21.0515 078 756	20.5119 702 231	19.9993 559 811	19.5117 068 832	212
54	21.0516 982 482	20.5121 176 363	19.9994 701 641	19.5117 953 538	216
55	21.0518 563 688	20.5122 394 927	19.9995 641 027	19.5118 677 932	220
56	21.0519 877 014	20.5123 402 232	19.9996 413 862	19.5119 271 063	224
57	21.0520 967 841	20.5124 234 901	19.9997 049 675	19.5119 756 717	228
58	21.0521 873 866	20.5124 923 212	19.9997 572 761	19.5120 154 368	232
59	21.0522 626 396	20.5125 492 192	19.9998 003 104	19.5120 479 964	236
60	21.0523 251 436	20.5125 962 529	19.9998 357 149	19.5120 746 561	240

Table 5. PRESENT WORTH OF ONE DOLLAR PER PERIOD
PAYABLE AT END OF EACH PERIOD

QUARTERS	21% NOMINAL ANNUAL RATE	21½% NOMINAL ANNUAL RATE	22% NOMINAL ANNUAL RATE	22½% NOMINAL ANNUAL RATE	QUARTERS
1	0.9501 187 648	0.9489 916 963	0.9478 672 986	0.9467 455 621	1
2	1.8528 444 322	1.8495 769 360	1.8463 197 143	1.8430 727 215	2
3	2.7105 410 282	2.7042 248 503	2.6979 333 785	2.6916 664 819	3
YEARS					
1	3.5254 546 586	3.5152 786 243	3.5051 501 218	3.4950 688 586	4
2	6.3983 957 133	6.3663 586 189	6.3345 659 879	6.3030 154 864	8
3	8.7395 945 382	8.6787 378 084	8.6185 178 487	8.5589 264 808	12
4	10.6474 693 722	10.5542 016 769	10.4621 620 317	10.3713 307 353	16
5	12.2022 225 795	12.0753 037 253	11.9503 824 849	11.8274 206 210	20
6	13.4692 121 601	13.3089 992 822	13.1516 989 525	12.9972 466 958	24
7	14.5016 992 389	14.3095 927 195	14.1214 217 191	13.9370 877 446	28
8	15.3430 870 327	15.1211 278 031	14.9041 981 727	14.6921 582 769	32
9	16.0287 454 143	15.7793 263 952	15.5360 684 322	15.2987 837 372	36
10	16.5874 977 753	16.3131 608 475	16.0461 246 854	15.7861 480 738	40
11	17.0428 326 903	16.7461 292 946	16.4578 506 329	16.1776 977 401	44
12	17.4138 913 190	17.0972 899 876	16.7902 027 114	16.4922 696 726	48
13	17.7162 720 532	17.3821 001 930	17.0584 828 739	16.7449 975 108	52
14	17.9626 862 350	17.6130 965 849	17.2750 431 129	16.9480 396 567	56
15	18.1634 925 105	17.8004 470 803	17.4498 541 638	17.1111 641 992	60
16	18.3271 322 815	17.9523 984 067	17.5909 645 710	17.2422 188 444	64
17	18.4604 845 614	18.0756 391 034	17.7048 712 543	17.3475 084 579	68
18	18.5691 551 519	18.1755 939 355	17.7968 186 363	17.4320 983 835	72
19	18.6577 122 973	18.2566 626 794	17.8710 401 025	17.5000 581 309	76
20	18.7298 787 222	18.3224 137 900	17.9309 529 127	17.5546 571 534	80
21	18.7886 881 255	18.3757 414 765	17.9793 155 363	17.5985 221 379	84
22	18.8366 127 099	18.4189 930 978	18.0183 546 558	17.6337 633 706	88
23	18.8756 671 069	18.4540 724 885	18.0498 676 867	17.6620 762 608	92
24	18.9074 930 673	18.4825 237 607	18.0753 055 329	17.6848 229 040	96
25	18.9334 284 763	18.5055 992 725	18.0958 393 882	17.7030 976 113	100
26	18.9545 635 946	18.5243 147 533	18.1124 146 600	17.7177 795 545	104
27	18.9717 868 906	18.5394 940 147	18.1257 944 970	17.7295 750 626	108
28	18.9858 223 892	18.5518 052 119	18.1365 949 254	17.7390 516 019	112
29	18.9972 601 084	18.5617 902 549	18.1453 132 121	17.7466 650 760	116
30	19.0065 808 616	18.5698 886 617	18.1523 507 590	17.7527 817 592	120
31	19.0141 764 705	18.5764 569 051	18.1580 315 847	17.7576 959 171	124
32	19.0203 662 357	18.5817 841 037	18.1626 172 424	17.7616 439 632	128
33	19.0254 103 597	18.5861 047 482	18.1663 188 620	17.7648 158 328	132
34	19.0295 208 851	18.5896 090 232	18.1693 068 714	17.7673 641 203	136
35	19.0328 706 083	18.5924 511 787	18.1717 188 425	17.7694 114 206	140
36	19.0356 003 434	18.5947 563 197	18.1736 658 261	17.7710 562 266	144
37	19.0378 248 417	18.5966 259 129	18.1752 374 638	17.7723 776 676	148
38	19.0396 376 157	18.5981 422 536	18.1765 061 160	17.7734 393 164	152
39	19.0411 148 700	18.5993 720 874	18.1775 301 934	17.7742 922 476	156
40	19.0423 187 046	18.6003 695 488	18.1783 568 457	17.7749 774 945	160
41	19.0432 997 259	18.6011 785 436	18.1790 241 334	17.7755 280 236	164
42	19.0440 991 734	18.6018 346 819	18.1795 627 791	17.7759 703 199	168
43	19.0447 506 542	18.6023 668 453	18.1799 975 830	17.7763 256 618	172
44	19.0452 815 547	18.6027 984 585	18.1803 485 640	17.7766 111 444	176
45	19.0457 141 928	18.6031 485 200	18.1806 318 817	17.7768 405 017	180
46	19.0460 667 554	18.6034 324 387	18.1808 605 805	17.7770 247 680	184
47	19.0463 540 636	18.6036 627 120	18.1810 451 900	17.7771 728 079	188
48	19.0465 881 949	18.6038 494 760	18.1811 942 099	17.7772 917 435	192
49	19.0467 789 917	18.6040 009 517	18.1813 145 012	17.7773 872 967	196
50	19.0469 344 746	18.6041 238 067	18.1814 116 024	17.7774 640 644	200
51	19.0470 611 797	18.6042 234 486	18.1814 899 841	17.7775 257 397	204
52	19.0471 644 335	18.6043 042 636	18.1815 532 551	17.7775 752 898	208
53	19.0472 485 763	18.6043 698 089	18.1816 043 286	17.7776 150 984	212
54	19.0473 171 455	18.6044 229 696	18.1816 455 559	17.7776 470 808	216
55	19.0473 730 235	18.6044 660 859	18.1816 788 353	17.7776 727 755	220
56	19.0474 185 592	18.6045 010 555	18.1817 056 990	17.7776 934 187	224
57	19.0474 556 669	18.6045 294 177	18.1817 273 838	17.7777 100 035	228
58	19.0474 859 064	18.6045 524 210	18.1817 448 881	17.7777 233 278	232
59	19.0475 105 490	18.6045 710 779	18.1817 590 179	17.7777 340 325	236
60	19.0475 306 307	18.6045 862 096	18.1817 704 237	17.7777 426 327	240

Table 6.   PARTIAL PAYMENT TO AMORTIZE 1
PAYABLE AT END OF EACH PERIOD

QUARTERS	5% NOMINAL ANNUAL RATE	5½% NOMINAL ANNUAL RATE	6% NOMINAL ANNUAL RATE	6½% NOMINAL ANNUAL RATE	QUARTERS
1	1.0125 000 000	1.0137 500 000	1.0150 000 000	1.0162 500 000	1
2	0.5093 944 099	0.5103 359 714	0.5112 779 156	0.5122 202 418	2
3	0.3417 011 728	0.3425 417 264	0.3433 829 602	0.3442 248 730	3
YEARS					
1	0.2578 610 233	0.2586 524 264	0.2594 447 860	0.2602 381 002	4
2	0.1321 331 365	0.1328 575 771	0.1335 840 246	0.1343 124 747	8
3	0.0902 583 123	0.0909 676 365	0.0916 799 929	0.0923 953 744	12
4	0.0693 467 221	0.0700 538 765	0.0707 650 778	0.0714 803 149	16
5	0.0568 203 896	0.0575 305 367	0.0582 457 359	0.0589 659 708	20
6	0.0484 866 480	0.0492 023 513	0.0499 241 020	0.0506 518 766	24
7	0.0425 486 329	0.0432 713 391	0.0440 010 765	0.0447 378 128	28
8	0.0381 079 056	0.0388 385 002	0.0395 770 970	0.0403 236 526	32
9	0.0346 653 285	0.0354 043 826	0.0361 523 955	0.0369 093 105	36
10	0.0319 214 139	0.0326 693 079	0.0334 271 017	0.0341 947 219	40
11	0.0296 855 745	0.0304 425 657	0.0312 103 801	0.0319 889 251	44
12	0.0278 307 483	0.0285 970 100	0.0293 749 996	0.0301 646 019	48
13	0.0262 689 655	0.0270 446 116	0.0278 328 700	0.0286 335 995	52
14	0.0249 373 877	0.0257 224 879	0.0265 210 635	0.0273 329 436	56
15	0.0237 899 301	0.0245 845 211	0.0253 934 274	0.0262 164 454	60
16	0.0227 920 267	0.0235 961 188	0.0244 153 423	0.0252 494 566	64
17	0.0219 172 421	0.0227 308 248	0.0235 603 297	0.0244 054 755	68
18	0.0211 450 133	0.0219 680 587	0.0228 077 911	0.0236 638 845	72
19	0.0204 591 042	0.0212 915 703	0.0221 414 609	0.0230 084 016	76
20	0.0198 465 240	0.0206 883 566	0.0215 483 231	0.0224 259 969	80
21	0.0192 967 547	0.0201 478 890	0.0210 178 380	0.0219 061 187	84
22	0.0188 011 891	0.0196 615 514	0.0205 413 794	0.0214 401 303	88
23	0.0183 527 152	0.0192 222 237	0.0201 118 190	0.0210 208 943	92
24	0.0179 454 053	0.0188 239 712	0.0197 232 141	0.0206 424 601	96
25	0.0175 742 788	0.0184 618 069	0.0193 705 712	0.0202 998 271	100
26	0.0172 365 201	0.0181 315 097	0.0190 496 632	0.0199 887 618	104
27	0.0169 243 373	0.0178 294 825	0.0187 568 877	0.0197 056 566	108
28	0.0166 388 506	0.0175 526 412	0.0184 891 557	0.0194 474 177	112
29	0.0163 760 042	0.0172 983 257	0.0182 438 030	0.0192 113 770	116
30	0.0161 334 957	0.0170 642 299	0.0180 185 199	0.0189 952 210	120
31	0.0159 093 190	0.0168 483 444	0.0178 112 938	0.0187 969 344	124
32	0.0157 017 181	0.0166 489 106	0.0176 203 629	0.0186 147 529	128
33	0.0155 091 496	0.0164 643 820	0.0174 441 787	0.0184 471 261	132
34	0.0153 302 508	0.0162 933 938	0.0172 813 742	0.0182 926 855	136
35	0.0151 638 147	0.0161 347 369	0.0171 307 386	0.0181 502 190	140
36	0.0150 087 677	0.0159 873 361	0.0169 911 952	0.0180 186 496	144
37	0.0148 641 521	0.0158 502 320	0.0168 617 839	0.0178 970 166	148
38	0.0147 291 110	0.0157 225 663	0.0167 416 453	0.0177 844 608	152
39	0.0146 028 746	0.0156 035 685	0.0166 300 085	0.0176 802 117	156
40	0.0144 847 505	0.0154 925 450	0.0165 261 798	0.0175 835 762	160
41	0.0143 741 133	0.0153 888 700	0.0164 295 334	0.0174 939 295	164
42	0.0142 703 972	0.0152 919 772	0.0163 395 032	0.0174 107 069	168
43	0.0141 730 889	0.0152 013 531	0.0162 555 763	0.0173 333 969	172
44	0.0140 817 220	0.0151 165 311	0.0161 772 867	0.0172 615 355	176
45	0.0139 958 712	0.0150 370 861	0.0161 042 104	0.0171 947 003	180
46	0.0139 151 484	0.0149 626 302	0.0160 359 605	0.0171 325 069	184
47	0.0138 391 985	0.0148 928 088	0.0159 721 837	0.0170 746 044	188
48	0.0137 676 961	0.0148 272 971	0.0159 125 567	0.0170 206 718	192
49	0.0137 003 425	0.0147 657 970	0.0158 567 829	0.0169 704 154	196
50	0.0136 368 629	0.0147 080 346	0.0158 045 903	0.0169 235 660	200
51	0.0135 770 043	0.0146 537 579	0.0157 557 286	0.0168 798 764	204
52	0.0135 205 333	0.0146 027 344	0.0157 099 676	0.0168 391 192	208
53	0.0134 672 342	0.0145 547 498	0.0156 670 947	0.0168 010 854	212
54	0.0134 169 075	0.0145 096 058	0.0156 269 142	0.0167 655 823	216
55	0.0133 693 685	0.0144 671 191	0.0155 892 448	0.0167 324 321	220
56	0.0133 244 456	0.0144 271 196	0.0155 539 191	0.0167 014 707	224
57	0.0132 819 798	0.0143 894 498	0.0155 207 820	0.0166 725 466	228
58	0.0132 418 232	0.0143 539 634	0.0154 896 896	0.0166 455 194	232
59	0.0132 038 379	0.0143 205 244	0.0154 605 087	0.0166 202 593	236
60	0.0131 678 958	0.0142 890 064	0.0154 331 152	0.0165 966 461	240

Table 6. PARTIAL PAYMENT TO AMORTIZE 1
PAYABLE AT END OF EACH PERIOD

QUARTERS	7% NOMINAL ANNUAL RATE	7½% NOMINAL ANNUAL RATE	8% NOMINAL ANNUAL RATE	8½% NOMINAL ANNUAL RATE	QUARTERS
1	1.0175 000 000	1.0187 500 000	1.0200 000 000	1.0212 500 000	1
2	0.5131 629 492	0.5141 060 372	0.5150 495 050	0.5159 933 519	2
3	0.3450 674 635	0.3459 107 305	0.3467 546 726	0.3475 992 886	3
YEARS					
1	0.2610 323 673	0.2618 275 854	0.2626 237 527	0.2634 208 674	4
2	0.1350 429 233	0.1357 753 662	0.1365 097 991	0.1372 462 178	8
3	0.0931 137 738	0.0938 351 837	0.0945 595 966	0.0952 870 051	12
4	0.0721 995 764	0.0729 228 507	0.0736 501 259	0.0743 813 898	16
5	0.0596 912 246	0.0604 214 797	0.0611 567 181	0.0618 969 215	20
6	0.0513 856 510	0.0521 253 999	0.0528 710 973	0.0536 227 162	24
7	0.0454 815 145	0.0462 321 462	0.0469 896 716	0.0477 540 528	28
8	0.0410 781 216	0.0418 404 564	0.0426 106 073	0.0433 885 228	32
9	0.0376 750 673	0.0384 496 033	0.0392 328 526	0.0400 247 469	36
10	0.0349 720 911	0.0357 591 280	0.0365 557 478	0.0373 618 618	40
11	0.0327 781 026	0.0335 778 099	0.0343 879 391	0.0352 083 782	44
12	0.0309 656 950	0.0317 781 508	0.0326 018 355	0.0334 366 095	48
13	0.0294 466 511	0.0302 718 678	0.0311 090 856	0.0319 581 340	52
14	0.0281 579 481	0.0289 958 877	0.0298 465 645	0.0307 097 729	56
15	0.0270 533 598	0.0279 039 451	0.0287 679 658	0.0296 451 775	60
16	0.0260 982 079	0.0269 613 304	0.0278 385 471	0.0287 295 710	64
17	0.0252 659 661	0.0261 414 915	0.0270 317 294	0.0279 363 465	68
18	0.0245 359 964	0.0254 237 690	0.0263 268 307	0.0272 447 986	72
19	0.0238 919 996	0.0247 918 453	0.0257 075 147	0.0266 385 715	76
20	0.0233 209 310	0.0242 326 606	0.0251 607 055	0.0261 045 729	80
21	0.0228 122 263	0.0237 356 371	0.0246 758 118	0.0256 321 981	84
22	0.0223 572 379	0.0232 921 161	0.0242 441 633	0.0252 127 654	88
23	0.0219 488 187	0.0228 949 407	0.0238 585 936	0.0248 390 990	92
24	0.0215 810 099	0.0225 381 438	0.0235 131 275	0.0245 052 164	96
25	0.0212 488 036	0.0222 167 105	0.0232 027 435	0.0242 060 903	100
26	0.0209 479 605	0.0219 263 956	0.0229 231 911	0.0239 374 657	104
27	0.0206 748 675	0.0216 635 810	0.0226 708 483	0.0236 957 179	108
28	0.0204 264 263	0.0214 251 648	0.0224 426 100	0.0234 777 400	112
29	0.0201 999 650	0.0212 084 719	0.0222 357 993	0.0232 808 547	116
30	0.0199 931 675	0.0210 111 841	0.0220 480 969	0.0231 027 431	120
31	0.0198 040 158	0.0208 312 819	0.0218 774 832	0.0229 413 873	124
32	0.0196 307 440	0.0206 669 987	0.0217 221 924	0.0227 950 237	128
33	0.0194 718 004	0.0205 167 829	0.0215 806 741	0.0226 621 053	132
34	0.0193 258 160	0.0203 792 659	0.0214 515 619	0.0225 412 696	136
35	0.0191 915 786	0.0202 532 368	0.0213 336 475	0.0224 313 129	140
36	0.0190 680 114	0.0201 376 202	0.0212 258 591	0.0223 311 686	144
37	0.0189 541 546	0.0200 314 585	0.0211 272 426	0.0222 398 886	148
38	0.0188 491 500	0.0199 338 964	0.0210 369 471	0.0221 566 279	152
39	0.0187 522 288	0.0198 441 677	0.0209 542 112	0.0220 806 320	156
40	0.0186 626 998	0.0197 615 848	0.0208 783 523	0.0220 112 251	160
41	0.0185 799 404	0.0196 855 287	0.0208 087 568	0.0219 478 010	164
42	0.0185 033 884	0.0196 154 413	0.0207 448 725	0.0218 898 150	168
43	0.0184 325 351	0.0195 508 183	0.0206 862 008	0.0218 367 763	172
44	0.0183 669 195	0.0194 912 031	0.0206 322 913	0.0217 882 425	176
45	0.0183 061 227	0.0194 361 815	0.0205 827 365	0.0217 438 138	180
46	0.0182 497 636	0.0193 853 775	0.0205 371 665	0.0217 031 287	184
47	0.0181 974 949	0.0193 384 489	0.0204 952 458	0.0216 658 597	188
48	0.0181 489 996	0.0192 950 838	0.0204 566 694	0.0216 317 100	192
49	0.0181 039 881	0.0192 549 979	0.0204 211 596	0.0216 004 099	196
50	0.0180 621 950	0.0192 179 315	0.0203 884 634	0.0215 717 146	200
51	0.0180 233 774	0.0191 836 470	0.0203 583 501	0.0215 454 013	204
52	0.0179 873 123	0.0191 519 270	0.0203 306 090	0.0215 212 673	208
53	0.0179 537 950	0.0191 225 722	0.0203 050 476	0.0214 991 277	212
54	0.0179 226 371	0.0190 954 001	0.0202 814 899	0.0214 788 144	216
55	0.0178 936 655	0.0190 702 428	0.0202 597 747	0.0214 601 735	220
56	0.0178 667 205	0.0190 469 464	0.0202 397 545	0.0214 430 649	224
57	0.0178 416 551	0.0190 253 692	0.0202 212 941	0.0214 273 605	228
58	0.0178 183 333	0.0190 053 809	0.0202 042 694	0.0214 129 432	232
59	0.0177 966 301	0.0189 868 615	0.0201 885 667	0.0213 997 061	236
60	0.0177 764 294	0.0189 697 006	0.0201 740 815	0.0213 875 512	240

Table 6. PARTIAL PAYMENT TO AMORTIZE 1
PAYABLE AT END OF EACH PERIOD

QUARTERS	9% NOMINAL ANNUAL RATE	9½% NOMINAL ANNUAL RATE	10% NOMINAL ANNUAL RATE	10½% NOMINAL ANNUAL RATE	QUARTERS
1	1.0225 000 000	1.0237 500 000	1.0250 000 000	1.0262 500 000	1
2	0.5169 375 773	0.5178 821 804	0.5188 271 605	0.5197 725 170	2
3	0.3484 445 772	0.3492 905 372	0.3501 371 672	0.3509 844 661	3
YEARS					
1	0.2642 189 277	0.2650 179 317	0.2658 178 777	0.2666 187 639	4
2	0.1379 846 181	0.1387 249 955	0.1394 673 458	0.1402 116 647	8
3	0.0960 174 015	0.0967 507 781	0.0974 871 270	0.0982 264 402	12
4	0.0751 166 300	0.0758 558 339	0.0765 989 886	0.0773 460 810	16
5	0.0626 420 708	0.0633 921 465	0.0641 471 287	0.0649 069 971	20
6	0.0543 802 289	0.0551 436 068	0.0559 128 204	0.0566 878 394	24
7	0.0485 252 506	0.0493 032 245	0.0500 879 327	0.0508 793 325	28
8	0.0441 741 493	0.0449 674 315	0.0457 683 123	0.0465 767 327	32
9	0.0408 252 151	0.0416 341 837	0.0424 515 767	0.0432 773 159	36
10	0.0381 773 781	0.0390 022 013	0.0398 362 332	0.0406 793 722	40
11	0.0360 390 105	0.0368 797 153	0.0377 303 683	0.0385 908 410	44
12	0.0342 823 279	0.0351 388 408	0.0360 059 938	0.0368 836 281	48
13	0.0328 188 359	0.0336 910 084	0.0345 744 635	0.0354 690 081	52
14	0.0315 853 000	0.0324 729 262	0.0333 724 260	0.0342 835 683	56
15	0.0305 353 275	0.0314 381 558	0.0323 533 959	0.0332 807 755	60
16	0.0296 341 061	0.0305 518 483	0.0314 824 869	0.0324 257 049	64
17	0.0288 549 998	0.0297 873 380	0.0307 330 027	0.0316 916 300	68
18	0.0281 772 792	0.0291 238 710	0.0300 841 652	0.0310 577 482	72
19	0.0275 845 689	0.0285 450 519	0.0295 195 594	0.0305 076 257	76
20	0.0270 637 600	0.0280 377 561	0.0290 260 451	0.0300 281 079	80
21	0.0266 042 345	0.0275 913 524	0.0285 929 793	0.0296 085 415	84
22	0.0261 972 998	0.0271 971 383	0.0282 116 510	0.0292 402 087	88
23	0.0258 357 716	0.0268 479 223	0.0278 748 628	0.0289 159 082	92
24	0.0255 136 609	0.0265 377 102	0.0275 766 173	0.0286 296 418	96
25	0.0252 259 358	0.0262 614 672	0.0273 118 787	0.0283 763 752	100
26	0.0249 683 384	0.0260 149 342	0.0270 763 891	0.0281 518 546	104
27	0.0247 372 426	0.0257 944 857	0.0268 665 260	0.0279 524 631	108
28	0.0245 295 416	0.0255 970 170	0.0266 791 895	0.0277 751 084	112
29	0.0243 425 594	0.0254 198 558	0.0265 117 132	0.0276 171 333	116
30	0.0241 739 796	0.0252 606 903	0.0263 617 930	0.0274 762 442	120
31	0.0240 217 877	0.0251 175 121	0.0262 274 291	0.0273 504 528	124
32	0.0238 842 248	0.0249 885 693	0.0261 068 791	0.0272 380 295	128
33	0.0237 597 491	0.0248 723 277	0.0259 986 195	0.0271 374 641	132
34	0.0236 470 043	0.0247 674 398	0.0259 013 140	0.0270 474 343	136
35	0.0235 447 937	0.0246 727 179	0.0258 137 867	0.0269 667 790	140
36	0.0234 520 579	0.0245 871 124	0.0257 350 004	0.0268 944 758	144
37	0.0233 678 567	0.0245 096 937	0.0256 640 380	0.0268 296 227	148
38	0.0232 913 536	0.0244 396 356	0.0256 000 866	0.0267 714 223	152
39	0.0232 218 027	0.0243 762 033	0.0255 424 243	0.0267 191 680	156
40	0.0231 585 374	0.0243 187 413	0.0254 904 089	0.0266 722 330	160
41	0.0231 009 607	0.0242 666 638	0.0254 434 681	0.0266 300 601	164
42	0.0230 485 373	0.0242 194 470	0.0254 010 911	0.0265 921 535	168
43	0.0230 007 860	0.0241 766 210	0.0253 628 212	0.0265 580 713	172
44	0.0229 572 741	0.0241 377 645	0.0253 282 501	0.0265 274 196	176
45	0.0229 176 114	0.0241 024 986	0.0252 970 116	0.0264 998 462	180
46	0.0228 814 461	0.0240 704 826	0.0252 687 776	0.0264 750 367	184
47	0.0228 484 604	0.0240 414 097	0.0252 432 532	0.0264 527 095	188
48	0.0228 183 668	0.0240 150 031	0.0252 201 739	0.0264 326 129	192
49	0.0227 909 052	0.0239 910 135	0.0251 993 016	0.0264 145 210	196
50	0.0227 658 400	0.0239 692 153	0.0251 804 222	0.0263 982 316	200
51	0.0227 429 575	0.0239 494 050	0.0251 633 427	0.0263 835 632	204
52	0.0227 220 639	0.0239 313 985	0.0251 478 896	0.0263 703 529	208
53	0.0227 029 831	0.0239 150 293	0.0251 339 062	0.0263 584 546	212
54	0.0226 855 551	0.0239 001 464	0.0251 212 513	0.0263 477 369	216
55	0.0226 696 348	0.0238 866 134	0.0251 097 976	0.0263 380 819	220
56	0.0226 550 897	0.0238 743 065	0.0250 994 301	0.0263 293 836	224
57	0.0226 417 995	0.0238 631 135	0.0250 900 451	0.0263 215 465	228
58	0.0226 296 548	0.0238 529 327	0.0250 815 488	0.0263 144 851	232
59	0.0226 185 556	0.0238 436 719	0.0250 738 565	0.0263 081 222	236
60	0.0226 084 112	0.0238 352 472	0.0250 668 918	0.0263 023 883	240

Table 6. PARTIAL PAYMENT TO AMORTIZE 1
PAYABLE AT END OF EACH PERIOD

QUARTERS	11% NOMINAL ANNUAL RATE	11½% NOMINAL ANNUAL RATE	12% NOMINAL ANNUAL RATE	12½% NOMINAL ANNUAL RATE	QUARTERS
1	1.0275 000 000	1.0287 500 000	1.0300 000 000	1.0312 500 000	1
2	0.5207 182 491	0.5216 643 561	0.5226 108 374	0.5235 576 923	2
3	0.3518 324 326	0.3526 810 654	0.3535 303 633	0.3543 803 250	3
YEARS					
1	0.2674 205 884	0.2682 233 494	0.2690 270 452	0.2698 316 739	4
2	0.1409 579 478	0.1417 061 906	0.1424 563 888	0.1432 085 380	8
3	0.0989 687 098	0.0997 139 277	0.1004 620 855	0.1012 131 750	12
4	0.0780 970 977	0.0788 520 250	0.0796 108 493	0.0803 735 563	16
5	0.0656 717 306	0.0664 413 080	0.0672 157 076	0.0679 949 071	20
6	0.0574 686 330	0.0582 551 694	0.0590 474 159	0.0598 453 396	24
7	0.0516 773 795	0.0524 820 286	0.0532 932 334	0.0541 109 465	28
8	0.0473 926 322	0.0482 159 486	0.0490 466 183	0.0498 845 760	32
9	0.0441 113 206	0.0449 535 082	0.0458 037 942	0.0466 620 918	36
10	0.0415 315 144	0.0423 925 527	0.0432 623 779	0.0441 408 783	40
11	0.0394 610 021	0.0403 407 166	0.0412 298 469	0.0421 282 525	44
12	0.0377 715 811	0.0386 696 862	0.0395 777 738	0.0404 956 713	48
13	0.0363 744 446	0.0372 905 715	0.0382 171 837	0.0391 540 731	52
14	0.0352 061 174	0.0361 398 334	0.0370 844 726	0.0380 397 885	56
15	0.0342 200 173	0.0351 708 400	0.0361 329 587	0.0371 060 861	60
16	0.0333 811 810	0.0343 485 894	0.0353 276 021	0.0363 178 885	64
17	0.0326 628 513	0.0336 462 949	0.0346 415 871	0.0356 483 530	68
18	0.0320 442 024	0.0330 431 080	0.0340 540 446	0.0350 765 920	72
19	0.0315 087 826	0.0325 225 610	0.0335 484 929	0.0345 861 124	76
20	0.0310 434 245	0.0320 714 758	0.0331 117 457	0.0341 637 230	80
21	0.0306 374 664	0.0316 791 846	0.0327 331 325	0.0337 987 540	84
22	0.0302 821 858	0.0313 369 633	0.0324 039 306	0.0334 824 878	88
23	0.0299 703 805	0.0310 376 114	0.0321 169 449	0.0332 077 392	92
24	0.0296 960 540	0.0307 751 378	0.0318 661 932	0.0329 685 390	96
25	0.0294 541 767	0.0305 445 208	0.0316 466 659	0.0327 598 935	100
26	0.0292 405 017	0.0303 415 239	0.0314 541 408	0.0325 775 995	104
27	0.0290 514 211	0.0301 625 521	0.0312 850 394	0.0324 180 991	108
28	0.0288 838 535	0.0300 045 384	0.0311 363 131	0.0322 783 663	112
29	0.0287 351 542	0.0298 648 540	0.0310 053 531	0.0321 558 160	116
30	0.0286 030 433	0.0297 412 364	0.0308 899 176	0.0320 482 312	120
31	0.0284 855 476	0.0296 317 304	0.0307 880 734	0.0319 537 039	124
32	0.0283 809 528	0.0295 346 412	0.0306 981 479	0.0318 705 875	128
33	0.0282 877 656	0.0294 484 947	0.0306 186 898	0.0317 974 563	132
34	0.0282 046 805	0.0293 720 055	0.0305 484 366	0.0317 330 737	136
35	0.0281 305 536	0.0293 040 499	0.0304 862 875	0.0316 763 642	140
36	0.0280 643 803	0.0292 436 434	0.0304 312 805	0.0316 263 909	144
37	0.0280 052 763	0.0291 899 217	0.0303 825 739	0.0315 823 364	148
38	0.0279 524 617	0.0291 421 248	0.0303 394 292	0.0315 434 861	152
39	0.0279 052 475	0.0290 995 831	0.0303 011 985	0.0315 092 147	156
40	0.0278 630 240	0.0290 617 062	0.0302 673 117	0.0314 789 743	160
41	0.0278 252 512	0.0290 279 723	0.0302 372 672	0.0314 522 845	164
42	0.0277 914 497	0.0289 979 205	0.0302 106 231	0.0314 287 233	168
43	0.0277 611 941	0.0289 711 423	0.0301 869 895	0.0314 079 202	172
44	0.0277 341 057	0.0289 472 761	0.0301 660 223	0.0313 895 494	176
45	0.0277 098 479	0.0289 260 012	0.0301 474 177	0.0313 733 240	180
46	0.0276 881 207	0.0289 070 332	0.0301 309 070	0.0313 589 916	184
47	0.0276 686 568	0.0288 901 193	0.0301 162 526	0.0313 463 301	188
48	0.0276 512 178	0.0288 750 350	0.0301 032 443	0.0313 351 434	192
49	0.0276 355 907	0.0288 615 809	0.0300 916 960	0.0313 252 590	196
50	0.0276 215 857	0.0288 495 795	0.0300 814 430	0.0313 165 244	200
51	0.0276 090 330	0.0288 388 729	0.0300 723 391	0.0313 088 056	204
52	0.0275 977 808	0.0288 293 206	0.0300 642 551	0.0313 019 838	208
53	0.0275 876 935	0.0288 207 975	0.0300 570 762	0.0312 959 545	212
54	0.0275 786 498	0.0288 131 923	0.0300 507 007	0.0312 906 255	216
55	0.0275 705 412	0.0288 064 056	0.0300 450 384	0.0312 859 151	220
56	0.0275 632 704	0.0288 003 491	0.0300 400 094	0.0312 817 515	224
57	0.0275 567 506	0.0287 949 439	0.0300 355 425	0.0312 780 709	228
58	0.0275 509 039	0.0287 901 198	0.0300 315 749	0.0312 748 174	232
59	0.0275 456 606	0.0287 858 141	0.0300 280 506	0.0312 719 412	236
60	0.0275 409 581	0.0287 819 711	0.0300 249 200	0.0312 693 985	240

Table 6.   PARTIAL PAYMENT TO AMORTIZE 1
            PAYABLE AT END OF EACH PERIOD

QUARTERS	**13%** NOMINAL ANNUAL RATE	**13½%** NOMINAL ANNUAL RATE	**14%** NOMINAL ANNUAL RATE	**14½%** NOMINAL ANNUAL RATE	QUARTERS
1	1.0325 000 000	1.0337 500 000	1.0350 000 000	1.0362 500 000	1
2	0.5245 049 200	0.5254 525 200	0.5264 004 914	0.5273 488 336	2
3	0.3552 309 493	0.3560 822 349	0.3569 341 806	0.3577 867 851	3
YEARS					
1	0.2706 372 337	0.2714 437 228	0.2722 511 395	0.2730 594 819	4
2	0.1439 626 337	0.1447 186 713	0.1454 766 465	0.1462 365 548	8
3	0.1019 671 878	0.1027 241 154	0.1034 839 493	0.1042 466 807	12
4	0.0811 401 319	0.0819 105 616	0.0826 848 306	0.0834 629 241	16
5	0.0687 788 839	0.0695 676 149	0.0703 610 768	0.0711 592 457	20
6	0.0606 489 063	0.0614 580 816	0.0622 728 303	0.0630 931 163	24
7	0.0549 351 193	0.0557 657 023	0.0566 026 452	0.0574 458 966	28
8	0.0507 297 552	0.0515 820 878	0.0524 415 048	0.0533 079 356	32
9	0.0475 283 128	0.0484 023 670	0.0492 841 628	0.0501 736 070	36
10	0.0450 279 400	0.0459 234 473	0.0468 272 823	0.0477 393 256	40
11	0.0430 357 906	0.0439 523 160	0.0448 776 816	0.0458 117 383	44
12	0.0414 232 032	0.0423 601 920	0.0433 064 580	0.0442 618 199	48
13	0.0401 010 288	0.0410 578 378	0.0420 242 854	0.0430 001 552	52
14	0.0390 055 322	0.0399 814 528	0.0409 672 981	0.0419 628 152	56
15	0.0380 899 328	0.0390 842 082	0.0400 886 213	0.0411 028 811	60
16	0.0373 191 174	0.0383 309 570	0.0393 530 765	0.0403 851 462	64
17	0.0366 662 182	0.0376 948 093	0.0387 337 550	0.0397 826 869	68
18	0.0361 103 320	0.0371 548 492	0.0382 097 323	0.0392 745 750	72
19	0.0356 349 575	0.0366 945 715	0.0377 645 038	0.0388 443 115	76
20	0.0352 269 026	0.0363 007 873	0.0373 848 887	0.0384 787 288	80
21	0.0348 755 020	0.0359 628 404	0.0370 602 452	0.0381 672 057	84
22	0.0345 720 479	0.0356 720 378	0.0367 819 002	0.0379 010 945	88
23	0.0343 093 692	0.0354 212 273	0.0365 427 259	0.0376 732 973	92
24	0.0340 815 142	0.0352 044 800	0.0363 368 213	0.0374 779 470	96
25	0.0338 835 102	0.0350 168 489	0.0361 592 702	0.0373 101 634	100
26	0.0337 111 771	0.0348 541 817	0.0360 059 536	0.0371 658 655	104
27	0.0335 609 823	0.0347 129 759	0.0358 734 032	0.0370 416 247	108
28	0.0334 299 266	0.0345 902 632	0.0357 586 865	0.0369 345 480	112
29	0.0333 154 526	0.0344 835 183	0.0356 593 142	0.0368 421 863	116
30	0.0332 153 719	0.0343 905 851	0.0355 731 662	0.0367 624 592	120
31	0.0331 278 056	0.0343 096 172	0.0354 984 319	0.0366 935 952	124
32	0.0330 511 359	0.0342 390 289	0.0354 335 608	0.0366 340 818	128
33	0.0329 839 661	0.0341 774 553	0.0353 772 225	0.0365 826 252	132
34	0.0329 250 879	0.0341 237 191	0.0353 282 727	0.0365 381 166	136
35	0.0328 734 538	0.0340 768 027	0.0352 857 262	0.0364 996 043	140
36	0.0328 281 541	0.0340 358 255	0.0352 487 328	0.0364 662 704	144
37	0.0327 883 973	0.0340 000 241	0.0352 165 585	0.0364 374 110	148
38	0.0327 534 945	0.0339 687 358	0.0351 885 682	0.0364 124 198	152
39	0.0327 228 444	0.0339 413 851	0.0351 642 125	0.0363 907 740	156
40	0.0326 959 223	0.0339 174 711	0.0351 430 155	0.0363 720 227	160
41	0.0326 722 699	0.0338 965 581	0.0351 245 643	0.0363 557 763	164
42	0.0326 514 861	0.0338 782 665	0.0351 085 009	0.0363 416 984	168
43	0.0326 332 200	0.0338 622 655	0.0350 945 146	0.0363 294 983	172
44	0.0326 171 644	0.0338 482 663	0.0350 823 355	0.0363 189 245	176
45	0.0326 030 499	0.0338 360 172	0.0350 717 289	0.0363 097 593	180
46	0.0325 906 404	0.0338 252 984	0.0350 624 911	0.0363 018 146	184
47	0.0325 797 290	0.0338 159 178	0.0350 544 449	0.0362 949 274	188
48	0.0325 701 339	0.0338 077 079	0.0350 474 361	0.0362 889 567	192
49	0.0325 616 957	0.0338 005 221	0.0350 413 306	0.0362 837 802	196
50	0.0325 542 745	0.0337 942 322	0.0350 360 118	0.0362 792 921	200
51	0.0325 477 473	0.0337 887 262	0.0350 313 780	0.0362 754 007	204
52	0.0325 420 060	0.0337 839 064	0.0350 273 410	0.0362 720 266	208
53	0.0325 369 559	0.0337 796 869	0.0350 238 237	0.0362 691 009	212
54	0.0325 325 136	0.0337 759 929	0.0350 207 592	0.0362 665 640	216
55	0.0325 286 057	0.0337 727 589	0.0350 180 890	0.0362 643 642	220
56	0.0325 251 678	0.0337 699 275	0.0350 157 625	0.0362 624 566	224
57	0.0325 221 435	0.0337 674 485	0.0350 137 353	0.0362 608 024	228
58	0.0325 194 827	0.0337 652 781	0.0350 119 689	0.0362 593 680	232
59	0.0325 171 419	0.0337 633 777	0.0350 104 298	0.0362 581 241	236
60	0.0325 150 824	0.0337 617 138	0.0350 090 886	0.0362 570 453	240

Table 6. PARTIAL PAYMENT TO AMORTIZE 1
PAYABLE AT END OF EACH PERIOD

QUARTERS	15% NOMINAL ANNUAL RATE	15½% NOMINAL ANNUAL RATE	16% NOMINAL ANNUAL RATE	16½% NOMINAL ANNUAL RATE	QUARTERS
1	1.0375 000 000	1.0387 500 000	1.0400 000 000	1.0412 500 000	1
2	0.5282 975 460	0.5292 466 278	0.5301 960 784	0.5311 458 971	2
3	0.3586 400 472	0.3594 939 656	0.3603 485 392	0.3612 037 667	3
YEARS					
1	0.2738 687 482	0.2746 789 366	0.2754 900 454	0.2763 020 727	4
2	0.1469 983 915	0.1477 621 521	0.1485 278 320	0.1492 954 268	8
3	0.1050 123 010	0.1057 808 013	0.1065 521 727	0.1073 264 062	12
4	0.0842 448 270	0.0850 305 238	0.0858 199 992	0.0866 132 375	16
5	0.0719 620 973	0.0727 696 072	0.0735 817 503	0.0743 985 014	20
6	0.0639 189 033	0.0647 501 542	0.0655 868 313	0.0664 288 965	24
7	0.0582 954 043	0.0591 511 151	0.0600 129 752	0.0608 809 300	28
8	0.0541 813 087	0.0550 615 513	0.0559 485 897	0.0568 423 494	32
9	0.0510 706 050	0.0519 750 610	0.0528 868 780	0.0538 059 578	36
10	0.0486 594 563	0.0495 875 521	0.0505 234 893	0.0514 671 434	40
11	0.0467 543 358	0.0477 053 222	0.0486 645 444	0.0496 318 487	44
12	0.0452 260 947	0.0461 990 989	0.0471 806 476	0.0481 705 556	48
13	0.0439 852 301	0.0449 792 922	0.0459 821 236	0.0469 935 063	52
14	0.0429 677 509	0.0439 818 520	0.0450 048 662	0.0460 365 422	56
15	0.0421 266 973	0.0431 597 810	0.0442 018 451	0.0452 526 049	60
16	0.0414 268 386	0.0424 778 288	0.0435 377 955	0.0446 064 212	64
17	0.0408 412 407	0.0419 090 564	0.0429 857 795	0.0440 710 613	68
18	0.0403 489 770	0.0414 325 446	0.0425 248 919	0.0436 256 408	72
19	0.0399 335 598	0.0410 318 234	0.0421 386 869	0.0432 537 458	76
20	0.0395 818 410	0.0406 937 705	0.0418 140 755	0.0429 423 276	80
21	0.0392 832 256	0.0404 078 238	0.0415 405 351	0.0426 809 105	84
22	0.0390 290 977	0.0401 654 056	0.0413 095 329	0.0424 610 138	88
23	0.0388 123 956	0.0399 594 965	0.0411 140 984	0.0422 757 221	92
24	0.0386 272 913	0.0397 843 139	0.0409 485 002	0.0421 193 615	96
25	0.0384 689 464	0.0396 350 665	0.0408 080 000	0.0419 872 521	100
26	0.0383 333 233	0.0395 077 652	0.0406 886 620	0.0418 755 164	104
27	0.0382 170 371	0.0393 990 737	0.0405 872 033	0.0417 809 291	108
28	0.0381 172 394	0.0393 061 921	0.0405 008 762	0.0417 007 988	112
29	0.0380 315 248	0.0392 267 626	0.0404 273 741	0.0416 328 730	116
30	0.0379 578 561	0.0391 587 944	0.0403 647 553	0.0415 752 620	120
31	0.0378 945 038	0.0391 006 024	0.0403 113 821	0.0415 263 772	124
32	0.0378 399 958	0.0390 507 577	0.0402 658 702	0.0414 848 811	128
33	0.0377 930 774	0.0390 080 461	0.0402 270 478	0.0414 496 452	132
34	0.0377 526 768	0.0389 714 346	0.0401 939 216	0.0414 197 169	136
35	0.0377 178 776	0.0389 400 427	0.0401 656 484	0.0413 942 907	140
36	0.0376 878 948	0.0389 131 198	0.0401 415 119	0.0413 726 850	144
37	0.0376 620 557	0.0388 900 247	0.0401 209 028	0.0413 543 227	148
38	0.0376 397 832	0.0388 702 096	0.0401 033 029	0.0413 387 145	152
39	0.0376 205 816	0.0388 532 060	0.0400 882 707	0.0413 254 458	156
40	0.0376 040 249	0.0388 386 131	0.0400 754 300	0.0413 141 648	160
41	0.0375 897 470	0.0388 260 875	0.0400 644 602	0.0413 045 727	164
42	0.0375 774 329	0.0388 153 355	0.0400 550 880	0.0412 964 162	168
43	0.0375 668 113	0.0388 061 050	0.0400 470 800	0.0412 894 800	172
44	0.0375 576 490	0.0387 981 802	0.0400 402 373	0.0412 835 811	176
45	0.0375 497 448	0.0387 913 760	0.0400 343 900	0.0412 785 642	180
46	0.0375 429 256	0.0387 855 336	0.0400 293 930	0.0412 742 972	184
47	0.0375 370 422	0.0387 805 168	0.0400 251 226	0.0412 706 680	188
48	0.0375 319 658	0.0387 762 087	0.0400 214 730	0.0412 675 811	192
49	0.0375 275 856	0.0387 725 092	0.0400 183 537	0.0412 649 554	196
50	0.0375 238 060	0.0387 693 322	0.0400 156 878	0.0412 627 220	200
51	0.0375 205 445	0.0387 666 038	0.0400 134 092	0.0412 608 222	204
52	0.0375 177 301	0.0387 642 605	0.0400 114 617	0.0412 592 061	208
53	0.0375 153 014	0.0387 622 481	0.0400 097 971	0.0412 578 315	212
54	0.0375 132 055	0.0387 605 198	0.0400 083 743	0.0412 566 621	216
55	0.0375 113 967	0.0387 590 353	0.0400 071 582	0.0412 556 674	220
56	0.0375 098 358	0.0387 577 604	0.0400 061 187	0.0412 548 212	224
57	0.0375 084 887	0.0387 566 655	0.0400 052 302	0.0412 541 013	228
58	0.0375 073 261	0.0387 557 250	0.0400 044 707	0.0412 534 890	232
59	0.0375 063 228	0.0387 549 172	0.0400 038 215	0.0412 529 681	236
60	0.0375 054 569	0.0387 542 235	0.0400 032 666	0.0412 525 249	240

Table 6. PARTIAL PAYMENT TO AMORTIZE 1
PAYABLE AT END OF EACH PERIOD

QUARTERS	**17%** NOMINAL ANNUAL RATE	**17½%** NOMINAL ANNUAL RATE	**18%** NOMINAL ANNUAL RATE	**18½%** NOMINAL ANNUAL RATE	QUARTERS
1	1.0425 000 000	1.0437 500 000	1.0450 000 000	1.0462 500 000	1
2	0.5320 960 832	0.5330 466 361	0.5339 975 550	0.5349 488 393	2
3	0.3620 596 468	0.3629 161 784	0.3637 733 601	0.3646 311 908	3
YEARS					
1	0.2771 150 167	0.2779 288 757	0.2787 436 479	0.2795 593 3.5	4
2	0.1500 649 316	0.1508 363 420	0.1516 096 533	0.1523 848 608	8
3	0.1081 034 928	0.1088 834 234	0.1096 661 886	0.1104 517 793	12
4	0.0874 102 226	0.0882 109 387	0.0890 153 694	0.0898 234 984	16
5	0.0752 198 348	0.0760 457 245	0.0768 761 443	0.0777 110 675	20
6	0.0672 763 108	0.0681 290 352	0.0689 870 299	0.0698 502 547	24
7	0.0617 549 240	0.0626 349 013	0.0635 208 051	0.0644 125 781	28
8	0.0577 427 548	0.0586 497 294	0.0595 631 962	0.0604 830 773	32
9	0.0547 322 015	0.0556 655 090	0.0566 057 796	0.0575 529 120	36
10	0.0524 183 886	0.0533 770 987	0.0543 431 466	0.0553 164 048	40
11	0.0506 070 805	0.0515 900 845	0.0525 807 056	0.0535 787 880	44
12	0.0491 686 377	0.0501 747 082	0.0511 885 821	0.0522 100 748	48
13	0.0480 132 229	0.0490 410 567	0.0500 767 923	0.0511 202 156	52
14	0.0470 766 300	0.0481 248 818	0.0491 810 518	0.0502 448 970	56
15	0.0463 117 784	0.0473 790 870	0.0484 542 558	0.0495 370 141	60
16	0.0456 833 932	0.0467 684 034	0.0478 611 494	0.0489 613 345	64
17	0.0451 645 597	0.0462 659 393	0.0473 748 725	0.0484 910 393	68
18	0.0447 344 223	0.0458 508 762	0.0469 746 524	0.0481 054 105	72
19	0.0443 766 067	0.0455 068 877	0.0466 442 194	0.0477 882 442	76
20	0.0440 781 123	0.0452 210 294	0.0463 706 935	0.0475 267 336	80
21	0.0438 285 180	0.0449 829 425	0.0461 437 861	0.0473 106 681	84
22	0.0436 194 021	0.0447 842 714	0.0459 552 152	0.0471 318 465	88
23	0.0434 439 110	0.0446 182 312	0.0457 982 710	0.0469 836 406	92
24	0.0432 964 344	0.0444 792 809	0.0456 674 877	0.0468 606 653	96
25	0.0431 723 562	0.0443 628 735	0.0455 583 922	0.0467 585 267	100
26	0.0430 678 618	0.0442 652 621	0.0454 673 100	0.0466 736 260	104
27	0.0429 797 880	0.0441 833 491	0.0453 912 122	0.0466 030 068	108
28	0.0429 055 028	0.0441 145 653	0.0453 275 957	0.0465 442 342	112
29	0.0428 428 109	0.0440 567 751	0.0452 743 866	0.0464 952 982	116
30	0.0427 898 768	0.0440 081 993	0.0452 298 637	0.0464 545 369	120
31	0.0427 451 631	0.0439 673 531	0.0451 925 960	0.0464 205 737	124
32	0.0427 073 800	0.0439 329 954	0.0451 613 921	0.0463 922 674	128
33	0.0426 754 436	0.0439 040 879	0.0451 352 588	0.0463 686 704	132
34	0.0426 484 426	0.0438 797 603	0.0451 133 678	0.0463 489 957	136
35	0.0426 256 093	0.0438 592 831	0.0450 950 272	0.0463 325 887	140
36	0.0426 062 969	0.0438 420 442	0.0450 796 590	0.0463 189 050	144
37	0.0425 899 601	0.0438 275 294	0.0450 667 799	0.0463 074 912	148
38	0.0425 761 385	0.0438 153 070	0.0450 559 856	0.0462 979 701	152
39	0.0425 644 438	0.0438 050 138	0.0450 469 379	0.0462 900 271	156
40	0.0425 545 476	0.0437 963 447	0.0450 393 537	0.0462 834 003	160
41	0.0425 461 728	0.0437 890 428	0.0450 329 958	0.0462 778 712	164
42	0.0425 390 849	0.0437 828 923	0.0450 276 658	0.0462 732 579	168
43	0.0425 330 860	0.0437 777 113	0.0450 231 971	0.0462 694 085	172
44	0.0425 280 084	0.0437 733 468	0.0450 194 506	0.0462 661 965	176
45	0.0425 237 104	0.0437 696 700	0.0450 163 094	0.0462 635 162	180
46	0.0425 200 724	0.0437 665 725	0.0450 136 756	0.0462 612 795	184
47	0.0425 169 927	0.0437 639 629	0.0450 114 673	0.0462 594 131	188
48	0.0425 143 857	0.0437 617 644	0.0450 096 156	0.0462 578 555	192
49	0.0425 121 788	0.0437 599 121	0.0450 080 630	0.0462 565 557	196
50	0.0425 103 105	0.0437 583 515	0.0450 067 611	0.0462 554 710	200
51	0.0425 087 289	0.0437 570 366	0.0450 056 695	0.0462 545 658	204
52	0.0425 073 900	0.0437 559 288	0.0450 047 541	0.0462 538 104	208
53	0.0425 062 564	0.0437 549 954	0.0450 039 866	0.0462 531 800	212
54	0.0425 052 968	0.0437 542 090	0.0450 033 429	0.0462 526 538	216
55	0.0425 044 844	0.0437 535 464	0.0450 028 032	0.0462 522 148	220
56	0.0425 037 966	0.0437 529 881	0.0450 023 506	0.0462 518 483	224
57	0.0425 032 142	0.0437 525 177	0.0450 019 711	0.0462 515 425	228
58	0.0425 027 213	0.0437 521 214	0.0450 016 529	0.0462 512 873	232
59	0.0425 023 039	0.0437 517 874	0.0450 013 861	0.0462 510 744	236
60	0.0425 019 505	0.0437 515 060	0.0450 011 623	0.0462 508 966	240

126

Table 6. PARTIAL PAYMENT TO AMORTIZE 1
PAYABLE AT END OF EACH PERIOD

QUARTERS	19% NOMINAL ANNUAL RATE	19½% NOMINAL ANNUAL RATE	20% NOMINAL ANNUAL RATE	20½% NOMINAL ANNUAL RATE	QUARTERS
1	1.0475 000 000	1.0487 500 000	1.0500 000 000	1.0512 500 000	1
2	0.5359 004 884	0.5368 525 015	0.5378 048 780	0.5387 576 173	2
3	0.3654 896 693	0.3663 487 943	0.3672 085 646	0.3680 689 790	3
YEARS					
1	0.2803 759 246	0.2811 934 256	0.2820 118 326	0.2828 311 439	4
2	0.1531 619 598	0.1539 409 457	0.1547 218 136	0.1555 045 590	8
3	0.1112 401 861	0.1120 313 995	0.1128 254 100	0.1136 222 081	12
4	0.0906 353 090	0.0914 507 845	0.0922 699 080	0.0930 926 624	16
5	0.0785 504 673	0.0793 943 163	0.0802 425 872	0.0810 952 521	20
6	0.0707 186 689	0.0715 922 314	0.0724 709 008	0.0733 546 351	24
7	0.0653 101 623	0.0662 134 994	0.0671 225 304	0.0680 371 960	28
8	0.0614 092 942	0.0623 417 680	0.0632 804 189	0.0642 251 672	32
9	0.0585 068 041	0.0594 673 534	0.0604 344 571	0.0614 080 120	36
10	0.0562 967 454	0.0572 840 403	0.0582 781 612	0.0592 789 799	40
11	0.0545 841 765	0.0555 967 156	0.0566 162 506	0.0576 426 272	44
12	0.0532 390 022	0.0542 751 814	0.0553 184 306	0.0563 685 693	48
13	0.0521 711 140	0.0532 292 771	0.0542 944 966	0.0553 665 665	52
14	0.0513 161 771	0.0523 946 552	0.0534 800 978	0.0545 722 749	56
15	0.0506 270 953	0.0517 242 377	0.0528 281 845	0.0539 386 844	60
16	0.0500 686 682	0.0511 828 665	0.0523 036 520	0.0534 307 543	64
17	0.0496 141 277	0.0507 438 343	0.0518 798 643	0.0530 219 316	68
18	0.0492 428 204	0.0503 865 626	0.0515 363 280	0.0526 918 184	72
19	0.0489 386 173	0.0500 950 066	0.0512 570 925	0.0524 245 681	76
20	0.0486 887 937	0.0498 565 325	0.0510 296 235	0.0522 077 547	80
21	0.0484 832 248	0.0496 611 096	0.0508 439 924	0.0520 315 596	84
22	0.0483 137 976	0.0495 007 197	0.0506 922 828	0.0518 881 748	88
23	0.0481 739 715	0.0493 689 164	0.0505 681 481	0.0517 713 589	92
24	0.0480 584 480	0.0492 604 924	0.0504 664 770	0.0516 761 013	96
25	0.0479 629 162	0.0491 712 245	0.0503 831 381	0.0515 983 654	100
26	0.0478 838 573	0.0490 976 768	0.0503 147 810	0.0515 348 895	104
27	0.0478 183 901	0.0490 370 458	0.0502 586 824	0.0514 830 318	108
28	0.0477 641 499	0.0489 870 392	0.0502 126 236	0.0514 406 485	112
29	0.0477 191 924	0.0489 457 791	0.0501 747 942	0.0514 059 972	116
30	0.0476 819 156	0.0489 117 246	0.0501 437 145	0.0513 776 595	120
31	0.0476 509 983	0.0488 836 099	0.0501 181 741	0.0513 544 800	124
32	0.0476 253 494	0.0488 603 937	0.0500 971 814	0.0513 355 163	128
33	0.0476 040 667	0.0488 412 191	0.0500 799 238	0.0513 199 993	132
34	0.0475 864 041	0.0488 253 802	0.0500 657 349	0.0513 073 010	136
35	0.0475 717 438	0.0488 122 950	0.0500 540 677	0.0512 969 083	140
36	0.0475 595 741	0.0488 014 836	0.0500 444 731	0.0512 884 020	144
37	0.0475 494 708	0.0487 925 502	0.0500 365 823	0.0512 814 392	148
38	0.0475 410 824	0.0487 851 680	0.0500 300 925	0.0512 757 394	152
39	0.0475 341 174	0.0487 790 674	0.0500 247 545	0.0512 710 734	156
40	0.0475 283 340	0.0487 740 255	0.0500 203 638	0.0512 672 536	160
41	0.0475 235 314	0.0487 698 586	0.0500 167 521	0.0512 641 263	164
42	0.0475 195 432	0.0487 664 146	0.0500 137 812	0.0512 615 660	168
43	0.0475 162 311	0.0487 635 680	0.0500 113 373	0.0512 594 698	172
44	0.0475 134 805	0.0487 612 152	0.0500 093 268	0.0512 577 536	176
45	0.0475 111 962	0.0487 592 705	0.0500 076 701	0.0512 563 484	180
46	0.0475 092 990	0.0487 576 630	0.0500 063 124	0.0512 551 980	184
47	0.0475 077 234	0.0487 563 343	0.0500 051 931	0.0512 542 560	188
48	0.0475 064 147	0.0487 552 360	0.0500 042 723	0.0512 534 847	192
49	0.0475 053 279	0.0487 543 282	0.0500 035 148	0.0512 528 533	196
50	0.0475 044 251	0.0487 535 778	0.0500 028 916	0.0512 523 362	200
51	0.0475 036 754	0.0487 529 575	0.0500 023 789	0.0512 519 129	204
52	0.0475 030 527	0.0487 524 447	0.0500 019 571	0.0512 515 662	208
53	0.0475 025 355	0.0487 520 209	0.0500 016 101	0.0512 512 824	212
54	0.0475 021 059	0.0487 516 705	0.0500 013 246	0.0512 510 500	216
55	0.0475 017 491	0.0487 513 809	0.0500 010 898	0.0512 508 598	220
56	0.0475 014 528	0.0487 511 415	0.0500 008 966	0.0512 507 040	224
57	0.0475 012 067	0.0487 509 436	0.0500 007 376	0.0512 505 764	228
58	0.0475 010 022	0.0487 507 800	0.0500 006 068	0.0512 504 720	232
59	0.0475 008 324	0.0487 506 448	0.0500 004 992	0.0512 503 864	236
60	0.0475 006 914	0.0487 505 330	0.0500 004 107	0.0512 503 164	240

Table 6.   PARTIAL PAYMENT TO AMORTIZE 1
PAYABLE AT END OF EACH PERIOD

QUARTERS	21% NOMINAL ANNUAL RATE	21½% NOMINAL ANNUAL RATE	22% NOMINAL ANNUAL RATE	22½% NOMINAL ANNUAL RATE	QUARTERS
1	1.0525 000 000	1.0537 500 000	1.0550 000 000	1.0562 500 000	1
2	0.5397 107 186	0.5406 641 814	0.5416 180 049	0.5425 721 884	2
3	0.3689 300 363	0.3697 917 353	0.3706 540 747	0.3715 170 534	3
YEARS					
1	0.2836 513 576	0.2844 724 720	0.2852 944 853	0.2861 173 958	4
2	0.1562 891 770	0.1570 756 628	0.1578 640 118	0.1586 542 191	8
3	0.1144 217 842	0.1152 241 284	0.1160 292 312	0.1168 370 826	12
4	0.0939 190 304	0.0947 489 948	0.0955 825 380	0.0964 196 423	16
5	0.0819 522 832	0.0828 136 520	0.0836 793 300	0.0845 492 886	20
6	0.0742 433 921	0.0751 371 293	0.0760 358 037	0.0769 393 721	24
7	0.0689 574 362	0.0698 831 909	0.0708 143 996	0.0717 510 012	28
8	0.0651 759 322	0.0661 326 333	0.0670 951 895	0.0680 635 194	32
9	0.0623 879 146	0.0633 740 614	0.0643 663 488	0.0653 646 732	36
10	0.0602 863 683	0.0613 001 986	0.0623 203 434	0.0633 466 755	40
11	0.0586 756 919	0.0597 152 920	0.0607 612 757	0.0618 134 926	44
12	0.0574 254 187	0.0584 888 015	0.0595 585 424	0.0606 344 681	48
13	0.0564 452 836	0.0575 304 474	0.0586 218 603	0.0597 193 281	52
14	0.0556 709 607	0.0567 759 335	0.0578 869 756	0.0590 038 742	56
15	0.0550 554 618	0.0561 783 643	0.0573 070 692	0.0584 413 771	60
16	0.0545 639 102	0.0557 028 636	0.0568 473 659	0.0579 971 759	64
17	0.0541 697 590	0.0553 230 784	0.0564 816 307	0.0576 451 657	68
18	0.0538 527 462	0.0550 188 348	0.0561 898 180	0.0573 654 404	72
19	0.0535 971 390	0.0547 745 236	0.0559 564 521	0.0571 426 673	76
20	0.0533 906 287	0.0545 779 618	0.0557 694 845	0.0569 649 405	80
21	0.0532 235 137	0.0544 195 727	0.0556 194 699	0.0568 229 532	84
22	0.0530 881 011	0.0542 917 843	0.0554 989 631	0.0567 093 920	88
23	0.0529 782 600	0.0541 885 809	0.0554 020 682	0.0566 184 850	92
24	0.0528 890 846	0.0541 051 651	0.0553 240 994	0.0565 456 610	96
25	0.0528 166 360	0.0540 376 988	0.0552 613 216	0.0564 872 895	100
26	0.0527 577 433	0.0539 831 035	0.0552 107 501	0.0564 404 810	104
27	0.0527 098 478	0.0539 389 047	0.0551 699 955	0.0564 029 311	108
28	0.0526 708 814	0.0539 031 102	0.0551 371 415	0.0563 727 995	112
29	0.0526 391 698	0.0538 741 138	0.0551 106 497	0.0563 486 151	116
30	0.0526 133 557	0.0538 506 190	0.0550 892 837	0.0563 292 003	120
31	0.0525 923 382	0.0538 315 786	0.0550 720 487	0.0563 136 121	124
32	0.0525 752 232	0.0538 161 467	0.0550 581 442	0.0563 010 948	128
33	0.0525 612 842	0.0538 036 352	0.0550 469 254	0.0562 910 423	132
34	0.0525 499 305	0.0537 934 928	0.0550 378 728	0.0562 829 688	136
35	0.0525 406 819	0.0537 852 696	0.0550 305 675	0.0562 764 841	140
36	0.0525 331 475	0.0537 786 020	0.0550 246 719	0.0562 712 755	144
37	0.0525 270 092	0.0537 731 955	0.0550 199 139	0.0562 670 915	148
38	0.0525 220 080	0.0537 688 112	0.0550 160 737	0.0562 637 305	152
39	0.0525 179 333	0.0537 652 559	0.0550 129 742	0.0562 610 306	156
40	0.0525 146 131	0.0537 623 727	0.0550 104 725	0.0562 588 617	160
41	0.0525 119 078	0.0537 600 345	0.0550 084 533	0.0562 571 193	164
42	0.0525 097 034	0.0537 581 382	0.0550 068 234	0.0562 557 195	168
43	0.0525 079 072	0.0537 566 003	0.0550 055 079	0.0562 545 950	172
44	0.0525 064 435	0.0537 553 531	0.0550 044 460	0.0562 536 915	176
45	0.0525 052 508	0.0537 543 416	0.0550 035 888	0.0562 529 658	180
46	0.0525 042 789	0.0537 535 212	0.0550 028 969	0.0562 523 827	184
47	0.0525 034 868	0.0537 528 558	0.0550 023 384	0.0562 519 142	188
48	0.0525 028 414	0.0537 523 162	0.0550 018 876	0.0562 515 379	192
49	0.0525 023 155	0.0537 518 786	0.0550 015 237	0.0562 512 355	196
50	0.0525 018 869	0.0537 515 236	0.0550 012 299	0.0562 509 926	200
51	0.0525 015 377	0.0537 512 357	0.0550 009 928	0.0562 507 975	204
52	0.0525 012 531	0.0537 510 022	0.0550 008 014	0.0562 506 407	208
53	0.0525 010 211	0.0537 508 129	0.0550 006 469	0.0562 505 147	212
54	0.0525 008 321	0.0537 506 593	0.0550 005 222	0.0562 504 135	216
55	0.0525 006 781	0.0537 505 347	0.0550 004 215	0.0562 503 322	220
56	0.0525 005 526	0.0537 504 337	0.0550 003 403	0.0562 502 669	224
57	0.0525 004 503	0.0537 503 517	0.0550 002 747	0.0562 502 144	228
58	0.0525 003 670	0.0537 502 853	0.0550 002 217	0.0562 501 723	232
59	0.0525 002 991	0.0537 502 314	0.0550 001 790	0.0562 501 384	236
60	0.0525 002 437	0.0537 501 877	0.0550 001 445	0.0562 501 112	240

128

Table 1.   FUTURE WORTH OF ONE DOLLAR WITH INTEREST
PAYABLE AT BEGINNING OF EACH PERIOD

HALF YEARS	5% NOMINAL ANNUAL RATE	5½% NOMINAL ANNUAL RATE	6% NOMINAL ANNUAL RATE	6½% NOMINAL ANNUAL RATE	HALF YEARS
1	1.0250 000 000	1.0275 000 000	1.0300 000 000	1.0325 000 000	1
YEARS					
1	1.0506 250 000	1.0557 562 500	1.0609 000 000	1.0660 562 500	2
2	1.1038 128 906	1.1146 212 594	1.1255 088 100	1.1364 759 282	4
3	1.1596 934 182	1.1767 683 610	1.1940 522 965	1.2115 472 662	6
4	1.2184 028 975	1.2423 805 519	1.2667 700 814	1.2915 775 353	8
5	1.2800 845 442	1.3116 510 326	1.3439 163 793	1.3768 943 039	10
6	1.3448 888 242	1.3847 837 755	1.4257 608 868	1.4678 467 782	12
7	1.4129 738 210	1.4619 941 259	1.5125 897 249	1.5648 072 320	14
8	1.4845 056 207	1.5435 094 358	1.6047 064 391	1.6681 725 297	16
9	1.5596 587 177	1.6295 697 338	1.7024 330 612	1.7783 657 513	18
10	1.6386 164 403	1.7204 284 313	1.8061 112 347	1.8958 379 240	20
11	1.7215 713 976	1.8163 530 690	1.9161 034 089	2.0210 698 679	22
12	1.8087 259 496	1.9176 261 048	2.0327 941 065	2.1545 741 643	24
13	1.9002 927 008	2.0245 457 453	2.1565 912 675	2.2968 972 540	26
14	1.9964 950 188	2.1374 268 240	2.2879 276 757	2.4486 216 732	28
15	2.0975 675 791	2.2566 017 284	2.4272 624 712	2.6103 684 386	30
16	2.2037 569 378	2.3824 213 785	2.5750 827 557	2.7827 995 888	32
17	2.3153 221 327	2.5152 562 605	2.7319 052 955	2.9666 208 941	34
18	2.4325 353 157	2.6554 975 174	2.8982 783 280	3.1625 847 456	36
19	2.5556 824 161	2.8035 581 008	3.0747 834 782	3.3714 932 342	38
20	2.6850 638 384	2.9598 739 872	3.2620 377 920	3.5942 014 341	40
21	2.8209 951 952	3.1249 054 612	3.4606 958 935	3.8316 209 026	42
22	2.9638 080 770	3.2991 384 713	3.6714 522 734	4.0847 234 108	44
23	3.1138 508 609	3.4830 860 607	3.8950 437 169	4.3545 449 216	46
24	3.2714 895 607	3.6772 898 779	4.1322 518 793	4.6421 898 296	48
25	3.4371 087 197	3.8823 217 716	4.3839 060 187	4.9488 354 816	50
26	3.6111 123 486	4.0987 854 749	4.6508 858 952	5.2757 369 953	52
27	3.7939 249 113	4.3273 183 825	4.9341 248 463	5.6242 323 972	54
28	3.9859 923 599	4.5685 934 281	5.2346 130 494	5.9957 480 985	56
29	4.1877 832 231	4.8233 210 654	5.5534 009 841	6.3918 047 339	58
30	4.3997 897 488	5.0922 513 606	5.8916 031 040	6.8140 233 853	60
31	4.6225 291 048	5.3761 762 005	6.2504 017 331	7.2641 322 176	62
32	4.8565 446 408	5.6759 316 248	6.6310 511 986	7.7439 735 513	64
33	5.1024 072 132	5.9924 002 874	7.0348 822 166	8.2555 114 043	66
34	5.3607 165 784	6.3265 140 559	7.4633 065 436	8.8008 395 294	68
35	5.6321 028 552	6.6792 567 553	7.9178 219 121	9.3821 899 856	70
36	5.9172 280 622	7.0516 670 647	8.4000 172 666	10.0019 422 729	72
37	6.2167 877 329	7.4448 415 765	8.9115 783 181	10.6626 330 721	74
38	6.5315 126 118	7.8599 380 247	9.4542 934 377	11.3669 666 280	76
39	6.8621 704 378	8.2981 786 942	10.0300 599 080	12.1178 258 173	78
40	7.2095 678 162	8.7608 540 200	10.6408 905 564	12.9182 839 489	80
41	7.5745 521 869	9.2493 263 869	11.2889 207 913	13.7716 173 431	82
42	7.9580 138 914	9.7650 341 413	11.9764 160 675	14.6813 187 412	84
43	8.3608 883 446	10.3094 958 261	12.7057 798 060	15.6511 116 023	86
44	8.7841 583 171	10.8843 146 528	13.4795 617 962	16.6849 653 430	88
45	9.2288 563 319	11.4911 832 216	14.3004 671 096	17.7871 115 850	90
46	9.6960 671 837	12.1318 885 061	15.1713 655 566	18.9620 614 746	92
47	10.1869 305 849	12.8083 171 147	16.0953 017 190	20.2146 241 479	94
48	10.7026 439 457	13.5224 608 458	17.0755 055 936	21.5499 264 143	96
49	11.2444 652 955	14.2764 225 533	18.1154 038 843	22.9734 337 410	98
50	11.8137 163 511	15.0724 223 383	19.2186 319 809	24.4909 726 235	100
51	12.4117 857 413	15.9128 040 863	20.3890 466 685	26.1087 544 339	102
52	13.0401 323 945	16.8000 423 691	21.6307 396 106	27.8334 008 440	104
53	13.7002 890 970	17.7367 497 315	22.9480 516 529	29.6719 709 285	106
54	14.3938 662 325	18.7256 843 837	24.3455 879 985	31.6319 900 581	108
55	15.1225 557 105	19.7697 583 236	25.8282 343 077	33.7214 807 014	110
56	15.8881 350 934	20.8720 459 111	27.4011 737 770	35.9489 952 610	112
57	16.6924 719 325	22.0357 929 210	29.0699 052 600	38.3236 510 792	114
58	17.5375 283 240	23.2644 261 000	30.8402 624 903	40.8551 677 558	116
59	18.4253 656 954	24.5615 632 578	32.7184 344 760	43.5539 069 308	118
60	19.3581 498 338	25.9310 239 192	34.7109 871 356	46.4309 146 955	120

129

Table 1. FUTURE WORTH OF ONE DOLLAR WITH INTEREST
PAYABLE AT BEGINNING OF EACH PERIOD

HALF YEARS	7% NOMINAL ANNUAL RATE	7½% NOMINAL ANNUAL RATE	8% NOMINAL ANNUAL RATE	8½% NOMINAL ANNUAL RATE	HALF YEARS
1	1.0350 000 000	1.0375 000 000	1.0400 000 000	1.0425 000 000	1

YEARS	7%	7½%	8%	8½%	HALF YEARS
1	1.0712 250 000	1.0764 062 500	1.0816 000 000	1.0868 062 500	2
2	1.1475 230 006	1.1586 504 150	1.1698 585 600	1.1811 478 250	4
3	1.2292 553 263	1.2471 785 483	1.2653 190 185	1.2836 788 384	6
4	1.3168 090 370	1.3424 707 843	1.3685 690 504	1.3951 101 846	8
5	1.4105 987 606	1.4450 439 426	1.4802 442 849	1.5162 144 681	10
6	1.5110 686 573	1.5554 543 314	1.6010 322 186	1.6478 313 602	12
7	1.6186 945 225	1.6743 007 639	1.7316 764 476	1.7908 734 212	14
8	1.7339 860 398	1.8022 278 066	1.8729 812 457	1.9463 324 272	16
9	1.8574 891 955	1.9399 292 750	2.0258 165 154	2.1152 862 464	18
10	1.9897 888 635	2.0881 519 961	2.1911 231 430	2.2989 063 131	20
11	2.1315 115 753	2.2476 998 596	2.3699 187 915	2.4984 657 493	22
12	2.2833 284 872	2.4194 381 770	2.5633 041 649	2.7153 481 917	24
13	2.4459 585 587	2.6042 983 752	2.7724 697 847	2.9510 573 857	26
14	2.6201 719 571	2.8032 830 479	2.9987 033 192	3.2072 276 109	28
15	2.8067 937 047	3.0174 713 933	3.2433 975 100	3.4856 350 127	30
16	3.0067 075 863	3.2480 250 670	3.5080 587 468	3.7882 099 170	32
17	3.2208 603 342	3.4961 944 822	3.7943 163 406	4.1170 502 141	34
18	3.4502 661 115	3.7633 255 919	4.1039 325 540	4.4744 359 043	36
19	3.6960 113 152	4.0508 671 879	4.4388 134 504	4.8628 449 060	38
20	3.9592 597 212	4.3603 787 590	4.8010 206 279	5.2849 702 366	40
21	4.2412 579 948	4.6935 389 485	5.1927 839 112	5.7437 386 842	42
22	4.5433 415 955	5.0521 546 588	5.6165 150 783	6.2423 311 004	44
23	4.8669 411 006	5.4381 708 507	6.0748 227 087	6.7842 044 544	46
24	5.2135 889 805	5.8536 810 923	6.5705 282 418	7.3731 158 024	48
25	5.5849 268 557	6.3009 389 132	7.1066 833 463	8.0131 483 360	50
26	5.9827 132 710	6.7823 700 270	7.6865 887 073	8.7087 396 937	52
27	6.4088 320 237	7.3005 854 869	8.3138 143 459	9.4647 127 288	54
28	6.8653 010 846	7.8583 958 468	8.9922 215 965	10.2863 089 481	56
29	7.3542 821 543	8.4588 264 045	9.7259 868 787	11.1792 248 542	58
30	7.8780 909 008	9.1051 336 094	10.5196 274 081	12.1496 514 417	60
31	8.4392 079 252	9.8008 227 243	11.3780 290 045	13.2043 171 222	62
32	9.0402 905 096	10.5496 668 355	12.3064 761 713	14.3505 343 753	64
33	9.6841 852 012	11.3557 273 172	13.3106 846 269	15.5962 504 500	66
34	10.3739 412 921	12.2233 758 575	14.3968 364 925	16.9501 024 656	68
35	11.1128 252 607	13.1573 181 691	15.5716 183 502	18.4214 772 977	70
36	11.9043 362 399	14.1626 195 105	16.8422 624 076	20.0205 766 614	72
37	12.7522 225 885	15.2447 321 575	18.2165 910 201	21.7584 878 442	74
38	13.6604 996 424	16.4095 249 739	19.7030 648 473	23.6472 605 797	76
39	14.6334 687 294	17.6633 152 414	21.3108 349 389	25.6999 905 934	78
40	15.6757 375 397	19.0129 029 216	23.0497 990 699	27.9309 104 018	80
41	16.7922 419 460	20.4656 075 354	24.9306 626 740	30.3554 879 929	82
42	17.9882 693 786	22.0293 078 612	26.9650 047 482	32.9905 340 725	84
43	19.2694 838 651	23.7124 846 650	29.1653 491 356	35.8543 186 208	86
44	20.6419 528 533	25.5242 666 964	31.5452 416 251	38.9686 975 666	88
45	22.1121 759 453	27.4744 801 987	34.1193 333 417	42.3492 504 572	90
46	23.6871 156 770	29.5737 022 013	36.9034 709 424	46.0254 300 797	92
47	25.3742 304 911	31.8333 178 852	39.9147 941 713	50.0207 250 695	94
48	27.1815 100 579	34.2655 823 298	43.1718 413 757	54.3628 366 351	96
49	29.1175 131 117	36.8836 869 797	46.6946 636 319	59.0818 706 228	98
50	31.1914 079 831	39.7018 311 880	50.5049 481 843	64.2105 462 545	100
51	33.4130 160 167	42.7352 992 272	54.6261 519 561	69.7844 229 853	102
52	35.7928 580 825	46.0005 431 838	59.0836 459 557	75.8421 470 531	104
53	38.3422 043 994	49.5152 721 864	63.9048 714 657	82.4257 194 307	106
54	41.0731 279 078	53.2985 484 519	69.1195 089 773	89.5807 870 381	108
55	43.9985 614 430	57.3708 906 696	74.7596 609 099	97.3569 592 329	110
56	47.1323 589 818	61.7543 852 848	80.8600 492 401	105.8081 517 753	112
57	50.4893 612 503	66.4728 062 855	87.4582 292 581	114.9929 606 503	114
58	54.0854 660 053	71.5517 441 407	94.5948 207 636	124.9750 683 408	116
59	57.9377 033 215	77.0187 445 915	102.3137 581 400	135.8236 853 669	118
60	62.0643 162 406	82.9034 580 454	110.6625 608 043	147.6140 301 548	120

130

Table 1.   FUTURE WORTH OF ONE DOLLAR WITH INTEREST
PAYABLE AT BEGINNING OF EACH PERIOD

HALF YEARS	9% NOMINAL ANNUAL RATE	9½% NOMINAL ANNUAL RATE	10% NOMINAL ANNUAL RATE	10½% NOMINAL ANNUAL RATE	HALF YEARS
1	1.0450 000 000	1.0475 000 000	1.0500 000 000	1.0525 000 000	1
YEARS					
1	1.0920 250 000	1.0972 562 500	1.1025 000 000	1.1077 562 500	2
2	1.1925 186 006	1.2039 712 782	1.2155 062 500	1.2271 239 094	4
3	1.3022 601 248	1.3210 650 098	1.3400 956 406	1.3593 541 802	6
4	1.4221 006 128	1.4495 468 386	1.4774 554 438	1.5058 330 891	8
5	1.5529 694 217	1.5905 243 284	1.6288 946 268	1.6680 960 159	10
6	1.6958 814 328	1.7452 127 601	1.7958 563 260	1.8478 437 872	12
7	1.8519 449 216	1.9149 456 086	1.9799 315 994	2.0469 605 043	14
8	2.0223 701 530	2.1011 860 374	2.1828 745 884	2.2675 332 921	16
9	2.2084 787 664	2.3055 395 120	2.4066 192 337	2.5118 741 764	18
10	2.4117 140 248	2.5297 676 391	2.6532 977 051	2.7825 443 181	20
11	2.6336 520 080	2.7758 033 531	2.9252 607 199	3.0823 808 593	22
12	2.8760 138 340	3.0457 675 779	3.2250 999 437	3.4145 266 618	24
13	3.1406 790 071	3.3419 875 110	3.5556 726 879	3.7824 632 504	26
14	3.4296 999 927	3.6670 166 838	3.9201 291 385	4.1900 473 060	28
15	3.7453 181 345	4.0236 569 752	4.3219 423 752	4.6415 510 910	30
16	4.0899 810 359	4.4149 827 639	4.7649 414 686	5.1417 072 308	32
17	4.4663 615 407	4.8443 674 313	5.2533 479 691	5.6957 583 205	34
18	4.8773 784 615	5.3155 124 413	5.7918 161 360	6.3095 118 781	36
19	5.3262 192 144	5.8324 792 481	6.3854 772 899	6.9894 012 174	38
20	5.8163 645 376	6.3997 243 080	7.0399 887 121	7.7425 528 823	40
21	6.3516 154 842	7.0221 374 953	7.7615 875 551	8.5768 613 463	42
22	6.9361 228 991	7.7050 842 550	8.5571 502 795	9.5010 717 618	44
23	7.5744 196 089	8.4544 518 556	9.4342 581 832	10.5248 716 258	46
24	8.2714 555 734	9.2767 001 389	10.4012 696 469	11.6589 923 240	48
25	9.0326 362 725	10.1789 172 068	11.4673 997 858	12.9153 216 156	50
26	9.8638 646 255	11.1688 805 234	12.6428 082 638	14.3070 282 404	52
27	10.7715 867 677	12.2551 239 598	13.9386 961 108	15.8486 999 522	54
28	11.7628 420 400	13.4470 113 594	15.3674 124 622	17.5564 964 265	56
29	12.8453 175 787	14.7548 172 579	16.9425 722 396	19.4483 186 445	58
30	14.0274 079 289	16.1898 154 538	18.6791 858 941	21.5439 965 304	60
31	15.3182 801 435	17.7643 761 931	20.5938 024 483	23.8654 968 066	62
32	16.7279 448 738	19.4920 728 052	22.7046 671 992	26.4371 532 468	64
33	18.2673 340 008	21.3877 987 109	25.0318 955 871	29.2859 217 414	66
34	19.9483 854 122	23.4678 958 093	27.5976 648 848	32.4416 628 460	68
35	21.7841 355 797	25.7502 953 511	30.4264 255 355	35.9374 547 781	70
36	23.7888 206 565	28.2546 725 134	33.5451 341 529	39.8099 401 395	72
37	25.9979 868 774	31.0026 160 070	36.9835 104 036	44.0997 100 017	74
38	28.3686 111 198	34.0178 141 800	40.7743 202 199	48.8517 293 775	76
39	30.9792 325 581	37.3262 592 204	44.9536 880 425	54.1158 085 413	78
40	33.8300 964 342	40.9564 712 187	49.5614 410 668	59.9471 251 354	80
41	36.9433 110 586	44.9397 440 227	54.6414 887 762	66.4068 025 383	82
42	40.3430 192 587	49.3104 150 023	60.2422 413 758	73.5625 505 543	84
43	44.0555 856 060	54.1061 610 513	66.4170 711 168	81.4893 751 425	86
44	48.1098 008 714	59.3683 233 771	73.2248 209 062	90.2703 646 227	88
45	52.5371 052 966	65.1422 638 775	80.7303 650 491	99.9975 606 005	90
46	57.3718 324 115	71.4777 561 787	89.0052 274 667	110.7729 227 400	92
47	62.6514 752 892	78.4294 147 031	98.1282 632 820	122.7093 974 960	94
48	68.4169 773 027	86.0571 654 668	108.1864 102 684	135.9321 020 099	96
49	74.7130 496 390	94.4267 626 657	119.2755 173 209	150.5796 355 771	98
50	81.5885 180 320	103.6103 555 023	131.5012 578 463	166.8055 324 333	100
51	89.0967 014 039	113.6871 101 396	144.9801 367 755	184.7798 710 876	102
52	97.2958 253 506	124.7438 921 451	159.8406 007 950	204.6910 570 714	104
53	106.2494 736 785	136.8760 153 055	176.2242 623 765	226.7477 977 900	106
54	116.0270 814 938	150.1880 632 691	194.2872 492 701	251.1812 901 756	108
55	126.7044 736 682	164.7947 910 974	214.2016 923 203	278.2476 440 751	110
56	138.3644 528 575	180.8221 144 991	236.1573 657 832	308.2305 667 720	112
57	151.0974 416 318	198.4081 952 723	260.3634 957 759	341.4443 367 827	114
58	165.0021 836 979	217.7046 323 138	287.0507 540 930	378.2370 980 981	116
59	180.1865 096 527	238.8777 684 602	316.4734 563 875	418.9945 094 001	118
60	196.7681 732 035	262.1101 244 290	348.9119 856 672	464.1437 865 036	120

Table 1.   FUTURE WORTH OF ONE DOLLAR WITH INTEREST
PAYABLE AT BEGINNING OF EACH PERIOD

HALF YEARS	11% NOMINAL ANNUAL RATE	11½% NOMINAL ANNUAL RATE	12% NOMINAL ANNUAL RATE	12½% NOMINAL ANNUAL RATE	HALF YEARS
1	1.0550 000 000	1.0575 000 000	1.0600 000 000	1.0625 000 000	1
YEARS					
1	1.1130 250 000	1.1183 062 500	1.1236 000 000	1.1289 062 500	2
2	1.2388 246 506	1.2506 088 688	1.2624 769 600	1.2744 293 213	4
3	1.3788 428 068	1.3985 637 143	1.4185 191 123	1.4387 112 260	6
4	1.5346 865 150	1.5640 225 427	1.5938 480 745	1.6241 700 950	8
5	1.7081 444 584	1.7490 561 846	1.7908 476 965	1.8335 357 713	10
6	1.9012 074 858	1.9559 804 629	2.0121 964 718	2.0698 899 918	12
7	2.1160 914 618	2.1873 851 765	2.2609 039 558	2.3367 117 485	14
8	2.3552 626 993	2.4461 665 141	2.5403 516 847	2.6379 284 974	16
9	2.6214 662 659	2.7355 633 012	2.8543 391 529	2.9779 739 677	18
10	2.9177 574 906	3.0591 975 370	3.2071 354 722	3.3618 534 245	20
11	3.2475 370 310	3.4211 197 256	3.6035 374 166	3.7952 173 425	22
12	3.6145 899 039	3.8258 595 712	4.0489 346 413	4.2844 445 781	24
13	4.0231 289 278	4.2784 826 701	4.5493 829 629	4.8367 362 620	26
14	4.4778 430 749	4.7846 539 104	5.1116 866 971	5.4602 217 957	28
15	4.9839 512 884	5.3507 083 721	5.7434 911 729	6.1640 785 116	30
16	5.5472 623 828	5.9837 306 145	6.4533 866 819	6.9586 667 572	32
17	6.1742 417 136	6.6916 433 445	7.2510 252 758	7.8556 823 939	34
18	6.8720 853 833	7.4833 065 749	8.1472 519 999	8.8683 289 525	36
19	7.6488 028 337	8.3686 285 134	9.1542 523 470	10.0115 119 815	38
20	8.5133 087 740	9.3586 895 705	10.2857 179 371	11.3020 584 479	40
21	9.4755 254 982	10.4658 810 385	11.5570 326 742	12.7589 644 197	42
22	10.5464 967 676	11.7040 601 771	12.9854 819 127	14.4036 746 769	44
23	11.7385 145 647	13.0887 236 464	14.5904 874 771	16.2603 983 657	46
24	13.0652 601 734	14.6372 014 583	16.3938 717 293	18.3564 653 425	48
25	14.5419 612 045	16.3688 738 733	18.4201 542 750	20.7227 284 531	50
26	16.1855 663 697	18.3054 139 580	20.6988 853 434	23.3940 176 678	52
27	18.0149 400 086	20.4710 588 380	23.2550 203 718	26.4096 527 578	54
28	20.0510 786 031	22.8929 130 427	26.1293 408 898	29.8140 220 586	56
29	22.3173 517 622	25.6012 877 363	29.3589 274 238	33.6572 358 395	58
30	24.8397 704 451	28.6300 800 836	32.9876 908 533	37.9958 638 970	60
31	27.6472 854 997	32.0171 974 955	37.0649 694 428	42.8937 682 275	62
32	30.7721 199 432	35.8050 320 667	41.6461 996 659	48.4230 430 380	64
33	34.2501 387 998	40.0409 911 416	46.7936 699 446	54.6650 759 296	66
34	38.1212 607 377	44.7780 906 499	52.5773 675 498	61.7117 458 737	68
35	42.4299 162 326	50.0756 186 368	59.0759 301 790	69.6667 756 152	70
36	47.2255 575 147	55.9998 772 942	66.3777 151 491	78.6472 584 094	72
37	52.5632 261 529	62.6250 127 773	74.5820 007 415	88.7853 815 637	74
38	58.5041 847 888	70.0339 431 952	83.8003 360 332	100.2303 721 559	76
39	65.1166 202 745	78.3193 963 873	94.1580 575 669	113.1506 935 666	78
40	72.4764 262 811	87.5850 704 762	105.7959 934 821	127.7365 251 592	80
41	80.6680 743 615	97.9469 317 202	118.8723 782 765	144.2025 616 055	82
42	89.7855 834 662	109.5346 659 110	133.5650 042 315	162.7911 730 625	84
43	99.9335 990 375	122.4933 014 800	150.0736 387 545	183.7759 727 151	86
44	111.2285 940 687	136.9850 246 282	168.6227 405 045	207.4658 441 979	88
45	123.8002 059 133	153.1912 091 981	189.4645 112 309	234.2094 881 765	90
46	137.7927 241 866	171.3146 866 913	212.8823 248 190	264.4005 550 117	92
47	153.3667 468 378	191.5822 848 437	239.1945 801 667	298.4834 390 562	94
48	170.7010 233 992	214.2476 665 299	268.7590 302 753	336.9598 198 721	96
49	189.9945 065 688	239.5945 045 283	301.9776 464 173	380.3960 466 524	98
50	211.4686 356 738	267.9400 318 797	339.3020 835 145	429.4314 745 412	100
51	235.3698 782 208	299.6390 122 763	381.2398 210 369	484.7878 755 563	102
52	261.9725 587 067	335.0881 801 724	428.3610 629 170	547.2800 626 397	104
53	291.5820 071 545	374.7312 061 879	481.3064 902 936	617.8278 832 144	106
54	324.5380 635 132	419.0642 499 500	540.7959 724 939	697.4697 587 850	108
55	361.2189 781 418	468.6421 698 706	607.6383 546 941	787.3779 698 784	110
56	402.0057 531 462	524.0854 675 799	682.7424 553 343	888.8759 113 080	112
57	447.4869 743 956	586.0880 539 287	767.1294 228 136	1003.4575 717 501	114
58	498.0641 896 767	655.4259 337 588	861.9466 194 734	1132.8095 243 585	116
59	554.3578 947 149	732.9669 181 346	968.4832 216 403	1278.8357 521 078	118
60	617.0141 957 650	819.6814 855 932	1088.1877 478 350	1443.6856 732 780	120

Table 1.   FUTURE WORTH OF ONE DOLLAR WITH INTEREST
PAYABLE AT BEGINNING OF EACH PERIOD

HALF YEARS	13% NOMINAL ANNUAL RATE	13½% NOMINAL ANNUAL RATE	14% NOMINAL ANNUAL RATE	14½% NOMINAL ANNUAL RATE	HALF YEARS
1	1.0650 000 000	1.0675 000 000	1.0700 000 000	1.0725 000 000	1
YEARS					
1	1.1342 250 000	1.1395 562 500	1.1449 000 000	1.1502 562 500	2
2	1.2864 663 506	1.2985 884 469	1.3107 960 100	1.3230 894 407	4
3	1.4591 422 965	1.4798 145 809	1.5007 303 518	1.5218 918 984	6
4	1.6549 956 713	1.6863 319 545	1.7181 861 798	1.7505 656 680	8
5	1.8771 374 653	1.9216 701 183	1.9671 513 573	2.0135 991 006	10
6	2.1290 962 415	2.1898 511 937	2.2521 915 890	2.3161 549 505	12
7	2.4148 741 846	2.4954 586 144	2.5785 341 502	2.6641 717 078	14
8	2.7390 106 720	2.8437 154 606	2.9521 637 486	3.0644 801 580	16
9	3.1066 543 794	3.2405 737 264	3.3799 322 757	3.5249 374 547	18
10	3.5236 450 635	3.6928 160 435	3.8696 844 625	4.0545 813 381	20
11	3.9966 063 222	4.2081 716 025	4.4304 017 411	4.6638 075 253	22
12	4.5330 508 058	4.7954 482 506	5.0723 669 534	5.3645 737 548	24
13	5.1414 995 502	5.4646 830 256	5.8073 529 249	6.1706 344 900	26
14	5.8316 173 273	6.2273 136 961	6.6488 383 638	7.0978 108 886	28
15	6.6143 661 630	7.0963 742 431	7.6122 550 427	8.1643 013 360	30
16	7.5021 794 613	8.0867 176 210	8.7152 707 983	9.3910 386 386	32
17	8.5091 594 995	9.2152 696 070	9.9781 135 370	10.8021 008 880	34
18	9.6513 014 333	10.5013 180 761	11.4239 421 885	12.4251 840 596	36
19	10.9467 473 682	11.9668 426 469	13.0792 714 117	14.2921 456 219	38
20	12.4160 745 337	13.6368 903 310	14.9744 578 392	16.4396 298 275	40
21	14.0826 221 379	15.5400 036 073	17.1442 567 801	18.9097 869 568	42
22	15.9728 620 944	17.7087 082 357	19.6284 595 875	21.7511 006 332	44
23	18.1168 195 090	20.1800 691 494	22.4726 233 818	25.0193 394 478	46
24	20.5485 496 076	22.9963 239 246	25.7289 065 098	28.7786 515 707	48
25	23.3066 786 787	26.2056 046 553	29.4570 250 631	33.1028 238 357	50
26	26.4350 176 243	29.8627 605 700	33.7253 479 947	38.0767 300 097	52
27	29.9832 578 650	34.0302 954 498	38.6121 509 191	43.7979 966 732	54
28	34.0077 606 519	38.7794 358 692	44.2070 515 873	50.3789 194 108	56
29	38.5724 523 254	44.1913 485 162	50.6126 533 623	57.9486 669 206	58
30	43.7498 397 388	50.3585 273 976	57.9464 268 345	66.6558 163 046	60
31	49.6221 619 777	57.3863 746 367	66.3428 640 829	76.6712 693 032	62
32	56.2826 966 692	65.3950 018 821	75.9559 450 885	88.1916 067 114	64
33	63.8372 416 296	74.5212 831 135	86.9619 615 318	101.4429 468 173	66
34	72.4057 953 873	84.9211 939 300	99.5627 497 577	116.6853 835 950	68
35	82.1244 632 732	96.7724 773 004	113.9893 921 976	134.2180 917 638	70
36	93.1476 193 560	110.2776 813 356	130.5064 551 271	154.3851 989 144	72
37	105.6503 585 641	125.6676 210 015	149.4168 404 750	177.5825 399 588	74
38	119.8312 779 424	143.2653 229 349	171.0673 406 598	204.2654 264 785	76
39	135.9156 312 242	163.1905 207 837	195.8549 983 214	234.9575 834 658	78
40	154.1589 068 252	185.9647 778 999	224.2343 875 782	270.2614 288 665	80
41	174.8508 860 939	211.9173 249 357	256.7259 503 383	310.8698 976 876	82
42	198.3202 462 798	241.4917 121 137	293.9255 405 423	357.5800 427 520	84
43	224.9397 813 367	275.1933 898 624	336.5153 513 669	411.3086 790 508	86
44	255.1323 234 066	313.5983 473 764	385.2764 257 799	473.1103 787 574	88
45	289.3774 596 066	357.3629 567 424	441.1029 798 754	544.1981 701 055	90
46	328.2191 491 223	407.2351 908 743	505.0188 016 594	625.9673 464 025	92
47	372.2743 644 133	464.0674 069 807	578.1960 260 198	720.0228 524 954	94
48	422.2428 909 767	528.8309 140 462	661.9766 301 901	828.2107 862 256	96
49	478.9184 430 180	602.6325 732 945	757.8970 439 046	952.6546 331 734	98
50	543.2012 710 321	686.7337 153 514	867.7163 255 664	1095.7969 458 992	100
51	616.1124 616 364	782.5716 974 144	993.4484 211 410	1260.4472 857 514	102
52	698.8101 567 995	891.7844 688 617	1137.3990 973 643	1449.8373 682 311	104
53	792.6079 500 959	1016.2385 651 442	1302.2082 265 724	1667.6844 942 914	106
54	898.9957 521 976	1158.0610 084 011	1490.8981 986 027	1918.2645 125 868	108
55	1019.6634 570 363	1319.6756 600 048	1706.9293 475 803	2206.4957 447 562	110
56	1156.5277 845 570	1503.8446 463 314	1954.2634 100 447	2538.0355 210 042	112
57	1311.7627 264 392	1713.7155 657 559	2237.4361 781 601	2919.3912 207 571	114
58	1487.8340 783 954	1952.8752 836 795	2561.6406 803 755	3358.0479 978 709	116
59	1687.5386 075 681	2225.4112 349 875	2932.8224 149 620	3862.6156 973 510	118
60	1914.0484 771 689	2535.9812 816 502	3357.7883 828 899	4442.9978 472 261	120

133

Table 1. FUTURE WORTH OF ONE DOLLAR WITH INTEREST
PAYABLE AT BEGINNING OF EACH PERIOD

HALF YEARS	15% NOMINAL ANNUAL RATE	15½% NOMINAL ANNUAL RATE	16% NOMINAL ANNUAL RATE	16½% NOMINAL ANNUAL RATE	HALF YEARS
1	1.0750 000 000	1.0775 000 000	1.0800 000 000	1.0825 000 000	1
YEARS					
1	1.1556 250 000	1.1610 062 500	1.1664 000 000	1.1718 062 500	2
2	1.3354 691 406	1.3479 355 125	1.3604 889 600	1.3731 298 875	4
3	1.5433 015 256	1.5649 615 547	1.5868 743 229	1.6090 421 843	6
4	1.7834 778 256	1.8169 301 460	1.8509 302 103	1.8854 856 881	8
5	2.0610 315 622	2.1094 672 553	2.1589 249 973	2.2094 239 135	10
6	2.3817 795 990	2.4491 046 675	2.5181 701 168	2.5890 167 508	12
7	2.7524 440 491	2.8434 258 259	2.9371 936 243	3.0338 260 099	14
8	3.1807 931 543	3.3012 351 553	3.4259 426 433	3.5550 562 799	16
9	3.6758 040 889	3.8327 546 480	3.9960 194 992	4.1658 371 678	18
10	4.2478 511 002	4.4498 521 011	4.6609 571 438	4.8815 540 297	20
11	4.9089 229 277	5.1663 061 009	5.4365 404 126	5.7202 355 218	22
12	5.6728 740 583	5.9981 136 726	6.3411 807 372	6.7030 077 359	24
13	6.5557 150 837	6.9638 474 621	7.3963 532 119	7.8546 263 587	26
14	7.5759 482 436	8.0850 704 275	8.6271 063 864	9.2041 002 586	28
15	8.7549 551 890	9.3868 172 981	10.0626 568 891	10.7854 222 086	30
16	10.1174 450 903	10.8981 535 507	11.7370 829 954	12.6384 251 529	32
17	11.6919 724 824	12.6528 243 858	13.6901 336 059	14.8097 855 844	34
18	13.5115 357 000	14.6900 081 921	15.9681 718 379	17.3541 993 089	36
19	15.6142 684 433	17.0551 913 235	18.6252 756 317	20.3357 592 139	38
20	18.0442 389 698	19.8011 837 216	21.7245 214 968	23.8295 697 454	40
21	20.8523 736 595	22.9892 980 581	25.3394 818 739	27.9236 387 624	42
22	24.0975 243 102	26.6907 187 286	29.5559 716 577	32.7210 944 246	44
23	27.8477 015 310	30.9880 912 609	34.4740 853 415	38.3427 829 535	46
24	32.1815 000 818	35.9773 676 295	40.2105 731 423	44.9303 127 073	48
25	37.1897 460 320	41.7699 486 764	46.9016 125 132	52.6496 212 449	50
26	42.9774 002 582	48.4951 714 754	54.7060 408 354	61.6951 552 349	52
27	49.6657 581 734	56.3031 971 778	63.8091 260 304	72.2947 684 990	54
28	57.3949 917 892	65.3683 638 184	74.4269 646 019	84.7154 615 694	56
29	66.3270 873 864	75.8930 789 455	86.8116 115 117	99.2701 073 387	58
30	76.6492 403 609	88.1123 389 874	101.2570 636 672	116.3253 322 177	60
31	88.5777 783 920	102.2989 762 665	118.1062 390 614	136.3107 513 260	62
32	102.3626 951 543	118.7697 508 140	137.7591 172 413	159.7297 903 460	64
33	118.2928 895 877	137.8924 230 060	160.6822 343 502	187.1723 666 386	66
34	136.7022 205 297	160.0939 649 376	187.4197 581 461	219.3297 490 544	68
35	157.9765 035 997	185.8700 938 799	218.6064 059 016	257.0119 707 529	70
36	182.5615 969 724	215.7963 406 826	254.9825 118 436	301.1682 336 531	72
37	210.9727 455 012	250.5409 002 596	297.4116 018 144	352.9108 184 961	74
38	243.8053 790 198	290.8795 510 821	346.9008 923 563	413.5431 028 064	76
39	281.7475 911 298	337.7129 768 035	404.6252 008 444	484.5923 925 129	78
40	325.5945 599 993	392.0868 767 749	471.9548 342 649	567.8483 942 491	80
41	376.2652 133 992	455.2153 144 787	550.4881 186 866	665.4082 974 335	82
42	434.8214 872 345	528.5078 252 055	642.0893 416 361	779.7296 017 345	84
43	502.4905 811 854	613.6008 882 375	748.9330 080 843	913.6920 206 225	86
44	580.6906 778 823	712.3944 662 492	873.5554 606 295	1070.6700 203 406	88
45	671.0606 646 278	827.0944 277 808	1018.9150 892 783	1254.6178 215 227	90
46	775.4944 805 605	960.2617 999 937	1188.4625 601 342	1470.1690 046 217	92
47	896.1808 090 977	1114.8699 514 289	1386.2227 301 405	1722.7532 281 719	94
48	1035.6489 475 135	1294.3709 815 461	1616.8901 924 359	2018.7329 999 796	96
49	1196.8218 149 703	1502.7727 993 937	1885.9407 204 572	2365.5639 464 573	98
50	1383.0772 099 251	1744.7286 124 261	2199.7612 563 413	2771.9826 172 333	100
51	1598.3186 007 197	2025.6408 235 805	2565.8015 293 965	3248.2265 557 654	102
52	1847.0569 329 567	2351.7816 564 321	2992.7509 038 880	3806.2921 794 618	104
53	2134.5051 681 481	2730.4332 017 530	3490.7446 542 950	4460.2369 652 195	106
54	2466.6875 349 411	3170.0500 124 428	4071.6045 647 697	5226.5335 523 253	108
55	2850.5657 825 663	3680.4478 772 587	4749.1195 643 474	6124.4846 824 494	110
56	3294.1850 824 782	4273.0229 882 965	5539.3730 598 548	7176.7094 289 235	112
57	3806.8426 359 389	4961.0063 958 060	6461.1247 370 146	8409.7129 632 465	114
58	4399.2825 211 568	5759.7594 318 207	7536.2558 932 539	9854.5542 110 383	116
59	5083.9208 635 119	6687.1166 988 403	8790.2888 738 913	11547.6282 154 585	118
60	5875.1060 478 959	7763.7842 818 329	10252.9929 425 068	13531.5829 155 506	120

Table 1.   FUTURE WORTH OF ONE DOLLAR WITH INTEREST
PAYABLE AT BEGINNING OF EACH PERIOD

HALF YEARS	**17%** NOMINAL ANNUAL RATE	**17½%** NOMINAL ANNUAL RATE	**18%** NOMINAL ANNUAL RATE	**18½%** NOMINAL ANNUAL RATE	HALF YEARS
1	1.0850 000 000	1.0875 000 000	1.0900 000 000	1.0925 000 000	1
YEARS					
1	1.1772 250 000	1.1826 562 500	1.1881 000 000	1.1935 562 500	2
2	1.3858 587 006	1.3986 758 057	1.4115 816 100	1.4245 765 219	4
3	1.6314 675 088	1.6541 526 833	1.6771 001 108	1.7003 122 113	6
4	1.9206 043 381	1.9562 940 094	1.9925 626 417	2.0294 182 668	8
5	2.2609 834 419	2.3136 233 370	2.3673 636 746	2.4222 248 562	10
6	2.6616 862 324	2.7362 210 996	2.8126 647 818	2.8910 616 160	12
7	3.1334 035 750	3.2360 089 849	3.3417 270 272	3.4506 446 609	14
8	3.6887 210 235	3.8270 862 510	3.9703 058 811	4.1185 385 016	16
9	4.3424 546 069	4.5261 274 741	4.7171 204 173	4.9157 073 694	18
10	5.1120 461 246	5.3528 529 455	5.6044 107 678	5.8671 732 539	20
11	6.0180 284 991	6.3305 849 913	6.6586 004 332	7.0028 013 071	22
12	7.0845 735 998	7.4869 059 061	7.9110 831 747	8.3582 372 676	24
13	8.3401 371 560	8.8544 360 631	9.3991 579 198	9.9760 263 297	26
14	9.8182 179 635	10.4717 541 502	11.1671 395 246	11.9069 485 760	28
15	11.5582 516 421	12.3844 854 942	13.2676 784 691	14.2116 128 913	30
16	13.6066 627 894	14.6465 891 727	15.7633 287 892	16.9623 593 890	32
17	16.0181 036 022	17.3218 802 263	18.7284 109 344	20.2455 300 634	34
18	18.8569 120 131	20.4488 299 114	22.2512 250 312	24.1641 789 418	36
19	22.1988 282 446	24.2276 947 812	26.4366 804 595	28.8413 068 021	38
20	26.1330 155 803	28.6530 346 560	31.4094 200 540	34.4237 219 918	40
21	30.7644 392 665	33.8866 905 174	37.3175 319 661	41.0866 485 316	42
22	36.2166 670 155	40.0763 063 323	44.3369 597 290	49.0392 261 464	44
23	42.6351 658 273	47.3964 941 608	52.6767 418 540	58.5310 748 622	46
24	50.1911 830 911	56.0537 600 473	62.5852 369 967	69.8601 302 210	48
25	59.0863 155 144	66.2923 296 559	74.3575 200 758	83.3819 950 511	50
26	69.5578 877 815	78.4010 379 947	88.3441 696 021	99.5211 013 307	52
27	81.8852 844 435	92.7214 775 909	104.9617 079 042	118.7840 325 002	54
28	96.3974 039 790	109.6576 349 821	124.7050 051 610	141.7754 243 908	56
29	113.4814 338 992	129.6872 873 718	148.1620 166 318	169.2169 438 780	58
30	133.5931 810 220	153.3754 809 558	176.0312 919 602	201.9699 409 715	60
31	157.2692 325 286	181.3904 711 491	209.1427 779 780	241.0624 853 586	62
32	185.1412 722 635	214.5225 743 949	248.4825 345 156	287.7216 360 404	64
33	217.9529 342 404	253.7064 633 743	295.2220 992 580	343.4119 569 562	66
34	256.5796 430 111	300.0475 345 750	350.7533 761 285	409.8814 875 498	68
35	302.0519 702 438	354.8530 920 622	416.7300 861 782	489.2166 112 243	70
36	355.5831 306 703	419.6692 271 591	495.1170 153 883	583.9075 439 306	72
37	418.6013 510 033	496.3244 344 324	588.2485 259 829	696.9264 984 806	74
38	492.7879 754 348	586.9811 944 092	698.8980 737 203	831.8209 780 521	76
39	580.1223 243 813	694.1969 782 005	830.3608 013 870	992.8251 272 352	78
40	682.9345 033 198	820.9963 950 000	986.5516 681 279	1184.9926 357 686	80
41	803.9675 706 706	970.9565 177 742	1172.1220 369 028	1414.3553 666 256	82
42	946.4507 233 827	1148.3077 942 239	1392.5981 920 442	1688.1126 875 570	84
43	1114.1854 528 342	1358.0533 897 626	1654.5459 119 677	2014.8574 489 380	86
44	1311.6469 697 127	1606.1103 292 364	1965.7659 980 089	2404.8457 010 390	88
45	1544.1036 039 201	1899.4764 190 610	2335.5265 822 343	2870.3186 167 607	90
46	1817.7573 651 248	2246.4276 587 301	2774.8391 323 526	3425.8867 245 261	92
47	2139.9094 141 591	2656.7517 107 701	3296.7863 731 482	4088.9885 118 501	94
48	2519.1548 600 834	3142.0240 154 404	3916.9118 899 373	4880.4377 944 969	96
49	2965.6120 801 617	3715.9343 395 107	4653.6830 164 345	5825.0770 323 580	98
50	3491.1926 810 683	4394.6729 712 119	5529.0407 918 259	6952.5570 987 023	100
51	4109.9193 039 707	5197.3874 561 099	6569.0533 647 683	8298.2679 786 380	102
52	4838.2997 526 169	6146.7227 586 399	7804.6923 026 812	9904.4496 100 783	104
53	5695.7674 262 744	7269.4600 875 228	9272.7549 248 156	11821.5177 349 190	106
54	6705.1998 083 959	8597.2724 066 344	11016.9601 261 734	14109.6463 769 984	108
55	7893.5288 444 388	10167.6119 446 587	13089.2503 259 066	16840.6566 185 563	110
56	9292.4594 938 945	12024.7969 098 627	15551.3383 122 097	20100.2709 611 818	112
57	10939.3156 277 000	14221.2012 204 298	18476.5450 487 363	23990.8040 324 120	114
58	12878.0358 398 191	16818.7925 058 490	21951.9831 724 036	28634.3740 954 106	116
59	15160.3457 415 310	19890.8500 744 954	26081.1512 071 327	34176.7361 664 154	118
60	17847.1380 155 739	23524.0381 584 150	30987.0157 491 944	40791.8570 560 261	120

Table 1.   FUTURE WORTH OF ONE DOLLAR WITH INTEREST
PAYABLE AT BEGINNING OF EACH PERIOD

HALF YEARS	19% NOMINAL ANNUAL RATE	19½% NOMINAL ANNUAL RATE	20% NOMINAL ANNUAL RATE	20½% NOMINAL ANNUAL RATE	HALF YEARS
1	1.0950 000 000	1.0975 000 000	1.1000 000 000	1.1025 000 000	1
YEARS					
1	1.1990 250 000	1.2045 062 500	1.2100 000 000	1.2155 062 500	2
2	1.4376 609 506	1.4508 353 063	1.4641 000 000	1.4774 554 438	4
3	1.7237 514 213	1.7475 401 941	1.7715 610 000	1.7958 563 260	6
4	2.0668 690 090	2.1049 230 860	2.1435 888 100	2.1828 745 884	8
5	2.4782 276 135	2.5353 930 128	2.5937 424 601	2.6532 977 051	10
6	2.9714 568 642	3.0538 967 302	3.1384 283 767	3.2250 999 437	12
7	3.5628 510 666	3.6784 376 983	3.7974 983 358	3.9201 291 385	14
8	4.2719 475 002	4.4307 011 979	4.5949 729 864	4.7649 414 686	16
9	5.1221 718 514	5.3368 072 847	5.5599 173 135	5.7918 161 360	18
10	6.1416 121 041	6.4282 177 295	6.7274 999 493	7.0399 887 121	20
11	7.3639 464 531	7.7428 284 315	8.1402 749 387	8.5571 502 795	22
12	8.8295 558 960	9.3262 852 385	9.8497 326 758	10.4012 696 469	24
13	10.5868 582 582	11.2335 688 590	11.9181 765 377	12.6428 082 638	26
14	12.6939 077 230	13.5309 039 005	14.4209 936 106	15.3674 124 622	28
15	15.2203 127 076	16.2980 583 163	17.4494 022 689	18.6791 858 941	30
16	18.2495 354 442	19.6311 131 048	21.1137 767 454	22.7046 671 992	32
17	21.8816 492 360	23.6457 984 292	25.5476 698 619	27.5976 648 848	34
18	26.2366 444 751	28.4815 119 942	30.9126 805 329	33.5451 341 529	36
19	31.4583 926 418	34.3061 592 065	37.4043 434 448	40.7743 202 199	38
20	37.7193 992 373	41.3219 831 777	45.2592 555 682	49.5614 410 668	40
21	45.2265 026 705	49.7725 869 099	54.7636 992 375	60.2422 413 758	42
22	54.2277 073 646	59.9513 921 201	66.2640 760 774	73.2248 209 062	44
23	65.0203 768 228	72.2118 265 048	80.1795 320 536	89.0052 274 667	46
24	77.9610 573 199	86.9795 963 490	97.0172 337 849	108.1864 102 684	48
25	93.4772 567 530	104.7674 674 248	117.3908 528 797	131.5012 578 463	50
26	112.0815 677 783	126.1930 693 099	142.0429 319 844	159.8406 007 950	52
27	134.3886 018 054	152.0003 406 904	171.8719 477 012	194.2872 992 701	54
28	161.1352 932 797	183.0853 603 638	207.9650 567 184	236.1573 657 832	56
29	193.2052 450 247	220.5274 608 417	251.6377 186 293	287.0507 540 930	58
30	231.6579 189 157	265.6267 048 804	304.4816 395 414	348.9119 856 672	60
31	277.7636 362 280	319.9490 261 953	368.4227 838 451	424.1046 992 784	62
32	333.0455 439 282	385.3806 017 337	445.7915 684 526	515.5019 126 273	64
33	399.3299 333 085	464.1933 434 170	539.4077 978 276	626.5957 966 854	66
34	478.8065 732 853	559.1237 833 542	652.6834 353 714	761.6311 070 948	68
35	574.1010 515 334	673.4680 915 738	789.7469 567 994	925.7673 708 682	70
36	688.3615 133 148	811.1965 254 762	955.5938 177 273	1125.2760 253 363	72
37	825.3626 635 023	977.0912 849 143	1156.2685 194 501	1367.7800 417 715	74
38	989.6304 676 058	1176.9125 594 999	1399.0849 085 346	1662.5451 893 985	76
39	1186.5916 714 211	1417.5985 336 211	1692.8927 393 268	2020.8340 686 213	78
40	1422.7530 788 256	1707.5062 937 374	2048.4002 145 855	2456.3364 406 221	80
41	1705.9165 103 389	2056.7020 027 211	2478.5642 596 484	2985.6922 956 789	82
42	2045.4365 438 091	2477.3104 166 650	2999.0627 541 746	3629.1276 459 746	84
43	2452.5295 519 407	2983.9358 800 631	3628.8659 325 512	4411.2273 357 299	86
44	2940.6442 460 157	3594.1694 171 353	4390.9277 783 870	5361.8743 967 505	88
45	3525.9059 670 790	4329.1995 264 983	5313.0226 118 483	6517.3918 409 652	90
46	4227.6494 021 769	5214.5478 871 643	6428.7573 603 364	7921.9305 163 922	92
47	5069.0573 244 452	6280.9555 210 137	7778.7964 060 071	9629.1560 547 405	94
48	6077.9264 584 429	7565.4501 810 330	9412.3436 512 685	11704.2993 667 624	96
49	7287.5857 718 345	9112.6320 271 178	11388.9358 180 349	14226.6490 321 707	98
50	8737.9975 300 739	10976.2222 306 136	13780.6123 398 223	17292.5808 151 600	100
51	10477.0774 884 968	13220.9282 781 630	16674.5409 311 849	21019.2400 594 571	102
52	12562.2778 356 449	15924.6907 418 491	20176.1945 267 338	25549.0176 625 204	104
53	15062.4851 818 841	19181.3895 278 744	24413.1953 773 479	31054.9906 501 540	106
54	18060.2962 952 086	23104.1035 700 092	29539.9664 065 909	37747.5352 289 537	108
55	21654.7467 653 625	27829.0371 507 234	35743.3593 519 750	45882.3649 928 884	110
56	25964.5827 403 388	33520.2491 795 286	43249.4648 158 898	55770.3014 136 371	112
57	31132.1838 202 347	40375.3496 382 996	52331.8524 272 266	67789.1499 326 597	114
58	37328.2667 050 569	48632.3609 852 670	63321.5414 369 442	82398.1354 253 349	116
59	44757.5249 860 309	58577.9827 590 103	76619.0651 387 025	100155.4485 978 410	118
60	53665.3913 963 757	70557.5463 456 202	92709.0688 178 300	121739.5737 422 295	120

Table 1.   FUTURE WORTH OF ONE DOLLAR WITH INTEREST
PAYABLE AT BEGINNING OF EACH PERIOD

HALF YEARS	21% NOMINAL ANNUAL RATE	21½% NOMINAL ANNUAL RATE	22% NOMINAL ANNUAL RATE	22½% NOMINAL ANNUAL RATE	HALF YEARS
1	1.1050 000 000	1.1075 000 000	1.1100 000 000	1.1125 000 000	1
YEARS					
1	1.2210 250 000	1.2265 562 500	1.2321 000 000	1.2376 562 500	2
2	1.4909 020 506	1.5044 402 344	1.5180 704 100	1.5317 929 932	4
3	1.8204 286 764	1.8452 805 723	1.8704 145 522	1.8958 331 717	6
4	2.2227 889 246	2.2633 404 189	2.3045 377 697	2.3463 897 739	8
5	2.7140 808 466	2.7761 143 367	2.8394 209 861	2.9040 239 686	10
6	3.3139 605 657	3.4050 603 904	3.4984 505 969	3.5941 834 149	12
7	4.0464 286 998	4.1764 981 035	4.3104 409 805	4.4483 635 671	14
8	4.9407 906 031	5.1227 098 519	5.3108 943 321	5.5055 449 711	16
9	6.0328 288 462	6.2832 917 858	6.5435 529 065	6.8139 721 431	18
10	7.3662 348 419	7.7068 108 105	8.0623 115 361	8.4333 552 103	20
11	8.9943 568 979	9.4528 369 672	9.9335 740 437	10.4375 947 845	22
12	10.9823 346 312	11.5944 362 623	12.2391 565 792	12.9181 544 200	24
13	13.4097 051 431	14.2212 282 628	15.0798 648 212	15.9882 345 563	26
14	16.3735 852 223	17.4431 364 084	18.5799 014 462	19.7879 384 251	28
15	19.9925 568 961	21.3949 879 813	22.8922 965 719	24.4906 656 664	30
16	24.4114 117 840	26.2421 562 271	28.2055 986 063	30.3110 254 287	32
17	29.8069 440 736	32.1874 807 338	34.7521 180 428	37.5146 300 658	34
18	36.3950 238 875	39.4797 556 658	42.8180 846 405	46.4302 163 673	36
19	44.4392 340 422	48.4241 410 604	52.7561 620 855	57.4646 474 759	38
20	54.2614 157 464	59.3949 328 685	65.0008 673 056	71.1214 801 026	40
21	66.2545 451 617	72.8512 261 282	80.0875 686 072	88.0239 443 582	42
22	80.8984 560 061	89.3561 267 277	98.6758 932 810	108.9433 848 846	44
23	98.7790 372 449	109.6003 157 137	121.5785 681 115	134.8344 611 986	46
24	120.6116 739 519	134.4309 522 406	149.7969 537 702	166.8787 136 178	48
25	147.2698 691 871	164.8871 246 641	184.5648 267 402	206.5384 829 010	50
26	179.8201 920 242	202.2433 333 013	227.4023 230 266	255.6236 442 280	52
27	219.5649 499 664	248.0628 244 816	280.1824 022 011	316.3742 009 266	54
28	268.0942 930 327	304.2630 077 606	345.2127 377 520	391.5625 071 155	56
29	327.3498 341 503	373.1956 938 125	425.3366 141 842	484.6197 841 972	58
30	399.7023 312 433	457.7455 107 188	524.0572 423 363	599.7927 047 853	60
31	488.0465 390 064	561.4506 170 816	645.6909 282 826	742.3371 897 819	62
32	595.9170 252 903	688.6507 634 478	795.5557 927 370	918.7582 625 410	64
33	727.6295 858 051	844.6688 979 742	980.2042 922 313	1137.1069 058 730	66
34	888.4539 150 076	1036.0339 159 908	1207.7097 084 581	1407.3474 689 719	68
35	1084.8244 415 722	1270.7538 748 705	1488.0191 317 913	1741.8123 908 948	70
36	1324.5977 637 707	1558.6511 074 342	1833.3883 722 800	2155.7649 919 184	72
37	1617.3669 845 081	1911.7732 573 928	2258.9178 134 862	2668.0960 157 789	74
38	1974.8455 222 590	2344.8974 374 380	2783.2126 379 964	3302.1857 095 289	76
39	2411.3357 538 163	2876.1486 074 985	3429.1962 912 753	4086.9707 820 591	78
40	2944.3012 388 035	3527.7580 504 561	4225.1127 504 804	5058.2649 319 829	80
41	3595.0654 201 101	4326.9936 852 748	5205.7614 198 668	6260.3932 072 244	82
42	4389.6647 545 899	5307.3011 483 843	6414.0186 454 179	7748.2147 803 789	84
43	5359.8904 069 732	6509.7033 941 829	7902.7123 730 194	9589.6264 492 783	86
44	6544.5601 841 744	7984.5173 837 813	9736.9319 147 973	11868.6611 101 146	88
45	7991.0715 988 816	9793.4597 003 106	11996.8738 122 217	14689.3226 020 653	90
46	9757.2981 990 244	12012.2292 045 391	14781.3482 240 383	18180.3319 267 123	92
47	11913.9050 334 637	14733.6748 072 599	18212.0991 468 376	22501.0014 361 701	94
48	14547.1758 934 851	18071.6809 203 122	22439.1273 588 187	27848.5050 587 349	96
49	17762.4654 453 426	22165.9331 808 147	27647.2488 188 005	34466.8763 390 998	98
50	21688.4143 703 994	27187.7638 800 107	34064.1752 696 441	42658.1449 190 640	100
51	26482.0961 566 170	33347.3217 105 513	41970.4703 497 285	52796.1196 724 853	102
52	32335.3014 596 332	40902.3658 648 374	51711.8165 179 004	65343.4474 883 994	104
53	39482.2114 647 487	50169.0524 913 030	63714.1291 317 051	80872.7261 805 643	106
54	48208.7672 537 448	61535.1648 897 858	78502.1785 031 739	100092.6350 119 141	108
55	58864.1100 360 037	75476.3410 903 473	96722.5341 337 605	123880.2753 014 643	110
56	71874.5499 567 114	92575.9778 914 973	119171.8343 062 064	153321.1969 785 779	112
57	87760.6223 608 935	113549.6442 826 779	146831.6170 486 769	189758.9376 980 180	114
58	107157.9139 182 100	139275.0258 801 933	180911.2353 656 748	234856.3352 353 126	116
59	130842.4918 419 824	170828.6534 622 653	222900.7330 940 479	290671.4111 560 799	118
60	159761.9536 013 566	209530.9525 832 256	274635.9932 451 764	359751.2887 136 420	120

Table 2. FUTURE WORTH OF ONE DOLLAR PER PERIOD WITH INTEREST
PAYABLE AT END OF EACH PERIOD

HALF YEARS	5% NOMINAL ANNUAL RATE	5½% NOMINAL ANNUAL RATE	6% NOMINAL ANNUAL RATE	6½% NOMINAL ANNUAL RATE	HALF YEARS
1	1.0000 000 000	1.0000 000 000	1.0000 000 000	1.0000 000 000	1
YEARS					
1	2.0250 000 000	2.0275 000 000	2.0300 000 000	2.0325 000 000	2
2	4.1525 156 250	4.1680 457 969	4.1836 270 000	4.1992 593 281	4
3	6.3877 367 285	6.4279 404 003	6.4684 098 843	6.5091 466 521	6
4	8.7361 159 004	8.8138 382 523	8.8923 360 463	8.9716 164 707	8
5	11.2033 817 679	11.3327 648 213	11.4638 793 115	11.5967 478 111	10
6	13.7955 529 699	13.9921 372 899	14.1920 295 615	14.3952 854 837	12
7	16.5189 528 390	16.7997 863 947	17.0863 241 618	17.3786 840 605	14
8	19.3802 248 264	19.7639 794 848	20.1568 813 033	20.5591 547 595	16
9	22.3863 487 083	22.8934 448 660	23.4144 353 747	23.9497 154 260	18
10	25.5446 576 116	26.1973 975 013	26.8703 744 890	27.5642 438 156	20
11	28.8628 559 032	29.6855 661 457	30.5367 802 954	31.4175 343 962	22
12	32.3490 379 833	33.3682 219 932	34.4264 702 153	35.5253 589 026	24
13	36.0117 080 312	37.2562 089 207	38.5530 422 515	39.9045 308 917	26
14	39.8598 007 503	41.3609 754 193	42.9309 225 246	44.5729 745 604	28
15	43.9027 031 633	45.6946 083 050	47.5754 157 063	49.5497 981 112	30
16	48.1502 775 109	50.2698 683 093	52.5027 585 228	54.8553 719 627	32
17	52.6128 853 099	55.1002 276 542	57.7301 765 169	60.5114 121 269	34
18	57.3014 126 287	60.1999 097 224	63.2759 442 668	66.5410 690 942	36
19	62.2272 966 430	65.5839 309 388	69.1594 492 726	72.9690 225 895	38
20	67.4025 535 356	71.2681 449 883	75.4012 597 333	79.8215 825 880	40
21	72.8398 078 083	77.2692 894 973	82.0231 964 511	87.1267 970 028	42
22	78.5523 230 786	83.6050 353 198	89.0484 091 149	94.9145 664 873	44
23	84.5540 344 345	90.2940 385 703	96.5014 572 300	103.2167 668 198	46
24	90.8595 824 277	97.3559 955 584	104.4083 959 753	112.0673 793 731	48
25	97.4843 487 881	104.8117 007 857	112.7968 672 902	121.5026 302 018	50
26	104.4444 939 455	112.6831 081 777	121.6961 965 082	131.5611 383 180	52
27	111.7569 964 515	120.9933 957 280	131.1374 948 756	142.2840 737 611	54
28	119.4396 943 969	129.7670 337 485	141.1537 683 135	153.7153 261 084	56
29	127.5113 289 257	139.0298 569 240	151.7800 328 038	165.9016 841 187	58
30	135.9915 899 526	148.8091 403 841	163.0534 368 015	178.8930 272 403	60
31	144.9011 641 940	159.1336 800 177	175.0133 911 027	192.7425 297 709	62
32	154.2617 856 313	170.0338 772 641	187.7017 066 209	207.5068 785 031	64
33	164.0962 885 289	181.5418 286 333	201.1627 405 541	223.2465 047 462	66
34	174.4286 631 356	193.6914 202 161	215.4435 514 539	240.0258 316 753	68
35	185.2841 142 069	206.5184 274 645	230.5940 637 374	257.9135 380 189	70
36	196.6891 224 886	220.0606 205 358	246.6672 422 190	276.9828 391 647	72
37	208.6715 093 146	234.3578 755 096	263.7192 772 701	297.3117 868 343	74
38	221.2605 044 736	249.4522 918 060	281.8097 812 559	318.9835 885 533	76
39	234.4868 175 126	265.3883 161 510	301.0019 969 344	342.0869 482 247	78
40	248.3827 126 492	282.2128 734 534	321.3630 185 477	366.7164 291 984	80
41	262.9820 874 770	299.9755 049 788	342.9640 263 772	392.9728 413 246	82
42	278.3205 556 556	318.7285 142 283	365.8805 355 839	420.9636 535 744	84
43	294.4355 337 856	338.5271 209 498	390.1926 602 006	450.8034 339 158	86
44	311.3663 326 835	359.4296 237 372	415.9853 932 069	482.6143 182 474	88
45	329.1542 532 756	381.4975 716 957	443.3489 036 532	516.5265 103 071	90
46	347.8426 873 477	404.7959 456 776	472.3788 518 856	552.6788 146 036	92
47	367.4772 233 947	429.3933 496 238	503.1767 239 655	591.2192 045 508	94
48	388.1057 578 290	455.3622 125 737	535.8501 864 550	632.3054 281 314	96
49	409.7786 118 191	482.7790 019 385	570.5134 628 101	676.1056 535 684	98
50	432.5486 540 425	511.7244 486 654	607.2877 326 952	722.7991 576 469	100
51	456.4714 296 534	542.2837 849 563	646.3015 556 163	772.5770 595 042	102
52	481.6052 957 796	574.5469 952 412	687.6913 203 534	825.6431 028 911	104
53	508.0115 638 784	608.6090 811 446	731.6017 217 629	882.2144 901 064	106
54	535.7546 492 998	644.5703 412 252	778.1862 666 183	942.5227 710 185	108
55	564.9022 284 206	682.5366 663 131	827.6078 102 553	1006.8147 908 116	110
56	595.5254 037 344	722.6198 513 143	880.0391 258 999	1075.3537 003 372	112
57	627.6988 772 984	764.9379 243 991	935.6635 086 672	1148.4200 332 051	114
58	661.5011 329 617	809.6154 945 464	994.6754 163 450	1226.3128 540 235	116
59	697.0146 278 178	856.7841 184 642	1057.2811 492 004	1309.3509 824 871	118
60	734.3259 933 511	906.5826 879 693	1123.6995 711 867	1397.8742 983 240	120

Table 2. FUTURE WORTH OF ONE DOLLAR PER PERIOD WITH INTEREST
PAYABLE AT END OF EACH PERIOD

HALF YEARS	7% NOMINAL ANNUAL RATE	7½% NOMINAL ANNUAL RATE	8% NOMINAL ANNUAL RATE	8½% NOMINAL ANNUAL RATE	HALF YEARS
1	1.0000 000 000	1.0000 000 000	1.0000 000 000	1.0000 000 000	1
YEARS					
1	2.0350 000 000	2.0375 000 000	2.0400 000 000	2.0425 000 000	2
2	4.2149 428 750	4.2306 777 344	4.2464 640 000	4.2623 017 656	4
3	6.5501 521 813	6.5914 279 550	6.6329 754 624	6.6747 961 983	6
4	9.0516 867 704	9.1325 542 472	9.2142 262 601	9.2967 102 258	8
5	11.7313 931 606	11.8678 384 702	12.0061 071 230	12.1462 227 778	10
6	14.6019 616 385	14.8121 155 033	15.0258 054 642	15.2430 908 288	12
7	17.6769 863 562	17.9813 537 034	18.2919 111 901	18.6087 863 820	14
8	20.9710 297 094	21.3927 415 098	21.8245 311 432	22.2666 453 449	16
9	24.4996 913 004	25.0647 806 658	25.6454 128 845	26.2420 293 274	18
10	28.2796 818 133	29.0173 865 636	29.7780 785 758	30.5625 014 857	20
11	32.3289 021 505	33.2719 962 557	34.2479 697 876	35.2580 176 303	22
12	36.6665 282 061	37.8516 847 196	39.0826 041 223	40.3611 339 232	24
13	41.3131 016 776	42.7812 900 052	44.3117 446 187	45.9072 326 048	26
14	46.2906 273 446	48.0875 479 447	49.9675 829 796	51.9347 673 151	28
15	51.6226 772 772	53.7992 371 548	56.0849 377 507	58.4855 297 104	30
16	57.3345 024 663	59.9473 351 187	62.7014 686 711	65.6049 392 238	32
17	63.4531 524 044	66.5651 861 926	69.8579 085 147	73.3423 579 793	34
18	70.0076 031 845	73.6886 824 501	77.5983 138 495	81.7514 330 416	36
19	77.0288 947 213	81.3564 583 436	85.9703 362 596	90.8904 683 761	38
20	84.5502 777 478	89.6101 002 389	95.0255 156 984	100.8228 290 966	40
21	92.6073 712 804	98.4943 719 603	104.8195 977 794	111.6173 808 049	42
22	101.2383 312 998	108.0574 575 679	115.4128 769 582	123.3489 670 674	44
23	110.4840 314 467	118.3512 226 852	126.8705 677 180	136.0989 283 398	46
24	120.3882 565 864	129.4314 957 935	139.2632 060 438	149.9556 659 380	48
25	130.9979 101 618	141.3583 710 189	152.6670 836 570	165.0152 549 644	50
26	142.3632 363 131	154.1965 340 546	167.1647 176 834	181.3821 104 406	52
27	154.5380 578 195	168.0156 129 847	182.8453 586 463	199.1697 112 651	54
28	167.5800 309 877	182.8905 559 143	199.8055 399 119	218.5013 870 136	56
29	181.5509 186 948	198.9020 374 521	218.1496 719 687	239.5111 730 400	58
30	196.5168 828 788	216.1368 962 512	237.9906 852 013	262.3447 398 047	60
31	212.5487 978 619	234.6886 059 804	259.4507 251 137	287.1604 028 744	62
32	229.7225 859 896	254.6577 822 811	282.6619 042 830	314.1302 205 964	64
33	248.1195 771 767	276.1527 284 585	307.7671 156 725	343.4411 870 581	66
34	267.8268 940 611	299.2900 228 673	334.9209 123 114	375.2965 286 021	68
35	288.9378 645 906	324.1951 511 770	364.2904 587 560	409.9171 128 881	70
36	311.5524 639 960	351.0031 869 466	396.0565 601 905	447.5429 802 687	72
37	335.7777 882 442	379.8595 241 992	430.4147 755 021	488.4350 080 997	74
38	361.7285 612 119	410.9206 659 701	467.5766 211 830	532.8767 195 215	76
39	389.5276 779 842	444.3550 731 044	507.7708 734 716	581.1762 492 555	78
40	419.3067 868 486	480.3440 779 088	551.2449 767 468	633.6684 800 424	80
41	451.2069 127 419	519.0828 676 115	598.2665 668 494	690.7173 645 381	82
42	485.3791 251 019	560.7815 429 649	649.1251 187 043	752.7184 487 635	84
43	521.9852 532 873	605.6662 577 321	704.1337 283 906	820.1016 146 065	86
44	561.1986 529 527	653.9804 452 369	763.6310 406 272	893.3340 603 895	88
45	603.2050 270 092	705.9861 386 308	827.9833 335 424	972.9235 401 691	90
46	648.2033 050 580	761.9653 920 356	897.5867 735 595	1059.4218 842 279	92
47	696.4065 854 607	822.2218 102 708	972.8698 542 819	1153.4288 251 657	94
48	748.0431 445 102	887.0821 954 618	1054.2960 343 913	1255.5961 561 203	96
49	803.3575 174 779	956.8983 194 588	1142.3665 907 976	1366.6322 499 475	98
50	862.6116 566 603	1032.0488 316 799	1237.3665 046 067	1487.3069 706 945	100
51	926.0861 719 059	1112.9413 127 255	1340.6537 989 026	1618.4570 114 193	102
52	994.0816 594 999	1200.0144 849 009	1452.0911 488 931	1760.9916 953 668	104
53	1066.9201 256 978	1293.7405 916 379	1572.6217 866 428	1915.8992 807 228	106
54	1144.9465 116 506	1394.6279 587 177	1702.9877 244 328	2084.2538 126 600	108
55	1228.5303 269 429	1503.2237 511 885	1843.9915 227 465	2267.2225 701 852	110
56	1318.0673 994 794	1620.1169 409 277	1996.5012 310 027	2466.0741 594 184	112
57	1413.9817 500 074	1745.9415 009 455	2161.4557 314 525	2682.1873 094 194	114
58	1516.7276 001 516	1881.3798 437 521	2339.8705 191 390	2917.0604 315 477	116
59	1626.7915 234 724	2027.1665 224 387	2532.8439 535 007	3172.3220 086 337	118
60	1744.6947 497 318	2184.0922 145 438	2741.5640 201 064	3449.7418 859 957	120

Table 2. FUTURE WORTH OF ONE DOLLAR PER PERIOD WITH INTEREST PAYABLE AT END OF EACH PERIOD

HALF YEARS	9% NOMINAL ANNUAL RATE	9½% NOMINAL ANNUAL RATE	10% NOMINAL ANNUAL RATE	10½% NOMINAL ANNUAL RATE	HALF YEARS
1	1.0000 000 000	1.0000 000 000	1.0000 000 000	1.0000 000 000	1
YEARS					
1	2.0450 000 000	2.0475 000 000	2.0500 000 000	2.0525 000 000	2
2	4.2781 911 250	4.2941 321 719	4.3101 250 000	4.3261 697 031	4
3	6.7168 916 633	6.7592 633 639	6.8019 128 125	6.8448 415 272	6
4	9.3800 136 186	9.4641 439 715	9.5491 088 758	9.6349 159 820	8
5	12.2882 093 718	12.4320 911 236	12.5778 925 355	12.7256 383 973	10
6	15.4640 318 393	15.6886 896 859	15.9171 265 204	16.1494 054 698	12
7	18.9321 093 693	19.2620 128 122	19.5986 319 888	19.9421 048 430	14
8	22.7193 367 340	23.1828 639 457	23.6574 917 676	24.1434 912 780	16
9	26.8550 836 970	27.4850 423 574	28.1323 846 738	28.7976 033 600	18
10	31.3714 227 742	32.2056 345 081	33.0659 541 029	33.9532 251 071	20
11	36.3033 779 550	37.3853 337 493	38.5052 143 984	39.6643 973 200	22
12	41.6891 963 113	43.0687 911 147	44.5019 988 743	45.9909 840 337	24
13	47.5706 446 018	49.3050 002 306	51.1134 537 589	52.9993 000 070	26
14	53.9933 331 713	56.1477 196 592	58.4025 827 692	60.7628 058 284	28
15	61.0070 696 564	63.6559 363 194	66.4388 475 030	69.3628 779 240	30
16	68.6662 452 415	71.8943 739 760	75.2988 293 721	78.8896 615 383	32
17	77.0302 564 599	80.9340 511 850	85.0669 593 827	89.4430 156 294	34
18	86.1639 658 106	90.8528 935 006	95.8363 227 194	101.1335 595 823	36
19	96.1382 047 643	101.7364 052 291	107.7095 457 982	114.0838 327 120	38
20	107.0303 230 577	113.6784 064 847	120.7997 742 425	128.4295 787 107	40
21	118.9247 885 371	126.7818 420 053	135.2317 511 023	144.3211 685 017	42
22	131.9138 422 022	141.1596 685 269	151.1430 055 903	161.9251 764 150	44
23	146.0982 135 309	156.9358 285 390	168.6851 636 633	181.4261 262 061	46
24	161.5879 016 311	174.2463 187 134	188.0253 929 388	203.0284 252 181	48
25	178.5030 282 787	193.2403 622 478	209.3479 957 151	226.9585 069 630	50
26	196.9747 694 560	214.0816 952 286	232.8561 652 759	253.4672 045 789	52
27	217.1463 726 152	236.9499 781 002	258.7739 222 166	282.8323 800 424	54
28	239.1742 675 551	262.0423 444 078	287.3482 492 439	315.3618 366 943	56
29	263.2292 795 269	289.5751 001 661	318.8514 447 913	351.3965 456 096	58
30	289.4979 539 753	319.7855 885 017	353.5837 178 825	391.3142 196 274	60
31	318.1840 031 899	352.9342 356 434	391.8760 489 654	435.5332 725 061	62
32	349.5098 860 835	389.3067 958 987	434.0933 439 844	484.5172 047 016	64
33	383.7185 333 503	429.2168 149 673	480.6379 117 428	538.7794 617 408	66
34	421.0752 313 819	473.0083 328 280	531.9532 976 964	598.8888 161 150	68
35	461.8696 795 498	521.0588 494 975	588.5285 107 103	665.4753 291 065	70
36	506.4182 368 104	573.7825 792 290	650.9026 830 581	739.2369 550 385	72
37	555.0663 750 528	631.6340 212 001	719.6702 080 715	820.9468 571 749	74
38	608.1913 582 171	695.1118 774 745	795.4864 043 989	911.4615 119 533	76
39	666.2051 679 570	764.7633 520 081	879.0737 608 497	1011.7296 865 007	78
40	729.5576 985 382	841.1888 677 618	971.2288 213 368	1122.8023 835 317	80
41	798.7402 457 462	925.0472 425 821	1072.8297 755 239	1245.8438 578 722	82
42	874.2893 168 610	1017.0613 684 685	1184.8448 275 151	1382.1438 200 820	84
43	956.7907 912 452	1118.0244 431 856	1308.3414 223 354	1533.1309 550 947	86
44	1046.8844 638 095	1228.8068 079 382	1444.4964 181 247	1700.3878 975 746	88
45	1145.2690 065 916	1350.3634 500 527	1594.6073 009 825	1885.6678 209 627	90
46	1252.7073 869 232	1483.7422 353 419	1760.1045 493 332	2090.9128 140 953	92
47	1370.0327 842 048	1630.0929 411 179	1942.5652 656 399	2318.2742 380 191	94
48	1498.1550 511 712	1790.6711 677 225	2143.7282 053 680	2570.1352 763 797	96
49	1638.0677 697 552	1966.8792 140 158	2365.5103 464 182	2849.1359 157 551	98
50	1790.8559 562 670	2160.2180 105 739	2610.0251 569 261	3158.2006 177 771	100
51	1957.7044 756 462	2372.3602 134 648	2879.6027 355 110	3500.5689 730 965	102
52	2139.9072 300 134	2605.1345 714 755	3176.8120 159 009	3879.8296 585 037	104
53	2338.8771 928 554	2860.5476 906 426	3504.4852 475 307	4299.9580 531 428	106
54	2556.1573 665 279	3140.8013 319 807	3865.7449 854 026	4765.3579 081 068	108
55	2793.4327 481 827	3448.3113 915 241	4264.0338 464 064	5280.9075 061 923	110
56	3052.5433 968 342	3785.7287 262 960	4703.1473 156 630	5852.0107 956 564	112
57	3335.4987 029 278	4155.9620 057 329	5187.2699 155 185	6484.6540 339 558	114
58	3644.4929 710 648	4562.2027 855 529	5721.0150 818 591	7185.4685 352 023	116
59	3981.9224 367 270	5007.9530 202 154	6309.4691 277 497	7961.8001 790 487	118
60	4350.4038 489 668	5497.0552 511 377	6958.2397 133 440	8821.7864 095 923	120

Table 2. FUTURE WORTH OF ONE DOLLAR PER PERIOD WITH INTEREST PAYABLE AT END OF EACH PERIOD

HALF YEARS	11% NOMINAL ANNUAL RATE	11½% NOMINAL ANNUAL RATE	12% NOMINAL ANNUAL RATE	12½% NOMINAL ANNUAL RATE	HALF YEARS
1	1.0000 000 000	1.0000 000 000	1.0000 000 000	1.0000 000 000	1
YEARS					
1	2.0550 000 000	2.0575 000 000	2.0600 000 000	2.0625 000 000	2
2	4.3422 663 750	4.3584 151 094	4.3746 160 000	4.3908 691 406	4
3	6.8880 510 320	6.9315 428 569	6.9753 185 376	7.0193 796 158	6
4	9.7215 729 999	9.8090 876 990	9.8974 679 088	9.9867 215 194	8
5	12.8753 537 882	13.0270 640 806	13.1807 949 424	13.3365 723 402	10
6	16.3855 906 502	16.6257 471 805	16.8699 411 973	17.1182 398 685	12
7	20.2925 720 334	20.6501 769 829	21.0150 659 292	21.3873 879 765	14
8	24.6411 399 875	25.1507 219 836	25.6725 280 781	26.2068 559 579	16
9	29.4812 048 346	30.1837 095 862	30.9056 525 485	31.6475 834 837	18
10	34.8683 180 110	35.8121 310 785	36.7855 912 035	37.7896 547 921	20
11	40.8643 096 542	42.1064 300 109	43.3922 902 763	44.7234 774 802	22
12	47.5379 982 528	49.1453 838 463	50.8155 773 545	52.5511 132 491	24
13	54.9659 805 054	57.0170 899 140	59.1563 827 155	61.3877 801 914	26
14	63.2335 104 520	65.8200 680 076	68.5281 116 191	71.3635 487 317	28
15	72.4354 779 708	75.6644 934 284	79.0581 862 152	82.6252 561 854	30
16	82.6774 978 685	86.6735 759 040	90.8897 780 314	95.3386 681 155	32
17	94.0771 220 651	98.9851 016 433	104.1837 545 961	108.6909 183 023	34
18	106.7651 887 865	112.7531 578 246	119.1208 666 642	125.8932 632 397	36
19	120.8873 242 490	128.1500 611 025	135.9042 057 839	144.1841 917 042	38
20	136.6056 140 723	145.3685 142 688	154.7619 656 188	164.8329 351 660	40
21	154.1004 636 028	164.6240 180 600	175.9505 445 692	188.1434 307 148	42
22	173.5726 685 015	186.1575 682 966	199.7580 318 780	214.4587 948 303	44
23	195.2457 193 589	210.2386 721 109	226.5081 246 181	244.1663 738 514	46
24	219.3683 667 895	237.1687 210 134	256.5645 288 209	277.7034 454 807	48
25	246.2174 764 458	267.2847 630 138	290.3359 045 832	315.5636 552 497	50
26	276.1012 067 211	300.9637 210 081	328.2814 223 897	358.3042 826 843	52
27	309.3625 456 108	338.6271 102 266	370.9170 061 970	406.5544 441 240	54
28	346.3832 473 284	380.7463 137 858	418.8223 481 630	461.1243 529 369	56
29	387.5882 138 577	427.8484 823 711	472.6487 903 959	522.5157 734 327	58
30	433.4503 717 290	480.5231 318 886	533.1281 808 889	591.9338 223 517	60
31	484.4960 999 937	539.4295 216 606	601.0828 240 467	670.3002 916 392	62
32	541.3112 716 955	605.3049 055 076	677.4366 610 989	758.7686 886 084	64
33	604.5479 781 788	678.9737 589 848	763.2278 324 107	858.6412 148 743	66
34	674.9320 134 125	761.3580 982 587	859.6227 924 967	971.3879 339 792	68
35	753.2712 042 284	853.4890 197 708	967.9321 696 493	1098.6684 098 437	70
36	840.4646 820 864	956.5196 051 161	1089.6285 858 180	1242.3561 345 501	72
37	937.5132 027 792	1071.7393 526 489	1226.3666 790 251	1404.5661 050 194	74
38	1045.5306 325 233	1200.5903 164 382	1380.0056 005 526	1587.6859 544 946	76
39	1165.7567 322 642	1344.6851 545 623	1552.6342 927 808	1794.4110 970 661	78
40	1299.5713 869 284	1505.8273 126 292	1746.5998 913 686	2027.7844 025 473	80
41	1448.5104 429 360	1686.0335 951 340	1964.5396 379 417	2291.2409 856 882	82
42	1614.2833 357 488	1887.5594 071 483	2209.4167 371 913	2588.6587 689 996	84
43	1798.7927 097 718	2112.9269 822 602	2484.5606 459 082	2924.4155 634 409	86
44	2004.1562 557 938	2364.9569 500 552	2793.7123 417 424	3303.4535 071 657	88
45	2232.7310 166 049	2646.8036 382 277	3141.0751 871 818	3731.3518 108 238	90
46	2487.1404 397 566	2961.9945 511 528	3531.3720 803 174	4214.4088 801 878	92
47	2770.3044 879 601	3314.4745 190 201	3969.9096 694 447	4759.7350 248 995	94
48	3085.4731 527 118	3708.6550 700 859	4462.6505 045 880	5375.3571 179 530	96
49	3436.2637 557 971	4149.4696 439 713	5016.2941 069 551	6070.3367 464 391	98
50	3826.7024 667 960	4642.4353 370 384	5638.3680 585 748	6854.9035 926 597	100
51	4261.2705 131 057	5193.7219 526 309	6337.3303 506 146	7740.6060 089 010	102
52	4744.9556 128 494	5810.2292 203 893	7122.6843 819 506	8740.4810 022 359	104
53	5283.3092 209 917	6499.6731 510 940	8005.1081 715 597	9869.2461 314 304	106
54	5882.5102 456 943	7270.6826 078 256	8996.5995 415 644	11143.5161 405 601	108
55	6549.4359 662 139	8132.9073 020 977	10110.6392 449 018	12582.0475 180 542	110
56	7291.7409 662 953	9097.1385 666 065	11362.3742 555 716	14206.0145 809 284	112
57	8117.9449 890 108	10175.4444 161 520	12768.8237 135 913	16039.3211 480 012	114
58	9037.5307 213 937	11381.3205 871 104	14349.1103 245 564	18108.9523 897 357	116
59	10061.0526 311 793	12729.8594 458 193	16124.7203 606 715	20445.3720 337 251	118
60	11200.2581 048 183	14237.9388 798 812	18119.7957 972 505	23082.9707 724 474	120

Table 2.   FUTURE WORTH OF ONE DOLLAR PER PERIOD WITH INTEREST
PAYABLE AT END OF EACH PERIOD

HALF YEARS	**13%** NOMINAL ANNUAL RATE	**13½%** NOMINAL ANNUAL RATE	**14%** NOMINAL ANNUAL RATE	**14½%** NOMINAL ANNUAL RATE	HALF YEARS
1	1.0000 000 000	1.0000 000 000	1.0000 000 000	1.0000 000 000	1
YEARS					
1	2.0650 000 000	2.0675 000 000	2.0700 000 000	2.0725 000 000	2
2	4.4071 746 250	4.4235 325 469	4.4399 430 000	4.4564 060 781	4
3	7.0637 276 390	7.1083 641 609	7.1532 907 407	7.1985 089 439	6
4	10.0768 564 814	10.1678 808 068	10.2598 025 690	10.3526 299 034	8
5	13.4944 225 426	13.6543 721 226	13.8164 479 613	13.9806 772 503	10
6	17.3707 114 084	17.6274 250 922	17.8884 512 709	18.1538 613 864	12
7	21.7672 951 472	22.1549 424 352	22.5504 878 600	22.9540 925 214	14
8	26.7540 103 383	27.3143 031 204	27.8880 535 509	28.4755 883 858	16
9	32.4100 673 760	33.1936 848 353	33.9990 325 105	34.8267 235 132	18
10	38.8253 086 695	39.8935 710 146	40.9954 923 212	42.1321 563 880	20
11	46.1016 357 257	47.5284 681 845	49.0057 391 586	50.5352 762 113	22
12	54.3546 277 809	56.2288 629 725	58.1766 707 627	60.2010 173 076	24
13	63.7153 776 948	66.1434 522 307	68.6764 703 562	71.3190 964 144	26
14	74.3325 742 659	77.4416 843 861	80.6976 909 108	84.1077 363 950	28
15	86.3748 640 468	90.3166 554 527	94.4607 863 237	98.8179 494 617	30
16	100.0335 301 735	104.9884 092 003	110.2181 542 621	115.7384 639 805	32
17	115.5255 307 610	121.7076 978 817	128.2587 648 146	135.2013 915 589	34
18	133.0969 451 274	140.7602 677 942	148.9134 598 363	157.5887 456 494	36
19	153.0268 825 871	162.4717 429 166	172.5610 201 665	183.3399 396 129	38
20	175.6319 159 024	187.2131 900 890	199.6351 119 887	212.9604 114 143	40
21	201.2711 098 144	215.4074 608 483	230.6322 397 158	247.0315 442 319	42
22	230.3517 245 292	247.5364 183 063	266.1208 512 507	286.2220 776 999	44
23	263.3356 847 541	284.1491 725 836	306.7517 625 969	331.3012 337 623	46
24	300.7469 170 403	325.8714 655 500	353.2700 929 972	383.1538 147 678	48
25	343.1796 719 800	373.4163 652 641	406.5289 294 724	442.7975 701 480	50
26	391.3079 634 515	427.5964 528 890	467.5049 713 530	511.4031 725 475	52
27	445.8962 748 458	489.3377 103 675	537.3164 417 021	590.3171 954 926	54
28	507.8117 023 369	559.6953 462 100	617.2435 941 047	681.0885 435 978	56
29	578.0377 280 831	639.8718 298 695	708.7521 908 905	785.4988 540 768	58
30	657.6898 421 351	731.2374 429 267	813.5203 833 505	905.5974 662 697	60
31	748.0332 611 957	835.3536 983 212	933.4694 868 980	1043.7416 455 609	62
32	850.5030 256 796	954.0000 278 825	1070.7992 155 495	1202.6428 511 917	64
33	966.7267 943 015	1089.2041 942 737	1228.0280 218 826	1385.4199 561 010	66
34	1098.5506 982 666	1243.2769 471 108	1408.0392 822 534	1595.6604 633 799	68
35	1248.0686 657 414	1418.8515 155 610	1614.1341 742 519	1837.4909 208 807	70
36	1417.6556 824 006	1618.9286 123 795	1850.0922 161 010	2115.6579 160 612	72
37	1610.0055 163 708	1846.9277 185 409	2120.2405 782 140	2435.6212 408 114	74
38	1828.1735 068 057	2106.7455 249 615	2429.5334 379 972	2803.6610 548 761	76
39	2075.6250 957 567	2402.8225 301 295	2783.6428 331 631	3227.0011 512 528	78
40	2356.2908 742 346	2740.2189 318 498	3189.0626 796 884	3713.9507 429 858	80
41	2674.6290 168 287	3124.7011 101 578	3653.2278 619 752	4274.0675 543 115	82
42	3035.6960 966 126	3562.8401 794 623	4184.6505 791 754	4918.3454 172 690	84
43	3445.2274 051 804	4062.1242 942 573	4793.0764 480 980	5659.4300 558 726	86
44	3909.7280 536 407	4631.0866 277 978	5489.6632 254 273	6511.8672 932 053	88
45	4436.5763 016 407	5279.4512 109 984	6287.1854 267 918	7492.3885 531 799	90
46	5034.1407 557 284	6018.2991 240 633	7200.2685 951 339	8620.2392 607 237	92
47	5711.9132 986 660	6860.2578 811 958	8245.6575 145 688	9917.5565 861 428	94
48	6480.6598 611 795	7819.7172 451 285	9442.5232 884 298	11409.8039 479 394	96
49	7352.5914 310 463	8913.0751 599 189	10812.8149 129 233	13126.2708 023 920	98
50	8341.5580 158 785	10159.0180 052 054	12381.6617 938 059	15100.6475 296 439	100
51	9463.2686 405 598	11578.8399 616 943	14177.8635 877 284	17371.6867 000 199	102
52	10735.5408 738 389	13196.8069 460 985	16234.2728 194 902	19983.9636 997 398	104
53	12178.5838 476 299	15040.5713 354 700	18588.6889 510 343	22988.7516 453 988	106
54	13815.3192 645 781	17141.6445 689 057	21284.2599 800 392	26445.0277 598 178	108
55	15671.7454 098 661	19535.9357 037 750	24370.4192 511 469	30420.6309 621 539	110
56	17777.3505 316 460	22264.3651 308 350	27903.7630 006 381	34993.5933 931 610	112
57	20165.5804 067 562	25373.5639 371 250	31949.0882 594 305	40253.6720 104 422	114
58	22874.3704 368 530	28916.6708 693 254	36580.5811 482 220	46304.1103 154 612	116
59	25946.7478 087 396	32954.2405 183 327	41883.1773 565 994	53263.6647 910 487	118
60	29431.5150 333 677	37555.2782 466 693	47954.1197 555 706	61268.9358 238 087	120

Table 2. FUTURE WORTH OF ONE DOLLAR PER PERIOD WITH INTEREST PAYABLE AT END OF EACH PERIOD

HALF YEARS	15% NOMINAL ANNUAL RATE	15½% NOMINAL ANNUAL RATE	16% NOMINAL ANNUAL RATE	16½% NOMINAL ANNUAL RATE	HALF YEARS
1	1.0000 000 000	1.0000 000 000	1.0000 000 000	1.0000 000 000	1
YEARS					
1	2.0750 000 000	2.0775 000 000	2.0800 000 000	2.0825 000 000	2
2	4.4729 218 750	4.4894 904 844	4.5061 120 000	4.5227 865 156	4
3	7.2440 203 418	7.2898 265 117	7.3359 290 368	7.3823 295 064	6
4	10.4463 710 075	10.5410 341 415	10.6366 276 285	10.7331 598 552	8
5	14.1470 874 955	14.3157 065 197	14.4865 624 659	14.6596 838 006	10
6	18.4237 279 870	18.6981 247 425	18.9771 264 602	19.2608 091 005	12
7	23.3659 206 550	23.7861 396 894	24.2149 203 032	24.6524 364 840	14
8	29.0772 420 569	29.6933 568 427	30.3242 830 417	30.9703 791 497	16
9	35.6773 878 520	36.5516 728 779	37.4502 437 398	38.3737 838 525	18
10	43.3046 813 365	44.5142 206 592	45.7619 642 981	47.0491 397 545	20
11	52.1189 723 695	53.7587 883 992	55.4567 551 573	57.2149 760 215	22
12	62.3049 874 445	64.4917 893 239	66.7647 592 155	69.1273 664 956	24
13	74.0762 011 156	76.9528 704 787	79.9544 151 490	83.0863 801 056	26
14	87.6793 099 142	91.4202 635 813	95.3388 298 297	99.4436 394 976	28
15	103.3994 025 196	108.2169 973 945	113.2832 111 134	118.6111 782 860	30
16	121.5659 345 367	127.7181 103 312	134.2135 374 427	141.0718 200 354	32
17	142.5596 330 990	150.3590 243 328	158.6266 700 732	167.3913 404 164	34
18	166.8204 760 000	176.6452 669 942	187.1021 479 733	198.2327 188 958	36
19	194.8569 125 775	207.1637 590 132	220.3159 453 961	234.3728 389 566	38
20	227.2565 195 974	242.5959 189 879	259.0565 187 100	276.7220 575 195	40
21	264.6983 154 597	283.7328 781 694	304.2435 234 233	326.3471 365 143	42
22	307.9669 908 031	331.4931 448 852	356.9496 457 210	384.4981 142 370	44
23	357.9693 537 469	386.9431 130 438	418.4260 667 690	452.6397 933 761	46
24	415.7533 344 237	451.3208 726 383	490.1321 642 793	532.4886 388 769	48
25	482.5299 470 934	526.0638 538 886	573.7701 564 154	626.0560 150 899	50
26	559.6986 701 098	612.8409 222 637	671.3255 104 429	735.6988 513 325	52
27	648.8767 756 457	713.5896 410 039	785.1140 753 806	864.1790 121 092	54
28	751.9332 238 555	830.5595 331 408	917.8370 575 239	1014.7328 675 084	56
29	871.0278 318 180	966.3623 089 736	1072.6451 438 959	1191.1528 162 267	58
30	1008.6565 381 447	1124.0301 804 828	1253.2132 958 402	1397.8828 147 596	60
31	1167.7037 118 935	1307.0835 647 291	1463.8279 882 680	1640.1303 191 029	62
32	1351.5026 020 569	1519.6096 879 228	1709.4889 655 158	1923.9974 587 393	64
33	1563.9051 945 020	1766.2538 452 389	1996.0279 293 777	2256.6347 471 348	66
34	1809.3629 403 964	2052.8253 540 339	2330.2469 768 261	2646.4212 006 597	68
35	2093.0200 479 956	2385.4205 661 918	2720.0800 737 700	3103.1754 030 656	70
36	2420.8212 929 649	2771.5656 862 272	3174.7813 980 453	3638.4028 321 585	72
37	2799.6366 066 826	3219.8825 839 953	3705.1450 226 800	4265.5856 787 410	74
38	3237.4050 535 975	3740.3813 042 847	4323.7611 544 540	5000.5224 582 592	76
39	3743.3012 150 636	4344.6835 716 577	5045.3150 105 551	5861.7259 698 535	78
40	4327.9274 666 579	5046.2822 809 670	5886.9354 283 115	6870.8896 272 616	80
41	5003.5361 786 566	5860.8427 674 669	6868.6014 835 825	8053.4339 082 854	82
42	5784.2864 964 600	6806.5525 832 964	8013.6167 704 506	9439.1466 876 907	84
43	6686.5410 824 716	7904.5275 901 607	9349.1626 010 536	11062.9335 833 028	86
44	7729.2090 384 312	9179.2834 354 740	10906.9432 578 690	12965.6972 162 491	88
45	8934.1421 950 371	10659.2829 391 068	12723.9386 159 783	15195.3675 336 083	90
46	10326.5930 741 397	12377.5716 128 214	14843.2820 016 771	17808.1091 469 293	92
47	11935.7441 213 027	14372.5155 023 082	17315.2841 267 562	20869.7360 990 539	94
48	13795.3193 001 804	16688.6578 264 018	20198.6274 054 485	24457.3696 967 220	96
49	15944.2908 662 710	19377.7135 405 638	23561.7590 057 151	28661.3811 691 794	98
50	18427.6961 323 345	22499.7240 313 043	27484.5157 042 661	33587.6680 876 768	100
51	21297.5813 429 290	26124.3977 236 194	32060.0191 174 559	39360.3218 880 652	102
52	24614.0924 394 223	30332.6665 346 079	37396.8862 986 006	46124.7536 904 466	104
53	28446.7355 753 074	35218.4929 258 457	43621.8081 786 877	54051.3571 541 758	106
54	32875.8337 992 186	40890.9679 024 876	50882.5570 596 214	63339.8006 342 455	108
55	37994.2104 342 174	47476.7468 033 375	59351.4945 543 424	74224.0567 569 628	110
56	43909.1344 330 425	55122.8772 683 423	69229.6632 481 849	86978.2961 081 637	112
57	50744.5684 791 847	64000.0825 265 284	80751.5592 126 829	101923.7934 938 970	114
58	58643.7669 487 579	74306.5733 138 153	94190.6986 656 734	119437.0207 398 578	116
59	67772.2781 801 583	86272.4735 334 227	109866.1109 236 414	139959.1298 843 450	118
60	78321.4139 719 455	100164.9584 752 634	128149.9117 813 353	164007.0656 430 372	120

143

Table 2.   FUTURE WORTH OF ONE DOLLAR PER PERIOD WITH INTEREST
PAYABLE AT END OF EACH PERIOD

	17% NOMINAL ANNUAL RATE	17½% NOMINAL ANNUAL RATE	18% NOMINAL ANNUAL RATE	18½% NOMINAL ANNUAL RATE	
HALF YEARS					HALF YEARS
1	1.0000 000 000	1.0000 000 000	1.0000 000 000	1.0000 000 000	1
YEARS					
1	2.0850 000 000	2.0875 000 000	2.0900 000 000	2.0925 000 000	2
2	4.5395 141 250	4.5562 949 219	4.5731 290 000	4.5900 164 531	4
3	7.4290 295 158	7.4760 306 662	7.5233 345 649	7.5709 428 252	6
4	10.8306 392 717	10.9290 743 926	11.0284 737 966	11.1288 461 274	8
5	14.8350 993 167	15.0128 381 371	15.1929 297 177	15.3754 038 507	10
6	19.5492 497 931	19.8425 268 531	20.1407 197 976	20.4439 093 623	12
7	25.0988 655 877	25.5543 883 986	26.0191 891 915	26.4934 557 938	14
8	31.6320 120 414	32.3095 571 545	33.0033 986 784	33.7139 297 468	16
9	39.3229 953 755	40.2985 997 035	41.3013 379 699	42.3319 715 613	18
10	48.3770 132 309	49.7468 908 056	51.1601 196 420	52.6180 892 318	20
11	59.0356 294 007	60.9209 713 293	62.8733 381 466	64.8951 492 657	22
12	71.5832 188 213	74.1360 674 987	76.7898 130 520	79.5485 110 008	24
13	86.3545 547 769	89.7649 835 777	93.3239 768 871	97.0381 224 832	26
14	103.7437 407 472	108.2486 188 593	112.9682 169 396	117.9129 575 780	28
15	124.2147 252 011	130.1084 056 479	136.3075 385 459	142.8282 474 733	30
16	148.3136 798 749	155.9610 191 170	164.0369 865 464	172.5660 474 483	32
17	176.6835 717 907	186.5357 740 151	196.9823 437 158	208.0597 844 697	34
18	210.0813 178 013	222.6951 989 875	236.1247 225 687	250.4235 561 274	36
19	249.3979 793 487	265.4593 689 276	282.6297 828 839	300.9871 005 631	38
20	295.6825 362 387	316.0346 817 833	337.8824 450 443	361.3375 350 465	40
21	350.1698 737 236	375.8478 916 277	403.5281 329 572	433.3691 733 143	42
22	414.3137 295 943	446.5863 580 829	481.5217 747 664	519.3429 853 666	44
23	489.8254 803 217	530.2456 475 514	574.1860 206 000	621.9575 660 780	46
24	578.7198 010 717	629.1858 291 120	684.2804 110 748	744.4338 402 272	48
25	683.3684 178 166	746.1980 532 108	815.0835 563 980	890.6161 627 146	50
26	806.5633 856 641	884.5832 913 675	970.4907 733 565	1065.0929 873 591	52
27	951.5915 816 884	1048.2454 581 814	1155.1300 878 248	1273.3408 918 936	54
28	1122.3223 997 532	1241.8015 426 523	1374.5000 573 447	1521.8964 799 002	56
29	1323.3109 870 494	1470.7118 556 774	1635.1335 181 312	1818.5615 554 378	58
30	1559.9197 767 293	1741.4340 680 640	1944.7921 328 917	2172.6480 105 026	60
31	1838.4615 591 601	2061.6053 845 612	2312.6975 330 886	2595.2701 119 854	62
32	2166.3679 089 823	2440.2579 930 849	2749.8059 390 625	3099.6933 625 984	64
33	2552.3874 616 517	2888.0738 671 343	3269.1344 362 002	3701.7508 860 128	66
34	3006.8193 295 429	3417.6861 094 281	3886.1486 236 495	4420.3404 059 436	68
35	3541.7878 852 211	4044.0353 378 533	4619.2231 797 579	5278.0174 186 614	70
36	4171.5662 431 794	4784.7911 675 331	5490.1890 598 704	6301.7031 776 285	72
37	4912.9570 706 269	5660.8506 792 278	6524.9836 220 320	7523.5297 133 034	74
38	5785.7408 874 688	6696.9279 361 055	7754.4230 413 362	8981.8484 113 739	76
39	6813.2038 162 504	7922.2511 794 348	9215.1200 154 116	10722.4338 079 479	78
40	8022.7588 625 854	9371.3873 714 284	10950.5740 903 105	12799.9203 866 875	80
41	9446.6773 020 071	11085.2173 459 909	13012.4670 766 979	15279.5174 770 333	82
42	11122.9496 868 553	13112.0890 768 445	15462.2021 338 247	18239.0560 816 974	84
43	13096.2994 451 082	15509.1815 972 869	18372.7323 551 972	21771.4318 804 104	86
44	15419.3761 142 675	18344.1180 484 163	21830.7333 112 098	25987.5210 923 131	88
45	18154.1600 461 186	21696.8733 606 974	25939.1842 470 483	31019.6607 217 371	90
46	21373.6160 602 919	25662.0303 854 873	30820.3438 039 181	37025.8024 273 088	92
47	25163.6401 665 772	30351.4481 230 864	36619.8485 905 351	44194.4703 983 796	94
48	29625.3512 950 988	35897.4173 193 189	43510.1321 104 148	52750.6788 594 260	96
49	34877.7891 783 727	42456.3924 515 508	51696.4779 603 838	62962.9949 444 108	98
50	41061.0903 655 098	50213.4053 852 793	61422.6754 647 320	75151.9686 346 199	100
51	48340.2271 055 373	59387.2852 126 843	72978.3707 196 481	89700.1943 636 545	102
52	56909.4088 543 162	70236.8315 273 136	86707.6922 520 139	107064.3201 089 546	104
53	66997.2638 385 223	83068.1152 859 745	103019.4991 646 177	127789.3809 180 434	106
54	78872.9389 223 044	98243.1132 186 783	122399.5569 574 823	152525.9067 783 615	108
55	92853.2805 228 099	116189.9193 675 275	145425.0036 211 847	182050.3418 222 307	110
56	109311.2881 634 648	137414.8218 270 024	172781.5368 023 295	217289.4157 965 599	112
57	128686.0662 082 349	162516.5853 763 409	205283.8338 748 477	259349.2327 828 327	114
58	151494.5392 919 893	192203.3429 239 881	243899.8130 267 065	309549.9902 206 549	116
59	178345.2440 180 121	227312.5722 799 478	289779.4578 570 300	369467.4180 153 016	118
60	209954.5648 891 043	268834.7218 104 570	344289.0638 799 374	440982.2384 435 258	120

144

Table 2.   FUTURE WORTH OF ONE DOLLAR PER PERIOD WITH INTEREST PAYABLE AT END OF EACH PERIOD

HALF YEARS	19% NOMINAL ANNUAL RATE	19½% NOMINAL ANNUAL RATE	20% NOMINAL ANNUAL RATE	20½% NOMINAL ANNUAL RATE	HALF YEARS
1	1.0000 000 000	1.0000 000 000	1.0000 000 000	1.0000 000 000	1
YEARS					
1	2.0950 000 000	2.0975 000 000	2.1000 000 000	2.1025 000 000	2
2	4.6069 573 750	4.6239 518 594	4.6410 000 000	4.6581 018 906	4
3	7.6188 570 666	7.6670 789 143	7.7156 100 000	7.7644 519 612	6
4	11.2302 000 942	11.3325 444 715	11.4358 881 000	11.5402 398 867	8
5	15.5602 906 680	15.7476 206 444	15.9374 246 010	16.1297 337 087	10
6	20.7521 775 182	21.0656 074 888	21.3842 837 672	21.7082 921 338	12
7	26.9773 796 487	27.4711 558 803	27.9749 833 583	28.4890 647 655	14
8	34.4415 526 333	35.1866 789 525	35.9497 298 636	36.7311 362 791	16
9	43.3912 826 462	44.4800 747 150	45.5991 731 349	46.7494 257 168	18
10	54.1222 326 748	55.6740 279 947	57.2749 994 933	58.9267 191 427	20
11	66.9889 100 329	69.1572 146 823	71.4027 493 868	73.7282 954 099	22
12	82.4163 778 522	85.3977 973 175	88.4973 267 581	91.7197 038 726	24
13	100.9142 974 543	104.9596 806 051	109.1817 653 773	113.5883 733 053	26
14	123.0937 655 051	128.5220 912 869	134.2099 361 065	140.1698 776 799	28
15	149.6875 021 848	156.9031 622 181	164.4940 226 889	172.4798 623 817	30
16	181.5740 573 071	191.0883 395 365	201.1377 674 535	211.7528 507 241	32
17	219.8068 340 627	232.2645 992 738	245.4766 986 188	259.4894 135 104	34
18	265.6488 892 120	281.8616 614 791	299.1268 053 287	317.5135 039 308	36
19	320.6146 593 874	341.6016 328 869	364.0434 344 477	388.0021 484 873	38
20	386.5199 919 720	413.5588 018 225	442.5925 556 818	473.7701 567 497	40
21	465.5421 333 742	500.2316 615 377	537.6369 923 749	577.9730 865 927	42
22	560.2916 564 690	604.6296 627 700	652.6407 607 737	704.6323 990 852	44
23	673.8987 033 977	730.3777 077 419	791.7953 205 361	858.5875 850 406	46
24	810.1163 928 415	881.8420 138 358	960.1723 378 487	1045.7210 757 893	48
25	973.4448 079 267	1064.2817 171 778	1163.9085 287 970	1273.1830 033 786	50
26	1169.2796 608 244	1284.0314 801 014	1410.4293 198 443	1549.6643 980 004	52
27	1404.0905 453 199	1548.7214 429 789	1708.7194 770 116	1885.7292 611 720	54
28	1685.6346 661 022	1867.5421 575 770	2069.6505 671 841	2294.2182 027 625	56
29	2023.2131 055 232	2251.5637 009 400	2506.3771 862 927	2790.7390 643 215	58
30	2427.9780 938 500	2714.1200 500 554	3034.8163 954 142	3394.2632 748 020	60
31	2913.3014 339 785	3271.2720 635 420	3674.2278 384 512	4127.8507 246 673	62
32	3495.2162 518 760	3942.3651 459 868	4447.9156 845 259	5019.5308 549 001	64
33	4192.9466 664 057	4750.7009 581 233	5384.0779 782 763	6103.3736 261 989	66
34	5029.5428 766 871	5724.3464 959 404	6516.8343 537 144	7420.7912 887 299	68
35	6032.6426 477 197	6897.1086 315 259	7887.4695 679 944	9022.1206 913 968	70
36	7235.3843 506 821	8309.7079 536 019	9545.9381 772 732	10968.5465 886 471	72
37	8677.5017 210 766	10011.1926 657 881	11552.6851 945 006	13334.4394 319 167	74
38	10406.6365 011 139	12060.6416 358 960	13980.8490 853 457	16210.1969 697 412	76
39	12479.9123 307 481	14529.2157 294 469	16918.9273 932 683	19705.6982 304 515	78
40	14965.8218 823 753	17502.6286 537 171	20474.0021 458 547	23954.5018 597 278	80
41	17946.4895 825 150	21084.1231 048 314	24775.6425 964 841	29118.9492 261 357	82
42	21520.3846 716 750	25398.0555 555 388	29980.6275 417 458	35396.3672 778 006	84
43	25805.5742 309 552	30594.2141 544 937	36278.6593 255 124	43026.6081 534 621	86
44	30943.6236 422 710	36853.0196 629 262	43899.2777 838 700	52301.2136 268 342	88
45	37104.2733 376 740	44391.7900 153 675	53120.2261 184 827	63574.5545 460 021	90
46	44491.0463 387 046	53472.2860 221 977	64277.5736 033 641	77277.3708 916 315	92
47	53347.9718 362 653	64409.8002 155 248	77777.9640 600 706	93933.2298 023 462	94
48	63967.6469 309 779	77584.1044 208 509	94113.4365 126 854	114178.5304 074 380	96
49	76700.9028 614 158	93452.6361 755 676	113879.3581 803 493	138786.8198 260 560	98
50	91968.3950 534 091	112566.3818 524 472	137796.1233 982 227	168698.3494 161 950	100
51	110274.4998 789 139	135589.0079 811 593	166735.4093 118 494	205056.0005 800 688	102
52	132223.9772 173 147	163319.9050 446 062	201751.9452 673 378	249248.9528 050 773	104
53	158541.9492 829 908	196721.9438 756 347	244121.9537 734 788	302965.7624 405 265	106
54	190097.8557 390 380	236956.9084 103 512	295389.6640 659 093	368258.8802 824 752	108
55	227934.1764 775 000	285415.7656 484 456	357423.5935 197 502	447623.0731 013 503	110
56	273300.8709 509 345	343787.1710 720 880	432484.6481 588 978	544090.7454 988 982	112
57	327696.6717 919 442	414095.8937 261 492	523308.5242 722 663	661347.8042 210 701	114
58	392918.5968 953 359	498783.1895 924 825	633205.4143 694 423	803874.4919 544 871	116
59	471121.3156 424 301	600789.5667 590 802	766180.6513 870 251	977116.5716 862 538	118
60	564888.3304 881 648	723656.8855 961 043	927080.6881 783 004	1187693.4023 632 145	120

Table 2. FUTURE WORTH OF ONE DOLLAR PER PERIOD WITH INTEREST PAYABLE AT END OF EACH PERIOD

HALF YEARS	21% NOMINAL ANNUAL RATE	21½% NOMINAL ANNUAL RATE	22% NOMINAL ANNUAL RATE	22½% NOMINAL ANNUAL RATE	HALF YEARS
1	1.0000 000 000	1.0000 000 000	1.0000 000 000	1.0000 000 000	1
YEARS					
1	2.1050 000 000	2.1075 000 000	2.1100 000 000	2.1125 000 000	2
2	4.6752 576 250	4.6924 672 969	4.7097 310 000	4.7270 488 281	4
3	7.8136 064 416	7.8630 750 909	7.9128 595 651	7.9629 615 262	6
4	11.6456 088 053	11.7520 038 970	11.8594 342 702	11.9679 091 014	8
5	16.3245 794 915	16.5219 938 298	16.7220 089 643	16.9246 574 988	10
6	22.0377 196 736	22.3726 547 945	22.7131 872 449	23.0594 081 325	12
7	29.0136 066 645	29.5488 195 672	30.0949 180 044	30.6521 205 964	14
8	37.5313 390 775	38.3507 893 203	39.1899 484 732	40.0492 886 319	16
9	47.9317 032 971	49.1469 003 333	50.3959 355 139	51.6797 523 834	18
10	60.6308 080 183	62.3889 377 719	64.2028 321 466	66.0742 685 357	20
11	76.1367 323 606	78.6310 415 550	81.2143 094 879	83.8897 314 174	22
12	95.0698 536 306	98.5528 954 633	102.1741 507 200	105.9391 503 996	24
13	118.1876 680 293	122.9881 698 861	127.9987 711 021	133.2287 516 118	26
14	146.4150 973 555	152.9594 084 498	159.8172 858 749	167.0038 971 120	28
15	180.8814 942 485	189.7208 184 304	199.0208 779 265	208.8059 170 350	30
16	222.9658 265 147	234.8107 556 010	247.3236 236 932	260.5424 482 554	32
17	274.3518 483 201	290.1160 998 496	306.8374 367 524	324.5744 894 736	34
18	337.0954 655 951	357.9512 154 962	380.1644 058 226	403.8241 454 875	36
19	413.7069 908 783	441.1548 005 619	470.5105 644 141	501.9079 775 635	38
20	507.2515 785 371	543.2086 778 467	581.8260 664 146	623.3020 453 563	40
21	621.4718 586 833	668.3834 988 671	718.9778 964 294	773.5461 720 731	42
22	760.9376 762 488	821.9174 579 323	887.9626 661 906	959.4967 545 298	44
23	931.2289 261 417	1010.2354 950 110	1096.1688 010 135	1189.6396 550 985	46
24	1139.1587 995 421	1241.2181 603 776	1352.6995 797 287	1474.4774 543 805	48
25	1393.0463 732 109	1524.5313 922 246	1668.7711 521 837	1827.0087 368 982	50
26	1703.0494 478 499	1872.0310 074 543	2058.2029 366 056	2263.3212 820 266	52
27	2081.5709 520 609	2298.2588 323 869	2538.0218 381 917	2803.3262 304 582	54
28	2543.7551 717 401	2821.0512 349 819	3129.2067 068 360	3471.6667 299 156	56
29	3108.0936 585 740	3462.2855 238 372	3857.6055 834 927	4298.8425 261 971	58
30	3797.1650 594 603	4248.7954 485 471	4755.0658 394 213	5322.6018 203 136	60
31	4638.5384 667 276	5213.4941 123 870	5860.8266 207 510	6589.6639 091 725	62
32	5665.8764 313 360	6396.7512 878 865	7223.2344 794 273	8157.8512 225 868	64
33	6920.2817 695 721	7848.0827 718 527	8901.8572 021 024	10098.7280 522 047	66
34	8451.9420 476 917	9628.2224 743 332	10970.0882 587 104	12500.8663 908 614	68
35	10322.1375 387 828	11811.6639 522 839	13518.3557 435 571	15473.8879 190 646	70
36	12605.6929 882 922	14489.7777 435 735	16658.0761 116 367	19153.4665 948 298	72
37	15393.9712 810 295	17774.6349 524 910	20526.5255 771 475	23707.5201 402 573	74
38	18798.5287 834 191	21803.6970 924 043	25292.8421 636 035	29343.8729 735 903	76
39	22955.5786 077 743	26745.5684 418 468	31165.4208 297 759	36319.7402 849 702	78
40	28031.4403 695 576	32807.0516 321 499	38401.0250 043 668	44953.4660 620 701	80
41	34229.1944 772 391	40241.8017 234 862	47316.0129 078 804	55639.0507 308 840	82
42	41796.8071 865 708	49360.9409 152 028	58300.1695 037 994	68864.1313 811 456	84
43	51037.0514 949 896	60546.0780 854 227	71833.7488 456 313	85232.2351 046 960	86
44	62319.6208 016 612	74265.2779 886 632	88508.4719 527 023	105490.3209 787 964	88
45	76095.9199 893 483	91092.6483 749 823	109053.3982 929 245	130562.8675 739 135	90
46	92917.1257 049 940	111732.3646 933 869	134366.8020 367 123	161594.0615 707 764	92
47	113456.2384 139 404	137048.1377 419 530	165555.4467 894 332	200000.0127 659 562	94
48	138535.0085 093 815	168099.3573 982 533	203982.9759 892 606	247533.3782 998 655	96
49	169156.8137 651 676	206185.4249 378 114	251329.5347 163 680	306363.3452 364 429	98
50	206546.8035 276 137	252900.1291 163 784	309665.2297 240 370	379174.6215 027 912	100
51	252200.9157 773 045	310198.3414 935 009	381540.6395 429 860	469289.9526 443 140	102
52	307945.7281 869 833	380477.8219 984 879	470098.3319 809 131	580821.7554 524 392	104
53	376011.5377 595 113	466679.5580 586 328	579210.2648 336 830	718859.7882 716 829	106
54	459121.5928 928 072	572410.8361 840 539	713647.0773 015 808	889703.4223 281 251	108
55	560601.0479 619 400	702096.1961 892 775	879286.6739 432 777	1101149.1137 907 936	110
56	684509.9995 877 277	861162.5850 231 844	1083371.2209 665 125	1362846.1953 651 368	112
57	835805.9272 466 052	1056266.4584 435 150	1334823.7913 516 079	1686737.2239 823 826	114
58	1020542.0373 162 862	1295572.3337 692 587	1644638.5033 243 161	2087602.9798 694 457	116
59	1246109.4461 141 183	1589094.4508 117 703	2026361.2099 458 898	2583736.9880 540 436	118
60	1521532.8914 414 918	1949115.8379 834 944	2496681.7567 743 308	3197780.3441 212 625	120

Table 3.   SINKING FUND FACTORS
PAYABLE AT END OF EACH PERIOD

HALF YEARS	5% NOMINAL ANNUAL RATE	5½% NOMINAL ANNUAL RATE	6% NOMINAL ANNUAL RATE	6½% NOMINAL ANNUAL RATE	HALF YEARS
1	1.0000 000 000	1.0000 000 000	1.0000 000 000	1.0000 000 000	1
YEARS					
1	0.4938 271 605	0.4932 182 491	0.4926 108 374	0.4920 049 200	2
2	0.2408 178 777	0.2399 205 884	0.2390 270 452	0.2381 372 337	4
3	0.1565 499 711	0.1555 708 264	0.1545 975 005	0.1536 299 692	6
4	0.1144 673 458	0.1134 579 478	0.1124 563 888	0.1114 626 337	8
5	0.0892 587 632	0.0882 397 205	0.0872 305 066	0.0862 310 724	10
6	0.0724 871 270	0.0714 687 098	0.0704 620 855	0.0694 671 878	12
7	0.0605 365 249	0.0595 245 664	0.0585 263 390	0.0575 417 561	14
8	0.0515 989 886	0.0505 970 977	0.0496 108 493	0.0486 401 319	16
9	0.0446 700 805	0.0436 806 259	0.0427 086 959	0.0417 541 496	18
10	0.0391 471 287	0.0381 717 306	0.0372 157 076	0.0362 788 839	20
11	0.0346 466 061	0.0336 864 049	0.0327 473 948	0.0318 293 596	22
12	0.0309 128 204	0.0299 686 330	0.0290 474 159	0.0281 489 063	24
13	0.0277 687 467	0.0268 411 636	0.0259 382 903	0.0250 598 109	26
14	0.0250 879 327	0.0241 773 795	0.0232 932 334	0.0224 351 193	28
15	0.0227 776 407	0.0218 844 200	0.0210 192 593	0.0201 817 169	30
16	0.0207 683 123	0.0198 926 322	0.0190 466 183	0.0182 297 552	32
17	0.0190 067 508	0.0181 487 453	0.0173 219 633	0.0165 258 003	34
18	0.0174 515 767	0.0166 113 206	0.0158 037 942	0.0150 283 128	36
19	0.0160 701 180	0.0152 476 374	0.0144 593 401	0.0137 044 456	38
20	0.0148 362 332	0.0140 315 144	0.0132 623 779	0.0125 279 400	40
21	0.0137 287 567	0.0129 417 522	0.0121 916 731	0.0114 775 251	42
22	0.0127 303 683	0.0119 610 021	0.0112 298 469	0.0105 357 906	44
23	0.0118 267 568	0.0110 749 283	0.0103 625 378	0.0096 883 484	46
24	0.0110 059 938	0.0102 715 811	0.0095 777 738	0.0089 232 032	48
25	0.0102 580 569	0.0095 409 195	0.0088 654 944	0.0082 302 745	50
26	0.0095 744 635	0.0088 744 446	0.0082 171 837	0.0076 010 288	52
27	0.0089 479 856	0.0082 649 139	0.0076 255 841	0.0070 281 935	54
28	0.0083 724 260	0.0077 061 174	0.0070 844 726	0.0065 055 322	56
29	0.0078 424 404	0.0071 926 996	0.0065 884 819	0.0060 276 664	58
30	0.0073 533 959	0.0067 200 173	0.0061 329 587	0.0055 899 328	60
31	0.0069 012 558	0.0062 840 249	0.0057 138 485	0.0051 882 685	62
32	0.0064 824 869	0.0058 811 810	0.0053 276 021	0.0048 191 174	64
33	0.0060 939 830	0.0055 083 724	0.0049 710 995	0.0044 793 534	66
34	0.0057 330 027	0.0051 628 513	0.0046 415 871	0.0041 662 182	68
35	0.0053 971 168	0.0048 421 829	0.0043 366 251	0.0038 772 684	70
36	0.0050 841 652	0.0045 442 024	0.0040 540 446	0.0036 103 320	72
37	0.0047 922 211	0.0042 669 784	0.0037 919 109	0.0033 634 724	74
38	0.0045 195 594	0.0040 087 826	0.0035 484 929	0.0031 349 575	76
39	0.0042 646 321	0.0037 680 634	0.0033 222 371	0.0029 232 334	78
40	0.0040 260 451	0.0035 434 245	0.0031 117 457	0.0027 269 026	80
41	0.0038 025 404	0.0033 336 055	0.0029 157 577	0.0025 447 051	82
42	0.0035 929 793	0.0031 374 664	0.0027 331 325	0.0023 755 020	84
43	0.0033 963 292	0.0029 539 731	0.0025 628 365	0.0022 182 617	86
44	0.0032 116 510	0.0027 821 858	0.0024 039 306	0.0020 720 479	88
45	0.0030 380 893	0.0026 212 487	0.0022 555 599	0.0019 360 091	90
46	0.0028 748 628	0.0024 703 805	0.0021 169 449	0.0018 093 692	92
47	0.0027 212 571	0.0023 288 670	0.0019 873 733	0.0016 914 200	94
48	0.0025 766 173	0.0021 960 540	0.0018 661 932	0.0015 815 142	96
49	0.0024 403 421	0.0020 713 411	0.0017 528 070	0.0014 790 588	98
50	0.0023 118 787	0.0019 541 767	0.0016 466 659	0.0013 835 102	100
51	0.0021 907 176	0.0018 440 529	0.0015 472 653	0.0012 943 693	102
52	0.0020 763 891	0.0017 405 017	0.0014 541 408	0.0012 111 771	104
53	0.0019 684 591	0.0016 430 908	0.0013 668 639	0.0011 335 112	106
54	0.0018 665 260	0.0015 514 211	0.0012 850 394	0.0010 609 823	108
55	0.0017 702 178	0.0014 651 228	0.0012 083 018	0.0009 932 313	110
56	0.0016 791 895	0.0013 838 535	0.0011 363 131	0.0009 299 266	112
57	0.0015 931 206	0.0013 072 956	0.0010 687 603	0.0008 707 615	114
58	0.0015 117 132	0.0012 351 542	0.0010 053 531	0.0008 154 526	116
59	0.0014 346 901	0.0011 671 552	0.0009 458 222	0.0007 637 372	118
60	0.0013 617 930	0.0011 030 433	0.0008 899 176	0.0007 153 719	120

147

Table 3.   SINKING FUND FACTORS
PAYABLE AT END OF EACH PERIOD

HALF YEARS	7% NOMINAL ANNUAL RATE	7½% NOMINAL ANNUAL RATE	8% NOMINAL ANNUAL RATE	8½% NOMINAL ANNUAL RATE	HALF YEARS
1	1.0000 000 000	1.0000 000 000	1.0000 000 000	1.0000 000 000	1
YEARS					
1	0.4914 004 914	0.4907 975 460	0.4901 960 784	0.4895 960 832	2
2	0.2372 511 395	0.2363 687 482	0.2354 900 454	0.2346 150 167	4
3	0.1526 682 087	0.1517 121 945	0.1507 619 025	0.1498 173 083	6
4	0.1104 766 465	0.1094 983 915	0.1085 278 320	0.1075 649 316	8
5	0.0852 413 679	0.0842 613 423	0.0832 909 443	0.0823 301 217	10
6	0.0684 839 493	0.0675 123 010	0.0665 521 727	0.0656 034 928	12
7	0.0565 707 287	0.0556 131 655	0.0546 689 731	0.0537 380 557	14
8	0.0476 848 306	0.0467 448 270	0.0458 199 992	0.0449 102 226	16
9	0.0408 168 408	0.0398 966 188	0.0389 933 281	0.0381 068 090	18
10	0.0353 610 768	0.0344 620 973	0.0335 817 503	0.0327 198 348	20
11	0.0309 320 742	0.0300 553 051	0.0291 988 111	0.0283 623 433	22
12	0.0272 728 303	0.0264 189 033	0.0255 868 313	0.0247 763 108	24
13	0.0242 053 963	0.0233 747 042	0.0225 673 805	0.0217 830 600	26
14	0.0216 026 452	0.0207 954 043	0.0200 129 752	0.0192 549 240	28
15	0.0193 713 316	0.0185 876 242	0.0178 300 991	0.0170 982 464	30
16	0.0174 415 048	0.0166 813 087	0.0159 485 897	0.0152 427 548	32
17	0.0157 596 583	0.0150 228 679	0.0143 147 715	0.0136 346 857	34
18	0.0142 841 628	0.0135 706 050	0.0128 868 780	0.0122 322 015	36
19	0.0129 821 414	0.0122 915 872	0.0116 319 191	0.0110 022 538	38
20	0.0118 272 823	0.0111 594 563	0.0105 234 893	0.0099 183 886	40
21	0.0107 982 765	0.0101 528 644	0.0095 402 007	0.0089 591 782	42
22	0.0098 776 816	0.0092 543 358	0.0086 645 444	0.0081 070 805	44
23	0.0090 510 817	0.0084 494 269	0.0078 820 488	0.0073 475 964	46
24	0.0083 064 580	0.0077 260 947	0.0071 806 476	0.0066 686 377	48
25	0.0076 337 096	0.0070 742 185	0.0065 502 004	0.0060 600 458	50
26	0.0070 242 854	0.0064 852 301	0.0059 821 236	0.0055 132 229	52
27	0.0064 708 970	0.0059 518 278	0.0054 691 025	0.0050 208 438	54
28	0.0059 672 981	0.0054 677 509	0.0050 048 662	0.0045 766 300	56
29	0.0055 080 966	0.0050 276 006	0.0045 840 087	0.0041 751 706	58
30	0.0050 886 213	0.0046 266 973	0.0042 018 451	0.0038 117 784	60
31	0.0047 048 020	0.0042 609 653	0.0038 542 964	0.0034 823 743	62
32	0.0043 530 765	0.0039 268 386	0.0035 377 955	0.0031 833 932	64
33	0.0040 303 148	0.0036 211 846	0.0032 492 100	0.0029 117 067	66
34	0.0037 337 550	0.0033 412 407	0.0029 857 795	0.0026 645 597	68
35	0.0034 609 517	0.0030 845 619	0.0027 450 623	0.0024 395 176	70
36	0.0032 097 323	0.0028 489 770	0.0025 248 919	0.0022 344 223	72
37	0.0029 781 601	0.0026 325 521	0.0023 233 403	0.0020 473 553	74
38	0.0027 645 038	0.0024 335 598	0.0021 386 869	0.0018 766 067	76
39	0.0025 672 117	0.0022 504 525	0.0019 693 922	0.0017 206 484	78
40	0.0023 848 887	0.0020 818 410	0.0018 140 755	0.0015 781 123	80
41	0.0022 162 781	0.0019 264 747	0.0016 714 957	0.0014 477 702	82
42	0.0020 602 452	0.0017 832 256	0.0015 405 351	0.0013 285 180	84
43	0.0019 157 629	0.0016 510 743	0.0014 201 848	0.0012 193 611	86
44	0.0017 819 002	0.0015 290 977	0.0013 095 329	0.0011 194 021	88
45	0.0016 578 111	0.0014 164 584	0.0012 077 538	0.0010 278 300	90
46	0.0015 427 259	0.0013 123 956	0.0011 140 984	0.0009 439 110	92
47	0.0014 359 428	0.0012 162 168	0.0010 278 867	0.0008 669 802	94
48	0.0013 368 213	0.0011 272 913	0.0009 485 002	0.0007 964 344	96
49	0.0012 447 758	0.0010 450 431	0.0008 753 757	0.0007 317 257	98
50	0.0011 592 702	0.0009 689 464	0.0008 080 000	0.0006 723 562	100
51	0.0010 798 131	0.0008 985 200	0.0007 459 047	0.0006 178 725	102
52	0.0010 059 536	0.0008 333 233	0.0006 886 620	0.0005 678 618	104
53	0.0009 372 773	0.0007 729 525	0.0006 358 808	0.0005 219 481	106
54	0.0008 734 032	0.0007 170 371	0.0005 872 033	0.0004 797 880	108
55	0.0008 139 807	0.0006 652 370	0.0005 423 018	0.0004 410 683	110
56	0.0007 586 865	0.0006 172 394	0.0005 008 762	0.0004 055 028	112
57	0.0007 072 227	0.0005 727 569	0.0004 626 512	0.0003 728 300	114
58	0.0006 593 142	0.0005 315 248	0.0004 273 741	0.0003 428 109	116
59	0.0006 147 069	0.0004 932 994	0.0003 948 131	0.0003 152 265	118
60	0.0005 731 662	0.0004 578 561	0.0003 647 553	0.0002 898 768	120

Table 3.   SINKING FUND FACTORS
PAYABLE AT END OF EACH PERIOD

HALF YEARS	9% NOMINAL ANNUAL RATE	9½% NOMINAL ANNUAL RATE	10% NOMINAL ANNUAL RATE	10½% NOMINAL ANNUAL RATE	HALF YEARS
1	1.0000 000 000	1.0000 000 000	1.0000 000 000	1.0000 000 000	1
YEARS					
1	0.4889 975 550	0.4884 004 884	0.4878 048 780	0.4872 107 186	2
2	0.2337 436 479	0.2328 759 246	0.2320 118 326	0.2311 513 576	4
3	0.1488 783 875	0.1479 451 156	0.1470 174 681	0.1460 954 203	6
4	0.1066 096 533	0.1056 619 598	0.1047 218 136	0.1037 891 770	8
5	0.0813 788 217	0.0804 369 909	0.0795 045 750	0.0785 815 194	10
6	0.0646 661 886	0.0637 401 861	0.0628 254 100	0.0619 217 842	12
7	0.0528 203 160	0.0519 156 544	0.0510 239 695	0.0501 451 581	14
8	0.0440 153 694	0.0431 353 090	0.0422 699 080	0.0414 190 304	16
9	0.0372 368 975	0.0363 834 258	0.0355 462 223	0.0347 251 119	18
10	0.0318 761 443	0.0310 504 673	0.0302 425 872	0.0294 522 832	20
11	0.0275 456 461	0.0267 484 572	0.0259 705 086	0.0252 115 264	22
12	0.0239 870 299	0.0232 186 689	0.0224 709 008	0.0217 433 921	24
13	0.0210 213 674	0.0202 819 186	0.0195 643 207	0.0188 681 737	26
14	0.0185 208 051	0.0178 101 623	0.0171 225 304	0.0164 574 362	28
15	0.0163 915 429	0.0157 094 539	0.0150 514 351	0.0144 169 335	30
16	0.0145 631 962	0.0139 092 942	0.0132 804 189	0.0126 759 322	32
17	0.0129 819 119	0.0123 557 388	0.0117 554 454	0.0111 803 028	34
18	0.0116 057 796	0.0110 068 041	0.0104 344 571	0.0098 879 146	36
19	0.0104 016 920	0.0098 293 231	0.0092 842 282	0.0087 654 839	38
20	0.0093 431 466	0.0087 967 454	0.0082 781 612	0.0077 863 683	40
21	0.0084 086 759	0.0078 875 648	0.0073 947 131	0.0069 289 905	42
22	0.0075 807 056	0.0070 841 765	0.0066 162 506	0.0061 756 919	44
23	0.0068 447 107	0.0063 720 312	0.0059 282 036	0.0055 118 853	46
24	0.0061 885 821	0.0057 390 022	0.0053 184 306	0.0049 254 187	48
25	0.0056 021 459	0.0051 749 023	0.0047 767 355	0.0044 060 917	50
26	0.0050 767 923	0.0046 711 140	0.0042 944 966	0.0039 452 836	52
27	0.0046 051 886	0.0042 203 000	0.0038 643 770	0.0035 356 631	54
28	0.0041 810 518	0.0038 161 771	0.0034 800 978	0.0031 709 607	56
29	0.0037 989 695	0.0034 533 356	0.0031 362 568	0.0028 457 878	58
30	0.0034 542 558	0.0031 270 953	0.0028 281 845	0.0025 554 911	60
31	0.0031 428 356	0.0028 333 891	0.0025 518 273	0.0022 960 358	62
32	0.0028 611 494	0.0025 686 682	0.0023 036 520	0.0020 639 102	64
33	0.0026 060 769	0.0023 298 248	0.0020 805 683	0.0018 560 470	66
34	0.0023 748 725	0.0021 141 277	0.0018 798 643	0.0016 697 590	68
35	0.0021 651 129	0.0019 191 690	0.0016 991 530	0.0015 026 853	70
36	0.0019 746 524	0.0017 428 204	0.0015 363 280	0.0013 527 462	72
37	0.0018 015 863	0.0015 831 953	0.0013 895 254	0.0012 181 056	74
38	0.0016 442 194	0.0014 386 173	0.0012 570 925	0.0010 971 390	76
39	0.0015 010 391	0.0013 075 940	0.0011 375 610	0.0009 884 063	78
40	0.0013 706 935	0.0011 887 937	0.0010 296 235	0.0008 906 287	80
41	0.0012 519 715	0.0010 810 259	0.0009 321 143	0.0008 026 688	82
42	0.0011 437 861	0.0009 832 248	0.0008 439 924	0.0007 235 137	84
43	0.0010 451 606	0.0008 944 348	0.0007 643 265	0.0006 522 600	86
44	0.0009 552 152	0.0008 137 976	0.0006 922 828	0.0005 881 011	88
45	0.0008 731 573	0.0007 405 414	0.0006 271 136	0.0005 303 161	90
46	0.0007 982 710	0.0006 739 715	0.0005 681 481	0.0004 782 600	92
47	0.0007 299 095	0.0006 134 620	0.0005 147 832	0.0004 313 554	94
48	0.0006 674 877	0.0005 584 480	0.0004 664 770	0.0003 890 846	96
49	0.0006 104 754	0.0005 084 196	0.0004 227 418	0.0003 509 836	98
50	0.0005 583 922	0.0004 629 162	0.0003 831 381	0.0003 166 360	100
51	0.0005 108 023	0.0004 215 211	0.0003 472 701	0.0002 856 678	102
52	0.0004 673 100	0.0003 838 573	0.0003 147 810	0.0002 577 433	104
53	0.0004 275 556	0.0003 495 834	0.0002 853 486	0.0002 325 604	106
54	0.0003 912 122	0.0003 183 901	0.0002 586 824	0.0002 098 478	108
55	0.0003 579 825	0.0002 899 970	0.0002 345 197	0.0001 893 614	110
56	0.0003 275 957	0.0002 641 499	0.0002 126 236	0.0001 708 814	112
57	0.0002 998 052	0.0002 406 182	0.0001 927 796	0.0001 542 102	114
58	0.0002 743 866	0.0002 191 924	0.0001 747 942	0.0001 391 698	116
59	0.0002 511 350	0.0001 996 824	0.0001 584 919	0.0001 255 997	118
60	0.0002 298 637	0.0001 819 156	0.0001 437 145	0.0001 133 557	120

Table 3.   SINKING FUND FACTORS
PAYABLE AT END OF EACH PERIOD

HALF YEARS	**11%** NOMINAL ANNUAL RATE	**11½%** NOMINAL ANNUAL RATE	**12%** NOMINAL ANNUAL RATE	**12½%** NOMINAL ANNUAL RATE	HALF YEARS
1	1.0000 000 000	1.0000 000 000	1.0000 000 000	1.0000 000 000	1
YEARS					
1	0.4866 180 049	0.4860 267 315	0.4854 368 932	0.4848 484 848	2
2	0.2302 944 853	0.2294 412 017	0.2285 914 924	0.2277 453 433	4
3	0.1451 789 476	0.1442 680 253	0.1433 626 285	0.1424 627 324	6
4	0.1028 640 118	0.1019 462 799	0.1010 359 426	0.1001 329 614	8
5	0.0776 677 687	0.0767 632 671	0.0758 679 582	0.0749 817 850	10
6	0.0610 292 312	0.0601 476 727	0.0592 770 294	0.0584 172 209	12
7	0.0492 791 154	0.0484 257 351	0.0475 849 090	0.0467 565 278	14
8	0.0405 825 380	0.0397 602 900	0.0389 521 436	0.0381 579 538	16
9	0.0339 199 163	0.0331 304 539	0.0323 565 406	0.0315 979 892	18
10	0.0286 793 300	0.0279 234 988	0.0271 845 570	0.0264 622 687	20
11	0.0244 712 319	0.0237 493 418	0.0230 455 685	0.0223 596 209	22
12	0.0210 358 037	0.0203 477 910	0.0196 790 050	0.0190 290 926	24
13	0.0181 930 713	0.0175 386 012	0.0169 043 467	0.0162 898 870	26
14	0.0158 143 996	0.0151 929 348	0.0145 925 515	0.0140 127 561	28
15	0.0138 053 897	0.0132 162 386	0.0126 489 115	0.0121 028 369	30
16	0.0120 951 895	0.0115 375 417	0.0110 023 374	0.0104 889 235	32
17	0.0106 295 769	0.0101 025 304	0.0095 984 254	0.0091 165 250	34
18	0.0093 663 488	0.0088 689 312	0.0083 948 348	0.0079 432 368	36
19	0.0082 721 659	0.0078 033 517	0.0073 581 240	0.0069 355 731	38
20	0.0073 203 434	0.0068 790 687	0.0064 615 359	0.0060 667 487	40
21	0.0064 892 731	0.0060 744 478	0.0056 834 152	0.0053 150 939	42
22	0.0057 612 757	0.0053 717 934	0.0050 060 565	0.0046 629 004	44
23	0.0051 217 512	0.0047 564 988	0.0044 148 527	0.0040 955 681	46
24	0.0045 585 424	0.0042 164 076	0.0038 976 549	0.0036 009 636	48
25	0.0040 614 501	0.0037 413 281	0.0034 442 864	0.0031 689 327	50
26	0.0036 218 603	0.0033 226 596	0.0030 461 669	0.0027 909 239	52
27	0.0032 324 534	0.0029 531 008	0.0026 960 209	0.0024 596 952	54
28	0.0028 869 756	0.0026 264 207	0.0023 876 472	0.0021 690 828	56
29	0.0025 800 578	0.0023 372 760	0.0021 157 359	0.0019 138 178	58
30	0.0023 070 692	0.0020 810 653	0.0018 757 215	0.0016 893 780	60
31	0.0020 640 001	0.0018 538 103	0.0016 636 642	0.0014 918 687	62
32	0.0018 473 659	0.0016 520 600	0.0014 761 528	0.0013 179 247	64
33	0.0016 541 284	0.0014 728 110	0.0013 102 248	0.0011 646 308	66
34	0.0014 816 307	0.0013 134 424	0.0011 633 009	0.0010 294 548	68
35	0.0013 275 431	0.0011 716 612	0.0010 331 302	0.0009 101 927	70
36	0.0011 898 180	0.0010 454 569	0.0009 177 439	0.0008 049 222	72
37	0.0010 666 516	0.0009 330 627	0.0008 154 168	0.0007 119 636	74
38	0.0009 564 521	0.0008 329 236	0.0007 246 347	0.0006 298 475	76
39	0.0008 578 119	0.0007 436 685	0.0006 440 667	0.0005 572 859	78
40	0.0007 694 845	0.0006 640 868	0.0005 725 410	0.0004 931 491	80
41	0.0006 903 644	0.0005 931 080	0.0005 090 251	0.0004 364 447	82
42	0.0006 194 699	0.0005 297 847	0.0004 526 081	0.0003 863 004	84
43	0.0005 559 284	0.0004 732 771	0.0004 024 856	0.0003 419 487	86
44	0.0004 989 631	0.0004 228 407	0.0003 579 467	0.0003 027 135	88
45	0.0004 478 820	0.0003 778 142	0.0003 183 623	0.0002 679 994	90
46	0.0004 020 682	0.0003 376 103	0.0002 831 761	0.0002 372 812	92
47	0.0003 609 712	0.0003 017 070	0.0002 518 949	0.0002 100 957	94
48	0.0003 240 994	0.0002 696 395	0.0002 240 821	0.0001 860 342	96
49	0.0002 910 137	0.0002 409 947	0.0001 993 504	0.0001 647 355	98
50	0.0002 613 216	0.0002 154 042	0.0001 773 563	0.0001 458 810	100
51	0.0002 346 718	0.0001 925 401	0.0001 577 952	0.0001 291 889	102
52	0.0002 107 501	0.0001 721 102	0.0001 403 965	0.0001 144 102	104
53	0.0001 892 753	0.0001 538 539	0.0001 249 202	0.0001 013 249	106
54	0.0001 699 955	0.0001 375 387	0.0001 111 531	0.0000 897 383	108
55	0.0001 526 849	0.0001 229 573	0.0000 989 057	0.0000 794 783	110
56	0.0001 371 415	0.0001 099 247	0.0000 880 098	0.0000 703 927	112
57	0.0001 231 839	0.0000 982 758	0.0000 783 157	0.0000 623 468	114
58	0.0001 106 497	0.0000 878 633	0.0000 696 907	0.0000 552 213	116
59	0.0000 993 932	0.0000 785 555	0.0000 620 166	0.0000 489 108	118
60	0.0000 892 837	0.0000 702 349	0.0000 551 883	0.0000 433 220	120

Table 3.   SINKING FUND FACTORS
PAYABLE AT END OF EACH PERIOD

HALF YEARS	13% NOMINAL ANNUAL RATE	13½% NOMINAL ANNUAL RATE	14% NOMINAL ANNUAL RATE	14½% NOMINAL ANNUAL RATE	HALF YEARS
1	1.0000 000 000	1.0000 000 000	1.0000 000 000	1.0000 000 000	1
YEARS					
1	0.4842 615 012	0.4836 759 371	0.4830 917 874	0.4825 090 470	2
2	0.2269 027 404	0.2260 636 696	0.2252 281 167	0.2243 960 677	4
3	0.1415 683 122	0.1406 793 430	0.1397 957 998	0.1389 176 575	6
4	0.0992 372 971	0.0983 489 106	0.0974 677 625	0.0965 938 133	8
5	0.0741 046 901	0.0732 366 154	0.0723 775 027	0.0715 272 931	10
6	0.0575 681 661	0.0567 297 830	0.0559 019 887	0.0550 846 995	12
7	0.0459 404 806	0.0451 366 553	0.0443 449 386	0.0435 652 161	14
8	0.0373 775 740	0.0366 108 553	0.0358 576 477	0.0351 177 994	16
9	0.0308 546 103	0.0301 262 124	0.0294 126 017	0.0287 135 825	18
10	0.0257 563 954	0.0250 666 956	0.0243 929 257	0.0237 348 402	20
11	0.0216 912 043	0.0210 400 217	0.0204 057 732	0.0197 881 574	22
12	0.0183 976 975	0.0177 844 606	0.0171 890 207	0.0166 110 150	24
13	0.0156 947 983	0.0151 186 545	0.0145 610 279	0.0140 214 900	26
14	0.0134 530 522	0.0129 129 423	0.0123 919 283	0.0118 895 127	28
15	0.0115 774 422	0.0110 721 549	0.0105 864 035	0.0101 196 190	30
16	0.0099 966 481	0.0095 248 610	0.0090 729 155	0.0086 401 700	32
17	0.0086 560 953	0.0082 164 072	0.0077 967 381	0.0073 963 736	34
18	0.0075 133 205	0.0071 042 775	0.0067 153 097	0.0063 456 308	36
19	0.0065 347 995	0.0061 549 164	0.0057 950 515	0.0054 543 489	38
20	0.0056 937 260	0.0053 415 040	0.0050 091 389	0.0046 957 084	40
21	0.0049 684 229	0.0046 423 647	0.0043 359 072	0.0040 480 660	42
22	0.0043 411 874	0.0040 398 096	0.0037 576 913	0.0034 937 906	44
23	0.0037 974 344	0.0035 192 782	0.0032 599 650	0.0030 184 011	46
24	0.0033 250 549	0.0030 686 946	0.0028 306 953	0.0026 099 179	48
25	0.0029 139 255	0.0026 779 758	0.0024 598 495	0.0022 583 683	50
26	0.0025 555 319	0.0023 386 536	0.0021 390 147	0.0019 554 044	52
27	0.0022 426 740	0.0020 435 785	0.0018 611 007	0.0016 940 045	54
28	0.0019 692 339	0.0017 866 863	0.0016 201 059	0.0014 682 379	56
29	0.0017 299 909	0.0015 628 130	0.0014 109 304	0.0012 730 763	58
30	0.0015 204 735	0.0013 675 449	0.0012 292 255	0.0011 042 434	60
31	0.0013 368 390	0.0011 970 977	0.0010 712 723	0.0009 580 915	62
32	0.0011 757 748	0.0010 482 180	0.0009 338 819	0.0008 315 021	64
33	0.0010 344 184	0.0009 181 015	0.0008 143 137	0.0007 218 028	66
34	0.0009 102 903	0.0008 043 260	0.0007 102 075	0.0006 266 997	68
35	0.0008 012 380	0.0007 047 954	0.0006 195 272	0.0005 442 204	70
36	0.0007 053 899	0.0006 176 925	0.0005 405 136	0.0004 726 662	72
37	0.0006 211 159	0.0005 414 397	0.0004 716 446	0.0004 105 729	74
38	0.0005 469 940	0.0004 746 658	0.0004 116 017	0.0003 566 765	76
39	0.0004 817 826	0.0004 161 772	0.0003 592 415	0.0003 098 852	78
40	0.0004 243 958	0.0003 649 343	0.0003 135 718	0.0002 692 551	80
41	0.0003 738 836	0.0003 200 306	0.0002 737 305	0.0002 339 692	82
42	0.0003 294 137	0.0002 806 750	0.0002 389 686	0.0002 033 204	84
43	0.0002 902 566	0.0002 461 766	0.0002 086 343	0.0001 766 962	86
44	0.0002 557 723	0.0002 159 320	0.0001 821 605	0.0001 535 658	88
45	0.0002 253 990	0.0001 894 136	0.0001 590 537	0.0001 334 688	90
46	0.0001 986 436	0.0001 661 599	0.0001 388 837	0.0001 160 061	92
47	0.0001 750 727	0.0001 457 671	0.0001 212 760	0.0001 008 313	94
48	0.0001 543 053	0.0001 278 819	0.0001 059 039	0.0000 876 439	96
49	0.0001 360 065	0.0001 121 947	0.0000 924 829	0.0000 761 831	98
50	0.0001 198 817	0.0000 984 347	0.0000 807 646	0.0000 662 223	100
51	0.0001 056 717	0.0000 863 644	0.0000 705 326	0.0000 575 649	102
52	0.0000 931 485	0.0000 757 759	0.0000 615 981	0.0000 500 401	104
53	0.0000 821 114	0.0000 664 868	0.0000 537 962	0.0000 434 995	106
54	0.0000 723 834	0.0000 583 375	0.0000 469 831	0.0000 378 143	108
55	0.0000 638 091	0.0000 511 877	0.0000 410 334	0.0000 328 724	110
56	0.0000 562 514	0.0000 449 148	0.0000 358 375	0.0000 285 767	112
57	0.0000 495 894	0.0000 394 111	0.0000 312 998	0.0000 248 425	114
58	0.0000 437 171	0.0000 345 821	0.0000 273 369	0.0000 215 964	116
59	0.0000 385 405	0.0000 303 451	0.0000 238 759	0.0000 187 745	118
60	0.0000 339 772	0.0000 266 274	0.0000 208 533	0.0000 163 215	120

Table 3.   SINKING FUND FACTORS
             PAYABLE AT END OF EACH PERIOD

HALF YEARS	**15%** NOMINAL ANNUAL RATE	**15½%** NOMINAL ANNUAL RATE	**16%** NOMINAL ANNUAL RATE	**16½%** NOMINAL ANNUAL RATE	HALF YEARS
1	1.0000 000 000	1.0000 000 000	1.0000 000 000	1.0000 000 000	1

YEARS					
1	0.4819 277 108	0.4813 477 738	0.4807 692 308	0.4801 920 768	2
2	0.2235 675 087	0.2227 424 256	0.2219 208 045	0.2211 026 314	4
3	0.1380 448 912	0.1371 774 758	0.1363 153 862	0.1354 585 973	6
4	0.0957 270 232	0.0948 673 523	0.0940 147 606	0.0931 692 077	8
5	0.0706 859 274	0.0698 533 459	0.0690 294 887	0.0682 142 953	10
6	0.0542 778 313	0.0534 482 990	0.0526 950 169	0.0519 188 989	12
7	0.0427 973 721	0.0420 412 901	0.0412 968 528	0.0405 639 419	14
8	0.0343 911 571	0.0336 775 665	0.0329 768 720	0.0322 889 169	16
9	0.0280 289 578	0.0273 585 289	0.0267 020 959	0.0260 594 578	18
10	0.0230 921 916	0.0224 647 312	0.0218 522 088	0.0212 543 737	20
11	0.0191 868 710	0.0186 016 097	0.0180 320 684	0.0174 779 414	22
12	0.0160 500 795	0.0155 058 498	0.0149 779 616	0.0144 660 509	24
13	0.0134 996 124	0.0129 949 668	0.0125 071 267	0.0120 356 670	26
14	0.0114 051 993	0.0109 384 939	0.0104 889 057	0.0100 559 473	28
15	0.0096 712 358	0.0092 406 925	0.0088 274 334	0.0084 309 086	30
16	0.0082 259 887	0.0078 297 432	0.0074 508 132	0.0070 885 879	32
17	0.0070 146 084	0.0066 507 481	0.0063 041 101	0.0059 740 247	34
18	0.0059 944 680	0.0056 610 631	0.0053 446 741	0.0050 445 759	36
19	0.0051 319 709	0.0048 270 991	0.0045 389 361	0.0042 667 060	38
20	0.0044 003 138	0.0041 220 809	0.0038 601 615	0.0036 137 343	40
21	0.0037 778 858	0.0035 244 417	0.0032 868 407	0.0030 642 218	42
22	0.0032 471 012	0.0030 166 536	0.0028 015 156	0.0026 007 930	44
23	0.0027 935 352	0.0025 843 592	0.0023 899 085	0.0022 092 622	46
24	0.0024 052 724	0.0022 157 185	0.0020 402 660	0.0018 779 743	48
25	0.0020 724 102	0.0019 009 099	0.0017 428 582	0.0015 973 012	50
26	0.0017 866 757	0.0016 317 448	0.0014 895 903	0.0013 592 518	52
27	0.0015 411 247	0.0014 013 656	0.0012 737 003	0.0011 571 677	54
28	0.0013 299 053	0.0012 040 076	0.0010 895 180	0.0009 854 810	56
29	0.0011 480 689	0.0010 348 086	0.0009 322 748	0.0008 395 228	58
30	0.0009 914 178	0.0008 896 558	0.0007 979 488	0.0007 153 675	60
31	0.0008 563 816	0.0007 650 620	0.0006 831 404	0.0006 097 076	62
32	0.0007 399 172	0.0006 580 637	0.0005 849 701	0.0005 197 512	64
33	0.0006 394 249	0.0005 661 380	0.0005 009 950	0.0004 431 377	66
34	0.0005 526 807	0.0004 871 335	0.0004 291 391	0.0003 778 688	68
35	0.0004 777 785	0.0004 192 133	0.0003 676 362	0.0003 222 506	70
36	0.0004 130 829	0.0003 608 069	0.0003 149 823	0.0002 748 459	72
37	0.0003 571 892	0.0003 105 703	0.0002 698 950	0.0002 344 344	74
38	0.0003 088 894	0.0002 673 524	0.0002 312 801	0.0001 999 791	76
39	0.0002 671 439	0.0002 301 664	0.0001 982 037	0.0001 705 982	78
40	0.0002 310 575	0.0001 981 657	0.0001 698 677	0.0001 455 416	80
41	0.0001 998 587	0.0001 706 239	0.0001 455 900	0.0001 241 706	82
42	0.0001 728 822	0.0001 469 173	0.0001 247 876	0.0001 059 418	84
43	0.0001 495 542	0.0001 265 098	0.0001 069 615	0.0000 903 919	86
44	0.0001 293 793	0.0001 089 410	0.0000 916 847	0.0000 771 266	88
45	0.0001 119 302	0.0000 938 149	0.0000 785 920	0.0000 658 095	90
46	0.0000 968 374	0.0000 807 913	0.0000 673 705	0.0000 561 542	92
47	0.0000 837 820	0.0000 695 772	0.0000 577 524	0.0000 479 163	94
48	0.0000 724 884	0.0000 599 209	0.0000 495 083	0.0000 408 875	96
49	0.0000 627 184	0.0000 516 057	0.0000 424 417	0.0000 348 902	98
50	0.0000 542 661	0.0000 444 450	0.0000 363 841	0.0000 297 728	100
51	0.0000 469 537	0.0000 382 784	0.0000 311 915	0.0000 254 063	102
52	0.0000 406 271	0.0000 329 678	0.0000 267 402	0.0000 216 803	104
53	0.0000 351 534	0.0000 283 942	0.0000 229 243	0.0000 185 009	106
54	0.0000 304 175	0.0000 244 553	0.0000 196 531	0.0000 157 879	108
55	0.0000 263 198	0.0000 210 629	0.0000 168 488	0.0000 134 727	110
56	0.0000 227 743	0.0000 181 413	0.0000 144 447	0.0000 114 971	112
57	0.0000 197 065	0.0000 156 250	0.0000 123 837	0.0000 098 113	114
58	0.0000 170 521	0.0000 134 578	0.0000 106 168	0.0000 083 726	116
59	0.0000 147 553	0.0000 115 912	0.0000 091 020	0.0000 071 449	118
60	0.0000 127 679	0.0000 099 835	0.0000 078 034	0.0000 060 973	120

Table 3.   SINKING FUND FACTORS
PAYABLE AT END OF EACH PERIOD

HALF YEARS	17% NOMINAL ANNUAL RATE	17½% NOMINAL ANNUAL RATE	18% NOMINAL ANNUAL RATE	18½% NOMINAL ANNUAL RATE	HALF YEARS
1	1.0000 000 000	1.0000 000 000	1.0000 000 000	1.0000 000 000	1
YEARS					
1	0.4796 163 070	0.4790 419 162	0.4784 688 995	0.4778 972 521	2
2	0.2202 878 926	0.2194 765 741	0.2186 686 621	0.2178 641 428	4
3	0.1346 070 840	0.1337 608 210	0.1329 197 833	0.1320 839 456	6
4	0.0923 306 533	0.0914 990 569	0.0906 743 778	0.0898 565 753	8
5	0.0674 077 051	0.0666 096 571	0.0658 200 899	0.0650 389 420	10
6	0.0511 528 581	0.0503 968 072	0.0496 506 585	0.0489 143 237	12
7	0.0398 424 382	0.0391 322 220	0.0384 331 730	0.0377 451 703	14
8	0.0316 135 439	0.0309 505 944	0.0302 999 097	0.0296 613 301	16
9	0.0254 304 127	0.0248 147 580	0.0242 122 907	0.0236 228 071	18
10	0.0206 709 744	0.0201 017 588	0.0195 464 750	0.0190 048 710	20
11	0.0169 389 233	0.0164 147 087	0.0159 049 930	0.0154 094 722	22
12	0.0139 697 546	0.0134 887 111	0.0130 225 607	0.0125 709 455	24
13	0.0115 801 651	0.0111 402 014	0.0107 153 599	0.0103 052 282	26
14	0.0096 391 357	0.0092 379 932	0.0088 520 473	0.0084 808 321	28
15	0.0080 505 753	0.0076 858 985	0.0073 363 514	0.0070 014 162	30
16	0.0067 424 664	0.0064 118 586	0.0060 961 861	0.0057 948 827	32
17	0.0056 598 358	0.0053 609 020	0.0050 765 971	0.0048 063 109	34
18	0.0047 600 615	0.0044 904 426	0.0042 350 500	0.0039 932 346	36
19	0.0040 096 556	0.0037 670 548	0.0035 381 975	0.0033 224 015	38
20	0.0033 820 056	0.0031 642 097	0.0029 596 092	0.0027 674 955	40
21	0.0028 557 568	0.0026 606 508	0.0024 781 420	0.0023 075 015	42
22	0.0024 136 299	0.0022 392 086	0.0020 767 493	0.0019 255 098	44
23	0.0020 415 434	0.0018 859 184	0.0017 415 959	0.0016 078 267	46
24	0.0017 279 519	0.0015 893 556	0.0014 613 892	0.0013 433 027	48
25	0.0014 633 395	0.0013 401 268	0.0012 268 681	0.0011 228 182	50
26	0.0012 398 282	0.0011 304 758	0.0010 304 065	0.0009 388 852	52
27	0.0010 508 710	0.0009 539 750	0.0008 657 034	0.0007 853 357	54
28	0.0008 910 096	0.0008 052 817	0.0007 275 373	0.0006 570 749	56
29	0.0007 556 803	0.0006 799 428	0.0006 115 709	0.0005 498 852	58
30	0.0006 410 586	0.0005 742 394	0.0005 141 938	0.0004 602 678	60
31	0.0005 439 330	0.0004 850 589	0.0004 323 955	0.0003 853 163	62
32	0.0004 616 021	0.0004 097 927	0.0003 636 620	0.0003 226 126	64
33	0.0003 917 900	0.0003 462 515	0.0003 058 914	0.0002 701 424	66
34	0.0003 325 773	0.0002 925 956	0.0002 573 242	0.0002 262 269	68
35	0.0002 823 433	0.0002 472 778	0.0002 164 866	0.0001 894 651	70
36	0.0002 397 181	0.0002 089 955	0.0001 821 431	0.0001 586 873	72
37	0.0002 035 434	0.0001 766 519	0.0001 532 571	0.0001 329 163	74
38	0.0001 728 387	0.0001 493 222	0.0001 289 587	0.0001 113 357	76
39	0.0001 467 738	0.0001 262 267	0.0001 085 173	0.0000 932 624	78
40	0.0001 246 454	0.0001 067 078	0.0000 913 194	0.0000 781 255	80
41	0.0001 058 573	0.0000 902 102	0.0000 768 494	0.0000 654 471	82
42	0.0000 899 042	0.0000 762 655	0.0000 646 738	0.0000 548 274	84
43	0.0000 763 574	0.0000 644 779	0.0000 544 285	0.0000 459 318	86
44	0.0000 648 535	0.0000 545 134	0.0000 458 070	0.0000 384 800	88
45	0.0000 550 838	0.0000 460 896	0.0000 385 517	0.0000 322 376	90
46	0.0000 467 867	0.0000 389 681	0.0000 324 460	0.0000 270 082	92
47	0.0000 397 399	0.0000 329 474	0.0000 273 076	0.0000 226 273	94
48	0.0000 337 549	0.0000 278 572	0.0000 229 832	0.0000 189 571	96
49	0.0000 286 715	0.0000 235 536	0.0000 193 437	0.0000 158 823	98
50	0.0000 243 540	0.0000 199 150	0.0000 162 806	0.0000 133 064	100
51	0.0000 206 867	0.0000 168 386	0.0000 137 027	0.0000 111 482	102
52	0.0000 175 718	0.0000 142 375	0.0000 115 330	0.0000 093 402	104
53	0.0000 149 260	0.0000 120 383	0.0000 097 069	0.0000 078 254	106
54	0.0000 126 786	0.0000 101 788	0.0000 081 700	0.0000 065 563	108
55	0.0000 107 697	0.0000 086 066	0.0000 068 764	0.0000 054 930	110
56	0.0000 091 482	0.0000 072 772	0.0000 057 877	0.0000 046 020	112
57	0.0000 077 708	0.0000 061 532	0.0000 048 713	0.0000 038 558	114
58	0.0000 066 009	0.0000 052 028	0.0000 041 000	0.0000 032 305	116
59	0.0000 056 071	0.0000 043 992	0.0000 034 509	0.0000 027 066	118
60	0.0000 047 629	0.0000 037 198	0.0000 029 045	0.0000 022 677	120

153

Table 3.   SINKING FUND FACTORS
PAYABLE AT END OF EACH PERIOD

HALF YEARS	19% NOMINAL ANNUAL RATE	19½% NOMINAL ANNUAL RATE	20% NOMINAL ANNUAL RATE	20½% NOMINAL ANNUAL RATE	HALF YEARS
1	1.0000 000 000	1.0000 000 000	1.0000 000 000	1.0000 000 000	1
YEARS					
1	0.4773 269 690	0.4767 580 453	0.4761 904 762	0.4756 242 568	2
2	0.2170 630 025	0.2162 652 273	0.2154 708 037	0.2146 797 179	4
3	0.1312 532 826	0.1304 277 693	0.1296 073 804	0.1287 920 905	6
4	0.0890 456 084	0.0882 414 362	0.0874 440 176	0.0866 533 114	8
5	0.0642 661 517	0.0635 016 567	0.0627 453 949	0.0619 973 037	10
6	0.0481 877 142	0.0474 707 411	0.0467 633 151	0.0460 653 465	12
7	0.0370 680 923	0.0364 018 174	0.0357 462 232	0.0351 011 874	14
8	0.0290 346 957	0.0284 198 461	0.0278 166 207	0.0272 248 588	16
9	0.0230 461 037	0.0224 819 766	0.0219 302 222	0.0213 906 371	18
10	0.0184 766 953	0.0179 616 966	0.0174 596 248	0.0169 702 304	20
11	0.0149 278 440	0.0144 598 073	0.0140 050 630	0.0135 633 137	22
12	0.0121 335 107	0.0117 099 039	0.0112 997 764	0.0109 027 827	24
13	0.0099 093 986	0.0095 274 680	0.0091 590 386	0.0088 037 179	26
14	0.0081 238 883	0.0077 807 635	0.0074 510 132	0.0071 342 004	28
15	0.0066 805 845	0.0063 733 578	0.0060 792 483	0.0057 977 783	30
16	0.0055 073 947	0.0052 331 817	0.0049 717 167	0.0047 224 866	32
17	0.0045 494 491	0.0043 054 344	0.0040 737 064	0.0038 537 218	34
18	0.0037 643 673	0.0035 478 397	0.0033 430 638	0.0031 494 723	36
19	0.0031 190 090	0.0029 273 865	0.0027 469 250	0.0025 770 396	38
20	0.0025 871 883	0.0024 180 358	0.0022 594 144	0.0021 107 281	40
21	0.0021 480 333	0.0019 990 738	0.0018 599 911	0.0017 301 844	42
22	0.0017 847 847	0.0016 539 050	0.0015 322 365	0.0014 191 797	44
23	0.0014 839 025	0.0013 691 546	0.0012 629 527	0.0011 647 035	46
24	0.0012 343 905	0.0011 339 900	0.0010 414 797	0.0009 562 779	48
25	0.0010 272 796	0.0009 396 008	0.0008 591 740	0.0007 854 330	50
26	0.0008 552 274	0.0007 787 971	0.0007 090 040	0.0006 453 010	52
27	0.0007 122 048	0.0006 456 939	0.0005 852 336	0.0005 302 988	54
28	0.0005 932 484	0.0005 354 631	0.0004 831 734	0.0004 358 783	56
29	0.0004 942 633	0.0004 441 358	0.0003 989 822	0.0003 583 280	58
30	0.0004 118 653	0.0003 684 435	0.0003 295 092	0.0002 946 147	60
31	0.0003 432 532	0.0003 056 915	0.0002 721 660	0.0002 422 568	62
32	0.0002 861 053	0.0002 536 548	0.0002 248 244	0.0001 992 218	64
33	0.0002 384 958	0.0002 104 953	0.0001 857 328	0.0001 638 438	66
34	0.0001 988 252	0.0001 746 924	0.0001 534 487	0.0001 347 565	68
35	0.0001 657 648	0.0001 449 883	0.0001 267 834	0.0001 108 387	70
36	0.0001 382 097	0.0001 203 412	0.0001 047 566	0.0000 911 698	72
37	0.0001 152 405	0.0000 998 882	0.0000 865 600	0.0000 749 938	74
38	0.0000 960 925	0.0000 829 143	0.0000 715 264	0.0000 616 896	76
39	0.0000 801 288	0.0000 688 268	0.0000 591 054	0.0000 507 467	78
40	0.0000 668 189	0.0000 571 343	0.0000 488 424	0.0000 417 458	80
41	0.0000 557 212	0.0000 474 291	0.0000 403 622	0.0000 343 419	82
42	0.0000 464 676	0.0000 393 731	0.0000 333 549	0.0000 282 515	84
43	0.0000 387 513	0.0000 326 859	0.0000 275 644	0.0000 232 414	86
44	0.0000 323 168	0.0000 271 348	0.0000 227 794	0.0000 191 200	88
45	0.0000 269 511	0.0000 225 267	0.0000 188 252	0.0000 157 296	90
46	0.0000 224 764	0.0000 187 013	0.0000 155 575	0.0000 129 404	92
47	0.0000 187 449	0.0000 155 256	0.0000 128 571	0.0000 106 459	94
48	0.0000 156 329	0.0000 128 892	0.0000 106 255	0.0000 087 582	96
49	0.0000 130 377	0.0000 107 006	0.0000 087 812	0.0000 072 053	98
50	0.0000 108 733	0.0000 088 836	0.0000 072 571	0.0000 059 277	100
51	0.0000 090 683	0.0000 073 752	0.0000 059 975	0.0000 048 767	102
52	0.0000 075 629	0.0000 061 230	0.0000 049 566	0.0000 040 121	104
53	0.0000 063 075	0.0000 050 833	0.0000 040 963	0.0000 033 007	106
54	0.0000 052 604	0.0000 042 202	0.0000 033 854	0.0000 027 155	108
55	0.0000 043 872	0.0000 035 037	0.0000 027 978	0.0000 022 340	110
56	0.0000 036 590	0.0000 029 088	0.0000 023 122	0.0000 018 379	112
57	0.0000 030 516	0.0000 024 149	0.0000 019 109	0.0000 015 121	114
58	0.0000 025 451	0.0000 020 049	0.0000 015 793	0.0000 012 440	116
59	0.0000 021 226	0.0000 016 645	0.0000 013 052	0.0000 010 234	118
60	0.0000 017 703	0.0000 013 819	0.0000 010 787	0.0000 008 420	120

Table 3.   SINKING FUND FACTORS
PAYABLE AT END OF EACH PERIOD

HALF YEARS	**21%** NOMINAL ANNUAL RATE	**21½%** NOMINAL ANNUAL RATE	**22%** NOMINAL ANNUAL RATE	**22½%** NOMINAL ANNUAL RATE	HALF YEARS
1	1.0000 000 000	1.0000 000 000	1.0000 000 000	1.0000 000 000	1
YEARS					
1	0.4750 593 824	0.4744 958 482	0.4739 336 493	0.4733 727 811	2
2	0.2138 919 564	0.2131 075 054	0.2123 263 515	0.2115 484 812	4
3	0.1279 818 746	0.1271 767 074	0.1263 765 636	0.1255 814 180	6
4	0.0858 692 763	0.0850 918 710	0.0843 210 542	0.0835 567 844	8
5	0.0612 573 206	0.0605 253 827	0.0598 014 271	0.0590 853 907	10
6	0.0453 767 456	0.0446 974 223	0.0440 272 864	0.0433 662 475	12
7	0.0344 665 871	0.0338 422 994	0.0332 282 015	0.0326 241 702	14
8	0.0266 443 997	0.0260 750 826	0.0255 167 470	0.0249 692 325	16
9	0.0208 630 182	0.0203 471 632	0.0198 428 701	0.0193 499 379	18
10	0.0164 932 653	0.0160 284 825	0.0155 756 369	0.0151 344 846	20
11	0.0131 342 647	0.0127 176 237	0.0123 131 011	0.0119 204 101	22
12	0.0105 185 815	0.0101 468 353	0.0097 872 113	0.0094 393 810	24
13	0.0084 611 196	0.0081 308 633	0.0078 125 750	0.0075 058 873	26
14	0.0068 298 968	0.0065 376 822	0.0062 571 454	0.0059 878 842	28
15	0.0055 284 815	0.0052 709 028	0.0050 245 985	0.0047 891 363	30
16	0.0044 849 922	0.0042 587 487	0.0040 432 854	0.0038 381 462	32
17	0.0036 449 545	0.0034 468 959	0.0032 590 547	0.0030 809 569	34
18	0.0029 665 187	0.0027 936 768	0.0026 304 409	0.0024 763 254	36
19	0.0024 171 697	0.0022 667 780	0.0021 253 508	0.0019 923 971	38
20	0.0019 714 084	0.0018 409 132	0.0017 187 267	0.0016 043 586	40
21	0.0016 090 833	0.0014 961 470	0.0013 908 633	0.0012 927 477	42
22	0.0013 141 681	0.0012 166 672	0.0011 261 735	0.0010 422 130	44
23	0.0010 738 498	0.0009 898 682	0.0009 122 683	0.0008 405 907	46
24	0.0008 778 407	0.0008 056 601	0.0007 392 624	0.0006 782 064	48
25	0.0007 178 512	0.0006 559 393	0.0005 992 433	0.0005 473 428	50
26	0.0005 871 820	0.0005 341 792	0.0004 858 607	0.0004 418 286	52
27	0.0004 804 064	0.0004 351 120	0.0003 940 076	0.0003 567 191	54
28	0.0003 931 196	0.0003 544 778	0.0003 195 698	0.0002 880 461	56
29	0.0003 217 406	0.0002 888 266	0.0002 592 282	0.0002 326 208	58
30	0.0002 633 544	0.0002 353 608	0.0002 103 020	0.0001 878 780	60
31	0.0002 155 851	0.0001 918 099	0.0001 706 244	0.0001 517 528	62
32	0.0001 764 952	0.0001 563 294	0.0001 384 421	0.0001 225 813	64
33	0.0001 445 028	0.0001 274 197	0.0001 123 361	0.0000 990 224	66
34	0.0001 183 160	0.0001 038 613	0.0000 911 570	0.0000 799 945	68
35	0.0000 968 792	0.0000 846 621	0.0000 739 735	0.0000 646 250	70
36	0.0000 793 292	0.0000 690 142	0.0000 600 309	0.0000 522 099	72
37	0.0000 649 605	0.0000 562 599	0.0000 487 175	0.0000 421 807	74
38	0.0000 531 957	0.0000 458 638	0.0000 395 369	0.0000 340 787	76
39	0.0000 435 624	0.0000 373 894	0.0000 320 868	0.0000 275 332	78
40	0.0000 356 742	0.0000 304 813	0.0000 260 410	0.0000 222 452	80
41	0.0000 292 148	0.0000 248 498	0.0000 211 345	0.0000 179 730	82
42	0.0000 239 253	0.0000 202 589	0.0000 171 526	0.0000 145 213	84
43	0.0000 195 936	0.0000 165 163	0.0000 139 210	0.0000 117 327	86
44	0.0000 160 463	0.0000 134 652	0.0000 112 984	0.0000 094 795	88
45	0.0000 131 413	0.0000 109 778	0.0000 091 698	0.0000 076 591	90
46	0.0000 107 623	0.0000 089 500	0.0000 074 423	0.0000 061 883	92
47	0.0000 088 140	0.0000 072 967	0.0000 060 403	0.0000 050 000	94
48	0.0000 072 184	0.0000 059 489	0.0000 049 024	0.0000 040 399	96
49	0.0000 059 117	0.0000 048 500	0.0000 039 788	0.0000 032 641	98
50	0.0000 048 415	0.0000 039 541	0.0000 032 293	0.0000 026 373	100
51	0.0000 039 651	0.0000 032 237	0.0000 026 210	0.0000 021 309	102
52	0.0000 032 473	0.0000 026 283	0.0000 021 272	0.0000 017 217	104
53	0.0000 026 595	0.0000 021 428	0.0000 017 265	0.0000 013 911	106
54	0.0000 021 781	0.0000 017 470	0.0000 014 013	0.0000 011 240	108
55	0.0000 017 838	0.0000 014 243	0.0000 011 373	0.0000 009 081	110
56	0.0000 014 609	0.0000 011 612	0.0000 009 230	0.0000 007 338	112
57	0.0000 011 964	0.0000 009 467	0.0000 007 492	0.0000 005 929	114
58	0.0000 009 799	0.0000 007 719	0.0000 006 080	0.0000 004 790	116
59	0.0000 008 025	0.0000 006 293	0.0000 004 935	0.0000 003 870	118
60	0.0000 006 572	0.0000 005 131	0.0000 004 005	0.0000 003 127	120

Table 4.   PRESENT WORTH OF ONE DOLLAR
PAYABLE AT END OF EACH PERIOD

HALF YEARS	5% NOMINAL ANNUAL RATE	5½% NOMINAL ANNUAL RATE	6% NOMINAL ANNUAL RATE	6½% NOMINAL ANNUAL RATE	HALF YEARS
1	0.9756 097 561	0.9732 360 097	0.9708 737 864	0.9685 230 024	1
YEARS					
1	0.9518 143 962	0.9471 883 306	0.9425 959 091	0.9380 368 062	2
2	0.9059 506 448	0.8971 657 337	0.8884 870 479	0.8799 130 498	4
3	0.8622 968 660	0.8497 849 136	0.8374 842 567	0.8253 908 270	6
4	0.8207 465 708	0.8049 063 537	0.7894 092 343	0.7742 469 752	8
5	0.7811 984 017	0.7623 979 055	0.7440 939 149	0.7262 721 599	10
6	0.7435 558 850	0.7221 343 994	0.7013 798 802	0.6812 700 173	12
7	0.7077 271 958	0.6839 972 763	0.6611 178 058	0.6390 563 512	14
8	0.6736 249 335	0.6478 742 383	0.6231 669 392	0.5994 583 787	16
9	0.6411 659 093	0.6136 589 182	0.5873 946 076	0.5623 140 230	18
10	0.6102 709 429	0.5812 505 663	0.5536 757 542	0.5274 712 502	20
11	0.5808 646 690	0.5505 537 536	0.5218 925 009	0.4947 874 469	22
12	0.5528 753 542	0.5214 780 908	0.4919 337 363	0.4641 288 365	24
13	0.5262 347 214	0.4939 379 623	0.4636 947 274	0.4353 699 314	26
14	0.5008 777 836	0.4678 522 739	0.4370 767 532	0.4083 930 200	28
15	0.4767 426 852	0.4431 442 143	0.4119 867 595	0.3830 876 842	30
16	0.4537 705 510	0.4197 410 286	0.3883 370 341	0.3593 503 478	32
17	0.4319 053 430	0.3975 738 042	0.3660 448 997	0.3370 838 525	34
18	0.4110 937 233	0.3765 772 679	0.3450 324 251	0.3161 970 605	36
19	0.3912 849 240	0.3566 895 937	0.3252 261 524	0.2966 044 807	38
20	0.3724 306 237	0.3378 522 208	0.3065 568 408	0.2782 259 198	40
21	0.3544 848 292	0.3200 096 811	0.2889 592 240	0.2609 861 532	42
22	0.3374 037 637	0.3031 094 356	0.2723 717 825	0.2448 146 176	44
23	0.3211 457 596	0.2871 017 203	0.2567 365 279	0.2296 451 220	46
24	0.3056 711 573	0.2719 393 992	0.2419 988 009	0.2154 155 769	48
25	0.2909 422 080	0.2575 778 255	0.2281 070 798	0.2020 677 397	50
26	0.2769 229 820	0.2439 747 106	0.2150 128 003	0.1895 469 772	52
27	0.2635 792 809	0.2310 899 988	0.2026 701 859	0.1778 020 411	54
28	0.2508 785 541	0.2188 857 502	0.1910 360 882	0.1667 848 588	56
29	0.2387 898 195	0.2073 260 284	0.1800 698 352	0.1564 503 363	58
30	0.2272 835 879	0.1963 767 947	0.1697 330 900	0.1467 561 738	60
31	0.2163 317 910	0.1860 058 083	0.1599 897 163	0.1376 626 925	62
32	0.2059 077 130	0.1761 825 311	0.1508 056 521	0.1291 326 724	64
33	0.1959 859 255	0.1668 780 375	0.1421 487 907	0.1211 311 996	66
34	0.1865 422 253	0.1580 649 298	0.1339 888 686	0.1136 255 236	68
35	0.1775 535 756	0.1497 172 591	0.1262 973 594	0.1065 849 233	70
36	0.1689 980 493	0.1418 104 387	0.1190 473 743	0.0999 805 810	72
37	0.1608 547 763	0.1343 211 927	0.1122 135 680	0.0937 854 649	74
38	0.1531 038 918	0.1272 274 663	0.1057 720 502	0.0879 742 180	76
39	0.1457 264 883	0.1205 083 714	0.0997 003 018	0.0825 230 545	78
40	0.1387 045 695	0.1141 441 231	0.0939 770 966	0.0774 096 625	80
41	0.1320 210 060	0.1081 159 814	0.0885 824 268	0.0726 131 125	82
42	0.1256 594 941	0.1024 061 960	0.0834 974 332	0.0681 137 722	84
43	0.1196 045 155	0.0969 979 538	0.0787 043 389	0.0638 932 253	86
44	0.1138 412 997	0.0918 753 299	0.0741 863 879	0.0599 341 970	88
45	0.1083 557 880	0.0870 232 404	0.0699 277 857	0.0562 204 827	90
46	0.1031 345 989	0.0824 273 978	0.0659 136 448	0.0527 368 821	92
47	0.0981 649 960	0.0780 742 693	0.0621 299 319	0.0494 691 364	94
48	0.0934 348 564	0.0739 510 368	0.0585 634 197	0.0464 038 708	96
49	0.0889 326 414	0.0700 455 591	0.0552 016 398	0.0435 285 387	98
50	0.0846 473 684	0.0663 463 362	0.0520 328 399	0.0408 313 714	100
51	0.0805 685 838	0.0628 424 754	0.0490 459 420	0.0383 013 293	102
52	0.0766 863 380	0.0595 236 594	0.0462 305 043	0.0359 280 566	104
53	0.0729 911 605	0.0563 801 156	0.0435 766 842	0.0337 018 394	106
54	0.0694 740 373	0.0534 025 876	0.0410 752 043	0.0316 135 658	108
55	0.0661 263 889	0.0505 823 078	0.0387 173 195	0.0296 546 883	110
56	0.0629 400 489	0.0479 109 717	0.0364 947 870	0.0278 171 891	112
57	0.0599 072 447	0.0453 807 133	0.0343 998 369	0.0260 935 472	114
58	0.0570 205 779	0.0429 840 820	0.0324 251 455	0.0244 767 077	116
59	0.0542 730 069	0.0407 140 209	0.0305 638 095	0.0229 600 527	118
60	0.0516 578 293	0.0385 638 455	0.0288 093 218	0.0215 373 745	120

156

Table 4.   PRESENT WORTH OF ONE DOLLAR
PAYABLE AT END OF EACH PERIOD

	7%	7½%	8%	8½%	
HALF YEARS	NOMINAL ANNUAL RATE	NOMINAL ANNUAL RATE	NOMINAL ANNUAL RATE	NOMINAL ANNUAL RATE	HALF YEARS
1	0.9661 835 749	0.9638 554 217	0.9615 384 615	0.9592 326 139	1
YEARS					
1	0.9335 107 004	0.9290 172 739	0.9245 562 130	0.9201 272 076	2
2	0.8714 422 277	0.8630 730 952	0.8548 041 910	0.8466 340 781	4
3	0.8135 006 443	0.8018 098 141	0.7903 145 257	0.7790 110 502	6
4	0.7594 115 562	0.7448 951 677	0.7306 902 050	0.7167 892 623	8
5	0.7089 188 137	0.6920 204 781	0.6755 641 688	0.6595 373 023	10
6	0.6617 832 983	0.6428 989 780	0.6245 970 496	0.6068 582 163	12
7	0.6177 817 903	0.5972 642 560	0.5774 750 828	0.5583 867 559	14
8	0.5767 059 117	0.5548 688 109	0.5339 081 757	0.5137 868 465	16
9	0.5383 611 396	0.5154 827 101	0.4936 281 210	0.4727 492 564	18
10	0.5025 658 844	0.4788 923 421	0.4563 869 462	0.4349 894 532	20
11	0.4691 506 308	0.4448 992 581	0.4219 553 867	0.4002 456 309	22
12	0.4379 571 339	0.4133 190 959	0.3901 214 743	0.3682 768 947	24
13	0.4088 376 708	0.3839 805 798	0.3606 892 329	0.3388 615 907	26
14	0.3816 543 404	0.3567 245 915	0.3334 774 713	0.3117 957 692	28
15	0.3562 784 106	0.3314 033 075	0.3083 186 680	0.2868 917 705	30
16	0.3325 897 086	0.3078 793 973	0.2850 579 401	0.2639 769 236	32
17	0.3104 760 518	0.2860 252 784	0.2635 520 896	0.2428 923 496	34
18	0.2898 327 166	0.2657 224 244	0.2436 687 219	0.2234 918 594	36
19	0.2705 619 422	0.2468 607 223	0.2252 854 307	0.2056 409 405	38
20	0.2525 724 682	0.2293 378 753	0.2082 890 447	0.1892 158 244	40
21	0.2357 791 017	0.2130 588 477	0.1925 749 303	0.1741 026 281	42
22	0.2201 023 143	0.1979 353 499	0.1780 463 483	0.1601 965 650	44
23	0.2054 678 656	0.1838 853 592	0.1646 138 575	0.1474 012 180	46
24	0.1918 064 511	0.1708 326 751	0.1521 947 647	0.1356 278 711	48
25	0.1790 533 745	0.1587 065 061	0.1407 126 153	0.1247 948 943	50
26	0.1671 482 411	0.1474 410 856	0.1300 967 228	0.1148 271 777	52
27	0.1560 346 716	0.1369 753 154	0.1202 817 333	0.1056 556 103	54
28	0.1456 600 355	0.1272 524 341	0.1112 072 239	0.0972 166 017	56
29	0.1359 752 018	0.1182 197 095	0.1028 173 297	0.0894 516 403	58
30	0.1269 343 059	0.1098 281 522	0.0950 604 010	0.0823 068 880	60
31	0.1184 945 328	0.1020 322 506	0.0878 886 844	0.0757 328 070	62
32	0.1106 159 143	0.0947 897 233	0.0812 580 292	0.0696 838 162	64
33	0.1032 611 396	0.0880 612 903	0.0751 276 157	0.0641 179 752	66
34	0.0963 953 788	0.0818 104 599	0.0694 597 039	0.0589 966 935	68
35	0.0899 861 175	0.0760 033 304	0.0642 194 008	0.0542 844 628	70
36	0.0840 030 036	0.0706 084 068	0.0593 744 460	0.0499 486 112	72
37	0.0784 177 027	0.0655 964 296	0.0548 950 130	0.0459 590 762	74
38	0.0732 037 646	0.0609 402 162	0.0507 535 253	0.0422 881 964	76
39	0.0683 364 976	0.0566 145 135	0.0469 244 871	0.0389 105 201	78
40	0.0637 928 517	0.0525 958 610	0.0433 843 261	0.0358 026 282	80
41	0.0595 513 097	0.0488 624 634	0.0401 112 483	0.0329 429 723	82
42	0.0555 917 848	0.0453 940 726	0.0370 851 038	0.0303 117 251	84
43	0.0518 955 260	0.0421 718 776	0.0342 872 631	0.0278 906 430	86
44	0.0484 450 288	0.0391 784 027	0.0317 005 022	0.0256 629 394	88
45	0.0452 239 527	0.0363 974 129	0.0293 088 962	0.0236 131 688	90
46	0.0422 170 438	0.0338 138 253	0.0270 977 221	0.0217 271 191	92
47	0.0394 100 621	0.0314 136 278	0.0250 533 673	0.0199 917 134	94
48	0.0367 897 147	0.0291 838 029	0.0231 632 464	0.0183 949 194	96
49	0.0343 435 923	0.0271 122 570	0.0214 157 234	0.0169 256 659	98
50	0.0320 601 109	0.0251 877 551	0.0198 000 401	0.0155 737 657	100
51	0.0299 284 566	0.0233 998 596	0.0183 062 501	0.0143 298 455	102
52	0.0279 385 345	0.0217 388 737	0.0169 251 573	0.0131 852 807	104
53	0.0260 809 209	0.0201 957 892	0.0156 482 593	0.0121 321 355	106
54	0.0243 468 187	0.0187 622 370	0.0144 676 954	0.0111 631 080	108
55	0.0227 280 158	0.0174 304 423	0.0133 761 976	0.0102 714 794	110
56	0.0212 168 460	0.0161 931 820	0.0123 670 466	0.0094 510 676	112
57	0.0198 061 527	0.0150 437 458	0.0114 340 298	0.0086 961 845	114
58	0.0184 892 555	0.0139 758 997	0.0105 714 033	0.0080 015 959	116
59	0.0172 599 179	0.0129 838 522	0.0097 738 566	0.0073 624 861	118
60	0.0161 123 180	0.0120 622 230	0.0090 364 798	0.0067 744 238	120

157

Table 4. PRESENT WORTH OF ONE DOLLAR
PAYABLE AT END OF EACH PERIOD

HALF YEARS	**9%** NOMINAL ANNUAL RATE	**9½%** NOMINAL ANNUAL RATE	**10%** NOMINAL ANNUAL RATE	**10½%** NOMINAL ANNUAL RATE	HALF YEARS
1	0.9569 377 990	0.9546 539 379	0.9523 809 524	0.9501 187 648	1
YEARS					
1	0.9157 299 512	0.9113 641 412	0.9070 294 785	0.9027 256 673	2
2	0.8385 613 436	0.8305 845 979	0.8227 024 748	0.8149 136 304	4
3	0.7678 957 383	0.7569 650 188	0.7462 153 966	0.7356 434 508	6
4	0.7031 851 270	0.6898 707 743	0.6768 393 620	0.6640 842 250	8
5	0.6439 276 820	0.6287 234 858	0.6139 132 535	0.5994 858 752	10
6	0.5896 638 649	0.5729 960 397	0.5568 374 182	0.5411 712 867	12
7	0.5399 728 622	0.5222 080 437	0.5050 679 530	0.4885 292 110	14
8	0.4944 693 228	0.4759 216 853	0.4581 115 220	0.4410 078 580	16
9	0.4528 003 688	0.4337 379 580	0.4155 206 549	0.3981 091 129	18
10	0.4146 428 597	0.3952 932 216	0.3768 894 829	0.3593 833 146	20
11	0.3797 008 857	0.3602 560 675	0.3418 498 711	0.3244 245 425	22
12	0.3477 034 735	0.3283 244 615	0.3100 679 103	0.2928 663 616	24
13	0.3184 024 849	0.2992 231 409	0.2812 407 350	0.2643 779 817	26
14	0.2915 706 919	0.2727 012 409	0.2550 936 371	0.2386 607 900	28
15	0.2670 000 155	0.2485 301 322	0.2313 774 487	0.2154 452 209	30
16	0.2444 999 112	0.2265 014 505	0.2098 661 666	0.1944 879 308	32
17	0.2238 958 917	0.2064 252 999	0.1903 547 996	0.1755 692 471	34
18	0.2050 281 740	0.1881 286 162	0.1726 574 146	0.1584 908 657	36
19	0.1877 504 398	0.1714 536 748	0.1566 053 647	0.1430 737 725	38
20	0.1719 287 011	0.1562 567 311	0.1420 456 823	0.1291 563 668	40
21	0.1574 402 611	0.1424 067 815	0.1288 396 211	0.1165 927 674	42
22	0.1441 727 626	0.1297 844 341	0.1168 613 344	0.1052 512 838	44
23	0.1320 233 169	0.1182 808 794	0.1059 966 752	0.0950 130 354	46
24	0.1208 977 055	0.1077 969 520	0.0961 421 090	0.0857 707 058	48
25	0.1107 096 500	0.0982 422 766	0.0872 037 270	0.0774 274 176	50
26	0.1013 801 424	0.0895 344 881	0.0790 963 510	0.0698 957 172	52
27	0.0928 368 328	0.0815 985 218	0.0717 427 220	0.0630 966 580	54
28	0.0850 134 684	0.0743 659 668	0.0650 727 637	0.0569 589 727	56
29	0.0778 493 793	0.0677 744 754	0.0590 229 149	0.0514 183 266	58
30	0.0712 890 083	0.0617 672 266	0.0535 355 237	0.0464 166 432	60
31	0.0652 814 801	0.0562 924 354	0.0485 582 982	0.0419 014 952	62
32	0.0597 802 066	0.0513 029 071	0.0440 438 079	0.0378 255 552	64
33	0.0547 425 256	0.0467 556 299	0.0399 490 321	0.0341 460 996	66
34	0.0501 293 703	0.0426 114 045	0.0362 349 497	0.0308 245 605	68
35	0.0459 049 659	0.0388 345 060	0.0328 661 676	0.0278 261 220	70
36	0.0420 365 521	0.0353 923 762	0.0298 105 828	0.0251 193 545	72
37	0.0384 941 298	0.0322 553 426	0.0270 390 774	0.0226 758 861	74
38	0.0352 502 276	0.0293 963 626	0.0245 252 403	0.0204 701 044	76
39	0.0322 796 892	0.0267 907 907	0.0222 451 159	0.0184 788 886	78
40	0.0295 594 783	0.0244 161 065	0.0201 769 759	0.0166 813 671	80
41	0.0270 684 996	0.0222 520 182	0.0183 011 119	0.0150 586 982	82
42	0.0247 874 358	0.0202 796 914	0.0165 996 480	0.0135 938 734	84
43	0.0226 985 974	0.0184 821 836	0.0150 563 700	0.0122 715 384	86
44	0.0207 857 855	0.0168 439 993	0.0136 565 715	0.0110 778 327	88
45	0.0190 341 663	0.0153 510 170	0.0123 869 129	0.0100 002 439	90
46	0.0174 301 562	0.0139 903 664	0.0112 352 951	0.0090 274 769	92
47	0.0159 613 161	0.0127 503 183	0.0101 907 439	0.0081 493 351	94
48	0.0146 162 552	0.0116 201 829	0.0092 433 051	0.0073 566 140	96
49	0.0133 845 427	0.0105 902 180	0.0083 839 502	0.0066 410 043	98
50	0.0122 566 266	0.0096 515 449	0.0076 044 900	0.0059 950 050	100
51	0.0112 237 601	0.0087 960 719	0.0068 974 966	0.0054 118 449	102
52	0.0102 779 333	0.0080 164 246	0.0062 562 327	0.0048 854 113	104
53	0.0094 118 113	0.0073 058 819	0.0056 745 875	0.0044 101 862	106
54	0.0086 186 775	0.0066 583 188	0.0051 470 182	0.0039 811 882	108
55	0.0078 923 812	0.0060 681 530	0.0046 684 972	0.0035 939 208	110
56	0.0072 272 898	0.0055 302 970	0.0042 344 646	0.0032 443 246	112
57	0.0066 182 457	0.0050 401 144	0.0038 407 842	0.0029 287 351	114
58	0.0060 605 259	0.0045 933 795	0.0034 837 045	0.0026 438 443	116
59	0.0055 498 050	0.0041 862 414	0.0031 598 227	0.0023 866 661	118
60	0.0050 821 227	0.0038 151 903	0.0028 660 523	0.0021 545 048	120

Table 4.   PRESENT WORTH OF ONE DOLLAR
PAYABLE AT END OF EACH PERIOD

HALF YEARS	11% NOMINAL ANNUAL RATE	11½% NOMINAL ANNUAL RATE	12% NOMINAL ANNUAL RATE	12½% NOMINAL ANNUAL RATE	HALF YEARS
1	0.9478 672 986	0.9456 264 775	0.9433 962 264	0.9411 764 706	1
YEARS					
1	0.8984 524 157	0.8942 094 350	0.8899 964 400	0.8858 131 488	2
2	0.8072 167 433	0.7996 105 137	0.7920 936 632	0.7846 649 346	4
3	0.7252 458 330	0.7150 192 657	0.7049 605 404	0.6950 665 164	6
4	0.6515 988 707	0.6393 769 736	0.6274 123 713	0.6156 990 595	8
5	0.5854 305 794	0.5717 369 223	0.5583 947 769	0.5453 943 226	10
6	0.5259 815 183	0.5112 525 503	0.4969 693 636	0.4831 174 623	12
7	0.4725 693 658	0.4571 668 542	0.4423 009 644	0.4279 518 005	14
8	0.4245 810 883	0.4088 029 144	0.3936 462 837	0.3790 853 319	16
9	0.3814 659 044	0.3655 554 231	0.3503 437 911	0.3357 987 715	18
10	0.3427 289 633	0.3268 831 084	0.3118 047 269	0.2974 549 672	20
11	0.3079 256 650	0.2923 019 597	0.2775 050 969	0.2634 895 211	22
12	0.2766 565 576	0.2613 791 702	0.2469 785 483	0.2334 024 823	24
13	0.2485 627 525	0.2337 277 201	0.2198 100 288	0.2067 509 878	26
14	0.2233 218 055	0.2090 015 325	0.1956 301 431	0.1831 427 435	28
15	0.2006 440 156	0.1868 911 423	0.1741 101 309	0.1622 302 503	30
16	0.1802 691 005	0.1671 198 228	0.1549 573 967	0.1437 056 889	32
17	0.1619 632 088	0.1494 401 223	0.1379 115 314	0.1272 963 888	34
18	0.1455 162 362	0.1336 307 674	0.1227 407 720	0.1127 608 150	36
19	0.1307 394 140	0.1194 938 930	0.1092 388 501	0.0998 850 126	38
20	0.1174 631 423	0.1068 525 665	0.0972 221 877	0.0884 794 575	40
21	0.1055 350 440	0.0955 485 732	0.0865 274 010	0.0783 762 668	42
22	0.0948 182 152	0.0854 404 356	0.0770 090 788	0.0694 267 277	44
23	0.0851 896 545	0.0764 016 437	0.0685 378 060	0.0614 991 083	46
24	0.0765 388 509	0.0683 190 706	0.0609 984 033	0.0544 767 188	48
25	0.0687 665 155	0.0610 915 575	0.0542 883 618	0.0482 561 938	50
26	0.0617 834 419	0.0546 286 471	0.0483 164 488	0.0427 459 710	52
27	0.0555 094 827	0.0488 494 517	0.0430 014 674	0.0378 649 431	54
28	0.0498 726 288	0.0436 816 406	0.0382 711 529	0.0335 412 645	56
29	0.0448 081 838	0.0390 605 352	0.0340 611 898	0.0297 112 931	58
30	0.0402 580 210	0.0349 282 991	0.0303 143 377	0.0263 186 541	60
31	0.0361 699 162	0.0312 332 146	0.0269 796 526	0.0233 134 099	62
32	0.0324 969 486	0.0279 290 352	0.0240 117 948	0.0206 513 250	64
33	0.0291 969 620	0.0249 744 068	0.0213 704 119	0.0182 932 152	66
34	0.0262 320 810	0.0223 323 502	0.0190 195 905	0.0162 043 706	68
35	0.0235 682 766	0.0199 697 982	0.0169 273 678	0.0143 540 445	70
36	0.0211 749 750	0.0178 571 820	0.0150 652 971	0.0127 150 014	72
37	0.0190 247 074	0.0159 680 606	0.0134 080 608	0.0112 631 154	74
38	0.0170 927 944	0.0142 787 905	0.0119 331 264	0.0099 770 157	76
39	0.0153 570 624	0.0127 682 292	0.0106 204 400	0.0088 377 717	78
40	0.0137 975 898	0.0114 174 710	0.0094 521 538	0.0078 286 144	80
41	0.0123 964 779	0.0102 096 103	0.0084 123 832	0.0069 346 896	82
42	0.0111 376 455	0.0091 295 298	0.0074 869 911	0.0061 428 392	84
43	0.0100 066 445	0.0081 637 117	0.0066 633 954	0.0054 414 077	86
44	0.0089 904 939	0.0073 000 680	0.0059 303 982	0.0048 200 705	88
45	0.0080 775 310	0.0065 277 897	0.0052 780 333	0.0042 696 818	90
46	0.0072 572 772	0.0058 372 112	0.0046 974 308	0.0037 821 403	92
47	0.0065 203 183	0.0052 196 893	0.0041 806 967	0.0033 502 696	94
48	0.0058 581 957	0.0046 674 954	0.0037 208 052	0.0029 677 129	96
49	0.0052 633 101	0.0041 737 184	0.0033 115 034	0.0026 288 391	98
50	0.0047 288 336	0.0037 321 784	0.0029 472 262	0.0023 286 602	100
51	0.0042 486 320	0.0033 373 491	0.0026 230 209	0.0020 627 579	102
52	0.0038 171 937	0.0029 842 891	0.0023 344 792	0.0018 272 180	104
53	0.0034 295 669	0.0026 685 795	0.0020 776 782	0.0016 185 738	106
54	0.0030 813 027	0.0023 862 689	0.0018 491 262	0.0014 337 539	108
55	0.0027 684 038	0.0021 338 242	0.0016 457 157	0.0012 700 381	110
56	0.0024 872 791	0.0019 080 857	0.0014 646 811	0.0011 250 164	112
57	0.0022 347 019	0.0017 062 283	0.0013 035 610	0.0009 965 543	114
58	0.0020 077 733	0.0015 257 254	0.0011 601 647	0.0008 827 609	116
59	0.0018 038 888	0.0013 643 181	0.0010 325 424	0.0007 819 612	118
60	0.0016 207 083	0.0012 199 861	0.0009 189 591	0.0006 926 716	120

Table 4. PRESENT WORTH OF ONE DOLLAR
PAYABLE AT END OF EACH PERIOD

HALF YEARS	13% NOMINAL ANNUAL RATE	13½% NOMINAL ANNUAL RATE	14% NOMINAL ANNUAL RATE	14½% NOMINAL ANNUAL RATE	HALF YEARS
1	0.9389 671 362	0.9367 681 499	0.9345 794 393	0.9324 009 324	1
YEARS					
1	0.8816 592 828	0.8775 345 666	0.8734 387 283	0.8693 714 987	2
2	0.7773 230 909	0.7700 669 156	0.7628 952 120	0.7558 068 028	4
3	0.6853 341 188	0.6757 603 371	0.6663 422 238	0.6570 768 929	6
4	0.6042 311 876	0.5930 030 546	0.5820 091 046	0.5712 439 232	8
5	0.5327 260 355	0.5203 806 785	0.5083 492 921	0.4966 231 857	10
6	0.4696 828 544	0.4566 520 332	0.4440 119 592	0.4317 500 432	12
7	0.4141 002 485	0.4007 279 440	0.3878 172 410	0.3753 511 822	14
8	0.3650 953 281	0.3516 526 227	0.3387 345 978	0.3263 196 198	16
9	0.3218 896 851	0.3085 873 319	0.2958 639 163	0.2836 929 769	18
10	0.2837 970 289	0.2707 960 506	0.2584 190 028	0.2466 345 885	20
11	0.2502 122 850	0.2376 328 949	0.2257 131 652	0.2144 170 819	22
12	0.2206 019 837	0.2085 310 794	0.1971 466 199	0.1864 080 998	24
13	0.1944 957 867	0.1829 932 304	0.1721 954 930	0.1620 578 891	26
14	0.1714 790 158	0.1605 828 851	0.1504 022 124	0.1408 885 099	28
15	0.1511 860 661	0.1409 170 325	0.1313 671 172	0.1224 844 550	30
16	0.1332 945 986	0.1236 595 671	0.1147 411 277	0.1064 844 943	32
17	0.1175 204 202	0.1085 155 446	0.1002 193 447	0.0925 745 844	34
18	0.1036 129 694	0.0952 261 414	0.0875 354 570	0.0804 817 052	36
19	0.0913 513 363	0.0835 642 307	0.0764 568 582	0.0699 685 006	38
20	0.0805 407 536	0.0733 305 010	0.0667 803 810	0.0608 286 203	40
21	0.0710 095 031	0.0643 500 494	0.0583 285 711	0.0528 826 688	42
22	0.0626 061 876	0.0564 693 927	0.0509 464 329	0.0459 746 850	44
23	0.0551 973 264	0.0495 538 441	0.0444 985 876	0.0399 690 808	46
24	0.0486 652 352	0.0434 852 111	0.0388 667 898	0.0347 479 797	48
25	0.0429 061 564	0.0381 597 759	0.0339 477 594	0.0302 089 032	50
26	0.0378 286 111	0.0334 865 224	0.0296 512 878	0.0262 627 594	52
27	0.0333 519 461	0.0293 855 809	0.0258 985 831	0.0228 320 945	54
28	0.0294 050 529	0.0257 868 630	0.0226 208 255	0.0198 495 722	56
29	0.0259 252 378	0.0226 288 636	0.0197 579 051	0.0172 566 524	58
30	0.0228 572 266	0.0198 576 101	0.0172 573 195	0.0150 024 417	60
31	0.0201 522 860	0.0174 257 392	0.0150 732 112	0.0130 426 953	62
32	0.0177 674 500	0.0152 916 885	0.0131 655 264	0.0113 389 475	64
33	0.0156 648 372	0.0134 189 853	0.0114 992 806	0.0098 577 578	66
34	0.0138 110 492	0.0117 756 234	0.0100 439 171	0.0085 700 537	68
35	0.0121 766 397	0.0103 335 166	0.0087 727 461	0.0074 505 604	70
36	0.0107 356 474	0.0090 680 180	0.0076 624 562	0.0064 773 049	72
37	0.0094 651 832	0.0079 574 993	0.0066 926 860	0.0056 311 842	74
38	0.0083 450 666	0.0069 829 807	0.0058 456 512	0.0048 955 911	76
39	0.0073 575 055	0.0061 278 069	0.0051 058 181	0.0042 560 874	78
40	0.0064 868 130	0.0053 773 624	0.0044 596 193	0.0037 001 210	80
41	0.0057 191 589	0.0047 188 214	0.0038 952 042	0.0032 167 798	82
42	0.0050 423 495	0.0041 409 289	0.0034 022 222	0.0027 965 767	84
43	0.0044 456 343	0.0036 338 082	0.0029 716 326	0.0024 312 640	86
44	0.0039 195 347	0.0031 887 923	0.0025 955 390	0.0021 136 717	88
45	0.0034 556 942	0.0027 982 755	0.0022 670 443	0.0018 375 659	90
46	0.0030 467 448	0.0024 555 835	0.0019 801 243	0.0015 975 274	92
47	0.0026 861 909	0.0021 548 594	0.0017 295 172	0.0013 888 448	94
48	0.0023 683 051	0.0018 909 636	0.0015 106 273	0.0012 074 221	96
49	0.0020 880 382	0.0016 593 859	0.0013 194 404	0.0010 496 984	98
50	0.0018 409 383	0.0014 561 685	0.0011 524 504	0.0009 125 778	100
51	0.0016 230 803	0.0012 778 382	0.0010 065 948	0.0007 933 692	102
52	0.0014 310 038	0.0011 213 472	0.0008 791 989	0.0006 897 325	104
53	0.0012 616 578	0.0009 840 209	0.0007 679 263	0.0005 996 338	106
54	0.0011 123 523	0.0008 635 124	0.0006 707 366	0.0005 213 045	108
55	0.0009 807 157	0.0007 577 619	0.0005 858 473	0.0004 532 073	110
56	0.0008 646 571	0.0006 649 623	0.0005 117 017	0.0003 940 055	112
57	0.0007 623 330	0.0005 835 274	0.0004 469 401	0.0003 425 372	114
58	0.0006 721 180	0.0005 120 655	0.0003 903 748	0.0002 977 921	116
59	0.0005 925 790	0.0004 493 552	0.0003 409 685	0.0002 588 919	118
60	0.0005 224 528	0.0003 943 247	0.0002 978 151	0.0002 250 733	120

Table 4. PRESENT WORTH OF ONE DOLLAR
PAYABLE AT END OF EACH PERIOD

HALF YEARS	**15%** NOMINAL ANNUAL RATE	**15½%** NOMINAL ANNUAL RATE	**16%** NOMINAL ANNUAL RATE	**16½%** NOMINAL ANNUAL RATE	HALF YEARS
1	0.9302 325 581	0.9280 742 459	0.9259 259 259	0.9237 875 289	1
YEARS					
1	0.8653 326 122	0.8613 218 060	0.8573 388 203	0.8533 833 985	2
2	0.7488 005 298	0.7418 752 535	0.7350 298 528	0.7282 632 248	4
3	0.6479 615 185	0.6389 933 331	0.6301 696 269	0.6214 877 458	6
4	0.5607 022 334	0.5503 788 917	0.5402 688 845	0.5303 673 246	8
5	0.4851 939 283	0.4740 533 410	0.4631 934 881	0.4526 066 699	10
6	0.4198 541 294	0.4083 124 798	0.3971 137 586	0.3862 470 182	12
7	0.3633 134 706	0.3516 884 425	0.3404 610 414	0.3296 167 930	14
8	0.3143 869 945	0.3029 169 244	0.2918 904 676	0.2812 894 990	16
9	0.2720 493 192	0.2609 089 524	0.2502 490 291	0.2400 477 886	18
10	0.2354 131 481	0.2247 265 701	0.2145 482 074	0.2048 527 977	20
11	0.2037 106 744	0.1935 618 952	0.1839 405 070	0.1748 179 767	22
12	0.1762 774 900	0.1667 190 811	0.1576 993 373	0.1491 867 590	24
13	0.1525 386 609	0.1435 987 800	0.1352 017 638	0.1273 135 034	26
14	0.1319 966 779	0.1236 847 606	0.1159 137 207	0.1086 472 302	28
15	0.1142 210 301	0.1065 323 813	0.0993 773 325	0.0927 177 426	30
16	0.0988 391 823	0.0917 586 631	0.0852 000 451	0.0791 237 823	32
17	0.0855 287 678	0.0790 337 374	0.0730 453 061	0.0675 229 222	34
18	0.0740 108 321	0.0680 734 814	0.0626 245 766	0.0576 229 408	36
19	0.0640 439 867	0.0586 331 740	0.0536 904 806	0.0491 744 611	38
20	0.0554 193 503	0.0505 020 313	0.0460 309 333	0.0419 646 687	40
21	0.0479 561 711	0.0434 985 008	0.0394 641 061	0.0358 119 516	42
22	0.0414 980 388	0.0374 662 073	0.0338 341 101	0.0305 613 250	44
23	0.0359 096 064	0.0322 704 613	0.0290 072 961	0.0260 805 274	46
24	0.0310 737 535	0.0277 952 520	0.0248 690 810	0.0222 566 891	48
25	0.0268 891 323	0.0239 406 567	0.0213 212 286	0.0189 934 890	50
26	0.0232 680 431	0.0206 206 096	0.0182 795 169	0.0162 087 282	52
27	0.0201 345 965	0.0177 609 807	0.0156 717 395	0.0138 322 595	54
28	0.0174 231 230	0.0152 979 200	0.0134 359 906	0.0118 042 206	56
29	0.0150 767 965	0.0131 764 321	0.0115 191 964	0.0100 735 259	58
30	0.0130 464 437	0.0113 491 483	0.0098 758 542	0.0085 965 798	60
31	0.0112 895 132	0.0097 752 689	0.0084 669 532	0.0073 361 785	62
32	0.0097 691 840	0.0084 196 523	0.0072 590 477	0.0062 605 729	64
33	0.0084 535 935	0.0072 520 301	0.0062 234 634	0.0053 426 690	66
34	0.0073 151 701	0.0062 463 316	0.0053 356 167	0.0045 593 450	68
35	0.0063 300 553	0.0053 801 017	0.0045 744 314	0.0038 908 694	70
36	0.0054 776 033	0.0046 339 989	0.0039 218 376	0.0033 204 033	72
37	0.0047 399 487	0.0039 913 643	0.0033 623 436	0.0028 335 771	74
38	0.0041 016 322	0.0034 378 491	0.0028 826 677	0.0024 181 276	76
39	0.0035 492 761	0.0029 610 944	0.0024 714 229	0.0020 635 900	78
40	0.0030 713 044	0.0025 504 552	0.0021 188 468	0.0017 610 334	80
41	0.0026 576 998	0.0021 967 626	0.0018 165 696	0.0015 028 367	82
42	0.0022 997 944	0.0018 921 196	0.0015 574 157	0.0012 824 959	84
43	0.0019 900 871	0.0016 297 238	0.0013 352 329	0.0010 944 607	86
44	0.0017 220 872	0.0014 037 167	0.0011 447 470	0.0009 339 946	88
45	0.0014 901 782	0.0012 090 518	0.0009 814 360	0.0007 970 555	90
46	0.0012 894 998	0.0010 413 827	0.0008 414 232	0.0006 801 939	92
47	0.0011 158 463	0.0008 969 656	0.0007 213 848	0.0005 804 662	94
48	0.0009 655 782	0.0007 725 760	0.0006 184 712	0.0004 953 602	96
49	0.0008 355 463	0.0006 654 366	0.0005 302 394	0.0004 227 322	98
50	0.0007 230 254	0.0005 731 550	0.0004 545 948	0.0003 607 526	100
51	0.0006 256 575	0.0004 936 709	0.0003 897 418	0.0003 078 603	102
52	0.0005 414 018	0.0004 252 095	0.0003 341 407	0.0002 627 229	104
53	0.0004 684 927	0.0003 662 423	0.0002 864 718	0.0002 242 033	106
54	0.0004 054 020	0.0003 154 524	0.0002 456 034	0.0001 913 314	108
55	0.0003 508 076	0.0002 717 061	0.0002 105 653	0.0001 632 790	110
56	0.0003 035 652	0.0002 340 264	0.0001 805 258	0.0001 393 396	112
57	0.0002 626 849	0.0002 015 720	0.0001 547 718	0.0001 189 101	114
58	0.0002 273 098	0.0001 736 184	0.0001 326 919	0.0001 014 759	116
59	0.0001 966 986	0.0001 495 413	0.0001 137 619	0.0000 865 979	118
60	0.0001 702 097	0.0001 288 032	0.0000 975 325	0.0000 739 012	120

Table 4.   PRESENT WORTH OF ONE DOLLAR
            PAYABLE AT END OF EACH PERIOD

	17% NOMINAL ANNUAL RATE	17½% NOMINAL ANNUAL RATE	18% NOMINAL ANNUAL RATE	18½% NOMINAL ANNUAL RATE	
HALF YEARS					HALF YEARS
1	0.9216 589 862	0.9195 402 299	0.9174 311 927	0.9153 318 078	1
YEARS					
1	0.8494 552 868	0.8455 542 344	0.8416 799 933	0.8378 323 183	2
2	0.7215 742 843	0.7149 619 633	0.7084 252 111	0.7019 629 936	4
3	0.6129 450 906	0.6045 391 155	0.5962 673 269	0.5881 272 824	6
4	0.5206 694 477	0.5111 706 089	0.5018 662 797	0.4927 520 444	8
5	0.4422 854 150	0.4322 224 729	0.4224 108 069	0.4128 435 878	10
6	0.3757 016 841	0.3654 675 421	0.3555 347 251	0.3458 937 002	12
7	0.3191 417 818	0.3090 226 278	0.2992 464 650	0.2898 009 208	14
8	0.2710 966 738	0.2612 953 914	0.2518 697 627	0.2428 045 773	16
9	0.2302 845 028	0.2209 394 246	0.2119 937 402	0.2034 295 219	18
10	0.1956 163 884	0.1868 162 661	0.1784 308 898	0.1704 398 280	20
11	0.1661 673 753	0.1579 632 848	0.1501 817 101	0.1427 999 962	22
12	0.1411 517 554	0.1335 665 243	0.1264 049 408	0.1196 424 519	24
13	0.1199 021 049	0.1129 377 402	0.1063 925 097	0.1002 403 128	26
14	0.1018 514 769	0.0954 949 845	0.0895 484 468	0.0839 845 737	28
15	0.0865 182 755	0.0807 461 885	0.0753 711 361	0.0703 649 901	30
16	0.0734 934 065	0.0682 752 816	0.0634 383 773	0.0589 540 628	32
17	0.0624 293 627	0.0577 304 534	0.0533 948 130	0.0493 936 191	34
18	0.0530 309 522	0.0488 142 294	0.0449 413 459	0.0413 835 704	36
19	0.0450 474 227	0.0412 750 783	0.0378 262 317	0.0346 724 927	38
20	0.0382 657 714	0.0349 003 173	0.0318 375 824	0.0290 497 350	40
21	0.0325 050 618	0.0295 101 110	0.0267 970 562	0.0243 388 068	42
22	0.0276 115 966	0.0249 523 993	0.0225 545 461	0.0203 918 389	44
23	0.0234 548 167	0.0210 986 069	0.0189 837 102	0.0170 849 417	46
24	0.0199 238 181	0.0178 400 164	0.0159 782 090	0.0143 143 163	48
25	0.0169 243 926	0.0150 847 014	0.0134 485 389	0.0119 929 968	50
26	0.0143 765 148	0.0127 549 332	0.0113 193 661	0.0100 481 203	52
27	0.0122 122 065	0.0107 849 878	0.0095 272 840	0.0084 186 399	54
28	0.0103 737 233	0.0091 192 921	0.0080 189 243	0.0070 534 086	56
29	0.0088 120 141	0.0077 108 560	0.0067 493 682	0.0059 095 737	58
30	0.0074 854 120	0.0065 199 470	0.0056 808 082	0.0049 512 318	60
31	0.0063 585 228	0.0055 129 688	0.0047 814 226	0.0041 483 020	62
32	0.0054 012 808	0.0046 615 141	0.0040 244 277	0.0034 755 815	64
33	0.0045 881 465	0.0039 415 630	0.0033 872 803	0.0029 119 545	66
34	0.0038 974 253	0.0033 328 053	0.0028 510 061	0.0024 397 296	68
35	0.0033 106 886	0.0028 180 676	0.0023 996 348	0.0020 440 843	70
36	0.0028 122 819	0.0023 828 290	0.0020 197 246	0.0017 125 999	72
37	0.0023 889 077	0.0020 148 111	0.0016 999 618	0.0014 348 715	74
38	0.0020 292 703	0.0017 036 321	0.0014 308 238	0.0012 021 818	76
39	0.0017 237 744	0.0014 405 133	0.0012 042 958	0.0010 072 267	78
40	0.0014 642 693	0.0012 180 321	0.0010 136 317	0.0008 438 871	80
41	0.0012 438 313	0.0010 299 122	0.0008 531 535	0.0007 070 359	82
42	0.0010 565 790	0.0008 708 467	0.0007 180 822	0.0005 923 775	84
43	0.0008 975 167	0.0007 363 481	0.0006 043 954	0.0004 963 130	86
44	0.0007 624 003	0.0006 226 222	0.0005 087 075	0.0004 158 271	88
45	0.0006 476 249	0.0005 264 609	0.0004 281 690	0.0003 483 934	90
46	0.0005 501 284	0.0004 451 512	0.0003 603 813	0.0002 918 952	92
47	0.0004 673 095	0.0003 763 995	0.0003 033 257	0.0002 445 593	94
48	0.0003 969 585	0.0003 182 662	0.0002 553 032	0.0002 048 997	96
49	0.0003 371 985	0.0002 691 113	0.0002 148 836	0.0001 716 715	98
50	0.0002 864 351	0.0002 275 482	0.0001 808 632	0.0001 438 320	100
51	0.0002 433 138	0.0001 924 044	0.0001 522 289	0.0001 205 071	102
52	0.0002 066 842	0.0001 626 883	0.0001 281 280	0.0001 009 647	104
53	0.0001 755 690	0.0001 375 618	0.0001 078 428	0.0000 845 915	106
54	0.0001 491 380	0.0001 163 160	0.0000 907 691	0.0000 708 735	108
55	0.0001 266 861	0.0000 983 515	0.0000 763 986	0.0000 593 801	110
56	0.0001 076 141	0.0000 831 615	0.0000 643 031	0.0000 497 506	112
57	0.0000 914 134	0.0000 703 175	0.0000 541 227	0.0000 416 826	114
58	0.0000 776 516	0.0000 594 573	0.0000 455 540	0.0000 349 231	116
59	0.0000 659 616	0.0000 502 744	0.0000 383 419	0.0000 292 597	118
60	0.0000 560 314	0.0000 425 097	0.0000 322 716	0.0000 245 147	120

Table 4. PRESENT WORTH OF ONE DOLLAR
PAYABLE AT END OF EACH PERIOD

HALF YEARS	19% NOMINAL ANNUAL RATE	19½% NOMINAL ANNUAL RATE	20% NOMINAL ANNUAL RATE	20½% NOMINAL ANNUAL RATE	HALF YEARS
1	0.9132 420 091	0.9111 617 312	0.9090 909 091	0.9070 294 785	1
YEARS					
1	0.8340 109 672	0.8302 157 004	0.8264 462 810	0.8227 024 748	2
2	0.6955 742 935	0.6892 581 092	0.6830 134 554	0.6768 393 620	4
3	0.5801 165 893	0.5722 329 039	0.5644 739 301	0.5568 374 182	6
4	0.4838 235 978	0.4750 767 411	0.4665 073 802	0.4581 115 220	8
5	0.4035 141 867	0.3944 161 694	0.3855 432 894	0.3768 894 829	10
6	0.3365 352 572	0.3274 504 963	0.3186 308 177	0.3100 679 103	12
7	0.2806 740 954	0.2718 545 432	0.2633 312 543	0.2550 936 371	14
8	0.2340 852 737	0.2256 979 100	0.2176 291 358	0.2098 661 666	16
9	0.1952 296 856	0.1873 779 484	0.1798 587 899	0.1726 574 146	18
10	0.1628 236 989	0.1555 641 147	0.1486 436 280	0.1420 456 823	20
11	0.1357 967 506	0.1291 517 704	0.1228 459 736	0.1168 613 344	22
12	0.1132 559 793	0.1072 238 275	0.1015 255 980	0.0961 421 090	24
13	0.0944 567 289	0.0890 189 051	0.0839 054 529	0.0790 963 510	26
14	0.0787 079 478	0.0739 048 926	0.0693 433 495	0.0650 727 637	28
15	0.0657 016 724	0.0613 570 022	0.0573 085 533	0.0535 355 237	30
16	0.0547 959 154	0.0509 395 466	0.0473 624 407	0.0440 438 079	32
17	0.0457 003 944	0.0422 908 113	0.0391 425 130	0.0362 349 497	34
18	0.0381 146 301	0.0351 104 955	0.0323 491 843	0.0298 105 828	36
19	0.0317 880 195	0.0291 492 847	0.0267 348 631	0.0245 252 403	38
20	0.0265 115 569	0.0242 001 938	0.0220 949 282	0.0201 769 759	40
21	0.0221 109 292	0.0200 913 808	0.0182 602 712	0.0165 996 480	42
22	0.0184 407 575	0.0166 801 798	0.0150 911 332	0.0136 565 715	44
23	0.0153 797 940	0.0138 481 472	0.0124 720 109	0.0112 352 951	46
24	0.0128 269 169	0.0114 969 492	0.0103 074 470	0.0092 433 051	48
25	0.0106 977 893	0.0095 449 477	0.0085 185 513	0.0076 044 900	50
26	0.0089 220 736	0.0079 243 655	0.0070 401 250	0.0062 562 327	52
27	0.0074 411 073	0.0065 789 326	0.0058 182 851	0.0051 470 182	54
28	0.0062 059 651	0.0054 619 332	0.0048 085 001	0.0042 344 646	56
29	0.0051 758 429	0.0045 345 827	0.0039 739 670	0.0034 837 045	58
30	0.0043 167 098	0.0037 646 817	0.0032 842 703	0.0028 660 523	60
31	0.0036 001 833	0.0031 254 979	0.0027 142 730	0.0023 579 083	62
32	0.0030 025 923	0.0025 948 374	0.0022 432 008	0.0019 398 570	64
33	0.0025 041 949	0.0021 542 748	0.0018 538 850	0.0015 959 252	66
34	0.0020 885 260	0.0017 885 127	0.0015 321 363	0.0013 129 716	68
35	0.0017 418 536	0.0014 848 513	0.0012 662 284	0.0010 801 850	70
36	0.0014 527 250	0.0012 327 469	0.0010 464 697	0.0008 886 708	72
37	0.0012 115 886	0.0010 234 458	0.0008 648 510	0.0007 311 117	74
38	0.0010 104 787	0.0008 496 808	0.0007 147 529	0.0006 014 874	76
39	0.0008 427 499	0.0007 054 183	0.0005 907 049	0.0004 948 452	78
40	0.0007 028 627	0.0005 856 494	0.0004 881 859	0.0004 071 104	80
41	0.0005 861 952	0.0004 862 153	0.0004 034 594	0.0003 349 307	82
42	0.0004 888 932	0.0004 036 636	0.0003 334 375	0.0002 755 483	84
43	0.0004 077 423	0.0003 351 278	0.0002 755 682	0.0002 266 943	86
44	0.0003 400 615	0.0002 782 284	0.0002 277 423	0.0001 865 019	88
45	0.0002 836 151	0.0002 309 896	0.0001 882 168	0.0001 534 356	90
46	0.0002 365 381	0.0001 917 712	0.0001 555 511	0.0001 262 319	92
47	0.0001 972 753	0.0001 592 114	0.0001 285 546	0.0001 038 513	94
48	0.0001 645 298	0.0001 321 798	0.0001 062 435	0.0000 854 387	96
49	0.0001 372 197	0.0001 097 378	0.0000 878 045	0.0000 702 906	98
50	0.0001 144 427	0.0000 911 060	0.0000 725 657	0.0000 578 283	100
51	0.0000 954 465	0.0000 756 377	0.0000 599 717	0.0000 475 755	102
52	0.0000 796 034	0.0000 627 956	0.0000 495 634	0.0000 391 404	104
53	0.0000 663 901	0.0000 521 339	0.0000 409 615	0.0000 322 009	106
54	0.0000 553 701	0.0000 432 824	0.0000 338 524	0.0000 264 918	108
55	0.0000 461 793	0.0000 359 337	0.0000 279 772	0.0000 217 949	110
56	0.0000 385 140	0.0000 298 327	0.0000 231 217	0.0000 179 307	112
57	0.0000 321 211	0.0000 247 676	0.0000 191 088	0.0000 147 516	114
58	0.0000 267 893	0.0000 205 624	0.0000 157 924	0.0000 121 362	116
59	0.0000 223 426	0.0000 170 713	0.0000 130 516	0.0000 099 845	118
60	0.0000 186 340	0.0000 141 728	0.0000 107 864	0.0000 082 143	120

Table 4.   PRESENT WORTH OF ONE DOLLAR
PAYABLE AT END OF EACH PERIOD

HALF YEARS	21% NOMINAL ANNUAL RATE	21½% NOMINAL ANNUAL RATE	22% NOMINAL ANNUAL RATE	22½% NOMINAL ANNUAL RATE	HALF YEARS
1	0.9049 773 756	0.9029 345 372	0.9009 009 009	0.8988 764 045	1
YEARS					
1	0.8189 840 503	0.8152 907 786	0.8116 224 332	0.8079 787 906	2
2	0.6707 348 746	0.6646 990 536	0.6587 309 741	0.6528 297 260	4
3	0.5493 211 643	0.5419 230 089	0.5346 408 361	0.5274 725 724	6
4	0.4498 852 720	0.4418 248 318	0.4339 264 963	0.4261 866 511	8
5	0.3684 488 623	0.3602 157 111	0.3521 844 788	0.3443 497 749	10
6	0.3017 537 415	0.2936 805 476	0.2858 408 236	0.2782 273 147	12
7	0.2471 315 014	0.2394 350 423	0.2319 948 248	0.2248 017 692	14
8	0.2023 967 580	0.1952 091 820	0.1882 922 042	0.1816 350 616	16
9	0.1657 597 166	0.1591 522 460	0.1528 221 769	0.1467 572 774	18
10	0.1357 545 641	0.1297 553 586	0.1240 339 071	0.1185 767 675	20
11	0.1111 808 227	0.1057 883 473	0.1006 687 015	0.0958 075 132	22
12	0.0910 553 205	0.0862 482 640	0.0817 049 764	0.0774 104 386	24
13	0.0745 728 552	0.0703 174 143	0.0663 135 918	0.0625 459 926	26
14	0.0610 739 790	0.0573 291 395	0.0538 215 987	0.0505 358 354	28
15	0.0500 186 147	0.0467 399 188	0.0436 828 169	0.0408 318 832	30
16	0.0409 644 476	0.0381 066 248	0.0354 539 542	0.0329 912 956	32
17	0.0335 492 293	0.0310 679 798	0.0287 752 245	0.0266 562 671	34
18	0.0274 762 837	0.0253 294 374	0.0233 546 178	0.0215 376 985	36
19	0.0225 026 381	0.0206 508 567	0.0189 551 317	0.0174 020 036	38
20	0.0184 293 017	0.0168 364 531	0.0153 844 101	0.0140 604 498	40
21	0.0150 933 041	0.0137 266 049	0.0124 863 324	0.0113 605 452	42
22	0.0123 611 753	0.0111 911 744	0.0101 341 875	0.0091 790 796	44
23	0.0101 236 055	0.0091 240 613	0.0082 251 339	0.0074 165 016	46
24	0.0082 910 714	0.0074 387 630	0.0066 757 032	0.0059 923 760	48
25	0.0067 902 552	0.0060 647 549	0.0054 181 505	0.0048 417 127	50
26	0.0055 611 107	0.0049 445 388	0.0043 974 925	0.0039 120 012	52
27	0.0045 544 610	0.0040 312 369	0.0035 691 035	0.0031 608 140	54
28	0.0037 300 309	0.0032 866 302	0.0028 967 645	0.0025 538 707	56
29	0.0030 548 358	0.0026 795 593	0.0023 510 790	0.0020 634 733	58
30	0.0025 018 618	0.0021 846 200	0.0019 081 885	0.0016 672 427	60
31	0.0020 489 849	0.0017 811 005	0.0015 487 286	0.0013 470 967	62
32	0.0016 780 860	0.0014 521 148	0.0012 569 829	0.0010 884 256	64
33	0.0013 743 256	0.0011 838 958	0.0010 201 955	0.0008 794 248	66
34	0.0011 255 508	0.0009 652 194	0.0008 280 135	0.0007 105 566	68
35	0.0009 218 081	0.0007 869 344	0.0006 720 344	0.0005 741 146	70
36	0.0007 549 462	0.0006 415 804	0.0005 454 382	0.0004 638 725	72
37	0.0006 182 889	0.0005 230 746	0.0004 426 899	0.0003 747 991	74
38	0.0005 063 687	0.0004 264 579	0.0003 592 970	0.0003 028 297	76
39	0.0004 147 079	0.0003 476 872	0.0002 916 135	0.0002 446 800	78
40	0.0003 396 392	0.0002 834 662	0.0002 366 801	0.0001 976 962	80
41	0.0002 781 591	0.0002 311 073	0.0001 920 949	0.0001 597 344	82
42	0.0002 278 078	0.0001 884 197	0.0001 559 085	0.0001 290 620	84
43	0.0001 865 710	0.0001 536 168	0.0001 265 388	0.0001 042 793	86
44	0.0001 527 987	0.0001 252 424	0.0001 027 018	0.0000 842 555	88
45	0.0001 251 397	0.0001 021 090	0.0000 833 550	0.0000 680 767	90
46	0.0001 024 874	0.0000 832 485	0.0000 676 528	0.0000 550 045	92
47	0.0000 839 355	0.0000 678 717	0.0000 549 086	0.0000 444 425	94
48	0.0000 687 419	0.0000 553 352	0.0000 445 650	0.0000 359 086	96
49	0.0000 562 985	0.0000 451 143	0.0000 361 700	0.0000 290 134	98
50	0.0000 461 076	0.0000 367 813	0.0000 293 564	0.0000 234 422	100
51	0.0000 377 614	0.0000 299 874	0.0000 238 263	0.0000 189 408	102
52	0.0000 309 260	0.0000 244 485	0.0000 193 379	0.0000 153 038	104
53	0.0000 253 279	0.0000 199 326	0.0000 156 951	0.0000 123 651	106
54	0.0000 207 431	0.0000 162 509	0.0000 127 385	0.0000 099 907	108
55	0.0000 169 883	0.0000 132 492	0.0000 103 389	0.0000 080 723	110
56	0.0000 139 131	0.0000 108 019	0.0000 083 912	0.0000 065 223	112
57	0.0000 113 946	0.0000 088 067	0.0000 068 105	0.0000 052 698	114
58	0.0000 093 320	0.0000 071 800	0.0000 055 276	0.0000 042 579	116
59	0.0000 076 428	0.0000 058 538	0.0000 044 863	0.0000 034 403	118
60	0.0000 062 593	0.0000 047 726	0.0000 036 412	0.0000 027 797	120

Table 5.   PRESENT WORTH OF ONE DOLLAR PER PERIOD
PAYABLE AT END OF EACH PERIOD

HALF YEARS	5% NOMINAL ANNUAL RATE	5½% NOMINAL ANNUAL RATE	6% NOMINAL ANNUAL RATE	6½% NOMINAL ANNUAL RATE	HALF YEARS
1	0.9756 097 561	0.9732 360 097	0.9708 737 864	0.9685 230 024	1
YEARS					
1	1.9274 241 523	1.9204 243 404	1.9134 696 955	1.9065 598 086	2
2	3.7619 742 080	3.7394 278 654	3.7170 984 028	3.6949 830 824	4
3	5.5081 253 616	5.4623 667 778	5.4171 914 439	5.3725 899 383	6
4	7.1701 371 675	7.0943 144 100	7.0196 921 895	6.9462 469 155	8
5	8.7520 639 310	8.6400 761 634	8.5302 028 368	8.4223 950 804	10
6	10.2577 645 982	10.1042 036 582	9.9540 039 936	9.8070 763 906	12
7	11.6909 121 696	11.4910 081 358	11.2960 783 394	11.1059 584 244	14
8	13.0550 026 599	12.8045 731 539	12.5611 020 260	12.3243 575 791	16
9	14.3533 636 264	14.0487 666 106	13.7535 130 795	13.4672 608 309	18
10	15.5891 622 856	15.2272 521 338	14.8774 748 605	14.5393 461 469	20
11	16.7654 132 404	16.3434 998 692	15.9369 166 372	15.5450 016 328	22
12	17.8849 858 326	17.4007 966 983	16.9355 421 220	16.4883 434 930	24
13	18.9506 111 434	18.4022 559 168	17.8768 424 187	17.3732 328 786	26
14	19.9648 886 553	19.3508 264 022	18.7641 082 277	18.2032 916 918	28
15	20.9302 925 928	20.2493 012 968	19.6004 413 495	18.9819 174 099	30
16	21.8491 779 586	21.1003 262 323	20.3887 655 288	19.7122 969 917	32
17	22.7237 862 783	21.9064 071 203	21.1318 366 752	20.3974 199 220	34
18	23.5562 510 680	22.6699 175 310	21.8322 524 981	21.0400 904 474	36
19	24.3486 030 391	23.3931 056 823	22.4924 615 874	21.6429 390 545	38
20	25.1027 750 521	24.0781 010 600	23.1147 719 742	22.2084 332 365	40
21	25.8206 068 313	24.7269 206 884	23.7013 591 990	22.7388 875 929	42
22	26.5038 494 527	25.3414 750 691	24.2542 739 174	23.2364 733 033	44
23	27.1541 696 159	25.9235 738 070	24.7754 490 691	23.7032 270 139	46
24	27.7731 537 094	26.4749 309 389	25.2667 066 350	24.1410 591 738	48
25	28.3623 116 805	26.9971 699 802	25.7297 640 070	24.5517 618 548	50
26	28.9230 807 191	27.4918 287 059	26.1662 399 915	24.9370 160 860	52
27	29.4568 287 630	27.9603 636 785	26.5776 604 690	25.2983 987 346	54
28	29.9648 578 351	28.4041 545 371	26.9654 637 279	25.6373 889 601	56
29	30.4484 072 196	28.8245 080 596	27.3310 054 934	25.9553 742 685	58
30	30.9086 564 851	29.2226 620 109	27.6755 636 661	26.2536 561 917	60
31	31.3467 283 617	29.5997 887 873	28.0003 427 902	26.5334 556 143	62
32	31.7636 914 805	29.9569 988 691	28.3064 782 639	26.7959 177 710	64
33	32.1605 629 797	30.2953 440 902	28.5950 403 091	27.0421 169 343	66
34	32.5383 109 860	30.6158 207 353	28.8670 377 124	27.2730 608 111	68
35	32.8978 569 766	30.9193 724 738	29.1234 213 521	27.4896 946 677	70
36	33.2400 780 265	31.2068 931 383	29.3650 875 220	27.6929 051 987	72
37	33.5658 089 485	31.4792 293 565	29.5928 810 651	27.8835 241 561	74
38	33.8758 443 293	31.7371 830 443	29.8075 983 270	28.0623 317 542	76
39	34.1709 404 681	31.9815 137 674	30.0099 899 397	28.2300 598 624	78
40	34.4518 172 213	32.2129 409 770	30.2007 634 458	28.3873 950 014	80
41	34.7191 597 585	32.4321 461 294	30.3805 857 723	28.5349 811 526	82
42	34.9736 202 342	32.6397 746 917	30.5500 855 616	28.6734 223 945	84
43	35.2158 193 781	32.8364 380 431	30.7098 553 696	28.8032 853 750	86
44	35.4463 480 101	33.0227 152 746	30.8604 537 370	28.9251 016 304	88
45	35.6657 684 808	33.1991 548 945	31.0024 071 421	29.0393 697 616	90
46	35.8746 160 415	33.3662 764 435	31.1362 118 409	29.1465 574 744	92
47	36.0734 001 605	33.5245 720 246	31.2623 356 027	29.2471 034 942	94
48	36.2626 057 446	33.6745 077 517	31.3812 193 446	29.3414 193 615	96
49	36.4426 943 435	33.8165 251 229	31.4932 786 734	29.4298 911 165	98
50	36.6141 052 645	33.9510 423 195	31.5989 053 383	29.5128 808 789	100
51	36.7772 566 467	34.0784 554 385	31.6984 686 006	29.5907 283 306	102
52	36.9325 464 811	34.1991 396 579	31.7923 165 242	29.6637 521 056	104
53	37.0803 535 811	34.3134 503 423	31.8807 771 932	29.7322 510 943	106
54	37.2210 385 067	34.4217 240 886	31.9641 598 578	29.7965 056 668	108
55	37.3549 444 442	34.5242 797 176	32.0427 560 164	29.8567 788 208	110
56	37.4823 980 433	34.6214 192 126	32.1168 404 340	29.9133 172 577	112
57	37.6037 102 137	34.7134 286 087	32.1866 721 029	29.9663 523 925	114
58	37.7191 768 839	34.8005 788 351	32.2524 951 484	30.0161 013 009	116
59	37.8290 797 230	34.8831 265 125	32.3145 396 818	30.0627 676 081	118
60	37.9336 868 273	34.9613 147 092	32.3730 226 051	30.1065 423 219	120

Table 5.   PRESENT WORTH OF ONE DOLLAR PER PERIOD
PAYABLE AT END OF EACH PERIOD

HALF YEARS	7% NOMINAL ANNUAL RATE	7½% NOMINAL ANNUAL RATE	8% NOMINAL ANNUAL RATE	8½% NOMINAL ANNUAL RATE	HALF YEARS
1	0.9661 835 749	0.9638 554 217	0.9615 384 615	0.9592 326 139	1
YEARS					
1	1.8996 942 752	1.8928 726 956	1.8860 946 746	1.8793 598 215	2
2	3.6730 792 086	3.6513 841 271	3.6298 952 243	3.6086 099 261	4
3	5.3285 530 198	5.2850 716 234	5.2421 368 567	5.1997 399 961	6
4	6.8739 555 367	6.8027 955 276	6.7327 448 750	6.6637 820 642	8
5	8.3166 053 226	8.2127 872 517	8.1108 957 794	8.0108 870 042	10
6	9.6633 343 346	9.5226 939 194	9.3850 737 605	9.2503 949 110	12
7	10.9205 202 778	10.7396 198 409	10.5631 229 295	10.3908 998 600	14
8	12.0941 168 081	11.8701 650 431	11.6522 956 079	11.4403 094 940	16
9	13.1896 817 271	12.9204 610 649	12.6592 969 747	12.4058 998 501	18
10	14.2124 033 020	13.8962 042 118	13.5903 263 450	13.2943 658 082	20
11	15.1671 248 355	14.8026 864 502	14.4511 153 337	14.1118 675 092	22
12	16.0583 676 030	15.6448 241 082	15.2469 631 414	14.8640 730 666	24
13	16.8903 522 631	16.4271 845 395	15.9827 691 766	15.5561 978 656	26
14	17.6670 188 458	17.1540 108 946	16.6630 632 180	16.1930 407 243	28
15	18.3920 454 114	17.8292 451 336	17.2920 333 007	16.7790 171 654	30
16	19.0688 654 684	18.4565 494 056	17.8735 514 984	17.3181 900 320	32
17	19.7006 842 338	19.0393 259 102	18.4111 977 611	17.8142 976 561	34
18	20.2904 938 121	19.5807 353 499	18.9082 819 537	18.2707 797 789	36
19	20.8410 873 645	20.0837 140 716	19.3678 642 323	18.6908 013 999	38
20	21.3550 723 373	20.5509 899 925	19.7927 738 834	19.0772 747 211	40
21	21.8348 828 092	20.9850 973 947	20.1856 267 413	19.4328 793 390	42
22	22.2827 910 189	21.3883 906 701	20.5488 412 919	19.7600 808 230	44
23	22.7009 181 254	21.7630 570 893	20.8846 535 613	20.0611 478 109	46
24	23.0912 442 535	22.1111 286 648	21.1951 308 814	20.3381 677 377	48
25	23.4556 178 706	22.4344 931 709	21.4821 846 167	20.5930 613 094	50
26	23.7957 645 412	22.7349 043 829	21.7475 819 311	20.8275 958 198	52
27	24.1132 950 978	23.0139 915 882	21.9929 566 671	21.0433 974 039	54
28	24.4097 132 702	23.2732 684 227	22.2198 194 037	21.2419 623 129	56
29	24.6864 228 058	23.5141 410 808	22.4295 667 564	21.4246 672 881	58
30	24.9447 341 182	23.7379 159 409	22.6234 899 745	21.5927 791 068	60
31	25.1858 704 924	23.9458 066 515	22.8027 828 906	21.7474 633 650	62
32	25.4109 738 780	24.1389 407 126	22.9685 492 702	21.8897 925 596	64
33	25.6211 102 971	24.3183 655 916	23.1218 096 063	22.0207 535 240	66
34	25.8172 748 928	24.4850 544 036	23.2635 074 023	22.1412 542 705	68
35	26.0003 966 420	24.6399 111 893	23.3945 149 799	22.2521 302 859	70
36	26.1713 427 543	24.7837 758 182	23.5156 388 498	22.3541 503 243	72
37	26.3309 227 794	24.9174 285 435	23.6276 246 762	22.4480 217 374	74
38	26.4798 924 403	25.0415 942 341	23.7311 618 678	22.5343 953 785	76
39	26.6189 572 128	25.1569 463 054	23.8268 878 215	22.6138 701 158	78
40	26.7487 756 660	25.2641 103 723	23.9153 918 468	22.6869 969 839	80
41	26.8699 625 812	25.3636 476 416	23.9972 187 933	22.7542 830 048	82
42	26.9830 918 632	25.4561 580 645	24.0728 724 050	22.8161 947 033	84
43	27.0886 992 585	25.5420 832 650	24.1428 184 218	22.8731 613 416	86
44	27.1872 848 921	25.6219 092 606	24.2074 874 462	22.9255 778 954	88
45	27.2793 156 359	25.6960 689 893	24.2672 775 945	22.9738 077 927	90
46	27.3652 273 200	25.7649 646 584	24.3225 569 476	23.0181 854 334	92
47	27.4454 267 965	25.8289 699 251	24.3736 658 169	23.0590 185 081	94
48	27.5202 938 659	25.8884 319 234	24.4209 188 396	23.0965 901 310	96
49	27.5901 830 763	25.9436 731 470	24.4646 069 153	23.1311 608 035	98
50	27.6554 254 020	25.9949 931 980	24.5049 989 972	23.1629 702 199	100
51	27.7163 298 112	26.0426 704 118	24.5423 437 474	23.1922 389 293	102
52	27.7731 847 289	26.0869 633 671	24.5768 710 682	23.2191 698 652	104
53	27.8262 594 029	26.1281 122 876	24.6087 935 172	23.2439 497 520	106
54	27.8758 051 790	26.1663 403 456	24.6383 076 158	23.2667 504 001	108
55	27.9220 566 912	26.2018 548 718	24.6655 950 589	23.2877 298 968	110
56	27.9652 329 727	26.2348 484 801	24.6908 238 341	23.3070 337 024	112
57	28.0055 384 935	26.2655 001 073	24.7141 492 549	23.3247 956 592	114
58	28.0431 641 285	26.2939 760 078	24.7357 149 176	23.3411 389 190	116
59	28.0782 880 613	26.3204 306 068	24.7556 535 851	23.3561 767 969	118
60	28.1110 766 284	26.3450 073 862	24.7740 880 039	23.3700 135 575	120

Table 5. PRESENT WORTH OF ONE DOLLAR PER PERIOD
PAYABLE AT END OF EACH PERIOD

HALF YEARS	9% NOMINAL ANNUAL RATE	9½% NOMINAL ANNUAL RATE	10% NOMINAL ANNUAL RATE	10½% NOMINAL ANNUAL RATE	HALF YEARS
1	0.9569 377 990	0.9546 539 379	0.9523 809 524	0.9501 187 648	1
YEARS					
1	1.8726 677 503	1.8660 180 792	1.8594 104 308	1.8528 444 322	2
2	3.5875 256 979	3.5666 400 435	3.5459 505 042	3.5254 546 586	4
3	5.1578 724 827	5.1165 259 195	5.0756 920 673	5.0353 628 414	6
4	6.5958 860 674	6.5290 363 299	6.4632 127 594	6.3983 957 133	8
5	7.9127 181 771	7.8163 476 671	7.7217 349 292	7.6288 404 722	10
6	9.1185 807 808	8.9895 570 585	8.8632 516 364	8.7395 945 382	12
7	10.2228 252 840	10.0587 780 279	9.8986 409 401	9.7423 007 437	14
8	11.2340 150 491	11.0332 276 785	10.8377 695 602	10.6474 693 722	16
9	12.1599 918 034	11.9213 061 475	11.6895 869 027	11.4645 883 263	18
10	13.0079 364 515	12.7306 690 187	12.4622 103 425	12.2022 225 795	20
11	13.7844 247 627	13.4682 933 168	13.1630 025 783	12.8681 039 529	22
12	14.4954 783 660	14.1405 376 518	13.7986 417 943	13.4692 121 601	24
13	15.1466 114 476	14.7531 970 329	14.3751 853 010	14.0118 479 676	26
14	15.7428 735 126	15.3115 528 236	14.8981 272 571	14.5016 992 389	28
15	16.2888 885 443	15.8204 182 693	15.3724 510 269	14.9439 005 548	30
16	16.7888 908 627	16.2841 799 892	15.8026 766 684	15.3430 870 327	32
17	17.2467 579 613	16.7068 357 908	16.1929 040 076	15.7034 429 124	34
18	17.6660 405 772	17.0920 291 325	16.5468 517 076	16.0287 454 143	36
19	18.0499 902 266	17.4430 805 316	16.8678 927 053	16.3224 043 325	38
20	18.4015 844 203	17.7630 161 884	17.1590 863 540	16.5874 977 753	40
21	18.7235 497 542	18.0545 940 735	17.4232 075 773	16.8268 044 304	42
22	19.0183 830 536	18.3203 277 024	17.6627 733 128	17.0428 326 903	44
23	19.2883 707 366	18.5625 078 029	17.8800 664 968	17.2378 469 454	46
24	19.5356 065 444	18.7832 220 622	18.0771 578 203	17.4138 913 190	48
25	19.7620 077 785	18.9843 731 236	18.2559 254 606	17.5728 110 936	50
26	19.9693 301 697	19.1676 949 880	18.4180 729 801	17.7162 720 532	52
27	20.1591 814 928	19.3347 679 614	18.5651 455 602	17.8457 779 436	54
28	20.3330 340 357	19.4870 322 784	18.6985 447 258	17.9626 862 350	56
29	20.4922 360 163	19.6258 005 169	18.8195 417 014	18.0682 223 504	58
30	20.6380 220 382	19.7522 689 136	18.9292 895 251	18.1634 925 105	60
31	20.7715 226 650	19.8675 276 749	19.0288 340 363	18.2494 953 294	62
32	20.8937 731 874	19.9725 703 772	19.1191 238 425	18.3271 322 815	64
33	21.0057 216 523	20.0683 025 293	19.2010 193 583	18.3972 171 509	66
34	21.1082 362 147	20.1555 493 799	19.2753 010 052	18.4604 845 614	68
35	21.2021 118 699	20.2350 630 310	19.3426 766 487	18.5175 976 767	70
36	21.2880 766 190	20.3075 289 214	19.4037 883 435	18.5691 551 519	72
37	21.3667 971 145	20.3735 717 353	19.4592 184 522	18.6156 974 081	74
38	21.4388 838 301	20.4337 607 877	19.5094 951 947	18.6577 122 973	76
39	21.5048 957 946	20.4886 149 317	19.5550 976 823	18.6956 402 163	78
40	21.5653 449 276	20.5386 070 316	19.5964 604 828	18.7298 787 222	80
41	21.6207 000 093	20.5841 680 388	19.6339 777 622	18.7607 867 003	82
42	21.6713 903 155	20.6256 907 070	19.6680 070 405	18.7886 881 255	84
43	21.7178 089 471	20.6635 329 778	19.6988 725 991	18.8138 754 582	86
44	21.7603 158 784	20.6980 210 664	19.7268 685 706	18.8366 127 099	88
45	21.7992 407 485	20.7294 522 737	19.7522 617 421	18.8571 382 106	90
46	21.8348 854 179	20.7580 975 490	19.7752 940 971	18.8756 671 069	92
47	21.8675 263 093	20.7842 038 257	19.7961 851 221	18.8923 936 172	94
48	21.8974 165 512	20.8079 961 501	19.8151 338 976	18.9074 930 673	96
49	21.9247 879 409	20.8296 796 214	19.8323 209 955	18.9211 237 286	98
50	21.9498 527 423	20.8494 411 596	19.8479 102 000	18.9334 284 763	100
51	21.9728 053 317	20.8674 511 169	19.8620 500 681	18.9445 362 879	102
52	21.9938 237 052	20.8838 647 462	19.8748 753 452	18.9545 635 946	104
53	22.0130 708 594	20.8988 235 394	19.8865 082 496	18.9636 155 017	106
54	22.0306 960 549	20.9124 564 470	19.8970 596 368	18.9717 869 906	108
55	22.0468 359 744	20.9248 809 902	19.9066 300 561	18.9791 634 130	110
56	22.0616 157 820	20.9362 042 734	19.9153 107 085	18.9858 223 892	112
57	22.0751 500 946	20.9465 239 076	19.9231 843 161	18.9918 336 179	114
58	22.0875 438 699	20.9559 288 522	19.9303 259 549	18.9972 601 084	116
59	22.0988 932 213	20.9645 001 814	19.9368 035 467	19.0021 587 406	118
60	22.1092 861 622	20.9723 117 835	19.9426 789 539	19.0065 808 616	120

167

Table 5. PRESENT WORTH OF ONE DOLLAR PER PERIOD
PAYABLE AT END OF EACH PERIOD

HALF YEARS	11% NOMINAL ANNUAL RATE	11½% NOMINAL ANNUAL RATE	12% NOMINAL ANNUAL RATE	12½% NOMINAL ANNUAL RATE	HALF YEARS
1	0.9478 672 986	0.9456 264 775	0.9433 962 264	0.9411 764 706	1
YEARS					
1	1.8463 197 143	1.8398 359 126	1.8333 926 664	1.8269 896 194	2
2	3.5051 501 218	3.4850 345 445	3.4651 056 127	3.4453 610 469	4
3	4.9955 303 086	4.9561 866 836	4.9173 243 260	4.8789 357 371	6
4	6.3345 659 879	6.2717 048 068	6.2097 048 110	6.1488 150 474	8
5	7.5376 258 286	7.4480 535 246	7.3600 870 514	7.2736 908 378	10
6	8.6185 178 487	8.4999 556 468	8.3838 439 404	8.2701 206 037	12
7	9.5896 478 954	9.4405 764 493	9.2949 839 270	9.1527 711 922	14
8	10.4621 620 317	10.2816 884 456	10.1058 952 715	9.9346 346 893	16
9	11.2460 744 653	11.0338 187 286	10.8276 034 812	10.6272 196 556	18
10	11.9503 824 849	11.7063 807 241	11.4699 212 186	11.2407 205 254	20
11	12.5831 697 266	12.3077 920 061	12.0415 817 182	11.7841 676 626	22
12	13.1516 989 525	12.8455 796 488	12.5503 575 278	12.2655 602 824	24
13	13.6624 954 089	13.3264 744 329	13.0031 661 870	12.6919 841 948	26
14	14.1214 217 191	13.7564 950 861	13.4061 642 818	13.0697 161 034	28
15	14.5337 451 711	14.1410 236 115	13.7648 311 515	13.4043 159 947	30
16	14.9041 981 727	14.4848 726 469	14.0840 433 887	13.7007 089 780	32
17	15.2370 325 668	14.7923 456 986	14.3681 411 433	13.9632 577 798	34
18	15.5360 684 322	15.0672 910 024	14.6209 871 336	14.1958 269 607	36
19	15.8047 379 279	15.3131 496 872	14.8460 191 648	14.4018 397 991	38
20	16.0461 246 854	15.5329 988 429	15.0462 968 715	14.5843 286 801	40
21	16.2629 992 007	15.7295 900 321	15.2245 433 175	14.7459 797 305	42
22	16.4578 506 329	15.9053 837 284	15.3831 820 198	14.8891 723 564	44
23	16.6329 153 729	16.0625 801 103	15.5243 699 002	15.0160 142 673	46
24	16.7902 027 114	16.2031 465 980	15.6500 266 110	15.1283 724 997	48
25	16.9315 179 007	16.3288 424 777	15.7618 606 364	15.2279 008 994	50
26	17.0584 828 739	16.4412 409 192	15.8613 925 208	15.3160 644 645	52
27	17.1725 548 608	16.5417 486 660	15.9499 755 436	15.3941 609 098	54
28	17.2750 431 129	16.6316 236 416	16.0288 141 186	15.4633 397 678	56
29	17.3671 239 307	16.7119 906 927	16.0989 801 696	15.5246 193 099	58
30	17.4498 541 638	16.7838 556 681	16.1614 277 052	15.5789 015 340	60
31	17.5241 833 416	16.8481 180 071	16.2170 057 896	15.6269 854 419	62
32	17.5909 645 710	16.9055 819 970	16.2664 700 869	15.6695 787 998	64
33	17.6509 643 278	16.9569 668 389	16.3104 931 354	15.7073 085 562	66
34	17.7048 712 543	17.0029 156 493	16.3496 734 918	15.7407 300 705	68
35	17.7533 040 626	17.0440 035 092	16.3845 438 695	15.7703 352 874	70
36	17.7968 186 363	17.0807 446 611	16.4155 783 816	15.7965 599 778	72
37	17.8359 144 101	17.1135 989 458	16.4431 989 868	15.8197 901 533	74
38	17.8710 401 025	17.1429 775 572	16.4677 812 271	15.8403 677 483	76
39	17.9025 988 657	17.1692 481 887	16.4896 593 335	15.8585 956 524	78
40	17.9309 529 127	17.1927 396 352	16.5091 307 703	15.8747 421 696	80
41	17.9564 276 748	17.2137 459 083	16.5264 602 797	15.8890 449 669	82
42	17.9793 155 363	17.2325 299 160	16.5418 834 814	15.9017 145 727	84
43	17.9998 791 908	17.2493 267 528	16.5556 100 760	15.9129 374 762	86
44	18.0183 546 558	17.2643 466 428	16.5678 266 963	15.9228 788 716	88
45	18.0349 539 820	17.2777 775 702	16.5786 994 450	15.9316 850 905	90
46	18.0498 676 867	17.2897 876 321	16.5883 761 525	15.9394 857 549	92
47	18.0632 669 407	17.3005 271 428	16.5969 883 878	15.9463 956 860	94
48	18.0753 055 329	17.3101 305 146	16.6046 532 465	15.9525 165 938	96
49	18.0861 216 351	17.3187 179 403	16.6114 749 435	15.9579 385 744	98
50	18.0958 393 882	17.3263 968 974	16.6175 462 295	15.9627 414 362	100
51	18.1045 703 270	17.3332 634 932	16.6229 496 525	15.9669 958 743	102
52	18.1124 146 600	17.3394 036 680	16.6277 586 797	15.9707 645 115	104
53	18.1194 624 200	17.3448 942 703	16.6320 386 967	15.9741 028 198	106
54	18.1257 944 970	17.3498 040 186	16.6358 478 967	15.9770 599 373	108
55	18.1314 835 669	17.3541 943 619	16.6392 380 711	15.9796 793 908	110
56	18.1365 949 254	17.3581 202 482	16.6422 553 143	15.9819 997 372	112
57	18.1411 872 379	17.3616 308 129	16.6449 406 499	15.9840 551 305	114
58	18.1453 132 121	17.3647 699 929	16.6473 305 891	15.9858 758 250	116
59	18.1490 202 036	17.3675 770 773	16.6494 576 265	15.9874 886 200	118
60	18.1523 507 590	17.3700 871 987	16.6513 506 822	15.9889 172 551	120

Table 5.   PRESENT WORTH OF ONE DOLLAR PER PERIOD
PAYABLE AT END OF EACH PERIOD

HALF YEARS	**13%** NOMINAL ANNUAL RATE	**13½%** NOMINAL ANNUAL RATE	**14%** NOMINAL ANNUAL RATE	**14½%** NOMINAL ANNUAL RATE	HALF YEARS
1	0.9389 671 362	0.9367 681 499	0.9345 794 393	0.9324 009 324	1
YEARS					
1	1.8206 264 189	1.8143 027 165	1.8080 181 675	1.8017 724 311	2
2	3.4257 986 016	3.4064 160 646	3.3872 112 565	3.3681 820 300	4
3	4.8410 135 569	4.8035 505 615	4.7665 396 598	4.7299 738 906	6
4	6.0887 509 594	6.0295 843 769	5.9712 985 062	5.9138 769 214	8
5	7.1888 302 228	7.1054 714 297	7.0235 815 409	6.9431 284 737	10
6	8.1587 253 171	8.0495 995 083	7.9426 862 966	7.8379 304 383	12
7	9.0138 423 303	8.8781 045 326	8.7454 679 855	8.6158 457 633	14
8	9.7677 641 828	9.6051 463 301	9.4466 486 029	9.2921 431 753	16
9	10.4324 663 826	10.2431 506 387	10.0590 869 097	9.8800 968 700	18
10	11.0185 072 474	10.8030 214 733	10.5940 142 455	10.3912 470 547	20
11	11.5351 956 158	11.2943 274 834	11.0612 404 974	10.8356 264 569	22
12	11.9907 387 122	11.7254 654 901	11.4693 340 007	11.2219 572 438	24
13	12.3923 725 118	12.1038 039 940	11.8257 786 713	11.5578 222 190	26
14	12.7464 766 795	12.4358 091 090	12.1371 112 510	11.8498 136 559	28
15	13.0586 759 060	12.7271 550 737	12.4090 411 835	12.1036 626 890	30
16	13.3339 292 521	12.9828 212 287	12.6465 553 179	12.3243 518 033	32
17	13.5766 089 199	13.2071 771 171	12.8540 093 615	12.5162 126 294	34
18	13.7905 697 017	13.4040 571 644	13.0352 077 574	12.6830 109 634	36
19	13.9792 102 111	13.5768 262 115	13.1934 734 539	12.8280 206 809	38
20	14.1455 268 673	13.7284 370 223	13.3317 088 426	12.9540 879 964	40
21	14.2921 614 912	13.8614 807 494	13.4524 489 847	13.0636 873 274	42
22	14.4214 432 685	13.9782 312 189	13.5579 081 009	13.1589 698 621	44
23	14.5354 257 475	14.0806 837 915	13.6500 201 772	13.2418 057 820	46
24	14.6359 194 582	14.1705 894 654	13.7304 744 320	13.3138 209 699	48
25	14.7245 206 711	14.2494 848 020	13.8007 462 940	13.3764 289 218	50
26	14.8026 367 530	14.3187 181 870	13.8621 244 598	13.4308 584 907	52
27	14.8715 085 216	14.3794 728 756	13.9157 345 269	13.4781 780 066	54
28	14.9322 299 558	14.4327 872 148	13.9625 596 357	13.5193 162 450	56
29	14.9857 655 719	14.4795 723 904	14.0034 584 991	13.5550 806 570	58
30	15.0329 657 448	14.5206 279 163	14.0391 811 504	13.5861 732 175	60
31	15.0745 802 154	14.5566 557 151	14.0703 826 976	13.6132 042 034	62
32	15.1112 699 997	14.5882 712 811	14.0976 353 372	13.6367 041 722	64
33	15.1436 178 886	14.6160 150 331	14.1214 388 481	13.6571 343 752	66
34	15.1721 377 051	14.6403 611 345	14.1422 297 564	13.6748 958 114	68
35	15.1972 824 661	14.6617 256 801	14.1603 893 409	13.6903 370 979	70
36	15.2194 515 781	14.6804 738 073	14.1762 506 253	13.7037 613 122	72
37	15.2389 971 814	14.6969 259 370	14.1901 044 854	13.7154 319 415	74
38	15.2562 297 440	14.7113 632 495	14.2022 049 833	13.7255 780 541	76
39	15.2714 229 928	14.7240 324 903	14.2127 740 268	13.7343 987 951	78
40	15.2848 182 616	14.7351 501 870	14.2220 054 387	13.7420 672 960	80
41	15.2966 283 247	14.7449 063 502	14.2300 685 114	13.7487 340 720	82
42	15.3070 407 765	14.7534 677 206	14.2371 111 114	13.7545 299 772	84
43	15.3162 210 113	14.7609 806 191	14.2432 623 909	13.7595 687 719	86
44	15.3243 148 505	14.7675 734 472	14.2486 351 567	13.7639 493 564	88
45	15.3314 508 589	14.7733 588 817	14.2533 279 384	13.7677 577 117	90
46	15.3377 423 870	14.7784 358 006	14.2574 267 957	13.7710 685 873	92
47	15.3432 893 712	14.7828 909 723	14.2610 068 965	13.7739 469 682	94
48	15.3481 799 213	14.7868 005 395	14.2641 338 951	13.7764 493 505	96
49	15.3524 917 201	14.7902 313 199	14.2668 651 367	13.7786 248 503	98
50	15.3562 932 576	14.7932 419 482	14.2692 507 090	13.7805 161 678	100
51	15.3596 449 184	14.7958 838 787	14.2713 343 602	13.7821 604 254	102
52	15.3625 999 413	14.7982 022 640	14.2731 543 019	13.7835 898 961	104
53	15.3652 052 647	14.8002 367 272	14.2747 439 094	13.7848 326 372	106
54	15.3675 022 722	14.8020 220 390	14.2761 323 342	13.7859 130 408	108
55	15.3695 274 502	14.8035 887 119	14.2773 450 381	13.7868 523 130	110
56	15.3713 129 672	14.8049 635 214	14.2784 042 608	13.7876 688 894	112
57	15.3728 871 848	14.8061 699 643	14.2793 294 268	13.7883 787 977	114
58	15.3742 751 084	14.8072 286 597	14.2801 375 027	13.7889 959 717	116
59	15.3754 987 841	14.8081 577 015	14.2808 433 074	13.7895 325 252	118
60	15.3765 776 491	14.8089 729 677	14.2814 597 846	13.7899 989 895	120

Table 5.   PRESENT WORTH OF ONE DOLLAR PER PERIOD
PAYABLE AT END OF EACH PERIOD

HALF YEARS	15% NOMINAL ANNUAL RATE	15½% NOMINAL ANNUAL RATE	16% NOMINAL ANNUAL RATE	16½% NOMINAL ANNUAL RATE	HALF YEARS
1	0.9302 325 581	0.9280 742 459	0.9259 259 259	0.9237 875 289	1
YEARS					
1	1.7955 651 704	1.7893 960 519	1.7832 647 462	1.7771 709 274	2
2	3.3493 262 696	3.3306 418 910	3.3121 268 400	3.2937 790 931	4
3	4.6938 464 205	4.6581 505 405	4.6228 796 640	4.5880 273 237	6
4	5.8573 035 548	5.8015 626 880	5.7466 389 437	5.6925 172 772	8
5	6.8640 809 560	6.7864 085 038	6.7100 813 989	6.6350 706 674	10
6	7.7352 782 745	7.6346 776 805	7.5360 780 169	7.4394 300 827	12
7	8.4891 537 259	8.3653 104 197	8.2442 369 830	8.1258 570 542	14
8	9.1415 067 396	8.9946 203 302	8.8513 691 555	8.7116 424 359	16
9	9.7060 090 770	9.5366 586 788	9.3718 871 360	9.2115 419 558	18
10	10.1944 913 592	10.0035 281 281	9.8181 474 074	9.6381 479 070	20
11	10.6171 910 085	10.4056 529 654	10.2007 436 621	10.0022 063 434	22
12	10.9829 668 002	10.7520 118 564	10.5287 582 837	10.3128 877 691	24
13	11.2994 845 215	11.0503 383 220	10.8099 779 524	10.5780 181 400	26
14	11.5733 776 282	11.3072 934 120	11.0510 784 914	10.8042 759 970	28
15	11.8103 862 656	11.5286 144 343	11.2577 833 431	10.9973 606 959	30
16	12.0154 775 689	11.7192 430 569	11.4349 994 368	11.1621 359 725	32
17	12.1929 497 622	11.8834 356 463	11.5869 336 736	11.3027 524 580	34
18	12.3465 222 388	12.0248 583 040	11.7171 927 928	11.4227 522 323	36
19	12.4794 135 111	12.1466 687 229	11.8288 689 925	11.5251 580 475	38
20	12.5944 086 629	12.2515 866 930	11.9246 133 337	11.6125 494 701	40
21	12.6939 177 181	12.3419 548 284	12.0066 986 743	11.6871 278 593	42
22	12.7800 261 487	12.4197 908 740	12.0770 736 234	11.7507 718 186	44
23	12.8545 385 819	12.4868 327 573	12.1374 087 992	11.8050 845 168	46
24	12.9190 166 203	12.5445 773 934	12.1891 364 877	11.8514 340 718	48
25	12.9748 115 698	12.5943 141 076	12.2334 846 431	11.8909 880 126	50
26	13.0230 927 591	12.6371 534 241	12.2715 060 383	11.9247 426 890	52
27	13.0648 720 469	12.6740 518 616	12.3041 032 564	11.9535 483 694	54
28	13.1010 250 270	12.7058 332 904	12.3320 501 170	11.9781 306 589	56
29	13.1323 093 798	12.7332 073 280	12.3560 100 454	11.9991 087 766	58
30	13.1593 807 505	12.7567 851 836	12.3765 518 222	12.0170 111 541	60
31	13.1828 064 904	12.7770 933 047	12.3941 630 849	12.0322 887 457	62
32	13.2030 775 471	12.7945 851 322	12.4092 619 040	12.0453 263 888	64
33	13.2206 187 536	12.8096 512 247	12.4222 067 079	12.0564 524 970	66
34	13.2357 977 316	12.8226 279 787	12.4333 047 907	12.0659 473 330	68
35	13.2489 325 963	12.8338 051 399	12.4428 196 079	12.0740 500 685	70
36	13.2602 986 231	12.8434 322 726	12.4509 770 301	12.0809 648 084	72
37	13.2701 340 168	12.8517 243 319	12.4579 707 048	12.0868 657 326	74
38	13.2786 449 036	12.8588 664 634	12.4639 666 537	12.0919 014 834	76
39	13.2860 096 516	12.8650 181 369	12.4691 072 134	12.0961 989 095	78
40	13.2923 826 082	12.8703 167 075	12.4735 144 147	12.0998 662 616	80
41	13.2978 973 354	12.8748 804 820	12.4772 928 796	12.1029 959 190	82
42	13.3026 694 087	12.8788 113 604	12.4805 323 042	12.1056 667 166	84
43	13.3067 988 393	12.8821 971 117	12.4833 095 886	12.1079 459 310	86
44	13.3103 721 703	12.8851 133 331	12.4856 906 624	12.1098 909 747	88
45	13.3134 642 901	12.8876 251 382	12.4877 320 494	12.1115 508 428	90
46	13.3161 400 023	12.8897 886 107	12.4894 822 097	12.1129 673 466	92
47	13.3184 553 833	12.8916 520 567	12.4909 826 901	12.1141 761 674	94
48	13.3204 589 579	12.8932 570 834	12.4922 691 101	12.1152 077 550	96
49	13.3221 927 164	12.8946 395 279	12.4933 720 080	12.1160 880 948	98
50	13.3236 929 942	12.8958 302 575	12.4943 175 652	12.1168 393 621	100
51	13.3249 912 335	12.8968 558 589	12.4951 282 280	12.1174 804 812	102
52	13.3261 146 423	12.8977 392 317	12.4958 232 408	12.1180 276 016	104
53	13.3270 867 646	12.8985 001 000	12.4964 191 022	12.1184 945 050	106
54	13.3279 279 737	12.8991 554 524	12.4969 299 573	12.1188 929 527	108
55	13.3286 558 993	12.8997 199 218	12.4973 679 332	12.1192 329 813	110
56	13.3292 857 971	12.9002 061 115	12.4977 434 269	12.1195 231 561	112
57	13.3298 308 683	12.9006 248 774	12.4980 653 523	12.1197 707 864	114
58	13.3303 025 361	12.9009 855 695	12.4983 413 514	12.1199 821 100	116
59	13.3307 106 856	12.9012 962 415	12.4985 779 762	12.1201 624 501	118
60	13.3310 638 708	12.9015 638 301	12.4987 808 438	12.1203 163 493	120

Table 5. PRESENT WORTH OF ONE DOLLAR PER PERIOD
PAYABLE AT END OF EACH PERIOD

HALF YEARS	17% NOMINAL ANNUAL RATE	17½% NOMINAL ANNUAL RATE	18% NOMINAL ANNUAL RATE	18½% NOMINAL ANNUAL RATE	HALF YEARS
1	0.9216 589 862	0.9195 402 299	0.9174 311 927	0.9153 318 078	1
YEARS					
1	1.7711 142 730	1.7650 944 643	1.7591 111 859	1.7531 641 261	2
2	3.2755 966 557	3.2575 775 626	3.2397 198 771	3.2220 216 903	4
3	4.5535 871 695	4.5195 529 661	4.4859 185 902	4.4526 780 286	6
4	5.6391 829 680	5.5866 216 123	5.5348 191 147	5.4837 616 816	8
5	6.5613 480 584	6.4888 860 244	6.4176 577 012	6.3476 368 890	10
6	7.3446 860 697	7.2517 995 186	7.1607 252 766	7.0714 194 568	12
7	8.0100 966 847	7.8968 842 540	7.7861 503 885	7.6778 278 835	14
8	8.5753 332 496	8.4423 383 836	8.3125 581 925	8.1858 964 615	16
9	9.0554 764 379	8.9035 494 326	8.7556 251 094	8.6115 727 361	18
10	9.4633 366 076	9.2935 283 880	9.1285 456 691	8.9682 180 761	20
11	9.8097 955 850	9.6232 767 450	9.4424 254 432	9.2670 270 682	22
12	10.1040 969 951	9.9020 968 646	9.7066 117 694	9.5173 788 987	24
13	10.3540 928 838	10.1378 543 973	9.9289 721 146	9.7271 317 533	26
14	10.5664 532 131	10.3372 001 774	10.1161 283 685	9.9028 694 737	28
15	10.7468 438 175	10.5057 578 459	10.2736 540 430	10.0501 082 154	30
16	10.9000 775 701	10.6482 824 962	10.4062 402 517	10.1734 695 918	32
17	11.0302 427 914	10.7687 948 178	10.5178 354 109	10.2768 257 397	34
18	11.1408 123 268	10.8706 945 216	10.6117 628 237	10.3634 208 607	36
19	11.2347 362 032	10.9568 562 476	10.6908 196 480	10.4359 730 517	38
20	11.3145 203 366	11.0297 106 599	10.7573 601 952	10.4967 596 221	40
21	11.3822 933 904	11.0913 130 167	10.8133 660 426	10.5476 885 753	42
22	11.4398 635 694	11.1434 011 503	10.8605 050 439	10.5903 584 982	44
23	11.4887 668 622	11.1874 444 923	10.9001 809 981	10.6261 087 387	46
24	11.5303 080 229	11.2246 855 266	10.9335 754 550	10.6560 614 455	48
25	11.5655 953 814	11.2561 748 408	10.9616 829 013	10.6811 567 913	50
26	11.5955 704 146	11.2828 007 638	10.9853 403 765	10.7021 824 831	52
27	11.6210 328 651	11.3053 144 257	11.0052 524 000	10.7197 984 872	54
28	11.6426 620 783	11.3243 509 479	11.0220 119 519	10.7345 577 447	56
29	11.6610 351 278	11.3404 473 598	11.0361 181 314	10.7469 235 276	58
30	11.6766 422 118	11.3540 577 491	11.0479 910 204	10.7572 839 802	60
31	11.6898 997 318	11.3655 660 714	11.0579 841 936	10.7659 643 023	62
32	11.7011 614 023	11.3752 969 820	11.0663 952 475	10.7732 369 566	64
33	11.7107 276 878	11.3835 249 947	11.0734 746 634	10.7793 302 214	66
34	11.7188 538 196	11.3904 822 257	11.0794 302 660	10.7844 353 556	68
35	11.7257 566 053	11.3963 649 418	11.0844 485 027	10.7887 126 020	70
36	11.7316 202 130	11.4013 390 973	11.0886 697 270	10.7922 962 173	72
37	11.7366 010 856	11.4055 450 155	11.0922 226 471	10.7952 986 860	74
38	11.7408 321 142	11.4091 013 475	11.0952 130 689	10.7978 142 513	76
39	11.7444 261 838	11.4121 084 191	11.0977 300 470	10.7999 218 733	78
40	11.7474 791 852	11.4146 510 612	11.0998 485 372	10.8016 877 070	80
41	11.7500 725 734	11.4168 010 030	11.1016 316 280	10.8031 671 796	82
42	11.7522 755 407	11.4186 188 954	11.1031 324 198	10.8044 067 296	84
43	11.7541 468 629	11.4201 560 220	11.1043 956 063	10.8054 452 646	86
44	11.7557 364 674	11.4214 557 459	11.1054 588 050	10.8063 153 828	88
45	11.7570 867 654	11.4225 547 330	11.1063 536 782	10.8070 443 959	90
46	11.7582 337 832	11.4234 839 861	11.1071 068 750	10.8076 551 867	92
47	11.7592 081 235	11.4242 697 201	11.1077 408 257	10.8081 669 269	94
48	11.7600 357 820	11.4249 341 007	11.1082 744 093	10.8085 956 795	96
49	11.7607 388 410	11.4254 958 706	11.1087 235 159	10.8089 549 022	98
50	11.7613 360 581	11.4259 708 775	11.1091 015 200	10.8092 558 706	100
51	11.7618 433 673	11.4263 725 216	11.1094 196 785	10.8095 080 316	102
52	11.7622 743 038	11.4267 121 335	11.1096 874 661	10.8097 193 003	104
53	11.7626 403 651	11.4269 992 937	11.1099 128 576	10.8098 963 080	106
54	11.7629 513 178	11.4272 421 033	11.1101 025 651	10.8100 446 108	108
55	11.7632 154 582	11.4274 474 120	11.1102 622 381	10.8101 688 637	110
56	11.7634 398 337	11.4276 210 116	11.1103 966 317	10.8102 729 668	112
57	11.7636 304 306	11.4277 677 995	11.1105 097 481	10.8103 601 877	114
58	11.7637 923 342	11.4278 919 166	11.1106 049 559	10.8104 332 642	116
59	11.7639 298 640	11.4279 968 643	11.1106 850 904	10.8104 944 901	118
60	11.7640 466 895	11.4280 856 033	11.1107 525 380	10.8105 457 871	120

171

Table 5.   PRESENT WORTH OF ONE DOLLAR PER PERIOD
PAYABLE AT END OF EACH PERIOD

HALF YEARS	19% NOMINAL ANNUAL RATE	19½% NOMINAL ANNUAL RATE	20% NOMINAL ANNUAL RATE	20½% NOMINAL ANNUAL RATE	HALF YEARS
1	0.9132 420 091	0.9111 617 312	0.9090 909 091	0.9070 294 785	1
YEARS					
1	1.7472 529 764	1.7413 774 316	1.7355 371 901	1.7297 319 532	2
2	3.2044 811 212	3.1870 963 157	3.1698 654 463	3.1527 867 119	4
3	4.4198 253 758	4.3873 548 317	4.3552 606 995	4.3235 373 836	6
4	5.4334 358 131	5.3838 282 962	5.3349 261 979	5.2867 168 586	8
5	6.2787 980 343	6.2111 162 115	6.1445 671 057	6.0791 269 964	10
6	6.9838 393 981	6.8979 436 275	6.8136 918 229	6.7310 447 777	12
7	7.5718 516 279	7.4681 585 318	7.3666 874 569	7.2673 791 498	14
8	8.0622 602 764	7.9415 598 979	7.8237 086 421	7.7086 227 651	16
9	8.4712 664 676	8.3345 851 446	8.2014 121 009	8.0716 349 793	18
10	8.8123 821 168	8.6608 808 752	8.5135 637 198	8.3702 860 263	20
11	9.0968 763 094	8.9317 767 136	8.7715 402 643	8.6159 869 818	22
12	9.3341 475 861	9.1566 786 919	8.9847 440 201	8.8181 257 660	24
13	9.5320 344 330	9.3433 958 453	9.1609 454 711	8.9844 258 439	26
14	9.6970 742 337	9.4984 113 576	9.3065 665 051	9.1212 413 296	28
15	9.8347 192 374	9.6271 076 697	9.4269 144 670	9.2337 997 683	30
16	9.9495 166 802	9.7339 533 686	9.5263 755 926	9.3264 018 744	32
17	10.0452 590 064	9.8226 583 454	9.6085 748 699	9.4025 858 562	34
18	10.1251 091 565	9.8963 026 098	9.6765 081 569	9.4652 626 066	36
19	10.1917 050 575	9.9574 432 343	9.7326 513 694	9.5168 269 243	38
20	10.2472 467 692	10.0082 031 408	9.7790 507 185	9.5592 490 160	40
21	10.2935 691 660	10.0503 448 121	9.8173 972 880	9.5941 497 759	42
22	10.3322 025 529	10.0853 314 892	9.8490 886 678	9.6228 627 174	44
23	10.3644 232 213	10.1143 779 779	9.8752 798 907	9.6464 849 254	46
24	10.3912 956 121	10.1384 928 288	9.8969 255 295	9.6659 185 744	48
25	10.4137 074 807	10.1585 133 567	9.9148 144 872	9.6819 074 147	50
26	10.4323 992 250	10.1751 347 132	9.9295 987 498	9.6950 611 440	52
27	10.4479 883 447	10.1889 340 244	9.9418 171 486	9.7058 827 497	54
28	10.4609 898 415	10.2003 904 292	9.9519 149 988	9.7147 857 114	56
29	10.4718 332 324	10.2099 017 163	9.9602 603 296	9.7221 102 001	58
30	10.4808 767 393	10.2177 981 362	9.9671 572 972	9.7281 360 751	60
31	10.4884 191 233	10.2243 538 680	9.9728 572 704	9.7330 935 773	62
32	10.4947 095 543	10.2297 965 395	9.9775 679 921	9.7371 721 267	64
33	10.4999 558 427	10.2343 151 307	9.9814 611 505	9.7405 275 594	66
34	10.5043 313 048	10.2380 665 362	9.9846 786 368	9.7432 880 821	68
35	10.5079 804 881	10.2411 810 119	9.9873 377 163	9.7455 591 710	70
36	10.5110 239 471	10.2437 666 985	9.9895 353 027	9.7474 276 015	72
37	10.5135 622 252	10.2459 133 761	9.9913 514 899	9.7489 647 638	74
38	10.5156 791 770	10.2476 955 816	9.9928 524 710	9.7502 293 911	76
39	10.5174 447 380	10.2491 751 965	9.9940 929 512	9.7512 698 031	78
40	10.5189 172 353	10.2504 035 961	9.9951 181 415	9.7521 257 526	80
41	10.5201 453 141	10.2514 234 327	9.9959 654 062	9.7528 299 444	82
42	10.5211 695 454	10.2522 701 171	9.9966 656 250	9.7534 092 848	84
43	10.5220 237 654	10.2529 730 477	9.9972 443 181	9.7538 859 095	86
44	10.5227 361 944	10.2535 566 318	9.9977 225 770	9.7542 780 298	88
45	10.5233 303 679	10.2540 411 325	9.9981 178 322	9.7546 006 282	90
46	10.5238 259 151	10.2544 433 725	9.9984 444 894	9.7548 660 307	92
47	10.5242 392 070	10.2547 773 185	9.9987 144 541	9.7550 843 779	94
48	10.5245 838 969	10.2550 545 657	9.9989 375 654	9.7552 640 128	96
49	10.5248 713 721	10.2552 847 407	9.9991 219 548	9.7554 117 988	98
50	10.5251 111 295	10.2554 758 356	9.9992 743 428	9.7555 333 827	100
51	10.5253 110 899	10.2556 344 856	9.9994 002 833	9.7556 334 102	102
52	10.5254 778 590	10.2557 661 993	9.9995 043 664	9.7557 157 029	104
53	10.5256 169 462	10.2558 755 501	9.9995 903 855	9.7557 834 054	106
54	10.5257 329 466	10.2559 663 348	9.9996 614 756	9.7558 391 044	108
55	10.5258 296 921	10.2560 417 057	9.9997 202 278	9.7558 849 281	110
56	10.5259 103 789	10.2561 042 799	9.9997 687 833	9.7559 226 274	112
57	10.5259 776 726	10.2561 562 299	9.9998 089 118	9.7559 536 427	114
58	10.5260 337 963	10.2561 993 596	9.9998 420 759	9.7559 791 591	116
59	10.5260 806 041	10.2562 351 646	9.9998 694 842	9.7560 001 514	118
60	10.5261 196 423	10.2562 648 941	9.9998 921 357	9.7560 174 219	120

172

Table 5.   PRESENT WORTH OF ONE DOLLAR PER PERIOD
PAYABLE AT END OF EACH PERIOD

HALF YEARS	21% NOMINAL ANNUAL RATE	21½% NOMINAL ANNUAL RATE	22% NOMINAL ANNUAL RATE	22½% NOMINAL ANNUAL RATE	HALF YEARS
1	0.9049 773 756	0.9029 345 372	0.9009 009 009	0.8988 764 045	1
YEARS					
1	1.7239 614 259	1.7182 253 158	1.7125 233 341	1.7068 551 951	2
2	3.1358 583 369	3.1190 785 712	3.1024 456 896	3.0859 579 912	4
3	4.2921 793 878	4.2611 813 125	4.2305 378 537	4.2002 438 005	6
4	5.2391 878 854	5.1923 271 456	5.1461 227 609	5.1005 631 010	8
5	6.0147 727 404	5.9514 817 568	5.8892 320 111	5.8280 020 006	10
6	6.6499 643 664	6.5704 135 109	6.4923 561 490	6.4157 572 028	12
7	7.1701 761 769	7.0750 228 625	6.9818 652 293	6.8906 509 403	14
8	7.5962 213 524	7.4864 262 136	7.3791 617 801	7.2743 550 079	16
9	7.9451 455 559	7.8218 395 721	7.7016 165 734	7.5843 797 565	18
10	8.2309 089 134	8.0952 989 902	7.9633 281 174	7.8348 731 778	20
11	8.4649 445 453	8.3182 479 321	8.1757 390 775	8.0372 665 494	22
12	8.6566 159 950	8.5000 161 486	8.3481 365 778	8.2007 961 010	24
13	8.8135 918 552	8.6482 100 993	8.4880 582 565	8.3329 245 104	26
14	8.9421 525 810	8.7690 312 607	8.6016 218 298	8.4396 814 627	28
15	9.0474 417 649	8.8675 356 395	8.6937 925 735	8.5259 388 160	30
16	9.1336 719 272	8.9478 453 512	8.7686 004 167	8.5956 329 280	32
17	9.2042 930 548	9.0133 211 185	8.8293 161 405	8.6519 442 923	34
18	9.2621 306 318	9.0667 029 078	8.8785 943 840	8.6974 426 803	36
19	9.3094 986 850	9.1102 245 884	8.9185 897 119	8.7342 044 128	38
20	9.3482 923 650	9.1457 074 133	8.9510 508 172	8.7639 071 130	40
21	9.3800 637 702	9.1746 362 332	8.9773 969 785	8.7879 062 647	42
22	9.4060 840 443	9.1982 216 333	8.9987 801 140	8.8072 970 704	44
23	9.4273 942 338	9.2174 505 925	9.0161 351 465	8.8229 644 300	46
24	9.4448 469 391	9.2331 277 856	9.0302 208 802	8.8356 233 244	48
25	9.4591 404 263	9.2459 092 566	9.0416 531 777	8.8458 514 425	50
26	9.4708 465 644	9.2563 298 720	9.0509 318 868	8.8541 155 450	52
27	9.4804 337 048	9.2648 257 037	9.0584 626 952	8.8607 927 645	54
28	9.4882 854 199	9.2717 522 769	9.0645 748 683	8.8661 878 163	56
29	9.4947 158 493	9.2773 994 482	9.0695 356 451	8.8705 469 037	58
30	9.4999 822 684	9.2820 035 348	9.0735 619 228	8.8740 689 539	60
31	9.5042 953 817	9.2857 572 042	9.0768 297 401	8.8769 146 957	62
32	9.5078 277 527	9.2888 175 363	9.0794 819 740	8.8792 139 948	64
33	9.5107 207 081	9.2913 125 968	9.0816 345 864	8.8810 717 797	66
34	9.5130 899 925	9.2933 467 966	9.0833 816 950	8.8825 728 304	68
35	9.5150 303 987	9.2950 052 609	9.0847 996 875	8.8837 856 476	70
36	9.5166 195 603	9.2963 573 916	9.0859 505 621	8.8847 655 782	72
37	9.5179 210 584	9.2974 597 713	9.0868 846 377	8.8855 573 413	74
38	9.5189 869 646	9.2983 585 313	9.0876 427 544	8.8861 970 691	76
39	9.5198 599 247	9.2990 912 820	9.0882 580 589	8.8867 139 556	78
40	9.5205 748 651	9.2996 886 870	9.0887 574 539	8.8871 315 889	80
41	9.5211 603 900	9.3001 757 457	9.0891 627 740	8.8874 690 278	82
42	9.5216 399 254	9.3005 728 402	9.0894 917 409	8.8877 416 712	84
43	9.5220 326 573	9.3008 965 876	9.0897 587 379	8.8879 619 613	86
44	9.5223 542 985	9.3011 605 360	9.0899 754 386	8.8881 399 511	88
45	9.5226 177 175	9.3013 757 306	9.0901 513 177	8.8882 837 630	90
46	9.5228 334 535	9.3015 511 768	9.0902 940 652	8.8883 999 600	92
47	9.5230 101 378	9.3016 942 165	9.0904 099 223	8.8884 938 447	94
48	9.5231 548 394	9.3018 108 354	9.0905 039 544	8.8885 697 016	96
49	9.5232 733 477	9.3019 059 137	9.0905 802 731	8.8886 309 923	98
50	9.5233 704 041	9.3019 834 302	9.0906 422 150	8.8886 805 139	100
51	9.5234 498 918	9.3020 466 287	9.0906 924 884	8.8887 205 263	102
52	9.5235 149 909	9.3020 981 538	9.0907 332 915	8.8887 528 555	104
53	9.5235 683 061	9.3021 401 618	9.0907 664 081	8.8887 789 768	106
54	9.5236 119 703	9.3021 744 105	9.0907 932 864	8.8888 000 823	108
55	9.5236 477 307	9.3022 023 332	9.0908 151 013	8.8888 171 350	110
56	9.5236 770 178	9.3022 250 982	9.0908 328 069	8.8888 309 133	112
57	9.5237 010 035	9.3022 436 584	9.0908 471 771	8.8888 420 458	114
58	9.5237 206 474	9.3022 587 903	9.0908 588 402	8.8888 510 407	116
59	9.5237 367 355	9.3022 711 273	9.0908 683 063	8.8888 583 083	118
60	9.5237 499 113	9.3022 811 854	9.0908 759 892	8.8888 641 805	120

Table 6. PARTIAL PAYMENT TO AMORTIZE 1
PAYABLE AT END OF EACH PERIOD

HALF YEARS	5% NOMINAL ANNUAL RATE	5½% NOMINAL ANNUAL RATE	6% NOMINAL ANNUAL RATE	6½% NOMINAL ANNUAL RATE	HALF YEARS
1	1.0250 000 000	1.0275 000 000	1.0300 000 000	1.0325 000 000	1
YEARS					
1	0.5188 271 605	0.5207 182 491	0.5226 108 374	0.5245 049 200	2
2	0.2658 178 777	0.2674 205 884	0.2690 270 452	0.2706 372 337	4
3	0.1815 499 711	0.1830 708 264	0.1845 975 005	0.1861 299 692	6
4	0.1394 673 458	0.1409 579 478	0.1424 563 888	0.1439 626 337	8
5	0.1142 587 632	0.1157 397 205	0.1172 305 066	0.1187 310 724	10
6	0.0974 871 270	0.0989 687 098	0.1004 620 855	0.1019 671 878	12
7	0.0855 365 249	0.0870 245 664	0.0885 263 390	0.0900 417 561	14
8	0.0765 989 886	0.0780 970 977	0.0796 108 493	0.0811 401 319	16
9	0.0696 700 805	0.0711 806 259	0.0727 086 959	0.0742 541 496	18
10	0.0641 471 287	0.0656 717 306	0.0672 157 076	0.0687 788 839	20
11	0.0596 466 061	0.0611 864 049	0.0627 473 948	0.0643 293 596	22
12	0.0559 128 204	0.0574 686 330	0.0590 474 159	0.0606 489 063	24
13	0.0527 687 467	0.0543 411 636	0.0559 382 903	0.0575 598 109	26
14	0.0500 879 327	0.0516 773 795	0.0532 932 334	0.0549 351 193	28
15	0.0477 776 407	0.0493 844 200	0.0510 192 593	0.0526 817 169	30
16	0.0457 683 123	0.0473 926 322	0.0490 466 183	0.0507 297 552	32
17	0.0440 067 508	0.0456 487 453	0.0473 219 633	0.0490 258 084	34
18	0.0424 515 767	0.0441 113 206	0.0458 037 942	0.0475 283 128	36
19	0.0410 701 180	0.0427 476 374	0.0444 593 401	0.0462 044 456	38
20	0.0398 362 332	0.0415 315 144	0.0432 623 779	0.0450 279 400	40
21	0.0387 287 567	0.0404 417 522	0.0421 916 731	0.0439 775 251	42
22	0.0377 303 683	0.0394 610 021	0.0412 298 469	0.0430 357 906	44
23	0.0368 267 568	0.0385 749 283	0.0403 625 378	0.0421 883 484	46
24	0.0360 059 938	0.0377 715 811	0.0395 777 738	0.0414 232 032	48
25	0.0352 580 569	0.0370 409 195	0.0388 654 944	0.0407 302 745	50
26	0.0345 744 635	0.0363 744 446	0.0382 171 837	0.0401 010 288	52
27	0.0339 479 856	0.0357 649 139	0.0376 255 841	0.0395 281 935	54
28	0.0333 724 260	0.0352 061 174	0.0370 844 726	0.0390 055 322	56
29	0.0328 424 404	0.0246 926 996	0.0365 884 819	0.0385 276 664	58
30	0.0323 533 959	0.0342 200 173	0.0361 329 587	0.0380 899 328	60
31	0.0319 012 558	0.0337 840 249	0.0357 138 485	0.0376 882 685	62
32	0.0314 824 869	0.0333 811 810	0.0353 276 021	0.0373 191 174	64
33	0.0310 939 830	0.0330 083 724	0.0349 710 995	0.0369 793 534	66
34	0.0307 330 027	0.0326 628 513	0.0346 415 871	0.0366 662 182	68
35	0.0303 971 168	0.0323 421 829	0.0343 366 251	0.0363 772 684	70
36	0.0300 841 652	0.0320 442 024	0.0340 540 446	0.0361 103 320	72
37	0.0297 922 211	0.0317 669 784	0.0337 919 109	0.0358 634 724	74
38	0.0295 195 594	0.0315 087 826	0.0335 484 929	0.0356 349 575	76
39	0.0292 646 321	0.0312 680 634	0.0333 222 371	0.0354 232 334	78
40	0.0290 260 451	0.0310 434 245	0.0331 117 457	0.0352 269 026	80
41	0.0288 025 404	0.0308 336 055	0.0329 157 577	0.0350 447 051	82
42	0.0285 929 793	0.0306 374 664	0.0327 331 325	0.0348 755 020	84
43	0.0283 963 292	0.0304 539 731	0.0325 628 365	0.0347 182 617	86
44	0.0282 116 510	0.0302 821 858	0.0324 039 306	0.0345 720 479	88
45	0.0280 380 893	0.0301 212 487	0.0322 555 599	0.0344 360 091	90
46	0.0278 748 628	0.0299 703 805	0.0321 169 449	0.0343 093 694	92
47	0.0277 212 571	0.0298 288 670	0.0319 873 733	0.0341 914 200	94
48	0.0275 766 173	0.0296 960 540	0.0318 661 932	0.0340 815 142	96
49	0.0274 403 421	0.0295 713 411	0.0317 528 070	0.0339 790 588	98
50	0.0273 118 787	0.0294 541 767	0.0316 466 659	0.0338 835 102	100
51	0.0271 907 176	0.0293 440 529	0.0315 472 653	0.0337 943 693	102
52	0.0270 763 891	0.0292 405 017	0.0314 541 408	0.0337 111 771	104
53	0.0269 684 591	0.0291 430 908	0.0313 668 639	0.0336 335 112	106
54	0.0268 665 260	0.0290 514 211	0.0312 850 394	0.0335 609 823	108
55	0.0267 702 178	0.0289 651 228	0.0312 083 018	0.0334 932 313	110
56	0.0266 791 895	0.0288 838 535	0.0311 363 131	0.0334 299 266	112
57	0.0265 931 206	0.0288 072 956	0.0310 687 603	0.0333 707 615	114
58	0.0265 117 132	0.0287 351 542	0.0310 053 531	0.0333 154 526	116
59	0.0264 346 901	0.0286 671 552	0.0309 458 222	0.0332 637 372	118
60	0.0263 617 930	0.0286 030 433	0.0308 899 176	0.0332 153 719	120

Table 6. PARTIAL PAYMENT TO AMORTIZE 1
PAYABLE AT END OF EACH PERIOD

HALF YEARS	7% NOMINAL ANNUAL RATE	7½% NOMINAL ANNUAL RATE	8% NOMINAL ANNUAL RATE	8½% NOMINAL ANNUAL RATE	HALF YEARS
1	1.0350 000 000	1.0375 000 000	1.0400 000 000	1.0425 000 000	1
YEARS					
1	0.5264 004 914	0.5282 975 460	0.5301 960 784	0.5320 960 832	2
2	0.2722 511 395	0.2738 687 482	0.2754 900 454	0.2771 150 167	4
3	0.1876 682 087	0.1892 121 945	0.1907 619 025	0.1923 173 083	6
4	0.1454 766 465	0.1469 983 915	0.1485 278 320	0.1500 649 316	8
5	0.1202 413 679	0.1217 613 423	0.1232 909 443	0.1248 301 217	10
6	0.1034 839 493	0.1050 123 010	0.1065 521 727	0.1081 034 928	12
7	0.0915 707 287	0.0931 131 655	0.0946 689 731	0.0962 380 557	14
8	0.0826 848 306	0.0842 448 270	0.0858 199 992	0.0874 102 226	16
9	0.0758 168 408	0.0773 966 188	0.0789 933 281	0.0806 068 090	18
10	0.0703 610 768	0.0719 620 973	0.0735 817 503	0.0752 198 348	20
11	0.0659 320 742	0.0675 553 051	0.0691 988 111	0.0708 623 433	22
12	0.0622 728 303	0.0639 189 033	0.0655 868 313	0.0672 763 108	24
13	0.0592 053 963	0.0608 747 042	0.0625 673 805	0.0642 830 600	26
14	0.0566 026 452	0.0582 954 043	0.0600 129 752	0.0617 549 240	28
15	0.0543 713 316	0.0560 876 242	0.0578 300 991	0.0595 982 464	30
16	0.0524 415 048	0.0541 813 087	0.0559 485 897	0.0577 427 548	32
17	0.0507 596 583	0.0525 228 679	0.0543 147 715	0.0561 346 857	34
18	0.0492 841 628	0.0510 706 050	0.0528 868 780	0.0547 322 015	36
19	0.0479 821 414	0.0497 915 872	0.0516 319 191	0.0535 022 538	38
20	0.0468 272 823	0.0486 594 563	0.0505 234 893	0.0524 183 886	40
21	0.0457 982 765	0.0476 528 644	0.0495 402 007	0.0514 591 782	42
22	0.0448 776 816	0.0467 543 358	0.0486 645 444	0.0506 070 805	44
23	0.0440 510 817	0.0459 494 269	0.0478 820 488	0.0498 475 964	46
24	0.0433 064 580	0.0452 260 947	0.0471 806 476	0.0491 686 377	48
25	0.0426 337 096	0.0445 742 185	0.0465 502 004	0.0485 600 458	50
26	0.0420 242 854	0.0439 852 301	0.0459 821 236	0.0480 132 229	52
27	0.0414 708 979	0.0434 518 278	0.0454 691 025	0.0475 208 438	54
28	0.0409 672 981	0.0429 677 509	0.0450 048 662	0.0470 766 300	56
29	0.0405 080 966	0.0425 276 006	0.0445 840 087	0.0466 751 706	58
30	0.0400 886 213	0.0421 266 973	0.0442 018 451	0.0463 117 784	60
31	0.0397 048 020	0.0417 609 653	0.0438 542 964	0.0459 823 743	62
32	0.0393 530 765	0.0414 268 386	0.0435 377 955	0.0456 833 932	64
33	0.0390 303 148	0.0411 211 846	0.0432 492 100	0.0454 117 067	66
34	0.0387 337 550	0.0408 412 407	0.0429 857 795	0.0451 645 597	68
35	0.0384 609 517	0.0405 845 619	0.0427 450 623	0.0449 395 176	70
36	0.0382 097 323	0.0403 489 770	0.0425 248 919	0.0447 344 223	72
37	0.0379 781 601	0.0401 325 521	0.0423 233 403	0.0445 473 553	74
38	0.0377 645 038	0.0399 335 598	0.0421 386 869	0.0443 766 067	76
39	0.0375 672 117	0.0397 504 525	0.0419 693 922	0.0442 206 484	78
40	0.0373 848 887	0.0395 818 410	0.0418 140 755	0.0440 781 123	80
41	0.0372 162 781	0.0394 264 747	0.0416 714 957	0.0439 477 702	82
42	0.0370 602 452	0.0392 832 256	0.0415 405 351	0.0438 285 180	84
43	0.0369 157 629	0.0391 510 743	0.0414 201 848	0.0437 193 611	86
44	0.0367 819 002	0.0390 290 977	0.0413 095 329	0.0436 194 021	88
45	0.0366 578 111	0.0389 164 584	0.0412 077 538	0.0435 278 300	90
46	0.0365 427 259	0.0388 123 956	0.0411 140 984	0.0434 439 110	92
47	0.0364 359 428	0.0387 162 168	0.0410 278 867	0.0433 669 802	94
48	0.0363 368 213	0.0386 272 913	0.0409 485 002	0.0432 964 344	96
49	0.0362 447 758	0.0385 450 431	0.0408 753 757	0.0432 317 257	98
50	0.0361 592 702	0.0384 689 464	0.0408 080 000	0.0431 723 562	100
51	0.0360 798 131	0.0383 985 200	0.0407 459 047	0.0431 178 725	102
52	0.0360 059 536	0.0383 333 233	0.0406 886 620	0.0430 678 618	104
53	0.0359 372 773	0.0382 729 525	0.0406 358 808	0.0430 219 481	106
54	0.0358 734 032	0.0382 170 371	0.0405 872 033	0.0429 797 880	108
55	0.0358 139 807	0.0381 652 370	0.0405 423 018	0.0429 410 683	110
56	0.0357 586 865	0.0381 172 394	0.0405 008 762	0.0429 055 028	112
57	0.0357 072 227	0.0380 727 569	0.0404 626 512	0.0428 728 300	114
58	0.0356 593 142	0.0380 315 248	0.0404 273 741	0.0428 428 109	116
59	0.0356 147 069	0.0379 932 994	0.0403 948 131	0.0428 152 265	118
60	0.0355 731 662	0.0379 578 561	0.0403 647 553	0.0427 898 768	120

Table 6. PARTIAL PAYMENT TO AMORTIZE 1
PAYABLE AT END OF EACH PERIOD

HALF YEARS	9% NOMINAL ANNUAL RATE	9½% NOMINAL ANNUAL RATE	10% NOMINAL ANNUAL RATE	10½% NOMINAL ANNUAL RATE	HALF YEARS
1	1.0450 000 000	1.0475 000 000	1.0500 000 000	1.0525 000 000	1
YEARS					
1	0.5339 975 550	0.5359 004 884	0.5378 048 780	0.5397 107 186	2
2	0.2787 436 479	0.2803 759 246	0.2820 118 326	0.2836 513 576	4
3	0.1938 783 875	0.1954 451 156	0.1970 174 681	0.1985 954 203	6
4	0.1516 096 533	0.1531 619 598	0.1547 218 136	0.1562 891 770	8
5	0.1263 788 217	0.1279 369 909	0.1295 045 750	0.1310 815 194	10
6	0.1096 661 886	0.1112 401 861	0.1128 254 100	0.1144 217 842	12
7	0.0978 203 160	0.0994 156 544	0.1010 239 695	0.1026 451 581	14
8	0.0890 153 694	0.0906 353 090	0.0922 699 080	0.0939 190 304	16
9	0.0822 368 975	0.0838 834 258	0.0855 462 223	0.0872 251 119	18
10	0.0768 761 443	0.0785 504 673	0.0802 425 872	0.0819 522 832	20
11	0.0725 456 461	0.0742 484 572	0.0759 705 086	0.0777 115 264	22
12	0.0689 870 299	0.0707 186 689	0.0724 709 008	0.0742 433 921	24
13	0.0660 213 674	0.0677 819 186	0.0695 643 207	0.0713 681 737	26
14	0.0635 208 051	0.0653 101 623	0.0671 225 304	0.0689 574 362	28
15	0.0613 915 429	0.0632 094 539	0.0650 514 351	0.0669 169 335	30
16	0.0595 631 962	0.0614 092 942	0.0632 804 189	0.0651 759 322	32
17	0.0579 819 119	0.0598 557 388	0.0617 554 454	0.0636 803 028	34
18	0.0566 057 796	0.0585 068 041	0.0604 344 571	0.0623 879 146	36
19	0.0554 016 920	0.0573 293 231	0.0592 842 282	0.0612 654 839	38
20	0.0543 431 466	0.0562 967 454	0.0582 781 612	0.0602 863 683	40
21	0.0534 086 759	0.0553 875 648	0.0573 947 131	0.0594 289 905	42
22	0.0525 807 056	0.0545 841 765	0.0566 162 506	0.0586 756 919	44
23	0.0518 447 107	0.0538 720 312	0.0559 282 036	0.0580 118 853	46
24	0.0511 885 821	0.0532 390 022	0.0553 184 306	0.0574 254 187	48
25	0.0506 021 459	0.0526 749 023	0.0547 767 355	0.0569 060 917	50
26	0.0500 767 923	0.0521 711 140	0.0542 944 966	0.0564 452 836	52
27	0.0496 051 886	0.0517 203 000	0.0538 643 770	0.0560 356 631	54
28	0.0491 810 518	0.0513 161 771	0.0534 800 978	0.0556 709 607	56
29	0.0487 989 695	0.0509 533 356	0.0531 362 568	0.0553 457 878	58
30	0.0484 542 558	0.0506 270 953	0.0528 281 845	0.0550 554 911	60
31	0.0481 428 356	0.0503 333 891	0.0525 518 273	0.0547 960 358	62
32	0.0478 611 494	0.0500 686 682	0.0523 036 520	0.0545 639 102	64
33	0.0476 060 769	0.0498 298 248	0.0520 805 683	0.0543 560 470	66
34	0.0473 748 725	0.0496 141 277	0.0518 798 643	0.0541 697 590	68
35	0.0471 651 129	0.0494 191 690	0.0516 991 530	0.0540 026 853	70
36	0.0469 746 524	0.0492 428 204	0.0515 363 280	0.0538 527 462	72
37	0.0468 015 863	0.0490 831 953	0.0513 895 254	0.0537 181 056	74
38	0.0466 442 194	0.0489 386 173	0.0512 570 925	0.0535 971 399	76
39	0.0465 010 391	0.0488 075 940	0.0511 375 610	0.0534 884 063	78
40	0.0463 706 935	0.0486 887 937	0.0510 296 235	0.0533 906 287	80
41	0.0462 519 715	0.0485 810 259	0.0509 321 143	0.0533 026 688	82
42	0.0461 437 861	0.0484 832 248	0.0508 439 924	0.0532 235 137	84
43	0.0460 451 606	0.0483 944 348	0.0507 643 265	0.0531 522 600	86
44	0.0459 552 152	0.0483 137 976	0.0506 922 828	0.0530 881 011	88
45	0.0458 731 573	0.0482 405 414	0.0506 271 136	0.0530 303 161	90
46	0.0457 982 710	0.0481 739 715	0.0505 681 481	0.0529 782 600	92
47	0.0457 299 095	0.0481 134 620	0.0505 147 832	0.0529 313 554	94
48	0.0456 674 877	0.0480 584 480	0.0504 664 770	0.0528 890 846	96
49	0.0456 104 754	0.0480 084 196	0.0504 227 418	0.0528 509 836	98
50	0.0455 583 922	0.0479 629 162	0.0503 831 381	0.0528 166 360	100
51	0.0455 108 023	0.0479 215 211	0.0503 472 701	0.0527 856 678	102
52	0.0454 673 100	0.0478 838 573	0.0503 147 810	0.0527 577 433	104
53	0.0454 275 556	0.0478 495 834	0.0502 853 486	0.0527 325 604	106
54	0.0453 912 122	0.0478 183 901	0.0502 586 824	0.0527 098 478	108
55	0.0453 579 825	0.0477 899 970	0.0502 345 351	0.0526 893 614	110
56	0.0453 275 957	0.0477 641 499	0.0502 126 236	0.0526 708 814	112
57	0.0452 998 052	0.0477 406 182	0.0501 927 796	0.0526 542 102	114
58	0.0452 743 866	0.0477 191 924	0.0501 747 942	0.0526 391 698	116
59	0.0452 511 350	0.0476 996 824	0.0501 584 919	0.0526 255 997	118
60	0.0452 298 637	0.0476 819 156	0.0501 437 145	0.0526 133 557	120

Table 6. PARTIAL PAYMENT TO AMORTIZE 1
PAYABLE AT END OF EACH PERIOD

HALF YEARS	11% NOMINAL ANNUAL RATE	11½% NOMINAL ANNUAL RATE	12% NOMINAL ANNUAL RATE	12½% NOMINAL ANNUAL RATE	HALF YEARS
1	1.0550 000 000	1.0575 000 000	1.0600 000 000	1.0625 000 000	1
YEARS					
1	0.5416 180 049	0.5435 267 315	0.5454 368 932	0.5473 484 848	2
2	0.2852 944 853	0.2869 412 017	0.2885 914 924	0.2902 453 433	4
3	0.2001 789 476	0.2017 680 253	0.2033 626 285	0.2049 627 324	6
4	0.1578 640 118	0.1594 462 799	0.1610 359 426	0.1626 329 614	8
5	0.1326 677 687	0.1342 632 671	0.1358 679 582	0.1374 817 850	10
6	0.1160 292 312	0.1176 476 727	0.1192 770 294	0.1209 172 209	12
7	0.1042 791 154	0.1059 257 351	0.1075 849 090	0.1092 565 278	14
8	0.0955 825 380	0.0972 602 900	0.0989 521 436	0.1006 579 538	16
9	0.0889 199 163	0.0906 304 539	0.0923 565 406	0.0940 979 892	18
10	0.0836 793 300	0.0854 234 988	0.0871 845 570	0.0889 622 687	20
11	0.0794 712 319	0.0812 493 418	0.0830 455 685	0.0848 596 209	22
12	0.0760 358 037	0.0778 477 910	0.0796 790 050	0.0815 290 926	24
13	0.0731 930 713	0.0750 386 012	0.0769 043 467	0.0787 898 870	26
14	0.0708 143 996	0.0726 929 348	0.0745 925 515	0.0765 127 561	28
15	0.0688 053 897	0.0707 162 386	0.0726 489 115	0.0746 028 369	30
16	0.0670 951 895	0.0690 375 417	0.0710 023 374	0.0729 889 235	32
17	0.0656 295 769	0.0676 025 304	0.0695 984 254	0.0716 165 250	34
18	0.0643 663 488	0.0663 689 312	0.0683 948 348	0.0704 432 368	36
19	0.0632 721 659	0.0653 033 517	0.0673 581 240	0.0694 355 731	38
20	0.0623 203 434	0.0643 790 687	0.0664 615 359	0.0685 667 487	40
21	0.0614 892 731	0.0635 744 478	0.0656 834 152	0.0678 150 939	42
22	0.0607 612 757	0.0628 717 934	0.0650 060 565	0.0671 629 004	44
23	0.0601 217 512	0.0622 564 988	0.0644 148 527	0.0665 955 681	46
24	0.0595 585 424	0.0617 164 076	0.0638 976 549	0.0661 009 636	48
25	0.0590 614 501	0.0612 413 281	0.0634 442 864	0.0656 689 327	50
26	0.0586 218 603	0.0608 226 596	0.0630 461 669	0.0652 909 239	52
27	0.0582 324 534	0.0604 531 008	0.0626 960 209	0.0649 596 952	54
28	0.0578 869 756	0.0601 264 207	0.0623 876 472	0.0646 690 828	56
29	0.0575 800 578	0.0598 372 760	0.0621 157 359	0.0644 138 178	58
30	0.0573 070 692	0.0595 810 653	0.0618 757 215	0.0641 893 780	60
31	0.0570 640 001	0.0593 538 103	0.0616 636 642	0.0639 918 687	62
32	0.0568 473 659	0.0591 520 600	0.0614 761 528	0.0638 179 247	64
33	0.0566 541 284	0.0589 728 110	0.0613 102 248	0.0636 646 308	66
34	0.0564 816 307	0.0588 134 424	0.0611 633 009	0.0635 294 548	68
35	0.0563 275 431	0.0586 716 612	0.0610 331 302	0.0634 101 927	70
36	0.0561 898 180	0.0585 454 569	0.0609 177 439	0.0633 049 222	72
37	0.0560 666 516	0.0584 330 627	0.0608 154 168	0.0632 119 636	74
38	0.0559 564 521	0.0583 329 236	0.0607 246 347	0.0631 298 475	76
39	0.0558 578 119	0.0582 436 685	0.0606 440 667	0.0630 572 859	78
40	0.0557 694 845	0.0581 640 868	0.0605 725 410	0.0629 931 491	80
41	0.0556 903 644	0.0580 931 080	0.0605 090 251	0.0629 364 447	82
42	0.0556 194 699	0.0580 297 847	0.0604 526 081	0.0628 863 004	84
43	0.0555 559 284	0.0579 732 771	0.0604 024 856	0.0628 419 487	86
44	0.0554 989 631	0.0579 228 407	0.0603 579 467	0.0628 027 135	88
45	0.0554 478 820	0.0578 778 142	0.0603 183 623	0.0627 679 994	90
46	0.0554 020 682	0.0578 376 103	0.0602 831 761	0.0627 372 812	92
47	0.0553 609 712	0.0578 017 070	0.0602 518 949	0.0627 100 957	94
48	0.0553 240 994	0.0577 696 395	0.0602 240 821	0.0626 860 342	96
49	0.0552 910 137	0.0577 409 947	0.0601 993 504	0.0626 647 355	98
50	0.0552 613 216	0.0577 154 042	0.0601 773 563	0.0626 458 810	100
51	0.0552 346 718	0.0576 925 401	0.0601 577 952	0.0626 291 889	102
52	0.0552 107 501	0.0576 721 102	0.0601 403 965	0.0626 144 102	104
53	0.0551 892 753	0.0576 538 539	0.0601 249 202	0.0626 013 249	106
54	0.0551 699 955	0.0576 375 387	0.0601 111 531	0.0625 897 383	108
55	0.0551 526 849	0.0576 229 573	0.0600 989 057	0.0625 794 783	110
56	0.0551 371 415	0.0576 099 247	0.0600 880 098	0.0625 703 927	112
57	0.0551 231 839	0.0575 982 758	0.0600 783 157	0.0625 623 468	114
58	0.0551 106 497	0.0575 878 633	0.0600 696 907	0.0625 552 213	116
59	0.0550 993 932	0.0575 785 555	0.0600 620 166	0.0625 489 108	118
60	0.0550 892 837	0.0575 702 349	0.0600 551 883	0.0625 433 220	120

Table 6. PARTIAL PAYMENT TO AMORTIZE 1
PAYABLE AT END OF EACH PERIOD

HALF YEARS	13% NOMINAL ANNUAL RATE	13½% NOMINAL ANNUAL RATE	14% NOMINAL ANNUAL RATE	14½% NOMINAL ANNUAL RATE	HALF YEARS
1	1.0650 000 000	1.0675 000 000	1.0700 000 000	1.0725 000 000	1
YEARS					
1	0.5492 615 012	0.5511 759 371	0.5530 917 874	0.5550 090 470	2
2	0.2919 027 404	0.2935 636 696	0.2952 281 167	0.2968 960 677	4
3	0.2065 683 122	0.2081 793 430	0.2097 957 998	0.2114 176 575	6
4	0.1642 372 971	0.1658 489 106	0.1674 677 625	0.1690 938 133	8
5	0.1391 046 901	0.1407 366 154	0.1423 775 027	0.1440 272 931	10
6	0.1225 681 661	0.1242 297 830	0.1259 019 887	0.1275 846 995	12
7	0.1109 404 806	0.1126 366 553	0.1143 449 386	0.1160 652 161	14
8	0.1023 775 740	0.1041 108 553	0.1058 576 477	0.1076 177 994	16
9	0.0958 546 103	0.0976 262 124	0.0994 126 017	0.1012 135 825	18
10	0.0907 563 954	0.0925 666 956	0.0943 929 257	0.0962 348 402	20
11	0.0866 912 043	0.0885 400 217	0.0904 057 732	0.0922 881 574	22
12	0.0833 976 975	0.0852 844 606	0.0871 890 207	0.0891 110 150	24
13	0.0806 947 983	0.0826 186 545	0.0845 610 279	0.0865 214 900	26
14	0.0784 530 522	0.0804 129 423	0.0823 919 283	0.0843 895 127	28
15	0.0765 774 422	0.0785 721 549	0.0805 864 035	0.0826 196 190	30
16	0.0749 966 481	0.0770 248 610	0.0790 729 155	0.0811 401 700	32
17	0.0736 560 953	0.0757 164 072	0.0777 967 381	0.0798 963 736	34
18	0.0725 133 205	0.0746 042 775	0.0767 153 097	0.0788 456 308	36
19	0.0715 347 995	0.0736 549 164	0.0757 950 515	0.0779 543 489	38
20	0.0706 937 260	0.0728 415 040	0.0750 091 389	0.0771 957 084	40
21	0.0699 684 229	0.0721 423 647	0.0743 359 072	0.0765 480 660	42
22	0.0693 411 874	0.0715 398 096	0.0737 576 913	0.0759 937 906	44
23	0.0687 974 344	0.0710 192 782	0.0732 599 650	0.0755 184 011	46
24	0.0683 250 549	0.0705 686 946	0.0728 306 953	0.0751 099 179	48
25	0.0679 139 255	0.0701 779 758	0.0724 598 495	0.0747 583 683	50
26	0.0675 555 319	0.0698 386 536	0.0721 390 147	0.0744 554 044	52
27	0.0672 426 740	0.0695 435 785	0.0718 611 007	0.0741 940 045	54
28	0.0669 692 339	0.0692 866 863	0.0716 201 059	0.0739 682 379	56
29	0.0667 299 909	0.0690 628 130	0.0714 109 304	0.0737 730 763	58
30	0.0665 204 735	0.0688 675 449	0.0712 292 255	0.0736 042 434	60
31	0.0663 368 390	0.0686 970 977	0.0710 712 723	0.0734 580 915	62
32	0.0661 757 748	0.0685 482 180	0.0709 338 819	0.0733 315 021	64
33	0.0660 344 184	0.0684 181 015	0.0708 143 137	0.0732 218 028	66
34	0.0659 102 903	0.0683 043 260	0.0707 102 075	0.0731 266 997	68
35	0.0658 012 380	0.0682 047 954	0.0706 195 272	0.0730 442 204	70
36	0.0657 053 899	0.0681 176 925	0.0705 405 136	0.0729 726 662	72
37	0.0656 211 159	0.0680 414 397	0.0704 716 446	0.0729 105 729	74
38	0.0655 469 940	0.0679 746 658	0.0704 116 017	0.0728 566 765	76
39	0.0654 817 826	0.0679 161 772	0.0703 592 415	0.0728 098 852	78
40	0.0654 243 958	0.0678 649 343	0.0703 135 718	0.0727 692 551	80
41	0.0653 738 836	0.0678 200 306	0.0702 737 305	0.0727 339 692	82
42	0.0653 294 137	0.0677 806 750	0.0702 389 686	0.0727 033 204	84
43	0.0652 902 566	0.0677 461 766	0.0702 086 343	0.0726 766 962	86
44	0.0652 557 723	0.0677 159 320	0.0701 821 605	0.0726 535 658	88
45	0.0652 253 990	0.0676 894 136	0.0701 590 537	0.0726 334 688	90
46	0.0651 986 436	0.0676 661 599	0.0701 388 837	0.0726 160 061	92
47	0.0651 750 727	0.0676 457 671	0.0701 212 760	0.0726 008 313	94
48	0.0651 543 053	0.0676 278 819	0.0701 059 039	0.0725 876 439	96
49	0.0651 360 065	0.0676 121 947	0.0700 924 829	0.0725 761 831	98
50	0.0651 198 817	0.0675 984 347	0.0700 807 646	0.0725 662 223	100
51	0.0651 056 717	0.0675 863 644	0.0700 705 326	0.0725 575 649	102
52	0.0650 931 485	0.0675 757 759	0.0700 615 981	0.0725 500 401	104
53	0.0650 821 114	0.0675 664 868	0.0700 537 962	0.0725 434 995	106
54	0.0650 723 834	0.0675 583 375	0.0700 469 831	0.0725 378 143	108
55	0.0650 638 091	0.0675 511 877	0.0700 410 334	0.0725 328 724	110
56	0.0650 562 514	0.0675 449 148	0.0700 358 375	0.0725 285 767	112
57	0.0650 495 894	0.0675 394 111	0.0700 312 998	0.0725 248 425	114
58	0.0650 437 171	0.0675 345 821	0.0700 273 369	0.0725 215 964	116
59	0.0650 385 405	0.0675 303 451	0.0700 238 759	0.0725 187 745	118
60	0.0650 339 772	0.0675 266 274	0.0700 208 533	0.0725 163 215	120

Table 6. PARTIAL PAYMENT TO AMORTIZE 1
PAYABLE AT END OF EACH PERIOD

HALF YEARS	15% NOMINAL ANNUAL RATE	15½% NOMINAL ANNUAL RATE	16% NOMINAL ANNUAL RATE	16½% NOMINAL ANNUAL RATE	HALF YEARS
1	1.0750 000 000	1.0775 000 000	1.0800 000 000	1.0825 000 000	1
YEARS					
1	0.5569 277 108	0.5588 477 738	0.5607 692 308	0.5626 920 768	2
2	0.2985 675 087	0.3002 424 256	0.3019 208 045	0.3036 026 314	4
3	0.2130 448 912	0.2146 774 758	0.2163 153 862	0.2179 585 973	6
4	0.1707 270 232	0.1723 673 523	0.1740 147 606	0.1756 692 077	8
5	0.1456 859 274	0.1473 533 459	0.1490 294 887	0.1507 142 953	10
6	0.1292 778 313	0.1309 812 990	0.1326 950 169	0.1344 188 989	12
7	0.1177 973 721	0.1195 412 901	0.1212 968 528	0.1230 639 419	14
8	0.1093 911 571	0.1111 775 665	0.1129 768 720	0.1147 889 169	16
9	0.1030 289 578	0.1048 585 289	0.1067 020 959	0.1085 594 578	18
10	0.0980 921 916	0.0999 647 312	0.1018 522 088	0.1037 543 737	20
11	0.0941 868 710	0.0961 016 097	0.0980 320 684	0.0999 779 414	22
12	0.0910 500 795	0.0930 058 498	0.0949 779 616	0.0969 660 509	24
13	0.0884 996 124	0.0904 949 668	0.0925 071 267	0.0945 356 670	26
14	0.0864 051 993	0.0884 384 939	0.0904 889 057	0.0925 559 473	28
15	0.0846 712 358	0.0867 406 925	0.0888 274 334	0.0909 309 086	30
16	0.0832 259 887	0.0853 297 432	0.0874 508 132	0.0895 885 879	32
17	0.0820 146 084	0.0841 507 481	0.0863 041 101	0.0884 740 247	34
18	0.0809 944 680	0.0831 610 631	0.0853 446 741	0.0875 445 759	36
19	0.0801 319 709	0.0823 270 991	0.0845 389 361	0.0867 667 060	38
20	0.0794 003 138	0.0816 220 809	0.0838 601 615	0.0861 137 343	40
21	0.0787 778 858	0.0810 244 417	0.0832 868 407	0.0855 642 218	42
22	0.0782 471 012	0.0805 166 536	0.0828 015 156	0.0851 007 930	44
23	0.0777 935 352	0.0800 843 592	0.0823 899 085	0.0847 092 622	46
24	0.0774 052 724	0.0797 157 185	0.0820 402 660	0.0843 779 743	48
25	0.0770 724 102	0.0794 009 099	0.0817 428 582	0.0840 973 012	50
26	0.0767 866 757	0.0791 317 448	0.0814 895 903	0.0838 592 518	52
27	0.0765 411 247	0.0789 013 656	0.0812 737 003	0.0836 571 677	54
28	0.0763 299 053	0.0787 040 076	0.0810 895 180	0.0834 854 810	56
29	0.0761 480 689	0.0785 348 086	0.0809 322 748	0.0833 395 228	58
30	0.0759 914 178	0.0783 896 558	0.0807 979 488	0.0832 153 675	60
31	0.0758 563 816	0.0782 650 620	0.0806 831 404	0.0831 097 076	62
32	0.0757 399 172	0.0781 580 637	0.0805 849 701	0.0830 197 512	64
33	0.0756 394 249	0.0780 661 380	0.0805 009 950	0.0829 431 377	66
34	0.0755 526 807	0.0779 871 335	0.0804 291 391	0.0828 778 688	68
35	0.0754 777 785	0.0779 192 133	0.0803 676 362	0.0828 222 506	70
36	0.0754 130 829	0.0778 608 069	0.0803 149 823	0.0827 748 459	72
37	0.0753 571 892	0.0778 105 703	0.0802 698 950	0.0827 344 344	74
38	0.0753 088 894	0.0777 673 524	0.0802 312 801	0.0826 999 791	76
39	0.0752 671 439	0.0777 301 664	0.0801 982 037	0.0826 705 982	78
40	0.0752 310 575	0.0776 981 657	0.0801 698 677	0.0826 455 416	80
41	0.0751 998 587	0.0776 706 239	0.0801 455 900	0.0826 241 706	82
42	0.0751 728 822	0.0776 469 173	0.0801 247 876	0.0826 059 418	84
43	0.0751 495 542	0.0776 265 098	0.0801 069 615	0.0825 903 919	86
44	0.0751 293 793	0.0776 089 410	0.0800 916 847	0.0825 771 266	88
45	0.0751 119 302	0.0775 938 149	0.0800 785 920	0.0825 658 095	90
46	0.0750 968 374	0.0775 807 913	0.0800 673 705	0.0825 561 542	92
47	0.0750 837 820	0.0775 695 772	0.0800 577 524	0.0825 479 163	94
48	0.0750 724 884	0.0775 599 209	0.0800 495 083	0.0825 408 875	96
49	0.0750 627 184	0.0775 516 057	0.0800 424 417	0.0825 348 902	98
50	0.0750 542 661	0.0775 444 450	0.0800 363 841	0.0825 297 728	100
51	0.0750 469 537	0.0775 382 784	0.0800 311 915	0.0825 254 063	102
52	0.0750 406 271	0.0775 329 678	0.0800 267 402	0.0825 216 803	104
53	0.0750 351 534	0.0775 283 942	0.0800 229 243	0.0825 185 009	106
54	0.0750 304 175	0.0775 244 553	0.0800 196 531	0.0825 157 879	108
55	0.0750 263 198	0.0775 210 629	0.0800 168 488	0.0825 134 727	110
56	0.0750 227 743	0.0775 181 413	0.0800 144 447	0.0825 114 971	112
57	0.0750 197 065	0.0775 156 250	0.0800 123 837	0.0825 098 113	114
58	0.0750 170 521	0.0775 134 578	0.0800 106 168	0.0825 083 726	116
59	0.0750 147 553	0.0775 115 912	0.0800 091 020	0.0825 071 449	118
60	0.0750 127 679	0.0775 099 835	0.0800 078 034	0.0825 060 973	120

Table 6.   PARTIAL PAYMENT TO AMORTIZE 1
PAYABLE AT END OF EACH PERIOD

HALF YEARS	17% NOMINAL ANNUAL RATE	17½% NOMINAL ANNUAL RATE	18% NOMINAL ANNUAL RATE	18½% NOMINAL ANNUAL RATE	HALF YEARS
1	1.0850 000 000	1.0875 000 000	1.0900 000 000	1.0925 000 000	1
YEARS					
1	0.5646 163 070	0.5665 419 162	0.5684 688 995	0.5703 972 521	2
2	0.3052 878 926	0.3069 765 741	0.3086 686 621	0.3103 641 428	4
3	0.2196 070 840	0.2212 608 210	0.2229 197 833	0.2245 839 456	6
4	0.1773 306 533	0.1789 990 569	0.1806 743 778	0.1823 565 753	8
5	0.1524 077 051	0.1541 096 571	0.1558 200 899	0.1575 389 420	10
6	0.1361 528 581	0.1378 968 072	0.1396 506 585	0.1414 143 237	12
7	0.1248 424 382	0.1266 322 220	0.1284 331 730	0.1302 451 703	14
8	0.1166 135 439	0.1184 505 944	0.1202 999 097	0.1221 613 301	16
9	0.1104 304 127	0.1123 147 580	0.1142 122 907	0.1161 228 071	18
10	0.1056 709 744	0.1076 017 588	0.1095 464 750	0.1115 048 710	20
11	0.1019 389 233	0.1039 147 087	0.1059 049 930	0.1079 094 722	22
12	0.0989 697 546	0.1009 887 111	0.1030 225 607	0.1050 709 455	24
13	0.0965 801 651	0.0986 402 014	0.1007 153 599	0.1028 052 282	26
14	0.0946 391 357	0.0967 379 932	0.0988 520 473	0.1009 808 321	28
15	0.0930 505 753	0.0951 858 985	0.0973 363 514	0.0995 014 162	30
16	0.0917 424 664	0.0939 118 586	0.0960 961 861	0.0982 948 827	32
17	0.0906 598 358	0.0928 609 020	0.0950 765 971	0.0973 063 109	34
18	0.0897 600 615	0.0919 904 426	0.0942 350 500	0.0964 932 346	36
19	0.0890 096 556	0.0912 670 548	0.0935 381 975	0.0958 224 015	38
20	0.0883 820 056	0.0906 642 097	0.0929 596 092	0.0952 674 955	40
21	0.0878 557 568	0.0901 606 508	0.0924 781 420	0.0948 075 015	42
22	0.0874 136 299	0.0897 392 086	0.0920 767 493	0.0944 255 098	44
23	0.0870 415 434	0.0893 859 184	0.0917 415 959	0.0941 078 267	46
24	0.0867 279 519	0.0890 893 556	0.0914 613 892	0.0938 433 027	48
25	0.0864 633 395	0.0888 401 268	0.0912 268 681	0.0936 228 182	50
26	0.0862 398 282	0.0886 304 758	0.0910 304 065	0.0934 388 852	52
27	0.0860 508 710	0.0884 539 750	0.0908 657 034	0.0932 853 357	54
28	0.0858 910 096	0.0883 052 817	0.0907 275 373	0.0931 570 749	56
29	0.0857 556 803	0.0881 799 428	0.0906 115 709	0.0930 498 852	58
30	0.0856 410 586	0.0880 742 394	0.0905 141 938	0.0929 602 678	60
31	0.0855 439 330	0.0879 850 589	0.0904 323 955	0.0928 853 163	62
32	0.0854 616 021	0.0879 097 927	0.0903 636 620	0.0928 226 126	64
33	0.0853 917 900	0.0878 462 515	0.0903 058 914	0.0927 701 424	66
34	0.0853 325 773	0.0877 925 956	0.0902 573 242	0.0927 262 269	68
35	0.0852 823 433	0.0877 472 778	0.0902 164 866	0.0926 894 651	70
36	0.0852 397 181	0.0877 089 955	0.0901 821 431	0.0926 586 873	72
37	0.0852 035 434	0.0876 766 519	0.0901 532 571	0.0926 329 163	74
38	0.0851 728 387	0.0876 493 222	0.0901 289 587	0.0926 113 357	76
39	0.0851 467 738	0.0876 262 267	0.0901 085 173	0.0925 932 624	78
40	0.0851 246 454	0.0876 067 078	0.0900 913 194	0.0925 781 255	80
41	0.0851 058 573	0.0875 902 102	0.0900 768 494	0.0925 654 471	82
42	0.0850 899 042	0.0875 762 655	0.0900 646 738	0.0925 548 274	84
43	0.0850 763 574	0.0875 644 779	0.0900 544 285	0.0925 459 318	86
44	0.0850 648 535	0.0875 545 134	0.0900 458 070	0.0925 384 800	88
45	0.0850 550 838	0.0875 460 896	0.0900 385 517	0.0925 322 376	90
46	0.0850 467 867	0.0875 389 681	0.0900 324 460	0.0925 270 082	92
47	0.0850 397 399	0.0875 329 474	0.0900 273 076	0.0925 226 273	94
48	0.0850 337 549	0.0875 278 572	0.0900 229 832	0.0925 189 571	96
49	0.0850 286 715	0.0875 235 536	0.0900 193 437	0.0925 158 823	98
50	0.0850 243 540	0.0875 199 150	0.0900 162 806	0.0925 133 064	100
51	0.0850 206 867	0.0875 168 386	0.0900 137 027	0.0925 111 482	102
52	0.0850 175 718	0.0875 142 375	0.0900 115 330	0.0925 093 402	104
53	0.0850 149 260	0.0875 120 383	0.0900 097 069	0.0925 078 254	106
54	0.0850 126 786	0.0875 101 788	0.0900 081 700	0.0925 065 563	108
55	0.0850 107 697	0.0875 086 066	0.0900 068 764	0.0925 054 930	110
56	0.0850 091 482	0.0875 072 772	0.0900 057 877	0.0925 046 022	112
57	0.0850 077 708	0.0875 061 532	0.0900 048 713	0.0925 038 558	114
58	0.0850 066 009	0.0875 052 028	0.0900 041 000	0.0925 032 305	116
59	0.0850 056 071	0.0875 043 992	0.0900 034 509	0.0925 027 066	118
60	0.0850 047 629	0.0875 037 198	0.0900 029 045	0.0925 022 677	120

Table 6. PARTIAL PAYMENT TO AMORTIZE 1
PAYABLE AT END OF EACH PERIOD

HALF YEARS	**19%** NOMINAL ANNUAL RATE	**19½%** NOMINAL ANNUAL RATE	**20%** NOMINAL ANNUAL RATE	**20½%** NOMINAL ANNUAL RATE	HALF YEARS
1	1.0950 000 000	1.0975 000 000	1.1000 000 000	1.1025 000 000	1
YEARS					
1	0.5723 269 690	0.5742 580 453	0.5761 904 762	0.5781 242 568	2
2	0.3120 630 025	0.3137 652 273	0.3154 708 037	0.3171 797 179	4
3	0.2262 532 826	0.2279 277 693	0.2296 073 804	0.2312 920 905	6
4	0.1840 456 084	0.1857 414 362	0.1874 440 176	0.1891 533 114	8
5	0.1592 661 517	0.1610 016 567	0.1627 453 949	0.1644 973 037	10
6	0.1431 877 142	0.1449 707 411	0.1467 633 151	0.1485 653 465	12
7	0.1320 680 923	0.1339 018 174	0.1357 462 232	0.1376 011 874	14
8	0.1240 346 957	0.1259 198 461	0.1278 166 207	0.1297 248 588	16
9	0.1180 461 037	0.1199 819 766	0.1219 302 222	0.1238 906 371	18
10	0.1134 766 953	0.1154 616 966	0.1174 596 248	0.1194 702 304	20
11	0.1099 278 440	0.1119 598 073	0.1140 050 630	0.1160 633 137	22
12	0.1071 335 107	0.1092 099 039	0.1112 997 764	0.1134 027 827	24
13	0.1049 093 986	0.1070 274 680	0.1091 590 386	0.1113 037 179	26
14	0.1031 238 883	0.1052 807 635	0.1074 510 132	0.1096 342 004	28
15	0.1016 805 845	0.1038 733 578	0.1060 792 483	0.1082 977 783	30
16	0.1005 073 947	0.1027 331 817	0.1049 717 167	0.1072 224 866	32
17	0.0995 494 491	0.1018 054 344	0.1040 737 064	0.1063 537 218	34
18	0.0987 643 673	0.1010 478 397	0.1033 430 638	0.1056 494 723	36
19	0.0981 190 090	0.1004 273 865	0.1027 469 250	0.1050 770 396	38
20	0.0975 871 883	0.0999 180 358	0.1022 594 144	0.1046 107 281	40
21	0.0971 480 333	0.0994 990 738	0.1018 599 911	0.1042 301 844	42
22	0.0967 847 847	0.0991 539 050	0.1015 322 365	0.1039 191 797	44
23	0.0964 839 025	0.0988 691 546	0.1012 629 527	0.1036 647 035	46
24	0.0962 343 905	0.0986 339 900	0.1010 414 797	0.1034 562 779	48
25	0.0960 272 796	0.0984 396 008	0.1008 591 740	0.1032 854 330	50
26	0.0958 552 274	0.0982 787 971	0.1007 090 040	0.1031 453 010	52
27	0.0957 122 048	0.0981 456 939	0.1005 852 336	0.1030 302 988	54
28	0.0955 932 484	0.0980 354 631	0.1004 831 734	0.1029 358 783	56
29	0.0954 942 633	0.0979 441 358	0.1003 989 822	0.1028 583 280	58
30	0.0954 118 653	0.0978 684 435	0.1003 295 092	0.1027 946 147	60
31	0.0953 432 532	0.0978 056 915	0.1002 721 660	0.1027 422 568	62
32	0.0952 861 053	0.0977 536 548	0.1002 248 244	0.1026 992 218	64
33	0.0952 384 958	0.0977 104 953	0.1001 857 328	0.1026 638 438	66
34	0.0951 988 252	0.0976 746 924	0.1001 534 487	0.1026 347 565	68
35	0.0951 657 648	0.0976 449 883	0.1001 267 834	0.1026 108 387	70
36	0.0951 382 097	0.0976 203 412	0.1001 047 566	0.1025 911 698	72
37	0.0951 152 405	0.0975 998 882	0.1000 865 600	0.1025 749 938	74
38	0.0950 960 925	0.0975 829 143	0.1000 715 264	0.1025 616 896	76
39	0.0950 801 288	0.0975 688 268	0.1000 591 054	0.1025 507 467	78
40	0.0950 668 189	0.0975 571 343	0.1000 488 424	0.1025 417 458	80
41	0.0950 557 212	0.0975 474 291	0.1000 403 622	0.1025 343 419	82
42	0.0950 464 676	0.0975 393 731	0.1000 333 549	0.1025 282 515	84
43	0.0950 387 513	0.0975 326 859	0.1000 275 644	0.1025 232 414	86
44	0.0950 323 168	0.0975 271 348	0.1000 227 794	0.1025 191 200	88
45	0.0950 269 511	0.0975 225 267	0.1000 188 252	0.1025 157 296	90
46	0.0950 224 764	0.0975 187 013	0.1000 155 575	0.1025 129 404	92
47	0.0950 187 449	0.0975 155 256	0.1000 128 571	0.1025 106 459	94
48	0.0950 156 329	0.0975 128 892	0.1000 106 255	0.1025 087 582	96
49	0.0950 130 377	0.0975 107 006	0.1000 087 812	0.1025 072 053	98
50	0.0950 108 733	0.0975 088 836	0.1000 072 571	0.1025 059 277	100
51	0.0950 090 683	0.0975 073 752	0.1000 059 975	0.1025 048 767	102
52	0.0950 075 629	0.0975 061 230	0.1000 049 566	0.1025 040 121	104
53	0.0950 063 075	0.0975 050 833	0.1000 040 963	0.1025 033 007	106
54	0.0950 052 604	0.0975 042 202	0.1000 033 854	0.1025 027 155	108
55	0.0950 043 873	0.0975 035 037	0.1000 027 978	0.1025 022 340	110
56	0.0950 036 590	0.0975 029 088	0.1000 023 122	0.1025 018 379	112
57	0.0950 030 516	0.0975 024 149	0.1000 019 109	0.1025 015 121	114
58	0.0950 025 451	0.0975 020 049	0.1000 015 793	0.1025 012 440	116
59	0.0950 021 226	0.0975 016 645	0.1000 013 052	0.1025 010 234	118
60	0.0950 017 703	0.0975 013 819	0.1000 010 787	0.1025 008 420	120

181

Table 6.   PARTIAL PAYMENT TO AMORTIZE 1
PAYABLE AT END OF EACH PERIOD

HALF YEARS	21% NOMINAL ANNUAL RATE	21½% NOMINAL ANNUAL RATE	22% NOMINAL ANNUAL RATE	22½% NOMINAL ANNUAL RATE	HALF YEARS
1	1.1050 000 000	1.1075 000 000	1.1100 000 000	1.1125 000 000	1
YEARS					
1	0.5800 593 824	0.5819 958 482	0.5839 336 493	0.5858 727 811	2
2	0.3188 919 564	0.3206 075 054	0.3223 263 515	0.3240 484 812	4
3	0.2329 818 746	0.2346 767 074	0.2363 765 636	0.2380 814 180	6
4	0.1908 692 763	0.1925 918 710	0.1943 210 542	0.1960 567 844	8
5	0.1662 573 206	0.1680 253 827	0.1698 014 271	0.1715 853 907	10
6	0.1503 767 456	0.1521 974 223	0.1540 272 864	0.1558 662 475	12
7	0.1394 665 871	0.1413 422 994	0.1432 282 015	0.1451 241 702	14
8	0.1316 443 997	0.1335 750 826	0.1355 167 470	0.1374 692 325	16
9	0.1258 630 182	0.1278 471 632	0.1298 428 701	0.1318 499 379	18
10	0.1214 932 653	0.1235 284 825	0.1255 756 369	0.1276 344 846	20
11	0.1181 342 647	0.1202 176 237	0.1223 131 011	0.1244 204 101	22
12	0.1155 185 815	0.1176 468 353	0.1197 872 113	0.1219 393 810	24
13	0.1134 611 196	0.1156 308 633	0.1178 125 750	0.1200 058 873	26
14	0.1118 298 968	0.1140 376 822	0.1162 571 454	0.1184 878 842	28
15	0.1105 284 815	0.1127 709 028	0.1150 245 985	0.1172 891 363	30
16	0.1094 849 922	0.1117 587 487	0.1140 432 854	0.1163 381 462	32
17	0.1086 449 545	0.1109 468 959	0.1132 590 547	0.1155 809 569	34
18	0.1079 665 187	0.1102 936 768	0.1126 304 409	0.1149 763 254	36
19	0.1074 171 697	0.1097 667 780	0.1121 253 508	0.1144 923 971	38
20	0.1069 714 084	0.1093 409 132	0.1117 187 267	0.1141 043 586	40
21	0.1066 090 833	0.1089 961 470	0.1113 908 633	0.1137 927 477	42
22	0.1063 141 681	0.1087 166 672	0.1111 261 735	0.1135 422 130	44
23	0.1060 738 498	0.1084 898 682	0.1109 122 683	0.1133 405 907	46
24	0.1058 778 407	0.1083 056 601	0.1107 392 624	0.1131 782 064	48
25	0.1057 178 512	0.1081 559 393	0.1105 992 433	0.1130 473 428	50
26	0.1055 871 820	0.1080 341 792	0.1104 858 607	0.1129 418 286	52
27	0.1054 804 064	0.1079 351 120	0.1103 940 076	0.1128 567 191	54
28	0.1053 931 196	0.1078 544 778	0.1103 195 698	0.1127 880 461	56
29	0.1053 217 406	0.1077 888 266	0.1102 592 282	0.1127 326 208	58
30	0.1052 633 544	0.1077 353 608	0.1102 103 020	0.1126 878 780	60
31	0.1052 155 851	0.1076 918 099	0.1101 706 244	0.1126 517 528	62
32	0.1051 764 952	0.1076 563 294	0.1101 384 421	0.1126 225 813	64
33	0.1051 445 028	0.1076 274 197	0.1101 123 361	0.1125 990 224	66
34	0.1051 183 160	0.1076 038 613	0.1100 911 570	0.1125 799 945	68
35	0.1050 968 792	0.1075 846 621	0.1100 739 735	0.1125 646 250	70
36	0.1050 793 292	0.1075 690 142	0.1100 600 309	0.1125 522 099	72
37	0.1050 649 605	0.1075 562 599	0.1100 487 175	0.1125 421 807	74
38	0.1050 531 957	0.1075 458 638	0.1100 395 369	0.1125 340 787	76
39	0.1050 435 624	0.1075 373 894	0.1100 320 868	0.1125 275 332	78
40	0.1050 356 742	0.1075 304 813	0.1100 260 410	0.1125 222 452	80
41	0.1050 292 148	0.1075 248 498	0.1100 211 345	0.1125 179 730	82
42	0.1050 239 253	0.1075 202 589	0.1100 171 526	0.1125 145 213	84
43	0.1050 195 936	0.1075 165 163	0.1100 139 210	0.1125 117 327	86
44	0.1050 160 463	0.1075 134 652	0.1100 112 984	0.1125 094 795	88
45	0.1050 131 413	0.1075 109 778	0.1100 091 698	0.1125 076 591	90
46	0.1050 107 623	0.1075 089 500	0.1100 074 423	0.1125 061 883	92
47	0.1050 088 140	0.1075 072 967	0.1100 060 403	0.1125 050 000	94
48	0.1050 072 184	0.1075 059 489	0.1100 049 024	0.1125 040 399	96
49	0.1050 059 117	0.1075 048 500	0.1100 039 788	0.1125 032 641	98
50	0.1050 048 415	0.1075 039 541	0.1100 032 293	0.1125 026 373	100
51	0.1050 039 651	0.1075 032 237	0.1100 026 210	0.1125 021 309	102
52	0.1050 032 473	0.1075 026 283	0.1100 021 272	0.1125 017 217	104
53	0.1050 026 595	0.1075 021 428	0.1100 017 265	0.1125 013 911	106
54	0.1050 021 781	0.1075 017 470	0.1100 014 013	0.1125 011 240	108
55	0.1050 017 838	0.1075 014 243	0.1100 011 373	0.1125 009 081	110
56	0.1050 014 609	0.1075 011 612	0.1100 009 230	0.1125 007 338	112
57	0.1050 011 964	0.1075 009 467	0.1100 007 492	0.1125 005 929	114
58	0.1050 009 799	0.1075 007 719	0.1100 006 080	0.1125 004 790	116
59	0.1050 008 025	0.1075 006 293	0.1100 004 935	0.1125 003 870	118
60	0.1050 006 572	0.1075 005 131	0.1100 004 005	0.1125 003 127	120

Table 1. FUTURE WORTH OF ONE DOLLAR WITH INTEREST PAYABLE AT BEGINNING OF EACH PERIOD

YEARS	5% NOMINAL ANNUAL RATE	5½% NOMINAL ANNUAL RATE	6% NOMINAL ANNUAL RATE	6½% NOMINAL ANNUAL RATE	YEARS
1	1.0500 000 000	1.0550 000 000	1.0600 000 000	1.0650 000 000	1
2	1.1025 000 000	1.1130 250 000	1.1236 000 000	1.1342 250 000	2
3	1.1576 250 000	1.1742 413 750	1.1910 160 000	1.2079 496 250	3
4	1.2155 062 500	1.2388 246 506	1.2624 769 600	1.2864 663 506	4
5	1.2762 815 625	1.3069 600 064	1.3382 255 776	1.3700 866 634	5
6	1.3400 956 406	1.3788 428 068	1.4185 191 123	1.4591 422 965	6
7	1.4071 004 227	1.4546 791 611	1.5036 302 590	1.5539 865 458	7
8	1.4774 554 438	1.5346 865 150	1.5938 480 745	1.6549 956 713	8
9	1.5513 282 160	1.6190 942 733	1.6894 789 590	1.7625 703 899	9
10	1.6288 946 268	1.7081 444 584	1.7908 476 965	1.8771 374 653	10
11	1.7103 393 581	1.8020 924 036	1.8982 985 583	1.9991 514 005	11
12	1.7958 563 260	1.9012 074 858	2.0121 964 718	2.1290 962 415	12
13	1.8856 491 423	2.0057 738 975	2.1329 282 601	2.2674 874 972	13
14	1.9799 315 994	2.1160 914 618	2.2609 039 558	2.4148 741 846	14
15	2.0789 281 794	2.2324 764 922	2.3965 581 931	2.5718 410 066	15
16	2.1828 745 884	2.3552 626 993	2.5403 516 847	2.7390 106 720	16
17	2.2920 183 178	2.4848 021 478	2.6927 727 858	2.9170 463 657	17
18	2.4066 192 337	2.6214 662 659	2.8543 391 529	3.1066 543 794	18
19	2.5269 501 954	2.7656 469 105	3.0255 995 021	3.3085 869 141	19
20	2.6532 977 051	2.9177 574 906	3.2071 354 722	3.5236 450 635	20
21	2.7859 625 904	3.0782 341 526	3.3995 636 005	3.7526 819 926	21
22	2.9252 607 199	3.2475 370 310	3.6035 374 166	3.9966 063 222	22
23	3.0715 237 559	3.4261 515 677	3.8197 496 616	4.2563 857 331	23
24	3.2250 999 437	3.6145 899 039	4.0489 346 413	4.5330 508 058	24
25	3.3863 549 409	3.8133 923 486	4.2918 707 197	4.8276 991 081	25
26	3.5556 726 879	4.0231 289 278	4.5493 829 629	5.1414 995 502	26
27	3.7334 563 223	4.2444 010 188	4.8223 459 407	5.4756 970 209	27
28	3.9201 291 385	4.4778 430 749	5.1116 866 971	5.8316 173 273	28
29	4.1161 355 954	4.7241 244 440	5.4183 878 990	6.2106 724 536	29
30	4.3219 423 752	4.9839 512 884	5.7434 911 729	6.6143 661 630	30
31	4.5380 394 939	5.2580 686 093	6.0881 006 433	7.0442 999 636	31
32	4.7649 414 686	5.5472 623 828	6.4533 866 819	7.5021 794 613	32
33	5.0031 885 420	5.8523 618 138	6.8405 898 828	7.9898 211 263	33
34	5.2533 479 691	6.1742 417 136	7.2510 252 758	8.5091 594 995	34
35	5.5160 153 676	6.5138 250 078	7.6860 867 923	9.0622 548 669	35
36	5.7918 161 360	6.8720 853 833	8.1472 519 999	9.6513 014 333	36
37	6.0814 069 428	7.2500 500 793	8.6360 871 198	10.2786 360 264	37
38	6.3854 772 899	7.6488 028 337	9.1542 523 470	10.9467 473 682	38
39	6.7047 511 544	8.0694 869 896	9.7035 074 879	11.6582 859 471	39
40	7.0399 887 121	8.5133 087 740	10.2857 179 371	12.4160 745 337	40
41	7.3919 881 477	8.9815 407 565	10.9028 610 134	13.2231 193 783	41
42	7.7615 875 551	9.4755 254 982	11.5570 326 742	14.0826 221 379	42
43	8.1496 669 329	9.9966 794 006	12.2504 546 346	14.9979 925 769	43
44	8.5571 502 795	10.5464 967 676	12.9854 819 127	15.9728 620 944	44
45	8.9850 077 935	11.1265 540 898	13.7646 108 274	17.0110 981 305	45
46	9.4342 581 832	11.7385 145 647	14.5904 874 771	18.1168 195 090	46
47	9.9059 710 923	12.3841 328 658	15.4659 167 257	19.2944 127 771	47
48	10.4012 696 469	13.0652 601 734	16.3938 717 293	20.5485 496 076	48
49	10.9213 331 293	13.7838 494 830	17.3775 040 330	21.8842 053 321	49
50	11.4673 997 858	14.5419 612 045	18.4201 542 750	23.3066 786 787	50
51	12.0407 697 750	15.3417 690 708	19.5253 635 315	24.8216 127 928	51
52	12.6428 082 638	16.1855 663 697	20.6968 853 434	26.4350 176 243	52
53	13.2749 486 770	17.0757 725 200	21.9386 984 640	28.1532 937 699	53
54	13.9386 961 108	18.0149 400 086	23.2550 203 718	29.9832 578 650	54
55	14.6356 309 164	19.0057 617 091	24.6503 215 941	31.9321 696 262	55
56	15.3674 124 622	20.0510 786 031	26.1293 408 898	34.0077 606 519	56
57	16.1357 830 853	21.1538 879 262	27.6971 013 432	36.2182 650 943	57
58	16.9425 722 396	22.3173 517 622	29.3589 274 238	38.5724 523 254	58
59	17.7897 008 515	23.5448 061 091	31.1204 630 692	41.0796 617 266	59
60	18.6791 858 941	24.8397 704 451	32.9876 908 533	43.7498 397 388	60

183

Table 1. FUTURE WORTH OF ONE DOLLAR WITH INTEREST
PAYABLE AT BEGINNING OF EACH PERIOD

YEARS	7% NOMINAL ANNUAL RATE	7½% NOMINAL ANNUAL RATE	8% NOMINAL ANNUAL RATE	8½% NOMINAL ANNUAL RATE	YEARS
1	1.0700 000 000	1.0750 000 000	1.0800 000 000	1.0850 000 000	1
2	1.1449 000 000	1.1556 250 000	1.1664 000 000	1.1772 250 000	2
3	1.2250 430 000	1.2422 968 750	1.2597 120 000	1.2772 891 250	3
4	1.3107 960 100	1.3354 691 406	1.3604 889 600	1.3858 587 006	4
5	1.4025 517 307	1.4356 293 262	1.4693 280 768	1.5036 566 902	5
6	1.5007 303 518	1.5433 015 256	1.5868 743 229	1.6314 675 088	6
7	1.6057 814 765	1.6590 491 401	1.7138 242 688	1.7701 422 471	7
8	1.7181 861 798	1.7834 778 256	1.8509 302 103	1.9206 043 381	8
9	1.8384 592 124	1.9172 386 625	1.9990 046 271	2.0838 557 068	9
10	1.9671 513 573	2.0610 315 622	2.1589 249 973	2.2609 834 419	10
11	2.1048 519 523	2.2156 089 293	2.3316 389 971	2.4531 670 345	11
12	2.2521 915 890	2.3817 795 990	2.5181 701 168	2.6616 862 324	12
13	2.4098 450 002	2.5604 130 690	2.7196 237 262	2.8879 295 622	13
14	2.5785 341 502	2.7524 440 491	2.9371 936 243	3.1334 035 750	14
15	2.7590 315 407	2.9588 773 528	3.1721 691 142	3.3997 428 788	15
16	2.9521 637 486	3.1807 931 543	3.4259 426 433	3.6887 210 235	16
17	3.1588 152 110	3.4193 526 408	3.7000 180 548	4.0022 623 105	17
18	3.3799 322 757	3.6758 040 889	3.9960 194 992	4.3424 546 069	18
19	3.6165 275 350	3.9514 893 956	4.3157 010 591	4.7115 632 485	19
20	3.8696 844 625	4.2478 511 002	4.6609 571 438	5.1120 461 246	20
21	4.1405 623 749	4.5664 399 328	5.0338 337 154	5.5465 700 452	21
22	4.4304 017 411	4.9089 229 277	5.4365 404 126	6.0180 284 991	22
23	4.7405 298 630	5.2770 921 473	5.8714 636 456	6.5295 609 215	23
24	5.0723 669 534	5.6728 740 583	6.3411 807 372	7.0845 735 998	24
25	5.4274 326 401	6.0983 396 127	6.8484 751 962	7.6867 623 558	25
26	5.8073 529 249	6.5557 150 837	7.3963 532 119	8.3401 371 560	26
27	6.2138 676 297	7.0473 937 149	7.9880 614 689	9.0490 488 143	27
28	6.6488 383 638	7.5759 482 436	8.6271 063 864	9.8182 179 635	28
29	7.1142 570 492	8.1441 443 618	9.3172 748 973	10.6527 664 904	29
30	7.6122 550 427	8.7549 551 890	10.0626 568 891	11.5582 516 421	30
31	8.1451 128 956	9.4115 768 281	10.8676 694 402	12.5407 030 317	31
32	8.7152 707 983	10.1174 450 903	11.7370 829 954	13.6066 627 894	32
33	9.3253 397 542	10.8762 534 720	12.6760 496 350	14.7632 291 265	33
34	9.9781 135 370	11.6919 724 824	13.6901 336 059	16.0181 036 022	34
35	10.6765 814 846	12.5688 704 186	14.7853 442 943	17.3796 424 084	35
36	11.4239 421 885	13.5115 357 000	15.9681 718 379	18.8569 120 131	36
37	12.2236 181 417	14.5249 008 775	17.2456 255 849	20.4597 495 342	37
38	13.0792 714 117	15.6142 684 433	18.6252 756 317	22.1988 282 446	38
39	13.9948 204 105	16.7853 385 766	20.1152 976 822	24.0857 286 454	39
40	14.9744 578 392	18.0442 389 698	21.7245 214 968	26.1330 155 803	40
41	16.0226 698 880	19.3975 568 925	23.4624 832 165	28.3543 219 046	41
42	17.1442 567 801	20.8523 736 595	25.3394 818 739	30.7644 392 665	42
43	18.3443 547 547	22.4163 016 839	27.3666 404 238	33.3794 166 042	43
44	19.6284 595 875	24.0975 243 102	29.5559 716 577	36.2166 670 155	44
45	21.0024 517 587	25.9048 386 335	31.9204 493 903	39.2950 837 118	45
46	22.4726 233 818	27.8477 015 310	34.4740 853 415	42.6351 658 273	46
47	24.0457 070 185	29.9362 791 458	37.2320 121 688	46.2591 549 227	47
48	25.7289 065 098	32.1815 000 818	40.2105 731 423	50.1911 830 911	48
49	27.5299 299 655	34.5951 125 879	43.4274 189 937	54.4574 336 538	49
50	29.4570 250 631	37.1897 460 320	46.9016 125 132	59.0863 155 144	50
51	31.5190 168 175	39.9789 769 844	50.6537 415 143	64.1086 523 331	51
52	33.7253 479 947	42.9774 002 582	54.7060 408 354	69.5578 877 815	52
53	36.0861 223 543	46.2007 052 776	59.0825 241 023	75.4703 082 429	53
54	38.6121 509 191	49.6657 581 734	63.8091 260 304	81.8852 844 435	54
55	41.3150 014 835	53.3906 900 364	68.9138 561 129	88.8455 336 212	55
56	44.2070 515 873	57.3949 917 892	74.4269 646 019	96.3974 039 790	56
57	47.3015 451 984	61.6996 161 734	80.3811 217 701	104.5911 833 172	57
58	50.6126 533 623	66.3270 873 864	86.8116 115 117	113.4814 338 992	58
59	54.1555 390 977	71.3016 189 403	93.7565 404 326	123.1273 557 806	59
60	57.9464 268 345	76.6492 403 609	101.2570 636 672	133.5931 810 220	60

Table 1.   FUTURE WORTH OF ONE DOLLAR WITH INTEREST
PAYABLE AT BEGINNING OF EACH PERIOD

YEARS	9% NOMINAL ANNUAL RATE	9½% NOMINAL ANNUAL RATE	10% NOMINAL ANNUAL RATE	10½% NOMINAL ANNUAL RATE	YEARS
1	1.0900 000 000	1.0950 000 000	1.1000 000 000	1.1050 000 000	1
2	1.1881 000 000	1.1990 250 000	1.2100 000 000	1.2210 250 000	2
3	1.2950 290 000	1.3129 323 750	1.3310 000 000	1.3492 326 250	3
4	1.4115 816 100	1.4376 609 506	1.4641 000 000	1.4909 020 506	4
5	1.5386 239 549	1.5742 387 409	1.6105 100 000	1.6474 467 659	5
6	1.6771 001 108	1.7237 914 213	1.7715 610 000	1.8204 286 764	6
7	1.8280 391 208	1.8875 516 063	1.9487 171 000	2.0115 736 874	7
8	1.9925 626 417	2.0668 690 090	2.1435 888 100	2.2227 889 246	8
9	2.1718 932 794	2.2632 215 648	2.3579 476 910	2.4561 817 616	9
10	2.3673 636 746	2.4782 276 135	2.5937 424 601	2.7140 808 466	10
11	2.5804 264 053	2.7136 592 367	2.8531 167 061	2.9990 593 355	11
12	2.8126 647 818	2.9714 568 642	3.1384 283 767	3.3139 605 657	12
13	3.0658 046 121	3.2537 452 663	3.4522 712 144	3.6619 264 251	13
14	3.3417 270 272	3.5628 510 666	3.7974 983 358	4.0464 286 998	14
15	3.6424 824 597	3.9013 219 180	4.1772 481 694	4.4713 037 132	15
16	3.9703 058 811	4.2719 475 002	4.5949 729 864	4.9407 906 031	16
17	4.3276 334 104	4.6777 825 127	5.0544 702 850	5.4595 736 165	17
18	4.7171 204 173	5.1221 718 514	5.5599 173 135	6.0328 288 462	18
19	5.1416 612 548	5.6087 781 773	6.1159 090 448	6.6662 758 750	19
20	5.6044 107 678	6.1416 121 041	6.7274 999 493	7.3662 348 419	20
21	6.1088 077 369	6.7250 652 540	7.4002 499 443	8.1396 895 003	21
22	6.6586 004 332	7.3639 464 531	8.1402 749 387	8.9943 568 979	22
23	7.2578 744 722	8.0635 213 662	8.9543 024 326	9.9387 643 721	23
24	7.9110 831 747	8.8295 558 960	9.8497 326 758	10.9823 346 312	24
25	8.6230 806 604	9.6683 637 061	10.8347 059 434	12.1354 797 675	25
26	9.3991 579 198	10.5868 582 582	11.9181 765 377	13.4097 051 431	26
27	10.2450 821 326	11.5926 097 927	13.1099 941 915	14.8177 241 831	27
28	11.1671 395 246	12.6939 077 230	14.4209 936 106	16.3735 852 223	28
29	12.1721 820 818	13.8998 289 567	15.8630 929 717	18.0928 116 707	29
30	13.2676 784 691	15.2203 127 076	17.4494 022 689	19.9925 568 961	30
31	14.4617 695 314	16.6662 424 148	19.1943 424 958	22.0917 753 702	31
32	15.7633 287 892	18.2495 354 442	21.1137 767 454	24.4114 117 840	32
33	17.1820 283 802	19.9832 413 114	23.2251 544 199	26.9746 100 214	33
34	18.7284 109 344	21.8816 492 360	25.5476 698 619	29.8069 440 736	34
35	20.4139 679 185	23.9604 059 134	28.1024 368 481	32.9366 732 013	35
36	22.2512 250 312	26.2366 444 751	30.9126 805 329	36.3950 238 875	36
37	24.2538 352 840	28.7291 257 003	34.0039 485 862	40.2165 013 957	37
38	26.4366 804 595	31.4583 926 418	37.4043 434 448	44.4392 340 422	38
39	28.8159 817 009	34.4469 399 428	41.1447 777 893	49.1053 536 167	39
40	31.4094 200 540	37.7193 992 373	45.2592 555 682	54.2614 157 464	40
41	34.2362 678 588	41.3027 421 649	49.7851 811 250	59.9588 643 998	41
42	37.3175 319 661	45.2265 026 705	54.7636 992 375	66.2545 451 617	42
43	40.6761 098 431	49.5230 204 243	60.2400 691 612	73.2112 724 037	43
44	44.3369 597 290	54.2277 073 646	66.2640 760 774	80.8984 560 061	44
45	48.3272 861 046	59.3793 395 642	72.8904 836 851	89.3927 938 868	45
46	52.6767 418 540	65.0203 768 228	80.1795 320 536	98.7790 372 449	46
47	57.4176 486 209	71.1973 126 209	88.1974 852 590	109.1508 361 556	47
48	62.5852 369 967	77.9610 573 199	97.0172 337 849	120.6116 739 519	48
49	68.2179 083 264	85.3673 577 653	106.7189 571 634	133.2758 997 169	49
50	74.3575 200 758	93.4772 567 530	117.3908 528 797	147.2698 691 871	50
51	81.0496 968 826	102.3575 961 446	129.1299 381 677	162.7332 054 518	51
52	88.3441 696 021	112.0815 677 783	142.0429 319 844	179.8201 920 242	52
53	96.2951 448 663	122.7293 167 173	156.2472 251 829	198.7013 121 868	53
54	104.9617 079 042	134.3886 018 054	171.8719 477 012	219.5649 499 664	54
55	114.4082 616 156	147.1555 189 769	189.0591 424 713	242.6192 697 129	55
56	124.7050 051 610	161.1352 932 797	207.9650 567 184	268.0942 930 327	56
57	135.9284 556 255	176.4431 461 413	228.7615 623 902	296.2441 938 012	57
58	148.1620 166 318	193.2052 450 247	251.6377 186 293	327.3498 341 503	58
59	161.4965 981 287	211.5597 433 021	276.8014 904 922	361.7215 667 360	59
60	176.0312 919 602	231.6579 189 157	304.4816 395 414	399.7023 312 433	60

ANNUAL
COMPOUNDING

Table 1.   FUTURE WORTH OF ONE DOLLAR WITH INTEREST
PAYABLE AT BEGINNING OF EACH PERIOD

	11% NOMINAL ANNUAL RATE	**11½%** NOMINAL ANNUAL RATE	**12%** NOMINAL ANNUAL RATE	**12½%** NOMINAL ANNUAL RATE	
YEARS					**YEARS**
1	1.1100 000 000	1.1150 000 000	1.1200 000 000	1.1250 000 000	1
2	1.2321 000 000	1.2432 250 000	1.2544 000 000	1.2656 250 000	2
3	1.3676 310 000	1.3861 958 750	1.4049 280 000	1.4238 281 250	3
4	1.5180 704 100	1.5456 084 006	1.5735 193 600	1.6018 066 406	4
5	1.6850 581 551	1.7233 533 667	1.7623 416 832	1.8020 324 707	5
6	1.8704 145 522	1.9215 390 039	1.9738 226 852	2.0272 865 295	6
7	2.0761 601 529	2.1425 159 893	2.2106 814 074	2.2806 973 457	7
8	2.3045 377 697	2.3889 053 281	2.4759 631 763	2.5657 845 140	8
9	2.5580 369 244	2.6636 294 408	2.7730 787 575	2.8865 075 782	9
10	2.8394 209 861	2.9699 468 265	3.1058 482 083	3.2473 210 255	10
11	3.1517 572 945	3.3114 907 116	3.4785 499 933	3.6532 361 537	11
12	3.4984 505 969	3.6923 121 434	3.8959 759 925	4.1098 906 729	12
13	3.8832 801 626	4.1169 280 399	4.3634 931 117	4.6236 270 070	13
14	4.3104 409 805	4.5903 747 645	4.8871 122 851	5.2015 803 828	14
15	4.7845 894 883	5.1182 678 624	5.4735 657 593	5.8517 779 307	15
16	5.3108 943 321	5.7068 686 665	6.1303 936 504	6.5832 501 720	16
17	5.8950 927 086	6.3631 585 632	6.8660 408 884	7.4061 564 435	17
18	6.5435 529 065	7.0949 217 980	7.6899 657 950	8.3319 259 990	18
19	7.2633 437 262	7.9108 378 047	8.6127 616 904	9.3734 167 488	19
20	8.0623 115 361	8.8205 841 523	9.6462 930 933	10.5450 938 424	20
21	8.9491 658 051	9.8349 513 298	10.8038 482 645	11.8632 305 728	21
22	9.9335 740 437	10.9659 707 327	12.1003 100 562	13.3461 343 943	22
23	11.0262 671 885	12.2270 573 670	13.5523 472 629	15.0144 011 936	23
24	12.2391 565 792	13.6331 689 642	15.1786 289 345	16.8912 013 428	24
25	13.5854 638 029	15.2009 833 950	17.0000 644 066	19.0026 015 107	25
26	15.0798 648 212	16.9490 964 855	19.0400 721 354	21.3779 266 995	26
27	16.7386 499 516	18.8982 425 813	21.3248 807 917	24.0501 675 370	27
28	18.5799 014 462	21.0715 404 782	23.8838 664 867	27.0564 384 791	28
29	20.6236 906 053	23.4947 676 331	26.7499 304 651	30.4384 932 890	29
30	22.8922 965 719	26.1966 659 110	29.9599 221 209	34.2433 049 501	30
31	25.4104 491 948	29.2092 824 907	33.5551 127 754	38.5237 180 689	31
32	28.2055 986 063	32.5683 499 772	37.5817 263 085	43.3391 828 275	32
33	31.3082 144 529	36.3137 102 245	42.0915 334 655	48.7565 806 809	33
34	34.7521 180 428	40.4897 869 003	47.1425 174 813	54.8511 532 661	34
35	38.5748 510 275	45.1461 123 939	52.7996 195 791	61.7075 474 243	35
36	42.8180 846 405	50.3379 153 192	59.1355 739 286	69.4209 908 523	36
37	47.5280 739 509	56.1267 755 809	66.2318 428 000	78.0986 147 089	37
38	52.7561 620 855	62.5813 547 727	74.1796 639 360	87.8609 415 475	38
39	58.5593 399 150	69.7782 105 715	83.0812 236 084	98.8435 592 409	39
40	65.0008 673 056	77.8027 047 873	93.0509 704 414	111.1990 041 461	40
41	72.1509 627 092	86.7500 158 378	104.2170 868 943	125.0988 796 643	41
42	80.0875 686 072	96.7262 676 592	116.7231 373 216	140.7362 396 224	42
43	88.8972 011 540	107.8497 884 400	130.7299 138 002	158.3282 695 752	43
44	98.6758 932 810	120.2525 141 106	146.4175 034 563	178.1193 032 720	44
45	109.5302 415 419	134.0815 532 333	163.9876 038 710	200.3842 161 811	45
46	121.5785 681 115	149.5009 318 551	183.6661 163 355	225.4322 432 037	46
47	134.9522 106 037	166.6935 390 184	205.7060 502 958	253.6112 736 041	47
48	149.7969 537 702	185.8632 960 056	230.3907 763 313	285.3126 828 047	48
49	166.2746 186 849	207.2375 750 462	258.0376 694 911	320.9767 681 552	49
50	184.5648 267 402	231.0698 961 765	289.0021 898 300	361.0988 641 746	50
51	204.8669 576 816	257.6429 342 368	323.6824 526 096	406.2362 221 965	51
52	227.4023 230 266	287.2718 716 740	362.5243 469 228	457.0157 499 710	52
53	252.4165 785 595	320.3081 369 165	406.0272 685 535	514.1427 187 174	53
54	280.1824 022 011	357.1435 726 620	454.7505 407 799	578.4105 585 571	54
55	311.0024 664 432	398.2150 835 181	509.3206 056 735	650.7118 783 767	55
56	345.2127 377 520	444.0098 181 227	570.4390 783 543	732.0508 631 738	56
57	383.1861 389 047	495.0709 472 068	638.8917 677 568	823.5572 210 706	57
58	425.3366 141 842	552.0041 061 355	715.5587 798 876	926.5018 737 044	58
59	472.1236 417 445	615.4845 783 411	801.4258 334 742	1042.3146 079 174	59
60	524.0572 423 363	686.2653 048 504	897.5969 334 911	1172.6039 339 071	60

186

Table 1. FUTURE WORTH OF ONE DOLLAR WITH INTEREST
PAYABLE AT BEGINNING OF EACH PERIOD

	13% NOMINAL ANNUAL RATE	13½% NOMINAL ANNUAL RATE	14% NOMINAL ANNUAL RATE	14½% NOMINAL ANNUAL RATE	
YEARS					YEARS
1	1.1300 000 000	1.1350 000 000	1.1400 000 000	1.1450 000 000	1
2	1.2769 000 000	1.2882 250 000	1.2996 000 000	1.3110 250 000	2
3	1.4428 970 000	1.4621 353 750	1.4815 440 000	1.5011 236 250	3
4	1.6304 736 100	1.6595 236 506	1.6889 601 600	1.7187 865 506	4
5	1.8424 351 793	1.8835 593 435	1.9254 145 824	1.9680 106 005	5
6	2.0819 517 526	2.1378 398 548	2.1949 726 239	2.2533 721 375	6
7	2.3526 054 804	2.4264 482 352	2.5022 687 913	2.5801 110 975	7
8	2.6584 441 929	2.7540 187 470	2.8525 864 221	2.9542 272 066	8
9	3.0040 419 380	3.1258 112 778	3.2519 485 212	3.3825 901 516	9
10	3.3945 673 899	3.5477 958 003	3.7072 213 141	3.8730 657 235	10
11	3.8358 611 506	4.0267 482 334	4.2262 322 981	4.4346 602 535	11
12	4.3345 231 002	4.5703 592 449	4.8179 048 198	5.0776 859 902	12
13	4.8980 111 032	5.1873 577 429	5.4924 114 946	5.8139 504 588	13
14	5.5347 525 466	5.8876 510 382	6.2613 491 038	6.6569 732 753	14
15	6.2542 703 777	6.6824 839 284	7.1379 379 784	7.6222 344 002	15
16	7.0673 255 268	7.5846 192 587	8.1372 492 954	8.7274 583 883	16
17	7.9860 778 453	8.6085 428 587	9.2764 641 967	9.9929 398 546	17
18	9.0242 679 652	9.7706 961 446	10.5751 691 843	11.4419 161 335	18
19	10.1974 228 006	11.0897 401 241	12.0556 928 700	13.1009 939 728	19
20	11.5230 877 647	12.5868 550 409	13.7434 898 719	15.0006 380 989	20
21	13.0210 891 741	14.2860 804 714	15.6675 784 539	17.1757 306 232	21
22	14.7138 307 668	16.2147 013 350	17.8610 394 375	19.6662 115 636	22
23	16.6266 287 665	18.4036 860 152	20.3615 849 587	22.5178 122 403	23
24	18.7880 905 061	20.8881 836 273	23.2122 068 529	25.7828 950 152	24
25	21.2305 422 719	23.7080 884 170	26.4619 158 123	29.5214 147 924	25
26	23.9905 127 672	26.9086 803 533	30.1665 840 261	33.8020 199 373	26
27	27.1092 794 270	30.5413 522 010	34.3899 057 897	38.7033 128 282	27
28	30.6334 857 525	34.6644 347 481	39.2044 926 003	44.3152 931 883	28
29	34.6158 389 003	39.3441 334 391	44.6931 215 643	50.7410 107 006	29
30	39.1158 979 573	44.6555 914 534	50.9501 585 833	58.0984 572 522	30
31	44.2009 646 918	50.6844 962 996	58.0831 807 850	66.5227 335 537	31
32	49.9470 901 017	57.5264 493 000	66.2148 260 949	76.1685 299 190	32
33	56.4402 118 150	65.2925 199 555	75.4849 017 482	87.2129 667 573	33
34	63.7774 393 509	74.1070 101 495	86.0527 879 929	99.8588 469 371	34
35	72.0685 064 665	84.1114 565 197	98.1001 783 119	114.3383 797 429	35
36	81.4374 123 072	95.4665 031 499	111.8342 032 756	130.9174 448 057	36
37	92.0242 759 071	108.3544 810 751	127.4909 917 342	149.9004 743 025	37
38	103.9874 317 750	122.9823 360 202	145.3397 305 769	171.6360 430 763	38
39	117.5057 979 058	139.5849 513 830	165.6872 928 577	196.5232 693 224	39
40	132.7815 516 335	158.4289 198 197	188.8835 138 578	225.0191 433 742	40
41	150.0431 533 459	179.8168 239 953	215.3272 057 979	257.6469 191 634	41
42	169.5487 632 808	204.0920 952 347	245.4730 146 096	295.0057 224 421	42
43	191.5901 025 073	231.6445 280 914	279.8392 366 549	337.7815 521 962	43
44	216.4968 158 333	262.9165 393 837	319.0167 297 866	386.7598 772 647	44
45	244.6414 018 916	298.4102 722 005	363.6790 719 567	442.8400 594 680	45
46	276.4447 841 375	338.6956 589 476	414.5941 420 307	507.0518 680 909	46
47	312.3826 060 754	384.4195 729 055	472.6373 219 150	580.5743 889 641	47
48	352.9923 448 652	436.3162 152 477	538.8065 469 831	664.7576 753 639	48
49	398.8813 496 977	495.2189 043 062	614.2394 635 607	761.1475 382 916	49
50	450.7359 251 584	562.0734 563 875	700.2329 884 592	871.5139 313 439	50
51	509.3315 954 290	637.9533 729 998	798.2656 068 435	997.8834 513 888	51
52	575.5447 028 348	724.0770 783 548	910.0227 918 015	1142.5765 518 402	52
53	650.3655 142 033	821.8274 839 327	1037.4259 826 538	1308.2501 518 570	53
54	734.9130 310 497	932.7741 942 636	1182.6656 202 253	1497.9464 238 763	54
55	830.4517 250 862	1058.6987 104 891	1348.2388 070 568	1715.1486 553 383	55
56	938.4104 493 474	1201.6230 364 052	1536.9922 400 448	1963.8452 103 624	56
57	1060.4038 077 626	1363.8421 463 199	1752.1711 536 510	2248.6027 658 649	57
58	1198.2563 027 717	1547.9608 360 731	1997.4751 151 622	2574.6501 669 154	58
59	1354.0296 221 320	1756.9355 489 429	2277.1216 312 849	2947.9744 411 181	59
60	1530.0534 730 092	1994.1218 480 502	2595.9186 596 648	3375.4307 350 802	60

Table 1.   FUTURE WORTH OF ONE DOLLAR WITH INTEREST
PAYABLE AT BEGINNING OF EACH PERIOD

YEARS	15% NOMINAL ANNUAL RATE	15½% NOMINAL ANNUAL RATE	16% NOMINAL ANNUAL RATE	16½% NOMINAL ANNUAL RATE	YEARS
1	1.1500 000 000	1.1550 000 000	1.1600 000 000	1.1650 000 000	1
2	1.3225 000 000	1.3340 250 000	1.3456 000 000	1.3572 250 000	2
3	1.5208 750 000	1.5407 988 750	1.5608 960 000	1.5811 671 250	3
4	1.7490 062 500	1.7796 227 006	1.8106 393 600	1.8420 597 006	4
5	2.0113 571 875	2.0554 642 192	2.1003 416 576	2.1459 995 512	5
6	2.3130 607 656	2.3740 611 732	2.4363 963 228	2.5000 894 772	6
7	2.6600 198 805	2.7420 406 550	2.8262 197 345	2.9126 042 409	7
8	3.0590 228 625	3.1670 569 566	3.2784 148 920	3.3931 839 407	8
9	3.5178 762 919	3.6579 507 848	3.8029 612 747	3.9530 592 909	9
10	4.0455 577 357	4.2249 331 565	4.4114 350 786	4.6053 140 739	10
11	4.6523 913 961	4.8797 977 958	5.1172 646 912	5.3651 908 961	11
12	5.3502 501 055	5.6361 664 541	5.9360 270 418	6.2504 473 939	12
13	6.1527 876 213	6.5097 722 545	6.8857 913 685	7.2817 712 139	13
14	7.0757 057 645	7.5187 869 539	7.9875 179 875	8.4832 634 642	14
15	8.1370 616 292	8.6841 989 318	9.2655 208 655	9.8830 019 358	15
16	9.3576 208 735	10.0302 497 662	10.7480 042 040	11.5136 972 552	16
17	10.7612 640 046	11.5849 384 800	12.4676 848 766	13.4134 573 023	17
18	12.3754 536 053	13.3806 039 444	14.4625 144 569	15.6266 777 572	18
19	14.2317 716 460	15.4545 975 558	16.7765 167 700	18.2050 795 871	19
20	16.3665 373 929	17.8500 601 769	19.4607 594 531	21.2089 177 190	20
21	18.8215 180 019	20.6168 195 043	22.5744 809 656	24.7083 891 426	21
22	21.6447 457 022	23.8124 265 275	26.1863 979 201	28.7852 733 512	22
23	24.8914 575 575	27.5033 526 393	30.3762 215 874	33.5348 434 541	23
24	28.6251 761 911	31.7663 722 983	35.2364 170 414	39.0680 926 240	24
25	32.9189 526 198	36.6901 600 046	40.8742 437 680	45.5143 279 070	25
26	37.8567 955 128	42.3771 348 053	47.4141 227 708	53.0241 920 117	26
27	43.5353 148 397	48.9455 907 001	55.0003 824 142	61.7731 836 936	27
28	50.0656 120 656	56.5321 572 586	63.8004 436 004	71.9657 590 030	28
29	57.5754 538 755	65.2946 416 337	74.0085 145 765	83.8401 092 385	29
30	66.2117 719 568	75.4153 110 870	85.8498 769 088	97.6737 272 629	30
31	76.1435 377 503	87.1046 843 054	99.5858 572 142	113.7898 922 613	31
32	87.5650 684 128	100.6059 103 728	115.5195 943 684	132.5652 244 844	32
33	100.6998 286 748	116.1998 264 805	134.0027 294 674	154.4384 865 243	33
34	115.8048 029 760	134.2107 995 850	155.4431 661 822	179.9208 368 008	34
35	133.1755 234 224	155.0134 735 207	180.3140 727 713	209.6077 748 729	35
36	153.1518 519 358	179.0405 619 164	209.1643 244 147	244.1930 577 269	36
37	176.1246 297 261	206.7918 490 135	242.6306 163 211	284.4849 122 519	37
38	202.5433 241 850	238.8445 856 106	281.4515 149 324	331.4249 227 734	38
39	232.9248 228 128	275.8654 963 802	326.4837 573 216	386.1100 350 311	39
40	267.8635 462 347	318.6246 483 191	378.7211 584 931	449.8181 908 112	40
41	308.0430 781 699	368.0114 688 086	439.3165 438 520	524.0381 922 950	41
42	354.2495 398 954	425.0532 464 739	509.6071 908 683	610.5044 940 237	42
43	407.3869 708 797	490.9364 996 774	591.1443 414 072	711.2377 355 376	43
44	468.4950 165 117	567.0316 571 274	685.7274 360 324	828.5919 619 013	44
45	538.7692 689 884	654.9215 639 821	795.4438 257 976	965.3096 356 151	45
46	619.5846 593 367	756.4544 063 993	922.7148 379 252	1124.5857 254 916	46
47	712.5223 582 372	873.6817 393 912	1070.3492 119 932	1310.1423 701 977	47
48	819.4007 119 727	1009.1024 089 969	1241.6050 859 121	1526.3158 612 803	48
49	942.3108 187 687	1165.5132 823 914	1440.2618 996 581	1778.1579 783 915	49
50	1083.6574 415 840	1346.1678 411 621	1670.7038 036 034	2071.5540 448 261	50
51	1246.2060 578 216	1554.8238 565 422	1938.0164 121 799	2413.3604 622 224	51
52	1433.1369 664 948	1795.8215 543 062	2248.0990 381 287	2811.5649 384 891	52
53	1648.1075 114 690	2074.1738 952 237	2607.7948 842 293	3275.4731 533 398	53
54	1895.3236 381 894	2395.6708 489 833	3025.0420 657 060	3815.9262 236 409	54
55	2179.6221 839 178	2766.9998 305 758	3509.0487 962 189	4445.5540 505 417	55
56	2506.5655 115 054	3195.8848 043 150	4070.4966 036 140	5179.0704 688 810	56
57	2882.5503 382 312	3691.2469 489 838	4721.7760 601 922	6033.6170 962 464	57
58	3314.9328 889 659	4263.3902 260 763	5477.2602 298 229	7029.1639 171 271	58
59	3812.1728 223 108	4924.2157 111 182	6353.6218 665 946	8188.9759 634 530	59
60	4383.9987 456 574	5687.4691 463 415	7370.2013 652 497	9540.1569 974 228	60

ANNUAL
COMPOUNDING

Table 1. FUTURE WORTH OF ONE DOLLAR WITH INTEREST PAYABLE AT BEGINNING OF EACH PERIOD

YEARS	17% NOMINAL ANNUAL RATE	17½% NOMINAL ANNUAL RATE	18% NOMINAL ANNUAL RATE	18½% NOMINAL ANNUAL RATE	YEARS
1	1.1700 000 000	1.1750 000 000	1.1800 000 000	1.1850 000 000	1
2	1.3689 000 000	1.3806 250 000	1.3924 000 000	1.4042 250 000	2
3	1.6016 130 000	1.6222 343 750	1.6430 320 000	1.6640 066 250	3
4	1.8738 872 100	1.9061 253 906	1.9387 777 600	1.9718 478 506	4
5	2.1924 480 357	2.2396 973 340	2.2877 577 568	2.3366 397 030	5
6	2.5651 642 018	2.6316 443 674	2.6995 541 530	2.7689 180 480	6
7	3.0012 421 161	3.0921 821 317	3.1854 739 006	3.2811 678 869	7
8	3.5114 532 758	3.6333 140 048	3.7588 592 027	3.8881 839 460	8
9	4.1084 003 327	4.2691 439 556	4.4354 538 592	4.6074 979 760	9
10	4.8068 283 892	5.0162 441 479	5.2338 355 538	5.4598 851 016	10
11	5.6239 892 154	5.8940 868 737	6.1759 259 535	6.4699 638 454	11
12	6.5800 673 820	6.9255 520 766	7.2875 926 251	7.6669 071 568	12
13	7.6986 788 370	8.1375 236 900	8.5993 592 976	9.0852 849 808	13
14	9.0074 542 393	9.5615 903 358	10.1472 439 712	10.7660 627 022	14
15	10.5387 214 599	11.2348 686 446	11.9737 478 860	12.7577 843 021	15
16	12.3303 041 081	13.2009 706 574	14.1290 225 055	15.1179 743 980	16
17	14.4264 558 065	15.5111 405 224	16.6722 465 565	17.9147 996 617	17
18	16.8789 532 936	18.2255 901 138	19.6732 509 367	21.2290 375 991	18
19	19.7483 753 535	21.4150 683 838	23.2144 361 053	25.1564 095 549	19
20	23.1055 991 636	25.1627 053 509	27.3930 346 042	29.8103 453 226	20
21	27.0335 510 215	29.5661 787 873	32.3237 808 330	35.3252 592 073	21
22	31.6292 546 951	34.7402 600 751	38.1420 613 829	41.8604 321 606	22
23	37.0062 279 933	40.8198 055 882	45.0076 324 318	49.6046 121 103	23
24	43.2972 867 521	47.9632 715 662	53.1090 062 695	58.7814 653 507	24
25	50.6578 255 000	56.3568 440 903	62.6686 273 981	69.6560 364 406	25
26	59.2696 558 350	66.2192 918 061	73.9489 803 297	82.5424 031 821	26
27	69.3454 973 270	77.8076 678 721	87.2597 967 891	97.8127 477 708	27
28	81.1342 318 726	91.4240 097 497	102.9665 602 111	115.9081 061 084	28
29	94.9270 512 909	107.4232 114 559	121.5005 410 491	137.3511 057 385	29
30	111.0646 500 103	126.2222 734 607	143.3706 384 379	162.7610 603 001	30
31	129.9456 405 121	148.3111 713 164	169.1773 533 568	192.8718 564 556	31
32	152.0363 993 992	174.2656 262 967	199.6292 769 610	228.5531 498 999	32
33	177.8825 872 970	204.7621 108 986	235.5625 468 139	270.8354 826 314	33
34	208.1226 271 375	240.5954 803 059	277.9638 052 405	320.9400 469 182	34
35	243.5034 737 509	282.6996 893 594	327.9972 901 837	380.3139 555 981	35
36	284.8990 642 885	332.1721 349 973	387.0368 024 168	450.6720 373 837	36
37	333.3319 052 176	390.3022 586 219	456.7034 268 518	534.0463 642 997	37
38	389.9983 291 046	458.6051 538 807	538.9100 436 852	632.8449 416 952	38
39	456.2980 450 523	538.8610 558 098	635.9138 515 485	749.9212 559 088	39
40	533.8687 127 112	633.1617 405 766	750.3783 448 272	888.6566 882 519	40
41	624.6263 938 722	743.9650 451 774	885.4464 468 961	1053.0581 755 785	41
42	730.8128 808 304	874.1589 280 835	1044.8268 073 374	1247.8739 380 605	42
43	855.0510 705 716	1027.1367 404 981	1232.8956 326 582	1478.7306 166 018	43
44	1000.4097 525 688	1206.8856 700 853	1454.8168 465 366	1752.2957 806 731	44
45	1170.4794 105 055	1418.0906 623 502	1716.6838 789 132	2076.4705 000 976	45
46	1369.4609 102 914	1666.2565 282 615	2025.6869 771 176	2460.6175 426 156	46
47	1602.2692 650 409	1957.8514 207 073	2390.3106 329 988	2915.8317 879 995	47
48	1874.6550 400 979	2300.4754 193 310	2820.5665 469 386	3455.2606 687 795	48
49	2193.3463 969 145	2703.0586 177 140	3328.2685 253 875	4094.4838 925 037	49
50	2566.2152 843 900	3176.0938 758 139	3927.3568 599 573	4851.9634 126 168	50
51	3002.4718 827 363	3731.9103 040 813	4634.2810 947 496	5749.5766 439 509	51
52	3512.8921 028 015	4384.9946 072 956	5468.4516 918 045	6813.2483 230 819	52
53	4110.0837 602 777	5152.3686 635 723	6452.7729 963 293	8073.6992 628 520	53
54	4808.7979 995 249	6054.0331 796 974	7614.2721 356 686	9567.3336 264 796	54
55	5626.2936 594 442	7113.4889 861 445	8984.8411 200 889	11337.2903 473 784	55
56	6582.7635 815 497	8358.3495 587 198	10602.1125 217 049	13434.6890 616 434	56
57	7701.8333 904 131	9821.0607 314 957	12510.4927 756 118	15920.1065 380 474	57
58	9011.1450 667 833	11539.7463 595 075	14762.3814 752 219	18865.3262 475 862	58
59	10543.0397 281 365	13559.2019 724 213	17419.6101 407 618	22355.4116 033 896	59
60	12335.3564 819 197	15932.0623 175 950	20555.1399 660 990	26491.1627 500 167	60

Table 1. FUTURE WORTH OF ONE DOLLAR WITH INTEREST
PAYABLE AT BEGINNING OF EACH PERIOD

YEARS	19% NOMINAL ANNUAL RATE	19½% NOMINAL ANNUAL RATE	20% NOMINAL ANNUAL RATE	20½% NOMINAL ANNUAL RATE	YEARS
1	1.1900 000 000	1.1950 000 000	1.2000 000 000	1.2050 000 000	1
2	1.4161 000 000	1.4280 250 000	1.4400 000 000	1.4520 250 000	2
3	1.6851 590 000	1.7064 898 750	1.7280 000 000	1.7496 901 250	3
4	2.0053 392 100	2.0392 554 006	2.0736 000 000	2.1083 766 006	4
5	2.3863 536 599	2.4369 102 037	2.4883 200 000	2.5405 938 038	5
6	2.8397 608 553	2.9121 076 935	2.9859 840 000	3.0614 155 335	6
7	3.3793 154 178	3.4799 686 937	3.5831 808 000	3.6890 057 179	7
8	4.0213 853 472	4.1585 625 890	4.2998 169 600	4.4452 518 901	8
9	4.7854 485 631	4.9694 822 938	5.1597 803 520	5.3565 285 275	9
10	5.6946 837 901	5.9385 313 411	6.1917 364 224	6.4546 168 757	10
11	6.7766 737 102	7.0965 449 526	7.4300 837 069	7.7778 133 352	11
12	8.0642 417 152	8.4803 712 184	8.9161 004 483	9.3722 650 689	12
13	9.5964 476 411	10.1340 436 060	10.6993 205 379	11.2935 794 080	13
14	11.4197 726 929	12.1101 821 092	12.8391 846 455	13.6087 631 867	14
15	13.5895 295 045	14.4716 676 205	15.4070 215 746	16.3985 596 399	15
16	16.1715 401 104	17.2936 428 064	18.4884 258 895	19.7602 643 661	16
17	19.2441 327 314	20.6659 031 537	22.1861 110 674	23.8111 185 612	17
18	22.9005 179 503	24.6957 542 687	26.6233 332 809	28.6923 978 662	18
19	27.2516 163 609	29.5114 263 511	31.9479 999 371	34.5743 394 288	19
20	32.4294 234 694	35.2661 544 895	38.3375 999 245	41.6620 790 117	20
21	38.5910 139 286	42.1430 546 150	46.0051 199 094	50.2028 052 091	21
22	45.9233 065 751	50.3609 502 649	55.2061 438 912	60.4943 802 769	22
23	54.6487 348 243	60.1813 355 666	66.2473 726 695	72.8957 282 337	23
24	65.0319 944 410	71.9166 960 021	79.4968 472 034	87.8393 525 216	24
25	77.3880 733 847	85.9404 517 225	95.3962 166 441	105.8464 197 885	25
26	92.0918 073 278	102.6988 398 083	114.4754 599 729	127.5449 358 452	26
27	109.5892 507 201	122.7251 135 710	137.3705 519 675	153.6916 476 934	27
28	130.4112 083 569	146.6565 107 173	164.8446 623 610	185.1984 354 706	28
29	155.1893 379 448	175.2545 303 072	197.8135 948 331	223.1641 147 420	29
30	184.6753 121 543	209.4291 637 171	237.3763 137 998	268.9127 582 642	30
31	219.7636 214 636	250.2678 506 419	284.8515 765 597	324.0398 737 083	31
32	261.5187 095 417	299.0700 815 171	341.8218 918 717	390.4680 478 185	32
33	311.2072 643 546	357.3887 474 129	410.1862 702 460	470.5139 976 213	33
34	370.3366 445 819	427.0795 531 584	492.2235 242 952	566.9693 671 337	34
35	440.7006 070 525	510.3600 660 243	590.6682 291 542	683.1980 873 961	35
36	524.4337 223 925	609.8802 788 990	708.8018 749 851	823.2536 953 123	36
37	624.0761 296 470	728.8069 332 843	850.5622 499 821	992.0207 028 513	37
38	742.6505 942 800	870.9242 852 748	1020.6746 999 785	1195.3849 469 358	38
39	883.7542 071 932	1040.7545 209 033	1224.8096 399 742	1440.4388 610 577	39
40	1051.6675 065 599	1243.7016 524 795	1469.7715 679 691	1735.7288 275 745	40
41	1251.4843 328 063	1486.2234 747 130	1763.7258 815 629	2091.5532 372 272	41
42	1489.2663 560 395	1776.0370 522 820	2116.4710 578 755	2520.3216 508 588	42
43	1772.2269 636 869	2122.3642 774 770	2539.7652 694 506	3036.9875 892 849	43
44	2108.9500 867 875	2536.2253 115 851	3047.7183 233 407	3659.5700 450 883	44
45	2509.6506 032 771	3030.7892 473 441	3657.2619 880 088	4409.7819 043 314	45
46	2986.4842 178 997	3621.7931 505 762	4388.7143 856 106	5313.7871 947 193	46
47	3553.9162 193 007	4328.0428 149 386	5266.4572 627 327	6403.1135 696 368	47
48	4229.1603 009 678	5172.0111 638 516	6319.7487 152 793	7715.7518 514 123	48
49	5032.7007 581 517	6180.5533 408 027	7583.6984 583 351	9297.4809 809 519	49
50	5988.9139 022 005	7385.7612 422 592	9100.4381 500 021	11203.4645 820 470	50
51	7126.8075 436 186	8825.9846 844 998	10920.5257 800 026	13500.1748 213 666	51
52	8480.9009 769 062	10547.0516 979 773	13104.6309 360 031	16267.7106 597 468	52
53	10092.2721 625 183	12603.7267 790 828	15725.5571 232 037	19602.5913 449 949	53
54	12009.8038 733 968	15061.4535 010 040	18870.6685 478 445	23621.1225 707 188	54
55	14291.1666 093 422	17998.4369 336 998	22644.8022 574 133	28463.4526 977 162	55
56	17007.0832 651 172	21508.1321 357 712	27173.7627 088 960	34298.4605 007 480	56
57	20238.4290 854 895	25702.2179 022 466	32608.5152 506 752	41329.6449 034 013	57
58	24083.7306 117 325	30714.1503 931 847	39130.2183 008 103	49802.2221 085 986	58
59	28659.6394 279 617	36703.4097 198 557	46956.2619 609 723	60011.6776 408 613	59
60	34104.9709 192 744	43860.5746 152 275	56347.5143 531 668	72314.0715 572 378	60

Table 1. FUTURE WORTH OF ONE DOLLAR WITH INTEREST
PAYABLE AT BEGINNING OF EACH PERIOD

YEARS	**21%** NOMINAL ANNUAL RATE	**21½%** NOMINAL ANNUAL RATE	**22%** NOMINAL ANNUAL RATE	**22½%** NOMINAL ANNUAL RATE	YEARS
1	1.2100 000 000	1.2150 000 000	1.2200 000 000	1.2250 000 000	1
2	1.4641 000 000	1.4762 250 000	1.4884 000 000	1.5006 250 000	2
3	1.7715 610 000	1.7936 133 750	1.8158 480 000	1.8382 656 250	3
4	2.1435 888 100	2.1792 402 506	2.2153 345 600	2.2518 753 906	4
5	2.5937 424 601	2.6477 769 045	2.7027 081 632	2.7585 473 535	5
6	3.1384 283 767	3.2170 489 390	3.2973 039 591	3.3792 205 081	6
7	3.7974 983 358	3.9087 144 609	4.0227 108 301	4.1395 451 224	7
8	4.5949 729 864	4.7490 880 699	4.9077 072 127	5.0709 427 749	8
9	5.5599 173 135	5.7701 420 050	5.9874 027 995	6.2119 048 993	9
10	6.7274 999 493	7.0107 225 361	7.3046 314 154	7.6095 835 016	10
11	8.1402 749 387	8.5180 278 813	8.9116 503 268	9.3217 397 894	11
12	9.8497 326 758	10.3494 038 758	10.8722 133 987	11.4191 312 421	12
13	11.9181 765 377	12.5745 257 091	13.2641 003 464	13.9884 357 715	13
14	14.4209 936 106	15.2780 487 365	16.1822 024 227	17.1358 338 201	14
15	17.4494 022 689	18.5628 292 149	19.7422 869 556	20.9913 964 297	15
16	21.1137 767 454	22.5538 374 961	24.0855 900 859	25.7144 606 263	16
17	25.5476 698 619	27.4029 125 577	29.3844 199 048	31.5002 142 673	17
18	30.9126 805 329	33.2945 387 577	35.8489 922 838	38.5877 624 774	18
19	37.4043 434 448	40.4528 645 906	43.7357 705 863	47.2700 090 348	19
20	45.2592 555 682	49.1502 304 775	53.3576 401 153	57.9057 610 676	20
21	54.7636 992 375	59.7175 300 302	65.0963 209 406	70.9345 573 079	21
22	66.2640 760 774	72.5567 989 867	79.4175 115 475	86.8948 327 021	22
23	80.1795 320 536	88.1565 107 688	96.8893 640 880	106.4461 700 601	23
24	97.0172 337 849	107.1101 605 841	118.2050 241 874	130.3965 583 236	24
25	117.3908 528 797	130.1388 451 097	144.2101 295 086	159.7357 839 464	25
26	142.0429 319 844	158.1186 968 083	175.9363 580 005	195.6763 353 344	26
27	171.8719 477 012	192.1142 166 221	214.6423 567 606	239.7035 107 846	27
28	207.9650 567 184	233.4187 731 958	261.8636 752 479	293.6368 007 112	28
29	251.6377 186 293	283.6038 094 329	319.4736 838 025	359.7050 808 712	29
30	304.4816 395 414	344.5786 284 610	389.7578 942 390	440.6387 240 672	30
31	368.4227 838 451	418.6630 335 801	475.5046 309 716	539.7824 369 823	31
32	445.7915 684 526	508.6755 857 998	580.1156 497 853	661.2334 853 034	32
33	539.4077 978 276	618.0408 367 468	707.7410 927 381	810.0110 194 966	33
34	652.6834 353 714	750.9196 166 474	863.4441 331 405	992.2634 988 834	34
35	789.7469 567 994	912.3673 342 265	1053.4018 424 314	1215.5227 861 321	35
36	955.5938 177 273	1108.5263 110 852	1285.1502 477 663	1489.0154 130 119	36
37	1156.2685 194 501	1346.8594 679 686	1567.8833 022 749	1824.0438 809 395	37
38	1399.0849 085 346	1636.4342 535 818	1912.8176 287 753	2234.4537 541 509	38
39	1692.8927 393 268	1988.2676 181 019	2333.6375 071 059	2737.2058 488 349	39
40	2048.4002 145 855	2415.7451 559 938	2847.0377 586 692	3353.0771 648 227	40
41	2478.5642 596 484	2935.1303 645 325	3473.3860 655 765	4107.5195 269 079	41
42	2999.0627 541 746	3566.1833 929 070	4237.5310 000 033	5031.7114 204 621	42
43	3628.8659 325 512	4332.9128 223 820	5169.7878 200 040	6163.8464 900 661	43
44	4390.9277 783 870	5264.4890 791 941	6307.1411 404 049	7550.7119 503 310	44
45	5313.0226 118 483	6396.3542 312 208	7694.7121 912 939	9249.6221 391 555	45
46	6428.7573 603 364	7771.5703 909 333	9387.5488 733 786	11330.7871 204 654	46
47	7778.7964 060 071	9442.4580 249 840	11452.8096 255 219	13880.2142 225 702	47
48	9412.3436 512 685	11472.5865 003 555	13972.4277 431 367	17003.2624 226 485	48
49	11388.9358 180 349	13939.1925 979 319	17046.3618 466 268	20828.9964 677 444	49
50	13780.6123 398 223	16936.1190 064 873	20796.5614 528 847	25515.5206 729 868	50
51	16674.5409 311 849	20577.3845 928 821	25371.8049 725 193	31256.5128 244 089	51
52	20176.1945 267 338	25001.5222 803 517	30953.6020 664 736	38289.2282 099 009	52
53	24413.1953 773 479	30376.8495 706 274	37763.3945 210 978	46904.3045 571 286	53
54	29539.9664 065 909	36907.8722 283 122	46071.3413 157 393	57457.7730 824 825	54
55	35743.3593 519 750	44843.0647 573 994	56207.0364 052 020	70385.7720 260 411	55
56	43249.4648 158 898	54484.3236 802 402	68572.5844 143 464	86222.5707 319 003	56
57	52331.8524 272 266	66198.4532 714 919	83658.5529 855 026	105622.6491 465 779	57
58	63321.5414 369 442	80431.1207 248 626	102063.4346 423 132	129387.7452 045 579	58
59	76619.0651 387 025	97723.8116 807 081	124517.3902 636 221	158499.9878 755 835	59
60	92709.0688 178 300	118734.4311 920 603	151911.2161 216 189	194162.4851 475 898	60

Table 1. FUTURE WORTH OF ONE DOLLAR WITH INTEREST
PAYABLE AT BEGINNING OF EACH PERIOD

YEARS	23% NOMINAL ANNUAL RATE	24% NOMINAL ANNUAL RATE	25% NOMINAL ANNUAL RATE	26% NOMINAL ANNUAL RATE	YEARS
1	1.2300 000 000	1.2400 000 000	1.2500 000 000	1.2600 000 000	1
2	1.5129 000 000	1.5376 000 000	1.5625 000 000	1.5876 000 000	2
3	1.8608 670 000	1.9066 240 000	1.9531 250 000	2.0003 760 000	3
4	2.2888 664 100	2.3642 137 600	2.4414 062 500	2.5204 737 600	4
5	2.8153 056 843	2.9316 250 624	3.0517 578 125	3.1757 969 376	5
6	3.4628 259 917	3.6352 150 774	3.8146 972 656	4.0015 041 414	6
7	4.2592 759 698	4.5076 666 959	4.7683 715 820	5.0418 952 181	7
8	5.2389 094 428	5.5895 067 030	5.9604 644 775	6.3527 879 748	8
9	6.4438 586 147	6.9309 883 117	7.4505 805 969	8.0045 128 483	9
10	7.9259 460 961	8.5944 255 065	9.3132 257 462	10.0856 861 889	10
11	9.7489 136 981	10.6570 876 280	11.6415 321 827	12.7079 645 980	11
12	11.9911 638 487	13.2147 886 588	14.5519 152 284	16.0120 353 934	12
13	14.7491 315 339	16.3863 379 369	18.1898 940 355	20.1751 645 957	13
14	18.1414 317 867	20.3190 590 417	22.7373 675 443	25.4207 073 906	14
15	22.3139 610 977	25.1956 332 118	28.4217 094 304	32.0300 913 122	15
16	27.4461 721 501	31.2425 851 826	35.5271 367 880	40.3579 150 534	16
17	33.7587 917 447	38.7408 056 264	44.4089 209 850	50.8509 729 673	17
18	41.5233 138 459	48.0385 989 767	55.5111 512 313	64.0722 259 387	18
19	51.0736 760 305	59.5678 627 312	69.3889 390 391	80.7310 046 828	19
20	62.8206 215 175	73.8641 497 866	86.7361 737 988	101.7210 659 004	20
21	77.2693 644 665	91.5915 457 354	108.4202 172 486	128.1685 430 344	21
22	95.0413 182 939	113.5735 167 119	135.5252 715 607	161.4923 642 234	22
23	116.9008 215 014	140.8311 607 228	169.4065 894 509	203.4803 789 215	23
24	143.7880 104 468	174.6306 392 963	211.7582 368 136	256.3852 774 411	24
25	176.8592 528 495	216.5419 927 274	264.6977 960 170	323.0454 495 758	25
26	217.5368 810 049	268.5120 709 819	330.8722 450 212	407.0372 664 654	26
27	267.5703 636 361	332.9549 680 176	413.5903 062 765	512.8669 557 465	27
28	329.1115 472 724	412.8641 603 418	516.9878 828 456	646.2123 642 405	28
29	404.8072 031 450	511.9515 588 239	646.2348 535 571	814.2275 789 431	29
30	497.9128 598 683	634.8199 329 416	807.7935 669 463	1025.9267 494 683	30
31	612.4328 176 381	787.1767 168 476	1009.7419 586 829	1292.6677 043 300	31
32	753.2923 656 948	976.0991 288 910	1262.1774 483 536	1628.7613 074 559	32
33	926.5496 098 046	1210.3629 198 249	1577.7218 104 420	2052.2392 473 944	33
34	1139.6560 200 597	1500.8500 205 828	1972.1522 630 525	2585.8214 517 169	34
35	1401.7769 046 734	1861.0540 255 227	2465.1903 288 157	3258.1350 291 633	35
36	1724.1855 927 483	2307.7069 916 481	3081.4879 110 196	4105.2501 367 458	36
37	2120.7482 790 804	2861.5566 696 437	3851.8598 887 745	5172.6151 722 997	37
38	2608.5203 832 689	3548.3302 703 582	4814.8248 609 681	6517.4951 170 976	38
39	3208.4800 714 208	4399.9295 352 441	6018.5310 762 101	8212.0438 475 429	39
40	3946.4304 878 475	5455.9126 237 027	7523.1638 452 626	10347.1752 479 041	40
41	4854.1095 000 525	6765.3316 533 914	9403.9548 065 783	13037.4408 123 592	41
42	5970.5546 850 645	8389.0112 502 053	11754.9435 082 229	16427.1754 235 726	42
43	7343.7822 626 294	10402.3739 502 546	14693.6793 852 786	20698.2410 337 014	43
44	9032.8521 830 341	12898.9436 983 157	18367.0992 315 982	26079.7837 024 638	44
45	11110.4081 851 320	15994.6901 859 115	22958.8740 394 978	32860.5274 651 044	45
46	13665.8020 677 123	19833.4158 305 302	28698.5925 493 723	41404.2646 060 315	46
47	16808.9365 432 861	24593.4356 298 575	35873.2406 867 153	52169.3734 035 997	47
48	20674.9919 482 419	30495.8601 810 233	44841.5508 583 941	65733.4104 885 357	48
49	25430.2400 963 376	37814.8666 244 689	56051.9385 729 927	82824.0972 155 549	49
50	31279.1953 184 952	46890.4346 143 414	70064.9232 162 408	104358.3624 915 992	50
51	38473.4102 417 491	58144.1389 217 833	87581.1540 203 011	131491.5367 394 150	51
52	47322.2945 973 515	72098.7322 630 113	109476.4425 253 763	165679.3362 916 629	52
53	58206.4223 547 423	89402.4280 061 340	136845.5531 567 204	208755.9637 274 953	53
54	71593.8994 963 330	110859.0107 276 062	171056.9414 459 005	263032.5142 966 441	54
55	88060.4963 804 896	137465.1733 022 317	213821.1768 073 756	331420.9680 137 715	55
56	108314.4105 480 022	170456.8148 947 673	267276.4710 092 195	417590.4196 973 521	56
57	133226.7249 740 427	211366.4504 695 114	334095.5887 615 244	526163.9288 186 637	57
58	163868.8717 180 725	262094.3985 821 941	417619.4859 519 055	662966.5503 115 162	58
59	201558.7122 132 292	324997.0542 419 207	522024.3574 398 819	835337.8533 925 104	59
60	247917.2160 222 720	402996.3472 599 817	652530.4467 998 524	1052525.6952 745 631	60

Table 1.   FUTURE WORTH OF ONE DOLLAR WITH INTEREST
PAYABLE AT BEGINNING OF EACH PERIOD

YEARS	27% NOMINAL ANNUAL RATE	28% NOMINAL ANNUAL RATE	29% NOMINAL ANNUAL RATE	30% NOMINAL ANNUAL RATE	YEARS
1	1.2700 000 000	1.2800 000 000	1.2900 000 000	1.3000 000 000	1
2	1.6129 000 000	1.6384 000 000	1.6641 000 000	1.6900 000 000	2
3	2.0483 830 000	2.0971 520 000	2.1466 890 000	2.1970 000 000	3
4	2.6014 464 100	2.6843 545 600	2.7692 288 100	2.8561 000 000	4
5	3.3038 369 407	3.4359 738 368	3.5723 051 649	3.7129 300 000	5
6	4.1958 729 147	4.3980 465 111	4.6082 736 627	4.8268 090 000	6
7	5.3287 586 017	5.6294 995 342	5.9446 730 249	6.2748 517 000	7
8	6.7675 234 241	7.2057 594 038	7.6686 282 021	8.1573 072 100	8
9	8.5947 547 486	9.2233 720 369	9.8925 303 808	10.6044 993 730	9
10	10.9153 385 307	11.8059 162 072	12.7613 641 912	13.7858 491 849	10
11	13.8624 799 340	15.1115 727 452	16.4621 598 066	17.9216 039 404	11
12	17.6053 495 162	19.3428 131 138	21.2361 861 505	23.2980 851 225	12
13	22.3587 938 856	24.7588 007 857	27.3946 801 342	30.2875 106 592	13
14	28.3956 682 347	31.6912 650 057	35.3391 373 731	39.3737 638 570	14
15	36.0624 986 581	40.5648 192 073	45.5874 872 113	51.1858 930 141	15
16	45.7993 732 958	51.9229 685 853	58.8078 585 026	66.5416 609 183	16
17	58.1652 040 856	66.4613 997 892	75.8621 374 683	86.5041 591 938	17
18	73.8698 091 887	85.0705 917 302	97.8621 573 341	112.4554 069 520	18
19	93.8146 576 697	108.8903 574 147	126.2421 829 610	146.1920 290 375	19
20	119.1446 152 405	139.3796 574 908	162.8524 160 197	190.0496 377 488	20
21	151.3136 613 555	178.4059 615 882	210.0796 166 654	247.0645 290 735	21
22	192.1683 499 214	228.3596 308 330	271.0027 054 984	321.1838 877 955	22
23	244.0538 044 002	292.3003 274 662	349.5934 900 929	417.5390 541 341	23
24	309.9483 315 883	374.1444 191 567	450.9756 022 199	542.8007 703 744	24
25	393.6343 811 171	478.9048 565 206	581.7585 268 636	705.6410 014 867	25
26	499.9156 640 188	612.9982 163 464	750.4684 996 541	917.3333 019 327	26
27	634.8928 933 038	784.6377 169 233	968.1043 645 538	1192.5332 925 125	27
28	806.3139 744 959	1004.3362 776 619	1248.8546 302 744	1550.2932 802 662	28
29	1024.0187 476 097	1285.5504 354 072	1611.0224 730 540	2015.3812 643 461	29
30	1300.5038 094 644	1645.5045 573 212	2078.2189 902 396	2619.9956 436 499	30
31	1651.6398 380 198	2106.2458 333 711	2680.9024 974 091	3405.9943 367 449	31
32	2097.5825 942 851	2695.9946 667 151	3458.3642 216 577	4427.7926 377 684	32
33	2663.9298 947 421	3450.8731 733 953	4461.2898 459 385	5756.1304 290 989	33
34	3383.1909 663 224	4417.1176 619 460	5755.0639 012 606	7482.9695 578 286	34
35	4296.6525 272 295	5653.9106 072 908	7424.0324 326 262	9727.8604 251 772	35
36	5456.7487 095 814	7237.0055 773 323	9577.0018 380 878	12646.2185 527 303	36
37	6930.0708 611 684	9263.3671 389 853	12354.3323 711 333	16440.0841 185 494	37
38	8801.1899 936 839	11857.1099 379 012	15937.0887 587 619	21372.1093 541 143	38
39	11177.5112 919 785	15177.1007 205 135	20558.8444 988 029	27783.7421 603 486	39
40	14195.4393 408 127	19426.6889 222 573	26520.9094 034 557	36118.8648 084 531	40
41	18028.2079 628 321	24866.1618 204 893	34211.9731 304 579	46954.5242 509 891	41
42	22895.8241 127 968	31828.6871 302 263	44133.4453 382 907	61040.8815 262 858	42
43	29077.6966 232 520	40740.7195 266 897	56932.1444 863 949	79353.1459 841 716	43
44	36928.6747 115 300	52148.1209 941 628	73442.4663 874 495	103159.0897 794 230	44
45	46899.4168 836 431	66749.5948 725 284	94740.7816 398 098	134106.8167 132 499	45
46	59562.2594 422 267	85439.4814 368 364	122215.6083 153 547	174338.8617 272 249	46
47	75644.0694 916 279	109362.5362 391 506	157658.1347 268 075	226640.5202 453 924	47
48	96067.9682 543 675	139984.0463 861 128	203378.9937 975 817	294632.6763 190 101	48
49	122006.3196 830 467	179179.5793 742 243	262358.9019 988 804	383022.4792 147 131	49
50	154948.0259 974 693	229349.8615 990 071	338442.9835 785 558	497929.2229 791 270	50
51	196783.9930 167 860	293567.8228 467 291	436591.4488 163 369	647307.9898 728 651	51
52	249915.6711 313 182	375766.8132 438 133	563202.9689 730 746	841500.3868 347 246	52
53	317392.9023 367 741	480981.5209 520 810	726531.8299 752 663	1093950.5028 851 420	53
54	403088.9859 677 032	615656.3468 186 637	937226.0606 680 935	1422135.6537 506 846	54
55	511923.0121 789 830	788040.1239 278 895	1209021.6182 618 406	1848776.3498 758 900	55
56	650142.2254 673 084	1008691.3586 276 986	1559631.8875 577 744	2403409.2548 386 570	56
57	825680.6263 434 817	1291124.9390 434 542	2011932.8749 495 289	3124432.0312 902 541	57
58	1048614.3954 562 218	1652639.9215 756 213	2595393.4086 848 923	4061761.6406 773 304	58
59	1331740.2822 294 016	2115379.1001 287 953	3348057.4972 035 110	5280290.1328 805 295	59
60	1691310.1584 313 401	2707685.2481 648 580	4318994.1713 925 293	6864377.1727 446 883	60

Table 2.   FUTURE WORTH OF ONE DOLLAR PER PERIOD WITH INTEREST
PAYABLE AT END OF EACH PERIOD

	5% NOMINAL ANNUAL RATE	5½% NOMINAL ANNUAL RATE	6% NOMINAL ANNUAL RATE	6½% NOMINAL ANNUAL RATE	
YEARS					YEARS
1	1.0000 000 000	1.0000 000 000	1.0000 000 000	1.0000 000 000	1
2	2.0500 000 000	2.0550 000 000	2.0600 000 000	2.0650 000 000	2
3	3.1525 000 000	3.1680 250 000	3.1836 000 000	3.1992 250 000	3
4	4.3101 250 000	4.3422 663 750	4.3746 160 000	4.4071 746 250	4
5	5.5256 312 500	5.5810 910 256	5.6370 929 600	5.6936 409 756	5
6	6.8019 128 125	6.8880 510 320	6.9753 185 376	7.0637 276 390	6
7	8.1420 084 531	8.2668 938 388	8.3938 376 499	8.5228 699 356	7
8	9.5491 088 758	9.7215 729 999	9.8974 679 088	10.0768 564 814	8
9	11.0265 643 196	11.2562 595 149	11.4913 159 834	11.7318 521 527	9
10	12.5778 925 355	12.8753 537 882	13.1807 949 424	13.4944 225 426	10
11	14.2067 871 623	14.5834 982 466	14.9716 426 389	15.3715 600 079	11
12	15.9171 265 204	16.3855 906 502	16.8699 411 973	17.3707 114 084	12
13	17.7129 828 465	18.2867 981 359	18.8821 376 691	19.4998 076 499	13
14	19.5986 319 888	20.2925 720 334	21.0150 659 292	21.7672 951 472	14
15	21.5785 635 882	22.4086 634 952	23.2759 698 850	24.1821 693 317	15
16	23.6574 917 676	24.6411 399 875	25.6725 280 781	26.7540 103 383	16
17	25.8403 663 560	26.9964 026 868	28.2128 797 628	29.4930 210 103	17
18	28.1323 846 738	29.4812 048 346	30.9056 525 485	32.4100 673 760	18
19	30.5390 039 075	32.1026 711 005	33.7599 917 015	35.5167 217 554	19
20	33.0659 541 029	34.8683 180 103	36.7855 912 035	38.8253 086 695	20
21	35.7192 518 080	37.7860 755 016	39.9927 266 758	42.3489 537 330	21
22	38.5052 143 984	40.8643 096 542	43.3922 902 763	46.1016 357 257	22
23	41.4304 751 184	44.1118 466 852	46.9958 276 929	50.0982 420 478	23
24	44.5019 988 743	47.5379 982 528	50.8155 773 545	54.3546 277 809	24
25	47.7270 988 180	51.1525 881 567	54.8645 119 957	58.8876 785 867	25
26	51.1134 537 589	54.9659 805 054	59.1563 827 155	63.7153 776 948	26
27	54.6691 264 468	58.9891 094 332	63.7057 656 784	68.8568 772 450	27
28	58.4025 827 692	63.2335 104 520	68.5281 116 191	74.3325 742 659	28
29	62.3227 119 076	67.7113 535 268	73.6397 983 162	80.1641 915 932	29
30	66.4388 475 030	72.4354 779 708	79.0581 862 152	86.3748 640 468	30
31	70.7607 898 782	77.4194 292 592	84.8016 773 881	92.9892 302 098	31
32	75.2988 293 721	82.6774 978 685	90.8897 780 314	100.0335 301 735	32
33	80.0637 708 407	88.2247 602 512	97.3431 647 133	107.5357 096 347	33
34	85.0669 593 827	94.0771 220 651	104.1837 545 961	115.5255 307 610	34
35	90.3203 073 518	100.2513 637 786	111.4347 798 719	124.0346 902 605	35
36	95.8363 227 194	106.7651 887 865	119.1208 666 642	133.0969 451 274	36
37	101.6281 388 554	113.6372 741 697	127.2681 186 640	142.7482 465 607	37
38	107.7095 457 982	120.8873 242 490	135.9042 057 839	153.0268 825 871	38
39	114.0950 230 881	128.5361 270 827	145.0584 581 309	163.9736 299 553	39
40	120.7997 742 425	136.6056 140 723	154.7619 656 188	175.6319 159 024	40
41	127.8397 629 546	145.1189 228 463	165.0476 835 559	188.0479 904 360	41
42	135.2317 511 023	154.1004 636 028	175.9505 445 692	201.2711 098 144	42
43	142.9933 386 575	163.5759 891 010	187.5075 772 434	215.3537 319 523	43
44	151.1430 055 903	173.5726 685 015	199.7580 318 780	230.3517 245 292	44
45	159.7001 558 699	184.1191 652 691	212.7435 137 907	246.3245 866 236	45
46	168.6851 636 633	195.2457 193 589	226.5081 246 181	263.3356 847 541	46
47	178.1194 218 465	206.9842 339 237	241.0986 120 952	281.4525 042 631	47
48	188.0253 929 388	219.3683 667 895	256.5645 288 209	300.7469 170 403	48
49	198.4266 625 858	232.4336 269 629	272.9584 005 502	321.2954 666 479	49
50	209.3479 957 151	246.2174 764 458	290.3359 045 832	343.1796 719 800	50
51	220.8153 955 008	260.7594 376 503	308.7560 588 582	366.4863 506 587	51
52	232.8561 652 759	276.1012 067 211	328.2814 223 897	391.3079 634 515	52
53	245.4989 735 397	292.2867 730 908	348.9783 077 331	417.7429 810 758	53
54	258.7739 222 166	309.3625 456 108	370.9170 061 970	445.8962 748 458	54
55	272.7126 183 275	327.3774 856 194	394.1720 265 689	475.8795 327 107	55
56	287.3482 492 439	346.3832 473 284	418.8223 481 630	507.8117 023 369	56
57	302.7156 617 060	366.4343 259 315	444.9516 890 528	541.8194 629 888	57
58	318.8514 447 913	387.5882 138 577	472.6487 903 959	578.0377 280 831	58
59	335.7940 170 309	409.9055 656 199	502.0077 178 197	616.6101 804 085	59
60	353.5837 178 825	433.4503 717 290	533.1281 808 889	657.6898 421 351	60

Table 2. FUTURE WORTH OF ONE DOLLAR PER PERIOD WITH INTEREST
PAYABLE AT END OF EACH PERIOD

YEARS	**7%** NOMINAL ANNUAL RATE	**7½%** NOMINAL ANNUAL RATE	**8%** NOMINAL ANNUAL RATE	**8½%** NOMINAL ANNUAL RATE	YEARS
1	1.0000 000 000	1.0000 000 000	1.0000 000 000	1.0000 000 000	1
2	2.0700 000 000	2.0750 000 000	2.0800 000 000	2.0850 000 000	2
3	3.2149 000 000	3.2306 250 000	3.2464 000 000	3.2622 250 000	3
4	4.4399 430 000	4.4729 218 750	4.5061 120 000	4.5395 141 250	4
5	5.7507 390 100	5.8083 910 156	5.8666 009 600	5.9253 728 256	5
6	7.1532 907 407	7.2440 203 418	7.3359 290 368	7.4290 295 158	6
7	8.6540 210 925	8.7873 218 674	8.9228 033 597	9.0604 970 246	7
8	10.2598 025 690	10.4463 710 075	10.6366 276 285	10.8306 392 717	8
9	11.9779 887 489	12.2298 488 331	12.4875 578 388	12.7512 436 098	9
10	13.8164 479 613	14.1470 874 955	14.4865 624 659	14.8350 993 167	10
11	15.7835 993 186	16.2081 190 577	16.6454 874 632	17.0960 827 586	11
12	17.8884 512 709	18.4237 279 870	18.9771 264 602	19.5492 497 931	12
13	20.1406 428 598	20.8055 075 860	21.4952 965 771	22.2109 360 255	13
14	22.5504 878 600	23.3659 206 550	24.2149 203 032	25.0988 655 877	14
15	25.1290 220 102	26.1183 647 041	27.1521 139 275	28.2322 691 626	15
16	27.8880 535 509	29.0772 420 569	30.3242 830 417	31.6320 120 414	16
17	30.8402 172 995	32.2580 352 112	33.7502 256 850	35.3207 330 649	17
18	33.9990 325 105	35.6773 878 520	37.4502 437 398	39.3229 953 755	18
19	37.3789 647 862	39.3531 919 410	41.4462 632 390	43.6654 499 824	19
20	40.9954 923 212	43.3046 813 365	45.7619 642 981	48.3770 132 309	20
21	44.8651 767 837	47.5525 324 368	50.4229 214 420	53.4890 593 555	21
22	49.0057 391 586	52.1189 723 695	55.4567 551 573	59.0356 294 007	22
23	53.4361 408 997	57.0278 952 972	60.8932 955 699	65.0536 578 998	23
24	58.1766 707 627	62.3049 874 445	66.7647 592 155	71.5832 188 213	24
25	63.2490 377 160	67.9778 615 029	73.1059 399 527	78.6677 924 211	25
26	68.6764 703 562	74.0762 011 156	79.9544 151 490	86.3545 547 769	26
27	74.4838 232 811	80.6319 161 992	87.3507 683 609	94.6946 919 329	27
28	80.6976 909 108	87.6793 099 142	95.3388 298 297	103.7437 407 472	28
29	87.3465 292 745	95.2552 581 578	103.9659 362 161	113.5619 587 107	29
30	94.4607 863 237	103.3994 025 196	113.2832 111 134	124.2147 252 011	30
31	102.0730 413 664	112.1543 577 086	123.3458 680 025	135.7729 768 432	31
32	110.2181 542 621	121.5659 345 367	134.2135 374 427	148.3136 798 749	32
33	118.9334 250 604	131.6833 796 269	145.9506 204 381	161.9203 426 642	33
34	128.2587 648 146	142.5596 330 990	158.6266 700 732	176.6835 717 907	34
35	138.2368 783 516	154.2516 055 814	172.3168 036 790	192.7016 753 929	35
36	148.9134 598 363	166.8204 760 000	187.1021 479 733	210.0813 178 013	36
37	160.3374 020 248	180.3320 117 000	203.0703 198 112	228.9382 298 144	37
38	172.5610 201 665	194.8569 125 775	220.3159 453 961	249.3979 793 487	38
39	185.6402 915 782	210.4711 810 208	238.9412 210 278	271.5968 075 933	39
40	199.6351 119 887	227.2565 195 974	259.0565 187 100	295.6825 362 387	40
41	214.6095 698 279	245.3007 585 672	280.7810 402 068	321.8155 518 190	41
42	230.6322 397 158	264.6983 154 597	304.2435 234 233	350.1698 737 236	42
43	247.7764 964 959	285.5506 891 192	329.5830 052 972	380.9343 129 901	43
44	266.1208 512 507	307.9669 908 031	356.9496 457 210	414.3137 295 943	44
45	285.7493 108 382	332.0645 151 134	386.5056 173 787	450.5303 966 098	45
46	306.7517 625 969	357.9693 537 469	418.4260 867 690	489.8254 803 217	46
47	329.2243 059 787	385.8170 552 779	452.9001 521 105	532.4606 461 490	47
48	353.2700 929 972	415.7533 344 237	490.1321 642 793	578.7198 010 717	48
49	378.9989 995 070	447.9348 345 055	530.3427 374 217	628.9109 841 627	49
50	406.5289 294 724	482.5299 470 934	573.7701 564 154	683.3684 178 166	50
51	435.9859 545 355	519.7196 931 254	620.6717 689 286	742.4547 333 310	51
52	467.5049 713 530	559.6986 701 098	671.3255 104 429	806.5633 856 641	52
53	501.2303 193 477	602.6760 703 681	726.0315 512 783	876.1212 734 656	53
54	537.3164 417 021	648.8767 756 457	785.1140 753 806	951.5915 816 884	54
55	575.9285 926 212	698.5425 338 191	848.9232 014 111	1033.4768 661 320	55
56	617.2435 941 047	751.9332 238 555	917.8370 575 239	1122.3223 997 532	56
57	661.4506 456 920	809.3282 156 447	992.2640 221 259	1218.7198 037 322	57
58	708.7521 908 905	871.0278 318 180	1072.6451 438 959	1323.3109 870 494	58
59	759.3648 442 528	937.3549 192 044	1159.4567 554 076	1436.7924 209 486	59
60	813.5203 833 505	1008.6565 381 447	1253.2132 958 402	1559.9197 767 293	60

Table 2. **FUTURE WORTH OF ONE DOLLAR PER PERIOD WITH INTEREST PAYABLE AT END OF EACH PERIOD**

YEARS	9% NOMINAL ANNUAL RATE	9½% NOMINAL ANNUAL RATE	10% NOMINAL ANNUAL RATE	10½% NOMINAL ANNUAL RATE	YEARS
1	1.0000 000 000	1.0000 000 000	1.0000 000 000	1.0000 000 000	1
2	2.0900 000 000	2.0950 000 000	2.1000 000 000	2.1050 000 000	2
3	3.2781 000 000	3.2940 250 000	3.3100 000 000	3.3260 250 000	3
4	4.5731 290 000	4.6069 573 750	4.6410 000 000	4.6752 576 250	4
5	5.9847 106 100	6.0446 183 256	6.1051 000 000	6.1661 596 756	5
6	7.5233 345 649	7.6188 570 666	7.7156 100 000	7.8136 064 416	6
7	9.2004 346 757	9.3426 484 879	9.4871 710 000	9.6340 351 179	7
8	11.0284 737 966	11.2302 000 942	11.4358 881 000	11.6456 088 053	8
9	13.0210 364 382	13.2970 691 032	13.5794 769 100	13.8683 977 299	9
10	15.1929 297 177	15.5602 906 680	15.9374 246 010	16.3245 794 915	10
11	17.5602 933 923	18.0385 182 814	18.5311 670 611	19.0386 603 381	11
12	20.1407 197 976	20.7521 775 182	21.3842 837 672	22.0377 196 736	12
13	22.9533 845 794	23.7236 343 824	24.5227 121 439	25.3516 802 393	13
14	26.0191 891 915	26.9773 796 487	27.9749 833 583	29.0136 066 645	14
15	29.3609 162 188	30.5402 307 154	31.7724 816 942	33.0600 353 642	15
16	33.0033 986 784	34.4415 526 333	35.9497 298 636	37.5313 390 775	16
17	36.9737 045 595	38.7135 001 335	40.5447 028 499	42.4721 296 806	17
18	41.3013 379 699	43.3912 826 462	45.5991 731 349	47.9317 032 971	18
19	46.0184 583 871	48.5134 544 976	51.1590 904 484	53.9645 321 433	19
20	51.1601 196 420	54.1222 326 748	57.2749 994 933	60.6308 080 183	20
21	56.7645 304 098	60.2638 447 789	64.0024 994 426	67.9970 428 603	21
22	62.8733 381 466	66.9889 100 329	71.4027 493 868	76.1367 323 606	22
23	69.5319 385 798	74.3528 564 861	79.5430 243 255	85.1310 892 585	23
24	76.7898 130 520	82.4163 778 522	88.4973 267 581	95.0698 536 306	24
25	84.7008 962 267	91.2459 337 482	98.3470 594 339	106.0521 882 618	25
26	93.3239 768 871	100.9142 974 543	109.1817 653 773	118.1876 680 293	26
27	102.7231 348 069	111.5011 557 124	121.0999 419 150	131.5973 731 724	27
28	112.9682 169 396	123.0937 655 051	134.2099 361 065	146.4150 973 555	28
29	124.1353 564 641	135.7876 732 281	148.6309 297 171	162.7886 825 778	29
30	136.3075 385 459	149.6875 021 848	164.4940 226 889	180.8814 942 485	30
31	149.5752 170 150	164.9078 148 923	181.9434 249 578	200.8740 511 446	31
32	164.0369 865 464	181.5740 573 071	201.1377 674 535	222.9658 265 147	32
33	179.8003 153 356	199.8235 927 513	222.2515 441 989	247.3772 382 988	33
34	196.9823 437 158	219.8068 340 627	245.4766 986 188	274.3518 483 201	34
35	215.7107 546 502	241.6884 832 986	271.0243 684 806	304.1587 923 938	35
36	236.1247 225 687	265.6488 892 120	299.1268 053 287	337.0954 655 951	36
37	258.3759 475 999	291.8855 336 871	330.0394 858 616	373.4904 894 826	37
38	282.6297 828 839	320.6146 593 874	364.0434 344 477	413.7069 908 783	38
39	309.0664 633 434	352.0730 520 292	401.4477 778 925	458.1462 249 205	39
40	337.8824 450 443	386.5199 919 720	442.5925 556 818	507.2515 785 371	40
41	369.2918 650 983	424.2393 912 093	487.8518 112 499	561.5129 942 835	41
42	403.5281 329 572	465.5421 333 742	537.6369 923 749	621.4718 586 833	42
43	440.8456 649 233	510.7686 360 447	592.4006 916 124	687.7264 038 450	43
44	481.5217 747 664	560.2916 564 690	652.6407 607 737	760.9376 762 488	44
45	525.8587 344 954	614.5193 638 335	718.9048 368 510	841.8361 322 549	45
46	574.1860 206 000	673.8987 033 977	791.7953 205 361	931.2289 261 417	46
47	626.8627 624 540	738.9190 802 205	871.9748 525 897	1030.0079 633 865	47
48	684.2804 110 748	810.1163 928 415	960.1723 378 487	1139.1587 995 421	48
49	746.8656 480 716	888.0774 501 614	1057.1895 716 336	1259.7704 734 941	49
50	815.0835 563 980	973.4448 079 267	1163.9085 287 970	1393.0463 732 109	50
51	889.4410 764 738	1066.9220 646 798	1281.2993 816 766	1540.3162 423 981	51
52	970.4907 733 565	1169.2796 608 244	1410.4293 198 443	1703.0494 478 499	52
53	1058.8349 429 585	1281.3612 286 027	1552.4722 518 287	1882.8696 398 741	53
54	1155.1300 878 248	1404.0905 453 199	1708.7194 770 116	2081.5709 520 609	54
55	1260.0917 957 290	1538.4791 471 253	1880.5914 247 128	2301.1359 020 273	55
56	1374.5000 573 447	1685.6346 661 022	2069.6505 671 841	2543.7551 717 401	56
57	1499.2050 625 057	1846.7699 593 819	2277.6156 239 025	2811.8494 647 729	57
58	1635.1335 181 312	2023.2131 055 232	2506.3771 862 927	3108.0936 585 740	58
59	1783.2955 347 630	2216.4183 505 479	2758.0149 049 220	3435.4434 927 243	59
60	1944.7921 328 917	2427.9780 938 500	3034.8163 954 142	3797.1650 594 603	60

Table 2.   FUTURE WORTH OF ONE DOLLAR PER PERIOD WITH INTEREST
PAYABLE AT END OF EACH PERIOD

YEARS	11% NOMINAL ANNUAL RATE	11½% NOMINAL ANNUAL RATE	12% NOMINAL ANNUAL RATE	12½% NOMINAL ANNUAL RATE	YEARS
1	1.0000 000 000	1.0000 000 000	1.0000 000 000	1.0000 000 000	1
2	2.1100 000 000	2.1150 000 000	2.1200 000 000	2.1250 000 000	2
3	3.3421 000 000	3.3582 250 000	3.3744 000 000	3.3906 250 000	3
4	4.7097 310 000	4.7444 208 750	4.7793 280 000	4.8144 531 250	4
5	6.2278 014 100	6.2900 292 756	6.3528 473 600	6.4162 597 656	5
6	7.9128 595 651	8.0133 826 423	8.1151 890 432	8.2182 922 363	6
7	9.7832 741 173	9.9349 216 462	10.0890 117 284	10.2455 787 659	7
8	11.8594 342 702	12.0774 376 355	12.2996 931 358	12.5262 761 116	8
9	14.1639 720 399	14.4663 429 636	14.7756 563 121	15.0920 606 256	9
10	16.7220 089 643	17.1299 724 044	17.5487 350 695	17.9785 682 037	10
11	19.5614 299 503	20.0999 192 309	20.6545 832 779	21.2258 892 292	11
12	22.7131 872 449	23.4114 099 425	24.1331 332 712	24.8791 253 829	12
13	26.2116 378 418	27.1037 220 858	28.0291 092 638	28.9890 160 557	13
14	30.0949 180 044	31.2206 501 257	32.3926 023 754	33.6126 430 627	14
15	34.4053 589 849	35.8110 248 902	37.2797 146 605	38.8142 234 455	15
16	39.1899 484 732	40.9292 927 525	42.7532 804 197	44.6660 013 762	16
17	44.5008 428 053	46.6361 614 191	48.8836 740 701	51.2492 515 482	17
18	50.3959 355 139	52.9993 199 823	55.7497 149 585	58.6554 079 918	18
19	56.9394 884 204	60.0942 417 802	63.4396 807 535	66.9873 339 907	19
20	64.2028 321 466	68.0050 795 850	72.0524 424 440	76.3607 507 396	20
21	72.2651 436 828	76.8256 637 372	81.6987 355 372	86.9058 445 820	21
22	81.2143 094 879	86.6606 150 670	92.5025 838 017	98.7690 751 548	22
23	91.1478 835 315	97.6265 857 997	104.6028 938 579	112.1152 095 491	23
24	102.1741 507 200	109.8536 431 667	118.1552 411 209	127.1296 107 428	24
25	114.4133 072 992	123.4868 121 308	133.3338 700 554	144.0208 120 856	25
26	127.9987 711 021	138.6877 955 259	150.3339 344 620	163.0234 135 963	26
27	143.0786 359 233	155.6368 920 114	169.3740 065 974	184.4013 402 959	27
28	159.8172 858 749	174.5351 345 927	190.6988 873 891	208.4515 078 329	28
29	178.3971 873 211	195.6066 750 708	214.5827 538 758	235.5079 463 120	29
30	199.0208 779 265	219.1014 427 040	241.3326 843 409	265.9464 396 010	30
31	221.9131 744 984	245.2981 086 149	271.2926 064 618	300.1897 445 511	31
32	247.3236 236 932	274.5073 911 057	304.8477 192 373	338.7134 626 200	32
33	275.5292 222 995	307.0757 410 828	342.4294 455 457	382.0526 454 475	33
34	306.8374 367 524	343.3894 513 073	384.5209 790 112	430.8092 261 284	34
35	341.5895 547 952	383.8792 382 077	431.6634 964 926	485.6603 793 945	35
36	380.1644 058 226	429.0253 506 016	484.4631 160 717	547.3679 268 188	36
37	422.9824 904 631	479.3632 659 207	543.5986 900 003	616.7889 176 711	37
38	470.5105 644 141	535.4900 415 016	609.8305 328 003	694.8875 323 800	38
39	523.2667 264 996	598.0713 962 743	684.0101 967 363	782.7484 739 275	39
40	581.8260 664 146	667.8496 068 459	767.0914 203 447	881.5920 331 685	40
41	646.8269 337 202	745.6523 116 331	860.1423 907 861	992.7910 373 145	41
42	718.9778 964 294	832.4023 274 709	964.3594 776 804	1117.8899 169 789	42
43	799.0654 650 366	929.1285 951 301	1081.0826 150 020	1258.6261 566 012	43
44	887.9626 661 906	1036.9783 835 701	1211.8125 288 023	1416.9544 261 764	44
45	986.6385 594 716	1157.2308 976 806	1358.2300 322 586	1595.0737 294 484	45
46	1096.1688 010 135	1291.3124 509 139	1522.2176 361 296	1795.4579 456 295	46
47	1217.7473 691 250	1440.8133 827 690	1705.8837 524 651	2020.8901 888 331	47
48	1352.6995 797 287	1607.5069 217 874	1911.5898 027 609	2274.5014 624 373	48
49	1502.4965 334 989	1793.3702 177 930	2141.9805 790 923	2559.8141 452 420	49
50	1668.7711 521 837	2000.6077 928 392	2400.0182 485 833	2880.7909 133 972	50
51	1853.3359 789 239	2231.6776 890 157	2689.0204 384 133	3241.8897 775 718	51
52	2058.2029 366 056	2489.3206 232 525	3012.7028 910 229	3648.1259 997 683	52
53	2285.6052 596 322	2776.5924 949 265	3375.2272 379 457	4105.1417 497 394	53
54	2538.0218 381 917	3096.9006 318 430	3781.2545 064 992	4619.2844 684 568	54
55	2818.2042 403 928	3454.0442 045 050	4236.0050 472 791	5197.6950 270 139	55
56	3129.2067 068 360	3852.2592 880 231	4745.3256 529 525	5848.4069 053 906	56
57	3474.4194 445 880	4296.2691 061 457	5315.7647 313 069	6580.4577 685 644	57
58	3857.6055 834 927	4791.3400 533 525	5954.6564 990 637	7404.0149 896 350	58
59	4282.9421 976 769	5343.3441 594 880	6670.2152 789 513	8330.5168 633 394	59
60	4755.0658 394 213	5958.8287 378 291	7471.6411 124 255	9372.8314 712 568	60

Table 2.   FUTURE WORTH OF ONE DOLLAR PER PERIOD WITH INTEREST
PAYABLE AT END OF EACH PERIOD

YEARS	13% NOMINAL ANNUAL RATE	13½% NOMINAL ANNUAL RATE	14% NOMINAL ANNUAL RATE	14½% NOMINAL ANNUAL RATE	YEARS
1	1.0000 000 000	1.0000 000 000	1.0000 000 000	1.0000 000 000	1
2	2.1300 000 000	2.1350 000 000	2.1400 000 000	2.1450 000 000	2
3	3.4069 000 000	3.4232 250 000	3.4396 000 000	3.4560 250 000	3
4	4.8497 970 000	4.8853 603 750	4.9211 440 000	4.9571 486 250	4
5	6.4802 706 100	6.5448 840 256	6.6101 041 600	6.6759 351 756	5
6	8.3227 057 893	8.4284 433 691	8.5355 187 424	8.6439 457 761	6
7	10.4046 575 419	10.5662 832 239	10.7304 913 663	10.8973 179 136	7
8	12.7572 630 224	12.9927 314 591	13.2327 601 576	13.4774 290 111	8
9	15.4157 072 153	15.7467 502 061	16.0853 465 797	16.4316 562 177	9
10	18.4197 491 532	18.8725 614 839	19.3372 951 008	19.8142 463 693	10
11	21.8143 165 432	22.4203 572 843	23.0445 164 150	23.6873 120 928	11
12	25.6501 776 938	26.4471 055 177	27.2707 487 131	28.1219 723 463	12
13	29.9847 007 940	31.0174 647 625	32.0886 535 329	33.1996 583 365	13
14	34.8827 118 972	36.2048 225 055	37.5810 650 275	39.0136 087 953	14
15	40.4174 644 438	42.0924 735 437	43.8424 141 313	45.6705 820 706	15
16	46.6717 348 215	48.7749 574 721	50.9803 521 097	53.2928 164 708	16
17	53.7390 603 483	56.3595 767 309	59.1176 014 051	62.0202 748 591	17
18	61.7251 381 936	64.9681 195 895	68.3940 656 018	72.0132 147 137	18
19	70.7494 061 588	74.7388 157 341	78.9692 347 861	83.4551 308 472	19
20	80.9468 289 594	85.8285 558 582	91.0249 276 561	96.5561 248 200	20
21	92.4699 167 241	98.4154 108 991	104.7684 175 280	111.5567 629 189	21
22	105.4910 058 983	112.7014 913 705	120.4359 959 819	128.7324 935 421	22
23	120.2048 366 650	128.9161 927 055	138.2970 354 193	148.3987 051 057	23
24	136.8314 654 315	147.3198 787 207	158.6586 203 780	170.9165 173 461	24
25	155.6195 559 376	168.2080 623 480	181.8708 272 310	196.6994 123 613	25
26	176.8500 982 095	191.9161 507 650	208.3327 430 433	226.2208 271 536	26
27	200.8406 109 767	218.8248 311 183	238.4993 270 694	260.0228 470 909	27
28	227.9498 904 037	249.3661 833 192	272.8892 328 591	298.7261 599 191	28
29	258.5833 761 562	284.0306 180 673	312.0937 254 594	343.0414 531 074	29
30	293.1992 150 565	323.3747 515 064	356.7868 470 237	393.7824 638 079	30
31	332.3151 130 138	368.0303 429 598	407.7370 056 070	451.8809 210 601	31
32	376.5160 777 056	418.7144 392 594	465.8201 863 920	518.4036 546 138	32
33	426.4631 678 073	476.2408 885 594	532.0350 124 868	594.5721 845 328	33
34	482.9033 796 223	541.5334 085 149	607.5199 142 350	681.7851 512 901	34
35	546.6808 189 732	615.6404 186 644	693.5727 022 279	781.6439 982 271	35
36	618.7493 254 397	699.7518 751 841	791.6728 805 398	895.9823 779 701	36
37	700.1867 377 469	795.2183 783 340	903.5070 838 154	1026.8998 227 757	37
38	792.2110 136 540	903.5728 594 091	1030.9980 755 495	1176.8002 970 782	38
39	896.1984 454 290	1026.5551 954 293	1176.3378 061 264	1348.4363 401 546	39
40	1013.7042 433 348	1166.1401 448 123	1342.0250 989 841	1544.9596 094 770	40
41	1146.4857 949 683	1324.5690 666 319	1530.9086 128 419	1769.9787 528 511	41
42	1296.5289 483 141	1504.3858 906 272	1746.2358 186 398	2027.6256 720 145	42
43	1466.0777 115 950	1708.4779 858 619	1991.7088 332 494	2322.6313 944 567	43
44	1657.6678 141 023	1940.1225 139 532	2271.5480 699 043	2660.4129 466 529	44
45	1874.1646 299 356	2203.0390 533 369	2590.5647 996 909	3047.1728 239 175	45
46	2118.8060 318 273	2501.4493 255 374	2954.2438 716 476	3490.0128 833 856	46
47	2395.2508 159 648	2840.1449 844 850	3368.8380 136 783	3997.0647 514 765	47
48	2707.6334 220 402	3224.5645 573 904	3841.4753 355 932	4577.6391 404 406	48
49	3060.6257 669 055	3660.8807 726 382	4380.2818 825 763	5242.3968 158 045	49
50	3459.5071 166 032	4156.0996 769 443	4994.5213 461 370	6003.5443 540 961	50
51	3910.2430 417 616	4718.1731 333 318	5694.7543 345 961	6875.0582 854 401	51
52	4419.5746 371 906	5356.1265 063 316	6493.0199 414 396	7872.9417 368 289	52
53	4995.1193 400 254	6080.2035 846 863	7403.0427 332 411	9015.5182 886 690	53
54	5645.4848 542 287	6902.0310 686 190	8440.4687 158 949	10323.7684 405 261	54
55	6380.3978 852 784	7834.8052 628 826	9623.1343 361 202	11821.7148 644 023	55
56	7210.8496 103 646	8893.5039 733 717	10971.3731 431 770	13536.8635 197 407	56
57	8149.2600 597 120	10095.1270 097 769	12508.3653 832 218	15500.7087 301 031	57
58	9209.6638 674 745	11458.9691 560 908	14260.5365 368 728	17749.3114 959 680	58
59	10407.9201 702 462	13006.9299 921 698	16258.0116 520 350	20323.9616 628 834	59
60	11761.9497 923 782	14763.8655 411 128	18535.1332 833 199	23271.9361 040 015	60

198

Table 2. FUTURE WORTH OF ONE DOLLAR PER PERIOD WITH INTEREST
PAYABLE AT END OF EACH PERIOD

	15% NOMINAL ANNUAL RATE	**15½%** NOMINAL ANNUAL RATE	**16%** NOMINAL ANNUAL RATE	**16½%** NOMINAL ANNUAL RATE	
YEARS					**YEARS**
1	1.0000 000 000	1.0000 000 000	1.0000 000 000	1.0000 000 000	1
2	2.1500 000 000	2.1550 000 000	2.1600 000 000	2.1650 000 000	2
3	3.4725 000 000	3.4890 250 000	3.5056 000 000	3.5222 250 000	3
4	4.9933 750 000	5.0298 238 750	5.0664 960 000	5.1033 921 250	4
5	6.7423 812 500	6.8094 465 756	6.8771 353 600	6.9454 518 256	5
6	8.7537 384 375	8.8649 107 948	8.9774 770 176	9.0914 513 769	6
7	11.0667 992 031	11.2389 719 680	11.4138 733 404	11.5915 408 540	7
8	13.7268 190 836	13.9810 126 231	14.2400 930 749	14.5041 450 949	8
9	16.7858 419 461	17.1480 695 797	17.5185 079 669	17.8973 290 356	9
10	20.3037 182 381	20.8060 203 645	21.3214 692 416	21.8503 883 265	10
11	24.3492 759 738	25.0309 535 210	25.7329 043 202	26.4557 024 004	11
12	29.0016 673 698	29.9107 513 168	30.8501 690 114	31.8208 932 964	12
13	34.3519 174 753	35.5469 177 709	36.7861 960 533	38.0713 406 903	13
14	40.5047 050 966	42.0566 900 254	43.6719 874 218	45.3531 119 042	14
15	47.5804 108 611	49.5754 769 793	51.6595 054 093	53.8363 753 684	15
16	55.7174 724 902	58.2596 759 111	60.9250 262 748	63.7193 773 042	16
17	65.0750 933 638	68.2899 256 773	71.6730 304 787	75.2330 745 594	17
18	75.8363 573 683	79.8748 641 573	84.1407 153 553	88.6465 318 617	18
19	88.2118 109 736	93.2554 681 017	98.6032 298 122	104.2732 096 189	19
20	102.4435 826 196	108.7100 656 575	115.3797 405 821	122.4782 892 060	20
21	118.8101 200 126	126.5601 258 344	134.8405 060 353	143.6872 069 250	21
22	137.6316 380 145	147.1769 453 387	157.4149 870 009	168.3955 960 677	22
23	159.2763 837 166	170.9893 718 662	183.6013 849 211	197.1808 694 188	23
24	184.1678 412 741	198.4927 245 054	213.9776 065 085	230.7157 128 729	24
25	212.7930 174 653	230.2590 968 038	249.2140 235 498	269.7838 054 970	25
26	245.7119 700 851	266.9492 568 084	290.0882 673 178	315.2981 334 040	26
27	283.5687 655 978	309.3263 916 137	337.5023 900 886	368.3223 254 156	27
28	327.1040 804 375	358.2719 823 138	392.5027 725 028	430.0955 091 092	28
29	377.1696 925 031	414.8041 395 724	456.3032 161 032	502.0612 681 122	29
30	434.7451 463 786	480.0987 812 061	530.3117 306 798	585.9013 773 508	30
31	500.9569 183 354	555.5140 922 931	616.1616 075 885	683.5751 046 136	31
32	577.1004 560 857	642.6187 765 985	715.7474 648 027	797.3649 968 749	32
33	664.6655 244 985	743.2246 869 711	831.2670 591 711	929.9302 213 593	33
34	765.3653 531 733	859.4245 134 518	965.2697 886 385	1084.3687 078 835	34
35	881.1701 561 493	993.6353 130 369	1120.7129 548 207	1264.2895 446 843	35
36	1014.3456 795 717	1148.6487 865 576	1301.0270 275 920	1473.8973 195 572	36
37	1167.4975 315 074	1327.6893 484 740	1510.1913 520 067	1718.0903 772 842	37
38	1343.6221 612 335	1534.4811 974 875	1752.8219 683 278	2002.5752 895 360	38
39	1546.1654 854 186	1773.3257 830 980	2034.2734 832 602	2334.0002 123 095	39
40	1779.0903 082 314	2049.1912 794 782	2360.7572 405 818	2720.1102 473 406	40
41	2046.9538 544 661	2367.8159 277 973	2739.4783 990 749	3169.9284 381 518	41
42	2354.9969 326 360	2735.8273 966 059	3178.7949 429 269	3693.9666 304 468	42
43	2709.2464 725 314	3160.8806 430 798	3688.4021 337 952	4304.4711 244 705	43
44	3116.6334 434 111	3651.8171 427 572	4279.5464 752 025	5015.7088 600 082	44
45	3585.1284 599 227	4218.8487 998 846	4965.2739 112 349	5844.3008 219 095	45
46	4123.8977 289 111	4873.7703 638 667	5760.7177 370 324	6809.6104 575 246	46
47	4743.4823 882 478	5630.2047 702 660	6683.4325 749 576	7934.1961 830 161	47
48	5456.0047 464 850	6503.8865 096 573	7753.7817 869 508	9244.3385 532 138	48
49	6275.4054 584 577	7512.9889 186 542	8995.3868 728 630	10770.6544 144 941	49
50	7217.7162 772 264	8678.5022 010 455	10435.6487 725 211	12548.8123 928 856	50
51	8301.3737 188 103	10024.6700 422 076	12106.3525 761 244	14620.3664 377 117	51
52	9547.5797 766 319	11579.4938 987 498	14044.3689 883 043	17033.7268 999 341	52
53	10980.7167 431 267	13375.3154 530 560	16292.4680 264 330	19845.2918 384 233	53
54	12628.8242 545 957	15449.4893 482 797	18900.2629 106 623	23120.7649 917 631	54
55	14524.1478 927 850	17845.1601 972 630	21925.3049 763 683	26936.6912 154 040	55
56	16703.7700 767 028	20612.1600 278 388	25434.3537 725 872	31382.2452 659 457	56
57	19210.3355 882 082	23808.0448 321 538	29504.8503 762 012	36561.3157 348 267	57
58	22092.8859 264 394	27499.2917 811 377	34226.6264 363 934	42594.9328 310 731	58
59	25407.8188 154 053	31762.6820 072 140	39703.8866 662 163	49624.0967 482 002	59
60	29219.9916 377 161	36686.8977 183 322	46057.5085 328 109	57813.0727 116 532	60

Table 2. FUTURE WORTH OF ONE DOLLAR PER PERIOD WITH INTEREST
PAYABLE AT END OF EACH PERIOD

	17% NOMINAL ANNUAL RATE	17½% NOMINAL ANNUAL RATE	18% NOMINAL ANNUAL RATE	18½% NOMINAL ANNUAL RATE	
YEARS					YEARS
1	1.0000 000 000	1.0000 000 000	1.0000 000 000	1.0000 000 000	1
2	2.1700 000 000	2.1750 000 000	2.1800 000 000	2.1850 000 000	2
3	3.5389 000 000	3.5556 250 000	3.5724 000 000	3.5892 250 000	3
4	5.1405 130 000	5.1778 593 750	5.2154 320 000	5.2532 316 250	4
5	7.0144 002 100	7.0839 847 656	7.1542 097 600	7.2250 794 756	5
6	9.2068 482 457	9.3236 820 996	9.4419 675 168	9.5617 191 786	6
7	11.7720 124 475	11.9553 264 670	12.1415 216 698	12.3306 372 267	7
8	14.7732 545 635	15.0475 085 988	15.3269 955 704	15.6118 051 136	8
9	18.2847 078 393	18.6808 226 036	19.0858 547 731	19.4999 890 596	9
10	22.3931 081 720	22.9499 665 592	23.5213 086 322	24.1074 870 356	10
11	27.1999 365 613	27.9662 107 070	28.7551 441 860	29.5673 721 372	11
12	32.8239 257 767	33.8602 975 808	34.9310 701 395	36.0373 359 826	12
13	39.4039 931 587	40.7858 496 574	42.2186 627 646	43.7042 431 394	13
14	47.1026 719 957	48.9233 733 475	50.8180 220 622	52.7895 281 202	14
15	56.1101 262 350	58.4849 636 833	60.9652 660 334	63.5555 908 224	15
16	66.6488 476 949	69.7198 323 278	72.9390 139 195	76.3133 751 246	16
17	78.9791 518 031	82.9208 029 852	87.0680 364 250	91.4313 495 226	17
18	93.4056 076 096	98.4319 435 076	103.7402 829 814	109.3461 491 843	18
19	110.2845 609 032	116.6575 336 214	123.4135 339 181	130.5751 867 834	19
20	130.0329 362 568	138.0726 020 052	146.6279 700 234	155.7315 963 383	20
21	153.1385 354 204	163.2353 073 561	174.0210 046 276	185.5419 416 609	21
22	180.1720 864 419	192.8014 861 434	206.3447 854 605	220.8672 008 682	22
23	211.8013 411 370	227.5417 462 185	244.4868 468 434	262.7276 330 288	23
24	248.8075 691 303	268.3615 518 067	289.4944 792 752	312.3322 451 391	24
25	292.1048 558 824	316.3248 233 729	342.6034 855 648	371.1137 104 898	25
26	342.7626 813 825	372.6816 674 632	405.2721 129 429	440.7697 469 305	26
27	402.0323 372 175	438.9009 592 692	479.2210 932 726	523.3121 501 126	27
28	471.3778 345 444	516.7086 271 413	566.4808 900 616	621.1248 978 834	28
29	552.5120 664 170	608.1326 368 911	669.4474 502 727	737.0330 039 918	29
30	647.4391 177 079	715.5558 483 470	790.9479 913 218	874.3841 097 303	30
31	758.5037 677 182	841.7781 218 078	934.3186 297 597	1037.1451 700 304	31
32	888.4494 082 303	990.0892 931 241	1103.4959 831 165	1230.0170 264 861	32
33	1040.4858 076 295	1164.3549 194 208	1303.1252 600 775	1458.5701 763 860	33
34	1218.3683 949 265	1369.1170 303 195	1538.6878 068 914	1729.4056 590 174	34
35	1426.4910 220 640	1609.7125 106 254	1816.6516 121 319	2050.3457 059 356	35
36	1669.9944 958 149	1892.4121 999 848	2144.6489 023 156	2430.6596 615 337	36
37	1954.8935 601 034	2224.5843 349 822	2531.6857 047 324	2881.3316 989 175	37
38	2288.2254 653 210	2614.8865 936 040	2988.3891 315 843	3415.3780 632 172	38
39	2678.2237 944 256	3073.4917 474 847	3527.2991 752 694	4048.2230 049 124	39
40	3134.5218 394 779	3612.3528 032 946	4163.2130 268 179	4798.1442 608 212	40
41	3668.3905 521 892	4245.5145 438 711	4913.5913 716 451	5686.8009 490 731	41
42	4293.0169 460 613	4989.4795 890 486	5799.0378 185 413	6739.8591 246 516	42
43	5023.8298 268 918	5863.6385 171 321	6843.8646 258 787	7987.7330 627 122	43
44	5878.8808 974 634	6890.7752 576 302	8076.7602 585 369	9466.4636 793 139	44
45	6879.2906 500 321	8097.6609 277 155	9531.5771 050 735	11218.7594 599 870	45
46	8049.7700 605 376	9515.7515 900 657	11248.2609 839 867	13295.2299 600 846	46
47	9419.2309 708 290	11182.0081 183 272	13273.9479 611 043	15755.8475 027 002	47
48	11021.5002 358 699	13139.8595 390 344	15664.2585 941 031	18671.6792 906 998	48
49	12896.1552 759 678	15440.3349 583 655	18484.8251 410 417	22126.9399 594 792	49
50	15089.5016 728 823	18143.3935 760 794	21813.0936 664 292	26221.4238 519 829	50
51	17655.7169 572 723	21319.4874 518 933	25740.4505 263 864	31073.3872 645 997	51
52	20658.1888 400 086	25051.3977 559 747	30374.7316 211 360	36822.9639 085 507	52
53	24171.0809 428 101	29436.3923 632 702	35843.1833 129 405	43636.2122 316 325	53
54	28281.1647 030 878	34588.7610 268 425	42295.9563 092 698	51709.9114 944 846	54
55	33089.9627 026 127	40642.7942 065 400	49910.2284 449 383	61277.2451 209 642	55
56	38716.2563 620 569	47756.2831 926 845	58895.0695 650 272	72614.5354 683 426	56
57	45299.0199 436 065	56114.6327 514 042	69497.1820 867 321	86049.2245 299 860	57
58	53000.8533 340 196	65935.6934 829 000	82007.6748 623 439	101969.3310 680 334	58
59	62011.9984 008 030	77475.4398 424 075	96770.0563 375 658	120834.6573 156 195	59
60	72555.0381 289 395	91034.6418 148 288	114189.6664 783 276	143190.0689 190 092	60

Table 2.   FUTURE WORTH OF ONE DOLLAR PER PERIOD WITH INTEREST
PAYABLE AT END OF EACH PERIOD

	19% NOMINAL ANNUAL RATE	19½% NOMINAL ANNUAL RATE	20% NOMINAL ANNUAL RATE	20½% NOMINAL ANNUAL RATE	
YEARS					YEARS
1	1.0000 000 000	1.0000 000 000	1.0000 000 000	1.0000 000 000	1
2	2.1900 000 000	2.1950 000 000	2.2000 000 000	2.2050 000 000	2
3	3.6061 000 000	3.6230 250 000	3.6400 000 000	3.6570 250 000	3
4	5.2912 590 000	5.3295 148 750	5.3680 000 000	5.4067 151 250	4
5	7.2965 982 100	7.3687 702 756	7.4416 000 000	7.5150 917 256	5
6	9.6829 518 699	9.8056 804 794	9.9299 200 000	10.0556 855 294	6
7	12.5227 127 252	12.7177 881 728	12.9159 040 000	13.1171 010 629	7
8	15.9020 281 430	16.1977 568 666	16.4990 848 000	16.8061 067 808	8
9	19.9234 134 901	20.3563 194 555	20.7989 017 600	21.2513 586 709	9
10	24.7088 620 533	25.3258 017 494	25.9586 821 120	26.6078 871 984	10
11	30.4035 458 434	31.2643 330 905	32.1504 185 344	33.0625 040 741	11
12	37.1802 195 536	38.3608 780 431	39.5805 022 413	40.8403 174 092	12
13	45.2444 612 688	46.8412 492 615	48.4966 026 895	50.2125 824 781	13
14	54.8409 089 099	56.9752 928 675	59.1959 232 274	61.5061 618 861	14
15	66.2606 816 027	69.0854 749 767	72.0351 078 729	75.1149 250 728	15
16	79.8502 111 073	83.5571 425 972	87.4421 294 475	91.5134 847 127	16
17	96.0217 512 176	100.8507 854 036	105.9305 553 370	111.2737 490 788	17
18	115.2658 839 490	121.5166 885 573	128.1166 664 044	135.0848 676 400	18
19	138.1664 018 993	146.2124 428 260	154.7399 996 853	163.7772 655 062	19
20	165.4180 182 602	175.7238 691 771	186.6879 996 224	198.3516 049 350	20
21	197.8474 417 296	210.9900 236 666	225.0255 995 468	240.0136 839 466	21
22	236.4384 556 582	253.1330 782 816	271.0307 194 562	290.2164 891 557	22
23	282.3617 622 333	303.4940 285 465	326.2368 633 475	350.7108 694 326	23
24	337.0104 970 576	363.6753 641 131	392.4842 360 170	423.6065 976 663	24
25	402.0424 914 986	435.5920 601 151	471.9810 832 203	511.4459 501 879	25
26	479.4305 648 833	521.5325 118 376	567.3772 998 644	617.2923 699 764	26
27	571.5223 722 111	624.2313 516 459	681.8527 598 373	744.8373 058 216	27
28	681.1116 229 313	746.9564 652 169	819.2233 118 048	898.5289 535 150	28
29	811.5228 312 882	893.6129 759 342	984.0679 741 657	1083.7273 889 856	29
30	966.7121 692 330	1068.8675 062 413	1181.8815 689 988	1306.8915 037 276	30
31	1151.3874 813 872	1278.2966 699 584	1419.2578 827 986	1575.8042 619 918	31
32	1371.1511 028 508	1528.5645 206 003	1704.1094 593 583	1899.8441 357 001	32
33	1632.6698 123 924	1827.6346 021 173	2045.9313 512 300	2290.3121 835 186	33
34	1943.8770 767 470	2185.0233 495 302	2456.1176 214 760	2760.8261 811 399	34
35	2314.2137 213 289	2612.1029 026 886	2948.3411 457 712	3327.7955 482 736	35
36	2754.9143 283 814	3122.4629 687 129	3539.0093 749 255	4010.9936 356 697	36
37	3279.3480 507 739	3732.3432 476 119	4247.8112 499 106	4834.2473 309 819	37
38	3903.4241 804 210	4461.1501 808 962	5098.3734 998 927	5826.2680 338 332	38
39	4646.0747 747 010	5332.0744 661 710	6119.0481 998 712	7021.6529 807 691	39
40	5529.8289 818 941	6372.8289 870 744	7343.8578 398 454	8462.0918 418 267	40
41	6581.4964 884 540	7616.5306 395 539	8813.6294 078 145	10197.8206 694 012	41
42	7832.9808 212 603	9102.7541 142 669	10577.3552 893 774	12289.3739 066 284	42
43	9322.2471 772 997	10878.7911 665 489	12693.8263 472 529	14809.6955 574 873	43
44	11094.4741 409 867	13001.1554 440 259	15233.5916 167 035	17846.6831 467 721	44
45	13203.4242 277 742	15537.3807 556 110	18281.3099 400 442	21506.2531 918 604	45
46	15713.0748 310 512	18568.1700 029 551	21938.5719 280 530	25916.0350 961 918	46
47	18699.5590 489 510	22189.9631 535 314	26327.2863 136 636	31229.8222 909 111	47
48	22253.4752 682 517	26518.0059 684 700	31593.7435 763 963	37632.9358 605 479	48
49	26482.6355 692 195	31690.0171 323 216	37913.4922 916 756	45348.6877 119 603	49
50	31515.3363 273 712	37870.5704 731 243	45497.1907 500 107	54646.1686 929 121	50
51	37504.2502 295 717	45256.3317 153 836	54597.6289 000 129	65849.6332 749 591	51
52	44631.0577 731 903	54082.3163 998 834	65518.1546 800 155	79349.8080 963 257	52
53	53111.9587 500 965	64629.3680 978 606	78622.7856 160 186	95617.5187 560 725	53
54	63204.2309 126 148	77233.0948 769 435	94348.3427 392 223	115220.1101 010 673	54
55	75214.0347 860 116	92294.5483 779 474	113219.0112 870 667	138841.2326 717 861	55
56	89505.7013 953 539	110292.9853 116 472	135863.8135 444 801	167304.6853 695 023	56
57	106512.7846 604 711	131801.1174 474 184	163037.5762 533 761	201603.1458 702 503	57
58	126751.2137 459 606	157503.3353 496 650	195646.0915 040 513	242932.7907 736 516	58
59	150834.9443 576 931	188221.4857 428 497	234776.3098 048 616	292735.0128 822 502	59
60	179494.5837 856 548	224920.8954 627 053	281732.5717 658 339	352746.6905 231 114	60

Table 2. FUTURE WORTH OF ONE DOLLAR PER PERIOD WITH INTEREST
PAYABLE AT END OF EACH PERIOD

	21% NOMINAL ANNUAL RATE	21½% NOMINAL ANNUAL RATE	22% NOMINAL ANNUAL RATE	22½% NOMINAL ANNUAL RATE	
YEARS					YEARS
1	1.0000 000 000	1.0000 000 000	1.0000 000 000	1.0000 000 000	1
2	2.2100 000 000	2.2150 000 000	2.2200 000 000	2.2250 000 000	2
3	3.6741 000 000	3.6912 250 000	3.7084 000 000	3.7256 250 000	3
4	5.4456 610 000	5.4848 383 750	5.5242 480 000	5.5638 906 250	4
5	7.5892 498 100	7.6640 786 256	7.7395 825 600	7.8157 660 156	5
6	10.1829 922 701	10.3118 555 301	10.4422 907 232	10.5743 133 691	6
7	13.3214 206 468	13.5289 044 691	13.7395 946 823	13.9535 338 772	7
8	17.1189 189 827	17.4376 189 300	17.7623 055 124	18.0930 789 996	8
9	21.7138 919 690	22.1867 069 999	22.6700 127 251	23.1640 217 745	9
10	27.2738 092 825	27.9568 490 049	28.6574 155 247	29.3759 266 737	10
11	34.0013 092 318	34.9675 715 410	35.9620 469 401	36.9855 101 753	11
12	42.1415 841 705	43.4855 994 223	44.8736 972 669	46.3072 499 648	12
13	51.9913 168 463	53.8250 032 980	55.7459 106 656	57.7263 812 068	13
14	63.9094 933 840	66.4095 290 071	69.0100 110 121	71.7148 169 784	14
15	78.3304 869 947	81.6875 777 437	85.1922 134 347	88.8506 507 985	15
16	95.7798 892 636	100.2504 069 585	104.9345 003 904	109.8420 472 282	16
17	116.8936 660 089	122.8042 444 546	129.0200 904 763	135.5565 078 545	17
18	142.4413 358 708	150.2071 570 124	158.4045 103 811	167.0567 221 218	18
19	173.3540 164 037	183.5016 957 700	194.2535 026 649	205.6444 845 992	19
20	210.7583 598 485	223.9545 603 606	237.9892 732 512	252.9144 936 340	20
21	256.0176 154 166	273.1047 908 381	291.3469 133 664	310.8202 547 016	21
22	310.7813 146 541	332.8223 208 683	356.4432 343 070	381.7548 120 095	22
23	377.0453 907 315	405.3791 198 550	435.8607 458 546	468.6496 447 116	23
24	457.2249 227 851	493.5356 306 238	532.7501 099 426	575.0958 147 717	24
25	554.2421 565 700	600.6457 912 079	650.9551 341 300	705.4923 730 953	25
26	671.6330 094 497	730.7846 363 176	795.1652 636 386	865.2281 570 418	26
27	813.6759 414 341	888.9033 331 259	971.1016 216 390	1060.9044 923 762	27
28	985.5478 891 353	1081.0175 497 480	1185.7439 783 996	1300.6080 031 608	28
29	1193.5129 458 537	1314.4363 229 438	1447.6076 536 475	1594.2448 038 720	29
30	1445.1506 644 829	1598.0401 323 767	1767.0813 374 500	1953.9498 847 432	30
31	1749.6323 040 244	1942.6187 608 377	2156.8392 316 890	2394.5886 088 104	31
32	2118.0550 878 695	2361.2817 944 178	2632.3438 626 606	2934.3710 457 928	32
33	2563.8466 563 221	2869.9573 802 177	3212.4595 124 459	3595.6045 310 962	33
34	3103.2544 541 497	3487.9982 169 645	3920.2006 051 840	4405.6155 505 928	34
35	3755.9378 895 211	4238.9178 336 118	4783.6447 383 245	5397.8790 494 762	35
36	4545.6848 463 206	5151.2851 678 383	5837.0465 807 559	6613.4018 356 083	36
37	5501.2786 640 479	6259.8114 789 236	7122.1968 285 222	8102.4172 486 202	37
38	6657.5471 834 980	7606.6709 468 922	8690.0801 307 970	9926.4611 295 597	38
39	8056.6320 920 325	9243.1052 004 740	10602.8977 595 724	12160.9148 837 107	39
40	9749.5248 313 594	11231.3728 185 759	12936.5352 666 783	14898.1207 325 455	40
41	11797.925C 459 448	13647.1179 745 697	15783.5730 253 475	18251.1978 973 683	41
42	14276.4893 055 932	16582.2483 391 022	19256.9590 909 240	22358.7174 242 762	42
43	17275.5520 597 678	20148.4317 320 092	23494.4900 909 273	27390.4288 447 383	43
44	20904.4179 923 191	24481.3445 543 911	28664.2779 109 313	33554.2753 348 044	44
45	25295.3457 707 061	29745.8336 335 852	34971.4190 513 361	41104.9872 851 354	45
46	30608.3683 825 543	36142.1878 648 060	42666.1312 426 301	50354.6094 242 909	46
47	37037.1257 428 907	43913.7582 557 393	52053.6801 160 087	61685.3965 447 563	47
48	44815.9221 488 978	53356.2162 807 233	63506.4897 415 306	75565.6107 673 265	48
49	54228.2658 001 663	64828.8027 810 788	77478.9174 846 673	92568.8731 899 750	49
50	65617.2016 182 013	78767.9953 790 108	94525.2793 312 942	113397.8696 577 193	50
51	79397.8139 580 235	95704.1143 854 981	115321.8407 841 789	138913.3903 307 062	51
52	96072.3548 892 085	116281.4989 783 801	140693.6457 566 982	170169.9031 551 151	52
53	116248.5494 159 423	141283.0212 587 319	171647.2478 231 718	208459.1313 650 160	53
54	140661.7447 932 902	171659.8708 293 592	209410.6423 442 696	255363.4359 221 446	54
55	170201.7111 998 811	208567.7430 576 715	255481.9836 600 089	312821.2090 046 271	55
56	205945.0705 518 561	253410.8078 150 708	311689.0200 652 109	383206.9810 306 682	56
57	249194.5353 677 459	307895.1314 953 111	380261.6044 795 573	469429.5517 625 685	57
58	301526.3877 949 725	374093.5847 668 029	463920.1574 650 599	575052.2009 091 464	58
59	364847.9292 319 168	454524.7054 916 656	565983.5921 073 731	704439.9461 137 043	59
60	441466.9943 706 193	552248.5171 723 737	690500.9823 709 952	862939.9339 892 878	60

Table 2. FUTURE WORTH OF ONE DOLLAR PER PERIOD WITH INTEREST
PAYABLE AT END OF EACH PERIOD

YEARS	23% NOMINAL ANNUAL RATE	24% NOMINAL ANNUAL RATE	25% NOMINAL ANNUAL RATE	26% NOMINAL ANNUAL RATE	YEARS
1	1.0000 000 000	1.0000 000 000	1.0000 000 000	1.0000 000 000	1
2	2.2300 000 000	2.2400 000 000	2.2500 000 000	2.2600 000 000	2
3	3.7429 000 000	3.7776 000 000	3.8125 000 000	3.8476 000 000	3
4	5.6037 670 000	5.6842 240 000	5.7656 250 000	5.8479 760 000	4
5	7.8926 334 100	8.0484 377 600	8.2070 312 500	8.3684 497 600	5
6	10.7079 390 943	10.9800 628 224	11.2587 890 625	11.5442 466 976	6
7	14.1707 650 860	14.6152 778 998	15.0734 863 281	15.5457 508 390	7
8	18.4300 410 558	19.1229 445 957	19.8418 579 102	20.5876 460 571	8
9	23.6689 504 986	24.7124 512 987	25.8023 223 877	26.9404 340 320	9
10	30.1128 091 133	31.6434 396 104	33.2529 029 846	34.9449 468 803	10
11	38.0387 552 093	40.2378 651 169	42.5661 287 308	45.0306 330 691	11
12	47.7876 689 075	50.8949 527 449	54.2076 609 135	57.7385 976 671	12
13	59.7788 327 562	64.1097 414 037	68.7595 761 418	73.7506 330 606	13
14	74.5279 642 901	80.4960 793 406	86.9494 701 773	93.9257 976 563	14
15	92.6693 960 768	100.8151 383 823	109.6868 377 216	119.3465 050 469	15
16	114.9833 571 745	126.0107 715 941	138.1085 471 520	151.3765 963 592	16
17	142.4295 293 246	157.2533 567 767	173.6356 839 400	191.7345 114 125	17
18	176.1883 210 693	195.9941 624 031	218.0446 049 250	242.5854 843 798	18
19	217.7116 349 152	244.0327 613 798	273.5557 561 563	306.6577 103 185	19
20	268.7853 109 457	303.6006 241 110	342.9446 951 954	387.3887 150 014	20
21	331.6059 324 633	377.4647 738 976	429.6808 689 942	489.1097 809 017	21
22	408.8752 969 298	469.0563 196 331	538.1010 862 428	617.2783 239 362	22
23	503.9166 152 237	582.6298 363 450	673.6263 578 034	778.7706 881 596	23
24	620.8174 367 251	723.4609 970 678	843.0329 472 543	982.2510 670 810	24
25	764.6054 471 719	898.0916 363 641	1054.7911 840 679	1238.6363 445 221	25
26	941.4647 000 214	1114.6336 290 914	1319.4889 800 848	1561.6817 940 979	26
27	1159.0015 810 263	1383.1457 000 734	1650.3612 251 061	1968.7190 605 633	27
28	1426.5719 446 624	1716.1006 680 910	2063.9515 313 826	2481.5860 163 098	28
29	1755.6834 919 348	2128.9648 284 328	2580.9394 142 282	3127.7983 805 503	29
30	2160.4906 950 798	2640.9163 872 567	3227.1742 677 853	3942.0259 594 934	30
31	2658.4035 549 481	3275.7363 201 983	4034.9678 347 316	4967.9527 089 617	31
32	3270.8363 725 862	4062.9130 370 459	5044.7097 934 145	6260.6204 132 917	32
33	4024.1287 382 810	5039.0121 659 369	6306.8872 417 681	7889.3817 207 476	33
34	4950.6783 480 856	6249.3765 857 617	7884.6090 522 101	9941.6209 681 420	34
35	6090.3343 681 453	7750.2251 063 445	9856.7613 152 626	12527.4424 198 589	35
36	7492.1112 728 187	9611.2791 318 672	12321.9516 440 783	15785.5174 490 222	36
37	9216.2968 655 670	11918.9861 235 154	15403.4395 550 979	19890.8275 857 679	37
38	11337.0451 446 474	14780.5427 931 591	19255.2994 438 724	25063.4427 580 676	38
39	13945.5655 279 163	18328.8730 635 172	24070.1243 048 404	31580.9378 751 652	39
40	17154.0455 993 371	22728.8025 987 614	30088.6553 810 506	39792.9817 227 081	40
41	21100.4760 871 846	28184.7152 224 641	37611.8192 263 132	50140.1569 706 122	41
42	25954.5855 872 370	34950.0468 758 555	47015.7740 328 915	63177.5977 829 714	42
43	31925.1402 723 016	43339.0581 260 608	58770.7175 411 144	79604.7732 065 440	43
44	39268.9225 349 309	53741.4320 763 154	73464.3969 263 930	100303.0142 402 454	44
45	48301.7747 179 650	66640.3757 746 311	91831.4961 579 912	126382.7979 427 092	45
46	59412.1829 030 970	82635.0659 605 426	114790.3701 974 890	159243.3254 078 136	46
47	73077.9849 708 093	102468.4817 910 728	143488.9627 468 613	200647.5900 138 451	47
48	89886.9215 140 954	127061.9174 209 303	179362.2034 335 766	252816.9634 174 449	48
49	110561.9134 623 374	157557.7776 019 536	224203.7542 919 707	318550.3739 059 805	49
50	135992.1535 586 750	195372.6442 264 224	280255.6928 649 634	401374.4711 215 355	50
51	167271.3488 771 702	242263.0788 407 638	350320.6160 812 042	505732.8336 131 347	51
52	205744.7591 189 194	300407.2177 625 471	437901.7701 015 053	637224.3703 525 497	52
53	253067.0537 162 708	372505.9500 255 584	547378.2126 268 816	802903.7066 442 126	53
54	311273.4760 710 131	461908.3780 316 924	684223.7657 836 020	1011659.6703 717 079	54
55	382867.3755 673 461	572767.3887 592 986	855280.7072 295 025	1274692.1846 683 520	55
56	470927.8719 478 357	710232.5620 615 302	1069101.8840 368 781	1606113.1526 821 235	56
57	579242.2824 958 379	880689.3769 562 975	1336378.3550 460 977	2023703.5723 794 756	57
58	712469.0074 698 806	1092055.8274 258 089	1670473.9438 076 221	2549867.5011 981 392	58
59	876337.8791 879 532	1354150.2260 080 030	2088093.4297 595 276	3212834.0515 096 554	59
60	1077896.5914 011 824	1679147.2802 499 237	2610117.7871 994 095	4048171.9049 021 658	60

Table 2. FUTURE WORTH OF ONE DOLLAR PER PERIOD WITH INTEREST
PAYABLE AT END OF EACH PERIOD

	27% NOMINAL ANNUAL RATE	**28%** NOMINAL ANNUAL RATE	**29%** NOMINAL ANNUAL RATE	**30%** NOMINAL ANNUAL RATE	
YEARS					YEARS
1	1.0000 000 000	1.0000 000 000	1.0000 000 000	1.0000 000 000	1
2	2.2700 000 000	2.2800 000 000	2.2900 000 000	2.3000 000 000	2
3	3.8829 000 000	3.9184 000 000	3.9541 000 000	3.9900 000 000	3
4	5.9312 830 000	6.0155 520 000	6.1007 890 000	6.1870 000 000	4
5	8.5327 294 100	8.6999 065 600	8.8700 178 100	9.0431 000 000	5
6	11.8365 663 507	12.1358 803 968	12.4423 229 749	12.7560 300 000	6
7	16.0324 392 654	16.5339 269 079	17.0505 966 376	17.5828 390 000	7
8	21.3611 978 670	22.1634 264 421	22.9952 696 625	23.8576 907 000	8
9	28.1287 212 911	29.3691 858 459	30.6638 978 647	32.0149 979 100	9
10	36.7234 760 398	38.5925 578 828	40.5564 282 454	42.6194 972 830	10
11	47.6388 145 705	50.3984 740 899	53.3177 924 366	56.4053 464 679	11
12	61.5012 945 045	65.5100 468 351	69.7799 522 432	74.3269 504 083	12
13	79.1066 440 207	84.8528 599 490	91.0161 383 937	97.6250 355 308	13
14	101.4654 379 063	109.6116 607 347	118.4108 185 279	127.9125 461 900	14
15	129.8611 061 411	141.3029 257 404	153.7499 559 010	167.2863 100 470	15
16	165.9236 047 991	181.8677 449 477	199.3374 431 123	218.4722 030 611	16
17	211.7229 780 949	233.7907 135 330	258.1453 016 149	285.0138 639 794	17
18	269.8881 821 805	300.2521 133 223	334.0074 390 832	371.5180 231 732	18
19	343.7579 913 693	385.3227 050 525	431.8695 964 173	483.9734 301 251	19
20	437.5726 490 390	494.2130 624 672	558.1117 793 783	630.1654 591 627	20
21	556.7172 642 795	633.5927 199 580	720.9641 953 980	820.2150 969 115	21
22	708.0309 256 350	811.9986 815 463	931.0438 120 634	1067.2796 259 850	22
23	900.1992 755 564	1040.3583 123 792	1202.0465 175 618	1388.4635 137 804	23
24	1144.2530 799 566	1332.6586 398 454	1551.6400 076 548	1806.0025 679 146	24
25	1454.2014 115 449	1706.8030 590 021	2002.6156 098 746	2348.8033 382 889	25
26	1847.8357 926 621	2185.7079 155 227	2584.3741 367 383	3054.4443 397 756	26
27	2347.7514 566 808	2798.7061 318 691	3334.8426 363 924	3971.7776 417 083	27
28	2982.6443 499 847	3583.3438 487 924	4302.9470 009 462	5164.3109 342 208	28
29	3788.9583 244 805	4587.6801 264 543	5551.8016 312 205	6714.6042 144 870	29
30	4812.9770 720 903	5873.2305 618 614	7162.8241 042 745	8729.9854 788 331	30
31	6113.4808 815 546	7518.7351 191 827	9241.0430 945 141	11349.9811 224 831	31
32	7765.1207 195 744	9624.9809 525 538	11921.9455 919 232	14755.9754 592 280	32
33	9862.7033 138 595	12320.9756 192 689	15380.3098 135 809	19183.7680 969 964	33
34	12526.6332 086 015	15771.8487 926 641	19841.5996 595 194	24939.8985 260 954	34
35	15909.8241 749 239	20188.9664 546 101	25596.6635 607 800	32422.8680 839 240	35
36	20206.4767 021 534	25842.8770 619 009	33020.6959 934 062	42150.7285 091 012	36
37	25663.2246 117 348	33079.8826 392 332	42597.6978 314 940	54796.9470 618 315	37
38	32593.2962 729 032	42343.2497 782 185	54952.0302 026 273	71237.0311 803 809	38
39	41394.4862 665 871	54200.3597 161 197	70889.1189 613 892	92609.1405 344 952	39
40	52751.9975 585 656	69377.4604 366 332	91447.9634 601 921	120392.8826 948 438	40
41	66767.4368 993 783	88804.1493 588 905	117968.8728 636 478	156511.7475 032 969	41
42	84795.6448 622 104	113670.3111 793 798	152180.8459 941 057	203466.2717 542 860	42
43	107691.4689 750 073	145498.9983 096 061	196314.2913 323 964	264507.1532 805 718	43
44	136769.1655 982 592	186239.7178 362 959	253246.4358 187 913	343860.2992 647 434	44
45	173697.8403 097 892	238387.8388 304 587	326688.9022 062 408	447019.3890 441 664	45
46	220597.2571 934 323	305137.4337 029 871	421429.6838 460 506	581126.2057 574 163	46
47	280159.5166 356 590	390576.9151 398 235	543645.2921 614 053	755465.0674 846 412	47
48	355803.5861 272 869	499939.4513 789 741	701303.4268 882 129	982105.5877 300 336	48
49	451871.5543 816 544	639923.4977 650 869	904682.4206 857 946	1276738.2640 490 436	49
50	573877.8740 647 011	819103.0771 393 112	1167041.3226 846 750	1659760.7432 637 567	50
51	728825.9000 621 704	1048452.9387 383 183	1505484.3062 632 308	2157689.9662 428 837	51
52	925609.8930 789 564	1342020.7615 850 475	1942075.7550 795 677	2804997.9561 157 488	52
53	1175525.5642 102 746	1717787.5748 288 607	2505278.7240 526 423	3646498.3429 504 735	53
54	1492918.4665 470 488	2198769.0957 809 417	3231810.5540 279 086	4740448.8458 356 155	54
55	1896007.4525 147 519	2814425.4425 996 054	4169036.6146 960 020	6162584.4995 863 001	55
56	2407930.4646 937 349	3602465.5665 274 949	5378058.2329 578 426	8011360.8494 621 901	56
57	3058072.6901 610 433	4611156.9251 551 935	6937696.1205 156 169	10414770.1043 008 472	57
58	3883753.3165 045 250	5902281.8641 986 476	8949628.9954 651 458	13539202.1355 911 012	58
59	4932367.7119 607 468	7554921.7861 742 690	11545022.4041 500 381	17600963.7762 684 316	59
60	6264107.9941 901 484	9670300.8863 030 643	14893079.9013 535 492	22881253.9091 489 610	60

Table 3. **SINKING FUND FACTORS**
PAYABLE AT END OF EACH PERIOD

YEARS	5% NOMINAL ANNUAL RATE	5½% NOMINAL ANNUAL RATE	6% NOMINAL ANNUAL RATE	6½% NOMINAL ANNUAL RATE	YEARS
1	1.0000 000 000	1.0000 000 000	1.0000 000 000	1.0000 000 000	1
2	0.4878 048 780	0.4866 180 04°	0.4854 368 932	0.4842 615 012	2
3	0.3172 085 646	0.3156 540 747	0.3141 098 128	0.3125 757 019	3
4	0.2320 118 326	0.2302 944 853	0.2285 914 924	0.2269 027 404	4
5	0.1809 747 981	0.1791 764 362	0.1773 964 004	0.1756 345 376	5
6	0.1470 174 681	0.1451 789 476	0.1433 626 285	0.1415 683 122	6
7	0.1228 198 184	0.1209 644 178	0.1191 350 181	0.1173 313 693	7
8	0.1047 218 136	0.1028 640 118	0.1010 359 426	0.0992 372 971	8
9	0.0906 900 800	0.0888 394 585	0.0870 222 350	0.0852 380 329	9
10	0.0795 045 750	0.0776 677 687	0.0758 679 582	0.0741 046 901	10
11	0.0703 888 915	0.0685 706 532	0.0667 929 381	0.0650 552 058	11
12	0.0628 254 100	0.0610 292 312	0.0592 770 294	0.0575 681 661	12
13	0.0564 557 652	0.0546 842 587	0.0529 601 053	0.0512 825 571	13
14	0.0510 239 695	0.0492 791 154	0.0475 849 090	0.0459 404 806	14
15	0.0463 422 876	0.0446 255 976	0.0429 627 640	0.0413 527 830	15
16	0.0422 699 080	0.0405 825 380	0.0389 521 436	0.0373 775 740	16
17	0.0386 991 417	0.0370 419 723	0.0354 448 042	0.0339 063 265	17
18	0.0355 462 223	0.0339 199 163	0.0323 565 406	0.0308 546 103	18
19	0.0327 450 104	0.0311 500 559	0.0296 208 604	0.0281 557 517	19
20	0.0302 425 872	0.0286 793 300	0.0271 845 570	0.0257 563 954	20
21	0.0279 961 071	0.0264 647 754	0.0250 045 467	0.0236 133 343	21
22	0.0259 705 086	0.0244 712 319	0.0230 455 685	0.0216 912 043	22
23	0.0241 368 219	0.0226 696 472	0.0212 784 847	0.0199 607 802	23
24	0.0224 709 008	0.0210 358 037	0.0196 790 050	0.0183 976 975	24
25	0.0209 524 573	0.0195 493 529	0.0182 267 182	0.0169 814 811	25
26	0.0195 643 207	0.0181 930 713	0.0169 043 467	0.0156 947 983	26
27	0.0182 918 599	0.0169 522 817	0.0156 971 663	0.0145 228 776	27
28	0.0171 225 304	0.0158 143 996	0.0145 925 515	0.0134 530 522	28
29	0.0160 455 149	0.0147 685 720	0.0135 796 135	0.0124 743 976	29
30	0.0150 514 351	0.0138 053 897	0.0126 489 115	0.0115 774 422	30
31	0.0141 321 204	0.0129 166 543	0.0117 922 196	0.0107 539 335	31
32	0.0132 804 189	0.0120 951 895	0.0110 023 374	0.0099 966 481	32
33	0.0124 900 437	0.0113 346 865	0.0102 729 350	0.0092 992 365	33
34	0.0117 554 454	0.0106 295 769	0.0095 984 254	0.0086 560 953	34
35	0.0110 717 072	0.0099 749 266	0.0089 738 590	0.0080 622 606	35
36	0.0104 344 571	0.0093 663 488	0.0083 948 348	0.0075 133 205	36
37	0.0098 397 945	0.0087 999 295	0.0078 574 274	0.0070 053 400	37
38	0.0092 842 282	0.0082 721 659	0.0073 581 240	0.0065 347 995	38
39	0.0087 646 242	0.0077 799 139	0.0068 937 724	0.0060 985 416	39
40	0.0082 781 612	0.0073 203 434	0.0064 615 359	0.0056 937 260	40
41	0.0078 222 924	0.0068 909 001	0.0060 588 551	0.0053 177 915	41
42	0.0073 947 131	0.0064 892 731	0.0056 834 152	0.0049 684 229	42
43	0.0069 933 328	0.0061 133 667	0.0053 331 178	0.0046 435 230	43
44	0.0066 162 506	0.0057 612 757	0.0050 060 565	0.0043 411 874	44
45	0.0062 617 347	0.0054 312 651	0.0047 004 958	0.0040 596 841	45
46	0.0059 282 036	0.0051 217 512	0.0044 148 527	0.0037 974 344	46
47	0.0056 142 109	0.0048 312 858	0.0041 476 805	0.0035 529 973	47
48	0.0053 184 306	0.0045 585 424	0.0038 976 549	0.0033 250 549	48
49	0.0050 396 453	0.0043 023 035	0.0036 635 619	0.0031 124 000	49
50	0.0047 767 355	0.0040 614 501	0.0034 442 864	0.0029 139 255	50
51	0.0045 286 697	0.0038 349 523	0.0032 388 028	0.0027 286 146	51
52	0.0042 944 966	0.0036 218 603	0.0030 461 669	0.0025 555 319	52
53	0.0040 733 368	0.0034 212 975	0.0028 655 076	0.0023 938 164	53
54	0.0038 643 770	0.0032 324 534	0.0026 960 209	0.0022 426 740	54
55	0.0036 668 637	0.0030 545 778	0.0025 369 634	0.0021 013 722	55
56	0.0034 800 978	0.0028 869 756	0.0023 876 472	0.0019 692 339	56
57	0.0033 034 300	0.0027 290 020	0.0022 474 350	0.0018 456 332	57
58	0.0031 362 568	0.0025 800 578	0.0021 157 359	0.0017 299 909	58
59	0.0029 780 161	0.0024 395 863	0.0019 920 012	0.0016 217 702	59
60	0.0028 281 845	0.0023 070 692	0.0018 757 215	0.0015 204 735	60

Table 3.   **SINKING FUND FACTORS**
PAYABLE AT END OF EACH PERIOD

YEARS	**7%** NOMINAL ANNUAL RATE	**7½%** NOMINAL ANNUAL RATE	**8%** NOMINAL ANNUAL RATE	**8½%** NOMINAL ANNUAL RATE	YEARS
1	1.0000 000 000	1.0000 000 000	1.0000 000 000	1.0000 000 000	1
2	0.4830 917 874	0.4819 277 108	0.4807 692 308	0.4796 163 070	2
3	0.3110 516 657	0.3095 376 282	0.3080 335 140	0.3065 392 485	3
4	0.2252 281 167	0.2235 675 087	0.2219 208 045	0.2202 878 926	4
5	0.1738 906 944	0.1721 647 178	0.1704 564 546	0.1687 657 519	5
6	0.1397 957 998	0.1380 448 912	0.1363 153 862	0.1346 070 840	6
7	0.1155 532 196	0.1138 003 154	0.1120 724 014	0.1103 692 212	7
8	0.0974 677 625	0.0957 270 232	0.0940 147 606	0.0923 306 533	8
9	0.0834 864 701	0.0817 671 595	0.0800 797 092	0.0784 237 233	9
10	0.0723 775 027	0.0706 859 274	0.0690 294 887	0.0674 077 051	10
11	0.0633 569 048	0.0616 974 737	0.0600 763 421	0.0584 929 316	11
12	0.0559 019 887	0.0542 778 313	0.0526 950 169	0.0511 528 581	12
13	0.0496 508 481	0.0480 641 963	0.0465 218 052	0.0450 228 662	13
14	0.0443 449 386	0.0427 973 721	0.0412 968 528	0.0398 424 382	14
15	0.0397 946 247	0.0382 872 363	0.0368 295 449	0.0354 204 614	15
16	0.0358 576 477	0.0343 911 571	0.0329 768 720	0.0316 135 439	16
17	0.0324 251 931	0.0310 000 282	0.0296 294 315	0.0283 119 832	17
18	0.0294 126 017	0.0280 289 578	0.0267 020 959	0.0254 304 127	18
19	0.0267 530 148	0.0254 108 994	0.0241 276 275	0.0229 014 015	19
20	0.0243 929 257	0.0230 921 916	0.0218 522 088	0.0206 709 744	20
21	0.0222 890 017	0.0210 293 742	0.0198 322 503	0.0186 954 120	21
22	0.0204 057 732	0.0191 868 710	0.0180 320 684	0.0169 389 233	22
23	0.0187 139 263	0.0175 352 780	0.0164 221 692	0.0153 719 258	23
24	0.0171 890 207	0.0160 500 795	0.0149 779 616	0.0139 697 546	24
25	0.0158 105 172	0.0147 106 716	0.0136 787 791	0.0127 116 825	25
26	0.0145 610 279	0.0134 996 124	0.0125 071 267	0.0115 801 651	26
27	0.0134 257 340	0.0124 020 369	0.0114 480 962	0.0105 602 540	27
28	0.0123 919 283	0.0114 051 993	0.0104 889 057	0.0096 391 357	28
29	0.0114 486 518	0.0104 981 081	0.0096 185 350	0.0088 057 657	29
30	0.0105 864 035	0.0096 712 358	0.0088 274 334	0.0080 505 753	30
31	0.0097 969 061	0.0089 162 831	0.0081 072 841	0.0073 652 359	31
32	0.0090 729 155	0.0082 259 887	0.0074 508 132	0.0067 424 664	32
33	0.0084 080 653	0.0075 939 728	0.0068 516 324	0.0061 758 763	33
34	0.0077 967 381	0.0070 146 084	0.0063 041 101	0.0056 598 358	34
35	0.0072 339 596	0.0064 829 147	0.0058 032 646	0.0051 893 685	35
36	0.0067 153 097	0.0059 944 680	0.0053 446 741	0.0047 600 615	36
37	0.0062 368 480	0.0055 453 271	0.0049 244 025	0.0043 679 904	37
38	0.0057 950 515	0.0051 319 709	0.0045 389 361	0.0040 096 556	38
39	0.0053 867 616	0.0047 512 443	0.0041 851 297	0.0036 819 284	39
40	0.0050 091 389	0.0044 003 138	0.0038 601 615	0.0033 820 056	40
41	0.0046 596 245	0.0040 766 282	0.0035 614 940	0.0031 073 700	41
42	0.0043 359 072	0.0037 778 858	0.0032 868 407	0.0028 557 568	42
43	0.0040 358 953	0.0035 020 052	0.0030 341 370	0.0026 251 245	43
44	0.0037 576 913	0.0032 471 012	0.0028 015 156	0.0024 136 299	44
45	0.0034 995 710	0.0030 114 630	0.0025 872 845	0.0022 196 061	45
46	0.0032 599 650	0.0027 935 352	0.0023 899 085	0.0020 415 434	46
47	0.0030 374 421	0.0025 919 020	0.0022 079 922	0.0018 780 731	47
48	0.0028 306 953	0.0024 052 724	0.0020 402 660	0.0017 279 519	48
49	0.0026 385 294	0.0022 324 676	0.0018 855 731	0.0015 900 501	49
50	0.0024 598 495	0.0020 724 102	0.0017 428 582	0.0014 633 395	50
51	0.0022 936 519	0.0019 241 141	0.0016 111 575	0.0013 468 835	51
52	0.0021 390 147	0.0017 866 757	0.0014 895 903	0.0012 398 282	52
53	0.0019 950 908	0.0016 592 661	0.0013 773 506	0.0011 413 945	53
54	0.0018 611 007	0.0015 411 247	0.0012 737 003	0.0010 508 710	54
55	0.0017 363 264	0.0014 315 521	0.0011 779 629	0.0009 676 075	55
56	0.0016 201 059	0.0013 299 053	0.0010 895 180	0.0008 910 096	56
57	0.0015 118 286	0.0012 355 927	0.0010 077 963	0.0008 205 332	57
58	0.0014 109 304	0.0011 480 689	0.0009 322 748	0.0007 556 803	58
59	0.0013 168 900	0.0010 668 318	0.0008 624 729	0.0006 959 948	59
60	0.0012 292 255	0.0009 914 178	0.0007 979 488	0.0006 410 586	60

Table 3.   SINKING FUND FACTORS
PAYABLE AT END OF EACH PERIOD

YEARS	9% NOMINAL ANNUAL RATE	9½% NOMINAL ANNUAL RATE	10% NOMINAL ANNUAL RATE	10½% NOMINAL ANNUAL RATE	YEARS
1	1.0000 000 000	1.0000 000 000	1.0000 000 000	1.0000 000 000	1
2	0.4784 688 995	0.4773 269 690	0.4761 904 762	0.4750 593 824	2
3	0.3050 547 573	0.3035 799 668	0.3021 148 036	0.3006 591 953	3
4	0.2186 686 621	0.2170 630 025	0.2154 708 037	0.2138 919 564	4
5	0.1670 924 570	0.1654 364 173	0.1637 974 808	0.1621 754 954	5
6	0.1329 197 833	0.1312 532 826	0.1296 073 804	0.1279 818 746	6
7	0.1086 905 168	0.1070 360 296	0.1054 054 997	0.1037 986 667	7
8	0.0906 743 778	0.0890 456 084	0.0874 440 176	0.0858 692 763	8
9	0.0767 988 021	0.0752 045 426	0.0736 405 391	0.0721 063 831	9
10	0.0658 200 899	0.0642 661 517	0.0627 453 949	0.0612 573 206	10
11	0.0569 466 567	0.0554 369 258	0.0539 631 420	0.0525 247 041	11
12	0.0496 506 585	0.0481 877 142	0.0467 633 151	0.0453 767 456	12
13	0.0435 665 597	0.0421 520 575	0.0407 785 238	0.0394 451 173	13
14	0.0384 331 730	0.0370 680 923	0.0357 462 232	0.0344 665 871	14
15	0.0340 588 827	0.0327 436 950	0.0314 737 769	0.0302 480 015	15
16	0.0302 999 097	0.0290 346 957	0.0278 166 207	0.0266 443 997	16
17	0.0270 462 485	0.0258 307 825	0.0246 641 344	0.0235 448 518	17
18	0.0242 122 907	0.0230 461 037	0.0219 302 222	0.0208 630 182	18
19	0.0217 304 107	0.0206 128 384	0.0195 468 682	0.0185 306 897	19
20	0.0195 464 750	0.0184 766 953	0.0174 596 248	0.0164 932 653	20
21	0.0176 166 348	0.0165 936 973	0.0156 243 898	0.0147 065 219	21
22	0.0159 049 930	0.0149 278 440	0.0140 050 630	0.0131 342 647	22
23	0.0143 818 800	0.0134 493 824	0.0125 718 127	0.0117 465 900	23
24	0.0130 225 607	0.0121 335 107	0.0112 997 764	0.0105 185 815	24
25	0.0118 062 505	0.0109 593 925	0.0101 680 722	0.0094 293 198	25
26	0.0107 153 599	0.0099 093 986	0.0091 590 386	0.0084 611 196	26
27	0.0097 349 054	0.0089 685 169	0.0082 576 423	0.0075 989 359	27
28	0.0088 520 473	0.0081 238 883	0.0074 510 132	0.0068 298 968	28
29	0.0080 557 226	0.0073 644 387	0.0067 280 747	0.0061 429 332	29
30	0.0073 363 514	0.0066 805 845	0.0060 792 483	0.0055 284 815	30
31	0.0066 855 995	0.0060 639 940	0.0054 962 140	0.0049 782 438	31
32	0.0060 961 861	0.0055 073 947	0.0049 717 167	0.0044 849 922	32
33	0.0055 617 255	0.0050 044 141	0.0044 994 063	0.0040 424 091	33
34	0.0050 765 971	0.0045 494 491	0.0040 737 064	0.0036 449 545	34
35	0.0046 358 375	0.0041 375 575	0.0036 897 051	0.0032 877 563	35
36	0.0042 350 500	0.0037 643 673	0.0033 430 638	0.0029 665 187	36
37	0.0038 703 293	0.0034 260 006	0.0030 299 405	0.0026 774 443	37
38	0.0035 381 975	0.0031 190 090	0.0027 469 250	0.0024 171 697	38
39	0.0032 355 500	0.0028 403 196	0.0024 909 840	0.0021 827 092	39
40	0.0029 596 092	0.0025 871 883	0.0022 594 144	0.0019 714 084	40
41	0.0027 078 853	0.0023 571 597	0.0020 498 028	0.0017 809 027	41
42	0.0024 781 420	0.0021 480 333	0.0018 599 911	0.0016 090 833	42
43	0.0022 683 675	0.0019 578 336	0.0016 880 466	0.0014 540 666	43
44	0.0020 767 493	0.0017 847 847	0.0015 322 365	0.0013 141 681	44
45	0.0019 016 514	0.0016 272 880	0.0013 910 047	0.0011 878 796	45
46	0.0017 415 959	0.0014 839 025	0.0012 629 527	0.0010 738 498	46
47	0.0015 952 455	0.0013 533 282	0.0011 468 221	0.0009 708 663	47
48	0.0014 613 892	0.0012 343 905	0.0010 414 797	0.0008 778 407	48
49	0.0013 389 289	0.0011 260 279	0.0009 459 041	0.0007 937 954	49
50	0.0012 268 681	0.0010 272 796	0.0008 591 740	0.0007 178 512	50
51	0.0011 243 016	0.0009 372 756	0.0007 804 577	0.0006 492 173	51
52	0.0010 304 065	0.0008 552 274	0.0007 090 040	0.0005 871 820	52
53	0.0009 444 343	0.0007 804 201	0.0006 441 339	0.0005 311 042	53
54	0.0008 657 034	0.0007 122 048	0.0005 852 336	0.0004 804 064	54
55	0.0007 935 930	0.0006 499 926	0.0005 317 476	0.0004 345 680	55
56	0.0007 275 373	0.0005 932 484	0.0004 831 734	0.0003 931 196	56
57	0.0006 670 202	0.0005 414 860	0.0004 390 556	0.0003 556 378	57
58	0.0006 115 709	0.0004 942 633	0.0003 989 822	0.0003 217 406	58
59	0.0005 607 595	0.0004 511 784	0.0003 625 796	0.0002 910 832	59
60	0.0005 141 938	0.0004 118 653	0.0003 295 092	0.0002 633 544	60

Table 3.   SINKING FUND FACTORS
PAYABLE AT END OF EACH PERIOD

YEARS	11% NOMINAL ANNUAL RATE	11½% NOMINAL ANNUAL RATE	12% NOMINAL ANNUAL RATE	12½% NOMINAL ANNUAL RATE	YEARS
1	1.0000 000 000	1.0000 000 000	1.0000 000 000	1.0000 000 000	1
2	0.4739 336 493	0.4728 132 388	0.4716 981 132	0.4705 882 353	2
3	0.2992 130 696	0.2977 763 551	0.2963 489 806	0.2949 308 756	3
4	0.2123 263 515	0.2107 738 808	0.2092 344 363	0.2077 079 108	4
5	0.1605 703 095	0.1589 817 720	0.1574 097 319	0.1558 540 390	5
6	0.1263 765 636	0.1247 912 454	0.1232 257 184	0.1216 797 811	6
7	0.1022 152 695	0.1006 550 465	0.0991 177 359	0.0976 030 757	7
8	0.0843 210 542	0.0827 990 200	0.0813 028 414	0.0798 321 856	8
9	0.0706 016 644	0.0691 259 707	0.0676 788 888	0.0662 600 042	9
10	0.0598 014 271	0.0583 772 102	0.0569 841 642	0.0556 217 819	10
11	0.0511 210 071	0.0497 514 437	0.0484 154 043	0.0471 122 783	11
12	0.0440 272 864	0.0427 142 151	0.0414 368 076	0.0401 943 390	12
13	0.0381 509 925	0.0368 953 016	0.0356 771 951	0.0344 958 241	13
14	0.0332 282 015	0.0320 300 825	0.0308 712 461	0.0297 507 101	14
15	0.0290 652 395	0.0279 243 614	0.0268 242 396	0.0257 637 513	15
16	0.0255 167 470	0.0244 323 792	0.0233 900 180	0.0223 883 932	16
17	0.0224 714 845	0.0214 425 881	0.0204 567 275	0.0195 124 801	17
18	0.0198 428 701	0.0188 681 666	0.0179 373 114	0.0170 487 264	18
19	0.0175 625 041	0.0166 405 294	0.0157 630 049	0.0149 281 952	19
20	0.0155 756 369	0.0147 047 839	0.0138 787 800	0.0130 957 330	20
21	0.0138 379 300	0.0130 164 837	0.0122 400 915	0.0115 067 060	21
22	0.0123 131 011	0.0115 392 673	0.0108 105 088	0.0101 246 265	22
23	0.0109 711 818	0.0102 431 115	0.0095 599 650	0.0089 193 964	23
24	0.0097 872 113	0.0091 030 208	0.0084 634 417	0.0078 659 881	24
25	0.0087 402 421	0.0080 980 307	0.0074 999 698	0.0069 434 409	25
26	0.0078 125 750	0.0072 104 398	0.0066 518 581	0.0061 340 882	26
27	0.0069 891 636	0.0064 252 118	0.0059 040 937	0.0054 229 541	27
28	0.0062 571 454	0.0057 295 054	0.0052 438 691	0.0047 972 788	28
29	0.0056 054 695	0.0051 123 000	0.0046 602 068	0.0042 461 412	29
30	0.0050 245 985	0.0045 640 959	0.0041 436 576	0.0037 601 556	30
31	0.0045 062 669	0.0040 766 723	0.0036 860 570	0.0033 312 264	31
32	0.0040 432 854	0.0036 428 892	0.0032 803 263	0.0029 523 480	32
33	0.0036 293 791	0.0032 565 256	0.0029 203 096	0.0026 174 403	33
34	0.0032 590 547	0.0029 121 454	0.0026 006 383	0.0023 212 131	34
35	0.0029 274 900	0.0026 049 859	0.0023 166 193	0.0020 590 521	35
36	0.0026 304 409	0.0023 308 646	0.0020 641 406	0.0018 269 247	36
37	0.0023 641 641	0.0020 861 006	0.0018 395 924	0.0016 213 002	37
38	0.0021 253 508	0.0018 674 484	0.0016 397 998	0.0014 390 818	38
39	0.0019 110 713	0.0016 720 412	0.0014 619 665	0.0012 775 496	39
40	0.0017 187 267	0.0014 973 431	0.0013 036 256	0.0011 343 115	40
41	0.0015 460 086	0.0013 411 076	0.0011 625 982	0.0010 072 613	41
42	0.0013 908 633	0.0012 013 421	0.0010 369 577	0.0008 945 425	42
43	0.0012 514 619	0.0010 762 773	0.0009 249 987	0.0007 945 171	43
44	0.0011 261 735	0.0009 643 403	0.0008 252 102	0.0007 057 390	44
45	0.0010 135 424	0.0008 641 318	0.0007 362 523	0.0006 269 303	45
46	0.0009 122 683	0.0007 744 059	0.0006 569 363	0.0005 569 610	46
47	0.0008 211 884	0.0006 940 524	0.0005 862 064	0.0004 948 314	47
48	0.0007 392 624	0.0006 220 813	0.0005 231 248	0.0004 396 568	48
49	0.0006 655 589	0.0005 576 093	0.0004 668 576	0.0003 906 534	49
50	0.0005 992 433	0.0004 998 481	0.0004 166 635	0.0003 471 269	50
51	0.0005 395 676	0.0004 480 934	0.0003 718 826	0.0003 084 621	51
52	0.0004 858 607	0.0004 017 160	0.0003 319 279	0.0002 741 133	52
53	0.0004 375 209	0.0003 601 537	0.0002 962 763	0.0002 435 969	53
54	0.0003 940 076	0.0003 229 035	0.0002 644 625	0.0002 164 837	54
55	0.0003 548 359	0.0002 895 157	0.0002 360 715	0.0001 923 930	55
56	0.0003 195 698	0.0002 595 879	0.0002 107 337	0.0001 709 867	56
57	0.0002 878 179	0.0002 327 601	0.0001 881 197	0.0001 519 651	57
58	0.0002 592 282	0.0002 087 099	0.0001 679 358	0.0001 350 619	58
59	0.0002 334 844	0.0001 871 487	0.0001 499 202	0.0001 200 406	59
60	0.0002 103 020	0.0001 678 182	0.0001 338 394	0.0001 066 913	60

Table 3.   SINKING FUND FACTORS
PAYABLE AT END OF EACH PERIOD

YEARS	13% NOMINAL ANNUAL RATE	13½% NOMINAL ANNUAL RATE	14% NOMINAL ANNUAL RATE	14½% NOMINAL ANNUAL RATE	YEARS
1	1.0000 000 000	1.0000 000 000	1.0000 000 000	1.0000 000 000	1
2	0.4694 835 681	0.4683 840 749	0.4672 897 196	0.4662 004 662	2
3	0.2935 219 701	0.2921 221 947	0.2907 314 804	0.2893 497 588	3
4	0.2061 941 974	0.2046 931 901	0.2032 047 833	0.2017 288 719	4
5	0.1543 145 434	0.1527 910 955	0.1512 835 465	0.1497 917 481	5
6	0.1201 532 321	0.1186 458 704	0.1171 574 957	0.1156 879 076	6
7	0.0961 108 038	0.0946 406 583	0.0931 923 773	0.0917 656 994	7
8	0.0783 867 196	0.0769 661 101	0.0755 700 238	0.0741 981 278	8
9	0.0648 689 020	0.0635 051 669	0.0621 683 838	0.0608 581 379	9
10	0.0542 895 558	0.0529 869 780	0.0517 135 408	0.0504 687 376	10
11	0.0458 414 545	0.0446 023 222	0.0433 942 714	0.0422 166 937	11
12	0.0389 860 847	0.0378 113 211	0.0366 693 269	0.0355 593 835	12
13	0.0333 503 411	0.0322 399 012	0.0311 636 635	0.0301 207 919	13
14	0.0286 674 959	0.0276 206 298	0.0266 091 448	0.0256 320 815	14
15	0.0247 417 797	0.0237 572 163	0.0228 089 630	0.0218 959 329	15
16	0.0214 262 445	0.0205 023 244	0.0196 154 000	0.0187 642 550	16
17	0.0186 084 385	0.0177 432 135	0.0169 154 359	0.0161 237 596	17
18	0.0162 008 548	0.0153 921 647	0.0146 211 516	0.0138 863 402	18
19	0.0141 343 943	0.0133 799 284	0.0126 631 593	0.0119 824 868	19
20	0.0123 537 884	0.0116 511 339	0.0109 860 016	0.0103 566 708	20
21	0.0108 143 279	0.0101 610 103	0.0095 448 612	0.0089 640 464	21
22	0.0094 794 811	0.0088 729 970	0.0083 031 654	0.0077 680 465	22
23	0.0083 191 328	0.0077 569 775	0.0072 308 130	0.0067 386 033	23
24	0.0073 082 605	0.0067 879 502	0.0063 028 406	0.0058 508 096	24
25	0.0064 259 276	0.0059 450 182	0.0054 984 079	0.0050 838 993	25
26	0.0056 545 063	0.0052 106 089	0.0048 000 136	0.0044 204 595	26
27	0.0049 790 727	0.0045 698 653	0.0041 928 839	0.0038 458 159	27
28	0.0043 869 291	0.0040 101 668	0.0036 644 905	0.0033 475 475	28
29	0.0038 672 246	0.0035 207 472	0.0032 041 657	0.0029 150 996	29
30	0.0034 106 503	0.0030 923 874	0.0028 027 939	0.0025 394 732	30
31	0.0030 091 921	0.0027 171 673	0.0024 525 613	0.0022 129 724	31
32	0.0026 559 291	0.0023 882 625	0.0021 467 511	0.0019 289 987	32
33	0.0023 448 684	0.0020 997 777	0.0018 795 755	0.0016 818 816	33
34	0.0020 708 076	0.0018 466 081	0.0016 460 366	0.0014 667 377	34
35	0.0018 292 209	0.0016 243 248	0.0014 418 099	0.0012 793 548	35
36	0.0016 161 634	0.0014 290 780	0.0012 631 480	0.0011 160 934	36
37	0.0014 281 904	0.0012 575 162	0.0011 067 982	0.0009 738 048	37
38	0.0012 622 899	0.0011 067 176	0.0009 699 339	0.0008 497 619	38
39	0.0011 158 243	0.0009 741 317	0.0008 500 959	0.0007 415 997	39
40	0.0009 864 810	0.0008 575 299	0.0007 451 425	0.0006 472 661	40
41	0.0008 722 306	0.0007 549 625	0.0006 532 069	0.0005 649 785	41
42	0.0007 712 901	0.0006 647 231	0.0005 726 603	0.0004 931 877	42
43	0.0006 820 921	0.0005 853 163	0.0005 020 814	0.0004 305 461	43
44	0.0006 032 572	0.0005 154 314	0.0004 402 284	0.0003 758 815	44
45	0.0005 335 711	0.0004 539 184	0.0003 860 162	0.0003 281 731	45
46	0.0004 719 639	0.0003 997 682	0.0003 384 961	0.0002 865 319	46
47	0.0004 174 928	0.0003 520 947	0.0002 968 383	0.0002 501 836	47
48	0.0003 693 262	0.0003 101 194	0.0002 603 167	0.0002 184 532	48
49	0.0003 267 306	0.0002 731 583	0.0002 282 958	0.0001 907 524	49
50	0.0002 890 585	0.0002 406 102	0.0002 002 194	0.0001 665 683	50
51	0.0002 557 386	0.0002 119 464	0.0001 756 002	0.0001 454 533	51
52	0.0002 262 661	0.0001 867 021	0.0001 540 115	0.0001 270 173	52
53	0.0002 001 954	0.0001 644 682	0.0001 350 796	0.0001 109 199	53
54	0.0001 771 327	0.0001 448 849	0.0001 184 768	0.0000 968 639	54
55	0.0001 567 300	0.0001 276 356	0.0001 039 162	0.0000 845 901	55
56	0.0001 386 799	0.0001 124 416	0.0000 911 463	0.0000 738 724	56
57	0.0001 227 105	0.0000 990 577	0.0000 799 465	0.0000 645 132	57
58	0.0001 085 816	0.0000 872 679	0.0000 701 236	0.0000 563 402	58
59	0.0000 960 807	0.0000 768 821	0.0000 615 081	0.0000 492 030	59
60	0.0000 850 199	0.0000 677 329	0.0000 539 516	0.0000 429 702	60

Table 3.   SINKING FUND FACTORS
PAYABLE AT END OF EACH PERIOD

YEARS	15% NOMINAL ANNUAL RATE	15½% NOMINAL ANNUAL RATE	16% NOMINAL ANNUAL RATE	16½% NOMINAL ANNUAL RATE	YEARS
1	1.0000 000 000	1.0000 000 000	1.0000 000 000	1.0000 000 000	1
2	0.4651 162 791	0.4640 371 230	0.4629 629 630	0.4618 937 644	2
3	0.2879 769 618	0.2866 130 223	0.2852 578 731	0.2839 114 480	3
4	0.2002 653 516	0.1988 141 185	0.1973 750 695	0.1959 481 019	4
5	0.1483 155 525	0.1468 548 125	0.1454 093 816	0.1439 791 140	5
6	0.1142 369 066	0.1128 042 936	0.1113 898 702	0.1099 934 387	6
7	0.0903 603 636	0.0889 761 095	0.0876 126 771	0.0862 698 077	7
8	0.0728 500 896	0.0715 255 774	0.0702 242 601	0.0689 458 078	8
9	0.0595 740 150	0.0583 156 020	0.0570 824 868	0.0558 742 591	9
10	0.0492 520 625	0.0480 630 117	0.0469 010 831	0.0457 657 770	10
11	0.0410 689 830	0.0399 505 356	0.0388 607 515	0.0377 990 342	11
12	0.0344 807 761	0.0334 327 944	0.0324 147 333	0.0314 258 934	12
13	0.0291 104 565	0.0281 318 343	0.0271 841 100	0.0262 664 771	13
14	0.0246 884 898	0.0237 774 299	0.0228 979 733	0.0220 492 036	14
15	0.0210 170 526	0.0201 712 633	0.0193 575 218	0.0185 748 018	15
16	0.0179 476 914	0.0171 645 308	0.0164 136 162	0.0156 938 131	16
17	0.0153 668 623	0.0146 434 484	0.0139 522 494	0.0132 920 262	17
18	0.0131 862 874	0.0125 195 831	0.0118 848 526	0.0112 807 572	18
19	0.0113 363 504	0.0107 232 318	0.0101 416 556	0.0095 901 910	19
20	0.0097 614 704	0.0091 987 802	0.0086 670 324	0.0081 647 123	20
21	0.0084 167 914	0.0079 013 828	0.0074 161 691	0.0069 595 618	21
22	0.0072 657 713	0.0067 945 424	0.0063 526 353	0.0059 383 976	22
23	0.0062 783 947	0.0058 483 167	0.0054 465 820	0.0050 714 859	23
24	0.0054 298 296	0.0050 379 680	0.0046 733 862	0.0043 343 385	24
25	0.0046 994 023	0.0043 429 337	0.0040 126 153	0.0037 066 717	25
26	0.0040 698 058	0.0037 460 303	0.0034 472 266	0.0031 716 014	26
27	0.0035 264 815	0.0032 328 312	0.0029 629 420	0.0027 150 133	27
28	0.0030 571 309	0.0027 911 756	0.0025 477 527	0.0023 250 650	28
29	0.0026 513 265	0.0024 107 763	0.0021 915 252	0.0019 917 888	29
30	0.0023 001 982	0.0020 829 047	0.0018 856 833	0.0017 067 719	30
31	0.0019 961 796	0.0018 001 344	0.0016 229 508	0.0014 628 970	31
32	0.0017 328 006	0.0015 561 326	0.0013 971 408	0.0012 541 308	32
33	0.0015 045 161	0.0013 454 881	0.0012 029 828	0.0010 753 495	33
34	0.0013 065 655	0.0011 635 693	0.0010 359 798	0.0009 221 956	34
35	0.0011 348 546	0.0010 064 055	0.0008 922 891	0.0007 909 581	35
36	0.0009 858 572	0.0008 705 881	0.0007 686 235	0.0006 784 733	36
37	0.0008 565 329	0.0007 531 882	0.0006 621 677	0.0005 820 416	37
38	0.0007 442 569	0.0006 516 861	0.0005 705 086	0.0004 993 570	38
39	0.0006 467 613	0.0005 639 122	0.0004 915 760	0.0004 284 490	39
40	0.0005 620 850	0.0004 879 974	0.0004 235 929	0.0003 676 322	40
41	0.0004 885 308	0.0004 223 301	0.0003 650 330	0.0003 154 645	41
42	0.0004 246 290	0.0003 655 201	0.0003 145 846	0.0002 707 117	42
43	0.0003 691 063	0.0003 163 675	0.0002 711 201	0.0002 323 166	43
44	0.0003 208 590	0.0002 738 363	0.0002 336 696	0.0001 993 736	44
45	0.0002 789 300	0.0002 370 315	0.0002 013 988	0.0001 711 069	45
46	0.0002 424 890	0.0002 051 800	0.0001 735 895	0.0001 468 513	46
47	0.0002 108 156	0.0001 776 134	0.0001 496 237	0.0001 260 367	47
48	0.0001 832 843	0.0001 537 542	0.0001 289 693	0.0001 081 743	48
49	0.0001 593 523	0.0001 331 028	0.0001 111 681	0.0000 928 449	49
50	0.0001 385 480	0.0001 152 273	0.0000 958 254	0.0000 796 888	50
51	0.0001 204 620	0.0000 997 539	0.0000 826 013	0.0000 683 977	51
52	0.0001 047 386	0.0000 863 596	0.0000 712 029	0.0000 587 071	52
53	0.0000 910 687	0.0000 747 646	0.0000 613 781	0.0000 503 898	53
54	0.0000 791 839	0.0000 647 271	0.0000 529 093	0.0000 432 512	54
55	0.0000 688 509	0.0000 560 376	0.0000 456 094	0.0000 371 241	55
56	0.0000 598 667	0.0000 485 151	0.0000 393 169	0.0000 318 652	56
57	0.0000 520 553	0.0000 420 026	0.0000 338 927	0.0000 273 513	57
58	0.0000 452 634	0.0000 363 646	0.0000 292 170	0.0000 234 770	58
59	0.0000 393 580	0.0000 314 835	0.0000 251 865	0.0000 201 515	59
60	0.0000 342 231	0.0000 272 577	0.0000 217 120	0.0000 172 971	60

Table 3.   SINKING FUND FACTORS
PAYABLE AT END OF EACH PERIOD

YEARS	17% NOMINAL ANNUAL RATE	17½% NOMINAL ANNUAL RATE	18% NOMINAL ANNUAL RATE	18½% NOMINAL ANNUAL RATE	YEARS
1	1.0000 000 000	1.0000 000 000	1.0000 000 000	1.0000 000 000	1
2	0.4608 294 931	0.4597 701 149	0.4587 155 963	0.4576 659 039	2
3	0.2825 736 811	0.2812 445 069	0.2799 238 607	0.2786 116 780	3
4	0.1945 331 137	0.1931 300 037	0.1917 386 709	0.1903 590 154	4
5	0.1425 638 643	0.1411 634 882	0.1397 778 418	0.1384 067 820	5
6	0.1086 148 021	0.1072 537 641	0.1059 101 292	0.1045 837 031	6
7	0.0849 472 428	0.0836 447 254	0.0823 619 994	0.0810 988 095	7
8	0.0676 898 916	0.0664 561 840	0.0652 443 589	0.0640 540 919	8
9	0.0546 905 102	0.0535 308 333	0.0523 948 239	0.0512 820 801	9
10	0.0446 565 967	0.0435 730 482	0.0425 146 413	0.0414 808 893	10
11	0.0367 647 916	0.0357 574 364	0.0347 763 862	0.0338 210 645	11
12	0.0304 655 819	0.0295 331 132	0.0286 278 089	0.0277 489 990	12
13	0.0253 781 386	0.0245 183 074	0.0236 862 073	0.0228 810 735	13
14	0.0212 302 181	0.0204 401 277	0.0196 780 583	0.0189 431 510	14
15	0.0178 220 950	0.0170 984 119	0.0164 027 825	0.0157 342 570	15
16	0.0150 040 103	0.0143 431 211	0.0137 100 839	0.0131 038 628	16
17	0.0126 615 693	0.0120 596 999	0.0114 852 711	0.0109 371 677	17
18	0.0107 059 953	0.0101 593 036	0.0096 394 570	0.0091 452 695	18
19	0.0090 674 523	0.0085 720 996	0.0081 028 390	0.0076 584 229	19
20	0.0076 903 593	0.0072 425 665	0.0068 199 812	0.0064 213 045	20
21	0.0065 300 350	0.0061 261 256	0.0057 464 327	0.0053 896 170	21
22	0.0055 502 493	0.0051 866 820	0.0048 462 577	0.0045 276 075	22
23	0.0047 214 054	0.0043 947 980	0.0040 901 996	0.0038 062 232	23
24	0.0040 191 703	0.0037 263 162	0.0034 542 973	0.0032 017 187	24
25	0.0034 234 282	0.0031 613 074	0.0029 188 261	0.0026 945 919	25
26	0.0029 174 705	0.0026 832 551	0.0024 674 779	0.0022 687 583	26
27	0.0024 873 621	0.0022 784 184	0.0020 867 195	0.0019 109 054	27
28	0.0021 214 404	0.0019 353 267	0.0017 652 846	0.0016 099 822	28
29	0.0018 099 152	0.0016 443 781	0.0014 937 692	0.0013 567 913	29
30	0.0015 445 468	0.0013 975 150	0.0012 643 056	0.0011 436 621	30
31	0.0013 183 850	0.0011 879 615	0.0010 702 987	0.0009 641 852	31
32	0.0011 255 565	0.0010 100 099	0.0009 062 108	0.0008 129 969	32
33	0.0009 610 895	0.0008 588 447	0.0007 673 859	0.0006 856 029	33
34	0.0008 207 698	0.0007 303 978	0.0006 499 044	0.0005 782 333	34
35	0.0007 010 209	0.0006 212 289	0.0005 504 633	0.0004 877 226	35
36	0.0005 988 044	0.0005 284 261	0.0004 662 768	0.0004 114 109	36
37	0.0005 115 368	0.0004 495 222	0.0003 949 937	0.0003 470 617	37
38	0.0004 370 199	0.0003 824 258	0.0003 346 284	0.0002 927 934	38
39	0.0003 733 818	0.0003 253 628	0.0002 835 030	0.0002 470 220	39
40	0.0003 190 279	0.0002 768 279	0.0002 401 991	0.0002 084 139	40
41	0.0002 725 991	0.0002 355 427	0.0002 035 171	0.0001 758 458	41
42	0.0002 329 364	0.0002 004 217	0.0001 724 424	0.0001 483 711	42
43	0.0001 990 513	0.0001 705 426	0.0001 461 163	0.0001 251 920	43
44	0.0001 701 004	0.0001 451 216	0.0001 238 120	0.0001 056 361	44
45	0.0001 453 638	0.0001 234 925	0.0001 049 144	0.0000 891 364	45
46	0.0001 242 272	0.0001 050 889	0.0000 889 026	0.0000 752 149	46
47	0.0001 061 658	0.0000 894 294	0.0000 753 355	0.0000 634 685	47
48	0.0000 907 317	0.0000 761 043	0.0000 638 396	0.0000 535 570	48
49	0.0000 775 425	0.0000 647 654	0.0000 540 984	0.0000 451 938	49
50	0.0000 662 712	0.0000 551 165	0.0000 458 440	0.0000 381 504	50
51	0.0000 566 389	0.0000 469 054	0.0000 388 494	0.0000 321 819	51
52	0.0000 484 070	0.0000 399 179	0.0000 329 221	0.0000 271 570	52
53	0.0000 413 718	0.0000 339 716	0.0000 278 993	0.0000 229 167	53
54	0.0000 353 592	0.0000 289 111	0.0000 236 429	0.0000 193 387	54
55	0.0000 302 206	0.0000 246 046	0.0000 200 360	0.0000 163 193	55
56	0.0000 258 289	0.0000 209 397	0.0000 169 794	0.0000 137 713	56
57	0.0000 220 755	0.0000 178 207	0.0000 143 891	0.0000 116 213	57
58	0.0000 188 676	0.0000 151 663	0.0000 121 940	0.0000 098 069	58
59	0.0000 161 259	0.0000 129 073	0.0000 103 338	0.0000 082 758	59
60	0.0000 137 826	0.0000 109 848	0.0000 087 574	0.0000 069 837	60

211

Table 3.   SINKING FUND FACTORS
PAYABLE AT END OF EACH PERIOD

YEARS	**19%** NOMINAL ANNUAL RATE	**19½%** NOMINAL ANNUAL RATE	**20%** NOMINAL ANNUAL RATE	**20½%** NOMINAL ANNUAL RATE	YEARS
1	1.0000 000 000	1.0000 000 000	1.0000 000 000	1.0000 000 000	1
2	0.4566 210 046	0.4555 808 656	0.4545 454 545	0.4535 147 392	2
3	0.2773 078 950	0.2760 124 482	0.2747 252 747	0.2734 463 122	3
4	0.1889 909 377	0.1876 343 389	0.1862 891 207	0.1849 551 857	4
5	0.1370 501 666	0.1357 078 539	0.1343 797 033	0.1330 655 748	5
6	0.1032 742 921	0.1019 817 036	0.1007 057 459	0.0994 462 284	6
7	0.0798 549 022	0.0786 300 248	0.0774 239 263	0.0762 363 570	7
8	0.0628 850 604	0.0617 369 435	0.0606 094 224	0.0595 021 805	8
9	0.0501 922 023	0.0491 247 940	0.0480 794 617	0.0470 558 149	9
10	0.0404 713 094	0.0394 854 232	0.0385 227 569	0.0375 828 412	10
11	0.0328 909 005	0.0319 853 296	0.0311 037 942	0.0302 457 430	11
12	0.0268 960 219	0.0260 682 250	0.0252 649 649	0.0244 856 079	12
13	0.0221 021 529	0.0213 487 047	0.0206 200 011	0.0199 153 270	13
14	0.0182 345 628	0.0175 514 675	0.0168 930 552	0.0162 585 336	14
15	0.0150 919 063	0.0144 748 227	0.0138 821 198	0.0133 129 335	15
16	0.0125 234 484	0.0119 678 578	0.0114 361 350	0.0109 273 513	16
17	0.0104 143 070	0.0099 156 392	0.0094 401 469	0.0089 868 456	17
18	0.0086 755 939	0.0082 293 223	0.0078 053 857	0.0074 027 537	18
19	0.0072 376 496	0.0068 393 632	0.0064 624 532	0.0061 058 536	19
20	0.0060 452 907	0.0056 907 465	0.0053 565 307	0.0050 415 524	20
21	0.0050 543 994	0.0047 395 606	0.0044 439 388	0.0041 664 291	21
22	0.0042 294 304	0.0039 504 912	0.0036 896 187	0.0034 457 036	22
23	0.0035 415 560	0.0032 949 577	0.0030 652 575	0.0028 513 516	23
24	0.0029 672 666	0.0027 497 051	0.0025 478 730	0.0023 606 809	24
25	0.0024 872 993	0.0022 957 260	0.0021 187 290	0.0019 552 408	25
26	0.0020 858 078	0.0019 174 260	0.0017 624 956	0.0016 199 779	26
27	0.0017 497 128	0.0016 019 702	0.0014 665 923	0.0013 425 751	27
28	0.0014 681 881	0.0013 387 661	0.0012 206 684	0.0011 129 302	28
29	0.0012 322 512	0.0011 190 527	0.0010 161 900	0.0009 227 413	29
30	0.0010 344 341	0.0009 355 697	0.0008 461 085	0.0007 651 745	30
31	0.0008 685 173	0.0007 822 910	0.0007 045 936	0.0006 345 966	31
32	0.0007 293 142	0.0006 542 086	0.0005 868 168	0.0005 263 590	32
33	0.0006 124 937	0.0005 471 553	0.0004 887 750	0.0004 366 217	33
34	0.0005 144 358	0.0004 576 610	0.0004 071 466	0.0003 622 104	34
35	0.0004 321 122	0.0003 828 333	0.0003 391 738	0.0003 004 992	35
36	0.0003 629 877	0.0003 202 600	0.0002 825 649	0.0002 493 148	36
37	0.0003 049 387	0.0002 679 282	0.0002 354 154	0.0002 068 574	37
38	0.0002 561 853	0.0002 241 574	0.0001 961 410	0.0001 716 365	38
39	0.0002 152 355	0.0001 875 443	0.0001 634 241	0.0001 424 166	39
40	0.0001 808 374	0.0001 569 162	0.0001 361 682	0.0001 181 741	40
41	0.0001 519 411	0.0001 312 934	0.0001 134 606	0.0000 980 602	41
42	0.0001 276 653	0.0001 098 569	0.0000 945 416	0.0000 813 711	42
43	0.0001 072 703	0.0000 919 220	0.0000 787 785	0.0000 675 233	43
44	0.0000 901 350	0.0000 769 162	0.0000 656 444	0.0000 560 328	44
45	0.0000 757 379	0.0000 643 609	0.0000 547 007	0.0000 464 981	45
46	0.0000 636 413	0.0000 538 556	0.0000 455 818	0.0000 385 861	46
47	0.0000 534 772	0.0000 450 654	0.0000 379 834	0.0000 320 207	47
48	0.0000 449 368	0.0000 377 102	0.0000 316 518	0.0000 265 725	48
49	0.0000 377 606	0.0000 315 557	0.0000 263 758	0.0000 220 514	49
50	0.0000 317 306	0.0000 264 057	0.0000 219 794	0.0000 182 995	50
51	0.0000 266 636	0.0000 220 964	0.0000 183 158	0.0000 151 861	51
52	0.0000 224 059	0.0000 184 903	0.0000 152 629	0.0000 126 024	52
53	0.0000 188 282	0.0000 154 728	0.0000 127 190	0.0000 104 583	53
54	0.0000 158 217	0.0000 129 478	0.0000 105 990	0.0000 086 790	54
55	0.0000 132 954	0.0000 108 349	0.0000 088 324	0.0000 072 025	55
56	0.0000 111 725	0.0000 090 668	0.0000 073 603	0.0000 059 771	56
57	0.0000 093 885	0.0000 075 872	0.0000 061 336	0.0000 049 602	57
58	0.0000 078 895	0.0000 063 491	0.0000 051 113	0.0000 041 164	58
59	0.0000 066 298	0.0000 053 130	0.0000 042 594	0.0000 034 161	59
60	0.0000 055 712	0.0000 044 460	0.0000 035 495	0.0000 028 349	60

Table 3. SINKING FUND FACTORS
PAYABLE AT END OF EACH PERIOD

YEARS	21% NOMINAL ANNUAL RATE	21½% NOMINAL ANNUAL RATE	22% NOMINAL ANNUAL RATE	22½% NOMINAL ANNUAL RATE	YEARS
1	1.0000 000 000	1.0000 000 000	1.0000 000 000	1.0000 000 000	1
2	0.4524 886 878	0.4514 672 686	0.4504 504 505	0.4494 382 022	2
3	0.2721 754 988	0.2709 127 729	0.2696 580 736	0.2684 113 404	3
4	0.1836 324 369	0.1823 207 780	0.1810 201 135	0.1797 303 483	4
5	0.1317 653 293	0.1304 788 284	0.1292 059 348	0.1279 465 120	5
6	0.0982 029 617	0.0969 757 574	0.0957 297 542	0.0945 687 881	6
7	0.0750 670 688	0.0739 158 150	0.0727 823 508	0.0716 664 329	7
8	0.0584 149 035	0.0573 472 791	0.0562 989 979	0.0552 697 526	8
9	0.0460 534 667	0.0450 720 334	0.0441 111 354	0.0431 703 963	9
10	0.0366 652 120	0.0357 694 102	0.0348 949 820	0.0340 414 793	10
11	0.0294 106 322	0.0285 979 253	0.0278 070 935	0.0270 376 154	11
12	0.0237 295 303	0.0229 961 186	0.0222 847 695	0.0215 948 907	12
13	0.0192 339 810	0.0185 752 752	0.0179 385 355	0.0173 231 022	13
14	0.0156 471 276	0.0150 580 800	0.0144 906 512	0.0139 441 198	14
15	0.0127 664 213	0.0122 417 634	0.0117 381 620	0.0112 548 416	15
16	0.0104 406 051	0.0099 750 219	0.0095 297 542	0.0091 039 818	16
17	0.0085 547 835	0.0081 430 410	0.0077 507 309	0.0073 769 974	17
18	0.0070 204 340	0.0066 574 724	0.0063 129 516	0.0059 859 908	18
19	0.0057 685 424	0.0054 495 409	0.0051 479 123	0.0048 627 611	19
20	0.0047 447 703	0.0044 651 915	0.0042 018 701	0.0039 539 055	20
21	0.0039 059 812	0.0036 615 982	0.0034 323 343	0.0032 172 935	21
22	0.0032 176 967	0.0030 046 062	0.0028 054 958	0.0026 194 824	22
23	0.0026 522 006	0.0024 668 266	0.0022 943 108	0.0021 337 902	23
24	0.0021 871 074	0.0020 261 962	0.0018 770 526	0.0017 388 407	24
25	0.0018 042 655	0.0016 648 747	0.0015 362 042	0.0014 174 498	25
26	0.0014 889 084	0.0013 683 922	0.0012 576 002	0.0011 557 645	26
27	0.0012 289 905	0.0011 249 817	0.0010 297 583	0.0009 425 919	27
28	0.0010 146 640	0.0009 250 544	0.0008 433 524	0.0007 688 712	28
29	0.0008 378 627	0.0007 607 824	0.0006 907 949	0.0006 272 562	29
30	0.0006 919 694	0.0006 257 665	0.0005 659 049	0.0005 117 839	30
31	0.0005 715 487	0.0005 147 690	0.0004 636 414	0.0004 176 083	31
32	0.0004 721 313	0.0004 234 988	0.0003 798 896	0.0003 407 885	32
33	0.0003 900 389	0.0003 484 372	0.0003 112 880	0.0002 781 173	33
34	0.0003 222 423	0.0002 866 974	0.0002 550 890	0.0002 269 830	34
35	0.0002 662 451	0.0002 359 093	0.0002 090 456	0.0001 852 579	35
36	0.0002 199 889	0.0001 941 263	0.0001 713 195	0.0001 512 081	36
37	0.0001 817 759	0.0001 597 492	0.0001 404 061	0.0001 234 200	37
38	0.0001 502 055	0.0001 314 636	0.0001 150 737	0.0001 007 408	38
39	0.0001 241 213	0.0001 081 888	0.0000 943 138	0.0000 822 307	39
40	0.0001 025 691	0.0000 890 363	0.0000 773 005	0.0000 671 226	40
41	0.0000 847 607	0.0000 732 755	0.0000 633 570	0.0000 547 909	41
42	0.0000 700 452	0.0000 603 055	0.0000 519 293	0.0000 447 253	42
43	0.0000 578 853	0.0000 496 317	0.0000 425 632	0.0000 365 091	43
44	0.0000 478 368	0.0000 408 474	0.0000 348 866	0.0000 298 025	44
45	0.0000 395 330	0.0000 336 182	0.0000 285 948	0.0000 243 279	45
46	0.0000 326 708	0.0000 276 685	0.0000 234 378	0.0000 198 592	46
47	0.0000 269 999	0.0000 227 719	0.0000 192 109	0.0000 162 113	47
48	0.0000 223 135	0.0000 187 427	0.0000 157 464	0.0000 132 335	48
49	0.0000 184 406	0.0000 154 252	0.0000 129 067	0.0000 108 028	49
50	0.0000 152 399	0.0000 126 955	0.0000 105 792	0.0000 088 185	50
51	0.0000 125 948	0.0000 104 489	0.0000 086 714	0.0000 071 987	51
52	0.0000 104 088	0.0000 085 998	0.0000 071 076	0.0000 058 765	52
53	0.0000 086 023	0.0000 070 780	0.0000 058 259	0.0000 047 971	53
54	0.0000 071 093	0.0000 058 255	0.0000 047 753	0.0000 039 160	54
55	0.0000 058 754	0.0000 047 946	0.0000 039 142	0.0000 031 967	55
56	0.0000 048 557	0.0000 039 462	0.0000 032 083	0.0000 026 096	56
57	0.0000 040 129	0.0000 032 479	0.0000 026 298	0.0000 021 302	57
58	0.0000 033 165	0.0000 026 731	0.0000 021 555	0.0000 017 390	58
59	0.0000 027 409	0.0000 022 001	0.0000 017 668	0.0000 014 196	59
60	0.0000 022 652	0.0000 018 108	0.0000 014 482	0.0000 011 588	60

Table 3.   SINKING FUND FACTORS
PAYABLE AT END OF EACH PERIOD

	23% NOMINAL ANNUAL RATE	**24%** NOMINAL ANNUAL RATE	**25%** NOMINAL ANNUAL RATE	**26%** NOMINAL ANNUAL RATE	
YEARS					YEARS
1	1.0000 000 000	1.0000 000 000	1.0000 000 000	1.0000 000 000	1
2	0.4484 304 933	0.4464 285 714	0.4444 444 444	0.4424 778 761	2
3	0.2671 725 133	0.2647 183 397	0.2622 950 820	0.2599 022 767	3
4	0.1784 513 881	0.1759 255 089	0.1734 417 344	0.1709 993 338	4
5	0.1267 004 241	0.1242 477 149	0.1218 467 396	0.1194 964 454	5
6	0.0933 886 522	0.0910 741 602	0.0888 194 987	0.0866 232 355	6
7	0.0705 678 200	0.0684 215 522	0.0663 416 530	0.0643 262 593	7
8	0.0542 592 389	0.0522 932 018	0.0503 985 063	0.0485 728 187	8
9	0.0422 494 441	0.0404 654 313	0.0387 562 013	0.0371 189 268	9
10	0.0332 084 594	0.0316 021 271	0.0300 725 624	0.0286 164 407	10
11	0.0262 889 780	0.0248 522 131	0.0234 928 576	0.0222 071 051	11
12	0.0209 259 004	0.0196 483 138	0.0184 475 770	0.0173 194 369	12
13	0.0167 283 293	0.0155 982 535	0.0145 434 288	0.0135 592 056	13
14	0.0134 177 823	0.0124 229 653	0.0115 009 326	0.0106 467 022	14
15	0.0107 910 491	0.0099 191 452	0.0091 168 642	0.0083 789 634	15
16	0.0086 969 108	0.0079 358 295	0.0072 406 815	0.0066 060 410	16
17	0.0070 210 160	0.0063 591 647	0.0057 591 848	0.0052 155 451	17
18	0.0056 757 451	0.0051 021 928	0.0045 862 176	0.0041 222 582	18
19	0.0045 932 318	0.0040 978 105	0.0036 555 619	0.0032 609 648	19
20	0.0037 204 414	0.0032 938 009	0.0029 159 221	0.0025 813 865	20
21	0.0030 156 276	0.0026 492 538	0.0023 273 086	0.0020 445 308	21
22	0.0024 457 335	0.0021 319 401	0.0018 583 869	0.0016 200 148	22
23	0.0019 844 553	0.0017 163 556	0.0014 845 025	0.0012 840 750	23
24	0.0016 107 795	0.0013 822 465	0.0011 861 933	0.0010 180 696	24
25	0.0013 078 641	0.0011 134 721	0.0009 480 549	0.0008 073 395	25
26	0.0010 621 747	0.0008 971 558	0.0007 578 692	0.0006 403 353	26
27	0.0008 628 116	0.0007 229 896	0.0006 059 280	0.0005 079 445	27
28	0.0007 009 811	0.0005 827 164	0.0004 845 075	0.0004 029 681	28
29	0.0005 695 787	0.0004 697 118	0.0003 874 558	0.0003 197 137	29
30	0.0004 628 578	0.0003 786 564	0.0003 098 686	0.0002 536 767	30
31	0.0003 761 656	0.0003 052 749	0.0002 478 335	0.0002 012 902	31
32	0.0003 057 322	0.0002 461 288	0.0001 982 275	0.0001 597 286	32
33	0.0002 485 010	0.0001 984 516	0.0001 585 568	0.0001 267 526	33
34	0.0002 019 925	0.0001 600 160	0.0001 268 294	0.0001 005 872	34
35	0.0001 641 946	0.0001 290 285	0.0001 014 532	0.0000 798 248	35
36	0.0001 334 737	0.0001 040 444	0.0000 811 560	0.0000 633 490	36
37	0.0001 085 034	0.0000 838 998	0.0000 649 206	0.0000 502 744	37
38	0.0000 882 064	0.0000 676 565	0.0000 519 338	0.0000 398 987	38
39	0.0000 717 074	0.0000 545 587	0.0000 415 453	0.0000 316 647	39
40	0.0000 582 953	0.0000 439 970	0.0000 332 351	0.0000 251 301	40
41	0.0000 473 923	0.0000 354 802	0.0000 265 874	0.0000 199 441	41
42	0.0000 385 288	0.0000 286 123	0.0000 212 695	0.0000 158 284	42
43	0.0000 313 233	0.0000 230 739	0.0000 170 153	0.0000 125 621	43
44	0.0000 254 654	0.0000 186 076	0.0000 136 120	0.0000 099 698	44
45	0.0000 207 032	0.0000 150 059	0.0000 108 895	0.0000 079 125	45
46	0.0000 168 316	0.0000 121 014	0.0000 087 115	0.0000 062 797	46
47	0.0000 136 840	0.0000 097 591	0.0000 069 692	0.0000 049 839	47
48	0.0000 111 251	0.0000 078 702	0.0000 055 753	0.0000 039 554	48
49	0.0000 090 447	0.0000 063 469	0.0000 044 602	0.0000 031 392	49
50	0.0000 073 534	0.0000 051 184	0.0000 035 682	0.0000 024 914	50
51	0.0000 059 783	0.0000 041 277	0.0000 028 545	0.0000 019 773	51
52	0.0000 048 604	0.0000 033 288	0.0000 022 836	0.0000 015 693	52
53	0.0000 039 515	0.0000 026 845	0.0000 018 269	0.0000 012 455	53
54	0.0000 032 126	0.0000 021 649	0.0000 014 615	0.0000 009 885	54
55	0.0000 026 119	0.0000 017 459	0.0000 011 692	0.0000 007 845	55
56	0.0000 021 235	0.0000 014 080	0.0000 009 354	0.0000 006 226	56
57	0.0000 017 264	0.0000 011 355	0.0000 007 483	0.0000 004 941	57
58	0.0000 014 036	0.0000 009 157	0.0000 005 986	0.0000 003 922	58
59	0.0000 011 411	0.0000 007 385	0.0000 004 789	0.0000 003 113	59
60	0.0000 009 277	0.0000 005 955	0.0000 003 831	0.0000 002 470	60

Table 3.   SINKING FUND FACTORS
PAYABLE AT END OF EACH PERIOD

YEARS	**27%** NOMINAL ANNUAL RATE	**28%** NOMINAL ANNUAL RATE	**29%** NOMINAL ANNUAL RATE	**30%** NOMINAL ANNUAL RATE	YEARS
1	1.0000 000 000	1.0000 000 000	1.0000 000 000	1.0000 000 000	1
2	0.4405 286 344	0.4385 964 912	0.4366 812 227	0.4347 826 087	2
3	0.2575 394 679	0.2552 062 066	0.2529 020 510	0.2506 265 664	3
4	0.1685 975 867	0.1662 357 835	0.1639 132 250	0.1616 292 226	4
5	0.1171 957 942	0.1149 437 633	0.1127 393 452	0.1105 815 484	5
6	0.0844 839 602	0.0824 002 847	0.0803 708 441	0.0783 942 967	6
7	0.0623 735 405	0.0604 816 996	0.0586 489 741	0.0568 736 368	7
8	0.0468 138 541	0.0451 193 773	0.0434 872 047	0.0419 152 051	8
9	0.0355 508 517	0.0340 492 925	0.0326 116 401	0.0312 353 605	9
10	0.0272 305 377	0.0259 117 316	0.0246 570 037	0.0234 634 396	10
11	0.0209 912 864	0.0198 418 706	0.0187 554 652	0.0177 288 158	11
12	0.0162 598 204	0.0152 648 341	0.0143 307 636	0.0134 540 701	12
13	0.0126 411 632	0.0117 851 066	0.0109 870 625	0.0102 432 741	13
14	0.0098 555 727	0.0091 231 170	0.0084 451 743	0.0078 178 414	14
15	0.0077 005 351	0.0070 769 943	0.0065 040 669	0.0059 777 755	15
16	0.0060 268 700	0.0054 985 011	0.0050 166 190	0.0045 772 413	16
17	0.0047 231 529	0.0042 773 299	0.0038 737 873	0.0035 086 013	17
18	0.0037 052 382	0.0033 305 344	0.0029 939 453	0.0026 916 595	18
19	0.0029 090 233	0.0025 952 273	0.0023 155 138	0.0020 662 291	19
20	0.0022 853 348	0.0020 234 188	0.0017 917 558	0.0015 868 848	20
21	0.0017 962 439	0.0015 783 010	0.0013 870 314	0.0012 191 924	21
22	0.0014 123 677	0.0012 315 291	0.0010 740 633	0.0009 369 616	22
23	0.0011 108 651	0.0009 612 073	0.0008 319 146	0.0007 202 206	23
24	0.0008 739 325	0.0007 503 797	0.0006 444 794	0.0005 537 091	24
25	0.0006 876 627	0.0005 858 907	0.0004 993 470	0.0004 257 487	25
26	0.0005 411 736	0.0004 575 177	0.0003 869 409	0.0003 273 918	26
27	0.0004 259 395	0.0003 573 080	0.0002 998 642	0.0002 517 764	27
28	0.0003 352 730	0.0002 790 689	0.0002 323 989	0.0001 936 367	28
29	0.0002 639 248	0.0002 179 751	0.0001 801 217	0.0001 489 291	29
30	0.0002 077 716	0.0001 702 640	0.0001 396 097	0.0001 145 477	30
31	0.0001 635 729	0.0001 330 011	0.0001 082 129	0.0000 881 059	31
32	0.0001 287 810	0.0001 038 963	0.0000 838 789	0.0000 677 692	32
33	0.0001 013 921	0.0000 811 624	0.0000 650 182	0.0000 521 274	33
34	0.0000 798 299	0.0000 634 041	0.0000 503 992	0.0000 400 964	34
35	0.0000 628 542	0.0000 495 320	0.0000 390 676	0.0000 308 424	35
36	0.0000 494 891	0.0000 386 954	0.0000 302 840	0.0000 237 244	36
37	0.0000 389 663	0.0000 302 299	0.0000 234 754	0.0000 182 492	37
38	0.0000 306 812	0.0000 236 165	0.0000 181 977	0.0000 140 376	38
39	0.0000 241 578	0.0000 184 501	0.0000 141 065	0.0000 107 981	39
40	0.0000 190 215	0.0000 144 139	0.0000 109 352	0.0000 083 061	40
41	0.0000 149 774	0.0000 112 607	0.0000 084 768	0.0000 063 893	41
42	0.0000 117 931	0.0000 087 974	0.0000 065 711	0.0000 049 148	42
43	0.0000 092 858	0.0000 068 729	0.0000 050 939	0.0000 037 806	43
44	0.0000 073 116	0.0000 053 694	0.0000 039 487	0.0000 029 082	44
45	0.0000 057 571	0.0000 041 948	0.0000 030 610	0.0000 022 370	45
46	0.0000 045 331	0.0000 032 772	0.0000 023 729	0.0000 017 208	46
47	0.0000 035 694	0.0000 025 603	0.0000 018 394	0.0000 013 237	47
48	0.0000 028 105	0.0000 020 002	0.0000 014 259	0.0000 010 182	48
49	0.0000 022 130	0.0000 015 627	0.0000 011 054	0.0000 007 832	49
50	0.0000 017 425	0.0000 012 208	0.0000 008 569	0.0000 006 025	50
51	0.0000 013 721	0.0000 009 538	0.0000 006 642	0.0000 004 635	51
52	0.0000 010 804	0.0000 007 451	0.0000 005 149	0.0000 003 565	52
53	0.0000 008 507	0.0000 005 821	0.0000 003 992	0.0000 002 742	53
54	0.0000 006 698	0.0000 004 548	0.0000 003 094	0.0000 002 110	54
55	0.0000 005 274	0.0000 003 553	0.0000 002 399	0.0000 001 623	55
56	0.0000 004 153	0.0000 002 776	0.0000 001 859	0.0000 001 248	56
57	0.0000 003 270	0.0000 002 169	0.0000 001 441	0.0000 000 960	57
58	0.0000 002 575	0.0000 001 694	0.0000 001 117	0.0000 000 739	58
59	0.0000 002 027	0.0000 001 324	0.0000 000 866	0.0000 000 568	59
60	0.0000 001 596	0.0000 001 034	0.0000 000 671	0.0000 000 437	60

Table 4.   PRESENT WORTH OF ONE DOLLAR
             PAYABLE AT END OF EACH PERIOD

	5% NOMINAL ANNUAL RATE	**5½%** NOMINAL ANNUAL RATE	**6%** NOMINAL ANNUAL RATE	**6½%** NOMINAL ANNUAL RATE	
YEARS					**YEARS**
1	0.9523 809 524	0.9478 672 986	0.9433 962 264	0.9389 671 362	1
2	0.9070 294 785	0.8984 524 157	0.8899 964 400	0.8816 592 828	2
3	0.8638 375 985	0.8516 136 642	0.8396 192 830	0.8278 490 918	3
4	0.8227 024 748	0.8072 167 433	0.7920 936 632	0.7773 230 909	4
5	0.7835 261 665	0.7651 343 538	0.7472 581 729	0.7298 808 365	5
6	0.7462 153 966	0.7252 458 330	0.7049 605 404	0.6853 341 188	6
7	0.7106 813 301	0.6874 368 086	0.6650 571 136	0.6435 062 148	7
8	0.6768 393 620	0.6515 988 707	0.6274 123 713	0.6042 311 876	8
9	0.6446 089 162	0.6176 292 613	0.5918 984 635	0.5673 532 278	9
10	0.6139 132 535	0.5854 305 794	0.5583 947 769	0.5327 260 355	10
11	0.5846 792 891	0.5549 105 018	0.5267 875 254	0.5002 122 399	11
12	0.5568 374 182	0.5259 815 183	0.4969 693 636	0.4696 828 544	12
13	0.5303 213 506	0.4985 606 809	0.4688 390 222	0.4410 167 647	13
14	0.5050 679 530	0.4725 693 658	0.4423 009 644	0.4141 002 485	14
15	0.4810 170 981	0.4479 330 481	0.4172 650 607	0.3888 265 244	15
16	0.4581 115 220	0.4245 810 883	0.3936 462 837	0.3650 953 281	16
17	0.4362 966 876	0.4024 465 292	0.3713 644 186	0.3428 125 147	17
18	0.4155 206 549	0.3814 659 044	0.3503 437 911	0.3218 896 851	18
19	0.3957 339 570	0.3615 790 563	0.3305 130 105	0.3022 438 358	19
20	0.3768 894 829	0.3427 289 633	0.3118 047 269	0.2837 970 289	20
21	0.3589 423 646	0.3248 615 766	0.2941 554 027	0.2664 760 835	21
22	0.3418 498 711	0.3079 256 650	0.2775 050 969	0.2502 122 850	22
23	0.3255 713 058	0.2918 726 683	0.2617 972 612	0.2349 411 126	23
24	0.3100 679 103	0.2766 565 576	0.2469 785 483	0.2206 019 837	24
25	0.2953 027 717	0.2622 337 039	0.2329 986 305	0.2071 380 129	25
26	0.2812 407 350	0.2485 627 525	0.2198 100 288	0.1944 957 867	26
27	0.2678 483 190	0.2356 045 047	0.2073 679 517	0.1826 251 519	27
28	0.2550 936 371	0.2233 218 055	0.1956 301 431	0.1714 790 158	28
29	0.2429 463 211	0.2116 794 364	0.1845 567 388	0.1610 131 604	29
30	0.2313 774 487	0.2006 440 156	0.1741 101 309	0.1511 860 661	30
31	0.2203 594 749	0.1901 839 010	0.1642 548 405	0.1419 587 475	31
32	0.2098 661 666	0.1802 691 005	0.1549 573 967	0.1332 945 986	32
33	0.1998 725 396	0.1708 711 853	0.1461 862 233	0.1251 592 475	33
34	0.1903 547 996	0.1619 632 088	0.1379 115 314	0.1175 204 202	34
35	0.1812 902 854	0.1535 196 292	0.1301 052 183	0.1103 478 124	35
36	0.1726 574 146	0.1455 162 362	0.1227 407 720	0.1036 129 694	36
37	0.1644 356 330	0.1379 300 817	0.1157 931 811	0.0972 891 731	37
38	0.1566 053 647	0.1307 394 140	0.1092 388 501	0.0913 513 363	38
39	0.1491 479 664	0.1239 236 151	0.1030 555 190	0.0857 759 026	39
40	0.1420 456 823	0.1174 631 423	0.0972 221 877	0.0805 407 536	40
41	0.1352 816 022	0.1113 394 714	0.0917 190 450	0.0756 251 208	41
42	0.1288 396 211	0.1055 350 440	0.0865 274 010	0.0710 095 031	42
43	0.1227 044 011	0.1000 332 170	0.0816 296 235	0.0666 755 897	43
44	0.1168 613 344	0.0948 182 152	0.0770 090 788	0.0626 061 876	44
45	0.1112 965 089	0.0898 750 855	0.0726 500 743	0.0587 851 526	45
46	0.1059 966 752	0.0851 896 545	0.0685 378 060	0.0551 973 264	46
47	0.1009 492 144	0.0807 484 877	0.0646 583 075	0.0518 284 755	47
48	0.0961 421 090	0.0765 388 509	0.0609 984 033	0.0486 652 352	48
49	0.0915 639 133	0.0725 486 738	0.0575 456 635	0.0456 950 565	49
50	0.0872 037 270	0.0687 665 155	0.0542 883 618	0.0429 061 564	50
51	0.0830 511 685	0.0651 815 312	0.0512 154 357	0.0402 874 708	51
52	0.0790 963 510	0.0617 834 419	0.0483 164 488	0.0378 286 111	52
53	0.0753 298 581	0.0585 625 042	0.0455 815 554	0.0355 198 226	53
54	0.0717 427 220	0.0555 094 827	0.0430 014 674	0.0333 519 461	54
55	0.0683 264 019	0.0526 156 234	0.0405 674 221	0.0313 163 813	55
56	0.0650 727 637	0.0498 726 288	0.0382 711 529	0.0294 050 529	56
57	0.0619 740 607	0.0472 726 339	0.0361 048 612	0.0276 103 783	57
58	0.0590 229 149	0.0448 081 838	0.0340 611 898	0.0259 252 378	58
59	0.0562 122 999	0.0424 722 121	0.0321 331 979	0.0243 429 463	59
60	0.0535 355 237	0.0402 580 210	0.0303 143 377	0.0228 572 266	60

Table 4.   PRESENT WORTH OF ONE DOLLAR
            PAYABLE AT END OF EACH PERIOD

	7% NOMINAL ANNUAL RATE	7½% NOMINAL ANNUAL RATE	8% NOMINAL ANNUAL RATE	8½% NOMINAL ANNUAL RATE	
YEARS					YEARS
1	0.9345 794 393	0.9302 325 581	0.9259 259 259	0.9216 589 862	1
2	0.8734 387 283	0.8653 326 122	0.8573 388 203	0.8494 552 868	2
3	0.8162 978 769	0.8049 605 695	0.7938 322 410	0.7829 080 984	3
4	0.7628 952 120	0.7488 005 298	0.7350 298 528	0.7215 742 843	4
5	0.7129 861 795	0.6965 586 324	0.6805 831 970	0.6650 454 233	5
6	0.6663 422 238	0.6479 615 185	0.6301 696 269	0.6129 450 906	6
7	0.6227 497 419	0.6027 549 009	0.5834 903 953	0.5649 263 508	7
8	0.5820 091 046	0.5607 022 334	0.5402 688 845	0.5206 694 477	8
9	0.5439 337 426	0.5215 834 729	0.5002 489 671	0.4798 796 753	9
10	0.5083 492 921	0.4851 939 283	0.4631 934 881	0.4422 854 150	10
11	0.4750 927 964	0.4513 431 891	0.4288 828 593	0.4076 363 272	11
12	0.4440 119 592	0.4198 541 294	0.3971 137 586	0.3757 016 841	12
13	0.4149 644 479	0.3905 619 808	0.3676 979 247	0.3462 688 333	13
14	0.3878 172 410	0.3633 134 706	0.3404 610 414	0.3191 417 818	14
15	0.3624 460 196	0.3379 660 191	0.3152 417 050	0.2941 398 911	15
16	0.3387 345 978	0.3143 869 945	0.2918 904 676	0.2710 966 738	16
17	0.3165 743 905	0.2924 530 182	0.2702 689 514	0.2498 586 855	17
18	0.2958 639 163	0.2720 493 192	0.2502 490 291	0.2302 845 028	18
19	0.2765 083 330	0.2530 691 342	0.2317 120 640	0.2122 437 814	19
20	0.2584 190 028	0.2354 131 481	0.2145 482 074	0.1956 163 884	20
21	0.2415 130 867	0.2189 889 749	0.1986 557 476	0.1802 916 022	21
22	0.2257 131 652	0.2037 106 744	0.1839 405 070	0.1661 673 753	22
23	0.2109 468 833	0.1894 983 017	0.1703 152 843	0.1531 496 546	23
24	0.1971 466 199	0.1762 774 900	0.1576 993 373	0.1411 517 554	24
25	0.1842 491 775	0.1639 790 605	0.1460 179 049	0.1300 937 838	25
26	0.1721 954 930	0.1525 386 609	0.1352 017 638	0.1199 021 049	26
27	0.1609 303 673	0.1418 964 287	0.1251 868 183	0.1105 088 524	27
28	0.1504 022 124	0.1319 966 779	0.1159 137 207	0.1018 514 769	28
29	0.1405 628 154	0.1227 876 073	0.1073 275 192	0.0938 723 289	29
30	0.1313 671 172	0.1142 210 301	0.0993 773 325	0.0865 182 755	30
31	0.1227 730 067	0.1062 521 210	0.0920 160 487	0.0797 403 461	31
32	0.1147 411 277	0.0988 391 823	0.0852 000 451	0.0734 934 065	32
33	0.1072 346 988	0.0919 434 254	0.0788 889 306	0.0677 358 586	33
34	0.1002 193 447	0.0855 287 678	0.0730 453 061	0.0624 293 627	34
35	0.0936 629 390	0.0795 616 445	0.0676 345 427	0.0575 385 832	35
36	0.0875 354 570	0.0740 108 321	0.0626 245 766	0.0530 309 522	36
37	0.0818 088 383	0.0688 472 857	0.0579 857 190	0.0488 764 537	37
38	0.0764 568 582	0.0640 439 867	0.0536 904 806	0.0450 474 227	38
39	0.0714 550 077	0.0595 758 016	0.0497 134 080	0.0415 183 620	39
40	0.0667 803 810	0.0554 193 503	0.0460 309 333	0.0382 657 714	40
41	0.0624 115 710	0.0515 528 840	0.0426 212 345	0.0352 679 921	41
42	0.0583 285 711	0.0479 561 711	0.0394 641 061	0.0325 050 618	42
43	0.0545 126 832	0.0446 103 918	0.0365 408 389	0.0299 585 823	43
44	0.0509 464 329	0.0414 980 388	0.0338 341 101	0.0276 115 966	44
45	0.0476 134 887	0.0386 028 268	0.0313 278 797	0.0254 484 761	45
46	0.0444 985 876	0.0359 096 064	0.0290 072 961	0.0234 548 167	46
47	0.0415 874 650	0.0334 042 850	0.0268 586 075	0.0216 173 426	47
48	0.0388 667 898	0.0310 737 535	0.0248 690 810	0.0199 238 181	48
49	0.0363 241 026	0.0289 058 172	0.0230 269 268	0.0183 629 660	49
50	0.0339 477 594	0.0268 891 323	0.0213 212 286	0.0169 243 926	50
51	0.0317 268 780	0.0250 131 463	0.0197 418 783	0.0155 985 185	51
52	0.0296 512 878	0.0232 680 431	0.0182 795 169	0.0143 765 148	52
53	0.0277 114 839	0.0216 446 912	0.0169 254 786	0.0132 502 440	53
54	0.0258 985 831	0.0201 345 965	0.0156 717 395	0.0122 122 065	54
55	0.0242 042 833	0.0187 298 572	0.0145 108 699	0.0112 554 898	55
56	0.0226 208 255	0.0174 231 230	0.0134 359 906	0.0103 737 233	56
57	0.0211 409 584	0.0162 075 563	0.0124 407 321	0.0095 610 353	57
58	0.0197 579 051	0.0150 767 965	0.0115 191 964	0.0088 120 141	58
59	0.0184 653 318	0.0140 249 270	0.0106 659 226	0.0081 216 720	59
60	0.0172 573 195	0.0130 464 437	0.0098 758 542	0.0074 854 120	60

Table 4. PRESENT WORTH OF ONE DOLLAR
PAYABLE AT END OF EACH PERIOD

YEARS	**9%** NOMINAL ANNUAL RATE	**9½%** NOMINAL ANNUAL RATE	**10%** NOMINAL ANNUAL RATE	**10½%** NOMINAL ANNUAL RATE	YEARS
1	0.9174 311 927	0.9132 420 091	0.9090 909 091	0.9049 773 756	1
2	0.8416 799 933	0.8340 109 672	0.8264 462 810	0.8189 840 503	2
3	0.7721 834 801	0.7616 538 514	0.7513 148 009	0.7411 620 365	3
4	0.7084 252 111	0.6955 742 935	0.6830 134 554	0.6707 348 746	4
5	0.6499 313 863	0.6352 276 653	0.6209 213 231	0.6069 998 865	5
6	0.5962 673 269	0.5801 165 893	0.5644 739 301	0.5493 211 643	6
7	0.5470 342 448	0.5297 868 395	0.5131 581 182	0.4971 232 256	7
8	0.5018 662 797	0.4838 235 978	0.4665 073 802	0.4498 852 720	8
9	0.4604 277 795	0.4418 480 345	0.4240 976 184	0.4071 359 928	9
10	0.4224 108 069	0.4035 141 867	0.3855 432 894	0.3684 488 623	10
11	0.3875 328 504	0.3685 061 066	0.3504 938 995	0.3334 378 844	11
12	0.3555 347 251	0.3365 352 572	0.3186 308 177	0.3017 537 415	12
13	0.3261 786 469	0.3073 381 344	0.2896 643 797	0.2730 803 091	13
14	0.2992 464 650	0.2806 740 954	0.2633 312 543	0.2471 315 014	14
15	0.2745 380 413	0.2563 233 748	0.2393 920 494	0.2236 484 176	15
16	0.2518 697 627	0.2340 852 737	0.2176 291 358	0.2023 967 580	16
17	0.2310 731 768	0.2137 765 057	0.1978 446 689	0.1831 644 869	17
18	0.2119 937 402	0.1952 296 856	0.1798 587 899	0.1657 597 166	18
19	0.1944 896 699	0.1782 919 503	0.1635 079 908	0.1500 087 933	19
20	0.1784 308 898	0.1628 236 989	0.1486 436 280	0.1357 545 641	20
21	0.1636 980 640	0.1486 974 419	0.1351 305 709	0.1228 548 091	21
22	0.1501 817 101	0.1357 967 506	0.1228 459 736	0.1111 808 227	22
23	0.1377 813 854	0.1240 152 974	0.1116 781 578	0.1006 161 292	23
24	0.1264 049 408	0.1132 559 793	0.1015 255 980	0.0910 553 205	24
25	0.1159 678 356	0.1034 301 181	0.0922 959 982	0.0824 030 050	25
26	0.1063 925 097	0.0944 567 289	0.0839 054 529	0.0745 728 552	26
27	0.0976 078 070	0.0862 618 528	0.0762 776 844	0.0674 867 468	27
28	0.0895 484 468	0.0787 779 478	0.0693 433 495	0.0610 739 790	28
29	0.0821 545 384	0.0719 433 313	0.0630 394 086	0.0552 705 692	29
30	0.0753 711 361	0.0657 016 724	0.0573 085 533	0.0500 186 147	30
31	0.0691 478 313	0.0600 015 273	0.0520 986 848	0.0452 657 146	31
32	0.0634 383 773	0.0547 959 154	0.0473 624 407	0.0409 644 476	32
33	0.0582 003 462	0.0500 419 319	0.0430 567 643	0.0370 718 983	33
34	0.0533 948 130	0.0457 003 944	0.0391 425 130	0.0335 492 293	34
35	0.0489 860 670	0.0417 355 200	0.0355 841 027	0.0303 612 934	35
36	0.0449 413 459	0.0381 146 301	0.0323 491 843	0.0274 762 837	36
37	0.0412 305 925	0.0348 078 814	0.0294 083 494	0.0248 654 151	37
38	0.0378 262 317	0.0317 880 195	0.0267 348 631	0.0225 026 381	38
39	0.0347 029 648	0.0290 301 548	0.0243 044 210	0.0203 643 783	39
40	0.0318 375 824	0.0265 115 569	0.0220 949 282	0.0184 293 017	40
41	0.0292 087 912	0.0242 114 675	0.0200 862 983	0.0166 781 011	41
42	0.0267 970 562	0.0221 109 292	0.0182 602 712	0.0150 933 041	42
43	0.0245 844 552	0.0201 926 294	0.0166 002 465	0.0136 590 988	43
44	0.0225 545 461	0.0184 407 575	0.0150 911 332	0.0123 611 753	44
45	0.0206 922 441	0.0168 408 744	0.0137 192 120	0.0111 865 840	45
46	0.0189 837 102	0.0153 797 940	0.0124 720 109	0.0101 236 055	46
47	0.0174 162 479	0.0140 454 740	0.0113 381 918	0.0091 616 339	47
48	0.0159 782 090	0.0128 269 169	0.0103 074 470	0.0082 910 714	48
49	0.0146 589 074	0.0117 140 793	0.0093 704 064	0.0075 032 320	49
50	0.0134 485 389	0.0106 977 893	0.0085 185 513	0.0067 902 552	50
51	0.0123 381 091	0.0097 696 706	0.0077 441 375	0.0061 450 274	51
52	0.0113 193 661	0.0089 220 736	0.0070 401 250	0.0055 611 107	52
53	0.0103 847 396	0.0081 480 124	0.0064 001 137	0.0050 326 794	53
54	0.0095 272 840	0.0074 411 073	0.0058 182 851	0.0045 544 610	54
55	0.0087 406 275	0.0067 955 317	0.0052 893 501	0.0041 216 842	55
56	0.0080 189 243	0.0062 059 651	0.0048 085 001	0.0037 300 309	56
57	0.0073 568 113	0.0056 675 480	0.0043 713 637	0.0033 755 936	57
58	0.0067 493 682	0.0051 758 429	0.0039 739 670	0.0030 548 358	58
59	0.0061 920 809	0.0047 267 972	0.0036 126 973	0.0027 645 573	59
60	0.0056 808 082	0.0043 167 098	0.0032 842 703	0.0025 018 618	60

Table 4.   PRESENT WORTH OF ONE DOLLAR
            PAYABLE AT END OF EACH PERIOD

	11% NOMINAL ANNUAL RATE	11½% NOMINAL ANNUAL RATE	12% NOMINAL ANNUAL RATE	12½% NOMINAL ANNUAL RATE	
YEARS					YEARS
1	0.9009 009 009	0.8968 609 865	0.8928 571 429	0.8888 888 889	1
2	0.8116 224 332	0.8043 596 292	0.7971 938 776	0.7901 234 568	2
3	0.7311 913 813	0.7213 987 706	0.7117 802 478	0.7023 319 616	3
4	0.6587 309 741	0.6469 944 131	0.6355 180 784	0.6242 950 770	4
5	0.5934 513 281	0.5802 640 476	0.5674 268 557	0.5549 289 573	5
6	0.5346 408 361	0.5204 161 862	0.5066 311 212	0.4932 701 843	6
7	0.4816 584 109	0.4667 409 742	0.4523 492 153	0.4384 623 860	7
8	0.4339 264 963	0.4186 017 705	0.4038 832 280	0.3897 443 431	8
9	0.3909 247 714	0.3754 275 969	0.3606 100 250	0.3464 394 161	9
10	0.3521 844 788	0.3367 063 649	0.3219 732 366	0.3079 461 477	10
11	0.3172 833 142	0.3019 788 026	0.2874 761 041	0.2737 299 090	11
12	0.2858 408 236	0.2708 330 068	0.2566 750 929	0.2433 154 747	12
13	0.2575 142 555	0.2428 995 577	0.2291 741 901	0.2162 804 219	13
14	0.2319 948 248	0.2178 471 370	0.2046 198 126	0.1922 492 640	14
15	0.2090 043 467	0.1953 785 982	0.1826 962 613	0.1708 882 346	15
16	0.1882 922 042	0.1752 274 423	0.1631 216 618	0.1519 006 530	16
17	0.1696 326 164	0.1571 546 568	0.1456 443 409	0.1350 228 027	17
18	0.1528 221 769	0.1409 458 805	0.1300 395 901	0.1200 202 690	18
19	0.1376 776 369	0.1264 088 614	0.1161 067 769	0.1066 846 836	19
20	0.1240 339 071	0.1133 711 762	0.1036 667 651	0.0948 308 299	20
21	0.1117 422 586	0.1016 781 849	0.0925 596 117	0.0842 940 710	21
22	0.1006 687 015	0.0911 911 972	0.0826 425 104	0.0749 280 631	22
23	0.0906 925 239	0.0817 858 271	0.0737 879 557	0.0666 027 228	23
24	0.0817 049 764	0.0733 505 176	0.0658 821 033	0.0592 024 202	24
25	0.0736 080 869	0.0657 852 176	0.0588 233 066	0.0526 243 735	25
26	0.0663 135 918	0.0590 001 951	0.0525 208 094	0.0467 772 209	26
27	0.0597 419 746	0.0529 149 732	0.0468 935 798	0.0415 797 519	27
28	0.0538 215 987	0.0474 573 751	0.0418 692 677	0.0369 597 795	28
29	0.0484 879 268	0.0425 626 682	0.0373 832 747	0.0328 531 373	29
30	0.0436 828 169	0.0381 727 966	0.0333 779 239	0.0292 027 887	30
31	0.0393 538 891	0.0342 356 920	0.0298 017 177	0.0259 580 344	31
32	0.0354 539 542	0.0307 046 565	0.0266 086 766	0.0230 738 084	32
33	0.0319 404 992	0.0275 378 086	0.0237 577 469	0.0205 100 519	33
34	0.0287 752 245	0.0246 975 861	0.0212 122 740	0.0182 311 572	34
35	0.0259 236 257	0.0221 503 015	0.0189 395 304	0.0162 054 731	35
36	0.0233 546 178	0.0198 657 412	0.0169 102 950	0.0144 048 650	36
37	0.0210 401 962	0.0178 168 083	0.0150 984 777	0.0128 043 244	37
38	0.0189 551 317	0.0159 792 003	0.0134 807 836	0.0113 816 217	38
39	0.0170 766 952	0.0143 311 213	0.0120 364 140	0.0101 169 971	39
40	0.0153 844 101	0.0128 530 236	0.0107 467 982	0.0089 928 863	40
41	0.0138 598 289	0.0115 273 754	0.0095 953 555	0.0079 936 767	41
42	0.0124 863 324	0.0103 384 533	0.0085 672 817	0.0071 054 904	42
43	0.0112 489 481	0.0092 721 554	0.0076 493 587	0.0063 159 915	43
44	0.0101 341 875	0.0083 158 345	0.0068 297 845	0.0056 142 146	44
45	0.0091 298 986	0.0074 581 475	0.0060 980 219	0.0049 904 130	45
46	0.0082 251 339	0.0066 889 215	0.0054 446 624	0.0044 359 227	46
47	0.0074 100 305	0.0059 990 328	0.0048 613 057	0.0039 430 424	47
48	0.0066 757 032	0.0053 802 984	0.0043 404 515	0.0035 049 266	48
49	0.0060 141 470	0.0048 253 798	0.0038 754 032	0.0031 154 903	49
50	0.0054 181 505	0.0043 276 949	0.0034 601 814	0.0027 693 247	50
51	0.0048 812 166	0.0038 813 407	0.0030 894 477	0.0024 616 219	51
52	0.0043 974 925	0.0034 810 230	0.0027 584 354	0.0021 881 084	52
53	0.0039 617 049	0.0031 219 937	0.0024 628 888	0.0019 449 852	53
54	0.0035 691 035	0.0027 999 944	0.0021 990 078	0.0017 288 758	54
55	0.0032 154 086	0.0025 112 057	0.0019 633 998	0.0015 367 785	55
56	0.0028 967 645	0.0022 522 024	0.0017 530 356	0.0013 660 253	56
57	0.0026 096 977	0.0020 199 125	0.0015 652 103	0.0012 142 447	57
58	0.0023 510 790	0.0018 115 807	0.0013 975 092	0.0010 793 286	58
59	0.0021 180 892	0.0016 247 361	0.0012 477 761	0.0009 594 032	59
60	0.0019 081 885	0.0014 571 624	0.0011 140 858	0.0008 528 029	60

Table 4. PRESENT WORTH OF ONE DOLLAR
PAYABLE AT END OF EACH PERIOD

YEARS	13% NOMINAL ANNUAL RATE	13½% NOMINAL ANNUAL RATE	14% NOMINAL ANNUAL RATE	14½% NOMINAL ANNUAL RATE	YEARS
1	0.8849 557 522	0.8810 572 687	0.8771 929 825	0.8733 624 454	1
2	0.7831 466 834	0.7762 619 108	0.7694 675 285	0.7627 619 611	2
3	0.6930 501 623	0.6839 311 989	0.6749 715 162	0.6661 676 516	3
4	0.6133 187 277	0.6025 825 541	0.5920 802 774	0.5818 058 092	4
5	0.5427 599 360	0.5309 097 393	0.5193 686 644	0.5081 273 443	5
6	0.4803 185 274	0.4677 618 848	0.4555 865 477	0.4437 793 400	6
7	0.4250 606 437	0.4121 250 087	0.3996 373 225	0.3875 802 096	7
8	0.3761 598 617	0.3631 057 345	0.3505 590 549	0.3384 979 997	8
9	0.3328 848 334	0.3199 169 467	0.3075 079 429	0.2956 314 408	9
10	0.2945 883 481	0.2818 651 513	0.2697 438 095	0.2581 933 980	10
11	0.2606 976 532	0.2483 393 403	0.2366 173 768	0.2254 964 175	11
12	0.2307 058 878	0.2188 011 809	0.2075 591 024	0.1969 401 026	12
13	0.2041 645 025	0.1927 763 709	0.1820 693 881	0.1720 000 896	13
14	0.1806 765 509	0.1698 470 228	0.1597 099 896	0.1502 184 189	14
15	0.1598 907 530	0.1496 449 540	0.1400 964 821	0.1311 951 257	15
16	0.1414 962 416	0.1318 457 744	0.1228 916 509	0.1145 808 958	16
17	0.1252 179 129	0.1161 636 779	0.1077 996 938	0.1000 706 513	17
18	0.1108 123 123	0.1023 468 528	0.0945 611 349	0.0873 979 488	18
19	0.0980 639 932	0.0901 734 386	0.0829 483 640	0.0763 300 863	19
20	0.0867 822 949	0.0794 479 635	0.0727 617 228	0.0666 638 308	20
21	0.0767 984 910	0.0699 982 057	0.0638 260 726	0.0582 216 863	21
22	0.0679 632 664	0.0616 724 280	0.0559 877 830	0.0508 486 343	22
23	0.0601 444 835	0.0543 369 409	0.0491 120 903	0.0444 092 876	23
24	0.0532 252 067	0.0478 739 568	0.0430 807 810	0.0387 854 040	24
25	0.0471 019 528	0.0421 796 976	0.0377 901 588	0.0338 737 153	25
26	0.0416 831 441	0.0371 627 292	0.0331 492 621	0.0295 840 308	26
27	0.0368 877 381	0.0327 424 927	0.0290 783 001	0.0258 375 815	27
28	0.0326 440 160	0.0288 480 111	0.0255 072 808	0.0225 655 734	28
29	0.0288 885 098	0.0254 167 499	0.0223 748 077	0.0197 079 243	29
30	0.0255 650 529	0.0223 936 123	0.0196 270 243	0.0172 121 610	30
31	0.0226 239 406	0.0197 300 548	0.0172 166 880	0.0150 324 550	31
32	0.0200 211 864	0.0173 833 082	0.0151 023 579	0.0131 287 817	32
33	0.0177 178 641	0.0153 156 901	0.0132 476 823	0.0114 661 849	33
34	0.0156 795 257	0.0134 940 001	0.0116 207 740	0.0100 141 353	34
35	0.0138 756 865	0.0118 889 868	0.0101 936 614	0.0087 459 697	35
36	0.0122 793 686	0.0104 748 783	0.0089 418 082	0.0076 384 014	36
37	0.0108 666 978	0.0092 289 676	0.0078 436 914	0.0066 710 930	37
38	0.0096 165 468	0.0081 312 490	0.0068 804 311	0.0058 262 821	38
39	0.0085 102 184	0.0071 640 961	0.0060 354 659	0.0050 884 560	39
40	0.0075 311 667	0.0063 119 789	0.0052 942 683	0.0044 440 663	40
41	0.0066 647 493	0.0055 612 149	0.0046 440 950	0.0038 812 806	41
42	0.0058 980 082	0.0048 997 488	0.0040 737 675	0.0033 897 648	42
43	0.0052 194 763	0.0043 169 593	0.0035 734 803	0.0029 604 932	43
44	0.0046 190 056	0.0038 034 884	0.0031 346 318	0.0025 855 836	44
45	0.0040 876 156	0.0033 510 911	0.0027 496 771	0.0022 581 516	45
46	0.0036 173 589	0.0029 525 032	0.0024 119 974	0.0019 721 848	46
47	0.0032 012 026	0.0026 013 244	0.0021 157 872	0.0017 224 322	47
48	0.0028 329 226	0.0022 919 157	0.0018 559 537	0.0015 043 076	48
49	0.0025 070 112	0.0020 193 090	0.0016 280 296	0.0013 138 057	49
50	0.0022 185 940	0.0017 791 269	0.0014 280 961	0.0011 474 286	50
51	0.0019 633 575	0.0015 675 127	0.0012 527 159	0.0010 021 210	51
52	0.0017 374 845	0.0013 810 684	0.0010 988 736	0.0008 752 149	52
53	0.0015 375 969	0.0012 168 004	0.0009 639 242	0.0007 643 798	53
54	0.0013 607 052	0.0010 720 708	0.0008 455 475	0.0006 675 806	54
55	0.0012 041 639	0.0009 445 558	0.0007 417 084	0.0005 830 398	55
56	0.0010 656 318	0.0008 322 077	0.0006 506 214	0.0005 092 051	56
57	0.0009 430 370	0.0007 332 227	0.0005 707 205	0.0004 447 206	57
58	0.0008 345 460	0.0006 460 112	0.0005 006 320	0.0003 884 023	58
59	0.0007 385 363	0.0005 691 728	0.0004 391 509	0.0003 392 160	59
60	0.0006 535 719	0.0005 014 739	0.0003 852 201	0.0002 962 585	60

Table 4. PRESENT WORTH OF ONE DOLLAR
PAYABLE AT END OF EACH PERIOD

YEARS	**15%** NOMINAL ANNUAL RATE	**15½%** NOMINAL ANNUAL RATE	**16%** NOMINAL ANNUAL RATE	**16½%** NOMINAL ANNUAL RATE	YEARS
1	0.8695 652 174	0.8658 008 658	0.8620 689 655	0.8583 690 987	1
2	0.7561 436 673	0.7496 111 392	0.7431 629 013	0.7367 975 096	2
3	0.6575 162 324	0.6490 139 734	0.6406 576 735	0.6324 442 143	3
4	0.5717 532 456	0.5619 168 600	0.5522 910 979	0.5428 705 702	4
5	0.4971 767 353	0.4865 081 039	0.4761 130 154	0.4659 833 221	5
6	0.4323 275 959	0.4212 191 376	0.4104 422 547	0.3999 856 842	6
7	0.3759 370 399	0.3646 918 940	0.3538 295 299	0.3433 353 512	7
8	0.3269 017 738	0.3157 505 576	0.3050 254 568	0.2947 084 560	8
9	0.2842 624 120	0.2733 771 061	0.2629 529 800	0.2529 686 317	9
10	0.2471 847 061	0.2366 901 352	0.2266 836 034	0.2171 404 564	10
11	0.2149 432 227	0.2049 265 240	0.1954 168 995	0.1863 866 579	11
12	0.1869 071 502	0.1774 255 619	0.1684 628 444	0.1599 885 475	12
13	0.1625 279 567	0.1536 152 051	0.1452 265 900	0.1373 292 254	13
14	0.1413 286 580	0.1330 001 776	0.1251 953 362	0.1178 791 634	14
15	0.1228 944 852	0.1151 516 689	0.1079 270 140	0.1011 838 312	15
16	0.1068 647 697	0.0996 984 146	0.0930 405 293	0.0868 530 740	16
17	0.0929 258 867	0.0863 189 737	0.0802 073 528	0.0745 519 949	17
18	0.0808 051 189	0.0747 350 422	0.0691 442 697	0.0639 931 286	18
19	0.0702 653 208	0.0647 056 642	0.0596 071 290	0.0549 297 242	19
20	0.0611 002 789	0.0560 222 201	0.0513 854 561	0.0471 499 778	20
21	0.0531 306 773	0.0485 040 867	0.0442 978 070	0.0404 720 840	21
22	0.0462 005 890	0.0419 948 802	0.0381 877 646	0.0347 399 862	22
23	0.0401 744 252	0.0363 592 037	0.0329 204 867	0.0298 197 307	23
24	0.0349 342 828	0.0314 798 300	0.0283 797 299	0.0255 963 353	24
25	0.0303 776 372	0.0272 552 641	0.0244 652 844	0.0219 711 033	25
26	0.0264 153 367	0.0235 976 312	0.0210 907 624	0.0188 593 161	26
27	0.0229 698 580	0.0204 308 496	0.0181 816 918	0.0161 882 542	27
28	0.0199 737 896	0.0176 890 472	0.0156 738 722	0.0138 954 972	28
29	0.0173 685 127	0.0153 151 924	0.0135 119 588	0.0119 274 654	29
30	0.0151 030 545	0.0132 599 068	0.0116 482 403	0.0102 381 677	30
31	0.0131 330 909	0.0114 804 388	0.0100 415 865	0.0087 881 268	31
32	0.0114 200 790	0.0099 397 739	0.0086 565 401	0.0075 434 565	32
33	0.0099 305 035	0.0086 058 648	0.0074 625 346	0.0064 750 699	33
34	0.0086 352 204	0.0074 509 652	0.0064 332 194	0.0055 579 999	34
35	0.0075 088 873	0.0064 510 521	0.0055 458 788	0.0047 708 154	35
36	0.0065 294 672	0.0055 853 265	0.0047 809 300	0.0040 951 205	36
37	0.0056 777 976	0.0048 357 805	0.0041 214 914	0.0035 151 249	37
38	0.0049 372 153	0.0041 868 230	0.0035 530 098	0.0030 172 746	38
39	0.0042 932 307	0.0036 249 550	0.0030 629 395	0.0025 899 353	39
40	0.0037 332 441	0.0031 384 891	0.0026 404 651	0.0022 231 204	40
41	0.0032 462 992	0.0027 173 066	0.0022 762 630	0.0019 082 579	41
42	0.0028 228 689	0.0023 526 464	0.0019 622 957	0.0016 379 896	42
43	0.0024 546 686	0.0020 369 233	0.0016 916 342	0.0014 059 996	43
44	0.0021 344 944	0.0017 635 700	0.0014 583 054	0.0012 068 666	44
45	0.0018 560 821	0.0015 269 004	0.0012 571 598	0.0010 359 370	45
46	0.0016 139 844	0.0013 219 917	0.0010 837 584	0.0008 892 163	46
47	0.0014 034 647	0.0011 445 816	0.0009 342 745	0.0007 632 758	47
48	0.0012 204 041	0.0009 909 797	0.0008 054 091	0.0006 551 724	48
49	0.0010 612 210	0.0008 579 911	0.0006 943 182	0.0005 623 797	49
50	0.0009 228 008	0.0007 428 494	0.0005 985 501	0.0004 827 294	50
51	0.0008 024 355	0.0006 431 597	0.0005 159 915	0.0004 143 600	51
52	0.0006 977 700	0.0005 568 482	0.0004 448 203	0.0003 556 738	52
53	0.0006 067 565	0.0004 821 197	0.0003 834 657	0.0003 052 994	53
54	0.0005 276 144	0.0004 174 196	0.0003 305 739	0.0002 620 596	54
55	0.0004 587 951	0.0003 614 023	0.0002 849 775	0.0002 249 438	55
56	0.0003 989 523	0.0003 129 024	0.0002 456 703	0.0001 930 848	56
57	0.0003 469 150	0.0002 709 112	0.0002 117 847	0.0001 657 381	57
58	0.0003 016 652	0.0002 345 551	0.0001 825 730	0.0001 422 644	58
59	0.0002 623 176	0.0002 030 780	0.0001 573 905	0.0001 221 154	59
60	0.0002 281 023	0.0001 758 251	0.0001 356 815	0.0001 048 201	60

221

Table 4.   PRESENT WORTH OF ONE DOLLAR
PAYABLE AT END OF EACH PERIOD

	17% NOMINAL ANNUAL RATE	17½% NOMINAL ANNUAL RATE	18% NOMINAL ANNUAL RATE	18½% NOMINAL ANNUAL RATE	
YEARS					YEARS
1	0.8547 008 547	0.8510 638 298	0.8474 576 271	0.8438 818 565	1
2	0.7305 135 510	0.7243 096 424	0.7181 844 298	0.7121 365 878	2
3	0.6243 705 564	0.6164 337 382	0.6086 308 727	0.6009 591 458	3
4	0.5336 500 482	0.5246 244 580	0.5157 888 752	0.5071 385 197	4
5	0.4561 111 523	0.4464 889 005	0.4371 092 162	0.4279 649 955	5
6	0.3898 385 917	0.3799 905 536	0.3704 315 392	0.3611 518 949	6
7	0.3331 953 776	0.3233 962 158	0.3139 250 332	0.3047 695 316	7
8	0.2847 823 740	0.2752 308 220	0.2660 381 637	0.2571 894 781	8
9	0.2434 037 384	0.2342 389 974	0.2254 560 710	0.2170 375 343	9
10	0.2080 373 833	0.1993 523 382	0.1910 644 669	0.1831 540 374	10
11	0.1778 097 293	0.1696 615 644	0.1619 190 398	0.1545 603 691	11
12	0.1519 741 276	0.1443 928 208	0.1372 195 252	0.1304 306 912	12
13	0.1298 924 168	0.1228 875 071	0.1162 877 332	0.1100 680 939	13
14	0.1110 191 596	0.1045 851 124	0.0985 489 265	0.0928 844 674	14
15	0.0948 881 706	0.0890 086 063	0.0835 160 394	0.0783 835 168	15
16	0.0811 010 005	0.0757 520 054	0.0707 763 046	0.0661 464 277	16
17	0.0693 170 945	0.0644 697 918	0.0599 799 191	0.0558 197 702	17
18	0.0592 453 799	0.0548 679 079	0.0508 304 399	0.0471 052 913	18
19	0.0506 370 768	0.0466 960 918	0.0430 766 440	0.0397 513 007	19
20	0.0432 795 528	0.0397 413 548	0.0365 056 305	0.0335 454 014	20
21	0.0369 910 708	0.0338 224 296	0.0309 369 750	0.0283 083 556	21
22	0.0316 162 998	0.0287 850 465	0.0262 177 754	0.0238 889 077	22
23	0.0270 224 785	0.0244 979 119	0.0222 184 538	0.0201 594 158	23
24	0.0230 961 355	0.0208 492 867	0.0188 291 981	0.0170 121 652	24
25	0.0197 402 867	0.0177 440 738	0.0159 569 475	0.0143 562 576	25
26	0.0168 720 399	0.0151 013 394	0.0135 228 369	0.0121 149 853	26
27	0.0144 205 470	0.0128 522 037	0.0114 600 313	0.0102 236 163	27
28	0.0123 252 538	0.0109 380 457	0.0097 118 909	0.0086 275 243	28
29	0.0105 344 050	0.0093 089 751	0.0082 304 160	0.0072 806 112	29
30	0.0090 037 649	0.0079 225 320	0.0069 749 288	0.0061 439 757	30
31	0.0076 955 256	0.0067 425 804	0.0059 109 566	0.0051 847 896	31
32	0.0065 773 723	0.0057 383 663	0.0050 092 853	0.0043 753 499	32
33	0.0056 216 857	0.0048 837 160	0.0042 451 570	0.0036 922 784	33
34	0.0048 048 596	0.0041 563 541	0.0035 975 907	0.0031 158 467	34
35	0.0041 067 176	0.0035 373 226	0.0030 488 057	0.0026 294 065	35
36	0.0035 100 150	0.0030 104 873	0.0025 837 336	0.0022 189 085	36
37	0.0030 000 129	0.0025 621 169	0.0021 896 048	0.0018 724 966	37
38	0.0025 641 135	0.0021 805 250	0.0018 555 973	0.0015 801 659	38
39	0.0021 915 500	0.0018 557 660	0.0015 725 401	0.0013 334 733	39
40	0.0018 731 197	0.0015 793 753	0.0013 326 611	0.0011 252 940	40
41	0.0016 009 570	0.0013 441 492	0.0011 293 738	0.0009 496 152	41
42	0.0013 683 393	0.0011 439 567	0.0009 570 964	0.0008 013 630	42
43	0.0011 695 208	0.0009 735 802	0.0008 110 987	0.0006 762 557	43
44	0.0009 995 904	0.0008 285 789	0.0006 873 717	0.0005 706 799	44
45	0.0008 543 508	0.0007 051 735	0.0005 825 184	0.0004 815 864	45
46	0.0007 302 143	0.0006 001 477	0.0004 936 597	0.0004 064 020	46
47	0.0006 241 148	0.0005 107 640	0.0004 183 557	0.0003 429 553	47
48	0.0005 334 315	0.0004 346 928	0.0003 545 387	0.0002 894 138	48
49	0.0004 559 243	0.0003 699 513	0.0003 004 565	0.0002 442 310	49
50	0.0003 896 789	0.0003 148 522	0.0002 546 242	0.0002 061 021	50
51	0.0003 330 589	0.0002 679 593	0.0002 157 832	0.0001 739 258	51
52	0.0002 846 657	0.0002 280 505	0.0001 828 671	0.0001 467 729	52
53	0.0002 433 040	0.0001 940 855	0.0001 549 721	0.0001 238 590	53
54	0.0002 079 522	0.0001 651 791	0.0001 313 323	0.0001 045 223	54
55	0.0001 777 369	0.0001 405 780	0.0001 112 986	0.0000 882 045	55
56	0.0001 519 119	0.0001 196 408	0.0000 943 208	0.0000 744 342	56
57	0.0001 298 392	0.0001 018 220	0.0000 799 329	0.0000 628 136	57
58	0.0001 109 737	0.0000 866 570	0.0000 677 397	0.0000 530 073	58
59	0.0000 948 493	0.0000 737 507	0.0000 574 066	0.0000 447 319	59
60	0.0000 810 678	0.0000 627 665	0.0000 486 496	0.0000 377 484	60

Table 4.   PRESENT WORTH OF ONE DOLLAR
PAYABLE AT END OF EACH PERIOD

YEARS	19% NOMINAL ANNUAL RATE	19½% NOMINAL ANNUAL RATE	20% NOMINAL ANNUAL RATE	20½% NOMINAL ANNUAL RATE	YEARS
1	0.8403 361 345	0.8368 200 837	0.8333 333 333	0.8298 755 187	1
2	0.7061 648 189	0.7002 678 525	0.6944 444 444	0.6886 933 765	2
3	0.5934 158 142	0.5859 982 029	0.5787 037 037	0.5715 297 730	3
4	0.4986 687 514	0.4903 750 652	0.4822 530 864	0.4742 985 668	4
5	0.4190 493 709	0.4103 557 031	0.4018 775 720	0.3936 087 691	5
6	0.3521 423 285	0.3433 938 938	0.3348 979 767	0.3266 462 815	6
7	0.2959 179 231	0.2873 589 069	0.2790 816 472	0.2710 757 522	7
8	0.2486 705 236	0.2404 677 046	0.2325 680 394	0.2249 591 305	8
9	0.2089 668 266	0.2012 282 046	0.1938 066 995	0.1866 880 751	9
10	0.1756 023 753	0.1683 918 030	0.1615 055 829	0.1549 278 632	10
11	0.1475 650 212	0.1409 136 427	0.1345 879 857	0.1285 708 408	11
12	0.1240 042 195	0.1179 193 663	0.1121 566 548	0.1066 977 932	12
13	0.1042 052 265	0.0986 772 940	0.0934 638 790	0.0885 458 865	13
14	0.0875 674 172	0.0825 751 414	0.0778 865 658	0.0734 820 635	14
15	0.0735 860 649	0.0691 005 367	0.0649 054 715	0.0609 809 655	15
16	0.0618 370 293	0.0578 247 169	0.0540 878 929	0.0506 066 104	16
17	0.0519 638 902	0.0483 888 845	0.0450 732 441	0.0419 971 870	17
18	0.0436 671 346	0.0404 927 903	0.0375 610 368	0.0348 524 374	18
19	0.0366 950 711	0.0338 851 802	0.0313 008 640	0.0289 231 846	19
20	0.0308 361 942	0.0283 557 993	0.0260 840 533	0.0240 026 428	20
21	0.0259 127 682	0.0237 287 024	0.0217 367 111	0.0199 192 056	21
22	0.0217 754 355	0.0198 566 547	0.0181 139 259	0.0165 304 611	22
23	0.0182 986 853	0.0166 164 475	0.0150 949 383	0.0137 182 250	23
24	0.0153 770 465	0.0139 049 769	0.0125 791 152	0.0113 844 191	24
25	0.0129 218 878	0.0116 359 640	0.0104 825 960	0.0094 476 507	25
26	0.0108 587 292	0.0097 372 083	0.0087 354 967	0.0078 403 740	26
27	0.0091 249 825	0.0081 482 915	0.0072 795 806	0.0065 065 344	27
28	0.0076 680 526	0.0068 186 540	0.0060 663 171	0.0053 996 136	28
29	0.0064 437 416	0.0057 059 866	0.0050 552 643	0.0044 810 072	29
30	0.0054 149 089	0.0047 748 842	0.0042 127 202	0.0037 186 782	30
31	0.0045 503 437	0.0039 957 190	0.0035 106 002	0.0030 860 400	31
32	0.0038 238 182	0.0033 436 979	0.0029 255 002	0.0025 610 290	32
33	0.0032 132 926	0.0027 980 735	0.0024 379 168	0.0021 253 353	33
34	0.0027 002 459	0.0023 414 841	0.0020 315 973	0.0017 637 637	34
35	0.0022 691 142	0.0019 594 010	0.0016 929 978	0.0014 637 043	35
36	0.0019 068 186	0.0016 396 661	0.0014 108 315	0.0012 146 924	36
37	0.0016 023 686	0.0013 721 055	0.0011 756 929	0.0010 080 435	37
38	0.0013 465 282	0.0011 482 054	0.0009 797 441	0.0008 365 506	38
39	0.0011 315 363	0.0009 608 414	0.0008 164 534	0.0006 942 329	39
40	0.0009 508 709	0.0008 040 514	0.0006 803 778	0.0005 761 269	40
41	0.0007 990 512	0.0006 728 463	0.0005 669 815	0.0004 781 136	41
42	0.0006 714 716	0.0005 630 513	0.0004 724 846	0.0003 967 748	42
43	0.0005 642 618	0.0004 711 726	0.0003 937 372	0.0003 292 737	43
44	0.0004 741 696	0.0003 942 867	0.0003 281 143	0.0002 732 561	44
45	0.0003 984 618	0.0003 299 471	0.0002 734 286	0.0002 267 686	45
46	0.0003 348 419	0.0002 761 063	0.0002 278 572	0.0001 881 897	46
47	0.0002 813 797	0.0002 310 513	0.0001 898 810	0.0001 561 740	47
48	0.0002 364 536	0.0001 933 484	0.0001 582 341	0.0001 296 050	48
49	0.0001 987 005	0.0001 617 978	0.0001 318 618	0.0001 075 560	49
50	0.0001 669 752	0.0001 353 957	0.0001 098 848	0.0000 892 581	50
51	0.0001 403 153	0.0001 133 018	0.0000 915 707	0.0000 740 731	51
52	0.0001 179 120	0.0000 948 132	0.0000 763 089	0.0000 614 715	52
53	0.0000 990 857	0.0000 793 416	0.0000 635 908	0.0000 510 137	53
54	0.0000 832 653	0.0000 663 947	0.0000 529 923	0.0000 423 350	54
55	0.0000 699 708	0.0000 555 604	0.0000 441 602	0.0000 351 328	55
56	0.0000 587 990	0.0000 464 940	0.0000 368 002	0.0000 291 558	56
57	0.0000 494 109	0.0000 389 071	0.0000 306 668	0.0000 241 957	57
58	0.0000 415 218	0.0000 325 583	0.0000 255 557	0.0000 200 794	58
59	0.0000 348 923	0.0000 272 454	0.0000 212 964	0.0000 166 634	59
60	0.0000 293 212	0.0000 227 995	0.0000 177 470	0.0000 138 286	60

Table 4.   PRESENT WORTH OF ONE DOLLAR
PAYABLE AT END OF EACH PERIOD

YEARS	**21%** NOMINAL ANNUAL RATE	**21½%** NOMINAL ANNUAL RATE	**22%** NOMINAL ANNUAL RATE	**22½%** NOMINAL ANNUAL RATE	YEARS
1	0.8264 462 810	0.8230 452 675	0.8196 721 311	0.8163 265 306	1
2	0.6830 134 554	0.6774 035 123	0.6718 624 026	0.6663 890 046	2
3	0.5644 739 301	0.5575 337 550	0.5507 068 874	0.5439 910 241	3
4	0.4665 073 802	0.4588 755 185	0.4513 990 880	0.4440 743 054	4
5	0.3855 432 894	0.3776 753 239	0.3699 992 525	0.3625 096 371	5
6	0.3186 308 177	0.3108 438 880	0.3032 780 758	0.2959 262 344	6
7	0.2633 312 543	0.2558 385 909	0.2485 885 867	0.2415 724 362	7
8	0.2176 291 358	0.2105 667 415	0.2037 611 366	0.1972 019 887	8
9	0.1798 587 899	0.1733 059 601	0.1670 173 251	0.1609 812 153	9
10	0.1486 436 280	0.1426 386 503	0.1368 994 468	0.1314 132 370	10
11	0.1228 459 736	0.1173 980 661	0.1122 126 613	0.1072 761 118	11
12	0.1015 255 980	0.0966 239 227	0.0919 775 913	0.0875 723 362	12
13	0.0839 054 529	0.0795 258 623	0.0753 914 682	0.0714 876 214	13
14	0.0693 433 495	0.0654 533 846	0.0617 962 854	0.0583 572 419	14
15	0.0573 085 533	0.0538 710 984	0.0506 526 930	0.0476 385 648	15
16	0.0473 624 407	0.0443 383 526	0.0415 186 008	0.0388 886 244	16
17	0.0391 425 130	0.0364 924 713	0.0340 316 400	0.0317 458 158	17
18	0.0323 491 843	0.0300 349 558	0.0278 947 869	0.0259 149 517	18
19	0.0267 348 631	0.0247 201 282	0.0228 645 794	0.0211 550 626	19
20	0.0220 949 282	0.0203 457 846	0.0187 414 585	0.0172 694 389	20
21	0.0182 602 712	0.0167 455 017	0.0153 618 513	0.0140 975 011	21
22	0.0150 911 332	0.0137 823 059	0.0125 916 814	0.0115 081 642	22
23	0.0124 720 109	0.0113 434 617	0.0103 210 503	0.0093 944 197	23
24	0.0103 074 470	0.0093 361 824	0.0084 598 773	0.0076 689 141	24
25	0.0085 185 513	0.0076 841 008	0.0069 343 256	0.0062 603 380	25
26	0.0070 401 250	0.0063 243 628	0.0056 838 735	0.0051 104 800	26
27	0.0058 182 851	0.0052 052 369	0.0046 589 127	0.0041 718 204	27
28	0.0048 085 001	0.0042 841 456	0.0038 187 809	0.0034 055 677	28
29	0.0039 739 670	0.0035 260 457	0.0031 301 483	0.0027 800 553	29
30	0.0032 842 703	0.0029 020 952	0.0025 656 953	0.0022 694 329	30
31	0.0027 142 730	0.0023 885 558	0.0021 030 289	0.0018 525 983	31
32	0.0022 432 008	0.0019 658 895	0.0017 237 942	0.0015 123 251	32
33	0.0018 538 850	0.0016 180 161	0.0014 129 461	0.0012 345 511	33
34	0.0015 321 363	0.0013 317 005	0.0011 581 525	0.0010 077 968	34
35	0.0012 662 284	0.0010 960 498	0.0009 493 053	0.0008 226 913	35
36	0.0010 464 697	0.0009 020 986	0.0007 781 191	0.0006 715 847	36
37	0.0008 648 510	0.0007 424 680	0.0006 378 026	0.0005 482 324	37
38	0.0007 147 529	0.0006 110 847	0.0005 227 890	0.0004 475 367	38
39	0.0005 907 049	0.0005 029 504	0.0004 285 156	0.0003 653 361	39
40	0.0004 881 859	0.0004 139 509	0.0003 512 423	0.0002 982 335	40
41	0.0004 034 594	0.0003 407 004	0.0002 879 035	0.0002 434 559	41
42	0.0003 334 375	0.0002 804 118	0.0002 359 865	0.0001 987 395	42
43	0.0002 755 682	0.0002 307 916	0.0001 934 315	0.0001 622 364	43
44	0.0002 277 423	0.0001 899 520	0.0001 585 504	0.0001 324 378	44
45	0.0001 882 168	0.0001 563 391	0.0001 299 594	0.0001 081 125	45
46	0.0001 555 511	0.0001 286 741	0.0001 065 241	0.0000 882 551	46
47	0.0001 285 546	0.0001 059 046	0.0000 873 148	0.0000 720 450	47
48	0.0001 062 435	0.0000 871 643	0.0000 715 695	0.0000 588 122	48
49	0.0000 878 045	0.0000 717 402	0.0000 586 635	0.0000 480 100	49
50	0.0000 725 657	0.0000 590 454	0.0000 480 849	0.0000 391 918	50
51	0.0000 599 717	0.0000 485 970	0.0000 394 138	0.0000 319 933	51
52	0.0000 495 634	0.0000 399 976	0.0000 323 064	0.0000 261 170	52
53	0.0000 409 615	0.0000 329 198	0.0000 264 807	0.0000 213 200	53
54	0.0000 338 524	0.0000 270 945	0.0000 217 055	0.0000 174 041	54
55	0.0000 279 772	0.0000 223 000	0.0000 177 914	0.0000 142 074	55
56	0.0000 231 217	0.0000 183 539	0.0000 145 831	0.0000 115 979	56
57	0.0000 191 088	0.0000 151 061	0.0000 119 534	0.0000 094 677	57
58	0.0000 157 924	0.0000 124 330	0.0000 097 978	0.0000 077 287	58
59	0.0000 130 516	0.0000 102 329	0.0000 080 310	0.0000 063 091	59
60	0.0000 107 864	0.0000 084 222	0.0000 065 828	0.0000 051 503	60

ANNUAL
COMPOUNDING

Table 4.   PRESENT WORTH OF ONE DOLLAR
PAYABLE AT END OF EACH PERIOD

	23% NOMINAL ANNUAL RATE	24% NOMINAL ANNUAL RATE	25% NOMINAL ANNUAL RATE	26% NOMINAL ANNUAL RATE	
YEARS					YEARS
1	0.8130 081 301	0.8064 516 129	0.8000 000 000	0.7936 507 937	1
2	0.6609 822 196	0.6503 642 040	0.6400 000 000	0.6298 815 823	2
3	0.5373 839 184	0.5244 872 613	0.5120 000 000	0.4999 060 177	3
4	0.4368 974 946	0.4229 735 978	0.4096 000 000	0.3967 508 077	4
5	0.3552 012 151	0.3411 077 401	0.3276 800 000	0.3148 815 934	5
6	0.2887 814 757	0.2750 868 872	0.2621 440 000	0.2499 060 265	6
7	0.2347 816 876	0.2218 442 639	0.2097 152 000	0.1983 381 163	7
8	0.1908 794 208	0.1789 066 644	0.1677 721 600	0.1574 112 034	8
9	0.1551 865 210	0.1442 795 681	0.1342 177 280	0.1249 295 265	9
10	0.1261 679 032	0.1163 544 904	0.1073 741 824	0.0991 504 179	10
11	0.1025 755 311	0.0938 342 664	0.0858 993 459	0.0786 908 078	11
12	0.0833 947 407	0.0756 727 955	0.0687 194 767	0.0624 530 221	12
13	0.0678 006 022	0.0610 264 480	0.0549 755 814	0.0495 658 905	13
14	0.0551 224 408	0.0492 148 774	0.0439 804 651	0.0393 380 084	14
15	0.0448 149 925	0.0396 894 173	0.0351 843 721	0.0312 206 416	15
16	0.0364 349 533	0.0320 075 946	0.0281 474 977	0.0247 782 870	16
17	0.0296 219 132	0.0258 125 763	0.0225 179 981	0.0196 653 071	17
18	0.0240 828 563	0.0208 165 938	0.0180 143 985	0.0156 073 866	18
19	0.0195 795 580	0.0167 875 756	0.0144 115 188	0.0123 868 148	19
20	0.0159 183 398	0.0135 383 674	0.0115 292 150	0.0098 308 054	20
21	0.0129 417 397	0.0109 180 383	0.0092 233 720	0.0078 022 265	21
22	0.0105 217 396	0.0088 048 696	0.0073 786 976	0.0061 922 432	22
23	0.0085 542 598	0.0071 007 013	0.0059 029 581	0.0049 144 788	23
24	0.0069 546 828	0.0057 263 720	0.0047 223 665	0.0039 003 800	24
25	0.0056 542 136	0.0046 180 419	0.0037 778 932	0.0030 955 397	25
26	0.0045 969 217	0.0037 242 274	0.0030 223 145	0.0024 567 775	26
27	0.0037 373 347	0.0030 034 092	0.0024 178 516	0.0019 498 234	27
28	0.0030 384 835	0.0024 221 042	0.0019 342 813	0.0015 474 789	28
29	0.0024 703 118	0.0019 533 098	0.0015 474 250	0.0012 281 579	29
30	0.0020 083 836	0.0015 752 498	0.0012 379 400	0.0009 747 285	30
31	0.0016 328 322	0.0012 703 628	0.0009 903 520	0.0007 735 940	31
32	0.0013 217 396	0.0010 244 861	0.0007 922 816	0.0006 139 635	32
33	0.0010 792 730	0.0008 261 985	0.0006 338 253	0.0004 872 726	33
34	0.0008 774 577	0.0006 662 891	0.0005 070 602	0.0003 867 243	34
35	0.0007 133 803	0.0005 373 299	0.0004 056 482	0.0003 069 241	35
36	0.0005 799 840	0.0004 333 306	0.0003 245 186	0.0002 435 905	36
37	0.0004 715 317	0.0003 494 601	0.0002 596 148	0.0001 933 258	37
38	0.0003 833 591	0.0002 818 227	0.0002 076 919	0.0001 534 332	38
39	0.0003 116 741	0.0002 272 764	0.0001 661 535	0.0001 217 724	39
40	0.0002 533 935	0.0001 832 874	0.0001 329 228	0.0000 966 447	40
41	0.0002 060 110	0.0001 478 124	0.0001 063 382	0.0000 767 022	41
42	0.0001 674 886	0.0001 192 036	0.0000 850 706	0.0000 608 747	42
43	0.0001 361 696	0.0000 961 319	0.0000 680 565	0.0000 483 133	43
44	0.0001 107 070	0.0000 775 257	0.0000 544 452	0.0000 383 439	44
45	0.0000 900 057	0.0000 625 207	0.0000 435 561	0.0000 304 316	45
46	0.0000 731 754	0.0000 504 200	0.0000 348 449	0.0000 241 521	46
47	0.0000 594 922	0.0000 406 613	0.0000 278 759	0.0000 191 683	47
48	0.0000 483 676	0.0000 327 913	0.0000 223 007	0.0000 152 130	48
49	0.0000 393 233	0.0000 264 446	0.0000 178 406	0.0000 120 738	49
50	0.0000 319 701	0.0000 213 263	0.0000 142 725	0.0000 095 824	50
51	0.0000 259 920	0.0000 171 986	0.0000 114 180	0.0000 076 051	51
52	0.0000 211 317	0.0000 138 699	0.0000 091 344	0.0000 060 358	52
53	0.0000 171 802	0.0000 111 854	0.0000 073 075	0.0000 047 903	53
54	0.0000 139 677	0.0000 090 205	0.0000 058 460	0.0000 038 018	54
55	0.0000 113 558	0.0000 072 746	0.0000 046 768	0.0000 030 173	55
56	0.0000 092 324	0.0000 058 666	0.0000 037 414	0.0000 023 947	56
57	0.0000 075 060	0.0000 047 311	0.0000 029 932	0.0000 019 005	57
58	0.0000 061 024	0.0000 038 154	0.0000 023 945	0.0000 015 084	58
59	0.0000 049 613	0.0000 030 770	0.0000 019 156	0.0000 011 971	59
60	0.0000 040 336	0.0000 024 814	0.0000 015 325	0.0000 009 501	60

Table 4.   PRESENT WORTH OF ONE DOLLAR
PAYABLE AT END OF EACH PERIOD

YEARS	27% NOMINAL ANNUAL RATE	28% NOMINAL ANNUAL RATE	29% NOMINAL ANNUAL RATE	30% NOMINAL ANNUAL RATE	YEARS
1	0.7874 015 748	0.7812 500 000	0.7751 937 984	0.7692 307 692	1
2	0.6200 012 400	0.6103 515 625	0.6009 254 252	0.5917 159 763	2
3	0.4881 899 528	0.4768 371 582	0.4658 336 629	0.4551 661 356	3
4	0.3844 015 376	0.3725 290 298	0.3611 113 666	0.3501 277 966	4
5	0.3026 783 761	0.2910 383 046	0.2799 312 919	0.2693 290 743	5
6	0.2383 294 300	0.2273 736 754	0.2170 010 015	0.2071 762 110	6
7	0.1876 609 685	0.1776 356 839	0.1682 178 306	0.1593 663 162	7
8	0.1477 645 421	0.1387 778 781	0.1304 014 191	0.1225 894 740	8
9	0.1163 500 332	0.1084 202 172	0.1010 863 714	0.0942 995 954	9
10	0.0916 141 993	0.0847 032 947	0.0783 615 282	0.0725 381 503	10
11	0.0721 371 648	0.0661 744 490	0.0607 453 707	0.0557 985 771	11
12	0.0568 009 172	0.0516 987 883	0.0470 894 347	0.0429 219 824	12
13	0.0447 251 316	0.0403 896 783	0.0365 034 377	0.0330 169 096	13
14	0.0352 166 391	0.0315 544 362	0.0282 972 385	0.0253 976 227	14
15	0.0277 296 371	0.0246 519 033	0.0219 358 438	0.0195 366 329	15
16	0.0218 343 599	0.0192 592 994	0.0170 045 301	0.0150 281 791	16
17	0.0171 924 094	0.0150 463 277	0.0131 818 063	0.0115 601 378	17
18	0.0135 373 302	0.0117 549 435	0.0102 184 545	0.0088 924 137	18
19	0.0106 593 151	0.0091 835 496	0.0079 212 825	0.0068 403 182	19
20	0.0083 931 615	0.0071 746 481	0.0061 405 291	0.0052 617 832	20
21	0.0066 087 886	0.0056 051 939	0.0047 601 001	0.0040 475 256	21
22	0.0052 037 706	0.0043 790 577	0.0036 900 001	0.0031 134 812	22
23	0.0040 974 571	0.0034 211 388	0.0028 604 652	0.0023 949 855	23
24	0.0032 263 442	0.0026 727 647	0.0022 174 149	0.0018 422 966	24
25	0.0025 404 285	0.0020 880 974	0.0017 189 262	0.0014 171 512	25
26	0.0020 003 374	0.0016 313 261	0.0013 325 010	0.0010 901 163	26
27	0.0015 750 688	0.0012 744 735	0.0010 329 465	0.0008 385 510	27
28	0.0012 402 117	0.0009 956 824	0.0008 007 337	0.0006 450 392	28
29	0.0009 765 446	0.0007 778 769	0.0006 207 238	0.0004 961 840	29
30	0.0007 689 328	0.0006 077 163	0.0004 811 812	0.0003 816 800	30
31	0.0006 054 589	0.0004 747 784	0.0003 730 087	0.0002 936 000	31
32	0.0004 767 393	0.0003 709 206	0.0002 891 540	0.0002 258 462	32
33	0.0003 753 853	0.0002 897 817	0.0002 241 504	0.0001 737 278	33
34	0.0002 955 789	0.0002 263 920	0.0001 737 600	0.0001 336 368	34
35	0.0002 327 393	0.0001 768 687	0.0001 346 977	0.0001 027 975	35
36	0.0001 832 593	0.0001 381 787	0.0001 044 168	0.0000 790 750	36
37	0.0001 442 987	0.0001 079 521	0.0000 809 433	0.0000 608 269	37
38	0.0001 136 210	0.0000 843 376	0.0000 627 467	0.0000 467 900	38
39	0.0000 894 654	0.0000 658 887	0.0000 486 409	0.0000 359 923	39
40	0.0000 704 452	0.0000 514 756	0.0000 377 061	0.0000 276 864	40
41	0.0000 554 686	0.0000 402 153	0.0000 292 295	0.0000 212 972	41
42	0.0000 436 761	0.0000 314 182	0.0000 226 586	0.0000 163 825	42
43	0.0000 343 906	0.0000 245 455	0.0000 175 648	0.0000 126 019	43
44	0.0000 270 792	0.0000 191 761	0.0000 136 161	0.0000 096 938	44
45	0.0000 213 222	0.0000 149 814	0.0000 105 551	0.0000 074 567	45
46	0.0000 167 892	0.0000 117 042	0.0000 081 823	0.0000 057 360	46
47	0.0000 132 198	0.0000 091 439	0.0000 063 428	0.0000 044 123	47
48	0.0000 104 093	0.0000 071 437	0.0000 049 169	0.0000 033 941	48
49	0.0000 081 963	0.0000 055 810	0.0000 038 116	0.0000 026 108	49
50	0.0000 064 538	0.0000 043 602	0.0000 029 547	0.0000 020 083	50
51	0.0000 050 817	0.0000 034 064	0.0000 022 905	0.0000 015 449	51
52	0.0000 040 013	0.0000 026 612	0.0000 017 756	0.0000 011 884	52
53	0.0000 031 507	0.0000 020 791	0.0000 013 764	0.0000 009 141	53
54	0.0000 024 808	0.0000 016 243	0.0000 010 670	0.0000 007 032	54
55	0.0000 019 534	0.0000 012 690	0.0000 008 271	0.0000 005 409	55
56	0.0000 015 381	0.0000 009 914	0.0000 006 412	0.0000 004 161	56
57	0.0000 012 111	0.0000 007 745	0.0000 004 970	0.0000 003 201	57
58	0.0000 009 536	0.0000 006 051	0.0000 003 853	0.0000 002 462	58
59	0.0000 007 509	0.0000 004 727	0.0000 002 987	0.0000 001 894	59
60	0.0000 005 913	0.0000 003 693	0.0000 002 315	0.0000 001 457	60

Table 5. PRESENT WORTH OF ONE DOLLAR PER PERIOD
PAYABLE AT END OF EACH PERIOD

YEARS	5% NOMINAL ANNUAL RATE	5½% NOMINAL ANNUAL RATE	6% NOMINAL ANNUAL RATE	6½% NOMINAL ANNUAL RATE	YEARS
1	0.9523 809 524	0.9478 672 986	0.9433 962 264	0.9389 671 362	1
2	1.8594 104 308	1.8463 197 143	1.8333 926 664	1.8206 264 189	2
3	2.7232 480 294	2.6979 333 785	2.6730 119 495	2.6484 755 107	3
4	3.5459 505 042	3.5051 501 218	3.4651 056 127	3.4257 986 016	4
5	4.3294 766 706	4.2702 844 756	4.2123 637 856	4.1556 794 381	5
6	5.0756 920 673	4.9955 303 086	4.9173 243 260	4.8410 135 569	6
7	5.7863 733 974	5.6829 671 172	5.5823 814 396	5.4845 197 718	7
8	6.4632 127 594	6.3345 659 879	6.2097 938 110	6.0887 509 594	8
9	7.1078 216 756	6.9521 952 492	6.8016 922 745	6.6561 041 872	9
10	7.7217 349 292	7.5376 258 286	7.3600 870 514	7.1888 302 228	10
11	8.3064 142 183	8.0925 363 304	7.8868 745 768	7.6890 424 627	11
12	8.8632 516 364	8.6185 178 487	8.3838 439 404	8.1587 253 171	12
13	9.3935 729 871	9.1170 785 296	8.8526 829 626	8.5997 420 818	13
14	9.8986 409 401	9.5896 478 954	9.2949 839 270	9.0138 423 303	14
15	10.3796 580 382	10.0375 809 435	9.7122 489 877	9.4026 688 547	15
16	10.8377 695 602	10.4621 620 317	10.1058 952 715	9.7677 641 828	16
17	11.2740 662 478	10.8646 085 609	10.4772 596 901	10.1105 766 975	17
18	11.6895 869 027	11.2460 744 653	10.8276 034 812	10.4324 663 826	18
19	12.0853 208 597	11.6076 535 216	11.1581 164 917	10.7347 102 184	19
20	12.4622 103 425	11.9503 824 849	11.4699 212 186	11.0185 072 474	20
21	12.8211 527 072	12.2752 440 615	11.7640 766 213	11.2849 833 309	21
22	13.1630 025 783	12.5831 697 266	12.0415 817 182	11.5351 956 158	22
23	13.4885 738 841	12.8750 423 949	12.3033 789 794	11.7701 367 285	23
24	13.7986 417 943	13.1516 989 525	12.5503 575 278	11.9907 387 122	24
25	14.0939 445 660	13.4139 326 564	12.7833 561 583	12.1978 767 251	25
26	14.3751 853 010	13.6624 954 089	13.0031 661 870	12.3923 725 118	26
27	14.6430 336 200	13.8980 999 136	13.2105 341 387	12.5749 976 637	27
28	14.8981 272 571	14.1214 217 191	13.4061 642 818	12.7464 766 795	28
29	15.1410 735 782	14.3331 011 555	13.5907 210 206	12.9074 898 399	29
30	15.3724 510 269	14.5337 451 711	13.7648 311 515	13.0586 759 060	30
31	15.5928 105 018	14.7239 290 722	13.9290 859 920	13.2006 346 535	31
32	15.8026 766 684	14.9041 981 727	14.0840 433 887	13.3339 292 521	32
33	16.0025 492 080	15.0750 693 580	14.2302 296 119	13.4590 884 997	33
34	16.1929 040 076	15.2370 325 668	14.3681 411 433	13.5766 089 199	34
35	16.3741 942 929	15.3905 521 960	14.4982 463 616	13.6869 567 323	35
36	16.5468 517 076	15.5360 684 322	14.6209 871 336	13.7905 697 017	36
37	16.7112 873 405	15.6739 985 140	14.7367 803 147	13.8878 588 748	37
38	16.8678 927 053	15.8047 379 279	14.8460 191 648	13.9792 102 111	38
39	17.0170 406 717	15.9286 615 431	14.9490 746 838	14.0649 861 137	39
40	17.1590 863 540	16.0461 246 854	15.0462 968 715	14.1455 268 673	40
41	17.2943 679 562	16.1574 641 568	15.1380 159 165	14.2211 519 881	41
42	17.4232 075 773	16.2629 992 007	15.2245 433 175	14.2921 614 912	42
43	17.5459 119 784	16.3630 324 177	15.3061 729 410	14.3588 370 809	43
44	17.6627 733 128	16.4578 506 329	15.3831 820 198	14.4214 432 685	44
45	17.7740 698 217	16.5477 257 184	15.4558 320 942	14.4802 284 211	45
46	17.8800 664 968	16.6329 153 729	15.5243 699 002	14.5354 257 475	46
47	17.9810 157 113	16.7136 638 606	15.5890 282 077	14.5872 542 230	47
48	18.0771 578 203	16.7902 027 114	15.6500 266 110	14.6359 194 582	48
49	18.1687 217 336	16.8627 513 853	15.7075 722 746	14.6816 145 148	49
50	18.2559 254 606	16.9315 179 007	15.7618 606 364	14.7245 206 711	50
51	18.3389 766 291	16.9966 994 320	15.8130 760 721	14.7648 081 419	51
52	18.4180 729 801	17.0584 828 739	15.8613 925 208	14.8026 367 530	52
53	18.4934 028 382	17.1170 453 781	15.9069 740 762	14.8381 565 756	53
54	18.5651 455 602	17.1725 548 608	15.9499 755 436	14.8715 085 216	54
55	18.6334 719 621	17.2251 704 841	15.9905 429 657	14.9028 249 030	55
56	18.6985 447 258	17.2750 431 129	16.0288 141 186	14.9322 299 558	56
57	18.7605 187 865	17.3223 157 468	16.0649 189 798	14.9598 403 341	57
58	18.8195 417 014	17.3671 239 307	16.0989 801 696	14.9857 655 719	58
59	18.8757 540 013	17.4095 961 428	16.1311 133 676	15.0101 085 182	59
60	18.9292 895 251	17.4498 541 638	16.1614 277 052	15.0329 657 448	60

Table 5. PRESENT WORTH OF ONE DOLLAR PER PERIOD
PAYABLE AT END OF EACH PERIOD

YEARS	7% NOMINAL ANNUAL RATE	7½% NOMINAL ANNUAL RATE	8% NOMINAL ANNUAL RATE	8½% NOMINAL ANNUAL RATE	YEARS
1	0.9345 794 393	0.9302 325 581	0.9259 259 259	0.9216 589 862	1
2	1.8080 181 675	1.7955 651 704	1.7832 647 462	1.7711 142 730	2
3	2.6243 160 444	2.6005 257 399	2.5770 969 872	2.5540 223 714	3
4	3.3872 112 565	3.3493 262 696	3.3121 268 400	3.2755 966 557	4
5	4.1001 974 359	4.0458 849 020	3.9927 100 371	3.9406 420 790	5
6	4.7665 396 598	4.6938 464 205	4.6228 796 640	4.5535 871 695	6
7	5.3892 894 016	5.2966 013 214	5.2063 700 592	5.1185 135 203	7
8	5.9712 985 062	5.8573 035 548	5.7466 389 437	5.6391 829 680	8
9	6.5152 322 488	6.3788 870 277	6.2468 879 109	6.1190 626 434	9
10	7.0235 815 409	6.8640 809 560	6.7100 813 989	6.5613 480 584	10
11	7.4986 743 373	7.3154 241 451	7.1389 642 583	6.9689 843 856	11
12	7.9426 862 966	7.7352 782 745	7.5360 780 169	7.3446 860 697	12
13	8.3576 507 444	8.1258 402 554	7.9037 759 416	7.6909 549 029	13
14	8.7454 679 855	8.4891 537 259	8.2442 369 830	8.0100 966 847	14
15	9.1079 140 051	8.8271 197 450	8.5594 786 879	8.3042 365 758	15
16	9.4466 486 029	9.1415 067 396	8.8513 691 555	8.5753 332 496	16
17	9.7632 229 934	9.4339 597 577	9.1216 381 069	8.8251 919 351	17
18	10.0590 869 097	9.7060 090 770	9.3718 871 360	9.0554 764 379	18
19	10.3355 952 427	9.9590 782 111	9.6035 992 000	9.2677 202 192	19
20	10.5940 142 455	10.1944 913 592	9.8181 474 074	9.4633 366 076	20
21	10.8355 273 323	10.4134 803 341	10.0168 031 550	9.6436 282 098	21
22	11.0612 404 974	10.6171 910 085	10.2007 436 621	9.8097 955 850	22
23	11.2721 873 808	10.8066 893 102	10.3710 589 464	9.9629 452 397	23
24	11.4693 340 007	10.9829 668 002	10.5287 582 837	10.1040 969 951	24
25	11.6535 831 783	11.1469 458 607	10.6747 761 886	10.2341 907 789	25
26	11.8257 786 713	11.2994 845 215	10.8099 779 524	10.3540 928 838	26
27	11.9867 090 386	11.4413 809 503	10.9351 647 707	10.4646 017 362	27
28	12.1371 112 510	11.5733 776 282	11.0510 784 914	10.5664 532 131	28
29	12.2776 740 664	11.6961 652 355	11.1584 060 106	10.6603 255 420	29
30	12.4090 411 835	11.8103 862 656	11.2577 833 431	10.7468 438 175	30
31	12.5318 141 902	11.9166 383 866	11.3497 993 918	10.8265 841 636	31
32	12.6465 553 179	12.0154 775 689	11.4349 994 368	10.9000 775 701	32
33	12.7537 900 168	12.1074 209 943	11.5138 883 674	10.9678 134 287	33
34	12.8540 093 615	12.1929 497 622	11.5869 336 736	11.0302 427 914	34
35	12.9476 723 004	12.2725 114 067	11.6545 682 163	11.0877 813 746	35
36	13.0352 077 574	12.3465 222 388	11.7171 927 928	11.1408 123 268	36
37	13.1170 165 957	12.4153 695 244	11.7751 785 119	11.1896 887 805	37
38	13.1934 734 539	12.4794 135 111	11.8288 689 925	11.2347 362 032	38
39	13.2649 284 616	12.5389 893 127	11.8785 824 004	11.2762 545 652	39
40	13.3317 088 426	12.5944 086 629	11.9246 133 337	11.3145 203 366	40
41	13.3941 204 137	12.6459 615 469	11.9672 345 683	11.3497 883 286	41
42	13.4524 489 847	12.6939 177 181	12.0066 986 743	11.3822 933 904	42
43	13.5069 616 680	12.7385 281 098	12.0432 395 133	11.4122 519 728	43
44	13.5579 081 009	12.7800 261 487	12.0770 736 234	11.4398 635 694	44
45	13.6055 215 896	12.8186 289 755	12.1084 015 032	11.4653 120 455	45
46	13.6500 201 772	12.8545 385 819	12.1374 087 992	11.4887 668 622	46
47	13.6916 076 423	12.8879 428 669	12.1642 674 067	11.5103 842 048	47
48	13.7304 744 320	12.9190 166 203	12.1891 364 877	11.5303 080 229	48
49	13.7667 985 346	12.9479 224 375	12.2121 634 145	11.5486 709 888	49
50	13.8007 462 940	12.9748 115 698	12.2334 846 431	11.5655 953 814	50
51	13.8324 731 720	12.9998 247 161	12.2532 265 214	11.5811 938 999	51
52	13.8621 244 598	13.0230 927 591	12.2715 060 383	11.5955 704 146	52
53	13.8898 359 437	13.0447 374 504	12.2884 315 169	11.6088 206 587	53
54	13.9157 345 269	13.0648 720 469	12.3041 032 564	11.6210 328 651	54
55	13.9399 388 102	13.0836 019 040	12.3186 141 263	11.6322 883 550	55
56	13.9625 596 357	13.1010 250 270	12.3320 501 170	11.6426 620 783	56
57	13.9837 005 941	13.1172 325 833	12.3444 908 490	11.6522 231 136	57
58	14.0034 584 991	13.1323 093 798	12.3560 100 454	11.6610 351 278	58
59	14.0219 238 310	13.1463 343 068	12.3666 759 680	11.6691 567 998	59
60	14.0391 811 504	13.1593 807 505	12.3765 518 222	11.6766 422 118	60

228

Table 5. **PRESENT WORTH OF ONE DOLLAR PER PERIOD**
PAYABLE AT END OF EACH PERIOD

YEARS	9% NOMINAL ANNUAL RATE	9½% NOMINAL ANNUAL RATE	10% NOMINAL ANNUAL RATE	10½% NOMINAL ANNUAL RATE	YEARS
1	0.9174 311 927	0.9132 420 091	0.9090 909 091	0.9049 773 756	1
2	1.7591 111 859	1.7472 529 764	1.7355 371 901	1.7239 614 259	2
3	2.5312 946 660	2.5089 068 277	2.4868 519 910	2.4651 234 623	3
4	3.2397 198 771	3.2044 811 212	3.1698 654 463	3.1358 583 369	4
5	3.8896 512 634	3.8397 087 865	3.7907 867 694	3.7428 582 235	5
6	4.4859 185 902	4.4198 253 758	4.3552 606 995	4.2921 793 878	6
7	5.0329 528 351	4.9496 122 153	4.8684 188 177	4.7893 026 134	7
8	5.5348 191 147	5.4334 358 131	5.3349 261 979	5.2391 878 854	8
9	5.9952 468 943	5.8752 838 476	5.7590 238 163	5.6463 238 782	9
10	6.4176 577 012	6.2787 980 343	6.1445 671 057	6.0147 727 404	10
11	6.8051 905 515	6.6473 041 409	6.4950 610 052	6.3482 106 248	11
12	7.1607 252 766	6.9838 393 981	6.8136 918 229	6.6499 643 664	12
13	7.4869 039 235	7.2911 775 325	7.1033 562 026	6.9230 446 754	13
14	7.7861 503 885	7.5718 516 279	7.3666 874 569	7.1701 761 769	14
15	8.0606 884 299	7.8281 750 026	7.6060 795 063	7.3938 245 944	15
16	8.3125 581 925	8.0622 602 764	7.8237 086 421	7.5962 213 524	16
17	8.5436 313 693	8.2760 367 821	8.0215 533 110	7.7793 858 393	17
18	8.7556 251 094	8.4712 664 676	8.2014 121 009	7.9451 455 559	18
19	8.9501 147 793	8.6495 584 179	8.3649 200 917	8.0951 543 493	19
20	9.1285 456 691	8.8123 821 168	8.5135 637 198	8.2309 089 134	20
21	9.2922 437 331	8.9610 795 588	8.6486 942 907	8.3537 637 225	21
22	9.4424 254 432	9.0968 763 094	8.7715 402 643	8.4649 445 453	22
23	9.5802 068 286	9.2208 916 067	8.8832 184 221	8.5655 606 744	23
24	9.7066 117 694	9.3341 475 861	8.9847 440 201	8.6566 159 950	24
25	9.8225 796 049	9.4375 777 042	9.0770 400 182	8.7390 190 000	25
26	9.9289 721 146	9.5320 344 330	9.1609 454 711	8.8135 918 552	26
27	10.0265 799 217	9.6182 962 859	9.2372 231 556	8.8810 786 020	27
28	10.1161 283 685	9.6970 742 337	9.3065 665 051	8.9421 525 810	28
29	10.1982 829 069	9.7690 175 650	9.3696 059 137	8.9974 231 502	29
30	10.2736 540 430	9.8347 192 374	9.4269 144 670	9.0474 417 649	30
31	10.3428 018 743	9.8947 207 648	9.4790 131 518	9.0927 074 795	31
32	10.4062 402 517	9.9495 166 802	9.5263 755 926	9.1336 719 272	32
33	10.4644 405 979	9.9995 586 120	9.5694 323 569	9.1707 438 255	33
34	10.5178 354 109	10.0452 590 064	9.6085 748 699	9.2042 930 548	34
35	10.5668 214 779	10.0869 945 264	9.6441 589 726	9.2346 543 482	35
36	10.6117 628 237	10.1251 091 565	9.6765 081 569	9.2621 306 318	36
37	10.6529 934 163	10.1599 170 379	9.7059 165 063	9.2869 960 469	37
38	10.6908 196 480	10.1917 050 575	9.7326 513 694	9.3094 986 850	38
39	10.7255 226 128	10.2207 352 123	9.7569 557 903	9.3298 630 633	39
40	10.7573 601 952	10.2472 467 692	9.7790 507 185	9.3482 923 650	40
41	10.7865 689 865	10.2714 582 367	9.7991 370 168	9.3649 704 661	41
42	10.8133 660 426	10.2935 691 660	9.8173 972 880	9.3800 637 702	42
43	10.8379 504 978	10.3137 617 954	9.8339 975 345	9.3937 228 690	43
44	10.8605 050 439	10.3322 025 529	9.8490 886 678	9.4060 840 443	44
45	10.8811 972 880	10.3490 434 273	9.8628 078 798	9.4172 706 283	45
46	10.9001 809 981	10.3644 232 213	9.8752 798 907	9.4273 942 338	46
47	10.9175 972 460	10.3784 686 952	9.8866 180 825	9.4365 558 677	47
48	10.9335 754 550	10.3912 956 121	9.8969 255 295	9.4448 469 391	48
49	10.9482 343 624	10.4030 096 914	9.9062 959 359	9.4523 501 711	49
50	10.9616 829 013	10.4137 074 807	9.9148 144 872	9.4591 404 263	50
51	10.9740 210 104	10.4234 771 513	9.9225 586 247	9.4652 854 537	51
52	10.9853 403 765	10.4323 992 250	9.9295 987 498	9.4708 465 644	52
53	10.9957 251 160	10.4405 472 374	9.9359 988 634	9.4758 792 438	53
54	11.0052 524 000	10.4479 883 447	9.9418 171 486	9.4804 337 048	54
55	11.0139 930 276	10.4547 838 764	9.9471 064 987	9.4845 553 890	55
56	11.0220 119 519	10.4609 898 415	9.9519 149 988	9.4882 854 199	56
57	11.0293 687 632	10.4666 573 895	9.9562 863 626	9.4916 610 135	57
58	11.0361 181 314	10.4718 332 324	9.9602 603 296	9.4947 158 493	58
59	11.0423 102 123	10.4765 600 296	9.9638 730 269	9.4974 804 066	59
60	11.0479 910 204	10.4808 767 393	9.9671 572 972	9.4999 822 684	60

Table 5. **PRESENT WORTH OF ONE DOLLAR PER PERIOD**
PAYABLE AT END OF EACH PERIOD

YEARS	11% NOMINAL ANNUAL RATE	11½% NOMINAL ANNUAL RATE	12% NOMINAL ANNUAL RATE	12½% NOMINAL ANNUAL RATE	YEARS
1	0.9009 009 009	0.8968 609 865	0.8928 571 429	0.8888 888 889	1
2	1.7125 233 341	1.7012 206 157	1.6900 510 204	1.6790 123 457	2
3	2.4437 147 154	2.4226 193 863	2.4018 312 682	2.3813 443 073	3
4	3.1024 456 896	3.0696 137 994	3.0373 493 466	3.0056 393 842	4
5	3.6958 970 176	3.6498 778 470	3.6047 762 023	3.5605 683 415	5
6	4.2305 378 537	4.1702 940 332	4.1114 073 235	4.0538 385 258	6
7	4.7121 962 646	4.6370 350 073	4.5637 565 389	4.4923 009 118	7
8	5.1461 227 609	5.0556 367 779	4.9676 397 668	4.8820 452 550	8
9	5.5370 475 324	5.4310 643 748	5.3282 497 918	5.2284 846 711	9
10	5.8892 320 111	5.7677 707 397	5.6502 230 284	5.5364 308 187	10
11	6.2065 153 254	6.0697 495 423	5.9376 991 325	5.8101 607 278	11
12	6.4923 561 490	6.3405 825 492	6.1943 742 255	6.0534 762 025	12
13	6.7498 704 045	6.5834 821 069	6.4235 484 156	6.2697 566 244	13
14	6.9818 652 293	6.8013 292 438	6.6281 682 282	6.4620 058 884	14
15	7.1908 695 759	6.9967 078 420	6.8108 644 895	6.6328 941 230	15
16	7.3791 617 801	7.1719 352 843	6.9739 861 513	6.7847 947 760	16
17	7.5487 943 965	7.3290 899 411	7.1196 304 922	6.9198 175 787	17
18	7.7016 165 734	7.4700 358 216	7.2496 700 824	7.0398 378 477	18
19	7.8392 942 103	7.5964 446 831	7.3657 768 592	7.1465 225 313	19
20	7.9633 281 174	7.7098 158 592	7.4694 436 243	7.2413 533 611	20
21	8.0750 703 760	7.8114 940 442	7.5620 032 360	7.3256 474 321	21
22	8.1757 390 775	7.9026 852 414	7.6446 457 464	7.4005 754 952	22
23	8.2664 316 013	7.9844 710 685	7.7184 337 022	7.4671 782 180	23
24	8.3481 365 778	8.0578 215 861	7.7843 158 055	7.5263 806 382	24
25	8.4217 446 647	8.1236 068 037	7.8431 391 121	7.5790 050 117	25
26	8.4880 582 565	8.1826 069 988	7.8956 599 215	7.6257 822 327	26
27	8.5478 002 310	8.2355 219 720	7.9425 535 013	7.6673 619 846	27
28	8.6016 218 298	8.2829 793 471	7.9844 227 690	7.7043 217 641	28
29	8.6501 097 565	8.3255 420 154	8.0218 060 438	7.7371 749 014	29
30	8.6937 925 735	8.3637 148 120	8.0551 839 677	7.7663 776 901	30
31	8.7331 464 626	8.3979 505 040	8.0849 856 854	7.7923 357 246	31
32	8.7686 004 167	8.4286 551 606	8.1115 943 620	7.8154 095 329	32
33	8.8005 409 160	8.4561 929 691	8.1353 521 089	7.8359 195 848	33
34	8.8293 161 405	8.4808 905 553	8.1565 643 830	7.8541 507 421	34
35	8.8552 397 662	8.5030 408 567	8.1755 039 134	7.8703 562 152	35
36	8.8785 943 840	8.5229 065 980	8.1924 142 084	7.8847 610 802	36
37	8.8996 345 802	8.5407 234 062	8.2075 126 860	7.8975 654 046	37
38	8.9185 897 119	8.5567 026 065	8.2209 934 697	7.9089 470 263	38
39	8.9356 664 071	8.5710 337 278	8.2330 298 836	7.9190 640 234	39
40	8.9510 508 172	8.5838 867 514	8.2437 766 818	7.9280 569 097	40
41	8.9649 106 461	8.5954 141 268	8.2533 720 373	7.9360 505 864	41
42	8.9773 969 785	8.6057 525 801	8.2619 393 190	7.9431 560 768	42
43	8.9886 459 266	8.6150 247 355	8.2695 886 777	7.9494 720 682	43
44	8.9987 801 140	8.6233 405 700	8.2764 184 623	7.9550 862 829	44
45	9.0079 100 126	8.6307 987 175	8.2825 164 842	7.9600 766 959	45
46	9.0161 351 465	8.6374 876 390	8.2879 611 466	7.9645 126 186	46
47	9.0235 451 770	8.6434 866 717	8.2928 224 523	7.9684 556 610	47
48	9.0302 208 802	8.6488 669 702	8.2971 629 038	7.9719 605 875	48
49	9.0362 350 272	8.6536 923 499	8.3010 383 070	7.9750 760 778	49
50	9.0416 531 777	8.6580 200 448	8.3044 984 884	7.9778 454 025	50
51	9.0465 343 943	8.6619 013 854	8.3075 879 361	7.9803 070 244	51
52	9.0509 318 868	8.6653 824 085	8.3103 463 715	7.9824 951 328	52
53	9.0548 935 917	8.6685 044 022	8.3128 092 603	7.9844 401 181	53
54	9.0584 626 952	8.6713 043 966	8.3150 082 681	7.9861 689 938	54
55	9.0616 781 038	8.6738 156 023	8.3169 716 679	7.9877 057 723	55
56	9.0645 748 683	8.6760 678 048	8.3187 247 035	7.9890 717 976	56
57	9.0671 845 660	8.6780 877 173	8.3202 899 138	7.9902 860 423	57
58	9.0695 356 451	8.6798 992 980	8.3216 874 231	7.9913 653 709	58
59	9.0716 537 343	8.6815 240 341	8.3229 351 992	7.9923 247 742	59
60	9.0735 619 228	8.6829 811 965	8.3240 492 850	7.9931 775 770	60

Table 5. **PRESENT WORTH OF ONE DOLLAR PER PERIOD**
PAYABLE AT END OF EACH PERIOD

YEARS	**13%** NOMINAL ANNUAL RATE	**13½%** NOMINAL ANNUAL RATE	**14%** NOMINAL ANNUAL RATE	**14½%** NOMINAL ANNUAL RATE	YEARS
1	0.8849 557 522	0.8810 572 687	0.8771 929 825	0.8733 624 454	1
2	1.6681 024 356	1.6573 191 795	1.6466 605 109	1.6361 244 065	2
3	2.3611 525 979	2.3412 503 784	2.3216 320 271	2.3022 920 581	3
4	2.9744 713 255	2.9438 329 325	2.9137 123 045	2.8840 978 673	4
5	3.5172 312 615	3.4747 426 718	3.4330 809 689	3.3922 252 116	5
6	3.9975 497 890	3.9425 045 567	3.8886 675 165	3.8360 045 516	6
7	4.4226 104 327	4.3546 295 653	4.2883 048 391	4.2235 847 612	7
8	4.7987 702 944	4.7177 352 999	4.6388 638 939	4.5620 827 609	8
9	5.1316 551 278	5.0376 522 466	4.9463 718 368	4.8577 142 017	9
10	5.4262 434 760	5.3195 173 979	5.2161 156 463	5.1159 075 997	10
11	5.6869 411 292	5.5678 567 382	5.4527 330 231	5.3414 040 172	11
12	5.9176 470 170	5.7866 579 191	5.6602 921 255	5.5383 441 198	12
13	6.1218 115 194	5.9794 342 900	5.8423 615 136	5.7103 442 095	13
14	6.3024 880 703	6.1492 813 128	6.0020 715 032	5.8605 626 284	14
15	6.4623 788 233	6.2989 262 667	6.1421 679 852	5.9917 577 540	15
16	6.6038 750 648	6.4307 720 412	6.2650 596 362	6.1063 386 498	16
17	6.7290 929 777	6.5469 357 191	6.3728 593 300	6.2064 093 011	17
18	6.8399 052 900	6.6492 825 719	6.4674 204 649	6.2938 072 499	18
19	6.9379 692 832	6.7394 560 105	6.5503 688 288	6.3701 373 362	19
20	7.0247 515 781	6.8189 039 740	6.6231 305 516	6.4368 011 670	20
21	7.1015 500 691	6.8889 021 797	6.6869 566 242	6.4950 228 532	21
22	7.1695 133 355	6.9505 746 077	6.7429 444 072	6.5458 714 875	22
23	7.2296 578 190	7.0049 115 486	6.7920 564 976	6.5902 807 751	23
24	7.2828 830 257	7.0527 855 054	6.8351 372 786	6.6290 661 792	24
25	7.3299 849 785	7.0949 652 030	6.8729 274 373	6.6629 398 945	25
26	7.3716 681 225	7.1321 279 322	6.9060 766 994	6.6925 239 253	26
27	7.4085 558 607	7.1648 704 248	6.9351 549 995	6.7183 615 068	27
28	7.4411 998 767	7.1937 184 360	6.9606 622 803	6.7409 270 802	28
29	7.4700 883 864	7.2191 351 859	6.9830 370 879	6.7606 350 045	29
30	7.4956 534 393	7.2415 287 981	7.0026 641 122	6.7778 471 655	30
31	7.5182 773 799	7.2612 588 530	7.0198 808 002	6.7928 796 205	31
32	7.5382 985 663	7.2786 421 612	7.0349 831 581	6.8060 084 022	32
33	7.5560 164 304	7.2939 578 513	7.0482 308 404	6.8174 745 871	33
34	7.5716 959 561	7.3074 518 513	7.0598 516 144	6.8274 887 224	34
35	7.5855 716 425	7.3193 408 382	7.0700 452 758	6.8362 346 920	35
36	7.5978 510 111	7.3298 157 165	7.0789 870 840	6.8438 730 935	36
37	7.6087 177 089	7.3390 446 841	7.0868 307 755	6.8505 441 864	37
38	7.6183 342 557	7.3471 759 331	7.0937 112 065	6.8563 704 685	38
39	7.6268 444 741	7.3543 400 292	7.0997 466 724	6.8614 589 245	39
40	7.6343 756 408	7.3606 520 081	7.1050 409 407	6.8659 029 908	40
41	7.6410 403 901	7.3662 132 230	7.1096 850 357	6.8697 842 714	41
42	7.6469 383 983	7.3711 129 718	7.1137 588 033	6.8731 740 362	42
43	7.6521 578 746	7.3754 299 311	7.1173 322 836	6.8761 345 294	43
44	7.6567 768 802	7.3792 334 195	7.1204 669 154	6.8787 201 130	44
45	7.6608 644 957	7.3825 845 106	7.1232 165 925	6.8809 782 647	45
46	7.6644 818 546	7.3855 370 137	7.1256 285 899	6.8829 504 495	46
47	7.6676 830 572	7.3881 383 381	7.1277 443 771	6.8846 728 816	47
48	7.6705 159 798	7.3904 302 538	7.1296 003 308	6.8861 771 892	48
49	7.6730 229 910	7.3924 495 628	7.1312 283 603	6.8874 909 949	49
50	7.6752 415 849	7.3942 286 897	7.1326 564 564	6.8886 384 235	50
51	7.6772 049 424	7.3957 962 024	7.1339 091 723	6.8896 405 446	51
52	7.6789 424 269	7.3971 772 708	7.1350 080 459	6.8905 157 594	52
53	7.6804 800 238	7.3983 940 712	7.1359 719 701	6.8912 801 393	53
54	7.6818 407 291	7.3994 661 420	7.1368 175 176	6.8919 477 199	54
55	7.6830 448 930	7.4004 106 978	7.1375 592 260	6.8925 307 597	55
56	7.6841 105 247	7.4012 429 056	7.1382 098 473	6.8930 399 648	56
57	7.6850 535 617	7.4019 761 283	7.1387 805 678	6.8934 846 854	57
58	7.6858 881 077	7.4026 221 394	7.1392 811 999	6.8938 730 877	58
59	7.6866 266 440	7.4031 913 123	7.1397 203 508	6.8942 123 037	59
60	7.6872 802 159	7.4036 927 861	7.1401 055 708	6.8945 085 622	60

Table 5.   PRESENT WORTH OF ONE DOLLAR PER PERIOD
PAYABLE AT END OF EACH PERIOD

YEARS	15% NOMINAL ANNUAL RATE	15½% NOMINAL ANNUAL RATE	16% NOMINAL ANNUAL RATE	16½% NOMINAL ANNUAL RATE	YEARS
1	0.8695 652 174	0.8658 008 658	0.8620 689 655	0.8583 690 987	1
2	1.6257 088 847	1.6154 120 050	1.6052 318 668	1.5951 666 083	2
3	2.2832 251 171	2.2644 259 784	2.2458 895 404	2.2276 108 226	3
4	2.8549 783 627	2.8263 428 384	2.7981 806 382	2.7704 813 928	4
5	3.3521 550 980	3.3128 509 424	3.2742 936 537	3.2364 647 148	5
6	3.7844 826 939	3.7340 700 800	3.6847 359 083	3.6364 503 990	6
7	4.1604 197 338	4.0987 619 740	4.0385 654 382	3.9797 857 502	7
8	4.4873 215 077	4.4145 125 316	4.3435 908 950	4.2744 942 062	8
9	4.7715 839 197	4.6878 896 377	4.6065 438 750	4.5274 628 379	9
10	5.0187 686 259	4.9245 797 729	4.8332 274 785	4.7446 032 944	10
11	5.2337 118 486	5.1295 062 969	5.0286 443 780	4.9309 899 522	11
12	5.4206 189 988	5.3069 318 588	5.1971 072 224	5.0909 784 998	12
13	5.5831 469 554	5.4605 470 639	5.3423 338 124	5.2283 077 251	13
14	5.7244 756 134	5.5935 472 415	5.4675 291 486	5.3461 868 885	14
15	5.8473 700 986	5.7086 989 104	5.5754 561 626	5.4473 707 198	15
16	5.9542 348 684	5.8083 973 250	5.6684 966 919	5.5342 237 938	16
17	6.0471 607 551	5.8947 162 987	5.7487 040 447	5.6087 757 887	17
18	6.1279 658 740	5.9694 513 409	5.8178 483 144	5.6727 689 173	18
19	6.1982 311 948	6.0341 570 051	5.8774 554 435	5.7276 986 415	19
20	6.2593 314 737	6.0901 792 252	5.9288 408 996	5.7748 486 193	20
21	6.3124 621 511	6.1386 833 118	5.9731 387 065	5.8153 207 032	21
22	6.3586 627 401	6.1806 781 921	6.0113 264 711	5.8500 606 895	22
23	6.3988 371 653	6.2170 373 957	6.0442 469 579	5.8798 804 202	23
24	6.4337 714 481	6.2485 172 257	6.0726 266 878	5.9054 767 555	24
25	6.4641 490 853	6.2757 724 898	6.0970 919 723	5.9274 478 588	25
26	6.4905 644 220	6.2993 701 211	6.1181 827 347	5.9463 071 749	26
27	6.5135 342 800	6.3198 009 706	6.1363 644 265	5.9624 954 291	27
28	6.5335 080 695	6.3374 900 178	6.1520 382 987	5.9763 909 263	28
29	6.5508 765 822	6.3528 052 103	6.1655 502 575	5.9883 183 917	29
30	6.5659 796 367	6.3660 651 171	6.1771 984 978	5.9985 565 594	30
31	6.5791 127 276	6.3775 455 559	6.1872 400 843	6.0073 446 862	31
32	6.5905 328 066	6.3874 853 298	6.1958 966 244	6.0148 881 426	32
33	6.6004 633 101	6.3960 911 946	6.2033 591 590	6.0213 632 126	33
34	6.6090 985 305	6.4035 421 599	6.2097 923 784	6.0269 212 125	34
35	6.6166 074 178	6.4099 932 120	6.2153 382 573	6.0316 920 279	35
36	6.6231 368 851	6.4155 785 385	6.2201 191 873	6.0357 871 484	36
37	6.6288 146 827	6.4204 143 191	6.2242 406 787	6.0393 022 733	37
38	6.6337 518 980	6.4246 011 421	6.2277 936 885	6.0423 195 479	38
39	6.6380 451 287	6.4282 260 970	6.2308 566 281	6.0449 094 832	39
40	6.6417 783 728	6.4313 645 862	6.2334 970 932	6.0471 326 036	40
41	6.6450 246 720	6.4340 818 928	6.2357 733 562	6.0490 408 614	41
42	6.6478 475 408	6.4364 345 392	6.2377 356 519	6.0506 788 510	42
43	6.6503 022 094	6.4384 714 625	6.2394 272 861	6.0520 848 507	43
44	6.6524 367 038	6.4402 350 325	6.2408 855 915	6.0532 917 173	44
45	6.6542 927 860	6.4417 619 329	6.2421 427 513	6.0543 276 543	45
46	6.6559 067 704	6.4430 839 246	6.2432 265 097	6.0552 168 707	46
47	6.6573 102 351	6.4442 285 061	6.2441 607 842	6.0559 801 465	47
48	6.6585 306 392	6.4452 194 858	6.2449 661 933	6.0566 353 189	48
49	6.6595 918 602	6.4460 774 769	6.2456 605 115	6.0571 976 986	49
50	6.6605 146 611	6.4468 203 263	6.2462 590 616	6.0576 804 280	50
51	6.6613 170 966	6.4474 634 860	6.2467 750 531	6.0580 947 880	51
52	6.6620 148 666	6.4480 203 342	6.2472 198 734	6.0584 504 618	52
53	6.6626 216 231	6.4485 024 538	6.2476 033 391	6.0587 557 612	53
54	6.6631 492 375	6.4489 198 735	6.2479 339 130	6.0590 178 208	54
55	6.6636 080 326	6.4492 812 757	6.2482 188 905	6.0592 427 646	55
56	6.6640 069 849	6.4495 941 781	6.2484 645 608	6.0594 358 494	56
57	6.6643 538 999	6.4498 650 893	6.2486 763 455	6.0596 015 875	57
58	6.6646 555 651	6.4500 996 444	6.2488 589 186	6.0597 438 519	58
59	6.6649 178 827	6.4503 027 224	6.2490 163 091	6.0598 659 673	59
60	6.6651 459 850	6.4504 785 476	6.2491 519 906	6.0599 707 874	60

Table 5.   PRESENT WORTH OF ONE DOLLAR PER PERIOD
PAYABLE AT END OF EACH PERIOD

YEARS	17% NOMINAL ANNUAL RATE	17½% NOMINAL ANNUAL RATE	18% NOMINAL ANNUAL RATE	18½% NOMINAL ANNUAL RATE	YEARS
1	0.8547 008 547	0.8510 638 298	0.8474 576 271	0.8438 818 565	1
2	1.5852 144 057	1.5753 734 722	1.5656 420 569	1.5560 184 443	2
3	2.2095 849 622	2.1918 072 103	2.1742 729 296	2.1569 775 902	3
4	2.7432 350 104	2.7164 316 684	2.6900 618 047	2.6641 161 098	4
5	3.1993 461 627	3.1629 205 688	3.1271 710 209	3.0920 811 053	5
6	3.5891 847 545	3.5429 111 224	3.4976 025 601	3.4532 330 003	6
7	3.9223 801 320	3.8663 073 382	3.8115 275 933	3.7580 025 319	7
8	4.2071 625 060	4.1415 381 602	4.0775 657 571	4.0151 920 100	8
9	4.4505 662 444	4.3757 771 576	4.3030 218 280	4.2322 295 443	9
10	4.6586 036 277	4.5751 294 958	4.4940 862 949	4.4153 835 817	10
11	4.8364 133 570	4.7447 910 603	4.6560 053 347	4.5699 439 508	11
12	4.9883 874 846	4.8891 838 811	4.7932 248 599	4.7003 746 420	12
13	5.1182 799 014	5.0120 713 882	4.9095 125 931	4.8104 427 359	13
14	5.2292 990 610	5.1166 565 006	5.0080 615 196	4.9033 272 033	14
15	5.3241 872 317	5.2056 651 069	5.0915 775 590	4.9817 107 201	15
16	5.4052 882 322	5.2814 171 122	5.1623 538 635	5.0478 571 477	16
17	5.4746 053 267	5.3458 869 040	5.2223 337 827	5.1036 769 179	17
18	5.5338 507 065	5.4007 548 119	5.2731 642 226	5.1507 822 092	18
19	5.5844 877 834	5.4474 509 038	5.3162 408 666	5.1905 335 099	19
20	5.6277 673 362	5.4871 922 585	5.3527 464 971	5.2240 789 113	20
21	5.6647 584 070	5.5210 146 881	5.3836 834 721	5.2523 872 669	21
22	5.6963 747 069	5.5497 997 346	5.4099 012 476	5.2762 761 746	22
23	5.7233 971 853	5.5742 976 464	5.4321 197 013	5.2964 355 904	23
24	5.7464 933 208	5.5951 469 331	5.4509 488 994	5.3134 477 556	24
25	5.7662 336 075	5.6128 910 069	5.4669 058 470	5.3278 040 132	25
26	5.7831 056 475	5.6279 923 463	5.4804 286 839	5.3399 189 985	26
27	5.7975 261 944	5.6408 445 501	5.4918 887 152	5.3501 426 147	27
28	5.8098 514 482	5.6517 825 958	5.5016 006 061	5.3587 701 390	28
29	5.8203 858 532	5.6610 915 709	5.5098 310 221	5.3660 507 502	29
30	5.8293 896 181	5.6690 141 029	5.5168 059 509	5.3721 947 259	30
31	5.8370 851 437	5.6757 566 833	5.5227 169 076	5.3773 795 155	31
32	5.8436 625 160	5.6814 950 496	5.5277 261 928	5.3817 548 654	32
33	5.8492 842 017	5.6863 787 656	5.5319 713 499	5.3854 471 438	33
34	5.8540 890 613	5.6905 351 197	5.5355 689 406	5.3885 629 906	34
35	5.8581 957 789	5.6940 724 423	5.5386 177 462	5.3911 923 971	35
36	5.8617 057 939	5.6970 829 296	5.5412 014 799	5.3934 113 056	36
37	5.8647 058 067	5.6996 450 465	5.5433 910 846	5.3952 838 022	37
38	5.8672 699 203	5.7018 255 715	5.5452 466 819	5.3968 639 681	38
39	5.8694 614 703	5.7036 813 374	5.5468 192 219	5.3981 974 414	39
40	5.8713 345 900	5.7052 607 127	5.5481 518 830	5.3993 227 354	40
41	5.8729 355 470	5.7066 048 619	5.5492 812 568	5.4002 723 505	41
42	5.8743 038 864	5.7077 488 186	5.5502 383 532	5.4010 737 135	42
43	5.8754 734 071	5.7087 223 988	5.5510 494 519	5.4017 499 692	43
44	5.8764 729 976	5.7095 509 777	5.5517 368 236	5.4023 206 491	44
45	5.8773 273 483	5.7102 561 513	5.5523 193 420	5.4028 022 356	45
46	5.8780 575 627	5.7108 562 989	5.5528 130 017	5.4032 086 376	46
47	5.8786 816 775	5.7113 670 629	5.5532 313 574	5.4035 515 929	47
48	5.8792 151 090	5.7118 017 557	5.5535 858 961	5.4038 410 067	48
49	5.8796 710 333	5.7121 717 070	5.5538 863 526	5.4040 852 377	49
50	5.8800 607 122	5.7124 865 591	5.5541 409 768	5.4042 913 398	50
51	5.8803 937 711	5.7127 545 184	5.5543 567 600	5.4044 652 657	51
52	5.8806 784 369	5.7129 825 688	5.5545 396 271	5.4046 120 385	52
53	5.8809 217 409	5.7131 766 543	5.5546 945 993	5.4047 358 975	53
54	5.8811 296 931	5.7133 418 335	5.5548 259 316	5.4048 404 198	54
55	5.8813 074 300	5.7134 824 115	5.5549 372 301	5.4049 286 243	55
56	5.8814 593 419	5.7136 020 523	5.5550 315 510	5.4050 030 585	56
57	5.8815 891 811	5.7137 038 743	5.5551 114 839	5.4050 658 722	57
58	5.8817 001 548	5.7137 905 313	5.5551 792 236	5.4051 188 795	58
59	5.8817 950 041	5.7138 642 820	5.5552 366 302	5.4051 636 114	59
60	5.8818 760 719	5.7139 270 485	5.5552 852 798	5.4052 013 598	60

233

Table 5.   PRESENT WORTH OF ONE DOLLAR PER PERIOD
PAYABLE AT END OF EACH PERIOD

YEARS	19% NOMINAL ANNUAL RATE	19½% NOMINAL ANNUAL RATE	20% NOMINAL ANNUAL RATE	20½% NOMINAL ANNUAL RATE	YEARS
1	0.8403 361 345	0.8368 200 837	0.8333 333 333	0.8298 755 187	1
2	1.5465 009 533	1.5370 879 361	1.5277 777 778	1.5185 688 952	2
3	2.1399 167 675	2.1230 861 390	2.1064 814 815	2.0900 986 682	3
4	2.6385 855 189	2.6134 612 042	2.5887 345 679	2.5643 972 350	4
5	3.0576 348 898	3.0238 169 073	2.9906 121 399	2.9580 060 042	5
6	3.4097 772 184	3.3672 108 011	3.3255 101 166	3.2846 522 856	6
7	3.7056 951 415	3.6545 697 080	3.6045 917 638	3.5557 280 378	7
8	3.9543 656 651	3.8950 374 126	3.8371 598 032	3.7806 871 683	8
9	4.1633 324 917	4.0962 656 172	4.0309 665 027	3.9673 752 434	9
10	4.3389 348 670	4.2646 574 203	4.1924 720 856	4.1223 031 066	10
11	4.4864 998 882	4.4055 710 630	4.3270 600 713	4.2508 739 474	11
12	4.6105 041 077	4.5234 904 293	4.4392 167 261	4.3575 717 406	12
13	4.7147 093 342	4.6221 677 232	4.5326 806 051	4.4461 176 270	13
14	4.8022 767 515	4.7047 428 646	4.6105 671 709	4.5195 996 905	14
15	4.8758 628 163	4.7738 434 014	4.6754 726 424	4.5805 806 560	15
16	4.9376 998 457	4.8316 681 183	4.7295 605 353	4.6311 872 664	16
17	4.9896 637 359	4.8800 570 028	4.7746 337 794	4.6731 844 534	17
18	5.0333 308 705	4.9205 497 931	4.8121 948 162	4.7080 368 908	18
19	5.0700 259 416	4.9544 349 733	4.8434 956 802	4.7369 600 754	19
20	5.1008 621 358	4.9827 907 726	4.8695 797 335	4.7609 627 181	20
21	5.1267 749 040	5.0065 194 750	4.8913 164 446	4.7808 819 238	21
22	5.1485 503 395	5.0263 761 297	4.9094 303 705	4.7974 123 849	22
23	5.1668 490 248	5.0429 925 772	4.9245 253 087	4.8111 306 099	23
24	5.1822 260 713	5.0568 975 541	4.9371 044 239	4.8225 150 289	24
25	5.1951 479 590	5.0685 335 181	4.9475 870 199	4.8319 626 796	25
26	5.2060 066 883	5.0782 707 264	4.9563 225 166	4.8398 030 536	26
27	5.2151 316 708	5.0864 190 179	4.9636 020 972	4.8463 095 881	27
28	5.2227 997 234	5.0932 376 719	4.9696 684 143	4.8517 092 017	28
29	5.2292 434 650	5.0989 436 585	4.9747 236 786	4.8561 902 089	29
30	5.2346 583 740	5.1037 185 427	4.9789 363 988	4.8599 088 870	30
31	5.2392 087 176	5.1077 142 617	4.9824 469 990	4.8629 949 270	31
32	5.2430 325 358	5.1110 579 595	4.9853 724 992	4.8655 559 560	32
33	5.2462 458 284	5.1138 560 331	4.9878 104 160	4.8676 812 913	33
34	5.2489 460 743	5.1161 975 172	4.9898 420 133	4.8694 450 550	34
35	5.2512 151 885	5.1181 569 182	4.9915 350 111	4.8709 087 594	35
36	5.2531 220 071	5.1197 965 843	4.9929 458 426	4.8721 234 517	36
37	5.2547 243 757	5.1211 686 898	4.9941 215 355	4.8731 314 952	37
38	5.2560 709 040	5.1223 168 952	4.9951 012 796	4.8739 680 458	38
39	5.2572 024 403	5.1232 777 366	4.9959 177 330	4.8746 622 787	39
40	5.2581 533 112	5.1240 817 879	4.9965 981 108	4.8752 384 056	40
41	5.2589 523 623	5.1247 546 342	4.9971 650 923	4.8757 165 191	41
42	5.2596 238 339	5.1253 176 856	4.9976 375 770	4.8761 132 939	42
43	5.2601 880 957	5.1257 888 582	4.9980 313 141	4.8764 425 675	43
44	5.2606 622 653	5.1261 831 449	4.9983 594 284	4.8767 158 237	44
45	5.2610 607 272	5.1265 130 920	4.9986 328 570	4.8769 425 923	45
46	5.2613 955 690	5.1267 891 983	4.9988 607 142	4.8771 307 820	46
47	5.2616 769 488	5.1270 202 496	4.9990 505 952	4.8772 869 560	47
48	5.2619 134 023	5.1272 135 980	4.9992 088 293	4.8774 165 610	48
49	5.2621 121 028	5.1273 753 958	4.9993 406 911	4.8775 241 170	49
50	5.2622 790 780	5.1275 107 915	4.9994 505 759	4.8776 133 751	50
51	5.2624 193 933	5.1276 240 933	4.9995 421 466	4.8776 874 482	51
52	5.2625 373 053	5.1277 189 065	4.9996 184 555	4.8777 489 197	52
53	5.2626 363 910	5.1277 982 481	4.9996 820 462	4.8777 999 333	53
54	5.2627 196 563	5.1278 646 428	4.9997 350 385	4.8778 422 683	54
55	5.2627 896 271	5.1279 202 032	4.9997 791 988	4.8778 774 011	55
56	5.2628 484 262	5.1279 666 972	4.9998 159 990	4.8779 065 569	56
57	5.2628 978 371	5.1280 056 044	4.9998 466 658	4.8779 307 526	57
58	5.2629 393 589	5.1280 381 627	4.9998 722 215	4.8779 508 321	58
59	5.2629 742 512	5.1280 654 081	4.9998 935 179	4.8779 674 955	59
60	5.2630 035 724	5.1280 882 076	4.9999 112 649	4.8779 813 241	60

ANNUAL
COMPOUNDING

Table 5.   PRESENT WORTH OF ONE DOLLAR PER PERIOD
PAYABLE AT END OF EACH PERIOD

YEARS	21% NOMINAL ANNUAL RATE	21½% NOMINAL ANNUAL RATE	22% NOMINAL ANNUAL RATE	22½% NOMINAL ANNUAL RATE	YEARS
1	0.8264 462 810	0.8230 452 675	0.8196 721 311	0.8163 265 306	1
2	1.5094 597 364	1.5004 487 798	1.4915 345 337	1.4827 155 352	2
3	2.0739 336 664	2.0579 825 348	2.0422 414 211	2.0267 065 593	3
4	2.5404 410 466	2.5168 580 534	2.4936 405 091	2.4707 808 648	4
5	2.9259 843 360	2.8945 333 773	2.8636 397 615	2.8332 905 019	5
6	3.2446 151 538	3.2053 772 652	3.1669 178 373	3.1292 167 362	6
7	3.5079 464 081	3.4612 158 562	3.4155 064 240	3.3707 891 724	7
8	3.7255 755 439	3.6717 825 977	3.6192 675 607	3.5679 911 612	8
9	3.9054 343 338	3.8450 885 577	3.7862 848 858	3.7289 723 765	9
10	4.0540 779 618	3.9877 272 080	3.9231 843 326	3.8603 856 134	10
11	4.1769 239 354	4.1051 252 741	4.0353 969 940	3.9676 617 252	11
12	4.2784 495 334	4.2017 491 968	4.1273 745 852	4.0552 340 614	12
13	4.3623 549 862	4.2812 750 591	4.2027 660 535	4.1267 216 828	13
14	4.4316 983 357	4.3467 284 437	4.2645 623 389	4.1850 789 247	14
15	4.4890 068 890	4.4005 995 421	4.3152 150 319	4.2327 174 896	15
16	4.5363 693 298	4.4449 378 948	4.3567 336 327	4.2716 061 139	16
17	4.5755 118 428	4.4814 303 661	4.3907 652 727	4.3033 519 297	17
18	4.6078 610 271	4.5114 653 219	4.4186 600 596	4.3292 668 814	18
19	4.6345 958 902	4.5361 854 501	4.4415 246 390	4.3504 219 440	19
20	4.6566 908 183	4.5565 312 346	4.4602 660 975	4.3676 913 829	20
21	4.6749 510 895	4.5732 767 363	4.4756 279 488	4.3817 888 840	21
22	4.6900 422 227	4.5870 590 422	4.4882 196 302	4.3932 970 481	22
23	4.7025 142 337	4.5984 025 039	4.4985 406 805	4.4026 914 679	23
24	4.7128 216 807	4.6077 386 863	4.5070 005 578	4.4103 603 819	24
25	4.7213 402 320	4.6154 227 871	4.5139 348 834	4.4166 207 199	25
26	4.7283 803 570	4.6217 471 499	4.5196 187 569	4.4217 312 000	26
27	4.7341 986 422	4.6269 523 867	4.5242 776 696	4.4259 030 204	27
28	4.7390 071 423	4.6312 365 323	4.5280 964 505	4.4293 085 881	28
29	4.7429 811 093	4.6347 625 780	4.5312 265 988	4.4320 886 433	29
30	4.7462 653 796	4.6376 646 733	4.5337 922 941	4.4343 580 762	30
31	4.7489 796 526	4.6400 532 290	4.5358 953 230	4.4362 106 744	31
32	4.7512 228 534	4.6420 191 185	4.5376 191 172	4.4377 229 995	32
33	4.7530 767 383	4.6436 371 346	4.5390 320 633	4.4389 575 506	33
34	4.7546 088 746	4.6449 688 351	4.5401 902 158	4.4399 653 475	34
35	4.7558 751 030	4.6460 648 848	4.5411 395 212	4.4407 880 387	35
36	4.7569 215 727	4.6469 669 834	4.5419 176 403	4.4414 596 235	36
37	4.7577 864 237	4.6477 094 514	4.5425 554 429	4.4420 078 559	37
38	4.7585 011 767	4.6483 205 361	4.5430 782 319	4.4424 553 926	38
39	4.7590 918 815	4.6488 234 865	4.5435 067 474	4.4428 207 286	39
40	4.7595 800 674	4.6492 374 374	4.5438 579 897	4.4431 189 621	40
41	4.7599 835 268	4.6495 781 078	4.5441 458 932	4.4433 624 181	41
42	4.7603 169 643	4.6498 585 496	4.5443 818 797	4.4435 611 576	42
43	4.7605 925 325	4.6500 893 413	4.5445 753 112	4.4437 233 940	43
44	4.7608 202 748	4.6502 792 932	4.5447 338 616	4.4438 558 318	44
45	4.7610 084 915	4.6504 356 323	4.5448 638 210	4.4439 639 443	45
46	4.7611 640 426	4.6505 643 064	4.5449 703 451	4.4440 521 995	46
47	4.7612 925 972	4.6506 702 110	4.5450 576 599	4.4441 242 445	47
48	4.7613 988 406	4.6507 573 753	4.5451 292 294	4.4441 830 567	48
49	4.7614 866 452	4.6508 291 155	4.5451 878 930	4.4442 310 667	49
50	4.7615 592 109	4.6508 881 609	4.5452 359 779	4.4442 702 585	50
51	4.7616 191 825	4.6509 367 073	4.5452 753 917	4.4443 022 519	51
52	4.7616 687 459	4.6509 767 555	4.5453 076 981	4.4443 283 689	52
53	4.7617 097 074	4.6510 096 753	4.5453 341 788	4.4443 496 889	53
54	4.7617 435 598	4.6510 367 698	4.5453 558 842	4.4443 670 930	54
55	4.7617 715 370	4.6510 590 698	4.5453 736 756	4.4443 813 004	55
56	4.7617 946 587	4.6510 774 237	4.5453 882 587	4.4443 928 983	56
57	4.7618 137 675	4.6510 925 298	4.5454 002 120	4.4444 023 659	57
58	4.7618 295 599	4.6511 049 628	4.5454 100 099	4.4444 100 946	58
59	4.7618 426 115	4.6511 151 957	4.5454 180 409	4.4444 164 038	59
60	4.7618 533 979	4.6511 236 179	4.5454 246 237	4.4444 215 541	60

Table 5.   PRESENT WORTH OF ONE DOLLAR PER PERIOD
             PAYABLE AT END OF EACH PERIOD

YEARS	23% NOMINAL ANNUAL RATE	24% NOMINAL ANNUAL RATE	25% NOMINAL ANNUAL RATE	26% NOMINAL ANNUAL RATE	YEARS
1	0.8130 081 301	0.8064 516 129	0.8000 000 000	0.7936 507 937	1
2	1.4739 903 497	1.4568 158 169	1.4400 000 000	1.4235 323 759	2
3	2.0113 742 680	1.9813 030 781	1.9520 000 000	1.9234 383 936	3
4	2.4482 717 626	2.4042 766 759	2.3616 000 000	2.3201 892 013	4
5	2.8034 729 777	2.7453 844 160	2.6892 800 000	2.6350 707 946	5
6	3.0922 544 534	3.0204 713 033	2.9514 240 000	2.8849 768 211	6
7	3.3270 361 410	3.2423 155 671	3.1611 392 000	3.0833 149 374	7
8	3.5179 155 618	3.4212 222 316	3.3289 113 600	3.2407 261 408	8
9	3.6731 020 828	3.5655 017 997	3.4631 290 880	3.3656 556 673	9
10	3.7992 699 860	3.6818 562 900	3.5705 032 704	3.4648 060 852	10
11	3.9018 455 171	3.7756 905 565	3.6564 026 163	3.5434 968 930	11
12	3.9852 402 578	3.8513 633 520	3.7251 220 931	3.6059 499 151	12
13	4.0530 408 600	3.9123 898 000	3.7800 976 744	3.6555 158 056	13
14	4.1081 633 008	3.9616 046 774	3.8240 781 396	3.6948 538 140	14
15	4.1529 782 933	4.0012 940 947	3.8592 625 116	3.7260 744 555	15
16	4.1894 132 466	4.0333 016 893	3.8874 100 093	3.7508 527 425	16
17	4.2190 351 598	4.0591 142 655	3.9099 280 075	3.7705 180 496	17
18	4.2431 180 161	4.0799 308 593	3.9279 424 060	3.7861 254 362	18
19	4.2626 975 741	4.0967 184 349	3.9423 539 248	3.7985 122 509	19
20	4.2786 159 139	4.1102 568 024	3.9538 831 398	3.8083 430 563	20
21	4.2915 576 536	4.1211 748 406	3.9631 065 119	3.8161 452 828	21
22	4.3020 793 932	4.1299 797 102	3.9704 852 095	3.8223 375 260	22
23	4.3106 336 530	4.1370 804 114	3.9763 881 676	3.8272 520 048	23
24	4.3175 883 357	4.1428 067 834	3.9811 105 341	3.8311 523 847	24
25	4.3232 425 494	4.1474 248 253	3.9848 884 273	3.8342 479 244	25
26	4.3278 394 710	4.1511 490 527	3.9879 107 418	3.8367 047 019	26
27	4.3315 768 057	4.1541 524 618	3.9903 285 934	3.8386 545 253	27
28	4.3346 152 892	4.1565 745 660	3.9922 628 748	3.8402 020 042	28
29	4.3370 856 010	4.1585 278 758	3.9938 102 998	3.8414 301 621	29
30	4.3390 939 845	4.1601 031 257	3.9950 482 398	3.8424 048 905	30
31	4.3407 268 167	4.1613 734 884	3.9960 385 919	3.8431 784 846	31
32	4.3420 543 225	4.1623 979 745	3.9968 308 735	3.8437 924 481	32
33	4.3431 335 955	4.1632 241 730	3.9974 646 988	3.8442 797 207	33
34	4.3440 110 533	4.1638 904 621	3.9979 717 590	3.8446 664 450	34
35	4.3447 244 336	4.1644 277 920	3.9983 774 072	3.8449 733 690	35
36	4.3453 044 175	4.1648 611 226	3.9987 019 258	3.8452 169 596	36
37	4.3457 759 492	4.1652 105 827	3.9989 615 406	3.8454 102 854	37
38	4.3461 593 083	4.1654 924 054	3.9991 692 325	3.8455 637 185	38
39	4.3464 709 824	4.1657 196 818	3.9993 353 860	3.8456 854 909	39
40	4.3467 243 759	4.1659 029 692	3.9994 683 088	3.8457 821 356	40
41	4.3469 303 869	4.1660 507 816	3.9995 746 470	3.8458 588 378	41
42	4.3470 978 755	4.1661 699 852	3.9996 597 176	3.8459 197 125	42
43	4.3472 340 452	4.1662 661 171	3.9997 277 741	3.8459 680 258	43
44	4.3473 447 522	4.1663 436 428	3.9997 822 193	3.8460 063 697	44
45	4.3474 347 579	4.1664 061 635	3.9998 257 754	3.8460 368 014	45
46	4.3475 079 332	4.1664 565 835	3.9998 606 203	3.8460 609 535	46
47	4.3475 674 254	4.1664 972 448	3.9998 884 963	3.8460 801 218	47
48	4.3476 157 930	4.1665 300 361	3.9999 107 970	3.8460 953 348	48
49	4.3476 551 163	4.1665 564 807	3.9999 286 376	3.8461 074 085	49
50	4.3476 870 864	4.1665 778 070	3.9999 429 101	3.8461 169 909	50
51	4.3477 130 784	4.1665 950 057	3.9999 543 281	3.8461 245 960	51
52	4.3477 342 100	4.1666 088 755	3.9999 634 625	3.8461 306 317	52
53	4.3477 513 903	4.1666 200 609	3.9999 707 700	3.8461 354 220	53
54	4.3477 653 580	4.1666 290 814	3.9999 766 160	3.8461 392 238	54
55	4.3477 767 138	4.1666 363 560	3.9999 812 928	3.8461 422 411	55
56	4.3477 859 462	4.1666 422 225	3.9999 850 342	3.8461 446 358	56
57	4.3477 934 522	4.1666 469 537	3.9999 880 274	3.8461 465 364	57
58	4.3477 995 546	4.1666 507 691	3.9999 904 219	3.8461 480 447	58
59	4.3478 045 159	4.1666 538 460	3.9999 923 375	3.8461 492 418	59
60	4.3478 085 495	4.1666 563 274	3.9999 938 700	3.8461 501 919	60

Table 5.　PRESENT WORTH OF ONE DOLLAR PER PERIOD
PAYABLE AT END OF EACH PERIOD

YEARS	27% NOMINAL ANNUAL RATE	28% NOMINAL ANNUAL RATE	29% NOMINAL ANNUAL RATE	30% NOMINAL ANNUAL RATE	YEARS
1	0.7874 015 748	0.7812 500 000	0.7751 937 984	0.7692 307 692	1
2	1.4074 028 148	1.3916 015 625	1.3761 192 236	1.3609 467 456	2
3	1.8955 927 676	1.8684 387 207	1.8419 528 865	1.8161 128 812	3
4	2.2799 943 052	2.2409 677 505	2.2030 642 531	2.1662 406 778	4
5	2.5826 726 812	2.5320 060 551	2.4829 955 450	2.4355 697 522	5
6	2.8210 021 112	2.7593 797 306	2.6999 965 465	2.6427 459 632	6
7	3.0086 630 797	2.9370 154 145	2.8682 143 772	2.8021 122 794	7
8	3.1564 276 218	3.0757 932 926	2.9986 157 963	2.9247 017 534	8
9	3.2727 776 550	3.1842 135 098	3.0997 021 676	3.0190 013 488	9
10	3.3643 918 543	3.2689 168 046	3.1780 636 958	3.0915 394 990	10
11	3.4365 290 191	3.3350 912 536	3.2388 090 665	3.1473 380 762	11
12	3.4933 299 363	3.3867 900 418	3.2858 985 012	3.1902 600 586	12
13	3.5380 550 680	3.4271 797 202	3.3224 019 389	3.2232 769 682	13
14	3.5732 717 071	3.4587 341 564	3.3506 991 775	3.2486 745 909	14
15	3.6010 013 441	3.4833 860 597	3.3726 350 213	3.2682 112 238	15
16	3.6228 357 041	3.5026 453 591	3.3896 395 514	3.2832 394 029	16
17	3.6400 281 134	3.5176 916 868	3.4028 213 577	3.2947 995 407	17
18	3.6535 654 436	3.5294 466 303	3.4130 398 121	3.3036 919 544	18
19	3.6642 247 588	3.5386 301 799	3.4209 610 947	3.3105 322 726	19
20	3.6726 179 203	3.5458 048 281	3.4271 016 238	3.3157 940 558	20
21	3.6792 267 089	3.5514 100 219	3.4318 617 239	3.3198 415 814	21
22	3.6844 304 794	3.5557 890 796	3.4355 517 239	3.3229 550 626	22
23	3.6885 279 366	3.5592 102 185	3.4384 121 891	3.3253 500 482	23
24	3.6917 542 808	3.5618 829 832	3.4406 296 039	3.3271 923 448	24
25	3.6942 947 093	3.5639 710 806	3.4423 485 302	3.3286 094 960	25
26	3.6962 950 467	3.5656 024 067	3.4436 810 312	3.3296 996 123	26
27	3.6978 701 155	3.5668 768 803	3.4447 139 776	3.3305 381 633	27
28	3.6991 103 272	3.5678 725 627	3.4455 147 113	3.3311 832 025	28
29	3.7000 868 718	3.5686 504 396	3.4461 354 352	3.3316 793 866	29
30	3.7008 558 045	3.5692 581 559	3.4466 166 164	3.3320 610 666	30
31	3.7014 612 634	3.5697 329 343	3.4469 896 251	3.3323 546 666	31
32	3.7019 380 027	3.5701 038 549	3.4472 787 792	3.3325 805 128	32
33	3.7023 133 879	3.5703 936 367	3.4475 029 296	3.3327 542 406	33
34	3.7026 089 669	3.5706 200 287	3.4476 766 896	3.3328 878 774	34
35	3.7028 417 062	3.5707 968 974	3.4478 113 873	3.3329 906 749	35
36	3.7030 249 655	3.5709 350 761	3.4479 158 041	3.3330 697 499	36
37	3.7031 692 642	3.5710 430 282	3.4479 967 474	3.3331 305 769	37
38	3.7032 828 852	3.5711 273 658	3.4480 594 941	3.3331 773 668	38
39	3.7033 723 505	3.5711 932 545	3.4481 081 349	3.3332 133 591	39
40	3.7034 427 957	3.5712 447 301	3.4481 458 410	3.3332 410 455	40
41	3.7034 982 643	3.5712 849 454	3.4481 750 706	3.3332 623 427	41
42	3.7035 419 404	3.5713 163 636	3.4481 977 291	3.3332 787 251	42
43	3.7035 763 310	3.5713 409 090	3.4482 152 939	3.3332 913 270	43
44	3.7036 034 103	3.5713 600 852	3.4482 289 100	3.3333 010 208	44
45	3.7036 247 325	3.5713 750 666	3.4482 394 651	3.3333 084 775	45
46	3.7036 415 216	3.5713 867 707	3.4482 476 474	3.3333 142 135	46
47	3.7036 547 415	3.5713 959 146	3.4482 539 902	3.3333 186 258	47
48	3.7036 651 508	3.5714 030 583	3.4482 589 071	3.3333 220 198	48
49	3.7036 733 470	3.5714 086 393	3.4482 627 187	3.3333 246 306	49
50	3.7036 798 008	3.5714 129 995	3.4482 656 734	3.3333 266 389	50
51	3.7036 848 825	3.5714 164 058	3.4482 679 639	3.3333 281 838	51
52	3.7036 888 839	3.5714 190 671	3.4482 697 395	3.3333 293 722	52
53	3.7036 920 346	3.5714 211 461	3.4482 711 159	3.3333 302 863	53
54	3.7036 945 154	3.5714 227 704	3.4482 721 828	3.3333 309 894	54
55	3.7036 964 688	3.5714 240 394	3.4482 730 099	3.3333 315 303	55
56	3.7036 980 069	3.5714 250 308	3.4482 736 511	3.3333 319 464	56
57	3.7036 992 181	3.5714 258 053	3.4482 741 482	3.3333 322 665	57
58	3.7037 001 717	3.5714 264 104	3.4482 745 335	3.3333 325 127	58
59	3.7037 009 226	3.5714 268 831	3.4482 748 321	3.3333 327 021	59
60	3.7037 015 139	3.5714 272 524	3.4482 750 637	3.3333 328 477	60

Table 6. PARTIAL PAYMENT TO AMORTIZE 1
PAYABLE AT END OF EACH PERIOD

YEARS	5% NOMINAL ANNUAL RATE	5½% NOMINAL ANNUAL RATE	6% NOMINAL ANNUAL RATE	6½% NOMINAL ANNUAL RATE	YEARS
1	1.0500 000 000	1.0550 000 000	1.0600 000 000	1.0650 000 000	1
2	0.5378 048 780	0.5416 180 049	0.5454 368 932	0.5492 615 012	2
3	0.3672 085 646	0.3706 540 747	0.3741 098 128	0.3775 757 019	3
4	0.2820 118 326	0.2852 944 853	0.2885 914 924	0.2919 027 404	4
5	0.2309 747 981	0.2341 764 362	0.2373 964 004	0.2406 345 376	5
6	0.1970 174 681	0.2001 789 476	0.2033 626 285	0.2065 683 122	6
7	0.1728 198 184	0.1759 646 178	0.1791 350 181	0.1823 313 693	7
8	0.1547 218 136	0.1578 640 118	0.1610 359 426	0.1642 372 971	8
9	0.1406 900 800	0.1438 394 585	0.1470 222 350	0.1502 380 329	9
10	0.1295 045 750	0.1326 677 687	0.1358 679 582	0.1391 046 901	10
11	0.1203 888 915	0.1235 706 532	0.1267 929 381	0.1300 552 058	11
12	0.1128 254 100	0.1160 292 312	0.1192 770 294	0.1225 681 661	12
13	0.1064 557 652	0.1096 842 587	0.1129 601 053	0.1162 825 571	13
14	0.1010 239 695	0.1042 791 154	0.1075 849 090	0.1109 404 806	14
15	0.0963 422 876	0.0996 255 976	0.1029 627 640	0.1063 527 830	15
16	0.0922 699 080	0.0955 825 380	0.0989 521 436	0.1023 775 740	16
17	0.0886 991 417	0.0920 419 723	0.0954 448 042	0.0989 063 265	17
18	0.0855 462 223	0.0889 199 163	0.0923 565 406	0.0958 546 103	18
19	0.0827 450 104	0.0861 500 559	0.0896 208 604	0.0931 557 517	19
20	0.0802 425 872	0.0836 793 300	0.0871 845 570	0.0907 563 954	20
21	0.0779 961 071	0.0814 647 754	0.0850 045 467	0.0886 133 343	21
22	0.0759 705 086	0.0794 712 319	0.0830 455 685	0.0866 912 043	22
23	0.0741 368 219	0.0776 696 472	0.0812 784 847	0.0849 607 802	23
24	0.0724 709 008	0.0760 358 037	0.0796 790 050	0.0833 976 975	24
25	0.0709 524 573	0.0745 493 529	0.0782 267 182	0.0819 814 811	25
26	0.0695 643 207	0.0731 930 713	0.0769 043 467	0.0806 947 983	26
27	0.0682 918 599	0.0719 522 817	0.0756 971 663	0.0795 228 776	27
28	0.0671 225 304	0.0708 143 996	0.0745 925 515	0.0784 530 522	28
29	0.0660 455 149	0.0697 685 720	0.0735 796 135	0.0774 743 976	29
30	0.0650 514 351	0.0688 053 897	0.0726 489 115	0.0765 774 422	30
31	0.0641 321 204	0.0679 166 543	0.0717 922 196	0.0757 539 335	31
32	0.0632 804 189	0.0670 951 895	0.0710 023 374	0.0749 966 481	32
33	0.0624 900 437	0.0663 346 865	0.0702 729 350	0.0742 992 365	33
34	0.0617 554 454	0.0656 295 769	0.0695 984 254	0.0736 560 953	34
35	0.0610 717 072	0.0649 749 266	0.0689 738 590	0.0730 622 606	35
36	0.0604 344 571	0.0643 663 488	0.0683 948 348	0.0725 133 205	36
37	0.0598 397 945	0.0637 999 295	0.0678 574 274	0.0720 053 400	37
38	0.0592 842 282	0.0632 721 659	0.0673 581 240	0.0715 347 995	38
39	0.0587 646 242	0.0627 799 139	0.0668 937 724	0.0710 985 416	39
40	0.0582 781 612	0.0623 203 434	0.0664 615 359	0.0706 937 260	40
41	0.0578 222 924	0.0618 909 001	0.0660 588 551	0.0703 177 915	41
42	0.0573 947 131	0.0614 892 731	0.0656 834 152	0.0699 684 229	42
43	0.0569 933 328	0.0611 133 667	0.0653 331 178	0.0696 435 230	43
44	0.0566 162 506	0.0607 612 757	0.0650 060 565	0.0693 411 874	44
45	0.0562 617 347	0.0604 312 651	0.0647 004 958	0.0690 596 841	45
46	0.0559 282 036	0.0601 217 512	0.0644 148 527	0.0687 974 344	46
47	0.0556 142 109	0.0598 312 858	0.0641 476 805	0.0685 529 973	47
48	0.0553 184 306	0.0595 585 424	0.0638 976 549	0.0683 250 549	48
49	0.0550 396 453	0.0593 023 035	0.0636 635 619	0.0681 124 000	49
50	0.0547 767 355	0.0590 614 501	0.0634 442 864	0.0679 139 255	50
51	0.0545 286 697	0.0588 349 523	0.0632 388 028	0.0677 286 146	51
52	0.0542 944 966	0.0586 218 603	0.0630 461 669	0.0675 555 319	52
53	0.0540 733 368	0.0584 212 975	0.0628 655 076	0.0673 938 164	53
54	0.0538 643 770	0.0582 324 534	0.0626 960 209	0.0672 426 740	54
55	0.0536 668 637	0.0580 545 778	0.0625 369 634	0.0671 013 722	55
56	0.0534 800 978	0.0578 869 756	0.0623 876 472	0.0669 692 339	56
57	0.0533 034 300	0.0577 290 020	0.0622 474 350	0.0668 456 332	57
58	0.0531 362 568	0.0575 800 578	0.0621 157 359	0.0667 299 909	58
59	0.0529 780 161	0.0574 395 863	0.0619 920 012	0.0666 217 702	59
60	0.0528 281 845	0.0573 070 692	0.0618 757 215	0.0665 204 735	60

Table 6.   PARTIAL PAYMENT TO AMORTIZE 1
PAYABLE AT END OF EACH PERIOD

YEARS	7% NOMINAL ANNUAL RATE	7½% NOMINAL ANNUAL RATE	8% NOMINAL ANNUAL RATE	8½% NOMINAL ANNUAL RATE	YEARS
1	1.0700 000 000	1.0750 000 000	1.0800 000 000	1.0850 000 000	1
2	0.5530 917 874	0.5569 277 108	0.5607 692 308	0.5646 163 070	2
3	0.3810 516 657	0.3845 376 282	0.3880 335 140	0.3915 392 485	3
4	0.2952 281 167	0.2985 675 087	0.3019 208 045	0.3052 878 926	4
5	0.2438 906 944	0.2471 647 178	0.2504 564 546	0.2537 657 519	5
6	0.2097 957 998	0.2130 448 912	0.2163 153 862	0.2196 070 840	6
7	0.1855 532 196	0.1888 003 154	0.1920 724 014	0.1953 692 212	7
8	0.1674 677 625	0.1707 270 232	0.1740 147 606	0.1773 306 533	8
9	0.1534 864 701	0.1567 671 595	0.1600 797 092	0.1634 237 233	9
10	0.1423 775 027	0.1456 859 274	0.1490 294 887	0.1524 077 051	10
11	0.1333 569 048	0.1366 974 737	0.1400 763 421	0.1434 929 316	11
12	0.1259 019 887	0.1292 778 313	0.1326 950 169	0.1361 528 581	12
13	0.1196 508 481	0.1230 641 963	0.1265 218 052	0.1300 228 662	13
14	0.1143 449 386	0.1177 973 721	0.1212 968 528	0.1248 424 382	14
15	0.1097 946 247	0.1132 872 363	0.1168 295 449	0.1204 204 614	15
16	0.1058 576 477	0.1093 911 571	0.1129 768 720	0.1166 135 439	16
17	0.1024 251 931	0.1060 000 282	0.1096 294 315	0.1133 119 832	17
18	0.0994 126 017	0.1030 289 578	0.1067 020 959	0.1104 304 127	18
19	0.0967 530 148	0.1004 108 994	0.1041 276 275	0.1079 014 015	19
20	0.0943 929 257	0.0980 921 916	0.1018 522 088	0.1056 709 744	20
21	0.0922 890 017	0.0960 293 742	0.0998 322 503	0.1036 954 120	21
22	0.0904 057 732	0.0941 868 710	0.0980 320 684	0.1019 389 233	22
23	0.0887 139 263	0.0925 352 780	0.0964 221 692	0.1003 719 258	23
24	0.0871 890 207	0.0910 500 795	0.0949 779 616	0.0989 697 546	24
25	0.0858 105 172	0.0897 106 716	0.0936 787 791	0.0977 116 825	25
26	0.0845 610 279	0.0884 996 124	0.0925 071 267	0.0965 801 651	26
27	0.0834 257 340	0.0874 020 369	0.0914 480 962	0.0955 602 540	27
28	0.0823 919 283	0.0864 051 993	0.0904 889 057	0.0946 391 357	28
29	0.0814 486 518	0.0854 981 081	0.0896 185 350	0.0938 057 657	29
30	0.0805 864 035	0.0846 712 358	0.0888 274 334	0.0930 505 753	30
31	0.0797 969 061	0.0839 162 831	0.0881 072 841	0.0923 652 359	31
32	0.0790 729 155	0.0832 259 887	0.0874 508 132	0.0917 424 664	32
33	0.0784 080 653	0.0825 939 728	0.0868 516 324	0.0911 758 763	33
34	0.0777 967 381	0.0820 146 084	0.0863 041 101	0.0906 598 358	34
35	0.0772 339 596	0.0814 829 147	0.0858 032 646	0.0901 893 685	35
36	0.0767 153 097	0.0809 944 680	0.0853 446 741	0.0897 600 615	36
37	0.0762 368 480	0.0805 453 271	0.0849 244 025	0.0893 679 904	37
38	0.0757 950 515	0.0801 319 709	0.0845 389 361	0.0890 096 556	38
39	0.0753 867 616	0.0797 512 443	0.0841 851 297	0.0886 819 284	39
40	0.0750 091 389	0.0794 003 138	0.0838 601 615	0.0883 820 056	40
41	0.0746 596 245	0.0790 766 282	0.0835 614 940	0.0881 073 700	41
42	0.0743 359 072	0.0787 778 858	0.0832 868 407	0.0878 557 568	42
43	0.0740 358 953	0.0785 020 052	0.0830 341 370	0.0876 251 245	43
44	0.0737 576 913	0.0782 471 012	0.0828 015 156	0.0874 136 299	44
45	0.0734 995 710	0.0780 114 630	0.0825 872 845	0.0872 196 061	45
46	0.0732 599 650	0.0777 935 352	0.0823 899 085	0.0870 415 434	46
47	0.0730 374 421	0.0775 919 020	0.0822 079 922	0.0868 780 731	47
48	0.0728 306 953	0.0774 052 724	0.0820 402 660	0.0867 279 519	48
49	0.0726 385 294	0.0772 324 676	0.0818 855 731	0.0865 900 501	49
50	0.0724 598 495	0.0770 724 102	0.0817 428 582	0.0864 633 395	50
51	0.0722 936 519	0.0769 241 141	0.0816 111 575	0.0863 468 835	51
52	0.0721 390 147	0.0767 866 757	0.0814 895 903	0.0862 398 282	52
53	0.0719 950 908	0.0766 592 661	0.0813 773 506	0.0861 413 945	53
54	0.0718 611 007	0.0765 411 247	0.0812 737 003	0.0860 508 710	54
55	0.0717 363 264	0.0764 315 521	0.0811 779 629	0.0859 676 075	55
56	0.0716 201 059	0.0763 299 053	0.0810 895 180	0.0858 910 096	56
57	0.0715 118 286	0.0762 355 927	0.0810 077 963	0.0858 205 332	57
58	0.0714 109 304	0.0761 480 689	0.0809 322 748	0.0857 556 803	58
59	0.0713 168 900	0.0760 668 318	0.0808 624 729	0.0856 959 948	59
60	0.0712 2º2 255	0.0759 914 178	0.0807 979 488	0.0856 410 586	60

Table 6.   PARTIAL PAYMENT TO AMORTIZE 1
             PAYABLE AT END OF EACH PERIOD

YEARS	9% NOMINAL ANNUAL RATE	9½% NOMINAL ANNUAL RATE	10% NOMINAL ANNUAL RATE	10½% NOMINAL ANNUAL RATE	YEARS
1	1.0900 000 000	1.0950 000 000	1.1000 000 000	1.1050 000 000	1
2	0.5684 688 995	0.5723 269 690	0.5761 904 762	0.5800 593 824	2
3	0.3950 547 573	0.3985 799 668	0.4021 148 036	0.4056 591 953	3
4	0.3086 686 621	0.3120 630 025	0.3154 708 037	0.3188 919 564	4
5	0.2570 924 570	0.2604 364 173	0.2637 974 808	0.2671 754 954	5
6	0.2229 197 833	0.2262 532 826	0.2296 073 804	0.2329 818 746	6
7	0.1986 905 168	0.2020 360 296	0.2054 054 997	0.2087 986 667	7
8	0.1806 743 778	0.1840 456 084	0.1874 440 176	0.1908 692 763	8
9	0.1667 988 021	0.1702 045 426	0.1736 405 391	0.1771 063 831	9
10	0.1558 200 899	0.1592 661 517	0.1627 453 949	0.1662 573 206	10
11	0.1469 466 567	0.1504 369 258	0.1539 631 420	0.1575 247 041	11
12	0.1396 506 585	0.1431 877 142	0.1467 633 151	0.1503 767 456	12
13	0.1335 665 597	0.1371 520 575	0.1407 785 238	0.1444 451 173	13
14	0.1284 331 730	0.1320 680 923	0.1357 462 232	0.1394 665 871	14
15	0.1240 588 827	0.1277 436 950	0.1314 737 769	0.1352 480 015	15
16	0.1202 999 097	0.1240 346 957	0.1278 166 207	0.1316 443 997	16
17	0.1170 462 485	0.1208 307 825	0.1246 641 344	0.1285 448 518	17
18	0.1142 122 907	0.1180 461 037	0.1219 302 222	0.1258 630 182	18
19	0.1117 304 107	0.1156 128 384	0.1195 468 682	0.1235 306 897	19
20	0.1095 464 750	0.1134 766 953	0.1174 596 248	0.1214 932 653	20
21	0.1076 166 348	0.1115 936 973	0.1156 243 898	0.1197 065 219	21
22	0.1059 049 930	0.1099 278 440	0.1140 050 630	0.1181 342 647	22
23	0.1043 818 800	0.1084 493 824	0.1125 718 127	0.1167 465 900	23
24	0.1030 225 607	0.1071 335 107	0.1112 997 764	0.1155 185 815	24
25	0.1018 062 505	0.1059 593 925	0.1101 680 722	0.1144 293 198	25
26	0.1007 153 599	0.1049 093 986	0.1091 590 386	0.1134 611 196	26
27	0.0997 349 054	0.1039 685 169	0.1082 576 423	0.1125 989 359	27
28	0.0988 520 473	0.1031 238 883	0.1074 510 132	0.1118 298 968	28
29	0.0980 557 226	0.1023 644 387	0.1067 280 747	0.1111 429 332	29
30	0.0973 363 514	0.1016 805 845	0.1060 792 483	0.1105 284 815	30
31	0.0966 855 995	0.1010 639 940	0.1054 962 140	0.1099 782 438	31
32	0.0960 961 861	0.1005 073 947	0.1049 717 167	0.1094 849 922	32
33	0.0955 617 255	0.1000 044 141	0.1044 994 063	0.1090 424 091	33
34	0.0950 765 971	0.0995 494 491	0.1040 737 064	0.1086 449 545	34
35	0.0946 358 375	0.0991 375 575	0.1036 897 051	0.1082 877 563	35
36	0.0942 350 500	0.0987 643 673	0.1033 430 638	0.1079 665 187	36
37	0.0938 703 293	0.0984 260 006	0.1030 299 405	0.1076 774 443	37
38	0.0935 381 975	0.0981 190 090	0.1027 469 250	0.1074 171 697	38
39	0.0932 355 500	0.0978 403 196	0.1024 909 840	0.1071 827 092	39
40	0.0929 596 092	0.0975 871 883	0.1022 594 144	0.1069 714 084	40
41	0.0927 078 853	0.0973 571 597	0.1020 498 028	0.1067 809 027	41
42	0.0924 781 420	0.0971 480 333	0.1018 599 911	0.1066 090 833	42
43	0.0922 683 675	0.0969 578 336	0.1016 880 466	0.1064 540 666	43
44	0.0920 767 493	0.0967 847 847	0.1015 322 365	0.1063 141 681	44
45	0.0919 016 514	0.0966 272 880	0.1013 910 047	0.1061 878 796	45
46	0.0917 415 959	0.0964 839 025	0.1012 629 527	0.1060 738 498	46
47	0.0915 952 455	0.0963 533 282	0.1011 468 221	0.1059 708 663	47
48	0.0914 613 892	0.0962 343 905	0.1010 414 797	0.1058 778 407	48
49	0.0913 389 289	0.0961 260 279	0.1009 459 041	0.1057 937 954	49
50	0.0912 268 681	0.0960 272 796	0.1008 591 740	0.1057 178 512	50
51	0.0911 243 016	0.0959 372 756	0.1007 804 577	0.1056 492 173	51
52	0.0910 304 065	0.0958 552 274	0.1007 090 040	0.1055 871 820	52
53	0.0909 444 343	0.0957 804 201	0.1006 441 339	0.1055 311 042	53
54	0.0908 657 034	0.0957 122 048	0.1005 852 336	0.1054 804 064	54
55	0.0907 935 930	0.0956 499 926	0.1005 317 476	0.1054 345 680	55
56	0.0907 275 373	0.0955 932 484	0.1004 831 734	0.1053 931 196	56
57	0.0906 670 202	0.0955 414 860	0.1004 390 556	0.1053 556 378	57
58	0.0906 115 709	0.0954 942 633	0.1003 989 822	0.1053 217 406	58
59	0.0905 607 595	0.0954 511 784	0.1003 625 796	0.1052 910 832	59
60	0.0905 141 938	0.0954 118 653	0.1003 295 092	0.1052 633 544	60

Table 6. PARTIAL PAYMENT TO AMORTIZE 1
PAYABLE AT END OF EACH PERIOD

YEARS	11% NOMINAL ANNUAL RATE	11½% NOMINAL ANNUAL RATE	12% NOMINAL ANNUAL RATE	12½% NOMINAL ANNUAL RATE	YEARS
1	1.1100 000 000	1.1150 000 000	1.1200 000 000	1.1250 000 000	1
2	0.5839 336 493	0.5878 132 388	0.5916 981 132	0.5955 882 353	2
3	0.4092 130 696	0.4127 763 551	0.4163 489 806	0.4199 308 756	3
4	0.3223 263 515	0.3257 738 808	0.3292 344 363	0.3327 079 108	4
5	0.2705 703 095	0.2739 817 720	0.2774 097 319	0.2808 540 390	5
6	0.2363 765 636	0.2397 912 454	0.2432 257 184	0.2466 797 811	6
7	0.2122 152 695	0.2156 550 465	0.2191 177 359	0.2226 030 757	7
8	0.1943 210 542	0.1977 990 200	0.2013 028 414	0.2048 321 856	8
9	0.1806 016 644	0.1841 259 707	0.1876 788 888	0.1912 600 042	9
10	0.1698 014 271	0.1733 772 102	0.1769 841 642	0.1806 217 819	10
11	0.1611 210 071	0.1647 514 437	0.1684 154 043	0.1721 122 783	11
12	0.1540 272 864	0.1577 142 151	0.1614 368 076	0.1651 943 390	12
13	0.1481 509 925	0.1518 953 016	0.1556 771 951	0.1594 958 241	13
14	0.1432 282 015	0.1470 300 825	0.1508 712 461	0.1547 507 101	14
15	0.1390 652 395	0.1429 243 614	0.1468 242 396	0.1507 637 513	15
16	0.1355 167 470	0.1394 323 792	0.1433 900 180	0.1473 883 932	16
17	0.1324 714 845	0.1364 425 881	0.1404 567 275	0.1445 124 801	17
18	0.1298 428 701	0.1338 681 666	0.1379 373 114	0.1420 487 264	18
19	0.1275 625 041	0.1316 405 294	0.1357 630 049	0.1399 281 952	19
20	0.1255 756 369	0.1297 047 839	0.1338 787 800	0.1380 957 330	20
21	0.1238 379 300	0.1280 164 837	0.1322 400 915	0.1365 067 060	21
22	0.1223 131 011	0.1265 392 673	0.1308 105 088	0.1351 246 265	22
23	0.1209 711 818	0.1252 431 115	0.1295 599 650	0.1339 193 964	23
24	0.1197 872 113	0.1241 030 208	0.1284 634 417	0.1328 659 881	24
25	0.1187 402 421	0.1230 980 307	0.1274 999 698	0.1319 434 409	25
26	0.1178 125 750	0.1222 104 398	0.1266 518 581	0.1311 340 882	26
27	0.1169 891 636	0.1214 252 118	0.1259 040 937	0.1304 229 541	27
28	0.1162 571 454	0.1207 295 054	0.1252 438 691	0.1297 972 788	28
29	0.1156 054 695	0.1201 123 000	0.1246 602 068	0.1292 461 412	29
30	0.1150 245 985	0.1195 640 959	0.1241 436 576	0.1287 601 556	30
31	0.1145 062 669	0.1190 766 723	0.1236 860 570	0.1283 312 264	31
32	0.1140 432 854	0.1186 428 892	0.1232 803 263	0.1279 523 480	32
33	0.1136 293 791	0.1182 565 256	0.1229 203 096	0.1276 174 403	33
34	0.1132 590 547	0.1179 121 454	0.1226 006 383	0.1273 212 131	34
35	0.1129 274 900	0.1176 049 859	0.1223 166 193	0.1270 590 521	35
36	0.1126 304 409	0.1173 308 646	0.1220 641 406	0.1268 269 247	36
37	0.1123 641 641	0.1170 861 006	0.1218 395 924	0.1266 213 002	37
38	0.1121 253 508	0.1168 674 484	0.1216 397 998	0.1264 390 818	38
39	0.1119 110 713	0.1166 720 412	0.1214 619 665	0.1262 775 496	39
40	0.1117 187 267	0.1164 973 431	0.1213 036 256	0.1261 343 115	40
41	0.1115 460 086	0.1163 411 076	0.1211 625 982	0.1260 072 613	41
42	0.1113 908 633	0.1162 013 421	0.1210 369 577	0.1258 945 425	42
43	0.1112 514 619	0.1160 762 773	0.1209 249 987	0.1257 945 171	43
44	0.1111 261 735	0.1159 643 403	0.1208 252 102	0.1257 057 390	44
45	0.1110 135 424	0.1158 641 318	0.1207 362 523	0.1256 269 303	45
46	0.1109 122 683	0.1157 744 059	0.1206 569 363	0.1255 569 610	46
47	0.1108 211 884	0.1156 940 524	0.1205 862 064	0.1254 948 314	47
48	0.1107 392 624	0.1156 220 813	0.1205 231 248	0.1254 396 568	48
49	0.1106 655 589	0.1155 576 093	0.1204 668 576	0.1253 906 534	49
50	0.1105 992 433	0.1154 998 481	0.1204 166 635	0.1253 471 269	50
51	0.1105 395 676	0.1154 480 934	0.1203 718 826	0.1253 084 621	51
52	0.1104 858 607	0.1154 017 160	0.1203 319 279	0.1252 741 133	52
53	0.1104 375 209	0.1153 601 537	0.1202 962 763	0.1252 435 969	53
54	0.1103 940 076	0.1153 229 035	0.1202 644 625	0.1252 164 837	54
55	0.1103 548 359	0.1152 895 157	0.1202 360 715	0.1251 923 930	55
56	0.1103 195 698	0.1152 595 879	0.1202 107 337	0.1251 709 867	56
57	0.1102 878 179	0.1152 327 601	0.1201 881 197	0.1251 519 651	57
58	0.1102 592 282	0.1152 087 099	0.1201 679 358	0.1251 350 619	58
59	0.1102 334 844	0.1151 871 487	0.1201 499 202	0.1251 200 406	59
60	0.1102 103 020	0.1151 678 182	0.1201 338 394	0.1251 066 913	60

Table 6.   PARTIAL PAYMENT TO AMORTIZE 1
             PAYABLE AT END OF EACH PERIOD

YEARS	13% NOMINAL ANNUAL RATE	13½% NOMINAL ANNUAL RATE	14% NOMINAL ANNUAL RATE	14½% NOMINAL ANNUAL RATE	YEARS
1	1.1300 000 000	1.1350 000 000	1.1400 000 000	1.1450 000 000	1
2	0.5994 835 681	0.6033 840 749	0.6072 897 196	0.6112 004 662	2
3	0.4235 219 701	0.4271 221 947	0.4307 314 804	0.4343 497 588	3
4	0.3361 941 974	0.3396 931 901	0.3432 047 833	0.3467 288 719	4
5	0.2843 145 434	0.2877 910 955	0.2912 835 465	0.2947 917 481	5
6	0.2501 532 321	0.2536 458 704	0.2571 574 957	0.2606 879 076	6
7	0.2261 108 038	0.2296 406 583	0.2331 923 773	0.2367 656 994	7
8	0.2083 867 196	0.2119 661 101	0.2155 700 238	0.2191 981 278	8
9	0.1948 689 020	0.1985 051 669	0.2021 683 838	0.2058 581 379	9
10	0.1842 895 558	0.1879 869 780	0.1917 135 408	0.1954 687 376	10
11	0.1758 414 545	0.1796 023 222	0.1833 942 714	0.1872 166 937	11
12	0.1689 860 847	0.1728 113 211	0.1766 693 269	0.1805 593 835	12
13	0.1633 503 411	0.1672 399 012	0.1711 636 635	0.1751 207 919	13
14	0.1586 674 959	0.1626 206 298	0.1666 091 448	0.1706 320 815	14
15	0.1547 417 797	0.1587 572 163	0.1628 089 630	0.1668 959 329	15
16	0.1514 262 445	0.1555 023 244	0.1596 154 000	0.1637 642 550	16
17	0.1486 084 385	0.1527 432 135	0.1569 154 359	0.1611 237 596	17
18	0.1462 008 548	0.1503 921 647	0.1546 211 516	0.1588 863 402	18
19	0.1441 343 943	0.1483 799 284	0.1526 631 593	0.1569 824 868	19
20	0.1423 537 884	0.1466 511 339	0.1509 860 016	0.1553 566 708	20
21	0.1408 143 279	0.1451 610 103	0.1495 448 612	0.1539 640 464	21
22	0.1394 794 811	0.1438 729 970	0.1483 031 654	0.1527 680 465	22
23	0.1383 191 328	0.1427 569 775	0.1472 308 130	0.1517 386 033	23
24	0.1373 082 605	0.1417 879 502	0.1463 028 406	0.1508 508 096	24
25	0.1364 259 276	0.1409 450 182	0.1454 984 079	0.1500 838 993	25
26	0.1356 545 063	0.1402 106 089	0.1448 000 136	0.1494 204 595	26
27	0.1349 790 727	0.1395 698 653	0.1441 928 839	0.1488 458 159	27
28	0.1343 869 291	0.1390 101 668	0.1436 644 905	0.1483 475 475	28
29	0.1338 672 246	0.1385 207 472	0.1432 041 657	0.1479 150 996	29
30	0.1334 106 503	0.1380 923 874	0.1428 027 939	0.1475 394 732	30
31	0.1330 091 921	0.1377 171 673	0.1424 525 613	0.1472 129 724	31
32	0.1326 559 291	0.1373 882 625	0.1421 467 511	0.1469 289 987	32
33	0.1323 448 684	0.1370 997 777	0.1418 795 755	0.1466 818 816	33
34	0.1320 708 076	0.1368 466 081	0.1416 460 366	0.1464 667 377	34
35	0.1318 292 209	0.1366 243 248	0.1414 418 099	0.1462 793 548	35
36	0.1316 161 634	0.1364 290 780	0.1412 631 480	0.1461 160 934	36
37	0.1314 281 904	0.1362 575 162	0.1411 067 982	0.1459 738 048	37
38	0.1312 622 899	0.1361 067 176	0.1409 699 339	0.1458 497 619	38
39	0.1311 158 243	0.1359 741 317	0.1408 500 959	0.1457 415 997	39
40	0.1309 864 810	0.1358 575 299	0.1407 451 425	0.1456 472 661	40
41	0.1308 722 306	0.1357 549 625	0.1406 532 069	0.1455 649 785	41
42	0.1307 712 901	0.1356 647 231	0.1405 726 603	0.1454 931 877	42
43	0.1306 820 921	0.1355 853 163	0.1405 020 814	0.1454 305 461	43
44	0.1306 032 572	0.1355 154 314	0.1404 402 284	0.1453 758 815	44
45	0.1305 335 711	0.1354 539 184	0.1403 860 162	0.1453 281 731	45
46	0.1304 719 639	0.1353 997 682	0.1403 384 961	0.1452 865 319	46
47	0.1304 174 928	0.1353 520 947	0.1402 968 383	0.1452 501 836	47
48	0.1303 693 262	0.1353 101 194	0.1402 603 167	0.1452 184 532	48
49	0.1303 267 306	0.1352 731 583	0.1402 282 958	0.1451 907 524	49
50	0.1302 890 585	0.1352 406 102	0.1402 002 194	0.1451 665 683	50
51	0.1302 557 386	0.1352 119 464	0.1401 756 002	0.1451 454 533	51
52	0.1302 262 661	0.1351 867 021	0.1401 540 115	0.1451 270 173	52
53	0.1302 001 954	0.1351 644 682	0.1401 350 796	0.1451 109 199	53
54	0.1301 771 327	0.1351 448 849	0.1401 184 768	0.1450 968 639	54
55	0.1301 567 300	0.1351 276 356	0.1401 039 162	0.1450 845 901	55
56	0.1301 386 799	0.1351 124 416	0.1400 911 463	0.1450 738 724	56
57	0.1301 227 105	0.1350 990 577	0.1400 799 465	0.1450 645 132	57
58	0.1301 085 816	0.1350 872 679	0.1400 701 236	0.1450 563 402	58
59	0.1300 960 807	0.1350 768 821	0.1400 615 081	0.1450 492 030	59
60	0.1300 850 199	0.1350 677 329	0.1400 539 516	0.1450 429 702	60

Table 6. **PARTIAL PAYMENT TO AMORTIZE 1**
PAYABLE AT END OF EACH PERIOD

YEARS	15% NOMINAL ANNUAL RATE	15½% NOMINAL ANNUAL RATE	16% NOMINAL ANNUAL RATE	16½% NOMINAL ANNUAL RATE	YEARS
1	1.1500 000 000	1.1550 000 000	1.1600 000 000	1.1650 000 000	1
2	0.6151 162 791	0.6190 371 230	0.6229 629 630	0.6268 937 644	2
3	0.4379 769 618	0.4416 130 223	0.4452 578 731	0.4489 114 480	3
4	0.3502 653 516	0.3538 141 185	0.3573 750 695	0.3609 481 019	4
5	0.2983 155 525	0.3018 548 125	0.3054 093 816	0.3089 791 140	5
6	0.2642 369 066	0.2678 042 936	0.2713 898 702	0.2749 934 387	6
7	0.2403 603 636	0.2439 761 095	0.2476 126 771	0.2512 698 077	7
8	0.2228 500 896	0.2265 255 774	0.2302 242 601	0.2339 458 078	8
9	0.2095 740 150	0.2133 156 020	0.2170 824 868	0.2208 742 591	9
10	0.1992 520 625	0.2030 630 117	0.2069 010 831	0.2107 657 770	10
11	0.1910 689 830	0.1949 505 356	0.1988 607 515	0.2027 990 342	11
12	0.1844 807 761	0.1884 327 944	0.1924 147 333	0.1964 258 934	12
13	0.1791 104 565	0.1831 318 343	0.1871 841 100	0.1912 664 771	13
14	0.1746 884 898	0.1787 774 299	0.1828 979 733	0.1870 492 036	14
15	0.1710 170 526	0.1751 712 633	0.1793 575 218	0.1835 748 018	15
16	0.1679 476 914	0.1721 645 308	0.1764 136 162	0.1806 938 131	16
17	0.1653 668 623	0.1696 434 484	0.1739 522 494	0.1782 920 262	17
18	0.1631 862 874	0.1675 195 831	0.1718 848 526	0.1762 807 572	18
19	0.1613 363 504	0.1657 232 318	0.1701 416 556	0.1745 901 910	19
20	0.1597 614 704	0.1641 987 802	0.1686 670 324	0.1731 647 123	20
21	0.1584 167 914	0.1629 013 828	0.1674 161 691	0.1719 595 618	21
22	0.1572 657 713	0.1617 945 424	0.1663 526 353	0.1709 383 976	22
23	0.1562 783 947	0.1608 483 167	0.1654 465 820	0.1700 714 859	23
24	0.1554 298 296	0.1600 379 680	0.1646 733 862	0.1693 343 385	24
25	0.1546 994 023	0.1593 429 337	0.1640 126 153	0.1687 066 717	25
26	0.1540 698 058	0.1587 460 303	0.1634 472 266	0.1681 716 014	26
27	0.1535 264 815	0.1582 328 312	0.1629 629 420	0.1677 150 133	27
28	0.1530 571 309	0.1577 911 756	0.1625 477 527	0.1673 250 650	28
29	0.1526 513 265	0.1574 107 763	0.1621 915 252	0.1669 917 888	29
30	0.1523 001 982	0.1570 829 047	0.1618 856 833	0.1667 067 719	30
31	0.1519 961 796	0.1568 001 344	0.1616 229 508	0.1664 628 970	31
32	0.1517 328 006	0.1565 561 326	0.1613 971 408	0.1662 541 308	32
33	0.1515 045 161	0.1563 454 881	0.1612 029 828	0.1660 753 495	33
34	0.1513 065 655	0.1561 635 693	0.1610 359 798	0.1659 221 956	34
35	0.1511 348 546	0.1560 064 055	0.1608 922 891	0.1657 909 581	35
36	0.1509 858 572	0.1558 705 881	0.1607 686 235	0.1656 784 733	36
37	0.1508 565 329	0.1557 531 882	0.1606 621 677	0.1655 820 416	37
38	0.1507 442 569	0.1556 516 861	0.1605 705 086	0.1654 993 570	38
39	0.1506 467 613	0.1555 639 122	0.1604 915 760	0.1654 284 490	39
40	0.1505 620 850	0.1554 879 974	0.1604 235 929	0.1653 676 322	40
41	0.1504 885 308	0.1554 223 301	0.1603 650 330	0.1653 154 645	41
42	0.1504 246 290	0.1553 655 201	0.1603 145 846	0.1652 707 117	42
43	0.1503 691 063	0.1553 163 675	0.1602 711 201	0.1652 323 166	43
44	0.1503 208 590	0.1552 738 363	0.1602 336 696	0.1651 993 736	44
45	0.1502 789 300	0.1552 370 315	0.1602 013 988	0.1651 711 069	45
46	0.1502 424 890	0.1552 051 800	0.1601 735 895	0.1651 468 513	46
47	0.1502 108 156	0.1551 776 134	0.1601 496 237	0.1651 260 367	47
48	0.1501 832 843	0.1551 537 542	0.1601 289 693	0.1651 081 743	48
49	0.1501 593 523	0.1551 331 028	0.1601 111 681	0.1650 928 449	49
50	0.1501 385 480	0.1551 152 273	0.1600 958 254	0.1650 796 888	50
51	0.1501 204 620	0.1550 997 539	0.1600 826 013	0.1650 683 977	51
52	0.1501 047 386	0.1550 863 596	0.1600 712 029	0.1650 587 071	52
53	0.1500 910 687	0.1550 747 646	0.1600 613 781	0.1650 503 898	53
54	0.1500 791 839	0.1550 647 271	0.1600 529 093	0.1650 432 512	54
55	0.1500 688 509	0.1550 560 376	0.1600 456 094	0.1650 371 241	55
56	0.1500 598 667	0.1550 485 151	0.1600 393 169	0.1650 318 652	56
57	0.1500 520 553	0.1550 420 026	0.1600 338 927	0.1650 273 513	57
58	0.1500 452 634	0.1550 363 646	0.1600 292 170	0.1650 234 770	58
59	0.1500 393 580	0.1550 314 835	0.1600 251 865	0.1650 201 515	59
60	0.1500 342 231	0.1550 272 577	0.1600 217 120	0.1650 172 971	60

Table 6.   PARTIAL PAYMENT TO AMORTIZE 1
PAYABLE AT END OF EACH PERIOD

YEARS	17% NOMINAL ANNUAL RATE	17½% NOMINAL ANNUAL RATE	18% NOMINAL ANNUAL RATE	18½% NOMINAL ANNUAL RATE	YEARS
1	1.1700 000 000	1.1750 000 000	1.1800 000 000	1.1850 000 000	1
2	0.6308 294 931	0.6347 701 149	0.6387 155 963	0.6426 659 039	2
3	0.4525 736 811	0.4562 445 069	0.4599 238 607	0.4636 116 780	3
4	0.3645 331 137	0.3681 300 037	0.3717 386 709	0.3753 590 154	4
5	0.3125 638 643	0.3161 634 882	0.3197 778 418	0.3234 067 820	5
6	0.2786 148 021	0.2822 537 641	0.2859 101 292	0.2895 837 031	6
7	0.2549 472 428	0.2586 447 254	0.2623 619 994	0.2660 988 095	7
8	0.2376 898 916	0.2414 561 840	0.2452 443 589	0.2490 540 919	8
9	0.2246 905 102	0.2285 308 333	0.2323 948 239	0.2362 820 801	9
10	0.2146 565 967	0.2185 730 482	0.2225 146 413	0.2264 808 893	10
11	0.2067 647 916	0.2107 574 364	0.2147 763 862	0.2188 210 645	11
12	0.2004 655 819	0.2045 331 132	0.2086 278 089	0.2127 489 990	12
13	0.1953 781 386	0.1995 183 074	0.2036 862 073	0.2078 810 735	13
14	0.1912 302 181	0.1954 401 277	0.1996 780 583	0.2039 431 510	14
15	0.1878 220 950	0.1920 984 119	0.1964 027 825	0.2007 342 570	15
16	0.1850 040 103	0.1893 431 211	0.1937 100 839	0.1981 038 628	16
17	0.1826 615 693	0.1870 596 999	0.1914 852 711	0.1959 371 677	17
18	0.1807 059 953	0.1851 593 036	0.1896 394 570	0.1941 452 695	18
19	0.1790 674 523	0.1835 720 996	0.1881 028 390	0.1926 584 229	19
20	0.1776 903 593	0.1822 425 665	0.1868 199 812	0.1914 213 045	20
21	0.1765 300 350	0.1811 261 256	0.1857 464 327	0.1903 896 170	21
22	0.1755 502 493	0.1801 866 820	0.1848 462 577	0.1895 276 075	22
23	0.1747 214 054	0.1793 947 980	0.1840 901 996	0.1888 062 232	23
24	0.1740 191 703	0.1787 263 162	0.1834 542 973	0.1882 017 187	24
25	0.1734 234 282	0.1781 613 074	0.1829 188 261	0.1876 945 919	25
26	0.1729 174 705	0.1776 832 551	0.1824 674 779	0.1872 687 583	26
27	0.1724 873 621	0.1772 784 184	0.1820 867 195	0.1869 109 054	27
28	0.1721 214 404	0.1769 353 267	0.1817 652 846	0.1866 099 822	28
29	0.1718 099 152	0.1766 443 781	0.1814 937 692	0.1863 567 913	29
30	0.1715 445 468	0.1763 975 150	0.1812 643 056	0.1861 436 621	30
31	0.1713 183 850	0.1761 879 615	0.1810 702 987	0.1859 641 852	31
32	0.1711 255 565	0.1760 100 099	0.1809 062 108	0.1858 129 969	32
33	0.1709 610 895	0.1758 588 447	0.1807 673 859	0.1856 856 029	33
34	0.1708 207 698	0.1757 303 978	0.1806 499 044	0.1855 782 333	34
35	0.1707 010 209	0.1756 212 289	0.1805 504 633	0.1854 877 226	35
36	0.1705 988 044	0.1755 284 261	0.1804 662 768	0.1854 114 109	36
37	0.1705 115 368	0.1754 495 222	0.1803 949 937	0.1853 470 617	37
38	0.1704 370 199	0.1753 824 258	0.1803 346 284	0.1852 927 934	38
39	0.1703 733 818	0.1753 253 628	0.1802 835 030	0.1852 470 220	39
40	0.1703 190 279	0.1752 768 279	0.1802 401 991	0.1852 084 139	40
41	0.1702 725 991	0.1752 355 427	0.1802 035 171	0.1851 758 458	41
42	0.1702 329 364	0.1752 004 217	0.1801 724 424	0.1851 483 711	42
43	0.1701 990 513	0.1751 705 426	0.1801 461 163	0.1851 251 920	43
44	0.1701 701 004	0.1751 451 216	0.1801 238 120	0.1851 056 361	44
45	0.1701 453 638	0.1751 234 925	0.1801 049 144	0.1850 891 364	45
46	0.1701 242 272	0.1751 050 889	0.1800 889 026	0.1850 752 149	46
47	0.1701 061 658	0.1750 894 294	0.1800 753 355	0.1850 634 685	47
48	0.1700 907 317	0.1750 761 043	0.1800 638 396	0.1850 535 570	48
49	0.1700 775 425	0.1750 647 654	0.1800 540 984	0.1850 451 938	49
50	0.1700 662 712	0.1750 551 165	0.1800 458 440	0.1850 381 368	50
51	0.1700 566 389	0.1750 469 054	0.1800 388 494	0.1850 321 819	51
52	0.1700 484 070	0.1750 399 179	0.1800 329 221	0.1850 271 570	52
53	0.1700 413 718	0.1750 339 716	0.1800 278 993	0.1850 229 167	53
54	0.1700 353 592	0.1750 289 111	0.1800 236 429	0.1850 193 387	54
55	0.1700 302 206	0.1750 246 046	0.1800 200 360	0.1850 163 193	55
56	0.1700 258 289	0.1750 209 397	0.1800 169 794	0.1850 137 713	56
57	0.1700 220 755	0.1750 178 207	0.1800 143 891	0.1850 116 213	57
58	0.1700 188 676	0.1750 151 663	0.1800 121 940	0.1850 098 069	58
59	0.1700 161 259	0.1750 129 073	0.1800 103 338	0.1850 082 758	59
60	0.1700 137 826	0.1750 109 848	0.1800 087 574	0.1850 069 837	60

Table 6. PARTIAL PAYMENT TO AMORTIZE 1
PAYABLE AT END OF EACH PERIOD

YEARS	19% NOMINAL ANNUAL RATE	19½% NOMINAL ANNUAL RATE	20% NOMINAL ANNUAL RATE	20½% NOMINAL ANNUAL RATE	YEARS
1	1.1900 000 000	1.1950 000 000	1.2000 000 000	1.2050 000 000	1
2	0.6466 210 046	0.6505 808 656	0.6545 454 545	0.6585 147 392	2
3	0.4673 078 950	0.4710 124 482	0.4747 252 747	0.4784 463 122	3
4	0.3789 909 377	0.3826 343 389	0.3862 891 207	0.3899 551 857	4
5	0.3270 501 666	0.3307 078 539	0.3343 797 033	0.3380 655 748	5
6	0.2932 742 921	0.2969 817 036	0.3007 057 459	0.3044 462 284	6
7	0.2698 549 022	0.2736 300 248	0.2774 239 263	0.2812 363 570	7
8	0.2528 850 604	0.2567 369 435	0.2606 094 224	0.2645 021 805	8
9	0.2401 922 023	0.2441 247 940	0.2480 794 617	0.2520 558 149	9
10	0.2304 713 094	0.2344 854 232	0.2385 227 569	0.2425 828 412	10
11	0.2228 909 005	0.2269 853 296	0.2311 037 942	0.2352 457 430	11
12	0.2168 960 219	0.2210 682 250	0.2252 649 649	0.2294 856 079	12
13	0.2121 021 529	0.2163 487 047	0.2206 200 011	0.2249 153 270	13
14	0.2082 345 628	0.2125 514 675	0.2168 930 552	0.2212 585 336	14
15	0.2050 919 063	0.2094 748 227	0.2138 821 198	0.2183 129 335	15
16	0.2025 234 484	0.2069 678 578	0.2114 361 350	0.2159 273 513	16
17	0.2004 143 070	0.2049 156 392	0.2094 401 469	0.2139 868 456	17
18	0.1986 755 939	0.2032 293 223	0.2078 053 857	0.2124 027 537	18
19	0.1972 376 496	0.2018 393 632	0.2064 624 532	0.2111 058 536	19
20	0.1960 452 907	0.2006 907 465	0.2053 565 307	0.2100 415 524	20
21	0.1950 543 994	0.1997 395 606	0.2044 439 388	0.2091 664 291	21
22	0.1942 294 304	0.1989 504 912	0.2036 896 187	0.2084 457 036	22
23	0.1935 415 560	0.1982 949 577	0.2030 652 575	0.2078 513 516	23
24	0.1929 672 666	0.1977 497 051	0.2025 478 730	0.2073 606 809	24
25	0.1924 872 993	0.1972 957 260	0.2021 187 290	0.2069 562 408	25
26	0.1920 858 078	0.1969 174 260	0.2017 624 956	0.2066 199 779	26
27	0.1917 497 128	0.1966 019 702	0.2014 665 923	0.2063 425 751	27
28	0.1914 681 881	0.1963 387 661	0.2012 206 684	0.2061 129 302	28
29	0.1912 322 512	0.1961 190 527	0.2010 161 900	0.2059 227 413	29
30	0.1910 344 341	0.1959 355 697	0.2008 461 085	0.2057 651 745	30
31	0.1908 685 173	0.1957 822 910	0.2007 045 936	0.2056 345 966	31
32	0.1907 293 142	0.1956 542 086	0.2005 868 168	0.2055 263 590	32
33	0.1906 124 937	0.1955 471 553	0.2004 887 750	0.2054 366 217	33
34	0.1905 144 358	0.1954 576 610	0.2004 071 466	0.2053 622 104	34
35	0.1904 321 122	0.1953 828 333	0.2003 391 738	0.2053 004 992	35
36	0.1903 629 877	0.1953 202 600	0.2002 825 649	0.2052 493 148	36
37	0.1903 049 387	0.1952 679 282	0.2002 354 154	0.2052 068 574	37
38	0.1902 561 853	0.1952 241 574	0.2001 961 410	0.2051 716 365	38
39	0.1902 152 355	0.1951 875 443	0.2001 634 241	0.2051 424 166	39
40	0.1901 808 374	0.1951 569 162	0.2001 361 682	0.2051 181 741	40
41	0.1901 519 411	0.1951 312 934	0.2001 134 606	0.2050 980 602	41
42	0.1901 276 653	0.1951 098 569	0.2000 945 416	0.2050 813 711	42
43	0.1901 072 703	0.1950 919 220	0.2000 787 785	0.2050 675 233	43
44	0.1900 901 350	0.1950 769 162	0.2000 656 444	0.2050 560 328	44
45	0.1900 757 379	0.1950 643 609	0.2000 547 007	0.2050 464 981	45
46	0.1900 636 413	0.1950 538 556	0.2000 455 818	0.2050 385 861	46
47	0.1900 534 772	0.1950 450 654	0.2000 379 834	0.2050 320 207	47
48	0.1900 449 368	0.1950 377 102	0.2000 316 518	0.2050 265 725	48
49	0.1900 377 606	0.1950 315 557	0.2000 263 758	0.2050 220 514	49
50	0.1900 317 306	0.1950 264 057	0.2000 219 794	0.2050 182 995	50
51	0.1900 266 636	0.1950 220 964	0.2000 183 158	0.2050 151 861	51
52	0.1900 224 059	0.1950 184 903	0.2000 152 629	0.2050 126 024	52
53	0.1900 188 282	0.1950 154 728	0.2000 127 190	0.2050 104 583	53
54	0.1900 158 217	0.1950 129 478	0.2000 105 990	0.2050 086 790	54
55	0.1900 132 954	0.1950 108 349	0.2000 088 324	0.2050 072 025	55
56	0.1900 111 725	0.1950 090 668	0.2000 073 603	0.2050 059 771	56
57	0.1900 093 885	0.1950 075 872	0.2000 061 336	0.2050 049 602	57
58	0.1900 078 895	0.1950 063 491	0.2000 051 113	0.2050 041 164	58
59	0.1900 066 298	0.1950 053 130	0.2000 042 594	0.2050 034 161	59
60	0.1900 055 712	0.1950 044 460	0.2000 035 495	0.2050 028 349	60

245

Table 6.   PARTIAL PAYMENT TO AMORTIZE 1
PAYABLE AT END OF EACH PERIOD

YEARS	21% NOMINAL ANNUAL RATE	21½% NOMINAL ANNUAL RATE	22% NOMINAL ANNUAL RATE	22½% NOMINAL ANNUAL RATE	YEARS
1	1.2100 000 000	1.2150 000 000	1.2200 000 000	1.2250 000 000	1
2	0.6624 886 878	0.6664 672 686	0.6704 504 505	0.6744 382 022	2
3	0.4821 754 988	0.4859 127 729	0.4896 580 736	0.4934 113 404	3
4	0.3936 324 369	0.3973 207 780	0.4010 201 135	0.4047 303 483	4
5	0.3417 653 293	0.3454 788 284	0.3492 059 348	0.3529 465 120	5
6	0.3082 029 617	0.3119 757 574	0.3157 644 282	0.3195 687 881	6
7	0.2850 670 688	0.2889 158 150	0.2927 823 508	0.2966 664 329	7
8	0.2684 149 035	0.2723 472 791	0.2762 989 979	0.2802 697 526	8
9	0.2560 534 667	0.2600 720 334	0.2641 111 354	0.2681 703 963	9
10	0.2466 652 120	0.2507 694 102	0.2548 949 820	0.2590 414 793	10
11	0.2394 106 322	0.2435 979 253	0.2478 070 935	0.2520 376 154	11
12	0.2337 295 303	0.2379 961 186	0.2422 847 695	0.2465 948 907	12
13	0.2292 339 810	0.2335 752 752	0.2379 385 355	0.2423 231 022	13
14	0.2256 471 276	0.2300 580 800	0.2344 906 512	0.2389 441 198	14
15	0.2227 664 213	0.2272 417 634	0.2317 381 620	0.2362 548 416	15
16	0.2204 406 051	0.2249 750 219	0.2295 297 542	0.2341 039 818	16
17	0.2185 547 835	0.2231 430 410	0.2277 507 309	0.2323 769 974	17
18	0.2170 204 340	0.2216 574 724	0.2263² 129 516	0.2309 859 908	18
19	0.2157 685 424	0.2204 495 409	0.2251 479 123	0.2298 627 611	19
20	0.2147 447 703	0.2194 651 915	0.2242 018 701	0.2289 539 055	20
21	0.2139 059 812	0.2186 615 982	0.2234 323 343	0.2282 172 935	21
22	0.2132 176 967	0.2180 046 062	0.2228 054 958	0.2276 194 824	22
23	0.2126 522 006	0.2174 668 266	0.2222 943 108	0.2271 337 902	23
24	0.2121 871 074	0.2170 261 962	0.2218 770 526	0.2267 388 407	24
25	0.2118 042 655	0.2166 648 747	0.2215 362 042	0.2264 174 498	25
26	0.2114 889 084	0.2163 683 922	0.2212 576 002	0.2261 557 645	26
27	0.2112 289 905	0.2161 249 817	0.2210 297 583	0.2259 425 919	27
28	0.2110 146 640	0.2159 250 544	0.2208 433 524	0.2257 688 712	28
29	0.2108 378 627	0.2157 607 824	0.2206 907 949	0.2256 272 562	29
30	0.2106 919 694	0.2156 257 665	0.2205 659 049	0.2255 117 839	30
31	0.2105 715 487	0.2155 147 690	0.2204 636 414	0.2254 176 083	31
32	0.2104 721 313	0.2154 234 988	0.2203 798 896	0.2253 407 885	32
33	0.2103 900 389	0.2153 484 372	0.2203 112 880	0.2252 781 173	33
34	0.2103 222 423	0.2152 866 974	0.2202 550 890	0.2252 269 830	34
35	0.2102 662 451	0.2152 359 093	0.2202 090 456	0.2251 852 579	35
36	0.2102 199 889	0.2151 941 263	0.2201 713 195	0.2251 512 081	36
37	0.2101 817 759	0.2151 597 492	0.2201 404 061	0.2251 234 200	37
38	0.2101 502 055	0.2151 314 636	0.2201 150 737	0.2251 007 408	38
39	0.2101 241 213	0.2151 081 888	0.2200 943 138	0.2250 822 307	39
40	0.2101 025 691	0.2150 890 363	0.2200 773 005	0.2250 671 226	40
41	0.2100 847 607	0.2150 732 755	0.2200 633 570	0.2250 547 909	41
42	0.2100 700 452	0.2150 603 055	0.2200 519 293	0.2250 447 253	42
43	0.2100 578 853	0.2150 496 317	0.2200 425 632	0.2250 365 091	43
44	0.2100 478 368	0.2150 408 474	0.2200 348 866	0.2250 298 025	44
45	0.2100 395 330	0.2150 336 182	0.2200 285 948	0.2250 243 279	45
46	0.2100 326 708	0.2150 276 685	0.2200 234 378	0.2250 198 592	46
47	0.2100 269 999	0.2150 227 719	0.2200 192 109	0.2250 162 113	47
48	0.2100 223 135	0.2150 187 420	0.2200 157 464	0.2250 132 335	48
49	0.2100 184 406	0.2150 154 252	0.2200 129 067	0.2250 108 028	49
50	0.2100 152 399	0.2150 126 955	0.2200 105 792	0.2250 088 185	50
51	0.2100 125 948	0.2150 104 489	0.2200 086 714	0.2250 071 987	51
52	0.2100 104 088	0.2150 085 998	0.2200 071 076	0.2250 058 765	52
53	0.2100 086 023	0.2150 070 780	0.2200 058 259	0.2250 047 971	53
54	0.2100 071 093	0.2150 058 255	0.2200 047 753	0.2250 039 160	54
55	0.2100 058 754	0.2150 047 946	0.2200 039 142	0.2250 031 967	55
56	0.2100 048 557	0.2150 039 462	0.2200 032 083	0.2250 026 096	56
57	0.2100 040 129	0.2150 032 479	0.2200 026 298	0.2250 021 302	57
58	0.2100 033 165	0.2150 026 731	0.2200 021 555	0.2250 017 390	58
59	0.2100 027 409	0.2150 022 001	0.2200 017 668	0.2250 014 196	59
60	0.2100 022 652	0.2150 018 108	0.2200 014 482	0.2250 011 588	60

Table 6.   PARTIAL PAYMENT TO AMORTIZE 1
PAYABLE AT END OF EACH PERIOD

YEARS	23% NOMINAL ANNUAL RATE	24% NOMINAL ANNUAL RATE	25% NOMINAL ANNUAL RATE	26% NOMINAL ANNUAL RATE	YEARS
1	1.2300 000 000	1.2400 000 000	1.2500 000 000	1.2600 000 000	1
2	0.6784 304 933	0.6864 285 714	0.6944 444 444	0.7024 778 761	2
3	0.4971 725 133	0.5047 183 397	0.5122 950 820	0.5199 022 767	3
4	0.4084 513 881	0.4159 255 089	0.4234 417 344	0.4309 993 338	4
5	0.3567 004 241	0.3642 477 149	0.3718 467 396	0.3794 964 454	5
6	0.3233 886 522	0.3310 741 602	0.3388 194 987	0.3466 232 355	6
7	0.3005 678 200	0.3084 215 522	0.3163 416 530	0.3243 262 593	7
8	0.2842 592 389	0.2922 932 018	0.3003 985 063	0.3085 728 187	8
9	0.2722 494 441	0.2804 654 313	0.2887 562 013	0.2971 189 268	9
10	0.2632 084 594	0.2716 021 271	0.2800 725 624	0.2886 164 407	10
11	0.2562 889 780	0.2648 522 131	0.2734 928 576	0.2822 071 051	11
12	0.2509 259 004	0.2596 483 138	0.2684 475 770	0.2773 194 369	12
13	0.2467 283 293	0.2555 982 535	0.2645 434 288	0.2735 592 056	13
14	0.2434 177 823	0.2524 229 653	0.2615 009 326	0.2706 467 022	14
15	0.2407 910 491	0.2499 191 452	0.2591 168 642	0.2683 789 634	15
16	0.2386 969 108	0.2479 358 295	0.2572 406 815	0.2666 060 410	16
17	0.2370 210 160	0.2463 591 647	0.2557 591 848	0.2652 155 451	17
18	0.2356 757 451	0.2451 021 928	0.2545 862 176	0.2641 222 582	18
19	0.2345 932 318	0.2440 978 105	0.2536 555 619	0.2632 609 648	19
20	0.2337 204 414	0.2432 938 009	0.2529 159 221	0.2625 813 865	20
21	0.2330 156 276	0.2426 492 538	0.2523 273 086	0.2620 445 308	21
22	0.2324 457 335	0.2421 319 401	0.2518 583 869	0.2616 200 148	22
23	0.2319 844 553	0.2417 163 556	0.2514 845 025	0.2612 840 750	23
24	0.2316 107 795	0.2413 822 445	0.2511 861 933	0.2610 180 696	24
25	0.2313 078 641	0.2411 134 721	0.2509 480 549	0.2608 073 395	25
26	0.2310 621 747	0.2408 971 558	0.2507 578 692	0.2606 403 353	26
27	0.2308 628 116	0.2407 229 896	0.2506 059 280	0.2605 079 445	27
28	0.2307 009 811	0.2405 827 164	0.2504 845 075	0.2604 029 681	28
29	0.2305 695 787	0.2404 697 118	0.2503 874 558	0.2603 197 137	29
30	0.2304 628 578	0.2403 786 564	0.2503 098 686	0.2602 536 767	30
31	0.2303 761 656	0.2403 052 749	0.2502 478 335	0.2602 012 902	31
32	0.2303 057 322	0.2402 461 288	0.2501 982 275	0.2601 597 286	32
33	0.2302 485 010	0.2401 984 516	0.2501 585 568	0.2601 267 526	33
34	0.2302 019 925	0.2401 600 160	0.2501 268 294	0.2601 005 872	34
35	0.2301 641 946	0.2401 290 285	0.2501 014 532	0.2600 798 248	35
36	0.2301 334 737	0.2401 040 444	0.2500 811 560	0.2600 633 490	36
37	0.2301 085 034	0.2400 838 998	0.2500 649 206	0.2600 502 744	37
38	0.2300 882 064	0.2400 676 565	0.2500 519 338	0.2600 398 987	38
39	0.2300 717 074	0.2400 545 587	0.2500 415 453	0.2600 316 647	39
40	0.2300 582 953	0.2400 439 970	0.2500 332 351	0.2600 251 301	40
41	0.2300 473 923	0.2400 354 802	0.2500 265 874	0.2600 199 441	41
42	0.2300 385 288	0.2400 286 123	0.2500 212 695	0.2600 158 284	42
43	0.2300 313 233	0.2400 230 739	0.2500 170 153	0.2600 125 621	43
44	0.2300 254 654	0.2400 186 076	0.2500 136 120	0.2600 099 698	44
45	0.2300 207 032	0.2400 150 059	0.2500 108 895	0.2600 079 125	45
46	0.2300 168 316	0.2400 121 014	0.2500 087 115	0.2600 062 797	46
47	0.2300 136 840	0.2400 097 591	0.2500 069 692	0.2600 049 839	47
48	0.2300 111 251	0.2400 078 702	0.2500 055 753	0.2600 039 554	48
49	0.2300 090 447	0.2400 063 469	0.2500 044 602	0.2600 031 392	49
50	0.2300 073 534	0.2400 051 184	0.2500 035 682	0.2600 024 914	50
51	0.2300 059 783	0.2400 041 277	0.2500 028 545	0.2600 019 773	51
52	0.2300 048 604	0.2400 033 288	0.2500 022 836	0.2600 015 693	52
53	0.2300 039 515	0.2400 026 845	0.2500 018 269	0.2600 012 455	53
54	0.2300 032 126	0.2400 021 649	0.2500 014 615	0.2600 009 885	54
55	0.2300 026 119	0.2400 017 459	0.2500 011 692	0.2600 007 845	55
56	0.2300 021 235	0.2400 014 080	0.2500 009 354	0.2600 006 225	56
57	0.2300 017 264	0.2400 011 355	0.2500 007 483	0.2600 004 941	57
58	0.2300 014 036	0.2400 009 157	0.2500 005 986	0.2600 003 922	58
59	0.2300 011 411	0.2400 007 385	0.2500 004 789	0.2600 003 113	59
60	0.2300 009 277	0.2400 005 955	0.2500 003 831	0.2600 002 470	60

Table 6.   PARTIAL PAYMENT TO AMORTIZE 1
PAYABLE AT END OF EACH PERIOD

YEARS	27% NOMINAL ANNUAL RATE	28% NOMINAL ANNUAL RATE	29% NOMINAL ANNUAL RATE	30% NOMINAL ANNUAL RATE	YEARS
1	1.2700 000 000	1.2800 000 000	1.2900 000 000	1.3000 000 000	1
2	0.7105 286 344	0.7185 964 912	0.7266 812 227	0.7347 826 087	2
3	0.5275 394 679	0.5352 062 066	0.5429 020 510	0.5506 265 664	3
4	0.4385 975 867	0.4462 357 835	0.4539 132 250	0.4616 292 226	4
5	0.3871 957 942	0.3949 437 633	0.4027 393 452	0.4105 815 484	5
6	0.3544 839 602	0.3624 002 847	0.3703 708 441	0.3783 942 967	6
7	0.3323 735 405	0.3404 816 996	0.3486 489 741	0.3568 736 368	7
8	0.3168 138 541	0.3251 193 773	0.3334 872 047	0.3419 152 051	8
9	0.3055 508 517	0.3140 492 925	0.3226 116 401	0.3312 353 605	9
10	0.2972 305 377	0.3059 117 316	0.3146 570 037	0.3234 634 396	10
11	0.2909 912 864	0.2998 418 706	0.3087 554 652	0.3177 288 158	11
12	0.2862 598 204	0.2952 648 341	0.3043 307 636	0.3134 540 701	12
13	0.2826 411 632	0.2917 851 066	0.3009 870 625	0.3102 432 741	13
14	0.2798 555 727	0.2891 231 170	0.2984 451 743	0.3078 178 414	14
15	0.2777 005 351	0.2870 769 943	0.2965 040 669	0.3059 777 755	15
16	0.2760 268 700	0.2854 985 011	0.2950 166 190	0.3045 772 413	16
17	0.2747 231 529	0.2842 773 299	0.2938 737 873	0.3035 086 013	17
18	0.2737 052 382	0.2833 305 344	0.2929 939 453	0.3026 916 595	18
19	0.2729 090 233	0.2825 952 273	0.2923 155 138	0.3020 662 291	19
20	0.2722 853 348	0.2820 234 188	0.2917 917 558	0.3015 868 848	20
21	0.2717 962 439	0.2815 783 010	0.2913 870 314	0.3012 191 924	21
22	0.2714 123 677	0.2812 315 291	0.2910 740 633	0.3009 369 616	22
23	0.2711 108 651	0.2809 612 073	0.2908 319 146	0.3007 202 206	23
24	0.2708 739 325	0.2807 503 797	0.2906 444 794	0.3005 537 091	24
25	0.2706 876 627	0.2805 858 907	0.2904 993 470	0.3004 257 487	25
26	0.2705 411 736	0.2804 575 177	0.2903 869 409	0.3003 273 918	26
27	0.2704 259 395	0.2803 573 080	0.2902 998 642	0.3002 517 764	27
28	0.2703 352 730	0.2802 790 689	0.2902 323 989	0.3001 936 367	28
29	0.2702 639 248	0.2802 179 751	0.2901 801 217	0.3001 489 291	29
30	0.2702 077 716	0.2801 702 640	0.2901 396 097	0.3001 145 477	30
31	0.2701 635 729	0.2801 330 011	0.2901 082 129	0.3000 881 059	31
32	0.2701 287 810	0.2801 038 963	0.2900 838 789	0.3000 677 692	32
33	0.2701 013 921	0.2800 811 624	0.2900 650 182	0.3000 521 274	33
34	0.2700 798 299	0.2800 634 041	0.2900 503 992	0.3000 400 964	34
35	0.2700 628 542	0.2800 495 320	0.2900 390 676	0.3000 308 424	35
36	0.2700 494 891	0.2800 386 954	0.2900 302 840	0.3000 237 244	36
37	0.2700 389 663	0.2800 302 299	0.2900 234 754	0.3000 182 492	37
38	0.2700 306 812	0.2800 236 165	0.2900 181 977	0.3000 140 376	38
39	0.2700 241 578	0.2800 184 501	0.2900 141 065	0.3000 107 981	39
40	0.2700 190 215	0.2800 144 139	0.2900 109 352	0.3000 083 061	40
41	0.2700 149 774	0.2800 112 607	0.2900 084 768	0.3000 063 893	41
42	0.2700 117 931	0.2800 087 974	0.2900 065 711	0.3000 049 148	42
43	0.2700 092 858	0.2800 068 729	0.2900 050 939	0.3000 037 806	43
44	0.2700 073 116	0.2800 053 694	0.2900 039 487	0.3000 029 082	44
45	0.2700 057 571	0.2800 041 948	0.2900 030 610	0.3000 022 370	45
46	0.2700 045 331	0.2800 032 772	0.2900 023 729	0.3000 017 208	46
47	0.2700 035 694	0.2800 025 603	0.2900 018 394	0.3000 013 237	47
48	0.2700 028 105	0.2800 020 002	0.2900 014 259	0.3000 010 182	48
49	0.2700 022 130	0.2800 015 627	0.2900 011 054	0.3000 007 832	49
50	0.2700 017 425	0.2800 012 208	0.2900 008 569	0.3000 006 025	50
51	0.2700 013 721	0.2800 009 538	0.2900 006 642	0.3000 004 635	51
52	0.2700 010 804	0.2800 007 451	0.2900 005 149	0.3000 003 565	52
53	0.2700 008 507	0.2800 005 821	0.2900 003 992	0.3000 002 742	53
54	0.2700 006 698	0.2800 004 548	0.2900 003 094	0.3000 002 110	54
55	0.2700 005 274	0.2800 003 553	0.2900 002 399	0.3000 001 623	55
56	0.2700 004 153	0.2800 002 776	0.2900 001 859	0.3000 001 248	56
57	0.2700 003 270	0.2800 002 169	0.2900 001 441	0.3000 000 960	57
58	0.2700 002 575	0.2800 001 694	0.2900 001 117	0.3000 000 739	58
59	0.2700 002 027	0.2800 001 324	0.2900 000 866	0.3000 000 568	59
60	0.2700 001 596	0.2800 001 034	0.2900 000 671	0.3000 000 437	60

Catalog

If you are interested in a list of fine Paperback
books, covering a wide range of subjects
and interests, send your name and address,
requesting your free catalog, to:

McGraw-Hill Paperbacks
1221 Avenue of Americas
New York, N.Y. 10020